Arthur Cox
Employment Law
Yearbook 2021

Disclaimer

This publication is a summary of selected developments in the area of employment law in 2021. Case reports and summaries of decisions are based solely on the publicly available copies of the relevant judgments, recommendations and determinations. There may be cases reported in this publication which, unknown to the authors and the publishers, have been appealed and/or overturned, or subsequently settled.

Whilst every care has been taken to ensure the accuracy of this work, this publication is not a definitive statement of the law and is not intended to constitute legal advice. The authors, editors and publishers do not accept any liability or responsibility for errors or omission. No responsibility for loss occasioned by any person acting or refraining from action as a result of any statement in the publication can be accepted by any of the authors, editors or the publishers.

Practice Areas Involved in the *Arthur Cox Employment Law Yearbook 2021*

Employment and Industrial Relations
Séamus Given
Kevin Langford
Cian Beecher
Louise O'Byrne
Grace Gannon
Niamh Fennelly
Emma Dunne
Sally Doyle
Sarah Lawn
Rachel Barry
Grace-Ann Meghen
Sarah Faulkner
Máille Brady Bates
Hannah O'Farrell
Declan MacQuillan
Ailbhe Moloney
Ciara McDermott
Mary Heavey, Arthur Cox Editor
Eamonn Butler
Katie Rooney
Sonam Gaitonde

Tax
Fintan Clancy
Ailish Finnerty
David Kilty
Caroline Devlin
Orlaith Kane
Susan Lynch
Anne Corrigan
Ciara Fagan
Dearbhla O'Gorman
Elaine Mooney
Dearbhla Ni Fhloinn
Cristina Susanu
Simona Prielaidaite

Nicola Cavey
Carl Grenville
Rachel Coyle
Ruth O'Sullivan

Pensions
Philip Smith
Sarah McCague
Michael Shovlin
Daniel Watters
Katie Lawless
Ross Neil
Doireann Nic Mhathúna
Enda Kerr

Technology and Innovation
Rob Corbet
Colin Rooney
Olivia Mullooly
Rachel Benson
Ian Duffy
Aoife MacArdle
Ciara Anderson
Caoimhe Stafford
Aoife Coll
Alison Peate
Siobhan O'Shea
David O'Connor
Isabel Cooke
Lorraine Sheridan

With input from:
Richard Willis
Leah O'Mahony

Arthur Cox Belfast
Rosemary Lundy
Chris Fullerton

Contents

Table of Cases

A

C

E

F

G

H

I

J

K

L

M

O

P

Q

R

T

U

V

W

X

Y

Z

Table of Statutes

Table of Statutory Instruments

GREAT BRITAIN

A

C

E

F

M

N

O

Table of EU Legislation

**TABLE OF AGREEMENTS,
CHARTERS, CONVENTIONS,
PROCEDURES AND TREATIES**

Chapter 1

Contract of Employment

INTRODUCTION

[1.01]   *Angard Staffing Solutions* is a case where the UK Employment Appeal Tribunal had to consider the scope of the obligation to inform an agency worker of vacant post within the hirers organisation and whether that gave an entitlement to be treated not less favourably in any ensuing selection process. The EAT also had to consider the scope of the obligation to make available the same basic working and employment conditions as an agency worker would be entitled to if he or she were employed directly.

There are two cases involving the non-payment of a bonus and the scope of the employer's entitlements and obligations under bonus clauses. They are *Meridian Global VAT Services (UK) Limited* (UK Employment Appeal Tribunal) and *Nair* (High Court of England and Wales).

The obligations of a new employer who has benefited from the misuse or disclosure of confidential information the property of a previous employer were explored by the Court of Appeal of England and Wales in *Trailfinders Limited.*

The extent to which the employer's contractual obligations can become relevant in a challenge to a disciplinary process were explored by the High Court of England and Wales in *Alderhey Children's NHS Foundation Trust.*

MD 5 Limited is an example of a case where it was necessary to adjudicate between employer and employee in relation to the ownership of copyright works.

AGENCY WORKERS

[1.02]   *Angard Staffing Solutions Ltd v Kocur*[1]*—UK Employment Appeal Tribunal—appeal from employment tribunal—agency workers—scope of Agency Workers Regulations*[2]*—Directive 2008/104/EC*[3]*—basic working conditions*

---

[1]   *Angard Staffing Solutions Ltd v Kocur* UKEAT/0105/19/JOJ, UKEAT/0209/19/JOJ. See also *Arthur Cox Employment Yearbook 2020* at **[5.09]** for decision in *Angard Staffing Solutions Ltd and Royal Mail Group Ltd v Kocur* UKEAT/0050/20/JOJ, where the EAT upheld the employment tribunal's decision that the claimant was an agency worker under reg 3 of the 2010 Regulations and Angard was a 'temporary work agency' under reg 4.

[2]   Agency Workers Regulations 2010 (SI 2010/93).

[3]   Directive 2008/104/EC on temporary agency work.

In the UK, the Agency Workers Regulations 2010 implement Directive 2008/104/EC (the Agency Workers Directive). The original claimants worked as agency workers for Royal Mail, through its wholly owned subsidiary, Angard Staffing Solutions Ltd. Angard provided agency workers only to Royal Mail. Mr Kocur and Ms Roberts (the claimants) were treated as agency workers and worked at the Leeds Mail Centre. The facts were not disputed before the employment tribunal. They alleged a broad range of breaches of their rights under the Agency Workers Regulations 2010 by both Angard and Royal Mail.

The claimants were successful in five out of 12 claims before the employment tribunal. In delivering its decision, the employment tribunal had regard to earlier litigation initiated by Mr Kocur in respect of his status as an agency worker and associated rights under the Agency Workers Directive. However, after the employment tribunal issued its decision, a decision of the Court of Appeal was subsequently issued in respect of Mr Kocur's claims.[4]

Both the claimants and Angard brought appeals to the EAT (comprising eight issues), which were heard together. One key issue in the judgment of the EAT concerned the scope of the right of an agency worker to be informed of vacant posts within the hirer (in this case Royal Mail) under reg 13(1) of the Agency Workers Regulations 2010, implementing art 6(1) of the Agency Workers Directive. The judgment also examined the right of agency workers to receive 'the same basic working and employment conditions' as if they were employed directly by the hirer.

The claimants argued that although they had been informed of internal vacancies, they were not given the same opportunity to apply and be considered for vacant positions in the same manner as directly employed workers of Royal Mail. There was an agreement in place at Royal Mail with the Communications Workers Union that, when permanent, fixed vacancies for particular shifts or duties became available at the Leeds Mail Office, they were offered first to the core grade of employees known as OPG. When new directly recruited OPG employees were recruited, they were not allocated a fixed shift or duty, but were used as a flexible resource by Royal Mail. When a fixed role became available, it was then filled on the basis of seniority from this pool of OPG employees.

While notice of such vacancies was provided to agency workers, they were informed of ineligibility to apply for these roles. They could apply for roles, once advertised externally and as such (and unlike their directly employed counterparts) were also in competition with external applicants. In considering the spirit of the Agency Workers Directive, and in particular the language of art 6(1), that agency workers should be provided with the same opportunity as other workers to find permanent employment, the employment tribunal found in the claimants' favour that Royal Mail had breached reg 13.

However, the EAT adopted a literal interpretation of the Agency Workers Directive, stating that 'to give them the same opportunity as other workers ... to find permanent employment' did not confer any additional rights on agency workers. The EAT concluded that reg 13(1) provides a right to be notified of the vacancies on the same

---

4 *Kocur v Angard Staffing Solutions Ltd* [2019] EWCA Civ 1185.

basis as directly-recruited employees, and a right to be given the same level of information about the vacancies as the directly-recruited employees. However, information in respect of vacancies is not provided to agency workers in order that they secure employment, nor does the Agency Workers Directive provide a right for an agency worker to apply and be considered for vacancies on the same basis as directly recruited employees of the hirer. The EAT commented that, in the present case, agency workers were ineligible for the open roles but that would not be the case in respect of every vacant post within Royal Mail.

Regulation 5(1) of the Agency Workers Regulations 2010 states that 'an agency worker (A) shall be entitled to the same basic working and employment conditions as A would be entitled to for doing the same job had A been recruited by the hirer'. Further, those basic working and employment conditions include terms relating to the duration of working time (reg 6(1)).

The claimants raised complaints in relation to the fact that their shifts were 12 minutes longer than those of direct employees of Royal Mail, that unlike directly recruited employees their breaks were not scheduled in advance, they did not receive certain training sessions during working time and that their payslips were not as detailed as direct employees of Royal Mail. Relying heavily on the rationale of the EAT and the Court of Appeal in relation Mr Koncur's earlier proceedings, the EAT held that agency workers were not entitled, under the Agency Workers Regulations 2010, to the same number of contractual hours as direct employees of the hirer. The EAT found that the Agency Workers Regulations 2010 were not drafted such that agency workers were entitled to equality of treatment 'in relation to the content of working time'; nor were hirers required to offer the same terms to agency workers as 'would have been offered to them if they had been direct employees'. It held that to do so would 'counter the flexibility which is at the heart of the relationship'. The EAT concluded that the differences in treatment raised by the claimants did not amount to a breach.

Finally, the EAT remitted one issue to the employment tribunal in relation to a six-month delay in implementing a pay increase for agency workers. It is for the employment tribunal to consider whether an implied term that any pay increase would be implemented within a reasonable period of time existed in respect of the agency workers and whether delayed implementation was a breach of that term.

BONUS

[1.03] *Ostilly v Meridian Global VAT Services (UK) Ltd[5]—UK Employment Appeal Tribunal—appeal from employment tribunal—contract of employment—bonus—entitlement to consider matters not mentioned in the bonus clause—exercise of discretion*

The claimant's letter of appointment in respect of his position as commercial director of the respondent described his bonus entitlement as follows: 'You will be entitled

---

5   *Ostilly v Meridian Global VAT Services (UK) Ltd* UKEAT/0017/20/OO.

to a maximum annual bonus of 20% of your salary which will be tied to your own performance and that of your market region. Further details on the bonus system will be forwarded to you shortly.' No further details were ever forwarded to the claimant and no documented bonus system was ever used. Ad hoc decisions on bonuses were made each year. The claimant was never assigned to work in a specific market region. In the following years, the claimant was paid a bonus each year, which exceeded the contractual ceiling of 20% of salary. By reason of a business downturn in 2018, the company decided to impose a pay freeze and to pay no bonuses in March 2018. The claimant took issue with that decision and claimed a contractual entitlement to at least £55,000 based on the pattern of previous bonuses. When his request was refused, the claimant resigned and claimed constructive dismissal on the grounds that the non-payment of a bonus was a breach of contract.

The employment tribunal found that, contrary to the claimant's assertion, the company was entitled to take account of its financial circumstances in exercising a discretion as to the level of bonus to be paid. The tribunal concluded that same was implicit in the bonus clause and that the decision to award a nil bonus was not irrational or perverse, therefore there was no breach of contract.

The EAT held that the employment tribunal did not misconstrue the bonus clause, and was correct to find that the employer's financial performance was a permissible consideration in deciding how much, if any, bonus to award the claimant for a particular year. The EAT concluded that in the absence of clear contrary words, the proposition that the employer, in exercising its discretion, could treat its own financial position and performance as a relevant consideration was inherent in the language of the clause. To displace it there must be express words and there were no such express words. The words 'maximum annual bonus' confer a discretion which must be exercised having regard to the claimant's performance and that of his market region (if any) but those words must not be read as requiring that that 'discretion be exercised as an abstract exercise, in a commercial vacuum'.

The EAT found that the employment tribunal was incorrect to consider how the clause had operated in practice, for the purpose of ascertaining its true meaning. It held that the meaning of the clause must be ascertained as of the date it came into existence. The fact that the claimant was awarded generous bonuses over and above his contractual entitlement for several years could not alter the meaning of the clause. The words 'tied to your own performance and that of your market region' meant that those factors could not be disregarded and were compulsory considerations but did not mean that other considerations that were inherently commercially relevant, such as market conditions and the employer's financial position, must be excluded.

However, the EAT found that the employment tribunal's financial miscalculation gave rise to concerns in its treatment of the issue of contractual discretion and the rationality of the respondent's decision not to pay a bonus to the claimant. The EAT also found that the tribunal's conclusion that the claimant would have resigned anyway was 'not justified' by any submissions or evidence and was procedurally unfair. The EAT concluded that in the exercise of the tribunal's discretion, the test to apply is a rationality test equivalent to that set out in *Wednesbury* namely that the employer must have regard to relevant considerations and disregard irrelevant considerations and the employer must not reach a decision no reasonable employer could reach. Therefore, the EAT remitted the case to a freshly constituted employment tribunal for further consideration of the manner in which the tribunal's discretion was exercised.

[1.04] *Nair v Lagardére Sports and Entertainment UK Ltd*[6]—*High Court of England and Wales—Master McCloud—trust and confidence—bonus payment*

This application was brought by the defendant seeking summary judgment to have the case struck out. The plaintiff had brought a claim against the defendant, his former employer, submitting that it had breached the implied term of trust and confidence in relation to the non-payment of bonuses amounting to at least US\$25m.

The plaintiff had been employed by World Sport Group (WSG) since 2006. The plaintiff alleged that, due to acts and omissions by WSG, in particular WSG Hong Kong and WSG Singapore, he had suffered a loss of reputation and other losses. The plaintiff moved to Lagardére Sports and Entertainment (LSE) in 2015 as part of a reorganisation, which the defendant argued, was a different legal entity; however, the plaintiff submitted that the defendant was still part of the same group.

An executive services agreement, which did not mention any liability for historical bonuses, was signed between the plaintiff and the defendant in 2015 to run until 2018 (the 2015 Agreement). The plaintiff argued that there was an implied term within the 2015 Agreement that the defendant would not conduct itself so as to 'destroy or seriously damage the relationship of trust and confidence' between the parties and that this term operated so as to require the defendant to take reasonable steps to ensure that the plaintiff's two previous employers within the WSG group paid bonuses and compensation due from them to the plaintiff.

The Court commented that WSG 'started to wriggle over paying the bonus' and that the 'new employer engaged in the same "wriggling" over the bonus in exactly the same way'.

As this was an application for summary judgment or strike out of the claim, the Court noted that 'the approach is to consider not whether the case would probably fail or probably succeed but rather to consider whether the claim is fanciful or there is an absence of reality about it'. The Court referred to the authorities on implied terms of trust and confidence and stated that the decision on whether the term was breached was 'fact sensitive' and required the Court to consider 'all the circumstances'.

The Court relied on *Malik v Bank of Credit and Commerce International SA (in liq)*[7] as clear authority that implied terms of trust and confidence 'can be breached … in many ways'. Although the defendant argued that the implied terms of trust and confidence

---

6   *Nair v Lagardére Sports and Entertainment UK Ltd* [2021] IRLR 54.
7   *Malik v Bank of Credit and Commerce International SA (in liq)* [1998] AC 20.

'must be interpreted negatively and not so as to impute positive obligations' the Court held that 'the application of the argued principle that there is a different treatment of positive versus negative conduct depends on [the] factual position'.

In concluding that summary judgment would be inappropriate and dismissing the defendant's application, the Court stated:

> The test is whether, on the facts, in all the circumstances the employer so conducted itself as to destroy or seriously undermine the relationship of trust and confidence between it and the employee without reasonable or probable cause. Conduct can take the form of failure to do something or the form of positively doing something and often the difference may be merely semantic.

CONFIDENTIALITY

[1.05]   ***Trailfinders Ltd v Travel Counsellors Ltd[8]—Court of Appeal of England and Wales—Lady Asplin J, Lewison & Arnold LJJ—appeal from High Court of England and Wales—contract of employment—duty of fidelity—confidential information—liability of the recipient***

Trailfinders Ltd is a travel agent, and a number of its employees left to join Travel Counsellors Ltd (TCL), a competitor. Before they left the employment of Trailfinders, two of the employees downloaded customer information, including a customer list, from Trailfinders system and emailed it to their personal accounts. The list consisted of the names, addresses, email addresses and telephone numbers of 313 individuals. Trailfinders issued High Court proceedings against the former employees and against TCL. The High Court of England and Wales held that the former employees had acted in breach of their contracts of employment and in breach of the equitable obligation of confidence to Trailfinders. It also concluded that TCL had infringed its equitable obligation of confidence. It did so on the basis that TCL knew that the persons concerned were employed by Trailfinders and TCL in a brochure issued to potential franchisees had stated 'if you're coming from a travel background already, feel free to bring your old customer contact list along with you'.

TCL appealed. The Court of Appeal dismissed the appeal on the basis that TCL ought to have known that it was in receipt of confidential information and accordingly had an equitable obligation of confidence, which it had infringed.

Both parties agreed that the test is that set out in *Primary Group (UK) Ltd v Royal Bank of Scotland plc.*[9] Specifically, an equitable obligation of confidence arises where

---

[8]   *Trailfinders Ltd v Travel Counsellors Ltd* [2021] EWCA Civ 38, [2021] IRLR 450. See *Arthur Cox Employment Law Yearbook 2020* at **[1.06]** for High Court of England and Wales decision in *Trailfinders Ltd v Travel Counsellors Ltd* [2020] IRLR 448.

[9]   *Primary Group (UK) Ltd v Royal Bank of Scotland plc* [2014] EWHC 1082 (Ch), [2014] RPC 26.

confidential information is disclosed in breach of an obligation of confidence and the recipient knew or had notice that that was the case; and also where confidential information was received, without being disclosed as a breach of confidence and where the recipient knew or had notice that the information was confidential.

Whether the recipient has notice is to be determined in an objective manner by reference to what a reasonable person in the position of the recipient would conclude. The Court of Appeal concluded that a reasonable person in TCL's position, if aware that the information was likely to be confidential would have made enquiries with regard to its provenance and TCL did not do so. Had it done so, it would have discovered that the information was confidential to Trailfinders. It was clear that the list of 313 customers must have come from a Trailfinders database and could not have been based on the recollection of the relevant employee. Accordingly the appeal was dismissed.

DISCIPLINARY PROCEDURE

[1.06] *Burn v Alder Hey Children's NHS Foundation Trust[10]—High Court of England and Wales (QB)—Thornton J—disciplinary procedure*

The claimant was employed by the defendant as a consultant paediatric neurosurgeon. She had been restricted from clinical duties while an internal investigation was conducted into allegations about her behaviour and clinical decision-making in relation to a patient who died (Patient A). The investigation was being conducted in line with the Maintaining High Professional Standards Policy (the MHPS Policy). This claim concerns the conduct of the disciplinary proceedings.

The Court set out the issues as follows:

1. Did the claimant have a contractual right under the MHPS Policy and/or under terms implied by law, notably the implied duty of mutual trust and confidence, to be consulted by the investigator about information gathered for the investigation; and be provided with the documents sought, before being interviewed about her treatment of Patient A under the investigation?
2. Did the defendant breach the terms of the claimant's contract by not consulting with her; not providing her with the documents she sought on grounds of their not being relevant; and by telling her that if she refused to be interviewed without sight of the documents, the investigation would conclude without her?
3. Did the investigator have discretion to decide on the relevance of the documents sought, and if so, did the investigator exercise that discretion lawfully?

Following the death of the patient there were a number of reviews and a number of meetings with the deceased patient's parents. In January 2020, an investigation was initiated and the claimant was informed that her duties would be restricted pending the

---

10   *Burn v Alder Hey Children's NHS Foundation Trust* [2021] EWHC 1674 (QB).

internal investigation. When the claimant was asked to attend a meeting to discuss the events in June 2020, her representative said she was not in a position to attend, as her representative did 'not consider that Ms Burn has received copies of all the necessary documentation to enable her to provide a meaningful response to all of the concerns raised'.

In its initial observation, the Court noted the defendant's internal disciplinary process was not 'an adjudicative process concerned with the determination of legal rights, such as occurs in a court or tribunal'. The reason for such process is for an employer to determine if the employee has breached their contract or acted in an inappropriate way, and if so, how their employment relationship should proceed.

Where the disciplinary process, such as the MHPS Policy in this case, has been contractually agreed, there is a 'panoply of safeguards' which are designed to ensure the employer 'has a duty to act fairly'.

The Court pointed out that the disciplinary proceedings in this case were 'in their infancy' and that there were safeguards protecting the claimant, including the 'opportunity to see any correspondence relating to the case'. It was not the Court's function to micromanage employment procedures and it was in the public interest to let the internal processes 'run their course'.

The Court considered the meaning of the words 'correspondence' and 'relating to the case' and found that they did impose a test of relevance. It concluded that it was the role of the investigator and not the Court to decide the issue of relevance. The MHPS Policy allowed the investigator a wide measure of discretion in conducting the investigation and the burden of proof lay with the claimant to prove that the investigator's exercise of that discretion 'lacked rationality'. The Court concluded:

> The defendant's decision not to disclose the documents sought did not breach the express terms of the claimant's contract. Nor was there a breach of the implied term of trust and confidence. The decision of the case investigator as to the relevance of the correspondence sought is primarily a matter for her discretion, subject to rationality review by the courts. There was no breach of any requirement to consult with the claimant about the information to be collected for the investigation and it has not therefore been necessary to consider the contractual status of the provision. The question of relief does not arise.

INTELLECTUAL PROPERTY

[1.07] *Penhallurick v MD5 Ltd[11]—High Court of England and Wales (Intellectual Property Enterprise Court)—Hacon J—Copyright, Designs and Patents Act 1988, s 11(2)—intellectual property rights—copyright—contract of employment*

This case concerned a claim for copyright infringement by the claimant who was employed by the respondent as a computer forensic analyst from November 2006.

---

[11]   *Penhallurick v MD5 Ltd* [2021] EWHC 293 (IPEC).

Prior to that (between 2002 and 2005) the claimant completed a master's degree at Cranfield University, during which time he developed a method of analysing the contents of the hard drive of a computer without damaging or corrupting the hard drive. He called this technique 'Virtual Forensic Computing' (VFC).

The method of analysis developed by the claimant was a manual one, however the claimant claimed that during 2005 and 2006 he also began to write software which would allow a computer to perform VFC automatically and began working on a graphical user interface and a user manual. By 2007 the claimant had created software that allowed a computer to perform VFC automatically and included a graphical user interface (known as 'VFC version 1').

The respondent submitted that this software, and the later versions which built on it, were all developed in the course of the claimant's duties. Accordingly, the respondent asserted ownership of the copyright in eight 'works' relating to the VFC software. The claimant claimed that VFC version 1 incorporated code written before his employment with the respondent and also that his work on the software and the later versions was done outside the scope of his employment, using his own computer and time at home. Accordingly, the claimant disputed the respondent's claim to ownership in the works.

In support of its claim, the respondent also relied on the fact that it had entered into an agreement with the claimant in 2008 (November 2008 Agreement) under which the claimant was given an annual bonus of 7.5% of the yearly sales of VFC software by the respondent. This agreement contained language recognising that the software developed by the claimant and sold by the respondent as VFC was the sole property of the respondent.

In addition, the respondent submitted that the claimant was estopped from denying the respondent's title to the software as he had made repeated representations to the respondent that it owned the software, which it relied on to its detriment by compensating the claimant above his normal remuneration and allowing him to work on the software instead of performing other duties.

While the Court held that the first and second works (ie the code the claimant developed before he began his employment with the respondent) were not relevant to the claimant's claim as they were created before his employment, it held that the respondent was entitled to ownership of the copyright in the remaining six works.

In so holding, the Court noted that the third to eighth works were created while the claimant was employed by the respondent, and so ownership turned on whether the works were created 'in the course of his employment' within the meaning of s 11(2) of the Copyright, Designs and Patents Act 1988. In examining whether the works were created in the course of the claimant's employment, the Court held that the fact that an employee might have worked on a work in their own time and/or using their own equipment did not displace the 'strong and primary indication' that it was work done in the course of their employment. Further, the Court held that the fact that work may have been done at home was not relevant to the analysis of whether it was done 'in the course of employment'.

In respect of the November 2008 Agreement, the Court held this was a binding agreement and:

> [I]f MD5 had not already been entitled to first ownership of the copyrights in the VFC software by reason of its status as Mr Penhallurick's employer, including copyrights in VFC software yet to be written by Mr Penhallurick while he remained employed by MD5, the effect of the November 2008 Agreement would have been to assign those copyrights to MD5. The consideration was the payments made to Mr Penhallurick under the November 2008 Agreement.

The Court held that the respondent was entitled to a declaration of ownership in the copyright in the third to eighth works and the claimant's claim of infringement of copyright was dismissed.

Chapter 2

Covid-19

INTRODUCTION

[2.01]   The Covid-19 pandemic continued into 2021, as Ireland began the year in a national lockdown, at the highest level of national restrictions. The lockdown saw the closure of all non-essential retail and services, restrictions on the movement of people to within 5km of their home and a restriction on household visits. Employees were required to work from home, unless attendance at the workplace was essential for work that was for an essential purpose and could not be done at home.

Adherence to the strict public health guidance, along with the rollout of the Covid-19 vaccine, resulted in a lower incidence of the disease in the community. Consequently, a limited number of restrictions were gradually lifted in March and April 2021, including the relaxation of restrictions to allow for travel within the county, some household visits and the resumption of construction projects.

On 29 April 2021 the Taoiseach, Micheál Martin, announced a re-opening plan which provided for the gradual lifting of the lockdown over the following months. He also noted that the continued rollout of the vaccine was a key priority for the Irish Government.

Restrictions were lifted on a phased basis over the following months, including the re-opening of the retail and hospitality industry, the lifting of restrictions on inter-county travel and an increase in the number of people permitted at gatherings. The gradual return to the workplace began on 20 September 2021.

However, a high incidence of Covid-19 in the community arising from the different variants of the disease saw a surge in cases in October 2021, resulting in new public health advice providing for restrictions on bars and restaurants, updated advice to close contacts and updated guidance on the return to the workplace. From 19 November 2021, all employees were advised to return to working from home unless necessary to attend the workplace in person. This remains the public health advice as at the time of writing.

This year presented many challenges for employers ranging from facilitating the continued remote working of employees to providing for the safe return of employees to the workplace, where permitted under public health advice.

This chapter will offer a brief summary of the continued impact of the Covid-19 pandemic on the Irish workforce, including an overview of the public health advice, the national vaccination rollout, the return of employees to the workplace and the impact of the pandemic on taxes. A brief overview of the first employment law cases from the Irish High Court and the Workplace Relations Commission (WRC) relating to Covid-19 is also provided. See further Covid-19 and Privacy at **[3.14, 3.15]**.[1]

GOVERNMENT GUIDANCE

The Resilience and Recovery 2020–2021: Plan for Living with Covid-19

[2.02]   The Resilience and Recovery 2020–2021: Plan for Living with Covid-19 (the Plan for Living with Covid-19) was published on 15 September 2020. It established the five-level framework for the management of Covid-19 risk in the community, and was intended to apply for 6–9 months from the date of its publication.

The lower levels of the Plan for Living with Covid-19 were activated when the incidence of the disease was low in the community, and the higher levels were used to deal with a higher incidence of the disease. Significantly, under all five levels of the Plan, employees were advised to work from home, with the lower levels advising that 'employees work from home if possible', and level five advising that employees 'work from home unless essential for work which is an essential health, social care or other essential service and cannot be done from home'.

Covid-19 Resilience and Recovery 2021—The Path Ahead

[2.03]   In February 2021, the Irish Government published Covid-19 Resilience and Recovery 2021—The Path Ahead (the Path Ahead Plan) to supplement the Plan for Living with Covid-19. The Path Ahead Plan set out the framework for the reinstatement of in-school education and childcare services in a phased manner from 1 March 2021.

The Path Ahead Plan also provided that when restrictions could be eased, the Irish Government would publish a National Economic Recovery Plan outlining how it will assist people with the return to work, support sectors which have been disproportionately affected by the pandemic, and how emergency supports will be phased out. It also stated that a new Pathways to Work 2021–2025 Strategy would be published, which would focus on assisting people back into employment, training and education as the economy recovers.

---

[1]   Please refer to **[3.14 and 3.15]** in the Data Privacy chapter.

National Economic Recovery Plan 2021

[2.04]   The Irish Government published the National Economic Recovery Plan 2021 in June 2021, which sought to increase job creation and economic growth following the Covid-19 pandemic. There were four pillars to the Economic Recovery Plan:

(a) Sustainable Public Finances;
(b) Helping People Back into Work;
(c) Re-building Sustainable Enterprises; and
(d) A Balanced and Inclusive Recovery.

Under the 'Helping People Back into Work' pillar, the plan detailed measures to actively decrease unemployment, which stood at 22.4% in April 2021. It also outlined the extension of existing emergency pandemic financial supports, such as the Covid Restrictions Support Scheme, the Employment Wage Subsidy Scheme and the Pandemic Unemployment Payment.[2]

Pathways to Work Strategy 2021–2025

[2.05]   The Pathways to Work Strategy 2021–2025 was published in July 2021, and established Ireland's national employment strategy, aiming to 'restore unemployment back to or below its pre-pandemic levels of 2019'. It contained 83 commitments under five Strands of Action from the Irish Government, seeking to reduce long term unemployment, reduce unemployment among the youth of Ireland, and to improve labour market transitions and outcomes.

The five Strands of Action provided the following framework for the achievement of the commitments: working for jobseekers, working for employers, working for work, working for all and working with evidence.

National Vaccine Rollout

[2.06]   The Irish Government published the Covid-19 Vaccine Allocation Strategy (the Allocation Strategy) on 8 December 2020. It was subsequently updated in April 2021. It established a provisional priority list of groups of the population to receive the Covid-19 vaccine. The nine cohorts identified in the Allocation Strategy are as follows:

(a) people aged 65 years and older who are residents of long-term care facilities (likely to include all staff and residents on site);
(b) frontline healthcare workers;
(c) people aged 70 and older;

---

[2]   Please see further at **[2.10]**.

(d) people aged 16–69 with a medical condition that puts them at very high risk of severe disease and death;

(e) people aged 65–69 whose underlying condition puts them at a high risk of severe disease and death;

(f) other people aged 65–69 and key workers essential to the vaccine programme;

(g) people aged 16–64 who have an underlying condition that puts them at high risk of severe disease and death;

(h) residents of long-term care facilities aged 16–64; and

(i) people aged 16–64 living or working in crowded settings, and in parallel, people aged 64 years and younger.

The vaccine was approved for 12–15 year olds on 27 July 2021.

The vaccine rollout began in December 2020, with the first vaccine being administered on 29 December 2020, before the widespread national rollout throughout 2021. The immunisation programme was largely seen as success, with nearly 90% of the eligible population being fully vaccinated as at the time of writing.

Covid-19: Reframing the Challenge, Continuing our Recovery & Reconnecting

[2.07] On 31 August 2021, the Irish Government published the Covid-19: Reframing the Challenge, Continuing our Recovery & Reconnecting (the Reframing the Challenge Plan), which set out its response plan to provide for the phased elimination of Covid-19 public health restrictions. It represented a shift in approach to the management of Covid-19, from an 'emergency footing to managing disease and protecting the most vulnerable', in circumstances where there was a reduction in the disease infection levels in the community, and a considerable uptake of the vaccine.

The Reframing the Challenge Plan provided for a return to the workplace on a 'phased and staggered basis' to commence from 20 September 2021. It advised employers to have long-term blended working and return to work policies in plan, having regard to public health advice. It noted that the Work Safely Protocol would be updated to reflect this.

It provided for the planned lifting of further restrictions from 22 October 2021, including the removal of requirements for physical distancing and cessation of the requirement for certification of immunity or testing being used as a prerequisite for access to, and engagement in, activities and events. It also contained updated guidance in relation to public transport, indoor and outdoor events and group activities.

On 19 October 2021, the Irish Government issued updated guidance under the Reframing the Challenge Plan, advising that the return to the workplace should continue on a 'phased and cautious basis for specific business requirements'. It was also announced that sector-specific guidance and protocols, including those regarding workplaces, would be reviewed and strengthened where appropriate.

On 18 November 2021, following a press conference held by the Taoiseach on 16 November, the Irish Government announced that, with effect from midnight 18 November 2021, employees should work from home unless it is necessary to attend the workplace in person. This effectively resulted in a return to the situation on working from home as it applied before 20 September 2021, ie, employees to work from home unless necessary to attend the workplace. This remains the advice as at the time of writing.

RETURN TO WORK

Covid-19 Work Safely Protocol

[2.08]   In November 2020, the Irish Government published the Work Safely Protocol to assist employers and workers in working together to suppress Covid-19 in the workplace by setting out health and safety practices and procedures to be implemented in the workplace.

The focus of the Work Safely Protocol was on the need for continued monitoring and review of workplace health and safety practice and procedures to manage and reduce the risk of Covid-19 in the workplace. It detailed the minimum public health infection prevention and control (IPC) measures required to be taken by employers and workers, in every place of work, to prevent and reduce the spread of Covid-19.

A revised version of the Work Safely Protocol was published in December 2020 and again in May 2021. The revised version of May 2021 contained more substantive changes introduced in line with updated public health guidance, including:

(a) **Additional IPC Measures**: It explored the practical and technical steps employers should take before establishing an Antigen Diagnostic Test or Rapid Antigen Diagnostic Tests regime in the workplace.
(b) **Vaccination**: In the context of the National Vaccination Roll Out Strategy, it detailed the significant role the Covid-19 vaccine plays in relation to the management and control of Covid-19 in the workplace. It noted that while the decision to get the vaccine is an employee's own individual choice, employers may wish to provide advice and information to employees in order to allow employees make an informed decision about vaccination, to encourage employees to consider the vaccine, and ultimately increase the uptake.
(c) **Occupational Health and Safety Measures**: In line with updated public health advice, it addressed the fundamental role that proper ventilation has in controlling and reducing the risks associated with Covid-19 in the workplace.

The following further revisions of the Work Safely Protocol were published:

(a) **September 2021**: This version of the Work Safely Protocol was updated to reflect updated public health advice, which provided that attendance at work for specific business requirements could commence on a phased and staggered basis. It advised employers to engage with staff in order to finalise their long-term arrangements for blended or remote working. Other key changes included updated advice regarding business travel, and best practice on the implementation of Covid-19 mitigation and prevention measures, including recommendations about the use of hand sanitisers, CO_2 monitors and cleaning agents.

(b) **October 2021**: There were no substantive changes contained in this version of the Work Safely Protocol, which stated that that the IPC measures as previously set out would continue for the foreseeable future. It was updated to reflect the public health advice at the time of its publication, noting that the return to workplaces should continue on a phased and cautious basis appropriate to each sector and for specific business requirements. It further advised that any such return should have regard to appropriate attendance levels, with the use of staggered arrangements such as non-fulltime attendance and flexible working hours.

(c) **November 2021**: The Work Safely Protocol was updated in November 2021. There were no substantive changes implemented, save for an update to reflect the public health advice that all employees should work from home unless it was necessary to attend in person. It also contained updated guidance in relation to asymptomatic close contacts.

The Work Safely Protocol is supplemented by guidance from the Labour Employer Economic Forum (the LEEF), which established a consultative stakeholder forum to oversee the implementation of the Work Safely Protocol. The LEEF guidance aims to assist employers and workers in keeping the workplace safe.

Health and Safety Authority

[2.09]   The Health and Safety Authority (the HSA) established a helpful resource on its website for employers and employees, containing guidance in relation to the safe return to the workplace. These resources include a template Covid-19 Response Plan, checklists and online training courses.

UNEMPLOYMENT AND WAGE SUBSIDY SCHEMES[3]

Pandemic Unemployment Payment

[2.10]   The Pandemic Unemployment Payment (the PUP) scheme was introduced on 15 March 2020. It provided for a social welfare payment for employees and self-employed people who, on or after 13 March 2020, lost their employment due to the Covid-19 public health emergency.

It had originally been scheduled to be closed to new applicants from 1 January 2021. This was extended and the scheme was closed to new applicants from 8 July 2021.

---

[3]   Please refer to Chapter 2 of *Arthur Cox Employment Yearbook 2020* for further detail.

As at the time of writing, existing claimants can continue to receive the PUP until such time as the Irish Government indicates otherwise.

The PUP weekly rates from 16 October 2020 to 7 September 2021 were as follows:

Average Weekly Earnings	Personal Rate
€400 or over	€350
€300–€399.99	€300
€200–€299.99	€250
Less than €200	€203

The weekly rates from 7 September 2021 to 9 November 2021 were as follows:

Average Weekly Earnings	Personal Rate
€400 or over	€300
€300–€399.99	€250
€200–€299.99	€203
Less than €200 (and were on the €203 rate of payment)	Moved to jobseeker's terms from 26 October 2021

From 9 November 2021, the PUP weekly rates are as follows:

Average Weekly Earnings	Personal Rate
€400 or over	€250
€300–€399.99	€203
€200–€299.99 Less than €200	Moved to jobseeker's terms on 9 November 2021

At the time of writing, the weekly PUP rates are intended to be as follows, from 8 February 2022:

Average Weekly Earnings	Personal Rate
€400 or over	€203
€300–€399.99 €200–€299.99 Less than €200	Moved to jobseeker's terms

Employment Wage Subsidy Scheme

[2.11]   The Employment Wage Subsidy Scheme (the EWSS) was introduced by s 28 of the Emergency Measures in the Public Interest (Covid-19) Act 2020 on 1 September 2020. The EWSS provides eligible employers with funding of up to 70% of an employee's net pay.

It was originally due to expire on 31 March 2021. This was extended until 30 April 2022 as part of Budget 2022. To avail of the scheme from 1 January 2022 to 30 April 2022, employers must be validly registered on or before 31 December 2021.

Covid-19 Restrictions Support Scheme

[2.12]   The Covid-19 Restrictions Support Scheme (the CRSS) was introduced by the Finance Bill 2020 as an additional support for businesses who were required to temporarily shut due to public health restrictions.

The CRSS was due to expire on 31 March 2021. This was extended and, as at the time of writing, it is due to operate until 31 December 2021.

Enhanced Illness Benefit for Covid-19 Absences

[2.13]   The Covid-19 Enhanced Illness Benefit was introduced in March 2020. It was originally due to operate until 31 March 2021. As per Budget 2022, it has been extended until January 2022.

Any worker who is advised to self-isolate by a medical doctor or who has tested positive for Covid-19 can claim this benefit at a rate of €350 per week. This benefit is also available to the self-employed and workers living in direct provision who are required to self-isolate or who have Covid-19.

SUSPENSION OF ENTITLEMENTS UNDER THE REDUNDANCY PAYMENTS ACTS 1967–2014

[2.14]   Entitlements under the Redundancy Payments Acts 1967–2014 (the RPA) in relation to temporary lay-off and short-time work were suspended by the Emergency Measures in the Public Interest (Covid-19) Act 2020. As a result of this suspension, employees who had been placed on temporary lay-off or short time could not make a claim for a statutory redundancy payment under the RPA.

This suspension was set to expire on 31 March 2021. This was extended to 30 June 2021 and again until 30 September 2021.

Since 30 September 2021, an employee on temporary lay-off or short time can make a claim for a redundancy payment under RPA in the normal course.

REMOTE WORKING

[2.15]   The majority of the workforce in Ireland continued to work remotely during the course of the 2021, in line with public health guidance.

In January 2021, the Making Remote Work: National Remote Work Strategy (the Remote Work Strategy) was published, which reflects the Irish Government's intention to 'ensure remote working is a permanent feature in the Irish workforce' and not simply a feature of life in a pandemic.

The Remote Work Strategy identifies a number of key actions to be taken by the Government in order to promote and facilitate remote working in Ireland, including:

1. mandating that home and remote working should be the norm for 20% of the public sector;
2. investing in remote working hubs across Ireland;
3. accelerating the provision of high-speed broadband throughout the country; and
4. reviewing tax arrangements for remote working and assessing the merits of further enhancement in Budget 2022.

Central to the Remote Work Strategy is the creation of an environment conducive to remote working. The Remote Work Strategy identifies that this environment can be created through the enhancement of employee rights, such as the right to disconnect;[4] and the right to request to work remotely. The Remote Work Strategy identifies the role of enhanced health and safety legislation in creating an environment that is supportive of long-term remote working, and signalled a welcome acceleration of remote working becoming a permanent fixture of the Irish workforce.

Employers also continued to grapple with the increased requests from employees to work remotely from outside of Ireland, and the tax, payroll, data protection and local mandatory employment protection considerations associated with such an arrangement.

INTERNATIONAL TRAVEL

[2.16]   The EU 'traffic lights' approach to travel continued to apply in 2021. This system involves the categorisation of countries as green, orange, red or grey, on the basis of the risk levels associated with Covid-19, and applies to countries in the EU, the EEA and the United Kingdom.

All passengers arriving into Ireland from overseas continue to be obliged to complete a Covid-19 Passenger Locator Form before entry.

In July 2021, in line with the EU, Ireland began operating under the EU Digital Covid Certificate for travel within the EU and the EEA. The EU Digital Covid-19 Certificate is evidence that the holder has been vaccinated against Covid-19, has received a negative Covid-19 test result or has recovered from Covid-19 in the last six months.

WRC AND LABOUR COURT HEARINGS

Virtual Hearings

[2.17]   In January 2021, the Workplace Relations Commission confirmed that all in-person adjudication hearings, conciliation meetings and mediations were postponed for the immediate future.

---

4   Please refer to **[15.67]** (ie, the Right to Disconnect Code in the Legislation Chapter).

Virtual hearings, through the platform Cisco WebEx, continued throughout 2021, in line with public health advice.

On 28 May 2021, the WRC published a notice to all parties, representatives and stakeholders on remote hearings, and confirmed that all cases will be considered amenable to remote hearing, 'unless the parties can demonstrate how holding a remote hearing might not be in the interests of justice or would breach fair procedures, both of which are subject to a high threshold'.

Face-to-face Hearings

[2.18] There was a resumption of face-to-face hearings this year, during the period permitted by public health advice.

In October 2021, the WRC issued guidance for visitors in face-to-face WRC and Labour Court hearings. This guidance stated that starting times of hearings would be staggered to reduce the possibility of congestion at the venue on any hearing day. Each hearing is allocated a time slot of 2.5 hours in duration. Hearing rooms may not contain more than 80% of persons permitted under HSA/HSE Social Distancing Guidelines.

Furthermore, each party is limited to three people in attendance at the hearing—including the named party, the representative(s) and/or witnesses. This means that where there are additional witnesses or party members they have to remain in the immediate vicinity outside the building until required.

WRC Inspections

[2.19] The WRC issued a notice on 8 July 2021 stating that WRC Inspectors were currently carrying out a programme of workplace inspections to monitor and give guidance to employers regarding obligations under the Work Safely Protocol.

COVID-19 AND EMPLOYMENT TAXES

[2.20] Revenue released online guidance throughout the course of 2020 detailing certain temporary measures and concessions in response to various issues arising out of the Covid-19 pandemic. Whereas some of these continue to be relevant,[5] it should be noted that certain of these temporary measures and concessions have ceased to apply. These measures as well as certain additional confirmations are noted below.

---

[5]   As to which we refer to Chapter 2 of the *Arthur Cox Employment Law Yearbook 2020.*

BENEFIT IN KIND

Tax treatment of reimbursements by an employer to an employee regarding holiday/flight cancellations or in relation to costs of assisting employees returning to the State

[2.21]   In 2020, Revenue allowed a concession on the tax treatment of reimbursements by an employer to an employee regarding:

— holiday and flight cancellations; and

— costs of assisting employees returning to the State.

No benefit in kind charge arose in 2020, provided that certain conditions were met.

Revenue have confirmed that this concessionary measure ceased to apply on 31 December 2020. From 1 January 2021 the provisions relating to costs of non-business travel apply in the usual manner.

Seasonal Parties

[2.22]   Revenue has confirmed that a benefit in kind charge will not arise where an employer incurs reasonable costs in hosting a virtual seasonal party for employees. Such reasonable costs include costs typically incurred in hosting a face-to-face event. This includes the cost of delivering or providing food and drink to the employees in advance of or during the event. Vouchers provided to employees to purchase food or drink for the event are not included. Such vouchers will be taxable unless they are covered by the Small Benefit Exemption. The event must be open to all employees.

Share Schemes Filing Obligations

[2.23]   The filing deadline for the 2020 Form ESA was extended to 14 September 2021 in recognition of the fact that this was the first year for filing this form. Note that Revenue has indicated that for subsequent years, the reporting date of 31 March following the relevant tax year will apply.

Special Assignee Relief Programme (SARP)

[2.24]   In 2020, the 90-day employer filing obligation, which is a requirement for an employee to be eligible to benefit from SARP relief, was extended for a further 60 days. Revenue stated that they anticipated that such an extension should provide sufficient time for employers to file the required return, but also clarified that exceptional cases may be submitted to Revenue for consideration on a case-by-case basis.

Revenue has confirmed that this concessionary measure ceased to apply on 31 December 2020. From 1 January 2021, all SARP 1A forms must be filed within the 90-day timeframe in the usual manner.

PAYE Dispensation Applications—Short-term Business Travellers

[2.25]　In 2020, given the unprecedented circumstances and the restrictions on travel as a consequence of Covid-19, Revenue confirmed that it would not strictly enforce the 30-day notification requirement for PAYE dispensations applicable to short-term business travellers from countries with which Ireland has a double taxation treaty and who were going to spend in excess of 60 workdays in the State in a tax year.

Revenue has confirmed that this concessionary measure ceased to apply on 31 December 2020. From 1 January 2021, the normal 30-day notification timeframe applies. Exceptional cases may be notified to Revenue as required.

Foreign Employments—Operation of PAYE

[2.26]　In 2020, Revenue stated that they would not seek to enforce Irish payroll obligations for foreign employers in genuine cases where an employee was working abroad for a foreign entity prior to Covid-19 but relocated temporarily to the State during the Covid-19 period and performed duties for his or her foreign employer while in the State.

Revenue has confirmed that this concessionary measure ceased to apply on 31 December 2020. From 1 January 2021 employers are required to operate PAYE on such employments in the usual manner.

PAYE Exclusion Order—Irish Contract of Employment

[2.27]　Regarding employees who are working abroad for a foreign employer under an Irish contract of employment where a PAYE exclusion order is in place, Revenue confirmed that, for the tax year 2020, the position would not be adversely impacted where the employee worked more than 30 days in the State due to Covid-19.

Revenue has confirmed that concessionary measures ceased to apply on 31 December 2020. From 1 January 2021 employers are required to operate PAYE on such employments in the usual manner.

Multi-state Workers

[2.28]　In response to the Covid-19 pandemic, Revenue confirmed that, for the tax year 2020, a foreign employer was permitted to continue to operate Irish payroll on the basis of a non-resident employee's established work pattern pre-Covid-19 where the employee could not return to the foreign jurisdiction as a result of the travel restrictions imposed by Covid-19 where certain conditions were satisfied.

Revenue has confirmed that this concessionary measure ceased to apply on 31 December 2020. From 1 January 2021 employers are required to operate PAYE on such employments in the usual manner.

Exemption in Respect of Re-training Costs as Part of a Redundancy Package

[2.29]   Where an employer pays the cost of re-training an employee as part of a redundancy package, the cost of re-training up to a maximum of €5,000 is exempt from income tax by virtue of s 201 of the Taxes Consolidation Act 1997, provided a number of conditions are satisfied. One such condition is that the re-training is completed within six months of the termination of employment. In 2020, having regard to the Covid-19 restrictions in place at that time, Revenue acknowledged that it may not have been possible to satisfy this condition. Therefore, where a termination took place during the Covid-19 crisis, Revenue was willing to extend this exemption once the re-training took place within six months of the required course/training becoming available following the end of the Covid-19 crisis.

Revenue has confirmed that this concessionary measure ceased to apply on 1 May 2021. From 2 May 2021, the individual must complete re-training within the usual six-month timeframe to avail of this exemption.

COVID-19 CASE LAW

Medical Profession

[2.30]   *Medical Council v Waters[6]—High Court—Irvine J—Medical Practitioners Act 2007, s 60—suspension from register of medical practitioners—Covid-19*

This case concerned an application by the Medical Council to suspend the defendant's registration from the Register of Medical Practitioners under s 60 of the Medical Practitioners Act 2007 (the 2007 Act) on an interim basis.

The defendant is a general practitioner. The Medical Council received a complaint from one of the defendant's patients regarding the defendant's attitude to, and opinions regarding, Covid-19, including alleging that the defendant subjected the complainant to a 'barrage of nonsense about the "hoax that is Covid-19"'; how 'the state and the government are scamming the people'; and how 'the wearing of masks was causing illness'.

---

[6]   *Medical Council v Waters* [2021] IEHC 252.

When notified of the complaint by the Medical Council, the defendant provided a lengthy response wherein he further expounded on his views on Covid-19, including the belief 'that the Covid 19 lockdown has caused considerably more damage to patients and the people of the country than Covid 19 virus, which is now generally accepted worldwide to have a pathogenicity and mortality similar to a winter flu' and that there was a 'propaganda machine worthy of Goebbels' surrounding Covid-19. The defendant followed up his response with additional emails referencing various articles, publications other documents supporting his views.

Over a series of letters exchanged between the defendant and the Medical Council from December–January 2021, the Medical Council sought assurances that the defendant would follow HSE guidance and best practice regarding public health measures. Those assurances were not forthcoming.

In February 2021, it was reported in an article in *The Irish Times* and on RTÉ's 'Live Line' radio programme that the defendant would not administer the Covid-19 vaccine and the defendant confirmed this in a fax to the HSE. When contacted by the HSE with a request to provide the name, address, date of birth, contact number and email addresses of his patients aged 70 and over, those details were not forthcoming.

The defendant was called to a meeting of the Medical Council wherein he reiterated his views on Covid-19 and confirmed that his practice did not comply with public health measures, including the wearing of masks.

The Medical Council brought an application under s 60 of the 2007 Act for an interim suspension of the defendant from the Register of Medical Practitioners. Section 60 allows the Medical Council to bring such an application 'if the Council considers that the suspension is necessary to protect the public until steps or further steps are taken'.

The Medical Council acknowledged that when invited, the defendant had signalled that he would undertake to cooperate with the HSE regarding the vaccination of patients and to refer Covid-19 patients to other general practitioners and not to share his personal views of Covid-19. However, the Council said that these proposed undertakings did not sufficiently protect the public.

The Court examined the case law on s 60, and noted that in *O'Ceallaigh v An Bord Altranais*,[7] the Supreme Court held that the criteria to be examined in applications under s 60 are:

(a)   the seriousness of the conduct complained of;
(b)   the strength of the case against the practitioner; and
(c)   whether the likely outcome, in terms of sanction, in the event of the misconduct being established would be a strike off either on a definite or permanent basis.

The Court noted that such an order could have significant adverse consequences for the medical practitioner in question, in terms of their livelihood and reputation. As such, before granting any such application the Court must be satisfied that the suspension

---

[7]   *O'Ceallaigh v An Bord Altranais* [2000] 4 IR 54.

is necessary in order to protect the public and must balance the constitutional right of the practitioner to earn a living against the right of the public to be protected from a practitioner who poses a risk to their care and welfare.

Applying the criteria listed in *O'Ceallaigh* to the facts of the case, the Court found the defendant's practices, most notably his failure to refer patients for Covid-19 testing and his failure to carry on his practice in compliance with public health guidelines (eg, regarding social distancing and the wearing of masks) posed significant risk to the public. It found that this risk, coupled with his unwillingness to remedy the situation and remove his patients from unnecessary risk, meant that it was 'likely that if found guilty of professional misconduct it is reasonable to conclude that he would be struck off the register either for a definite period or on a permanent basis', which satisfied the requirements under s 60. Further, the Court held that the undertakings offered by the defendant were not satisfactory so as to permit the Court to impose any less restrictive measures.

The Court found that the fact that the Medical Council had not acted with the utmost urgency in bringing the application was not fatal to the application as 'the significance of those risks cannot be determined by the speed with which the application is brought'. It also found that the adverse effects of the order on the defendant would be limited in view of his age (71), meaning that it would not have the same financial impact on him as on a medical practitioner in the early stages of their career; noting also that the defendant had not advanced any case of financial hardship. The Court held that 'a suspension, although carrying with it serious negative consequences for the Respondent, is not disproportionate in the circumstances' and granted the order sought.

Dismissal

[2.31] *An Operations Coordinator v A Facilities Management Service Provider[8]— Workplace Relations Commission—Safety, Health and Welfare at Work Act 2005— constructive dismissal—health and safety—Covid-19—sharing an office—working from home*

The claimant was employed as an operations coordinator by a facilities management company responsible for the management of student residences on a university campus. The claimant was one of three operations coordinators. Their role involved checking students in and managing front-of-house staff. The three coordinators shared an office with the university's accommodation manager.

In March 2020, as a result of the Covid-19 pandemic, only 10% of the student population remained in the residences. Some of these students had to self-isolate and have food brought to their rooms. On 18 April 2020, the claimant went on certified sick leave and returned to work on 11 May 2020. She resigned the following day.

---

[8]   *An Operations Coordinator v A Facilities Management Service Provider* ADJ-00028293.

Prior to her resignation, the claimant and her two colleagues, all of whom had family members in the 'at risk' category living at home with them, sought permission from the respondent to work from home. They suggested a rotating system, whereby one of them would be in the office each day, with the others working from home. They contended their work could be done from home. The respondent facilities management company refused the request. They were provided with letters from the respondent and the university confirming that they were essential workers, which they could use to travel to work during Government travel restrictions. The claimant alleged that they never received any document relating to health and safety guidelines implemented by the respondent in response to the pandemic.

Evidence was given at the hearing that the three operations coordinators had raised concerns about Covid-19 in the early weeks of the pandemic. On 30 April 2020, they each submitted a formal grievance asking that their concerns relating to Covid-19 be addressed and that their request to work in rotation be considered. They pointed out that the client's (the university) staff were permitted to work from home. They claimed the office they shared did not have enough room to allow for social distancing and that their concerns were brought to the respondent's attention numerous times but nothing was done.

In its response of 4 May 2020, the respondent stated the roles were not suitable for home working. The respondent also said that it had taken Covid-19 precautions, which included dispatching two senior managers to the site, providing personal protective equipment (PPE), changing the physical layout of the office, installing screens, warning tape and moving desks. Photographs of the claimant's office were submitted as evidence by both the claimant and the respondent.

The Adjudication Officer found the three operations coordinators' roles were interchangeable and that all three were not always required on the site at the same time, as the coordinator on site could discharge the staff management functions. Another important function, which involved access to emails and IT systems, could be effectively managed remotely, using a laptop which had been supplied by the client university.

The respondent argued that the client university required the claimant to be on site, but the Adjudication Officer noted that staff of other outsourced providers worked from home during the period. It was also noted that the university's own staff, including the individual who shared an office with the coordinators, worked from home. The university provided laptops for the coordinators, which clearly suggested that it intended them to be used to facilitate working from home.

The Adjudication Officer stated that, as an infectious disease, Covid-19 constituted a biological hazard. An employer's duties under the Safety, Health and Welfare at Work Act 2005 (the 2005 Act) and the general principles underpinning health and safety were central to the claimant's claim.

Referring to s 8 of the 2005 Act, the Adjudication Officer noted that it requires employers to ensure, in so far as reasonably practicable, the safety, health and welfare of employees at work and to provide safe systems of work. The general principles of health and safety are set out in the third Schedule of the 2005 Act. Section 19 of the

2005 Act requires the employer to prepare a written risk assessment of hazards, including any unusual risks to a particular employee.

The Adjudication Officer noted that the:

> health and safety duties imposed on employer and employee [in s 13 of the 2005 Act] are an implied term in every contract of employment. Through the contract of employment, employers and employees are bound to comply with the statutory regime and relevant health and safety policies.

Applying the general principles, the Adjudication Officer said the most effective way of addressing the risk was to eliminate it, while the use of PPE was a last resort and was the least effective measure.

The Adjudication Officer referred to both the 'contract test' and the 'reasonableness test' for constructive dismissal claims as established by *Western Excavating (ECC) Ltd v Sharp*[9] and *Conway v Ulster Bank*,[10] and found that the question was whether the claimant was constructively dismissed, either following a repudiation of her contract of employment or if it was reasonable for her to resign.

The Adjudication Officer noted that the proposal of the coordinators that they rotate attendance at the office was not even trialled by the respondent. Rotating the work would have eliminated the risk of transmission between the three coordinators and would have reduced the risk between them and others working on the campus; nor was there any objection from the client university to the proposal to rotate attendance at the workplace. In fact, the proposal was facilitated by the client, which had provided laptops.

The Adjudication Officer concluded that the respondent did not adequately consider mitigation of the risk and this amounted to a repudiation of the employment contract by the respondent, entitling the claimant to resign.

In upholding the claimant's claim for constructive dismissal, the Adjudication Officer noted that the claimant took up new employment five weeks after her resignation on higher pay than in her previous role, and awarded her five weeks' loss of wages covering the period from when she was constructively dismissed to when she took up new employment, amounting €3,712.50.

Temporary Wage Subsidy Scheme

[2.32] *A Financial Controller v A Hotel*[11]*—Workplace Relations Commission— Payment of Wages Act 1991—Emergency Measures in the Public Interest (Covid-19) Act 2020—Temporary Wage Subsidy Scheme—unlawful deduction*

The claimant was employed by the respondent as a financial controller. The claimant brought a complaint under the Payment of Wages Act 1991 (the 1991 Act) in respect

---

9   *Western Excavating (ECC) Ltd v Sharp* [1978] IRLR 27.
10 *Conway v Ulster Bank* UD474/1981.
11 *A Financial Controller v A Hotel* ADJ-0003054.

of the manner in which the respondent applied a deduction to his gross pay for the purposes of the Temporary Wage Subsidy Scheme (TWSS).

The claimant objected to the adjustment of his gross pay, such that his net pay would remain the same, before the implementation of the TWSS.

The claimant noted that he would receive a non-taxable amount in his weekly wages while the company was in receipt of the TWSS, such that, at the end of the tax year, the claimant would have a tax liability. The claimant contended that if he had continued to receive his full gross pay for the relevant period, although he would have received an increase in net pay, such increase could have been used by the claimant to pay the tax due to the Revenue Commissioners as a result of the application of the TWSS.

The claimant referred to a 10% pay reduction for the months of May, June and July and confirmed that he had consented to same, but did not give the respondent permission to reduce his gross pay for the purposes of the TWSS.

The respondent referred to the Emergency Measures in the Public Interest (Covid-19) Act 2020 (the 2020 Act) and the provisions in relation to the calculation of the TWSS and stated that payments made under the TWSS to employees are taxable in the hands of the employee, but are not subject to payroll tax deductions by the employer. The respondent also contended that the TWSS had a stated purpose of supplementing net weekly pay.

The respondent stated that it was clear from s 28(18) of the 2020 Act that any tax liability arising from the respondent's application of the TWSS would lie with the claimant. The respondent stated that there was no contravention of the 1991 Act, and that the respondent was required to reduce the claimant's gross pay in order to comply with the Revenue Commissioners' guidance in availing of necessary financial support during the pandemic.

Additionally, the respondent contended that the reduction in the claimant's gross wage was required such that the respondent did not increase the claimant's net wages through the application of the TWSS, which it was prohibited from doing.

The Adjudication Officer noted that the pay reduction in May, June and July was consented to by the claimant and was therefore outside of the scope of the complaint.

In respect of the reduction in the claimant's gross wages, the Adjudication Officer noted that the respondent had argued that no evidence of loss was presented by the claimant, and that to the extent that the claimant had a revenue liability, a statement of liability would have been available from the Revenue Commissioners in respect of the TWSS at that point.

The Adjudication Officer found that the respondent had ensured that there was no deficit in net pay to the claimant and the claimant had not produced evidence of a deduction having been made. The deduction in the claimant's gross pay was authorised by statute.

The Adjudication Officer also found that the claimant's assertion that he was entitled to an increase in net pay in order to defray the costs of a potential tax liability was unsustainable as such would have resulted in an increase in the claimant's net pay and could not be deemed to be 'wages property payable'.

The claimant's complaint was not upheld.

Unpaid Layoff/Covid-19

[2.33] *A Production Operator v Manufacturing Company[12]—Workplace Relations Commission—Payment of Wages Act 1991—short time—implied by custom and practice*

The claimant was employed as a production operator by the respondent. In March 2019, the claimant was advised that she was being put on short time due to a supply chain delay. As such, the claimant's hours of work were reduced below her contracted 39 hours per week.

The claimant received payment in respect of hours worked, as opposed to contracted hours, and alleged this constituted an unlawful deduction contrary to the Payment of Wages Act 1991. The claimant's contract of employment did not provide for a reduction in pay during any period of short time.

The respondent contended that there was a term implied in the claimant's contract by custom and practice and/or by prior agreement that allowed for payment in respect of hours worked.

The respondent referred to a period of short time working in 2008 and 2009 during which time the claimant was on short time, but no issues in relation to payment were raised by the claimant or her trade union. The claimant alleged that short time working during this period was under protest, and also alleged that the respondent introduced express contractual provisions permitting lay off and short time into employment contracts after that date. A witness for the respondent denied that such clauses were introduced in response to trade union protestations, but instead claimed that it was to cover expected volatility in production demands due to new products and systems.

The respondent's stated position was that the claimant was entitled to be paid only for the actual number of hours worked. As such, when the claimant's weekly working hours were reduced from a five-day week to a three-day week, the claimant was entitled to receive payment only in respect of the days on which she worked.

The Adjudication Officer noted that the respondent had contended there was no deduction, as the claimant was being paid for the hours worked. The Adjudication Officer examined the phrase 'properly payable' and considered *Lawe v Irish Country (Pig Meats) Ltd*[13] in which White J held: 'An employer's fundamental obligation is to pay the agreed remuneration for the times of work during which the employee is prepared to work.'

---

12   *A Production Operator v Manufacturing Company* ADJ-00023697.
13   *Lawe v Irish Country (Pig Meats) Ltd* (1998) 9 ELR 266.

The Adjudication Officer found that it was clear that the claimant was prepared to work in this instance, and therefore the existence of an implied contractual term permitting unpaid short time fell to be considered. The Adjudication Officer considered the UK EAT decision in *International Packaging Corporation (UK) Ltd v Balfour Reduction.*[14] Notably, the EAT found that:

> a reduction in working hours is plainly a variation of a contract of employment and, unless expressly catered for within that contract, or allowed by implication again within the terms of the contract, any actual deduction of wages, even if related to the hours worked, is not authorised by the statute and can only be achieved by agreement.

In light of the *Lawe* and *International Packaging Corporation* decisions, the Adjudication Officer found that the obvious purpose of s 5 of the Payment of Wages Act 1991 was to prevent an employer from reducing wages in the absence of an express contractual term or implied term permitting the employer to do so.

The Adjudication Officer preferred the claimant's evidence in relation to the introduction of the short time and lay off clause, ie that the reason for the introduction was 'in response to the contractual deficit which became glaringly obvious in the dispute that ensued prior to the onset of short-time working in 2009'.

In relation to there being a custom and practice of short-time working, the Adjudication Officer noted that the respondent submitted no reasonable evidence to prove the existence of such a term. On that basis, the Adjudication Officer concluded that no implied term existed, or could be construed, in the claimant's contract of employment to authorise the deduction.

The Adjudication Officer found that the wages properly payable were the 39-hour week referred to in the contract of employment and ordered that the respondent pay the claimant such sum, less any payment received by the claimant from the Department of Social Protection during the relevant period.

LEGISLATION

[2.34]   *SI 572/2020 Social Welfare (Consolidated Claims, Payments and Control) (Amendment) (No. 15) (Covid-19 Pandemic Unemployment Payment – New Band of Payment and Reference Period) Regulations 2020*

These Regulations were made under the Social Welfare (Covid-19) (Amendment) Act 2020 and specify a variation in the reference period for calculating of reckonable earnings of employed contributors to take account of people who have lost employment due to the public health crisis caused by Covid-19 and to specify an additional band for people who became unemployed as a result of the public health crisis caused by Covid-19 whose average weekly earnings were previously €400 or more.

---

14   *International Packaging Corporation (UK) Ltd v Balfour Reduction* UKEAT31/02/2310.

SI 573/2020 Social Welfare (Consolidated Claims, Payments and Control) (Amendment) (No. 16) (Covid-19 Pandemic Unemployment Payment – Ancillary Provisions) Regulations 2020

These Regulations provide: (i) for ancillary matters arising from the insertion by the Social Welfare (Covid-19) (Amendment) Act 2020 of provisions dealing with the Covid-19 pandemic unemployment payment into the Social Welfare Consolidation Act 2005; (ii) that as respects the prescribed time for making a claim for Covid-19 pandemic unemployment payment and the circumstances under which late claims may be accepted, the same provisions will apply as apply to jobseeker's benefit; and (iii) that where a decision made by a deciding officer relates to the non-approval of a claim for the Covid-19 pandemic unemployment payment, or the rate at which the Covid-19 pandemic unemployment payment is paid is less than the maximum rate, the claimant must be advised of the decision in writing and the reasons for that decision.

The Regulations also specify the social welfare payments which may be paid concurrently with Covid-19 pandemic unemployment payment.

SI 574/2020 Social Welfare (Consolidated Claims, Payments and Control) (Amendment) (No. 17) (Persons Regarded as Genuinely Seeking Employment) Regulations 2020

These Regulations make provisions in relation to the impact on employers and employees arising out of public health restrictions related to Covid-19. The Regulations define the concept of persons regarded as genuinely seeking employment.

The Regulations also outline factors to be considered in determining whether a person has taken steps which are reasonable in the circumstances:

— where a person's occupation immediately prior to the onset of Covid-19 was an occupation where, due to Covid-19 the opportunity to work in the person's normal occupation is temporarily curtailed; and

— where the person has a reasonable expectation of returning to that occupation within a period of 12 months,

such persons will not be required to seek employment outside of that occupation or employment for the period during which they are in receipt of Covid-19 pandemic unemployment payment.

SI 685/2020—Public Service Pay and Pensions Act 2017 (Section 42) (Payments to General Practitioners) (Amendment) (No. 2) Regulations 2020

These Regulations apply to payments to be made in respect of services rendered by a general practitioner to or on behalf of the Health Service Executive under and in accordance with the terms of the General Medical Services Scheme and the National Immunisation Programmes.

SI 50/2021 Emergency Measures in the Public Interest (Covid-19) Act 2021 (Covid-19: Employment Wage Subsidy Scheme) (Date Adjustment) (No. 2) Order 2021

This Order is made under the powers conferred on the Minister for Finance under s 28B(21)(aa) of the Emergency Measures in the Public Interest (Covid-19) Act 2020.

This Order extends the date on which the Employment Wage Subsidy Scheme will end to 30 June 2021.

SI 220/2021 Taxes Consolidation Act 1997 (Covid Restrictions Support Scheme) (Date Adjustment) Order 2021

This Order is made pursuant to the powers vested in the Minister for Finance under subs (2)(a)(ii) of s 484 of the Taxes Consolidation Act 1997. The Order extends the Covid Restrictions Support Scheme to 30 June 2021.

SI 231/2021 Safety, Health and Welfare At Work (Chemical Agents) (Amendment) Regulations 2021

These Regulations give further effect to Directive 98/24/EC, Directive 2000/39/EC, Directive 2006/15/EC, Directive 2009/161/EU, Directive (EU) 2017/164 and Directive (EU) 2019/1831.

SI 241/2021 Health Act 1947 (Exempted Traveller) (Covid-19) (Amendment) (No. 6) Regulations 2021

These Regulations are made under ss 5, 31A and 38G of the Health Act 1947 as amended. They amend SI 134/2021 to exempt persons providing essential services from the requirement to undergo mandatory quarantine in a designated facility.

SI 276/2021 Health Act 1947 (Section 31A – Temporary Restrictions) (Covid-19) (Restrictions upon Travel to the State from Certain States) (No. 5) (Amendment) Regulations 2021

These Regulations amend the Health Act 1947 (Section 31A – Temporary Restrictions) (Covid-19) (Restrictions upon Travel to the State from Certain States) (No. 5) Regulations 2021. These Regulations include those carrying out essential repair and maintenance within the scope of essential workers who are exempted from travel restrictions imposed under SI 135/2021.

SI 284/2021 Redundancy Payments Act 1967 (Section 12A(2)) (Covid-19) (No. 2) Order 2021

This Order extended, until 30 September 2021, the emergency period during which s 12 of the Redundancy Payments Act 1967 would not have effect.

This Order provided that any employee who had been laid off or kept on short-time due to the effects of measures taken by his or her employer in order to comply with, or as a consequence of, government policy to prevent, limit, minimise or slow the spread of infection of Covid-19 will not be entitled to claim redundancy during the period 13 March 2020 to 30 September 2021.

SI 325/2021 Health (Preservation and Protection and Other Emergency Measures in the Public Interest) Act 2020 (Continuation of Sections 4, 5 and 6 of Part 2) Order 2021

This Order extended, until 8 February 2022, the operation of the amendments effected by Pt 2 of the Health (Preservation and Protection and other Emergency Measures in the Public Interest) Act 2020 as respects ss 4, 5 and 6. This amended and extended the

Social Welfare Acts to provide for amendments in relation to entitlement to illness benefit for persons who have been diagnosed with, or are a probable source of infection with Covid-19.

SI 332/2021 Social Welfare (Consolidated Claims, Payments and Control) (Amendment) (No. 13) (Covid-19 Pandemic Unemployment Payment) Regulation 2021

The Order inserted art 52L stating that applications for Covid-19 pandemic unemployment payments would cease on 8 July 2021. The last date on which applications for the payment were accepted was 7 July 2021.

Chapter 3

Data Protection and Privacy

FINES AND THE GDPR

[3.01]   It is reported that a total of €984.47 million in fines were issued by data protection authorities under the General Data Protection Regulation (EU) 2016/679 (GDPR) in the third quarter of 2021. This amounted to a figure almost 20 times higher than the combined total of quarter one and quarter two of 2021, and triple the total amount of fines in all of 2020.[1]

The figure is attributed in the most part to the fines imposed on Amazon EuropeCore S.á.r.l (€746 million) and WhatsApp Ireland (€225 million) by the Luxembourg DPA and the Irish Data Protection Commission (DPC) respectively. Below, we look at the decision in respect of WhatsApp Ireland Ltd (WhatsApp) and some other fines imposed by data protection authorities that are of particular relevance to employers.

[3.02]   *In the matter of WhatsApp Ireland Ltd[2]—data processing activities—transparency obligations—mutual assistance request from German Federal Data Protection Authority*

Following the entry into force of the GDPR on 25 May 2018, the Irish DPC received complaints from both users and non-users of WhatsApp's services concerning its data processing activities. It also received a mutual assistance request, under art 61 GDPR, from the German Federal Data Protection Authority in relation to the transparency obligations that are placed on data controllers by the GDPR in the context of the possible sharing of personal data between WhatsApp and a variety of Facebook companies. Having carried out a preliminary examination of these complaints, the DPC decided to launch an own volition inquiry into WhatsApp in December 2018 under s 110 of the Data Protection Act 2018 to assess the extent to which WhatsApp complied with its transparency obligations under arts 12, 13 and 14 of the GDPR (the Decision).

---

[1]   See *https://finbold.com/gdpr-fines-q3-2021/* [last accessed 4 November 2021].
[2]   *In the matter of WhatsApp Ireland Ltd*, DPC Inquiry Reference IN-18-12-2.

One-Stop-Shop

In its Decision,[3] the DPC noted that WhatsApp determines the means and purposes of processing in respect of the personal data of individuals, in relation to the delivery of its services across the EU and as such, acts as the controller of such data. The Decision sets out the basis on which the DPC is competent, under art 56(1) and art 4(23)(a) of the GDPR, to act as the lead supervisory authority (LSA) for the purpose of the cross-border processing activities carried out by WhatsApp. As the LSA in the investigation under the One-Stop-Shop system, in accordance with art 60 of the GDPR, the DPC circulated its draft decision to other EU regulators for comment in December 2020. Objections to the content and proposed outcome of the decision were raised by eight EU regulators, triggering the dispute resolution process set out in art 65 of the GDPR. The European Data Protection Board (EDPB) adopted a binding decision under art 65 of the GDPR in July 2021. It required the DPC to reassess and increase its proposed fine. As a result the amount of the fine was significantly increased from the range of €30–€50 million that was initially proposed. On 2 September 2021, the DPC announced a conclusion to the GDPR investigation it conducted into WhatsApp. It imposed a fine of €225 million on WhatsApp and a reprimand, along with an order for WhatsApp to bring its processing into compliance by taking a range of specified remedial actions.

Investigation

The DPC investigated WhatsApp's compliance with arts 12, 13 and 14 GDPR under four main categories:

(a) transparency in the context of non-users;
(b) transparency in the context of users;
(c) transparency in the context of any sharing of personal data between WhatsApp and the Facebook Companies[4]; and
(d) the extent of compliance with the principle of transparency under art 5(1)(a) of the GDPR.

The DPC's ultimate finding was that WhatsApp had failed to comply with their transparency obligations on almost all counts.[5]

Non-user Data

One of the main issues considered in the Decision was WhatsApp's collection of non-user data. WhatsApp's contact feature allows users to consent to WhatsApp accessing

---

3   Decision of the Data Protection Commission dated 20 August 2021 made under Section 111 of the Data Protection Act 2018 and Articles 60 and 65 of the General Data Protection Regulation, further to an own-volition inquiry commenced under Section 110 of the Data Protection Act 2018, DPC Inquiry Reference IN-18-12-2.
4   Throughout the Decision the DPC uses 'The Facebook Companies' to collectively refer to those members of the Facebook family of companies that process personal data which has been shared with them by WhatsApp, whether as processors or as controllers and for whatever purpose.
5   WhatsApp was found to be compliant with art 13(1)(a), 13(1)(b) and 13(2)(b) and broadly compliant with art 13(2)(d) of the GDPR.

the phone numbers in their contact list in order to determine which of their contacts is already using the service, thereby providing WhatsApp with access to user and non-user data. The non-user data goes through a 'lossy hashing process', which takes the data (in this case the non-user phone numbers) and generates a new value for it. This new value is what is stored by WhatsApp, and is subsequently used to update relevant users' contact lists when any of these non-users join the service.

The DPC found that this stored data, both prior to and after the lossy hashing process, falls under the definition of 'personal data' in light of the broad interpretation set out in Recital 26 of the GDPR, which provides that 'all means reasonably likely to be used' to identify a natural person should be taken into account when assessing whether data is personal data. The DPC concluded that despite the lossy hashing process, the core purpose of storing this data was to ultimately use it to identify individuals and update contact lists. The Commission further determined that WhatsApp is processing this data as a controller and not a processor. The DPC found that WhatsApp had not sufficiently communicated to non-users that WhatsApp processes this data or how the data would be used should the non-user decide to join the service. The Commission also found that WhatsApp appeared to be the only party who could exert influence over the data, and that the lack of transparency had the effect of denying the data subject their rights under the GDPR, such as the right to restrict processing or the right to erasure.

User Data

In order for WhatsApp as a controller to comply with its transparency obligations to users of its services under art 13 (or art 14 as relevant) and art 12(1) of the GDPR, there are two main elements that needed to be met:

(a)   the data controller must provide the required information; and
(b)   the data controller must provide the required information in a 'concise, transparent, intelligible and easily accessible form, using clear and plain language, in particular for any information addressed specifically to a child'.

In the Decision, the DPC analysed WhatsApp's compliance with each subsection of art 13 in detail and found that WhatsApp had failed to meet its transparency obligations on a number of counts under the GDPR. WhatsApp sought to rely on its privacy policy and related documents as evidence of compliance. Throughout the Decision, vagueness of language, use of excessive links, and lack of detailed explanations were cited as reoccurring reasons as to why WhatsApp was not in compliance when processing user data.

Sharing with Facebook Companies

The DPC also considered WhatsApp's compliance with the obligations of transparency under arts 13 and 14 of the GDPR, by reference to WhatsApp's relationship with the Facebook Companies and considered any sharing of user data in the context of that relationship. The DPC ultimately found that WhatsApp had failed to meet the transparency obligations under the following headings:

(a)   providing information on the purpose of the processing for which the personal data is intended as well as the legal basis for the processing under art 13(1)(c) of the GDPR. In particular they considered the extent to which personal data that had been shared with the Facebook Companies had been identified to the user.

(b) providing information on the legitimate interests pursued by the controller or by the third party if they are relying on this legal basis of processing under art 12(1)(d) of the GDPR.

(c) providing information about the recipients or categories of recipients of the personal data, if any under art 12(1)(e) of the GDPR.

Article 5

WhatsApp's compliance with the transparency principle in art 5(1)(a) of the GDPR was not within the scope of the DPC's initial inquiry. During the course of the art 60 procedures, the Hungarian and Italian Supervisory Authorities raised objections about the absence of a finding under this provision, and the EDPB required the DPC to amend its decision accordingly. The EDPB emphasised the difference between obligations stemming from the principle of transparency and the principle itself. The DPC subsequently also found WhatsApp to be in contravention of the transparency obligations under art 5 of the GDPR.

WhatsApp has challenged the decision of the DPC in the High Court, and we can expect this case to produce greater insight into how the DPC will exercise its powers to impose fines going forward.

Key lessons for Employers

Some key points for employers to note from the Decision are:

— Review all Privacy Notices which support the processing of employee data and re-assess them against the 'concise, transparent, intelligible and easily accessible form, using clear and plain language' standard.

— In particular, ensure that any intra-group disclosures of personal data relating to employees are clearly identified in the relevant Privacy Notices.

— Review employee data capture points which come from external sources (ie, not from the employees themselves). Ensure that these sources are clearly explained in the Privacy Notices and ensure that there is a clear lawful basis to continue to collect, store and use the personal data in the manner intended.

FINES ISSUED BY EUROPEAN DATA PROTECTION AUTHORITIES

Video Surveillance

[3.03]   The data regulator for the German state of Lower Saxony imposed a fine of €10.4 million on notebooksbilliger.de AG (NBB) in January 2021. It found that NBB had conducted employee video-monitoring over a two-year period in the company's sales-rooms, warehouses and common areas without a valid legal basis. The company argued that the cameras were installed to prevent and investigate potential criminal offences and to track the flow of goods in the warehouses. Lower Saxony rejected this claim and explained that video surveillance of employees may take place only if there are reasonable grounds for suspecting specific individuals and in such event, an employee could be monitored for limited periods of time only. Lower Saxony stated that video surveillance should not to be used as a 'deterrent' for the prevention of crime. The storage of data relating to the video-monitoring for 60 days was also found to be longer than was necessary.

This case bears much similarity to the fine imposed last year by the Data Protection Authority of Hamburg on fashion-retailer H&M, the country's largest GDPR fine to date (€35.2 million), for similar surveillance activities found to be in breach of employee privacy rights.[6]

Algorithms

[3.04] The Italian DPA (the Garante) fined Foodinho s.r.l. €2.6 million in July for numerous privacy violations regarding the algorithms used for management of the food delivery company's staff. In particular, the Garante identified that Foodinho had not adequately informed the staff about the functioning of the algorithm system and could not guarantee the accuracy and correctness of the results of the algorithmic system used for the evaluation of the delivery staff. The Garante took issue with Foodinho for failing to provide a process for delivery staff to challenge decisions made by algorithms which ultimately dictate the amount of work staff receive.

Facial Recognition

[3.05] An investigation conducted by the Spanish DPA found that facial recognition systems in place at the supermarket chain Mercadona S.A were in breach of a number of key provisions of the GDPR, including the principle of data minimisation, the principle of necessity and proportionality. The facial recognition system, installed for tracking individuals with criminal convictions, or restraining orders issued against them for attacking Mercadona staff, was found to unlawfully capture biometric information from those who entered Mercadona supermarkets, including minors and company employees. The Spanish DPA imposed a fine of €3,150,000 (later reduced to €2,250,000 due to voluntary payment).

Access to Personal Data

[3.06] Capio St Göran's Hospital AB was the subject of a €2,944,000 fine following an investigation into several hospitals by the Swedish DPA. The hospitals were found to

---

[6] *Arthur Cox Employment Law Yearbook 2020* at **[3.15]** addressed the fine issued to Hennes & Mauritz (H&M) by the Hamburg Commissioner for Data Protection and Freedom of Information.

have processed personal data in violation of the GDPR by making them accessible to a large number of employees. Hospitals were criticised for failing to undertake the necessary risk analysis regarding access to personal data held within their medical record systems. The catalogue of obligations under art 32 GDPR also includes protecting data from unauthorised internal access. The Swedish DPA found that suitable safeguards and protective measures were not adopted by the hospitals, which was particularly troublesome due to the sensitive nature of the personal patient data that was stored.

FINES ISSUED BY THE DATA PROTECTION COMMISSION

[3.07]   The DPC issued a number of fines in the past year, with the landmark WhatsApp decision being the most widely publicised and which is a significant development in data protection law in Ireland generally. The DPC imposed a number of fines on public bodies, most notably TUSLA who received three separate fines for instances of infringement. The DPC also imposed a number of other fines that offer insight from an employment law perspective.

[3.08]   *Irish Credit Bureau DAC[7]—€90,000—23 March 2021*

The DPC imposed a €90,000 fine against the Irish Credit Bureau (ICB), acting as data controller. The fine follows a data breach reported by the controller to the DPA on 31 August 2018. The controller is a credit-reporting agency that maintains a database of credit contract performance between financial institutions and borrowers. The data breach occurred when the controller made a code change to its database that contained a technical error. As a result, between 28 June 2018 and 30 August 2018, the ICB database inaccurately updated the records of 15,120 closed accounts. The controller disclosed 1,062 inaccurate account records to financial institutions or affected individuals before the issue was resolved. Employers should be aware that a technical error that could result in inaccurate records of employees, in particular where this could prejudice the employees in some way, could result in a fine under GDPR. Employers have an obligation as data controller to ensure data processed is accurate.

[3.09]   *University College Dublin[8]—€70,000—17 December 2020*

The DPC fined University College Dublin (UCD) €70,000 as a result of seven personal data breaches. Unauthorised third parties were able to access UCD email accounts, and login credentials for UCD email accounts were posted online. It was found that the controller did not take appropriate technical and organisational measures to protect data security when processing personal data in its email service. In addition, the controller stored certain personal data in an email account in a form that allowed identification of the data subjects for longer than necessary for the purpose for which the personal data was processed. Also, the DPC found that the controller did not notify the DPC of

---

[7]   *In the matter of Irish Credit Bureau DAC* DPC Case Reference IN-19-7-2.
[8]   *In the matter of University College Dublin* DPC Case Reference IN-19-7-4.

a personal data breach in a timely manner. Employers are likely to store some personal data in an email account form, for example, where payslips are sent to employee email accounts. This fine reminds employers that they must take appropriate steps to ensure the security of this data, eg, by requiring passwords to open documents containing personal data, especially where it is of a sensitive nature.

[3.10]   *Twitter[9]—€450,000—15 December 2020*

In its first fine imposed against so-called 'Big-Tech', the DPC fined Twitter International Company €450,000 for violating art 33(1) of the GDPR and art 33(5) of the GDPR by failing to notify the DPA in a timely manner of a data breach and not adequately documenting that breach. The data breach concerned the privacy settings of user posts on the social media platform Twitter. There, users have the option to set the visibility of their posts to private or public. Private posts can only be seen by subscribers of the respective user profile, while public posts are visible to the public. A programming bug in Twitter's Android app resulted in some private posts being visible to the public. Twitter's legal team became aware of the error on 2 January 2019, and it was not until 8 January that the company informed the DPC. Consequently, the company failed to inform the DPC within the 72-hour period required by art 33(1) of the GDPR. Furthermore, the DPC found that Twitter had failed to adequately document the incident in accordance with art 33(5) of the GDPR. The decision by the DPC to impose an administrative fine on Twitter International Company was confirmed in the Dublin Circuit Court on 18 October 2021.

The Twitter and UCD decisions both serve as a reminder to employers that the DPC will take a dim view of any delay in reporting data breaches and of any failures to properly document any breach—as such it is essential that employers have procedures in place for managing data breaches to ensure they meet the 72-hour deadline for reporting and are compliant with their obligations in respect of breach documentation.

2020 ANNUAL REPORT OF THE DATA PROTECTION COMMISSION

[3.11]   Overall the number of complaints made to the DPC in 2020 fell to 4,660 complaints (a decrease from 7,215 complaints received in 2019). Similarly the number of cross-border complaints initiated through the One-Stop-Shop process fell to 354 complaints in 2020, compared with 457 in 2019.

Despite this however, the Annual Report showed a clear increase in the activity of the DPC compared to the previous year, across a range of areas, and reflecting the proactive, rather than simply reactive role that the DPC is establishing. The number of DPC staff grew to 145 with two recruitment competitions ongoing as of December 2020

---

[9]   *In the matter of Twitter International Company, Decision of the Data Protection Commission made under Section 111 of the Data Protection Act 2018* DPC Case Reference IN-19-1-1, available: at *https://dataprotection.ie/en/dpc-guidance/law/decisions/twitter-december-2020* [last accessed 4 November 2021].

and its budget was increased to €16.9 million, making it one of the top three resourced EU DPAs per capita. (It was announced in October 2021 that the DPC is to be allocated an additional €4.1 million under Budget 2022, an increase of 22% on 2021, and for the coming year its budget will be €23.2 million. The DPC welcomed this increase as critical to the DPC's role as the EU lead supervisory authority in respect of many of the world's largest internet platforms.)

In the months leading up the publication of the 2020 Annual Report, the DPC came under increasing pressure to deliver decisions in relation to its higher profile cross-border investigations. However, as the Report and some of the case studies outline, the detailed process to be followed under the Data Protection Act 2018 along with the One-Stop-Shop mechanism that applies for most of those cases, illustrates the inevitability of delays resulting from those processes.

From an employment context, the Annual Report included a case study involving a complaint received by the DPC from an individual whose photograph had been included in an article within a workplace newsletter without their consent. This was not the purpose for which the photograph had originally been obtained. The individual's employer, who was the data controller, informed the employee of the error and also told the individual that they, the employer, should have obtained consent to use the photograph in the workplace newsletter. The DPC recommended that a consent information leaflet be distributed to staff in advance of using photography, audio and/or video, and that a consent form for photography, audio and video be completed and signed prior to images or recordings being obtained, which the employer then implemented. The DPC was happy with this response and issued no further action. This case study is helpful for employers who process images or recordings of their employees, and also serves to illustrate the practical resolution that can be achieved through constructive engagement with the DPC.

As expected, several of the DPC's large-scale inquiries were concluded in 2020 with decisions being published. The DPC noted that 'a number of the inquiries that progressed in 2020 were cross-border in nature and so, as required by the Article 60 procedure laid down in the GDPR, the DPC transmitted a draft decision for consideration by its fellow EU supervisory authorities before the decision could be finalised'. The Twitter decision[10] was the first look at what the 2019 DPC Report described as 'the crystallisation in practical terms of many theoretical legal and procedural issues which have been raised during those first novel inquiries' and gives a valuable insight into the approach of the DPC moving forward.

At the end of 2020, the DPC had 83 statutory inquiries open, 27 of which were cross-border. We expect the 2021 Annual Report will include a number of significant decisions by the DPC. While 2020 gave us a taste of the DPC's views on what constitutes an 'effective, proportionate and dissuasive' fine under art 83 GDPR, 2021 is likely to give us a fuller understanding of the corrective powers and administrative fines that the DPC will utilise in the coming years.

---

[10]   DPC Case Reference IN-19-1-1, *In the matter of Twitter International Company, Decision of the Data Protection Commission* made under Section 111 of the Data Protection Act 2018, available at *https:// dataprotection.ie/en/dpc-guidance/law/decisions/twitter-december-2020* [last accessed 4 November 2021].

DATA PROTECTION COMMISSION GUIDANCE

[3.12]　The DPC has published new or updated guidance in 2021 on a number of aspects of the GDPR and its implementation into Irish law. Below we refer to some of the guidance published by the DPC relevant to employees, employers and employment law generally.

Redacting Documents and Records[11]

[3.13]　This note provides guidance on the approach to be taken in redacting documents and records when responding to subject access requests (SAR) under art 15 GDPR. Article 15(4) GDPR states that the data subject's right to a copy of his or her data 'shall not adversely affect the rights and freedoms of others'. As such, redaction may be necessary to ensure that a response to a SAR does not accidentally disclose another individual's personal data. When processing these requests, the DPC recommends that the controller work on a copy of a document, to avoid alteration or destruction of the original and to keep records of all the redactions to help prevent mistakes or omissions.

In relation to hard copy paper records, the DPC suggests cutting out, covering with tape, and blocking out with white correction fluid or a black marking pen and then photocopying the document, as techniques for redaction. Once all of the information subject to redaction is completely removed or covered, a further photocopy or scan of the redacted document should be prepared for provision to the data subject.

In relation to electronic documents and records, the DPC advises controllers to use search functions with caution as these have limitations when it comes to scanning of text which is stored in an image format. Furthermore, search functions also lack contextual analysis, and in cases where a data subject may be referred to in a document in variety of ways certain relevant documents may be omitted from the search. The DPC further warns of the concealed information found within electronic documents such as hidden content, file properties and metadata which if not redacted or erased may lead to disclosure of third party data. To combat this, the DPC suggests working from print outs or exporting the document into plain text or CSV format.

Processing Covid-19 Vaccination Data in the Context of Employment and the Work Safely Protocol[12]

[3.14]　In November 2021, the Department of Enterprise, Trade and Employment and the Department of Health published the Covid-19 National Protocol for Employers and Workers (the Protocol), which built upon the previous versions of the Work Safety

---

11　Redacting Documents and Records (August 2021).
12　Processing Covid-19 Vaccination Data in the context of Employment and the Work Safely Protocol (Version Last updated November 2021).

Protocol and introduced changes to reflect new restrictions and how these restrictions affect workplaces following the rise of Covid-19 cases. The DPC published guidance for employers on the implementation of the Protocol in a manner that complies with their obligations as data controllers under data protection legislation. The DPC notes that the updated Protocol sets out a number of requirements that will require employers to process personal data, namely requiring:

— employers to keep a log of contacts to facilitate contact tracing;

— employees to complete a pre-Return to Work form, which contains their personal data.

However, as a general position, the DPC considers that, in the absence of clear advice from public health authorities in Ireland, it is not necessary for all employers and managers of workplaces to establish the vaccination status of employees and workers, including for the purposes of pre-Return to Work forms, as the processing of vaccine data is likely to represent unnecessary and excessive data collection for which no clear legal basis exists. Employers should only process Covid-19 vaccination data where necessary to achieve a specific, legitimate purpose in line with general and sector-specific public health advice.

The Guidelines:

(a) Advise that the processing of health data in response to the Covid-19 pandemic, in all contexts, should be guided by the Government's public health policies.

(b) Advise that according to the Protocol there are limited set of circumstances in which vaccination should be offered as a workplace health and safety measure (as provided for under the Safety, Health and Welfare at Work (Biological Agents) Regulations 2013[13] and 2020[14]). An example of such exception being the provision of frontline healthcare services, where vaccination can be considered a necessary safety measure, based on relevant sector-specific guidance.

(c) Advise that Covid-19 vaccination should not in general be considered a necessary workplace safety measure and consequently, the processing of vaccine data is unlikely to be necessary or proportionate in the employment context, given the voluntary nature of the vaccination and it being special category data under GDPR. Furthermore, processing of personal data in the context of employment takes place in a situation where there is an imbalance between the data subject (employee) and data controller (employer). As such, employees should not be asked to consent to the processing of vaccine data as this consent is not likely to be freely given.

(d) Outline that the Medical Officer of Health in the course of carrying out their public health duties under the Infectious Diseases Regulations 1981,[15] as amended, may require access to the vaccination status of employees. This limited type of processing is permissible under data protection law where carried out on a case-by-case basis, subject to the determination of necessity and at the request of the Medical Officer of Health.

---

[13] Safety, Health and Welfare at Work (Biological Agents) Regulations 2013 (SI 572/2013).
[14] Safety, Health and Welfare at Work (Biological Agents) (Amendment) Regulations 2013 (SI 539/2020).
[15] Infectious Diseases Regulations 1981 (SI 390/1981).

Vaccine Certificate Check Guidance[16]

[3.15]   The Guidelines outline relevant legal bases and obligations for data controllers and data rights for data subjects in relation to checking vaccine certificates. The DPC notes that it is the responsibility of the owner/operator of a premises, as a data controller, to establish whether they have 'an identified legal basis' to ask for, and verify, the vaccination status of attendees or patrons. Examples of an identified legal basis are set out in the Guidelines:

— Under s 53 of the Data Protection Act 2018, special categories of personal data, including data revealing vaccination status, may be processed where necessary for public interest purposes in the area of public health. However, the determination of necessity in this context should be made with strict reference to the up-to-date advice of the public health authorities.

— Under Health Act 1947 (Sections 31AB and 31AD) (Covid-19) (Operation of certain indoor premises) Regulations 2021[17] operators of relevant indoor premises are under legal obligation to verify patrons' vaccination status.

The DPC notes that processing of personal data in this context should be limited to verification of vaccination status by the premises owner/operator, and that there is currently no requirement for any further processing of data subjects' information for public health purposes. Furthermore, owners/operators of premises/events are not required to demonstrate that they have carried out a data protection impact assessment, as the scope of the processing is limited and based upon public health requirements.

Garda Vetting—Some Data Protection Considerations[18]

[3.16]   These Guidelines outline how relevant organisations as provided for in National Vetting Bureau (Children and Vulnerable Persons) Acts 2012 to 2016 (the National Vetting Bureau Acts), must ensure they are processing the personal data contained in a vetting disclosure in accordance with data protection law, and in particular with data protection principles. Some of the most relevant provisions are set down below.

Data controllers must identify a lawful basis under art 6 of the GDPR for any processing of personal data they undertake in relation to the vetting process. Article 6(1)(c) provides that processing is lawful when 'necessary for compliance with a legal obligation to which the controller is subject'.

Where data controllers are processing special categories of personal data, they must also identify a lawful basis under art 9 GDPR (processing of special categories of personal data).

---

16   Vaccine Certificate Check Guidance (Version Last Updated: November 2021).
17   Health Act 1947 (Sections 31AB and 31AD) (Covid-19) (Operation of certain indoor premises) Regulations 2021 (SI 385/2021).
18   Garda Vetting—some data protection considerations (April 2021).

In circumstances where data controllers process personal data relating to criminal convictions and offences, they must ensure that it is either under the control of an official authority or authorised by EU or Member State law. Section 55(1)(b)(v) of the Data Protection Act 2018 provides that the processing of criminal offence data is permitted when authorised by the law of the State, and garda vetting under the National Vetting Bureau Acts is included within this provision.

Relevant organisations must take 'suitable and specific measures' to safeguard the personal data of individuals undergoing vetting, as outlined in s 36 of the Data Protection Act 2018. Some relevant measures outlined in the Guidelines include:

— limitations on access to the personal data undergoing processing within a workplace;

— strict time limits for the erasure of personal data and mechanisms to ensure that such time limits are observed;

— targeted training for those involved in the processing;

— the appointment of a Data Protection Officer where it is not mandatory under the GDPR; and

— logging mechanisms to permit the verification of whether and by whom the personal data has been consulted and/or erased.

In accordance with art 5(1)(b) GDPR ('purpose limitation'), vetting disclosures may only be used for the purpose for which they were provided to an organisation and should not be shared with any other organisation. The sole exception to this is where relevant organisations have a joint employment agreement in writing in accordance with s 12(3A) of the National Vetting Bureau Acts. Furthermore, it is an offence for a relevant organisation to use or disclose information contained within a vetting disclosure in a manner that is not foreseen by the National Vetting Bureau Acts.

Vetting disclosures and all accompanying information such as identity documentation submitted as part of the vetting application should be routinely deleted one year after they are received, unless the relevant organisation has a compatible lawful purpose for retaining the information. With regard to all unsuccessful employment applications, the vetting disclosure and all other personal data collected in the recruitment process should not be kept beyond the statutory period in which a claim arising from the recruitment process may be brought.

Data subjects undergoing the vetting process have a right to make a subject access request to receive a copy of their personal data from the relevant organisation. If, following the receipt of a garda vetting disclosure, a data subject believes that some of the information captured therein is inaccurate, they have a right to request the rectification of their personal data under the Law Enforcement Directive,[19] the rules for which are primarily found in Pt 5 of the Data Protection Act 2018 (which implements the Directive in Irish law).

---

[19] Directive (EU) 2016/680 on the protection of natural persons with regard to the processing of personal data by competent authorities for the purposes of the prevention, investigation, detection or prosecution of criminal offences or the execution of criminal penalties, and on the free movement of such data.

Guidance for Drivers on the Use of Dash Cams[20]

[3.17]   This guidance outlines data protection requirements for data controllers who use dash cams in their vehicles. The DPC notes a distinction between those who collect or otherwise process personal information of individuals in a purely personal capacity and those who use dash cams in a commercial non-personal use. The former are likely to fall under the 'personal' or 'household exemption', which is not subject to data protection obligations, whereas the latter would not be able to avail of these exemptions. The DPC further notes that any audio recordings inside a vehicle would require a very strong justification as to the proportionality and necessity for same, due to the high risk potential for recording of passengers' private conversation. As a guide for identifying what could fall under the 'personal' or 'household exemption' the DPC highlights *Rynes v Urad* (2014),[21] in which the ECJ noted that a fixed CCTV camera which covered both a private dwelling but also a public street could not amount to 'purely "personal or household activity"'.

As such, those who use dash cams in a commercial non-personal capacity are considered data controllers and need to be compliant with the GDPR and the Data Protection Act 2018 and process data in accordance with the principles of data protection. The DPC specifically highlights the following obligations:

(a) Personal data must be processed in a transparent manner:
   1. There should be a clear sign indication that recording is taking place.
   2. A policy detailing contact details, the legal basis for collecting the images or audio of others, the purposes for which the data is being used, and how long it will be retained for should be made available.
   3. This information could be provided on request in written, digital, or verbal form, including through a policy available online, once the individuals whose personal data is processed are made aware of how to access it.
   4. In the event of an accident, the controller should advise the other party that they have recorded footage of the accident for the purpose of transparency and allow a person to make a Subject Access Request.

(b) Personal data should only be retained for as long as required and for the purpose that it was obtained.

(c) Personal data must be kept securely.

(d) Data subjects have a right to access their data, which includes the right of an individual to confirmation as to whether or not their personal data is processed or stored.

The DPC notes that publication of dash cam footage to social media platforms could represent a further act of processing and data controllers could risk infringing the data protection rights of recorded individuals. Furthermore, following the ECJ reasoning in *Buivids*,[22] publication of material to an indefinite audience, such as on a fully public

---

[20]   Guidance for Drivers on the Use of Dash Cams (Version Last Updated: June 2021).
[21]   *Rynes v Urad* (Case C-212/13).
[22]   *Buivids* (Case C-345/17).

social media channel, cannot be considered to fall within the personal or household exemption. The DPC advises data controllers to ensure that they have appropriate legal basis for any use of recordings involving personal data which do not fall within the exceptions.

Under s 41 of the Data Protection Act 2018, law enforcement authorities, such as An Garda Síochána, may request a copy of dash cam footage from controllers in relation to the investigation of a crime. However, the relevant law enforcement authority should be in a position to demonstrate that the footage is necessary for the investigation or prosecution of a criminal offence and, a request for such footage should be obtained in writing.

In relation to third party disclosure requests, the DPC noted the decision of the ECJ in *Rīgas*,[23] where it was held that there was no obligation on the controller to grant the request for disclosure of the footage to a third party on the basis of legitimate interests, however if there was a national law in place to allow for such disclosure of personal data contained in dash cam footage to another third party for a civil liability claim, then that would be permissible. No such provision currently exists under Irish legislation.

EUROPEAN DATA PROTECTION BOARD GUIDELINES AND OPINIONS

[3.18]   The EDPB has published guidance on a number of topics in 2021 that may be of relevance to employers, employees and employment law generally. In the section below on EDPB guidance, we discuss guidance specifically addressed to employers and then some of the other important, but generally applicable, guidance. The EDPS also published their 2020 Annual Report, details of which are below.

Guidelines on Examples Regarding Data Breach Notifications[24]

[3.19]   The GDPR introduced a requirement to notify breaches to the national supervisory authority and the data subject in some cases. The Article 29 Working Party produced general guidance on these obligations in 2017. The nature and timing of that guidance meant that not all practical issues were addressed in sufficient detail. This EDPB practice-oriented and case-based guidance is based on the experiences of supervisory authorities since the application of the GDPR. The guidance clarifies that the controller must document any breaches and relevant facts, its effects, and remedial actions taken, and notify the breach to the supervisory authority unless the rights of the data subject are unlikely to be at risk. The Guidelines emphasise that it is better to prevent a breach by preparing in advance and by providing training on data protection issues, focusing on personal data breach management (ie, identification of a personal

---

23   *Rīgas* (Case C-13/16).
24   Guidelines 01/2021 on Examples Regarding Data Breach Notifications (adopted 14 January 2021).

data breach incident and further actions to be taken, etc). The Guidelines advise that internal documentation of the breach must be carried out in every case.

The Guidelines provide case-examples of specific breach situations, detailing particular risks like ransomware, data exfiltration attacks, human risk, lost/stolen devices, mis-postal and social engineering. These Guidelines will be of significant assistance to controllers when assessing their obligations under the GDPR and are particularly helpful to employers who might need guidance around procedures to put in place to deal with data breaches, advising them that it is better to deal proactively with a data breach.

Guidelines on the Concepts of Controller and Processor in the GDPR[25]

[3.20]   In relation to assessing the entities that can be controllers, these Guidelines note that while a controller can be a natural person, in practice the role of controller is typically undertaken by an organisation rather than an individual within the organisation. The Guidelines note further that, in identifying the data controller, it can be helpful to consider traditional roles and professional expertise that normally imply a position of responsibility. For example, when an employer processes personal data as part of its interactions with its own employees, it will generally be the one to determine the purpose and means of the processing, thereby acting as controller within the meaning of the GDPR.

The Guidelines provide other examples of controller-processor relationships, including the relationship between an employer and a company hired as a payroll administrator. Notwithstanding the fact that the payroll administrator may decide on certain detailed matters in relation to the data processing, provided it acts within the parameters of its instructions by the employer, it will be considered a data processor, and the employer will be considered a data controller. However, if the employer's instructions require the payroll administrator to transmit information to a bank in order to carry out the actual payments, then both the bank and the payroll administrator would be seen as controllers in circumstances where the bank decides independently of the employer which data is to be processed to provide the service and the applicable length of storage. The employer in this instance cannot have any influence on the purpose and means of the bank's processing of data. These Guidelines will be especially helpful to employers as they navigate the outsourcing of certain business functions, or are the provider of outsourced functions to other businesses.

Guidelines on Virtual Voice Assistants[26]

[3.21]   A virtual voice assistant (VVA) understands voice commands and executes them. VVAs are available on most smartphones and use a microphone and speaker. The device stores voice and other data that are transferred to remote VVA servers.

---

[25]   Guidelines 07/2020 on the concepts of controller and processor in the GDPR (adopted 7 July 2021).
[26]   Guidelines 02/20201 on Virtual Voice Assistants (adopted 7 July 2021).

These Guidelines identify some of the compliance challenges and provide recommendations as to how to address them.

Controllers providing VVA services through screenless terminal devices must inform users of the service about the GDPR, when setting up the VVA for the first time. Therefore, it is recommend that VVA providers/designers and developers develop voice-based interfaces to facilitate the provision of this information to users.

The Guidelines consider four of the most common purposes for which VVAs process personal data: executing requests, improving the VVA machine learning model, biometric identification and profiling for personalised content or advertising. Generally, the data is processed to provide a service requested by the user and as such is exempt from the requirement for prior consent under art 5(3) of the GDPR; although such consent is necessary to store or gain access to the information for any other purpose other than executing the user's request. The Guidelines note that some VVA services retain personal data until users require their deletion and state that this is not in line with the storage limitation principle. The Guidelines advise that VVA services very likely fall into the category of activities that require a Data Protection Impact Assessment and controllers should ensure that users can exercise their data subject rights using easy-to-follow voice commands. This is relevant to employers who use such software for dictations or other work-stream management purposes.

Addendum to Guidelines on Certification and Identifying Certification Criteria in Accordance with Articles 42 and 43 GDPR[27]

[3.22] These Guidelines should be read in line with the EDPB Guidelines 1/2018 on certification and identifying certification criteria according to Articles 42 and 43 and Guidelines 4/2018 on the accreditation of certification bodies under Article 43. They aim to refine elements from the previous Guidelines to help stakeholders involved in the drafting of certification criteria and Supervisory Authorities (SAs) and the EDPB to be able to provide consistent evaluations in the context of certification criteria approval. The recommendations should not be seen as exhaustive. The assessment of certification criteria will be carried out on a case-by-case basis, meaning that certain certification mechanisms may require additional measures that are not mentioned or detailed in the guidance. It is up to the stakeholders to make this assessment each time and consider what extra measures are required, if any.

Guidelines 8/2020 on the Targeting of Social Media Users

[3.23] The Guidelines offer guidance around the targeting of social media users by social media providers or targeters. Targeters are legal or natural persons who

---

[27] Guidelines 1/2018 on certification and identifying certification criteria in accordance with Articles 42 and 43 GDPR (adopted 6 April 2021).

communicate specific messages to users of social media in order to advance commercial, political, or other interests. Where joint responsibility exists, the Guidelines help clarify how the distribution of responsibilities will fall between targeters and social media providers. Practical examples are provided.

Guidelines 03/2021 on the Application of Article 65(1)(a) GDPR

[3.24]   The Guidelines offer clarification on the art 65(1) dispute resolution mechanism meant to ensure the correct and consistent application of the GDPR in cases involving cross-border processing of personal data. They clarify the application of the relevant provisions of the GDPR and Rules of Procedure,[28] set out the main stages of the procedure and clarify the competence of the EDPB when adopting a legally binding decision on the basis of the mechanism. The Guidelines also include a description of the applicable procedural safeguards and remedies.

The European Data Protection Supervisor (EDPS)

[3.25]   The EDPS published its 2020 Annual Report on 19 April 2021. In its report, the EDPS confirms its support of European Union Institutions (EUI) as employers. The EDPS worked closely with the data protection officers of EUIs to provide helpful guidelines and best practices for ongoing compliance. In their guidelines published on 15 July 2020 entitled; 'Orientations from the EDPS: Reactions of EU institutions as employers to the Covid-19 crisis' the EDPS seeks to guide EUIs on appropriate practices regarding teleworking tools, staff management, health data and replying to data subject access requests.

The Annual Report notes that the EDPS addressed an EUI's question about the data protection provisions to be included in agreements with service providers providing payroll services for employees located in a country outside of the EU with which there is no adequacy decision. It advises the EUI employer, as a data controller, to ensure that the service provider, as a data processor, demonstrates appropriate guarantees and safeguards for the processing.

In May 2020, the EDPS launched a consultation in relation to payroll services for local employees in a third country. The consultation relates to the data protection provisions of a future framework agreement between an institution and the service provider concerning payroll-related services for local employees of the institution based in a third country. The service provider will be a private company that applies the third country's law, including their data protection law and is not bound by the GDPR.

---

[28]   EDPB Rules of Procedure. Adopted on 25 May 2018, as last modified and adopted on 8 October 2020.

Guidelines on Restrictions under Article 23 GDPR[29]

[3.26]   Article 23 provides that, under Union or Member State law, the application of certain provisions of the GDPR, mainly relating to the rights of the data subjects and controllers' obligations, may be restricted in the situations therein listed. These Guidelines provide an analysis of the criteria to apply restrictions, the assessments that need to be observed, how data subjects can exercise their rights once the restriction is lifted and the consequences for infringements of art 23 of the GDPR. They provide details on the requirements that need to be met in order for a measure to be lawfully relied on. Restrictions should be seen as an exception to the general rule and should be interpreted narrowly.

Any restrictions must have a basis in national legislation that is sufficiently clear in its terms to give citizens an adequate indication of the circumstances under which controllers are empowered to resort to such restrictions. The conditions specified in art 23(1) are exhaustive, and the link between the restriction and the objective pursued should be clearly stated in the legislative measure. Any measures adopted must comply with the conditions set out in art 23(2), namely that the legislative provisions must cover: the purpose of processing, the categories of personal data, the scope of restrictions, safeguards, specifications of the controller, storage periods, risks, and rights of data subjects to be informed. As a rule, all of these requirements should be included in the legislative measure. Frequently this issue arises in the context of disputed SARs from employees where employers have attempted to apply some of the exceptions or restrictions on access rights set out in ss 60 and 162 of the Data Protection Act 2018.

GDPR CASE LAW

[3.27]   *Orange Romania SA v The Romanian National Supervisory Authority[30]— ECJ—referral from Romania—Data Protection Directive 95/46[31]—data processing— valid consent—transparency*

Orange Romania is a mobile telecommunications service on the Romanian market. On 28 March 2018, the National Romanian Data Protection Authority imposed a fine on Orange Romania for storing copies of customers' identity documents without demonstrating that those customers had given their valid consent and ordered Orange Romania to destroy the copies of these documents. Orange Romania disagreed with the Romanian Data Protection Authority's determination and challenged the decision in the Regional Court in Bucharest.

The Romanian Court considered the contracts concluded between Orange Romania and their customers. It was found that in certain contracts, but not all of them, Orange Romania had pre-ticked the box to indicate consent to the collection and storage of

---

29   Guidelines 10/2020 on restrictions under Article 23 GDPR (adopted 15 December 2020).
30   *Orange Romania SA v The Romanian National Supervisory Authority* (Case C-61/19).
31   Directive 95/46/EC of the European Parliament and of the Council of 24 October 1995 on the protection of individuals with regard to the processing of personal data and on the free movement of such data.

customer's identity documents. The customer did not need to consent to the disclosure of their identity in order to conclude the contract, but Orange Romania had not made this sufficiently clear. Further the only way a customer could refuse consent to this use of their data was to fill out a separate handwritten additional form before the conclusion of the contract.

The Romanian Court decided to stay the proceedings and refer the following two questions to the European Court of Justice (ECJ):

(1) For the purposes of Article 2(h) of Directive 95/46, what conditions must be fulfilled in order for an indication of wishes to be regarded as specific and informed?

(2) For the purposes of Article 2(h) of Directive 95/46, what conditions must be fulfilled in order for an indication of wishes to be regarded as freely given?

The ECJ assessed the questions posed, both under the Directive 95/46 and the GDPR, and came to the same conclusion under both, ie, that the burden of proof rests with the controller to show that the data subjects have given valid consent.

It was further determined that in order for consent to be 'freely given', 'informed' and 'specific' it must be an active rather than passive behaviour. A pre-ticked box does not give the data subject autonomy to give active consent. Additionally, the requirement for the data subject to fill out a separate handwritten form to refuse consent was an apparent deviation from the regular procedure Orange Romania used in contracts. The ECJ found that Orange Romania also had not met its transparency requirements. It was not sufficiently clear that if the customer refused consent, the contract would still be concluded or if the customer gave consent how their data would be processed.

[3.28] *Carey v Airbnb Ireland Unlimited Company*[32]*—Court of Appeal— Costello J—Tax Authorities—Data Protection Acts 1988 to 2018—request for records—Directive 2011/16/EU*[33]*—GDPR*

This case concerned an appeal to the Court of Appeal following a determination by the High Court. On 6 March 2015, the Austrian Federal Ministry of Finance submitted a request for information to the Revenue Commissioners, as the Irish competent authority under Directive 2011/16/EU. The Austrian tax authority sought the names, addresses and dates of birth of hosts of 365 rental properties hosted on Airbnb Ireland Unlimited Company (Airbnb), if available. Each of the rental properties was located in Austria.

Ms Carey, a Principal Officer in the International Tax Division of the Revenue Commissioners, determined that there were reasonable grounds to suspect that the information was relevant to a liability. She wrote a letter to Airbnb requesting the information sought by the Austrian tax authority. Airbnb ultimately stated that it couldn't disclose this information because of concerns that voluntary compliance with this particular request by the Austrian tax authority would place it in breach of its data privacy obligations. However the High Court ordered Airbnb to furnish the necessary information to Ms Carey.

---

[32] *Carey v Airbnb Ireland Unlimited Company* [2021] IECA 103.
[33] Directive 2011/16/EU on administrative cooperation in the field of taxation.

Airbnb raised a number of grounds of appeal, including that the disclosures were not in compliance with the provisions of the GDPR and the Data Protection Acts 1988 to 2018. Airbnb queried whether its compliance with this order from the High Court would result in a breach of its obligations as a data controller and secondly, whether the onward transfer of the requested information to the Austrian tax authority would constitute a breach by Ms Carey as the data controller of such data.

The Court ultimately found that the request for information received from the Austrian tax authority was a valid request which complied with the requirements of Directive 2011/16/EU. As the Austrian tax authority had exhausted all the usual sources for this information prior to sending the request and the request was not manifestly devoid of foreseeable relevance to the ongoing investigation, the Court was satisfied that this disclosure would not be in contravention of the GDPR or the Data Protection Acts 1988 to 2018.

[3.29]   *Data Protection Commissioner v Facebook Ireland Ltd[34]—High Court—Costello J—EU-Privacy Shield—standard contractual clauses—transfers of data outside of the EU*

Following the judgment of the ECJ on 16 July 2020, in which it addressed 11 questions posed by the Irish High Court in the context of a preliminary reference made on 4 May 2018,[35] the DPC initiated an own volition inquiry into Facebook's data transfers to the US. This inquiry was the subject of judicial review proceedings brought separately by Facebook and by Max Schrems. In May 2021, in a lengthy judgment, the Irish High Court dismissed Facebook's challenge and lifted the court-imposed stay halting the inquiry. We now await the outcome of the re-commenced inquiry to include the conclusion of the cooperation and consistency process with other European data protection authorities.

[3.30]   *Doolin v The Data Protection Commissioner[36]—Data Protection Commissioner—Data Protection Act 1988—CCTV—processing interpretation*

On 19 November 2015, Our Lady's Hospice and Care Services (OLHCS) found a threatening graffiti message in a staff room. The message was reported to An Garda Síochána who advised OLHCS to review the CCTV footage accessing the staff room.

Upon review of the CCTV footage, OLHCS found that a number of employees were accessing the staff room and taking unauthorised rest breaks. Subsequently, Mr Doolin was invited to an investigation meeting followed by disciplinary proceedings, not related to the graffiti, but as a result of the unauthorised rest breaks that had come to OLHCS attention following the review of the CCTV camera footage.

Mr Doolin acknowledged that the use of the CCTV footage from the staff room was permissible for the security purposes, ie, to prevent crime, promote staff security and public safety. However, he contended that the use of that information derived from

---

[34]   *Data Protection Commissioner v Facebook Ireland Ltd* [2020] IEHC 537.
[35]   *Arthur Cox Employment Law Yearbook 2020* at **[3.02]** addressed the decision in *Data Protection Commissioner v. Facebook Ireland Ltd, Maximillian Schrems* (Case C-311/18).
[36]   *Doolin v The Data Protection Commissioner* [2020] IEHC 90, see also *Arthur Cox Employment Law Yearbook 2020* at **[3.45]**.

the viewing of the CCTV footage was unlawfully processed for the purpose of disciplinary action against him by OLHCS. The DPC concluded that OLHCS had a lawful basis, under the legitimate interest provision set out in s 2A(d) of the Data Protection Act 1988, for the very limited processing of the appellant's personal data and that the limited viewing of the appellant's personal images was only used for the security purpose it was originally collected for. The High Court allowed Mr Doolin to appeal this determination and ultimately, concluded that the DPC had made an error in their finding as a result of an incorrect interpretation of the term 'processing' having regard to the terms of s 2(1)(c)(ii) of the Data Protection Act 1988.

The finding and order of the High Court was subject to an appeal to the Court of Appeal on 15 June 2021.

[3.31] *Lloyd v Google LLC[37]—UK Supreme Court—Data Protection Act 1998—GDPR[38]—'loss of control' of personal data is not compensable—representative action*

In a judgment that is set to alter the landscape of non-material damage claims in the UK and beyond, the UK Supreme Court in *Lloyd v Google LLC* rejected the idea that non-material breaches of the Data Protection Act 1998 (the DPA 1998) entitle claimants to compensation for 'loss of control' of their personal data. The DPA 1998 has since been replaced by the UK General Data Protection Regulation supplemented by the Data Protection Act 2018, but was in force at the time of the alleged breaches by Google. The decision comes in the wake of a number of preliminary references to the Court of Justice of the European Union (the ECJ) by Austrian and German courts under art 267 TFEU on the interpretation of art 82 of the GDPR, and sets the tone for a new line of jurisprudence in increasingly prevalent data protection claims.

Richard Lloyd, a former executive of Consumers International and Which?, filed a representative action against Google in 2017 on behalf of over four million Apple iPhone users (the claimants) alleging that Google had breached its duties as a data controller under the DPA 1998 in a period between 2011 and 2012. Lloyd, who runs the 'Google You Owe Us' campaign, on behalf of the claimants, accused Google of bypassing the privacy settings on Apple's iPhone Safari browser to track iPhone users' internet activity, including time spent on relevant websites and advertisements viewed, with an aim to targeting advertising, without the users' consent. Google disabled the 'Safari Workaround' after *The Wall Street Journal* broke the story in early 2012 and was fined $25m by the Federal Trade Commission in the US later that year.

In the wake of this fine, the Court of Appeal of England and Wales in *Vidal-Hall v Google Inc*,[39] paved the way for *Lloyd* when it ruled that three users could sue Google in the UK for damages for breaches of their individual privacy rights by the 'Safari Workaround'.

---

37 *Lloyd v Google LLC* [2021] UKSC 50.
38 Regulation (EU) 2016/679 on the protection of natural persons with regard to the processing of personal data and on the free movement of such data.
39 *Vidal-Hall v Google Inc* [2014] EWHC 13 (QB).

In the present case, Lloyd sought permission from the UK courts to serve the claims on Google LLC in the US. In this claim, Lloyd sought confirmation that:

1. the DPA 1998 allowed for compensation to be paid to claimants for loss of control of their personal data without the need for identification of specific financial loss or evidence of material damage and distress; and

2. a representative action under r 19.6 of the Civil Procedure Rules (the CPR) could proceed on behalf of 4.6 million identifiable members with the 'same interest'.

Google LLC opposed the application on the grounds that:

1. damages cannot be awarded under the DPA 1998 without proof that a breach caused an individual to suffer financial damage or distress; and

2. the claim was not suitable to proceed as a representative action.

The claim was initially rejected by the High Court in October 2018 on the basis that 'vindicatory' damages could not be awarded where it could not be shown that material damage or distress had been caused.

The High Court decision was overturned by the Court of Appeal of England and Wales in October 2019, which held that control over personal data had value to an individual, and in that instance damages could be awarded absent proof of distress or economic loss. The Court of Appeal also held that the representative class had the 'same interest' in that they had all suffered the same alleged loss of control over their personal data.

The UK Supreme Court considered a number of elements that have far-reaching consequences in respect of data protection claims for non-material damage in the UK and other common law jurisdictions, including Ireland, with similar data protection legislation in place.

The Supreme Court unanimously held that, for claimants to be awarded compensation under s 13 of the DPA 1998, which required claimants to suffer 'damage by reason of any contravention' of the Act, the damage must be caused by, and be distinct from, the contravention itself.

This moves UK jurisprudence away from the reasoning in cases such as *Johnson v Medical Defence Union*[40] where 'damage' for the purposes of the DPA 1998 did not go beyond monetary loss or material damage, towards the *Vidal-Hall* line of reasoning where the Court of Appeal held that there was a fundamental right to the protection of personal data under art 8 of the Charter of Fundamental Rights rejecting pecuniary loss as the sole basis for claiming under the provisions of the DPA 1998.

However, the above jurisprudence is peripheral to the *Lloyd* judgment and instead *Lloyd* segues from judgments such as *Gulati v Mirror Group Newspapers*,[41] where misuse of private information was found to be compensable *per se*, to distinguishing

---

[40] *Johnson v Medical Defence Union* [2007] EWCA Civ 262.
[41] *Gulati v Mirror Group Newspapers* [2015] EWHC CH 1482.

the tort of misuse of private information from claims for damages under the DPA 1998. Google submitted to the Supreme Court that 'it is an important point of reference in this case that under the general law, a claim in tort of breach of statutory duty is not actionable *per se*; it requires proof of harm'.

In respect of the DPA 1998, the Supreme Court held that, on the proper interpretation of s 13, the term 'damage' refers to material damage or mental distress distinct from, and caused by, unlawful processing of personal data in contravention of the Act, and does not refer to the act of unlawful processing itself.

Further, the Supreme Court held that it was necessary to prove what specifically amounted to unlawful processing by Google of personal data relating to a given individual in order to recover compensation in such claims. The Supreme Court emphasised that the right to such compensation is a qualified right and is subject to the defence of reasonable care taken by a defendant, as opposed to the strict liability operation of misuse of private information.

As it was not held that the alleged damage was compensable without evidence, the Supreme Court did not elaborate on the issue of quantum. However the Court did find that 'user damages' (which are a category of damages available for the wrongful use of another's property rights) were not available for such a breach, as damages under the DPA 1998 arise from an infringement of the claimant's right to have personal data processed in accordance with the DPA 1998, and not the infringement itself. Therefore the principles applying to an award of 'user damages' do not apply to a claim for damages under the DPA.

The Supreme Court held that representative actions are a 'flexible tool of convenience in the administration of justice' and that the 'same interest' requirement for members of a certain class must be interpreted purposely and pragmatically, in keeping with the overriding objective of the CPR of dealing with cases justly, so that Google would be able to identify 'who is, and who is not, in the class'.

The Court was at pains to note that there is no bar to a representative claim where each represented person has in law a separate cause of action, nor where the relief claimed consists of or includes damages, but in instances where the assessment of individual harm would vary across the large number of claimants, such actions are not the appropriate vehicle in that regard.

The Court acknowledged representative actions could be taken in two stages, the first being a claim by a representative to assess liability of a defendant for the alleged breach, and the second, an assessment of compensation in separate individual claims. However, the claimant did not propose such a two-stage procedure in *Lloyd*, likely because the proceedings would not be economic if it was necessary to prove loss on an individual basis.

In *obiter* comments, the Supreme Court in *Lloyd* stated that 'EU law therefore does not provide a basis for giving a wider meaning to the term "damage" in section 13 of the DPA 1998 than was given to that term by the Court of Appeal in *Vidal-Hall*'.

As to whether this is the case in respect of 'damage' as defined in art 82 of the GDPR which states that: 'Any person who has suffered material or non-material damage as a result of an infringement of this Regulation shall have the right to receive compensation from the controller or processor for the damage suffered', is yet to be decided by a court.

There have been two recent referrals to the ECJ on various aspects of art 82, by the German and Austrian courts.

The Austrian Supreme Court requested a preliminary ruling by the ECJ under art 267 TFEU on the interpretation and application of the claim for damages under art 82 GDPR. In particular, clarification was sought on:

1. whether a claim for damages, in addition to the violation of a GDPR provision, requires the claimant to have suffered specific damages or whether said violation is sufficient to qualify for the award;
2. whether additional requirements of EU law, beyond the principles of effectiveness and equivalence must be considered by national courts in its assessment of damages; and
3. whether the threshold for non-pecuniary/non-material damages requires that the infringement has consequences of a certain degree or weight that extend beyond anger or annoyance caused by said infringement.

In Germany, the Magistrate Court dismissed a plaintiff's claim for a breach of the GDPR following receipt of an unsolicited advertisement via email. The Magistrate Court held the plaintiff was not entitled to compensation under art 82 because he failed to show that he suffered any relevant damages from the unsolicited email that met the *de minimis* threshold of impairment. Ultimately, the plaintiff filed a constitutional complaint arguing that the decision violated his right to a trial before a legal judge under the German Constitution, and that the Magistrate Court had wrongly applied its own interpretation of the law, rather than referring to the ECJ the question of whether it is necessary to meet a *de minimis* threshold of impairment to be entitled to compensation for non-material damage under art 82.

The Federal Constitutional Court ruled that the Magistrate Court was obliged to turn to the ECJ in circumstances where the proceeding clearly raised the question of EU law, ie, under what circumstances does art 82 entitle a claimant alleging non-material damage to monetary compensation, particularly in light of Recital 146 sentence 3 of the GDPR's broad interpretation of the concept of damages?

The Future of Data Protection in Ireland

Although there is provision in Ord 15, r 9 of the Rules of the Superior Courts 1986 for representative actions to be taken in Ireland, the current trend, in the absence of any statutory provision for actions involving groups of claimants, is to progress class actions through test cases.

In addition, s 117 of the Data Protection Act 2018, which implements the GDPR in Ireland, expressly provides that 'damage' includes 'material and non-material damage'. The Supreme Court noted *obiter* in *Murphy v Callinan*,[42] which concerned the pre-GDPR Data Protection Act 1988 (as amended) but was decided close to the introduction of the new Act, that 'the Data Protection Act 2018 implementing GDPR permits an individual to seek compensation from the court for breaches of data subject rights even in the absence of any material damage or financial loss'. In *Murphy*, the defendant insurance company cancelled a motor insurance policy, and returned premia, upon receiving information about the applicant's convictions for road traffic offences from a member of An Garda Síochána. The applicant claimed that the defendant had not rectified errors in his data and sought damages under s 7 of the Data Protection Act 1988 (as amended), the predecessor to s 117 of the 2018 Act. The Supreme Court ruled that the applicant was not entitled to damages, as he had not provided any evidence of loss.

As of yet, the Irish courts have not issued any decision on a data protection action under s 117 of the Data Protection Act 2018. In light of this most recent judgment in the UK, it remains to be seen whether the courts in Ireland will follow suit, particularly once the ECJ opines on the scope of art 82 for 'bare breach' claims.

GDPR AND INTERNATIONAL DATA TRANSFERS

New Standard Contractual Clauses

[3.32]   On 4 June 2021, the European Commission issued two decisions containing new sets of Standard Contractual Clauses (SCCs) for the transfer of personal data under the GDPR. Each of these decisions came into force on 27 June 2021.

Commission Implementing Decision 2021/914 on standard contractual clauses for the transfer of personal data to third countries (the Third Country SCCs), will replace the SCCs adopted under the (now repealed) Data Protection Directive EU/95/46 (the Previous SCCs) and, caters for a broader range of transfer scenarios. Commission Implementing Decision 2021/915 provides new standard contractual clauses (the Intra EU SCCs) that can be used between controllers and processors to meet the requirements contained in art 28(3) and 28(4) of the GDPR (and art 29(3) and 29(4) of Regulation (EU) 2018/1725). Importantly, the Intra EU SCCs are enabling rather than mandatory, and controllers and processors may choose to negotiate their own contracts containing the compulsory terms referred to art 28 of the GDPR.

Improvements

Each set of SCCs may be entered into by more than two parties and each contains a mechanism for new parties to accede to the clauses, as data exporters or

---

[42]   *Murphy v Callinan* [2018] IESC 59.

importers, throughout the lifecycle of the contract. In recognition of the complexity of modern processing chains, the Third Country SCCs helpfully take a range of different data transfer scenarios into account. Data importers and exporters can build SCCs applicable to their situation by combining general clauses with one of four modules:

Module one provides for a controller to controller (C2C) transfer where personal data is transferred from a controller within or outside the EU/European Economic Area (EEA) to a controller in a third country, ie, outside the EEA, for example data transfers between customers and service providers where both entities are acting as controller.

Module two provides for a controller to processor (C2P) where personal data is transferred from a controller within or outside the EU/EEA to a processor in a third country, for example the transfer of personal data from a customer acting as a controller within the EU/EEA, to a service provider acting as a processor in a third country.

Module three provides for a processor to processor (P2P) transfer where personal data is transferred from a processor within or outside the EU/EEA to a processor/sub-processor in a third country, for example service provider arrangements where data is transferred from a processor within the EU/EEA to a processor/sub-processor in a third country.

Module four provides for a processor to controller (P2C) where personal data is transferred from a processor within or outside the EU/EEA to a controller in a third country, for example the provision of service by a service provider acting as a processor within the EU/EEA, to a controller in a third country.

Other Key Changes in the Third Country SCCs

Third-party beneficiary rights under Irish law: The Third Country SCCs are required to be governed by the law of an EU Member State that allows for third-party beneficiary rights. If Member State laws do not allow for third-party beneficiary rights, then the clauses must be governed by the law of another Member State that does allow for them. Third-party beneficiary rights do not generally exist in Ireland as the principle of privity of contract prevails in the Irish law. However, to overcome this difficulty, in June 2021 the Irish Department of Justice introduced the European Union (Enforcement of data subjects' rights on transfer of personal data outside the European Union) Regulations 2021.[43] The Regulations amend the Data Protection Act 2018 to provide an express right on the part of individuals to enforce third-party beneficiary rights conferred on data subjects under binding corporate rules and under standard data protection clauses adopted by the Commission or by a Supervisory Authority and approved by the Commission.

Liability: Clause 12 provides that each party is liable to the other party (or parties) for any damages it causes them through any breach of the Third Country SCCs.

---

[43]   European Union (Enforcement of data subjects' rights on transfer of personal data outside the European Union) Regulations 2021 (SI 297/2021).

Warranty: Both the data exporter and the data importer must 'warrant that they have no reason to believe' that the laws in the destination country would prevent the data importer from complying with its obligations under the SCCs. To support this warranty, the parties must undertake a 'transfer risk assessment'.

Timing

From 27 September 2021 the Third Country SCCs must be used for any new data transfers of personal data from the EU/EEA to third countries. Data transfer agreements based on the Previous SCCs, and concluded before 27 September 2021, remain valid until 27 December 2022, provided the processing and subject matter do not change, and the existing clauses ensure appropriate safeguards are in place within the meaning of *Schrems II* (Case C-311/18)[44] and otherwise. They must however, be replaced with the Third Country SSCs from 27 December 2022.

EDPB Recommendations on supplementary measures

[3.33]   The final version of the 'European Data Protection Board Recommendations on measures that supplement transfer tools to ensure compliance with the EU level of protection of personal data' was adopted on 18 June 2021. The Recommendations are detailed and substantive, with the stated aim to assist controllers and processors acting as data exporters with their duty to identify and implement appropriate supplementary measures where they are needed.

Law and practice in the third country

The basic tenet of the EDPB Recommendations was elucidated in the judgment of the Court of Justice of the European Union (CJEU) in *Schrems II*. In its judgment, the Court clarified that the level of protection in third countries does not need to be identical to that guaranteed within the EEA but essentially equivalent. While the validity of standard contractual clauses, as a transfer tool that may serve to ensure contractually an essentially equivalent level of protection for data transferred to third countries, the Recommendations state that the clauses, and other transfer tools mentioned under art 46 of the GDPR, are not considered to be enough in themselves to ensure essential equivalence. In the absence of an adequacy decision under art 45(3) of the GDPR, controllers or processors, acting as exporters, are responsible for verifying, on a case-by-case basis and, where appropriate, in collaboration with the importer in the third country, if the law or practice of the third country impinges on the effectiveness of the appropriate safeguards contained in the art 46 GDPR transfer tools.[45]

---

44   *Arthur Cox Employment Law Yearbook 2020* at **[3.02]** addressed the decision in *Data Protection Commissioner v Facebook Ireland LTD, Maximillian Schrems* (Case C-311/18).

45   In line with the principle of accountability in art 5.2 GDPR, which requires controllers to be responsible for, and be able to demonstrate compliance with the GDPR principles relating to processing of personal data.

Modifications

Following a consultation on a draft version of the Recommendations, which opened in 2020, the final version of the Recommendations now includes a subjective element in that the exporter may consider in its assessment the practical experience of the importer, among other elements and with certain caveats. The practices of third country public authorities must be examined in the exporters' legal assessment to determine whether the legislation and/or practices of the third country impinge, in practice, on the effectiveness of the art 46 GDPR transfer tool. The Recommendations also clarify that the legislation of the third country of destination allowing its authorities to access the data transferred, even without the importer's intervention, may also impinge on the effectiveness of the transfer tool.

Steps

The steps, as set out in the Recommendations, are as follows.

1.   Know your transfers.
2.   Verify the transfer tool your transfer relies on, among those listed under Chap V of the GDPR.
3.   Assess if there is anything in the law and/or practices in force of the third country that may impinge on the effectiveness of the appropriate safeguards of the transfer tools you are relying on, in the context of your specific transfer.
4.   Identify and adopt supplementary measures that are necessary to bring the level of protection of the data transferred up to the EU standard of essential equivalence.
5.   Take any formal procedural steps the adoption of your supplementary measure may require, depending on the art 46 GDPR transfer tool you are relying on.
6.   Re-evaluate at appropriate intervals the level of protection afforded to the personal data you transfer to third countries and monitor if there have been or there will be any developments that may affect it.

The Recommendations contain guidance for data exporters undertaking each of the six steps. They anticipate that the data importer will assist in the assessment process at step three by providing the exporter with the relevant sources and information on the third country. Sources and information to determine whether the relevant art 46 transfer tool can be effectively applied should be 'relevant, objective, reliable, verifiable' and importantly 'publicly available or otherwise accessible'. Annex 3 of the Recommendations provides a non-exhaustive list of examples of resources of information that may be used in the assessment. Annex 2 contains a non-exhaustive list of examples of technical, contractual and organisational measures that could be considered for the purposes of step four.

GDPR AND BREXIT

[3.34]   On 28 June 2021, on the basis that the UK offers an equivalent level of protection to personal data as under EU law, the European Commission adopted two UK adequacy decisions under the General Data Protection Regulation (EU) 2016/679 and the Law Enforcement Directive, creating a means for personal data to flow freely from the EU to the UK and much hoped for clarity around the future relationship with the UK.

However, since its departure from the EU, the UK and the UK Information Commissioner's Office (ICO) have launched a number of consultations on the future scope and application of the UK GDPR, ie the retained UK version of the General Data Protection Regulation (EU) 2016/679. The ICO's consultation on international transfers, which was launched on 11 August 2021, provides an indication of the ICO's expectations when it comes to assessing risk in the context of international data transfers. The UK Government's plans for data protection reform are set out in a consultation document entitled 'Data: A new direction'. The European Commission and EU exporters of personal data to the UK will be monitoring these initiatives as they unfold, to ensure that the level of protection to personal data offered by the UK remains equivalent as under EU law, bearing in mind in particular, that the current adequacy decisions in respect of the UK (referred to above) include sunset clauses that limit the decisions to four years, after which they will be reviewed.

Privacy Case Law

Private Life

[3.35] ***Špadijer v Montenegro[46]—European Court of Human Rights—European Convention on Human Rights, art 8—bullying—obligations to protect individuals***

The applicant claimed that, in breach of her rights under art 8 of the European Convention on Human Rights (to respect for her right to family life, her home and her correspondence), the relevant domestic bodies in Montenegro failed to protect her from bullying at work. She further complained that in breach of her rights under art 13 of the Convention, she did not have any effective domestic remedy.

The applicant worked as a prison guard in a woman's prison. She reported her colleagues for indecent behaviour at work, and they were ultimately disciplined for their conduct by temporary reductions in their salaries. Subsequently, she was informed by another colleague that her colleagues had all taken against her, and her car windscreen was smashed, which she reported to the police and ministerial authorities. A number of other incidents were reported by the applicant, including a colleague verbally insulting her and spitting near her. This incident was not investigated by her employer and the applicant was transferred to another role. The applicant made allegations of further bullying and requested her employer to deal with these allegations on 16 August 2013. She went on sick leave in September 2013. She requested that her complaints be dealt with by a mediator, who dismissed her request as unfounded, finding that even if her allegations were true, the conduct did not constitute bullying as it was not continuous

---

[46]   *Špadijer v Montenegro* (Application No. 31549/18).

and the employer could not be responsible for behaviour outside of the workplace, ie the damage to her car. The mediator further found she was transferred due to failure to do her job properly.

On 20 November 2013, the applicant instituted civil proceedings against her employer. Shortly before the domestic Court was due to rule in the civil proceedings, the applicant was physically assaulted in a car park—her assailant told her to 'be careful what you're doing'. The incident was reported to the police and efforts were made to find the perpetrator. The domestic Court ultimately ruled against the applicant, on the basis that the events complained of did not satisfy the definition of bullying, being 'a form of systematic psychological ill-treatment, rather than being sporadic and individual', as it was in the case of the applicant. In particular, the applicant could not show that the alleged bullying had occurred at least once a week for at least six months.

The applicant appealed the decision to the High Court and subsequently to the Supreme Court; both upheld the decision. In the interim period, the applicant retired, owing to a complete loss of working capacity caused by illness. It was specified in the relevant administrative authorities' findings that the first time the applicant's psychological problems had appeared was in 2013, following workplace incidents.

The applicant lodged a constitutional appeal. Her complaints concerned a violation of her dignity and integrity and the lack of an effective remedy. The appeal was dismissed, with the Constitutional Court finding that she had not been bullied at work. There was no reference made to the alleged failure of domestic authorities to act on criminal complaints.

The applicant made a complaint to the European Court of Human Rights (the ECtHR) that her rights had been violated by continuous active and passive bullying at work, and the failure of domestic bodies to protect her from such bullying.

The Government of Montenegro submitted that the claim was ill-founded and there had been no violation of art 8. The lack of frequency of complaints was replied upon, and there had been no causal connection between the psychological harm suffered by the applicant and the actions of the respondent. The alleged criminal damage was said to be unrelated to her bullying claim, and the complaints in relation to said damage and her assault had been duly processed.

The ECtHR observed that the concept of private life is a broad term and extends to other values such as dignity, but that for art 8 to be engaged, the breach must be sufficiently serious. In this case, the ECtHR was satisfied that a causal connection between the psychological problems suffered by the applicant and the alleged incidents in question were clearly established, that art 8 therefore applied, and the complaint was admissible.

In considering the merits of the complaint, the ECtHR observed that the issue was whether the remedies used by the applicant were sufficient and accessible, and secured an effective defence to the applicant's art 8 rights. It noted that the respondent enjoyed a wide margin of appreciation in making this assessment.

The ECtHR found that in the civil proceedings taken by the applicant, her art 8 rights were not sufficiently protected by the domestic courts due to the requirement of proof that the incidents occurred every week for six months. Having regard to the margin of appreciation, the ECtHR found that this approach was inadequate, and that bullying complaints should be examined on a case-by-case basis, not by such a limited rule. The courts had not examined all incidents, and failed to take into account the context and background to the incidents, most notably that the incidents had commenced after the applicant made a report which led to her colleagues receiving disciplinary sanction. It noted that art 8 takes on a particular importance where an attack on such rights may have been triggered by whistleblowing activities. The ECtHR identified specific procedural failures in the manner in which the criminal proceedings were dealt with.

Taking everything into account, the ECtHR found that a violation of the applicant's art 8 rights had occurred, and that Montenegro had failed to comply with its positive obligations under art 8 of the European Convention on Human Rights. The applicant was awarded €4,500 in respect of non-pecuniary damage and €1,000 in respect of costs and expenses.

[3.36] *Vavřička v Czech Republic*[47]*—European Court of Human Rights—Czech Public Health Protection Act—European Convention on Human Rights, art 8 (right to private life)—compulsory vaccination—mandatory approach to a pressing social need—wide margin of appreciation*

In the Czech Republic, the Public Health Protection Act, together with the relevant implementing ministerial decree, place a duty on parents to ensure their children receive certain specified vaccinations. A failure to vaccinate children against diseases well known to medical science constitutes a minor offence, for which a fine may be imposed. In addition, nursery and pre-school facilities may legitimately refuse to accept children who have not received the necessary vaccinations.

This case before the European Court of Human Rights (the ECtHR) originated with six applications brought against the Czech Republic between 2013 and 2015. Five of these applications were made by children who had been refused admission to nursery/pre-school facilities or who had their enrolment cancelled. One application (by Mr Vavřička) was lodged by a father who had been fined for failure to vaccinate his two children. The applicants relied on several provisions of the European Convention on Human Rights (the ECHR), including arts 2 and 9 and in particular art 8 and the right to respect for private life.

Rejecting the Czech Government's claims to the contrary, the ECtHR decided that although none of the applicants had in fact been compulsorily vaccinated, the legal duty imposed by statute constituted an interference in their private lives. Drawing on jurisprudence of the constitutional Court, the ECtHR found that the direct consequences for each of the relevant children in this case were intrinsically linked to the duty that had been enshrined in Czech law, such that the ECtHR was satisfied 'that, in their regard, there has been an interference with their right to respect for private life'.

---

[47] *Vavřička v Czech Republic* Application No. 47621/13.

Having established that there had been an interference, the ECtHR assessed whether such an interference by the Czech Government could be justified. In doing so, the ECtHR drew upon established principles of case law whereby an interference will be considered 'necessary in a democratic society' for the achievement of a legitimate aim if it answers a 'pressing social need' and, in particular, if the reasons adduced by the national authorities to justify it are 'relevant and sufficient' and if it is proportionate to the legitimate aim pursued. The ECtHR found that the vaccination duty imposed by the Public Health Protection Act was legitimate as there was a pressing social need to protect both the individual and public health of residents and to protect the best interests of children. The ECtHR ruled (16:1) in favour of the Czech Government, granting the State a wide margin of appreciation in the assessment of the need for the compulsory vaccination of children.

Turning to the second limb of the test, proportionality, the ECtHR noted that there were exceptions to the compulsory vaccination rule. These exceptions included, for example, cases where a medical contraindication to vaccination existed and circumstances where a secular conscientious objection was made. The ECtHR acknowledged that there were existing safeguards within the legal system and that the vaccines available were generally safe for use. It took into account the fact that (although not directly applicable to any of the applicants in this case) generally, compensation for any injury caused by compulsory vaccination was available through the courts system.

The ECtHR also found that the permitted exclusion of children from pre-school and nursery did not constitute a breach of art 8 on the basis that they were permitted to enrol in primary school thereafter and because the loss of this opportunity was 'the direct consequence of the choice made by their respective parents to decline to comply with a legal duty'. The ECtHR did not address the allegation that the provisions of the Public Health Protection Act amounted to an interference with a child's right to education under art 2.

Surveillance

[3.37] *Gerrard v Eurasian Natural Resources Corporate Ltd & Diligence International LLC[48]—High Court of England and Wales—Protection from Harassment Act 1997—harassment—surveillance—covert—private investigator*

The claimant was a partner in a law firm and had been instructed by Eurasian Natural Resources Corporate Ltd (ENRC) in relation to a corruption investigation by the Serious Fraud Office in the UK. In 2017, ENRC brought proceedings against the claimant and Dechert LLP in the UK Commercial Court alleging that the claimant had secretly leaked confidential and privileged information to the Serious Fraud Office and the media in order to trigger an investigation into ENRC, resulting in a significant amount of work and revenue for both Dechert LLP and the claimant. ENRC sought damages for breach of fiduciary duty and negligence.

---

[48] *Gerrard v Eurasian Natural Resources Corporate Ltd, Diligence International LLC* [2020] EWHC (QB) 3241.

In the context of the Commercial Court proceedings, ENRC instructed Diligence International to conduct covert surveillance of the claimant and his wife. The surveillance activities included:

— the installation and operation of a video camera at Mr and Mrs Gerrard's home, monitoring access to the property;

— obtaining information about Mr and Mrs Gerrard's travel arrangements and attempting surveillance while they were on holiday;

— surveillance of the claimant while at his place of work; and

— following and observing the claimant while at a lunch engagement.

The claimant brought separate proceedings alleging a breach of data protection law, misuse of private information, harassment and trespass arising out of the covert surveillance conducted by Diligence International at the instruction of ENRC.

ENRC and Diligence International brought an application to the High Court seeking to have the harassment claim (among others) struck out on the basis that it had no prospect of success.

The claimant's claim of harassment was brought under s 3 of the Protection from Harassment Act 1997. Harassment is not defined in the legislation, but has been developed through jurisprudence. The High Court referred to *Thomas v News Group Newspapers Ltd*,[49] and specifically looked to the mental element of the offence of harassment, which had been stated as being that the conduct in question be 'calculated' to cause harm to the victim.

ENRC and Diligence International argued that the surveillance was reasonable and necessary in pursuit of the legitimate aim of investigating and preventing wrongdoing, and that the surveillance was not calculated to harass the claimant. They also claimed that these actions could not constitute harassment, as the 'calculated' requirement was not met in circumstances where the surveillance was covert; ie, they did not intend their actions to be discovered and therefore, the surveillance was not calculated to cause harm.

The High Court examined the mental element of harassment and looked to the jurisprudence establishing the definition. The Court determined that a wholly subjective test was 'infelicitous, convoluted and unworkable' and instead found that 'calculated' should be interpreted as 'likely to produce a certain result'. In this instance, 'likely' was to be construed as 'sufficiently likely in all the circumstances' as opposed to a higher threshold of 'more likely than not'.

On that basis, the fact that ENRC or Diligence International did not intend to cause distress to the claimant was irrelevant. Therefore, the application to strike out the harassment claim on the basis that it had no prospect of success was dismissed.

---

[49] *Thomas v News Group Newspapers Ltd* [2001] EWCA Civ 1233.

Chapter 4

Employment Equality

INTRODUCTION

Age

[4.01]   The European Court of Justice considered age discrimination in two cases, *AB* which considered whether a labour reserve scheme in Greece constituted indirect discrimination on the grounds of age and *GN* in which a maximum age for recruitment had to be considered. Two age related equal pay cases are reported, namely *Dr Oliver Lynn* and *the Department of Education and Skills* which considered the post 2011 entrant primary teacher scale. Mandatory retirement ages featured in *Pat O'Donnell & Co, Gordon v Garda Commissioner and Others*, and *The University of Oxford.* Age discrimination in the context of pension schemes was considered in *London Fire Commissioner.*

Burden of Proof

[4.02]   In *Royal Mail Group Limited* the UK Supreme Court addressed the burden of proof in discrimination cases and that issue arose for the UK EAT in *Medrysa*.

Disability

[4.03]   The disability discrimination cases fall into two categories. Firstly, there a number of cases on whether a disability exists and whether the employer had actual or constructive knowledge of the disability. They are *Szpital* (ECJ), *Sullivan* (EWCA), *Bennett* (UK EAT), *Primaz* (UK EAT), *Stott* (UK EAT), *All Answers* (EWCA), *Elliot* (UK EAT) and *Reed* (UK EAT). In the second category are cases where the question of reasonable accommodation was addressed. Those cases are *X* (ECJ), *United Parcel Services* (Labour Court), *R & B Burke* (Labour Court), *Mallon* (UK EAT), *Brightman* (UK EAT), *Aleem* (UK EAT), and *Markden* (UK EAT).

Gender

[4.04]   The European Court of Human Rights considered gender discrimination in cases involving *Romania* and *Croatia*. The European Court of Justice in *Tesco Stores Limited*, examined the law relating to work of equal value carried out in different establishments within an employer's operation. The UK Supreme Court considered similar questions in *Asda Stores*. Gender discrimination in a social security context was considered by the European Court of Justice in *BT*. The implications of pregnancy, maternity leave and parental leave in a gender discrimination context were considered by the WRC in *O'Rourke*, by the Court of Appeal of England and Wales in *Geldart* and in the *Motherhood Plan* and were considered by the UK EAT in *Town*, in *Cumming*, in *Price* and in *De Lacey*. Discrimination in circumstances where the claimant suffered from severe menopausal symptoms was considered by the UK EAT in *Rooney*.

Harassment

[4.05] Harassment on the various grounds featured in *CPL Solutions LTD*, (Labour Court), in *Driscoll* (UK EAT), and *Allay* (UK EAT). The Labour Court had to consider harassment in *MBCC Foods Ireland*.

Religious Belief

[4.06] Discrimination on the grounds of religious belief featured in the European Court of Justice in *IX* and was considered by the Labour Court in *Tipperary Education and Training Board*. In the context of school admission policy, it was considered by the WRC in *A Student v. A Community School*. The removal of a magistrate because of an objection to same sex couple adoptions was considered by the Court of Appeal of England and Wales in *Page*. The entitlement of a fostering agency to accept only heterosexual, married, evangelical Christians to act as carers was considered by the Court of Appeal of England and Wales in *Cornerstone*. In *CDG Europe*, the UK EAT had to consider the termination of a consultancy agreement with the claimant because she expressed gender critical opinions.

Remedies

[4.07] The availability of an effective remedy in discrimination cases was considered by the European Court of Justice in *Braathens Regional Aviation*. The absence of interim relief was considered by the UK Supreme Court in *Anwar*. The Court of Appeal of England and Wales had to consider various matters relating to remedies in *Wisbey*. In *Stormsure*, the UK EAT and the Court of Appeal of England and Wales had to consider whether the absence of interim remedies infringed EU law and the European Convention on Human Rights.

Sexual Orientation

[4.08] *Plaistow* is a case where the UK EAT applied the law relating to sexual orientation discrimination.

Victimisation

[4.09] In *Knox*, the UK EAT considered whether the actions of the employer constituted victimisation.

AGE

[4.10] *AB v Olympiako Athlitiko Kentro Athinon[1]—European Court of Justice—request for preliminary ruling from Greece—Directive 2000/78[2]—employment equality—age*

This preliminary ruling, based on the interpretation of Directive 2000/78, was requested from the Greek courts. The applicant, a former employee of the respondent, was placed on a labour reserve scheme in 2012, having fulfilled the legal criteria of eligibility, which resulted in his pay being reduced by 60%. The respondent terminated his contract a year later in 2013, but refused to pay him severance, arguing that the severance pay could be offset against the amount paid to the employee during the assignment to the labour reserve.

The applicant objected to this and the hearings and appeals eventually reached the Court of Cassation, Greece (the referring Court), which found that there had been no direct discrimination but referred a number of questions to the ECJ on indirect discrimination on grounds of age.

The ECJ summarised the questions from the referring Court as:

> the referring court asks, in essence, whether Article 2 and Article 6(1) of Directive 2000/78 must be interpreted as precluding national legislation under which public-sector workers who, during a given period, fulfil the conditions for drawing a full pension are placed under a labour reserve system until the termination of their contract of employment, something which entails a reduction in their pay, the loss of potential advancement and the partial or even total cancellation of the severance pay to which they would have been entitled on termination of their employment relationship.

The ECJ initially established: (1) that the legislation in question came within the scope of Directive 2000/78; and (2) the application of the scheme was 'based on a criterion which is inextricably linked to the age of the workers concerned'.

The ECJ then sought to establish whether the legislation pursued a legitimate employment-policy objective and whether the means to achieve that objective were appropriate and necessary.

In considering the purpose of the legislation, the ECJ stated that budgetary concerns cannot 'in themselves constitute an aim' pursued by social policy 'in order to justify such a difference in treatment'. However, the ECJ noted that both the Greek Government and the European Commission stated that the objective was not purely budgetary; it also involved streamlining the public sector in light of the 'acute economic crisis' in Greece; instead of terminating the employment of workers, the labour reserve system maintained a high level of employment. Placing workers nearing retirement on the labour reserve system also ensured a 'balanced age structure' in the civil service.

The ECJ considered other objectives of the legislation and noted that it had had the effect of avoiding the potential dismissal of younger workers in the sector. Therefore, it formed

---

[1]   *AB v Olympiako Athlitiko Kentro Athinon* (Case C-511/19).
[2]   Directive 2000/78 on establishing a general framework for equal treatment in employment and occupation.

part of an employment policy which meant the next question was whether this objective was appropriate and necessary to justify a difference of treatment on the grounds of age.

The ECJ concluded that the legislation in question 'does not appear to prejudice unreasonably the legitimate interests of the workers affected. Therefore, in a context where there is an acute economic crisis, it does not go beyond what is necessary to achieve the employment-policy objectives pursued by the national legislature'.

[4.11] *Ministero della Giustizia v GN[3]—European Court of Justice—request for preliminary ruling from Italy—Charter of Fundamental Rights of the European Union—Directive 2000/78/EC[4]—access to employment—age discrimination*

The Italian Ministry of Justice held a competition to fill 500 notarial positions, under legislation which required candidates to be less than 50 years of age. The applicant challenged the legislation in a regional court on the ground that, as she was over the age of 50, she was excluded from the competition. That Court adopted a measure to allow her to take part in the competition and she passed all the necessary tests. Subsequently, the Court declared her action inadmissible on the ground that, as she had passed, she no longer had any interest in bringing proceedings. In appealing this, the Ministry of Justice argued that her case should have been dismissed on its merits. The Appeal Court referred the following question to the ECJ for a preliminary ruling:

> Do Article 21 of [the Charter], Article 10 TFEU and Article 6 of [Directive 2000/78], in so far as they prohibit discrimination on the basis of age for access to employment, preclude a Member State from imposing an age limit on access to the profession of notary?

The ECJ found that as the legislation affected recruitment conditions in accessing the profession of notary, it did fall within the scope of Directive 2000/78; the ECJ then noted that the result of the legislation in question was 'that certain persons are treated less favourably than others in comparable situations on the ground that they have reached 50 years of age' and this was, therefore, a difference in treatment on the ground of age.

The ECJ considered the aims of the legislation put forward by the Italian Government, namely:

> (i) ensuring that the profession of notary is practised in a stable manner for a significant period before retirement, so as to preserve the viability of the social welfare system; (ii) safeguarding the proper functioning of notarial privileges, which entail a high degree of professionalism; and (iii) facilitating the natural turnover and rejuvenation of that profession.

In considering each of the aims put forward the ECJ concluded, in relation to the first aim, that the right to a pension for retiring notaries was contingent on their having practised as a notary for 20 years and bore no relation to the age of 50, therefore 'there appeared to be no connection between the conditions laid down to safeguard the viability of the social welfare system for notaries and that age limit'.

In terms of the second stated aim of safeguarding the professionalism of the role, candidates had to have a law degree, relevant experience and to have completed a 120-day training period. The age limit of 50 had no bearing on this aim.

---

3   *Ministero della Giustizia v GN* (Case C-914/19).
4   Directive 2000/78/EC establishing a general framework for equal treatment in employment and occupation.

Finally, the third aim purported to facilitate 'the natural turnover and rejuvenation of the profession'; however, a notary could work until 75 years of age. The Court observed that, as a significant number of the notarial posts were not filled following the competition, the measure did not provide young candidates access to the profession, and in fact denied candidates over the age of 50 access also. Therefore, in fixing the age limit, the legislation went beyond the third aim asserted by the Italian Government.

The ECJ noted that although the aims had potential to be legitimate, the evidence did not support the conclusion that the legislation in question was pursuing these aims. The Court held that the legislation in question was precluded by art 21 of the Charter and art 6(1) of Directive 2000/78.

Equal Pay

[4.12] *Dr Oliver Lynn v Dr Katherine O'Reilly[5]—Labour Court—appeal from Workplace Relations Commission—Employment Equality Acts 1998 to 2021— employment equality—age—comparators—equal pay*

This was an appeal against the decision of an Adjudication Officer in a claim made by the claimant against her employer, Dr Oliver Lynn, alleging that she was discriminated against on grounds of age in relation to an entitlement to equal pay. The complaint was not upheld by the Adjudication Officer.

The claimant had worked as a locum for a number of years in the respondent's practice and subsequently, in 2011, became his employee. In 2018, the claimant discovered that two younger, female employees of the respondent were being paid more than she was and she alleged that the respondent had discriminated against her on grounds of age. The claimant submitted that she and the two named comparators were all qualified GPs and carried out 'like work'.

The respondent submitted that the claimant had failed to discharge the burden of proof that she was discriminated against on grounds of age. He submitted that the claimant had named two comparators but had inflated the differentiation in hourly pay between them and had failed to mention the additional benefits which she received but they did not. It was submitted that, unlike the two named comparators, the claimant was not required to work out of hours; she received supplementary leave; she had certain medical organisation membership fees paid; and she was paid 50% of fees for any medical legal reports.

The respondent also submitted that the claimant had not carried out the additional two years of training necessary for GPs, which the two comparators had done; nor had she applied at the relevant time to be exempted from this requirement, which resulted in the claimant being unable to be listed on the specialist register and unable to apply for a public patients' list.

The respondent sought to rely on variances in qualifications and training between the claimant and the two comparators to justify any differentiation in pay. He also referred to the claimant's refusal to attend out-of-hours calls, which resulted in other doctors in the practice having to cover the claimant's hours.

---

[5] *Dr Oliver Lynn v Dr Katherine O'Reilly* EDA217.

The respondent explained that he had struggled to recruit and find suitable doctors in recent years and that the two comparators had negotiated their pay and refused to work for less.

The Court considered the various arguments put forward by the parties and held that the determination of the case centred on the questions considered in *Enderby v Frenchay Health Authority*.[6] This case had been referred to by both parties in the course of the hearing and the Court noted that the following extract from the judgment was of most significance to the respondent's argument:

> "The state of the employment market, which may lead an employer to increase the pay of a particular job in order to attract candidates, may constitute an objectively justified ground ..." for paying more to such candidates than to other employees. However, as the Complainant's representative pointed out, this does not afford an employer "carte blanche" to pay wildly different rates of pay and any difference must be proportionate.

The Court noted that the witness evidence given on behalf of the respondent showed that the market for doctors was different between the time when the claimant was recruited by the respondent and the time when the two comparators were recruited—doctors were in a better position to negotiate their pay at the time when the two comparators were recruited. The Court also noted that no evidence had been presented on the claimant's behalf to rebut this.

The Court then turned to consider whether any differentiation in pay was disproportionate. Evidence was given on behalf of the respondent that out-of-hours availability was seen negatively by those who were required to be available and the Court held that the fact that the claimant was not required to work out of hours, unlike the two comparators, was a significantly positive element of her contractual relationship with the respondent. Evidence had been given that the claimant had delayed signing a contract of employment with the respondent for several years until he agreed to drop the requirement that she participate in out-of-hours work. The Court noted that this indicated the value which the claimant placed on not working such hours.

The Court ultimately held that the grounds for the respondent paying differing rates of pay to the two comparators did not fall within the discriminatory grounds set out in the Employment Equality Acts 1998 to 2021. It held that there were market conditions at the time when the comparators were hired which justified them being paid more than the claimant and the differences in pay were proportionate, taking all elements of the claimant's remuneration package into account.

[4.13]   *Department of Education & Skills, Department of Finance, Department of Public Expenditure & Reform, Government of Ireland, Ireland & Attorney General v Horgan & Keegan[7]—Labour Court—appeal from Workplace*

---

6   *Enderby v Frenchay Health Authority* (Case C-127/92).
7   *Department of Education & Skills, Department of Finance, Department of Public Expenditure & Reform, Government of Ireland, Ireland & Attorney General v Horgan & Keegan* EDA2121.

Relations Commission—preliminary reference to the ECJ from Ireland—Directive
2000/78/EC[8]—salary trackers for teachers—indirect age discrimination

The claimants, Ms Keegan and Mr Horgan, challenged the common basic salary scale
for national school teachers established in the Haddington Road Agreement on the basis
of age discrimination. Their comparators were teachers who had entered the workforce
prior to 2011, before the scale was put into practice. They argued that those who joined
after 2011 would earn approximately €100,000 less over the course of their career
compared to those that joined before, which was confirmed in a report, and that 70% of
teachers recruited after 2011 were 25 years of age or under. The respondent argued that
the scale did not discriminate on the basis of age and that the claimants failed to show
'particular disadvantage'; thus, it did not require justification.

The Labour Court posed the following questions for the ECJ:

(1) Did the introduction of salary scales, alongside the decision to leave the pay of
those who were already in employment unaltered, constitute indirect discrimination
on grounds of age within the meaning of art 2(b) of Directive 2000/78/EC where:

   (i) The new and pre-existing salary scales applied regardless of age?
   (ii) There was no difference in the age profile of those in the higher paid group
        compared to the lower paid group at the time of recruitment?
   (iii) The introduction of the scales had resulted in a substantial difference in pay
         between two groups who worked for the same value?
   (iv) The average age of those placed on the reduced salary scale was lower than
        those placed on the previous salary scale?
   (v) When the scales were introduced, statistics showed that 70% of teachers
        appointed were 25 or under?
   (vi) Teachers who entered after 2011 suffered a clear financial disadvantage to
        those appointed prior to 2011?

(2) If the answer to (i) was in the affirmative, could it be justified by the need to
achieve medium to long term structural reduction in the cost of the public service
given the budgetary constraints and the need to maintain good industrial relations?

(3) Would the answer to question (ii) be different if the State could have achieved
equivalent savings by reducing the pay of all teachers by a lesser amount than the
amount forgone by teachers recruited after 2011?

(4) Would the answer to questions (ii) or (iii) be different if the decision not to reduce
the salary scales of those that were already in employment was taken in compliance with a previous trade-union agreement and industrial relations consequences
would flow from a failure to comply with such agreement?

In relation to question 1, the ECJ held that for the purpose of Directive 2000/78/EC,
there must be no direct or indirect discrimination on the grounds of age and that indirect

---

[8] Directive 2000/78/EC establishing a general framework for equal treatment in employment and
     occupation.

discrimination occurs where an apparently neutral provision would put persons of a particular age at a disadvantage. However, these measures could potentially be justified by the State pursuing a legitimate aim and doing it through appropriate and necessary means. It was held that the difference in treatment of the salary scales resulted from the date of recruitment, not from age. Further, irrespective of the year of recruitment, both the teachers recruited before and after 2011 were on average 25 years of age or under. The ECJ held that the provision should be interpreted as not constituting indirect discrimination on the grounds of age. It was unnecessary to answer the remaining questions.

The appeal failed and the decision of the WRC was upheld.

Mandatory Retirement Age

[4.14] *Pat O'Donnell & Co v O'Keeffe[9]—Labour Court—appeal from Workplace Relations Commission—Employment Equality Acts 1998 to 2021—mandatory retirement age*

This was an appeal from a finding from the Adjudication Officer that the claimant's claim of age discrimination was not well founded. The claimant was employed as a service engineer with the respondent. The respondent's retirement plan set the normal retirement age at 65. In July 2019, the claimant wrote to the respondent seeking to work beyond his 65th birthday, but this request was refused on the basis that it was company policy that all service engineers retire on their 65th birthday due to succession planning. SIPTU, which represented the claimant in the Labour Court, wrote to the respondent on the claimant's behalf, requesting to extend the claimant's contract for one year, to bring him up to the State pension age of 66, but the respondent rejected his application. The claimant alleged that he was discriminated against on grounds of age, however the respondent submitted that the mandatory retirement age was objectively justified for that category of worker.

The claimant submitted that there was no objective legitimate aim for the mandatory retirement age and noted that office employees often continued to work for the respondent beyond the age of 65. He also submitted that another service engineer was permitted to stay on beyond retirement age. The respondent pointed out that the claimant was aware of the mandatory retirement age for service engineers, and that although it was not provided for in the claimant's contract, it had been 'universally employed'. The respondent asserted that the individual referenced by the claimant had not worked as a service engineer for a period before his retirement and continued providing cover for the warehouse manager after his retirement.

On the balance of probabilities, the Court found there was a mandatory retirement age in place for service engineers. In deciding whether such a mandatory retirement age was objectively justified the Court noted:

> the undisputed evidence of the Respondent's witnesses concerning the nature of the job, the fact that it is safety critical, the training period required to qualify service engineers, the investment required by the Respondent in terms of training apprentices to the standard they required.

---

[9]   *Pat O'Donnell & Co v O'Keeffe* EDA2133.

Taking all of the above into account the Court found that the mandatory retirement age was justifiable and that the legitimate aim was 'to ensure a through flow of appropriately qualified service engineers and to ensure that employees are not required to continue working until they are unable to perform the duties'.

The Court confirmed the decision of the WRC and rejected the appeal.

[4.15] *Gordon v Garda Commissioner & Minister for Justice and Equality[10]— Workplace Relations Commission—Employment Equality Acts 1998 to 2021— Directive 2000/78/EC[11]—age discrimination—mandatory retirement of claimant as chief superintendent of An Garda Síochána in 2008—objective justification— whether mandatory retirement age of 60 is appropriate and necessary*

The claimant, who held the rank of chief superintendent at the time of his retirement, claimed that he was discriminated against on grounds of age by the requirement to retire at age 60, the mandatory retirement age in An Garda Síochána. The claimant claimed that the mandatory retirement age was unlawfully discriminatory, being less favourable treatment on the age ground contrary to the Employment Equality Act 1998, as amended, and contrary to art 2(2) of Directive 2000/78/EC.

The background was that although there had been a relatively complex set of mandatory retirement age provisions in An Garda Síochána, by 1998 the common mandatory retirement age was 60. However, the regulations empowered the Garda Commissioner, if satisfied that it was in the interests of the efficiency of An Garda Síochána, to extend the retirement age of any applicant for extension by reason of their experience or some special qualification. The Commissioner was, in those circumstances, empowered with the consent of the Minister for Justice and Equality to extend the age by such period not exceeding five years as the Commissioner should determine.

The claimant had applied for such an extension but his application was denied by the Commissioner, who did not give reasons for that decision.

The respondents contented that the compulsory retirement age was objectively and reasonably justified by legitimate aims and was appropriate and necessary to achieve those aims. The aims cited as justifying the compulsory retirement age of 60 included:

1.   the need to maintain stability in the Force at a time of particular change for An Garda Síochána;
2.   the related importance of maintaining equality and fairness for all members in terms of an equal retirement age (of 60);
3.   the need to ensure maximum operational and administrative efficiency at a time when An Garda Síochána was already going through a time of significant change;
4.   the need to avoid internal unease in the event that the then policy of retirement at age 60 for all members would be changed for a particular group;

---

10   *Gordon v Garda Commissioner & Minister for Justice and Equality* DEC-E2020-004. *Duggan v Garda Commissioner* DEC-E2020-005; *Murphy v Garda Commissioner* DEC-E2020-006 and *Brislane v Garda Commissioner* DEC-E2020-007 are identical in all respects save that Brislane was a superintendent rather than a chief superintendent.
11   Directive 2000/78/EC establishing a general framework for equal treatment in employment and occupation.

5.   the risk of claims from other ranks for changes in their retirement age;

6.   the risk of creating a serious hiatus in the succession process through stagnation in the promotion process if the retirement age for this group of senior officers was to be increased;

7.   the risk of creating a loss of morale amongst suitably skilled and competent members in the middle ranks (eg, sergeants and inspectors) who would be seeking and expecting promotional opportunities based on the compulsory retirement age of 60 for Superintendents and Chief Superintendents;

8.   the maintenance of motivation within the force and senior ranks by preventing the blocking of the Superintendent and Chief Superintendent ranks; and

9.   the creation of a competitive pool of candidates from which Assistant and Deputy Commissioners might be chosen.

The respondents also highlighted the possibility of individual assessment provided for in the regulations permitting an extension of the mandatory retirement age in any case, and the claimant's entitlement to a pension on retirement. The respondents contended that the High Court had, in *Donnellan v Minister for Justice, Equality & Law Reform*,[12] determined the matter and upheld the mandatory retirement age.

The claimant contended that it was for the respondents to establish that the fixed retirement age relied on was objectively justified by a legitimate aim and that the means of achieving that aim were both appropriate and necessary. The burden of proof was on the respondents and cogent evidence was required to discharge the burden; mere denials of discriminatory motive, in the absence of independent corroboration, had to approached with caution since discrimination was usually covert and subconscious.

After an extensive survey of decisions from the European Court of Justice and domestic legislation, the Adjudication Officer concluded on the evidence that the respondents met the test of objective justification. The Adjudication Officer noted in particular the evidence from Garda HR to the effect that, had the claim to increase the retirement age (from 60 to 63) of superintendents and chief superintendents been acceded to, the relevant staff association for sergeants and inspectors was ready to lodge a similar claim for equality and parity. Furthermore, the evidence from Garda HR was to the effect that, the extension of the retirement age for chief superintendents from 60 to 63 would have a negative impact on morale and promotional opportunities for the lower ranks. Promotional opportunities were by way of competitive process and the extension of the retirement age could result in many capable members leaving the job to source work externally by reason of the reduced number of promotional opportunities.

There was evidence to the effect that there would have been much unease and disquiet among officers in the middle ranks seeking promotion had the mandatory retirement age for superintendents and chief superintendents been extended. Indeed, it was noted that the claimant himself had the benefit of being promoted by reason of members being compulsorily retired at age 60.

The Adjudication Officer noted that, in *Donnellan*, the High Court held that where multiple reasons are given for an early retirement age, it is enough if one or more amount to a legitimate aim. The fact was also noted that in *Donnellan* the Court had

---

[12]   *Donnellan v Minister for Justice, Equality and Law Reform* [2008] IEHC 467.

considered that Mr Donnellan had the benefit of a generous pension and lump sum on retirement to be relevant.

The Adjudication Officer accepted in particular that the following aims justified a compulsory retirement age of 60:

[i] the risk of creating a serious hiatus in the succession process through stagnation in the promotion process if the retirement age for this group of senior officers was to be increased and

[ii] the risk of creating a loss of morale amongst suitably skilled and competent members in the middle ranks (eg Sergeants and Inspectors) who would be seeking and expecting promotional opportunities based on the compulsory retirement age of 60 for Superintendents and Chief Superintendents.

The Adjudication Officer concluded that, having considered all of the reasons put forward to justify a retirement age of 60, she was:

satisfied that it was a legitimate aim and a legitimate employment policy to have succession planning as part of the rationale for having a retirement age of 60 to ensure there was a sufficient pool of suitably qualified candidates for promotion through a competitive process.

Accordingly, the Adjudication Officer concluded that the respondents had met the test of objective justification.

The Adjudication Officer found that the fact that there was a legal power to extend the age of retirement 'goes the heart of the issue of proportionality' and that 'the fact the respondent has a policy that enables a member over 60 to remain in certain circumstances clearly tempers the existence of an absolute retirement age'.

The Adjudication Officer also found, in this context, that it was relevant that 'access to a pension is a significant factor, in that it goes to the issue of proportionality' and the decision of the European Court of Justice in *Palacios de la Villa*[13] was cited in support of the proposition. The Adjudication Officer observed that members of the force, on attaining 30 years' service, can retire on a full pension and it was noted that the claimant had 30 years' service and accordingly had access to a pension which he described at the hearing as being a good and generous pension.

The Adjudication Officer found that the respondents had established objective justification for having a legitimate employment policy with a legitimate aim and the means to achieve the aim were appropriate and necessary. Accordingly, the claim was dismissed.

[4.16] *Pitcher v Chancellor Masters and Scholars of the University of Oxford and Chancellor Masters and Scholars of the University of Oxford v Ewart*[14]*—UK Employment Appeal Tribunal—appeal from employment tribunal—mandatory retirement—proportionality of Employer Justified Retirement Age policy*

In *Pitcher v Chancellor Masters and Scholars of the University of Oxford*, the claimant was an associate professor of English literature at Oxford University and an official

---

13   *Palacios de la Villa v Cortefiel Servicios SA* (Case C-411/05); [2007] ECR I-8531.

14   *Pitcher v Chancellor Masters and Scholars of the University of Oxford and Chancellor Masters and Scholars of the University of Oxford v Ewart* EA-2019-000638-RN (previously UKEAT/0083/20/RN) and EA-2020-000128-RN (previously UKEAT/0032/20/RN).

fellow and tutor in English at St John's College. He was compulsorily retired at age 67 from both employments by operation of the Employer Justified Retirement Age (EJRA) policy, after his application to have his employment extended under the EJRA policy was refused. An employment tribunal dismissed his claims of direct age discrimination and unfair dismissal, finding that the EJRA policy was justified and the dismissal fair. The claimant appealed this decision.

In *Chancellor Masters and Scholars of the University of Oxford v Ewart*, the claimant was an associate professor in atomic and laser physics at Oxford University. The EJRA policy was also applied to him but he initially obtained an extension of his employment, vacating his substantive post and taking up a fixed-term position. Upon his application for a further extension, the claimant was unsuccessful and also faced compulsory retirement. An employment tribunal upheld his claims of direct age discrimination and unfair dismissal, finding that the respondent had not shown the EJRA policy to be justified. The university appealed against the decision.

The EAT held that the university had the following legitimate aims in relation to mandatory retirement ages: (1) inter-generational fairness; (2) succession planning; and (3) equality and diversity. The aim of the EJRA policy was to facilitate measures in achieving those aims by ensuring vacancy creation was not delayed and that recruitment into senior academic roles could take place from a younger, more diverse cohort. In the *Pitcher* case, the employment tribunal acknowledged the limited evidence demonstrating the policy's impact but noted that the EJRA policy was relatively new. The EAT held that the tribunal was entitled to give due consideration to evidence from a survey of retirees that indicated that around a quarter would have continued in employment for a further three years had it not been for the EJRA policy. In these circumstances, the EAT was satisfied that it was not perverse of the tribunal to find that, absent the EJRA policy, turnover would have been significantly lower. The tribunal also had regard to the mitigating effects of the extension provisions and the availability of post-retirement opportunities for senior academics.

However, in the *Ewart* case, a statistical analysis was available which showed that the rate of vacancies created by the EJRA policy was trivial (between approximately 2% and 4%). The EAT found that the tribunal had acted reasonably in finding that there was insufficient evidence to show that the EJRA policy was contributing to the university's stated legitimate aims. The EAT also found that the tribunal was entitled to hold that the discriminatory impact of the policy was severe and not significantly mitigated by the extension provisions. Evidence was given of the very restrictive rules governing a second extension under the EJRA policy. The tribunal took into account that there was no financial detriment to the university as a result of the extension (the substantive post already having been vacated); nor was there any financial impediment to the refilling of the applicant's permanent role. Therefore, these factors could not be considered as part of the legitimate aims.

The EAT stated that, although the two tribunals had reached different conclusions on proportionality on the evidence before them, neither had erred in law. It stated that the nature of the proportionality test meant that it was possible for two differently constituted tribunals to reach different conclusions when considering the same measure adopted by the same employer in respect of the same legitimate aims. It emphasised that the role of the EAT is not to find a single answer, but to decide whether a particular decision is wrong in law. The EAT also pointed out that the presentation of the claims and the evidence before the tribunals differed in two significant respects. First, the tribunal in the *Ewart* case had the benefit of statistical analysis that was not available to the tribunal hearing the earlier case. Second, there was a difference in the evidence of the detriment suffered by those to whom the EJRA policy applied, and the extent to which any ongoing working relationship might mitigate that detriment. Both appeals were dismissed.

[4.17] *London Fire Commissioner v Sargeant[15]—UK Employment Appeal Tribunal—appeal from employment tribunal—Equality Act 2010, Sch 22, para 1(1)—employment equality—age discrimination—pension schemes*

The claimants were members of the Fire and Rescue Authorities (the FRA) pension scheme. The public sector pension schemes, including the FRA's pension scheme, underwent reforms following the publication of the Independent Public Service Pensions Commission Report conducted by Lord Hutton.

The appeal centred on whether the FRA was permitted to rely on para 1(1) of Sch 22 of the Equality Act 2010 as a defence to a claim of age discrimination in implementing the transitional measures arising from these reforms.

The FRA operated the Firefighters' Pension Scheme 1992 (the 1992 Scheme), which was overhauled in 2015. The relevant transitional measures, namely the Firefighters' Pension Scheme (England) Regulations 2014[16] and the Firefighters' Pension Scheme (Wales) 2015,[17] (the Regulations) established a new scheme (the 2015 Scheme). Under the Regulations, with effect from 1 April 2015, members of the Firefighters' Pension Scheme who were born on or after 2 April 1971 ceased to accrue benefits under the 1992 Scheme and automatically joined the 2015 Scheme. Their comparators were members who were born on or before 1 April 1967, who remained part of the 1992 Scheme until retirement. Those born between 2 April 1967 and 1 April 1971 had tapered protection.

The claimants challenged the transitional measures as discrimination on the grounds of age. At the employment tribunal, the FRA sought to rely on para 1(1) of Sch 22 of the Equality Act 2010 as a defence to any claim of age discrimination. Paragraph (1) states that an act of a person does not constitute age discrimination in contravention of the Equality Act 2010 if that person is acting by virtue of 'a requirement of an enactment'. The FRA submitted that they had been acting in response to the Regulations in implementing the transitional measures contained in the Regulations. This constituted a 'classic case within paragraph 1(1) of Schedule 22', and as such the FRA was fully protected by the defence contained therein. The employment tribunal rejected this submission, and found that no such defence existed for the FRA.

---

15   *London Fire Commissioner v Sargeant.*
16   Firefighters' Pension Scheme (England) Regulations 2014 (SI 2014/2848).
17   Firefighters' Pension Scheme (Wales) 2015 (SI 2015/622 (W.50)).

The FRA's appeal of this decision was stayed while a preliminary issue of whether the transitional measures were objectively justified was determined. The Court of Appeal ultimately held that the transitional measures were discriminatory on the grounds of age, and there was no objective justification for this discrimination.[18] The stay on the FRA's Sch 22 appeal was thereafter lifted.

The FRA appealed the employment tribunal's finding that there was no defence available under Sch 22 on a number of grounds. It submitted that the employment tribunal had erred in its interpretation of ss 61 and 62 of the Equality Act 2010, which contain a 'non-discrimination rule' in relation to occupational pension schemes. The FRA submitted that there was nothing in these sections providing 'that any discriminatory provisions in any scheme are automatically erased or disapplied'.

It also submitted that the employment tribunal had erred in its decision that the FRA's application was inconsistent with EU law. The FRA submitted that it was not their case that the claimants could not bring any claim for age discrimination under the Equality Act 2010—rather it was their submission that an effective remedy for any such discrimination lay with the Department for Communities and Local Government and the Welsh Ministers, as opposed to the FRA.

In response to these grounds of appeal, the claimants submitted that the employment tribunal had correctly determined that the principle of non-discrimination as contained in s 61 had the effect that discriminatory rules were overridden or modified as a matter of law, in order to adhere to the principle of non-discrimination as contained therein. As such 'there was no statutory requirement for the FRAs to provide discriminatory pensions under the scheme as modified'. Furthermore, the claimants argued that it is recognised that it is not possible to rely on national law as a defence to any discrimination protected on an EU level, and Sch 22 should not be construed so as to exclude any claim against the FRAs.

The EAT rejected all grounds of appeal. It rejected the FRA's submission that it had no choice but to implement the transitional measures. The EAT held that the effect of s 61 was in fact to prohibit the FRA from acting in a discriminatory manner, noting that the

> way in which section 61 works is clear. It prohibits the FRAs from acting in a manner which discriminates on the grounds of age and it prioritises that obligation over other provisions which would oblige them to act in that way. In this way it gives effect to the UK Government's obligations under EU Directive 2000/78.

The EAT also upheld the employment tribunal's finding in relation to EU law, ultimately determining that EU law is such that any discriminatory provisions of the Regulations should be overridden or amended to the effect that the FRA would not be in contravention of the Equality Act 2010 by applying them.

The EAT upheld the decision of the employment tribunal in full.

---

18 *McCloud v Lord Chancellor; Secretary of State for the Home Department v Sargeant* [2019] EWCA Civ 2844. See *Arthur Cox Employment Law Yearbook 2019* at **[4.05]**.

BURDEN OF PROOF

[4.18] *Royal Mail Group Ltd v Efobi[19]—UK Supreme Court—Hodge, Briggs, Hamblen & Leggatt LJJ, Arden LJ—Equality Act 2010, s 136—burden of proof*

The respondent identified as a black African and was a citizen of Ireland. He held qualifications in IT from Trinity College Dublin and was employed as a postman by the appellant. The respondent made several unsuccessful applications for IT roles within Royal Mail between 2011 and 2015. He brought proceedings in the employment tribunal for both direct and indirect discrimination of grounds of race, which were not upheld, as he had failed to establish any discrimination on how the appellant dealt with his applications. He also brought complaints of harassment and victimisation and was successful in some of these claims. The respondent appealed the finding that there had been no direct discrimination regarding his job applications and the EAT upheld his appeal. The EAT found that the tribunal had erred in placing the initial burden of proof on the respondent and in its assessment of the evidence. The appellant appealed this finding to the Court of Appeal, which was bound by its finding in *Ayodele v Citylink Ltd*,[20] and upheld the appeal.

This appeal by the respondent to the UK Supreme Court related to two key issues. The first was whether the respondent bore the initial burden of proof under s 136 of the Equality Act 2010 (the 2010 Act), and the second was whether adverse inferences could be drawn against Royal Mail arising from a failure to call relevant individuals involved in the allegedly discriminatory conduct (ie those who processed his applications) to give evidence.

On the first matter, having considered the authorities and the wording of s 136, the Supreme Court held that the respondent bore the burden of proof at the first stage of the claim, namely:

> the [respondent] has the burden of proving, on the balance of probabilities, those matters which he or she wishes the tribunal to find as facts from which the inference could properly be drawn (in the absence of any other explanation) that an unlawful act was committed. This is not the whole picture since ... along with those facts which the [respondent] proves, the tribunal must also take account of any facts proved by the [appellant] which would prevent the necessary inference from being drawn.

The Court upheld the finding in *Ayodele* that, despite the change of language in s 136, the law remains unchanged in this area and the claimant's appeal on this ground was rejected.

On the second issue, the Court held that, despite the fact that no adverse inferences could be drawn at the first stage, adverse inferences could be drawn if the respondent failed to call relevant witnesses. Whether such inferences can be drawn depends very

---

19 *Royal Mail Group Ltd v Efobi* [2021] UKSC 33. See *Arthur Cox Employment Law Yearbook 2019* at **[4.36]** for Court of Appeal of England and Wales decision.
20 *Ayodele v Citylink Ltd* [2017] EWCA Civ 1913.

much on the circumstances of each case. The Court stated that 'tribunals should be free to draw, or to decline to draw, inferences from the facts of the case before them using their common sense without the need to consult law books when doing so'.

The Court pointed out that to succeed in an appeal on the ground that no reasonable tribunal could have omitted to draw such an inference would be 'extremely hard'. It considered the arguments that the successful candidates were of a different race to the respondent and that the recruiters were aware of the claimant's race when rejecting his applications and concluded that the tribunal could not be 'faulted for not drawing the adverse inferences contended for from the fact that no evidence was adduced from the actual decision-makers'. The Court found that if such inferences had been drawn, they were not sufficient in themselves to shift the burden of proof to Royal Mail.

The appeal was dismissed in its entirety.

[4.19]   *Medrysa v London Borough of Tower Hamlets[21]—UK Employment Appeal Tribunal—appeal from employment tribunal—employment equality—race discrimination—burden of proof*

The claimant, who described his race as white Polish, was employed by as a debt recovery officer by a local authority. He asserted before the employment tribunal that he had been discriminated against on the grounds of race, citing a number of alleged incidents of discrimination. He was unsuccessful because he could not establish a difference in treatment between himself and someone of another race, nor was there any evidence to suggest that his race had any impact on how he was treated in circumstances where he relied on a hypothetical comparator. Where a difference in treatment did arise, all he had established was a difference in race and a difference in treatment—he had not established facts that would allow the employment tribunal to conclude that discrimination had occurred.

The claimant appealed to the EAT on the grounds that the employment tribunal hadn't appropriately considered whether he raised preliminary facts sufficient to shift the burden of proof to the local authority to prove that the difference in treatment suffered by the claimant arose from matters other than the claimant's race.

Three incidents were relevant for the purpose of the hearing—failure to progress certain procedures in respect of the claimant's duties, refusal of special leave, and failure to follow an anti-discrimination procedure.

The claimant's argument in respect of the anti-discrimination procedure was that he had been treated less favourably when compared to black and Asian colleagues. He asserted that their complaints had been treated in accordance with the anti-discrimination procedure, but his was not, and this was enough to require the employment tribunal to request evidence as to why the difference in treatment had occurred. He stated that two black employees were treated more favourably than him in respect of special leave, and that the employment tribunal should have obliged the local authority to demonstrate this

---

[21]   *Medrysa v London Borough of Tower Hamlets* UKEAT/0208/20/VP.

was not due to his race. He stated that a manager had failed to follow advice given by HR in respect of procedures related to the claimant's duties, and that the employment tribunal hadn't followed up on why this was the case.

The EAT noted the importance of considering evidence as a whole when determining whether a burden of proof had shifted, and that the employment tribunal had clearly taken such an overview, when it stated:

> There was no direct evidence of the Claimant's actual nationality or colour being a factor in this claim. The Claimant was not asserting that any alleged discriminators had a propensity to disfavour Polish people or white people. The Claimant sought to rely on inferences from the treatment of alleged comparators.

The EAT noted that the claimant was labouring under a misunderstanding that the burden of proof could be shifted merely by highlighting a difference in treatment and a difference of race between him and a comparator/hypothetical character. It rules that this is not sufficient and that 'something more' is needed to shift the burden of proof. It emphasised that this 'may not be a great deal', and cited potential examples as including the explanation for the adverse treatment, or factual evidence.

The EAT emphasised the importance of carefully considering all the evidence before dismissing a complaint on the basis that the burden of proof had not been shifted. It found that the employment tribunal had engaged in careful consideration of the evidence and was entitled to reach its conclusion. Further, the EAT emphasised that the presence of unimportant factual errors in the decision of the employment tribunal did not invalidate that decision, noting the conditions in which employment tribunals consider these complaints, and the fact that there was no evidence to suggest that the claimant had met the test.

The appeal was dismissed.

DISABILITY

[4.20] *Szpital Kliniczny im. dra J. Babinskiego, Samodzielny Publiczny Zaklad Opieki Zdrowotnej w Krakowie[22]—European Court of Justice—request for a preliminary ruling from Poland—Directive 2000/78/EC,[23] art 2—concept of 'discrimination'*

This was a request for a preliminary ruling from Poland to the ECJ on the interpretation of art 2 of Directive 2000/78/EC, which established a general framework for equal treatment in employment and occupation.

The case concerned a psychologist, VL, who in 2011 submitted a disability certificate to her employer, the hospital, for her 'moderate and permanent' disability.

---

[22]　*Szpital Kliniczny im. dra J. Babinskiego, Samodzielny Publiczny Zaklad Opieki Zdrowotnej w Krakowie* (Case C-16/19).

[23]　Directive 2000/78/EC establishing a general framework for equal treatment in employment and occupation.

After a meeting in 2013, the director of the hospital launched an initiative in an effort to reduce the amount of contributions payable by the hospital to the State Fund for the Rehabilitation of Persons with Disabilities (the State Fund) whereby the hospital would grant a monthly allowance to workers who submitted a disability certificate. In Poland, at the time, employers who employed more people with disabilities were required to pay less in contributions to the State Fund. The aim of this initiative was to encourage workers with disabilities who had not yet submitted a disability certificate to do so. However, the workers who had submitted their disability certificates before this date in 2013 did not receive the allowance. VL was one of 16 workers who did not receive the allowance.

VL was unsuccessful in the District Court in arguing that she had been the subject of discrimination in relation to pay and she appealed to the Regional Court, which referred the following question to the ECJ:

> Should Article 2 of [Directive 2000/78] be interpreted as meaning that the differing treatment of individual members of a group distinguished by a protected characteristic (disability) amounts to a breach of the principle of equal treatment if the employer treats individual members of that group differently on the basis of an apparently neutral criterion, that criterion cannot be objectively justified by a legitimate aim, and the measures taken in order to achieve that aim are not appropriate and necessary?

The ECJ noted that the scope of the Directive covered all persons in both public and private sectors and the concept of pay for this provision must be interpreted broadly. It stated that the Directive 'is intended to protect a worker who has a disability, for the purposes of that directive, against any discrimination on the basis of that disability, not only as compared with workers who do not have disabilities, but also as compared with other workers who have disabilities'.

In considering those who had submitted their disability certificates before 2013 and those who had submitted their disability certificates after 2013, the ECJ stated that 'those two categories of workers with disabilities were in a comparable situation'.

The ECJ commented 'that the employer does not appear to have given workers with disabilities who had already submitted their certificates the opportunity to resubmit their certificates, or to file new ones, in order to receive such an allowance' and ruled that:

— the practice adopted by an employer and consisting in the payment of an allowance to workers with disabilities who have submitted their disability certificates after a date chosen by that employer, and not to workers with disabilities who have submitted those certificates before that date, may constitute direct discrimination if it is established that that practice is based on a criterion that is inextricably linked to disability, inasmuch as it is such as to make it impossible for a clearly identified group of workers, consisting of all the workers with disabilities whose disabled status was necessarily known to the employer when that practice was introduced, to satisfy that temporal condition;

— that practice, although apparently neutral, may constitute discrimination indirectly based on disability if it is established that, without being objectively justified by a legitimate aim and without the means of achieving that aim being appropriate and necessary, it puts workers with disabilities at a particular disadvantage depending on the nature of their disabilities, including whether they are visible or require reasonable adjustments to be made to working conditions.

[4.21] *Sullivan v Bury Street Capital Ltd[24]—Court of Appeal of England and Wales—Jackson & Singh LJJ, Laing LJ—appeal from the Employment Appeal Tribunal—Equality Act 2010—actual or constructive knowledge*

The appellant contended that the employment tribunal and subsequently the EAT erred in finding that: (a) he did not have a disability within the meaning of the Equality Act 2010; and (b) that the respondent employer did not have knowledge (actual or constructive) of the disability.

The appellant was employed as a senior sales executive with the respondent in 2009, just as the global financial crisis started. In 2013, the appellant had a relationship with a Ukrainian woman. After it ended, he began to have paranoid delusions that he was being monitored and followed by a Russian gang. The question that arose was whether this potential persistent delusional disorder constituted a disability. The appellant had 'major episodes' in 2013 and 2017.

In 2017, the appellant's employment was terminated on the grounds of his 'lacking the skillset to fulfil his role effectively and his attitude'. The issues with capability included timekeeping, lack of communication, unauthorised absences, and poor record-keeping. The appellant brought a claim for unfair dismissal, discrimination, and unlawful deduction of wages.

The appellant's claim for unfair dismissal was upheld by the employment tribunal, as it was deemed procedurally unfair, and the claim for deduction of wages was dismissed. In dismissing the appellant's claim under the employment equality legislation, the employment tribunal found that the appellant's condition did not qualify as a disability under the Equality Act 2010. It found that the paranoid delusions that the appellant began suffering in May 2013 did give rise to a substantial adverse effect but this did not last beyond September 2013. Although the appellant maintained his delusional belief in the existence of the Russian gang beyond this point, it no longer had the relevant effect on his ability to carry out normal day-to-day activities. The employment tribunal also found that the respondent did not have actual or constructive knowledge of the appellant's disability.

The EAT upheld the employment tribunal's findings but granted permission to appeal to the Court of Appeal on three grounds, ie, the employment tribunal erred in finding that:

1. there was no substantial adverse effect throughout the period from 2013 to 2017;
2. the appellant did not have a recurring condition; and
3. the respondent did not have actual or constructive knowledge of the disability.

The Court noted that the questions for the appeal came down to whether the employment tribunal's reasons were adequate, and concluded:

> [H]owever dressed-up, the present appeal is in substance an attempt to challenge the findings of fact which were made by the ET. There being no perversity challenge (and in my view any such challenge would have failed in any event), I have reached the conclusion that this appeal must be dismissed.

---

[24] *Sullivan v Bury Street Capital Ltd* [2021] EWCA Civ 1694. See *Arthur Cox Employment Law Yearbook 2020* at [4.06] for EAT decision in *Sullivan v Bury Street Capital Ltd* UKEAT/0317/19/BA.

[4.22]   *Bennett v MiTAC Europe Ltd*[25]—**UK Employment Appeal Tribunal—appeal from employment tribunal—disability discrimination—actual or deemed knowledge**

The claimant worked for a manager who was diagnosed with cancer. As a result of the diagnosis, the work of both the manager and the claimant came to an end and both were dismissed. The claimant brought a claim of direct disability discrimination before the employment tribunal, who found that the employer had discharged the burden of proof that the claimant had not been the subject of direct discrimination as a result of his manager's disability, but had been dismissed due to poor performance.

The claimant appealed and the EAT allowed the appeal on the basis that the employment tribunal erred in finding that the burden of proof had properly been discharged. The EAT was persuaded by the fact that the decision maker was not called to give evidence on behalf of the employer. The EAT also found that the employment tribunal had wrongly found that, in order for there to be actual or deemed knowledge of a disability such as cancer, a medical diagnosis was required.

[4.23]   *Primaz v Carl Room Restaurants t/a McDonalds Restaurants Ltd*[26]—**UK Employment Appeal Tribunal—appeal from employment tribunal—Equality Act 2010, s 6(4)—employment equality—discrimination on the ground of disability—cancer**

The within proceedings comprised appeals by both the claimant and the respondent in respect of certain aspects of the preliminary findings of the employment tribunal relating to a claim of discrimination on the ground of disability.

The claimant had an operation to remove an 'astrocytic' tumour on her brain in 2008. At no time was the claimant told that her tumour was cancerous, nor did her medical records include the word 'cancer'. However, the claimant contended that she still had cancer in 2018/2019, at the time of the alleged discrimination. The claimant submitted that the employment tribunal erred in concluding that the claimant's tumour was not cancer and further erred in concluding that she did not have cancer at the time of the alleged discrimination but was discriminated against on grounds of epilepsy and vitiligo.

Despite the absence of material specific to the claimant indicating that her tumour was cancerous, the claimant referred to material produced by Public Health England to the effect that tumours of the type which the claimant had had removed were now considered to be cancer. However, the claimant did provide the pathology report which described her tumour as 'low grade'. The respondent relied on caselaw stating that it is insufficient to show that the tumour may have turned into cancer, had it not been removed. The EAT noted that once cancer is determined to have existed, it is classified as a disability under UK law regardless of its stage. The EAT allowed this ground of the claimant's appeal and concluded that the claimant had cancer at the time the operation occurred.

---

25   *Bennett v MiTAC Europe Ltd* EA-2020-000349-LA (previously UKEAT/0185/20/LA).
26   *Primaz v Carl Room Restaurants t/a McDonalds Restaurants Ltd* EA-2020-000110-JOJ and EA-2020-000278-JOJ (previously UKEAT/0137/20/JOJ and UKEAT/0172/20/JOJ respectively).

Conversely, the EAT upheld the finding of the employment tribunal that the claimant did not have cancer in 2018/2019 on the basis that there was no evidence that she had suffered from cancer after the operation. The claimant sought to rely on material which merely suggested that epilepsy and vitiligo, from which she suffered, might be caused by cancer.

The employment tribunal had also concluded that the claimant's epilepsy and vitiligo amounted to disabilities as the claimant did not participate in activities such as coffee drinking, wearing cosmetics, and she avoided sun exposure and did not take any medications as she believed these actions would be harmful to her given her epilepsy and vitiligo; however, these beliefs were not substantiated by medical evidence.

By way of appeal the respondent contended that the employment tribunal erred in concluding that the claimant's epilepsy and vitiligo were sufficient to amount to a mental or physical impairment that had a significant adverse effect on the claimant's ability to carry out normal day-to-day activities. The respondent submitted that the employment tribunal had incorrectly taken account of the claimant's subjective beliefs that certain behaviours would trigger her conditions and her resulting abstinence from such behaviours.

The EAT accepted the respondent's submission that the test is an objective one and the claimant's subjective beliefs, unsupported by any evidence, that engaging in certain activities would exacerbate her epilepsy and/or vitiligo and her decision not to engage in such activities was not sufficient evidence of disability; and the employment tribunal had erred in taking account of such subjective beliefs. The EAT found that the claimant was acting in accordance with her own unsubstantiated beliefs and so the chain of causation required was fractured such that it could not be said that her epilepsy had an adverse effect on the claimant's ability to carry out normal day-to-day activities. In terms of the claimant's vitiligo and her exposure to the sun, the EAT found that the employment tribunal would have to make further detailed findings as to whether this amounted to a disability.

The EAT therefore substituted the employment tribunal's finding and concluded that the claimant did have cancer in 2008, but dismissed the claimant's appeal against the finding that she did not at the time of the alleged incidents in 2018/2019 have cancer. The EAT allowed the respondent's appeals against the employment tribunal finding that the claimant's vitiligo and epilepsy amounted to a disability and remitted those particular questions for fresh consideration. The EAT ruled that, on remission, the employment tribunal would not be considering the claimant's behaviours in determining her causation case but would be examining more specific evidence of the impact of her actual conditions on her day-to-day activities such as her exposure to the sun in respect of vitiligo and the frequency and impact of her epileptic seizures.

[4.24]   *Stott v Ralli Ltd*[27]*—UK Employment Appeal Tribunal—appeal from employment tribunal—Equality Act 2010, s 15—disability—knowledge of employer— specificity of claims*

The claimant was employed as a paralegal by the respondent from October 2017 until her dismissal on account of her poor performance in January 2018. She brought a

---

[27]   *Stott v Ralli Ltd* EA-2019-000772-VP (previously UKEAT/0223/20/VP).

discriminatory dismissal claim under s 15 of the Equality Act 2010 (the 2010 Act) arising from her dismissal.

The claimant's poor performance quickly became evident following commencing work, and the respondent made a decision to dismiss her due to her performance. On 8 January 2018, the respondent held a meeting with the claimant, at which she was informed of her dismissal. The claimant did not appeal her dismissal.

Shortly following the dismissal the claimant lodged a number of grievances including allegations that she was dismissed due to her mental health issues and a heart condition. She was informed by way of letter that her grievances were unsuccessful. This letter contained a statement confirming that the claimant had never previously informed the respondent of her disabilities. The claimant appealed the outcome of the grievance procedure and the appeal was ultimately dismissed.

She brought a claim of discriminatory dismissal under s 15 of the 2010 Act on grounds of disability, citing a mental health impairment and a heart condition. Reliance on the heart condition was withdrawn before the hearing.

The employment tribunal found that the claimant had suffered from anxiety and depression which amounted to a disability. However, it dismissed her claim that she had been discriminatorily dismissed on the grounds of her disability. It held that while the dismissal constituted unfavourable treatment, she had been dismissed because of her poor performance. The employment tribunal also found that the respondent could not have known or could not reasonably have known about her disability, in circumstances where the claimant had never disclosed her mental health issues before her dismissal.

The claimant appealed the employment tribunal's findings on three grounds: (1) the employment tribunal erred in failing to determine whether her poor performance arose due to her disabilities; (2) the employment tribunal erred in not treating the grievance procedure and appeal as part of the dismissal decision, and failing to consider the respondent's knowledge of the claimant's disability in this context; and (3) the employment tribunal erred in that it failed to adequately conduct a balancing exercise as to whether the dismissal was a proportionate means for the respondent to achieve a legitimate aim. To be successful in the appeal before the EAT, the claimant was required to succeed on all three grounds.

The EAT upheld the first ground of appeal, finding that the employment tribunal had failed to address the question of whether the claimant's poor performance arose from her disability of anxiety and depression.

In relation to the respondent's knowledge of the disability, the EAT held that the respondent did not have actual or constructive knowledge of the claimant's disability at the time of the dismissal and such information only came to light after the dismissal, during the grievance procedure. It then considered whether the employment tribunal had erred in not considering whether the respondent had or should reasonably have had knowledge of the claimant's disability at the time of the appeal of the grievance outcome. The EAT ultimately held that this argument had not been advanced by the claimant. The EAT noted that the specificity of the claimant's claims had been considered at multiple preliminary hearings and there was no reference to a complaint relating to discriminatory treatment after the date of her dismissal. The claimant therefore failed on ground two of her appeal.

The third ground of appeal also failed. The EAT held that the employment tribunal had properly performed the balancing exercise in determining whether the respondent's dismissal of the claimant was a proportionate means of achieving a legitimate aim. It held that the employment tribunal had correctly interpreted the law and made sufficient findings of fact to support its conclusion.

As only one of three grounds succeeded, the EAT dismissed the appeal.

[4.25] *All Answers Ltd v W[28]—Court of Appeal of England and Wales—Lewison, Lewis & Newey LJJ—appeal from UK Employment Appeal Tribunal—Equality Act 2010—whether depression is a disability—long-term adverse effect*

This case concerned disability discrimination claims brought by two employees of the appellant. The respondents claimed that in August 2018 they had each been suffering from depression and that the appellant's decision to alter where they sat in the office gave rise to direct discrimination. The matter was heard before the employment tribunal, which found that both of the respondents fell within the definition of disability under the Equality Act 2010. The appellant appealed the decision to the EAT but was unsuccessful; it subsequently appealed to the Court of Appeal on the basis that the tribunal had 'failed to assess whether the claimants' mental impairments had a "long term" substantial adverse effect as at the date of the alleged discrimination'. The appellant also submitted that, in relation to one of the respondents, Ms R, the tribunal had considered events which had occurred after the dates of the alleged discrimination and that the tribunal should have considered whether, on the date of the alleged discrimination, it 'had been likely that the effect of the impairment would have been long term'.

Section 6 of the Equality Act 2010 sets out that a person has a disability if that person has a physical or mental impairment and that impairment has a substantial and long-term adverse effect on the person's ability to carry out day-to-day activities. Schedule 1 of the Equality Act 2010 states that the effect of an impairment is 'long term' if it has lasted for at least 12 months; is likely to last for at least 12 months; or is likely to last for the rest of the life of the person affected. It also states that if the impairment no longer has a substantial adverse effect on a person's ability to carry out day-to-day activities, it is treated as continuing to have such an effect if the effect is likely to recur.

Before the Court of Appeal, the appellant accepted that in August 2018 both of the respondents were suffering from a mental impairment and that this impairment had a substantial adverse effect on each of their abilities to carry out day-to-day activities. However, the appellant submitted that there was a requirement under Sch 1 of the Equality Act 2010 that the adverse effect be long term, ie, likely to last for 12 months and that the tribunal had failed to assess whether the adverse effect of the respondents' impairments were long term as at the time of the alleged discrimination.

---

[28]   *All Answers Ltd v W* [2021] EWCA Civ 606.

In considering the Equality Act 2010, the Court stated that the question to be considered was whether, at the time of the alleged discrimination, 'the effect of an impairment is likely to last at least 12 months' and this question needs to be assessed in accordance with the facts and circumstances which existed on the date of the alleged discrimination. The Court also stated that, in making such an assessment, a tribunal cannot give consideration to events which occurred after the date of the alleged discrimination.

The Court found that the tribunal had failed to assess whether the effect of the mental impairments suffered by the respondents, as at the date of the alleged discrimination, were likely to last at least 12 months.

First, the Court noted that in its decision the tribunal had referred to the issue as being whether each of the respondents 'are disabled'. It stated that the language used by the tribunal suggested that it had considered whether the respondents were disabled as at the date of the hearing as opposed to as at the date of the alleged discrimination.

Second, the Court noted that the tribunal's decision was articulated in the present tense and did not seem to consider matters as at the date of the alleged discrimination.

Third, the Court stated that the tribunal's decision did not make any reference to the dates of the alleged discrimination.

In finding that the tribunal had failed to address one of the requirements of the definition of disability as set out under the Equality Act 2010, the Court held that the tribunal's decision was 'legally flawed' and, accordingly, it allowed the appeal and remitted the issue to the tribunal to determine.

[4.26]   *Elliott   v   Dorset   County   Council[29]—UK   Employment   Appeal Tribunal—appeal   from   employment   tribunal—Equality   Act   2010—disability discrimination—substantial adverse effect*

The claimant was employed by the respondent as an Information Systems Manager for 34 years. In 2018, the claimant's new line manager instigated a disciplinary process against the claimant in which it was alleged that the claimant had exaggerated the number of hours he had worked. The allegations were denied by the claimant, who claimed that he had agreed with his previous line manager that he would record having worked from 9.00 am to 5.00 pm each day, regardless of whether that was actually the case on the day in question. In addition, the claimant argued that he, in fact, worked longer hours than were provided for in his contract of employment. During the investigation, the claimant submitted that he had difficulty communicating and engaging with his new line manager, as well as with the time management rules implemented by the new line manager.

In the course of the disciplinary process, during which the claimant was represented by a trade union official, the official requested that the claimant be medically assessed to determine whether he was on the autism spectrum, in light of the difficulties identified by the claimant in his dealings and interactions with his new line manager.

---

[29]   *Elliott v Dorset County Council* UKEAT/0197/20/LA.

Following an assessment, it was confirmed that the claimant was on the autism spectrum and, specifically, had Asperger's Syndrome.

While the disciplinary process was ongoing, the respondent announced a proposal to restructure the claimant's department. The claimant accepted redundancy arising from the restructure and received an *ex gratia* severance package, which included that no further steps would be taken in relation to the disciplinary process. Following his acceptance of the severance package, the claimant made a complaint of unfair dismissal and disability discrimination against the respondent.

The employment tribunal concluded that Asperger's Syndrome did not have a 'substantial' adverse effect on the claimant's ability to perform his duties of employment, by reference to the definition in the Equality Act 2010 (the 2010 Act). As the employment tribunal determined that this limb of the test for disability had not been satisfied, it concluded that the claimant was not disabled for the purposes of the 2010 Act. In doing so, the employment tribunal placed emphasis on what the claimant could do. A key extract from the employment tribunal's ruling noted that:

> Whilst [the respondent] reports that he does not find it easy to speak in public or to socialise for example and whilst he clearly has to prepare mentally for doing these things, he clearly is not prevented from doing them or substantially adversely impacted when he does them.

The claimant appealed the employment tribunal's ruling to the EAT, asserting that the employment tribunal had placed too much emphasis on what the claimant could do, in comparison to others, and had not considered the effect of Asperger's Syndrome on matters with which the claimant struggled, such as accepting organisational and operational changes in the workplace.

The EAT held that, when asked to rule on whether an individual suffers from a disability under the 2010 Act, employment tribunals must adhere to the statutory definition of 'substantial' in preference to any non-statutory definition when determining whether a disability can be said to have a 'substantial adverse effect' on the individual, as envisaged by s 6 of the 2010 Act.

'Substantial' is defined in the 2010 Act to mean 'more than minor or trivial'. As such, and by reference to this definition, the EAT held that if the adverse effect of an individual's disability has more than a minor or trivial influence on his/her ability to perform his/her duties of employment, then the 'substantial adverse effect' part of the definition of disability will be satisfied. The EAT noted in this context that it is what a person cannot do, or what he/she can only do with difficulty, that is the focus of the test—not what they can do without difficulty.

The EAT concluded that the employment tribunal had erred in the approach it had taken in determining whether the claimant's diagnosis of Asperger's Syndrome had a 'substantial adverse effect' on his ability to perform his duties of employment. The EAT held that the employment tribunal could not make such a determination by comparing the claimant to others, and that the correct approach is to consider the manner in which the claimant performed his duties in light of having Asperger's Syndrome, against how he would perform them if he did not have Asperger's Syndrome. The EAT stressed that the fact that the claimant might be just as proficient as others at a given activity was irrelevant if he would have been even more proficient at it were it not for his having Asperger's Syndrome.

The EAT remitted the question of whether the claimant was disabled within the meaning of the 2010 Act to a freshly constituted employment tribunal.

[4.27]   *Seccombe v Reed In Partnership Ltd[30]—UK Employment Appeal Tribunal—appeal from employment tribunal—disability—actual or constructive knowledge of employer*

This case concerned an appeal against an employment tribunal decision which found that the claimant was not disabled or, if he was, the respondent did not possess actual or constructive knowledge of the claimant's disability.

The claimant had been employed by the respondent from November 2016 until March 2018. The claimant's employment had come to an end when he was summarily dismissed, and he alleged that his dismissal amounted to discrimination on disability grounds and/or that the respondent had failed to make reasonable adjustments. The claimant submitted that at the time of his dismissal he was disabled by reason of severe anxiety and depression.

The claimant's GP records noted that in 2008 the claimant had seemed depressed, and he was referred to counselling at that time. They also noted that in 2015 he had suffered from stress. Both of these instances were prior to the claimant's employment with the respondent.

Between 2011 and 2015, the claimant had worked with one of the respondent's employees, Mr Atter, in another company. During that time, Mr Atter had never been made aware of the claimant having any mental health concerns.

In November 2016, the claimant began working for the respondent. In a questionnaire for the respondent, he had answered 'no' to the question of whether he 'had any health-related issues or impairment for which the respondent might need to make reasonable adjustments'.

In 2017, the claimant had undergone performance management and had not referred to any mental health concerns which may have given rise to his performance issues.

In December 2017, a traumatic event occurred which resulted in the claimant being extremely upset and he was later signed off work due to ill-health. The claimant returned to work in February 2018. In completing a document ahead of a performance review meeting in March 2018, the claimant stated that the issues which had led to his absence were 'ongoing and unlikely to be resolved fully for the foreseeable future (police investigation and psychological/emotional recovery)'. However, at no stage did the claimant refer to 'severe anxiety and depression' which he relied on in his claim; nor did he make any other reference to suffering from any mental health condition.

---

[30]   *Seccombe v Reed In Partnership Ltd* EA-2019-000478-OO.

On 28 March 2018, the claimant was dismissed on poor performance grounds. The minutes from the meeting referred to the claimant being very upset and aggressive about the dismissal and stating he was being dismissed because of the traumatic event which had occurred in 2017. He made no reference to any disability or mental health concerns.

On appeal, the EAT first considered the tribunal's finding that the respondent did not have knowledge of, and could not be reasonably expected to have knowledge of, the claimant's disability. It also considered the definition of disability and noted that the claimant 'had to establish that he had at some stage prior to the alleged discrimination had a mental impairment that had a substantial and long-term adverse effect on his ability to carry out normal day-to-day activities'. With regard to the requirement that the impairment had a long-term effect, the EAT noted that the fact that a person has an impairment which is long term will not suffice, rather the substantial adverse effect on the person's ability to carry out day-to-day activities must be long term.

The claimant had signed a document which stated that he had no such impairment upon the commencement of his employment with the respondent. The respondent was also not aware of the claimant's previous periods of impairment, nor had he ever suggested to the respondent, even in his dismissal meeting, that he suffered from a mental impairment. On this basis the tribunal had found that the respondent did not have knowledge of the disability, nor could it reasonably be expected to have knowledge of the disability and the EAT concluded that the tribunal had applied the correct legal test in this regard.

The EAT then considered the allegation that the tribunal had failed to consider a number of specific pieces of evidence. It stated that tribunal decisions 'have to be kept reasonably concise' and therefore it is not possible for the tribunal to refer to every specific piece of evidence which may be relevant to the case. It stated that the tribunal needs to 'form a view on the totality of the evidence' and it found that there had been no perversity or error of law in the tribunal's decision.

The EAT found that, on the evidence before the tribunal, it was entitled to conclude that, while the claimant had suffered from an impairment for a period of time in 2018 which had a substantial adverse effect on his ability to carry out day-to-day activities, the respondent did not know and could not reasonably have been expected to know that the effects were long term. It stated that this conclusion was 'sufficient to defeat the disability discrimination claims brought by the claimant'.

[4.28] *X v Tartu Vangla*[31]*—European Court of Justice—request for preliminary ruling from Estonia—Directive 2000/78,*[32] *art 2(2)—disability—dismissal— proportionate—legitimate aim—reasonable accommodation*

The applicant was employed for almost 15 years as a prison officer by the respondent prison. His duties included supervising persons under electronic surveillance by means of a surveillance system, passing on information on those persons, monitoring

---

[31]   *X v Tartu Vangla* (Case C-795/19).
[32]   Directive 2000/78/EC establishing a general framework for equal treatment in employment and occupation.

surveillance and signalling equipment, responding to and communicating information, particularly in the event of alarms, and identifying breaches of the prison's internal regulations. The applicant had a hearing impairment since his childhood. He was dismissed by the governor of the prison on the grounds that his level of auditory acuity did not meet the minimum standards of sound perception prescribed by national regulations. The applicant instituted proceedings, claiming that his dismissal was unlawful as constituting discrimination on the grounds of disability contrary to national law.

That action was dismissed at first instance but his appeal was upheld by the Estonian Court of Appeal and he was awarded compensation. The Estonian Court of Appeal raised issues with regard to the constitutionality of the relevant national regulations and referred the matter to the Supreme Court of Estonia which in turn, referred to the European Court of Justice (the ECJ) the following question:

> Should Article 2(2), read in combination with Article 4(1), of [Directive 2000/78] be interpreted as precluding provisions of national law which provide that impaired hearing below the prescribed standard constitutes an absolute impediment to work as a prison officer and that the use of corrective aids to address compliance with the requirement is not permitted?

The applicant had been subjected to auditory tests and had failed them. The national regulations did not allow the claimant to use hearing aids during those tests.

The ECJ noted that Directive 2000/78/EC (the Directive) applied because the case concerned a prison officer's conditions of recruitment and dismissal. The ECJ noted that under the relevant Estonian regulations, persons with a reduced level of auditory acuity below the prescribed minimum standards of sound perception could not be recruited or continue in the employment as prison officers. They were therefore treated less favourably than other persons in a comparable situation, namely other workers employed as prison officers whose level of auditory acuity met those standards. It followed that the Estonian regulations established a difference of treatment based directly on disability within the meaning of art 2(2)(a) of the Directive.

The ECJ noted that art 4(1) of Directive 2000/78 entitles Member States to provide that a difference in treatment which is based on a characteristic relating to any of the grounds referred to in art 1 of the Directive does not to constitute discrimination if 'such a characteristic constitutes a genuine and determining occupational requirement, provided that the objective is legitimate and the requirement is proportionate'. The ECJ observed that it has previously held that it is not the ground on which the difference of treatment is based, but a characteristic related to that ground which must constitute a genuine and determining occupational requirement. The ECJ stated that art 4(1), read in the light of Recital 23 to the Directive refers to 'very limited circumstances' in which such a difference of treatment may be justified and must be interpreted strictly.

The ECJ also noted that Recital 18 of Directive 2000/78 specifies that the Directive does not require prison services to recruit or maintain in employment persons who do not have the necessary capacity to perform the range of functions necessary with regard to the 'legitimate objective of preserving the occupational capacity of those services', ie, ensuring the occupational capacity and proper functioning of those services constitutes a legitimate objective under art 4(1) of the Directive.

Furthermore art 2(5) of Directive 2000/78 provides that the Directive is to be without prejudice to national laws which are necessary 'for public security, for the maintenance of public order and the prevention of criminal offences, for the protection of health and for the protection of the rights and freedoms of others'.

The ECJ observed that the impugned Estonian regulations, by providing for minimum standards of sound perception, non-compliance with which constituted an absolute medical impediment to performing the duties of a prison officer, sought to protect persons in public order by ensuring that prison officers were physically capable of performing all the tasks that were required of them. The ECJ pointed out that the impugned regulations required that a prison officer's 'level of auditory acuity must be sufficient to communicate by telephone and to hear the sound of an alarm and radio messages'.

The ECJ stated that it has already held that the possession of particular physical capacities may be regarded as a 'genuine and determining occupational requirement' within the meaning of art 4(1) for the purposes of employment in certain professions such a firefighter or prison officer. Therefore, by reason of the nature of a prison officer's duties and of the context at which they are carried out, the fact that his or her auditory acuity must satisfy minimum standards of sound perception laid down by national legislation may be regarded as a 'genuine and determining occupational requirement'. The ECJ noted that, as the impugned regulations sought to preserve the safety of persons in public order, it must be held that the national regulations pursued legitimate objectives.

However, it was still necessary to ascertain whether the requirement that a prison officer's auditory acuity must meet minimum standards of sound perception without the use of corrective aids being permitted during the assessment was an absolute medical impediment in performing his/her duties resulting in his/her dismissal was proportionate.

The ECJ observed that it was apparent from the information contained in the reference that compliance with the minimum standards of sound perception was assessed without, for the prison officer concerned, any possibility of using a hearing aid; but that in assessing visual acuity, an officer may use corrective devices such as contact lenses or spectacles. The ECJ noted however that the wearing, loss, or deterioration of contact lenses or spectacles may also hinder the performance of the prison officer's duties and create risks for him/her comparable to those resulting from the use, loss or deterioration of a hearing aid, particularly in situations of physical confrontation that the officer may encounter.

The ECJ observed that the national regulations applied an absolute ban on all prison officers who failed to meet the minimum prescribed medical standards, irrespective of their individual roles or the actual duties they performed, nor did the regulations take account of corrective measures such as hearing aids worn inside the ears or under head gear.

The ECJ noted that art 5 of Directive 2000/78 must be read in the light of Recitals 20 and 21, and that employers are obliged to take appropriate measures to enable a person with a disability to have access to or participate in employment, unless such measures would impose a disproportionate burden on the employer. The ECJ has previously held that 'reasonable accommodation' should be read broadly to encompass the elimination of the 'barriers that hinder the full and effective participation of persons with disabilities in professional life on an equal basis with other workers'. The ECJ noted that the obligation is also enshrined in the United Nations Convention on the Rights of Persons with Disabilities.

The ECJ concluded that the regulations, by providing for minimum standards of sound perception, non-compliance with which constituted 'an absolute medical impediment to the exercise of the duties of a prison officer, without allowing it to be ascertained whether that officer is capable of fulfilling his/her duties where appropriate after the adoption of reasonable accommodation measures', appeared to impose a requirement beyond that which was necessary to attain the objective pursued by the impugned regulations. However, that was for the referring Court to ascertain.

The ECJ held that the answer to the question referred was that art 2(2)(a), art 4(1) and art 5 of Directive 2000/78 'must be interpreted as precluding national legislation which imposes an absolute bar to the continued employment of a prison officer whose auditory acuity does not meet the minimum standards of sound perception prescribed by that legislation, without allowing it to be ascertained whether that officer is capable of fulfilling those duties', after the adoption of reasonable accommodation measures.

[4.29] *United Parcel Service of Ireland Ltd v Roberts*[33]*—Labour Court—appeal from Workplace Relations Commission—Employment Equality Acts 1998 to 2021— discriminatory dismissal—disability—reasonable accommodation*

The claimant was employed by the respondent from October 1986 until he was dismissed in August 2019, on the grounds of incapability. The claimant had a history of stress-related health issues. In January 2016, he went on sick leave and was advised to remove himself from work-related stressors. In April 2016, the respondent arranged a medical assessment which stated that he was not fit to return to work but that he might be in a position to do so in three months, provided his treatments were successful. He continued to be unfit to return to work during 2016 and 2017. In May 2018, he was admitted to hospital for 10 weeks.

On 3 December 2018, he was declared fit to return to work, subject to him being facilitated with reduced travel requirements and being able to maintain proximity to his support network. The claimant's role required extensive travel, both in Ireland and abroad, which he was unable to do after he returned from sick leave. It was agreed with the respondent that he should be eased back into work and this was facilitated by allowing him to make package deliveries locally in the run up to Christmas.

There were discussions regarding a role in a different team based in Dublin. However, he was later advised that it was not available as there were concerns regarding his senior grading level, when compared to other members of the team. He was put on paid leave and asked to remain at home. In February 2019, he was told that there was no

---

[33]   *United Parcel Service of Ireland Ltd v Roberts* EDA2136.

suitable role for him in Ireland. The respondent proposed a lower-level role, which the claimant declined as his pension was based on final salary. At this time, the claimant, reluctantly, raised the possibility of a severance package but he was advised that the company was not open to this.

In March 2019, the claimant attended another medical assessment that found he was not fit to return to his role but was fit for alternative roles which would minimise travel and responsibilities. Before a meeting with the respondent in May 2019, he was told that if a solution could not be found, the respondent might terminate his contract on grounds of capability. After this meeting, the company wrote to him advising him that he was being dismissed. He appealed the decision but his appeal was unsuccessful.

The claimant then brought two complaints to the WRC. The WRC did not uphold his complaint of discriminatory dismissal but found that the respondent had breached the Employment Equality Acts 1998 to 2021 by failing to provide the claimant with reasonable accommodation due to his disability and awarded the claimant €20,100. The claimant appealed the decision to the Labour Court.

The Labour Court found that there was no dispute about the claimant's disability, which meant that he was unable to travel to the extent required in his job. He was assessed as medically fit to return, subject to him not being required to engage in travel and subject to adjustments in responsibilities. However, the Court found that he was not accommodated and, as a result of his inability to travel which, in turn, was due to his disability, he was dismissed.

The Court first considered whether the respondent made the efforts required by s 16 of the Employment Equality Acts 1998 to 2021 to provide the claimant with reasonable accommodation to facilitate him in returning to work. The Court referred to the Supreme Court decision on reasonable accommodation in *Nano Nagle v Daly*,[34] and stated that there is no requirement on the employer to find another distinct and separate job for an employee with a disability. However, the Court noted that 'there is a requirement on employers to explore alternative modes of accommodation to establish if the position held by the employee with a disability is capable of adaptation so as to accommodate that employee'.

The Court found that the evidence was clear that the respondent had not undertaken an assessment to establish whether the claimant's role could have been done without the requirement for travel which would allow him to return to the role. There appeared to have been a simple assumption that it was not possible. The Court noted that the evidence before it was that there had been periods in the past during which travel was curtailed for budgetary reasons, and indeed during the pandemic, and that it had still been possible to do the job in those circumstances.

The Court further stated that the respondent should have had a time-limited trial where the job was performed without the previous level of international travel; if this trial did not prove viable, the respondent would have been able to prove so to the Court. As a

---

[34]   *Nano Nagle v Daly* [2019] IESC 63.

result of the respondent's failure to consider whether reasonable accommodation could have been provided, as required by s 16 of the Acts, the Court found that the claimant's rights were breached and he was discriminatorily dismissed.

In assessing compensation, the Court noted that while there was no obligation on the respondent to provide alternative employment, this had been explored. The Court stated that the claimant's refusal to show flexibility and consider anything other than employment at his existing salary level hampered the respondent's ability to find alternative employment for him. The Court set aside the decision of the WRC and awarded the claimant €75,000 in compensation, which was close to one year's salary but did not include an unguaranteed bonus.

[4.30]   ***R & B Burke Catering Services Ltd v Oglesby***[35]***—Labour Court—appeal from the Workplace Relations Commission—Employment Equality Acts 1998 to 2021—reasonable accommodation—transfer of undertakings***

This was a double appeal from the decision of the Workplace Relations Commission in which the claimant appealed the quantum of the award, and the respondent appealed the decision in its entirety.

The claimant had worked for the predecessor of the respondent and subsequently came under the employment of the respondent, following a transfer of undertakings on 31 August 2018. The claimant suffered from Achilles tendonitis which the parties did not dispute amounted to a disability under the Employment Equality Acts 1998 to 2021. The claimant had attended an occupational health assessment with the predecessor, who had advised that she should not spend more than three or four hours a day on her feet, should not lift anything above 5kg and that her duties should be varied between standing and sitting. The predecessor had made reasonable accommodations to facilitate those requirements such as providing a chair for the claimant so she could sit while working at the till, and temporarily reducing her hours.

After the transfer of the business to the respondent, the chair at the till was removed and the claimant's duties were altered such that she was required to lift heavy pots and trays. The claimant raised the matter with the respondent, and submitted a letter from her GP stating that her condition was worsening. This was not acknowledged by the respondent. The claimant also raised the issue with the respondent through her union but the respondent declined to make reasonable accommodation. The claimant went on certified sick leave in January 2019 and remained on sick leave until her resignation in April 2021.

The claimant brought a claim to the WRC, submitting that the respondent had discriminated against her on grounds of disability in failing to provide reasonable accommodation when her employment transferred to them.

The respondent maintained that, on the transfer, it had not received any documentation relating to the reasonable accommodations that had been made for the claimant or the

---

[35]   *R & B Burke Catering Services Ltd v Oglesby* EDA2129.

requirement for the claimant to have light duties, and that it only became aware of the matter when the claimant raised the issue in October 2018. The respondent confirmed to the Labour Court that on obtaining knowledge of the claimant's reasonable accommodation requirement, it did not carry out an assessment. The respondent submitted that the chair at the till was removed as it was identified as a hazard after a trip incident and that the heaviest pot the claimant was required to lift was 4kg, therefore below the limit suggested. The respondent submitted that there was not much scope to provide seated duties given the nature of the job.

The Labour Court concluded that the reasonable accommodations required were minimal and had been in place prior to the transfer of undertakings. It held that the defence that to provide a reasonable accommodation would put a disproportionate burden on the respondent was not open to the respondent as they had failed to perform an assessment or properly consider whether any reasonable accommodation was feasible. The respondent's appeal failed. The claimant's appeal on quantum was upheld, and she was awarded compensation of €5,000.

[4.31] *Mallon v AECOM Ltd[36]—UK Employment Appeal Tribunal—appeal from employment tribunal—Equality Act 2010—discrimination—access to employment—reasonable adjustment—reasonable accommodation—strike out*

The claimant, who had dyspraxia, requested the respondent to allow him to make a job application orally rather than through an online process, contending that he would be at a material disadvantage to other candidates were he forced to go through the application process online. The respondent refused and the claimant subsequently brought a claim to the employment tribunal.

The employment tribunal dismissed the claim on the basis that the claimant had no reasonable prospect of success since he could not demonstrate that he was actually left at a material disadvantage by the respondent's failure to put in place a reasonable adjustment to allow him to make his job application orally. The claimant appealed the employment tribunal's decision to strike out the claim, arguing that the employment tribunal had erred in law by failing to consider physical features and auxiliary aids when deciding an issue of reasonable adjustment.

Section 20 of the Equality Act 2010 places certain obligations on an employer to make reasonable adjustments to help a disabled candidate or employee, in circumstances where the candidate or employee would be placed at a significant disadvantage by: (a) an employer's provision, criterion or practice (PCP); (b) a physical feature of the employer's premises; or (c) an employer's failure to provide an auxiliary aid.

The EAT overturned the decision of the employment tribunal, concluding that it had indeed erred in dismissing the claim. In doing so, the EAT stressed that the decision to strike out a claim must be reserved for use in only 'the most obvious and plain cases', and that claims of discrimination, by their nature, could only very rarely be said to be obvious and plain. The EAT noted that it was important to consider, in all claims

---

[36]   *Mallon v AECOM Ltd* UKEAT/0175/20/LA, [2021] IRLR 438.

involving reasonable adjustments, not only the PCP limb, but also the other limbs in s 20, ie, the physical features of the workplace and the provision of auxiliary aids, which it held that the employment tribunal had failed to do. The EAT also noted that while a candidate or employee's family or friends might be prepared or in a position to provide assistance to him/her, that could not automatically be assumed, and it was not something that could absolve an employer from making a reasonable adjustment itself.

The EAT remitted the claim to a freshly constituted employment tribunal.

[4.32] *Brightman v TIAA Ltd*[37]*—UK Employment Appeal Tribunal—appeal from employment tribunal—Equality Act 2010—dismissal due to capability—medical evidence—reasonable adjustments*

The claimant had numerous long-term health conditions, including severe asthma and a slipped disc. There was no dispute that, due to her conditions, she qualified as having a disability under the Equality Act 2010. The claimant's absences from work as a result of her conditions were accommodated by the respondent prior to 2015. However, despite making adjustments to her working hours and type of work, her absences due to illness increased. The respondent sought medical opinions in respect of the claimant's condition in 2016 and was informed that her absence levels were unlikely to improve.

The respondent did not consider that further accommodations were possible; it noted that unacceptable levels of absence were likely to continue and that no alternative roles were available. The claimant was dismissed due to capability in early 2017. She brought a claim that her dismissal had been unfair, that she had been discriminated against on grounds of disability and that the respondent had failed to make reasonable adjustments for her.

The employment tribunal dismissed her claims. It accepted that her dismissal had been within the respondent's range of reasonable responses. In doing so, the employment tribunal permitted the respondent to introduce medical evidence at the hearing that post-dated the claimant's dismissal. The claimant appealed that decision to the EAT.

The EAT noted several aspects of the claimant's case. The claimant attended work throughout the dismissal and appeal processes, the report provided by her own GP was over a year old and the occupational health report the respondent had obtained was six months old at the time of her dismissal. Since the date of the occupational health report, she had been receiving new treatment and further, that report was an assessment of her fitness to work and not an assessment of her long-term prognosis.

The EAT found that the employment tribunal had erred in law in relying on medical evidence that post-dated the claimant's dismissal, which was irrelevant in determining whether the respondent had been reasonable in its original decision to dismiss.

The EAT also found that the employment tribunal's assessment of the reasonable adjustments that the respondent could have made for the claimant was also defective. The conclusion that it would not have been reasonable for the respondent to wait

---

[37]   *Brightman v TIAA Ltd* [2021] UKEAT0318/19/0207.

another 12 months for the claimant's health to improve was based on medical evidence showing that her health had not in fact improved after her dismissal and the tribunal should have considered what reasonable adjustments could have been made for her on the basis of medical information available at the date of her dismissal.

The claimant's case was remitted to be heard by a freshly constituted employment tribunal.

[4.33] *Aleem v E-Act Academy Trust Ltd[38]—UK Employment Appeal Tribunal— appeal from employment tribunal—disability—reasonable adjustment*

This case concerned an appeal against a decision of the employment tribunal which dismissed the claimant's claim that the respondent had failed to make reasonable adjustments.

The claimant was employed as a science teacher with the respondent. As a result of poor mental health, the claimant became unable to carry out her role and had significant periods of absence from work. In March 2016, the claimant continued to be unable to carry out her role as a teacher but was facilitated by the respondent in returning to work in the role of cover supervisor. This role attracted a lower rate of pay; however, the respondent continued to pay her at her teachers' rate of pay temporarily during a proba-tion period and then pending the outcome of a grievance and a grievance appeal, which the claimant had raised. These processes came to an end in November 2016.

In November 2016, it was indicated by Occupational Health that the claimant contin-ued to be long-term unfit to return to her role as a teacher but that she was able for the role of cover supervisor. The respondent then offered her the role of cover supervisor, on the lower rate of pay.

The claimant claimed that the respondent's decision not to continue to pay her at her teachers' rate of pay, following her acceptance of the supervisor role, constituted a failure to make reasonable adjustments.

Her argument that the respondent had failed to comply with its duty of reasonable adjustment was said to result from the application of the provision, criterion or practice (PCP) of obliging her to either work as a science teacher for four days a week or in the role of cover supervisor at a lower rate of pay. The tribunal held that this PCP had been applied. It then considered whether this application had placed the claimant at a 'substantial disadvantage in comparison with people who are not disabled' and it found that there was a substantial disadvantage to the claimant. However, on the question as to whether the respondent had failed to make reasonable adjustments, the tribunal found that the suggested adjustments were not reasonable.

The EAT noted that the claimant alleged that the respondent had failed to comply with the duty of reasonable adjustment because it had stopped paying her at the teachers' rate from November 2016. The tribunal had found that the respondent had made every effort to ensure that the claimant was aware that, from November 2016, she would be

---

[38]   *Aleem v E-Act Academy Trust Ltd* UKEAT/0099/20/RN.

paid at the cover supervisor's rate of pay and not the teachers' rate. It had paid her at the teachers' rate for a defined period during her probation and pending the outcome of the grievance and grievance appeal but had not made any commitment to pay her at the teachers' rate after those periods.

The EAT concluded that the respondent was not obliged to pay the claimant at the teachers' rate after November 2016, when they had offered her continued employment as a cover supervisor at the cover supervisor rate of pay. It stated that the claimant had been able to decline that offer if she had so wished but that, by accepting it, she had accepted it on the terms under which it was made—at the lower rate of pay.

A further ground of appeal raised by the claimant was that the tribunal had erred in concluding that 'it would not be reasonable to expect the respondent to continue to pay the claimant indefinitely at teachers' rates from 21 November 2016'.

The EAT stated that the tribunal had plenty of evidence in relation to the likely cost to the respondent of continuing to pay the claimant at teachers' rates, potentially until her retirement, in addition to the cost of employing another teacher to perform her former role in parallel with her. It stated that the respondent had never alleged that it could not afford to pay her at her previous rates, rather it had submitted that it was not reasonable to expect it to pay the considerable sums involved in such a scenario. The EAT found that there was more than sufficient evidence to show that such an adjustment would not be reasonable.

The EAT noted that the tribunal had concluded that, while it was reasonable for the respondent to continue to pay the claimant a teachers' rate from March to November 2016, in an effort to help the claimant to return to work, those arguments in favour of that adjustment no longer existed after November 2016. By that time the claimant had finished her probationary period in the role of cover supervisor and the grievance had been heard and finalised.

The EAT dismissed the appeal and upheld the decision of the tribunal.

[4.34] *Martin v City and County of Swansea*[39]*—UK Employment Appeal Tribunal—appeal from employment tribunal—disability—reasonable adjustments*

The claimant's role with the respondent had been made redundant and she was redeployed in April 2015. She was subsequently absent from work due to stress-related illness and, during the course of 2016, she went through a redeployment process for 19 weeks.

The claimant was later redeployed but went through further periods of sick leave and was ultimately referred to Occupational Health in March 2017. The resulting Occupational Health report stated that the claimant had a 'chronic medical condition' and suffered from 'work-related stress'.

---

[39] *Martin v City and County of Swansea* UKEAT/0253/20/AT.

The claimant was later placed on the redeployment list again and given a supernumerary position. During the redeployment process, she was advised that she could set out any positions which were of interest to her to HR directly.

In October 2017, the claimant attended a final absence review meeting and was dismissed. She appealed this decision, but the appeal was dismissed on the basis that the claimant had received appropriate support in line with the respondent's Management of Absence Policy.

The tribunal found that, at the final absence review meeting, there was no indication that another extension of the redeployment process would be successful and that the claimant had accepted that she had 'disengaged from the redeployment process'. It noted that the redeployment period had already been extended from a period of 12 weeks to a period of 29 weeks and the claimant had expressed a wish to leave the respondent's employment. The tribunal stated that, in the circumstances, there were no grounds to suggest that a further extension of the redeployment period would have prevented the claimant's dismissal.

The tribunal also found that the claim of failure to make reasonable adjustments failed as the Management of Absence Policy allowed discretion, meaning that it could not put employees with disabilities at a substantial disadvantage when compared to non-disabled employees.

On appeal, the claimant submitted that the tribunal had failed to apply the correct legal test in relation to her reasonable adjustments claim.

The EAT stated that the 'first requirement' of a reasonable adjustments claim was to begin with the identification of the correct 'provision, criterion or practice' (PCP).

The EAT stated that it was clear that the tribunal in its consideration of the PCP had appreciated that the PCP asserted was the application of the Management of Absence Policy and the asserted substantial disadvantage was the increased risk of dismissal. The tribunal had concluded that:

> [T]the application of the Management of Absence Policy, as a PCP, does not place the Claimant at a substantial disadvantage in comparison with non-disabled persons. As such no duty to make adjustments in respect of its application arises and the complaints of failure to make adjustment are not well founded and are dismissed.

In considering the relevant case law, the EAT stated that the terms of the Management of Absence Policy needed to be distinguished from the application of the policy. It found that an absence management policy could give rise to disabled employees being at a substantial disadvantage when compared with non-disabled employees even where there is a discretion within the policy. This was because it was more likely that the policy would be applied to disabled employees, as they were more likely to be out on sick leave.

In the case before it, the EAT found that, due to her disability, the claimant was at a higher risk of absence and therefore the application of the Policy put her at a disadvantage and at greater risk of being dismissed. It stated that the question to be considered was whether the respondent had taken reasonable steps to avoid the disadvantage to the claimant.

The EAT then referred to the tribunal's findings that:

1. The respondent only had the necessary knowledge to require it to make reasonable adjustments from 14 March 2017.
2. The claimant was placed in a supernumerary position within Employee Services which gave her a good opportunity to seek redeployment.
3. The redeployment period was extended to 29 weeks.
4. Placing the claimant into the specific roles that she identified would not have been reasonable, and she had accepted the reasons given as to why this was the case for each role during the internal proceedings.
5. The claimant did not request specific training during the redeployment period (save for one, which was deemed too specialist to be a reasonable step).
6. In June 2017 the claimant had contacted the principal HR officer, and suggested that there should be an 'exit strategy'.
7. By the end of August 2017, the claimant had disengaged and had not applied for some suitable roles.
8. There was no real prospect of the claimant reverting to her substantive role on medical grounds, due to her stress reaction.
9. A further extension to the redeployment period would have had no real prospect of resulting in successful redeployment.

Accordingly, the EAT found that the employment tribunal had not erred in law in its conclusion that the respondent had made all reasonable adjustments and it dismissed the appeal.

GENDER

[4.35] ***Napotnik v Romania[40]—European Court of Human Rights—gender— maternity—European Convention on Human Rights, Protocol 12—prohibition on general discrimination***

The applicant was a Romanian diplomat who worked for the Ministry of Foreign Affairs (the MFA). In 2007, she was posted as consular officer to the Romanian embassy in Slovenia, and was tasked with offering consular assistance to Romanian nationals in Slovenia. The applicant became pregnant in 2007, and was off work due to pregnancy-related illness from December 2007 to January 2008; she then commenced maternity leave in June 2008, and returned to work in December 2008. On 19 January 2009, the applicant informed the ambassador, her immediate superior, that she was pregnant again with a due date of July 2009.

---

[40]   *Napotnik v Romania* [2020] ECHR 747.

Following this disclosure, the ambassador concluded the applicant's annual performance review and noted that, while the applicant's performance in the role was satisfactory, 'because of her maternity leave and because of frequent absences due to medical appointments from February to June, these circumstances mean that she is not best suited for consular activity, which has a certain specificity, particularly since Mrs Napotnik is the head of the consular section'. The MFA thereafter decided to terminate the applicant's posting in Slovenia, and she was required to return to the office in Bucharest.

The applicant issued civil proceedings in Romania against the MFA alleging that the termination of her posting in Slovenia was due to her pregnancy, and, as such, was discriminatory and unlawful. The Bucharest County Court dismissed her action, finding that the MFA was entitled to use its discretion to terminate a posting abroad, and the early termination of her posting had not been done on discriminatory grounds. This decision was upheld by the Bucharest Court of Appeal.

The applicant brought an application to the European Court of Human Rights (the ECtHR) alleging that she had been discriminated against as her posting abroad had been terminated due to her pregnancy and without any valid reason. The applicant relied on Protocol 12 to the European Convention on Human Rights (the ECHR) which contains a general prohibition on discrimination, providing the following:

1. The enjoyment of any right set forth by law shall be secured without discrimination on any ground such as sex …
2. No one shall be discriminated against by any public authority on any ground such as those mentioned in paragraph 1.

Before considering the submissions of each party, the ECtHR first considered the applicability of art 1 of Protocol 12 and reiterated that, while art 14 of the ECHR prevents discrimination in the enjoyment of 'the rights and freedoms set forth in [the] Convention', art 1 of Protocol 12 contains a general prohibition of discrimination, which extends beyond the protection of 'any right set forth by law'. The Explanatory Report to art 1 establishes that the article offers protection in relation to discrimination arising in 'four categories of cases in particular where a person is discriminated against', namely:

i. in the enjoyment of any right specifically granted to an individual under national law;
ii. in the enjoyment of a right which may be inferred from a clear obligation of a public authority under national law, that is, where a public authority is under an obligation under national law to behave in a particular manner;
iii. by a public authority in the exercise of discretionary power (for example, granting certain subsidies);
iv. by any other act or omission by a public authority (for example, the behaviour of law enforcement officers when controlling a riot).

The ECtHR noted that the domestic laws of Romania governed the diplomatic postings abroad and the MFA enjoyed discretionary power to decide on early termination of any such posting. Therefore, the ECtHR found that this case fell into the third category above.

The applicant submitted that the main reason for the early termination of her posting was her pregnancy, noting that it was terminated as soon as she informed her superior of her second pregnancy. She further submitted that the MFA could not allege that they acted to protect her pregnancy as the work presented no danger to her. Furthermore, she submitted that the MFA had exercised its discretion in an 'improper and unreasonable manner'.

The respondent argued that the applicant should have been aware when she accepted the Slovenian posting that the nature of the role was such that 'her long, repeated and unpredictable absences' would impact the running of the embassy. Furthermore, while the respondent conceded that the applicant's pregnancy had played a role in the decision to terminate her posting, it argued that the actual reason her posting was terminated was to ensure the proper functioning of the embassy. The respondent further argued that the applicant was not discriminated against as the same decision would have been taken in circumstances of long, repeated absences, regardless of the reasons for such absences.

The ECtHR found that the jurisprudence of art 14 ECHR was applicable to the interpretation of the application of art 1 of Protocol 12. Article 14 ECHR provides for the 'protection against different treatment, without objective and reasonable justification, of individuals in analogous, or relevantly similar, situations'. The jurisprudence of the ECtHR has established that only differences in treatment on the basis of identifiable characteristics can constitute discrimination. Furthermore, the ECtHR noted that art 14 does not prohibit treating groups differently in order to amend any 'factual inequalities' between them.

In relation to the specific case of pregnancy and motherhood, the ECtHR noted that the jurisprudence of the ECtHR has indirectly acknowledged the need for protection in this area. Furthermore, in terms of different treatment on the basis of sex, the ECtHR noted that contracting parties enjoy a narrow margin of appreciation, and 'very weighty' reasons are required in order to justify any difference of treatment on the basis of gender. Any action taken which constitutes different treatment on the basis of sex must be proportionate. What is proportionate in these circumstances is a measure that not only fulfils the aim it seeks to achieve, but is also necessary to achieve the aim.

In applying these principles to the facts at hand, the ECtHR found that the applicant had been treated differently because of her pregnancy. This treatment could constitute a form of direct discrimination on the grounds of gender if the respondent could not justify these actions. The question therefore was whether there were any sufficient and relevant objective reasons to justify this treatment, and whether the decision of the MFA was proportionate in light of these reasons.

The ECtHR found that the MFA had made the decision to terminate her posting abroad in order to ensure the efficient running of the consular in Slovenia and ensure consular assistance to Romanian nationals in Slovenia. In considering if the decision was proportionate, the ECtHR noted that it was evident that the applicant's absences impacted on the operation of the consular. For example, during her absence, queries had to be re-directed to neighbouring countries. The ECtHR further noted that Romanian law permitted employers to change work conditions when an employee becomes pregnant, as the MFA had done here. The applicant had not been dismissed—rather her post abroad was terminated and she was required to return to Bucharest.

In considering the above, the ECtHR found that the termination of the applicant's post abroad was 'necessary for ensuring and maintaining the functional capacity of the diplomatic mission, and ultimately the protection of the rights of others'. The respondent had provided sufficient weighty reasons to justify its decision to terminate her post abroad, and accordingly, there had been no breach of art 1 of Protocol 12. The application was dismissed.

[4.36] *Jurčić v Croatia[41]—European Court of Human Rights—European Convention on Human Rights, art 14—direct discrimination—sex discrimination*

This case concerned the question of whether the rejection by the Croatian Health Insurance Fund of an employee's applications to be registered as an insured employee, and for salary compensation during pregnancy-related sick leave amounted to discrimination on the basis of sex.

The applicant underwent in vitro fertilisation (IVF) at a time when she was unemployed. Ten days later, the applicant took up a new role and entered into an employment contract. The company's headquarters were 360 km from where the applicant resided and the role involved travelling within and outside Croatia; however part of the applicant's role could be performed remotely.

Shortly after taking up this new role, the applicant applied and was registered as an insured employee with the Croatian Health Insurance Fund. Subsequently the applicant discovered that she was pregnant with twins and her doctor prescribed a period of sick leave due to pregnancy-related complications. The applicant made a request to the Health Insurance Fund for salary compensation during this sick leave.

The Health Insurance Fund rejected this request and also re-examined and rejected the applicant's application to be registered as an insured employee, as it found that when the applicant took up her employment she was not medically fit to do so, on the basis that she had undergone IVF ten days earlier and her employment was 'fictitious and aimed solely at obtaining pecuniary advantages related to the status of employed persons, including salary compensation during her absence from work due to pregnancy-related complications'.

The applicant challenged the decision before the Central Office of the Croatian Health Insurance Fund which dismissed her appeal. The applicant subsequently challenged the decision before the High Administrative Court and the Constitutional Court of Croatia, both of which dismissed her appeals.

The applicant referred the matter to the ECtHR, arguing that the treatment amounted to discrimination on the basis of sex and on the basis of the medical procedure she had undergone (IVF), contrary to art 14 ECHR (non-discrimination) read in conjunction with art 1 of Protocol 1.

---

[41]   *Jurčić v Croatia* Application no. 54711/15, [2021] IRLR 511.

The Croatian Government argued that the treatment in this case could be justified by reference to the 'legitimate aim' of 'preventing individuals from "cheating the system"'. In support of its contention that the applicant's entry into the employment contract was fraudulent, it pointed to the fact that she had entered into the contract despite the fact that she had been advised to rest following her IVF and that the company with which she contracted was headquartered around 360 km from the applicant's place of residence and she had never registered her residence in that district (which the Government argued indicated that she never intended to work there).

The ECtHR noted that, as only women can become pregnant, difference in treatment on the grounds of pregnancy is *prima facie* direct discrimination on the basis of sex unless it can be justified by reference to a legitimate aim and the difference in treatment is proportionate. The Court reiterated that:

> for the purposes of Article 14, a difference in treatment is discriminatory if it "has no objective and reasonable justification", that is, if it does not pursue a "legitimate aim" or if there is not a "reasonable relationship of proportionality" between the means employed and the aim sought to be realised.

Where differences in treatment are based on sex, States are only allowed a narrow margin of appreciation in assessing whether their measures are justified and proportionate.

The ECtHR held that the treatment of the applicant was due to her pregnancy and so amounted to direct discrimination on the basis of sex. In relation to the question of whether this difference in treatment could be justified, the Court held that it could not. It noted that although the Government had argued that the treatment 'pursued the legitimate aim of the protection of public resources from fraudulent use, and the overall stability of the healthcare system', the Court found that:

> a woman's pregnancy as such cannot be considered fraudulent behaviour. Furthermore, the Court considers that the financial obligations imposed on the State during a woman's pregnancy by themselves cannot constitute sufficiently weighty reasons to justify difference in treatment on the basis of sex.

While the Court accepted that the national body was entitled to check whether an individual's application for status as an insured employee was valid, it appeared from the Administrative Court's case law that 'such review in practice frequently targeted pregnant women and that women who concluded an employment contract at an advanced stage of their pregnancies or with close family members, were automatically put in the "suspicious" category of employees', an approach which the Court found was 'problematic'.

The Court found that the Croatian authorities' conclusion that the applicant was not medically fit to take up her role because she had recently undergone IVF was unlawful and 'tantamount to discouraging the applicant from seeking employment due to her possible prospective pregnancy'. The applicant had no way of knowing that she was pregnant at the time she entered into her employment contract and even if she had, asking a woman about her pregnancy status would also amount to direct discrimination on the basis of sex.

In addition, the Court noted that the applicant had contributed to the Health Insurance Fund during 14 years of employment before she became pregnant, so it could not be said that she had failed to contribute to the fund.

The Court held that 'a refusal to employ or recognise an employment-related benefit to a pregnant woman based on her pregnancy, amounts to direct discrimination on grounds of sex, which cannot be justified by the financial interests of the State'. It awarded the applicant €7,500 in respect of non-pecuniary damage by way of compensation, plus costs.

[4.37]   *K v Tesco Stores Ltd[42]—European Court of Justice—request for preliminary ruling from UK—Treaty on the Functioning of the European Union, art 157—equal pay—direct effect—work of equal value—single employer, different establishments*

The claimants were female employees or former employees of Tesco Stores, who used to work in the stores. They submitted that their work, and that of the male employees employed by Tesco Stores in its distribution centres, was of equal value, and that they were entitled to compare their work even though their work was carried out in different establishments.

Tesco Stores submitted that the female claimants did not have a right to compare themselves with male workers at its distribution centres because: (a) there were not common terms of employment; (b) art 157 TFEU was not directly effective in these types of claims; and (c) Tesco Stores could not be classified as a 'single source' for the terms and conditions of employment in the stores and the distribution centres.

Having established that it had jurisdiction to consider the matter under the Withdrawal Agreement, the European Court of Justice (ECJ) considered whether art 157 is directly effective in claims made on the basis that claimants are performing work of equal value to their comparators.

In particular, it considered the argument of Tesco Stores, that it could not have direct effect in circumstances where the workers performed different work. Tesco Stores argued that unlike the concept of 'equal work', the concept of 'work of equal value' required definition by national and EU law and accordingly it was necessary to have regard to provisions more explicit than those contained in art 157 TFEU.

The ECJ rejected this argument, noting that 'the very wording of Article 157 TFEU cannot support that interpretation'. The ECJ found that art 157 TFEU imposes a clear and precise obligation to achieve a specific result, and that applies both to 'equal work' and to 'work of equal value'. It found that the criterion laid down by art 157 is clear, in contrast to other types of discrimination which can only be identified by referring to other explicit implementing provisions. The ECJ found that courts are in a position to establish all the facts in deciding whether lower pay is being received by female

---

[42]   *K v Tesco Stores Ltd* (Case C-624/19).

workers in circumstances where they are performing the same tasks as male workers—the question as to whether workers do perform 'equal work' or 'work of equal value' is a matter of fact to be determined by national courts.

The ECJ went further and observed that where one single source determines the pay conditions of workers of different sexes performing equal work or work of equal value, this comes within the scope of art 157 TFEU, and 'the work and the pay of those workers can be compared on the basis of [art 157], even if they perform their work in different establishments'.

The ECJ found that in the case before it, Tesco was the employer of all the workers in question (those in the stores and those in the distribution centres). Accordingly, it followed that there was a single source to which the pay conditions of the workers could be attributed, and that Tesco Stores could therefore be responsible for any discrimination prohibited under art 157—the latter being a matter for the referring EAT to determine.

[4.38]   *Instituto Nacional de la Seguridad Social (INSS) v BT[43]—European Court of Justice—request for preliminary ruling from Spain—Directive 79/7/EEC[44]—equal treatment—social security—early retirement pension*

This case concerned an application for an early retirement pension made by a domestic worker. Her request was refused because she had not satisfied one of the criteria for persons wishing to take early retirement, namely that the amount of the pension to be received on foot of the application must be higher than the amount of minimum pension which would be due to the person concerned if they were to retire at age 65.

The applicant challenged the decision, and the Social Court of Barcelona upheld her challenge on the basis that this provision constituted indirect discrimination against women contrary to Directive 79/7/EEC, as it effectively prohibited domestic workers (the majority of whom were women) from obtaining an early retirement pension due to the contribution levels applicable to that particular scheme.

The INSS appealed that decision to the High Court of Spain, arguing that the rule was necessary to prevent a pension supplement being paid to such applicants, which would entail costs to the national budget. It argued that it would be incompatible with EU trends if a worker could voluntarily reduce their age of retirement without any reduction to the amount of their pension, due to the receipt of a pension supplement.

The ECJ noted that the legislation would be justified if it were to reflect a legitimate social policy objective, was appropriate to achieve that objective and was necessary to do so. It also observed that a broad margin of discretion was attributable to Member States in the present context.

In considering the question of a legitimate social policy, the ECJ recalled that case law had demonstrated that the provision of supplements meant to ensure a minimum

---

[43]   *Instituto Nacional de la Seguridad Social (INSS) v BT* (Case C-843/19).
[44]   Directive 79/7/EEC on the progressive implementation of the principle of equal treatment for men and women in matters of social security.

pension safety net was a legitimate objective of social policy that was unrelated to sex discrimination. The Court noted the submissions of the INSS and Spanish Government that the rule was necessary to maintain the viability of the Spanish social security system and achieve a balance between time spent in work and time spent in retirement, in circumstances where unrestricted access to early retirement pensions would have serious consequences for the funding of the scheme. It found that these objectives were consistent with those of the European Union, as set out in various Green and White papers.

It noted that while cost cannot justify gender discrimination, the objective of ensuring the long-term funding of retirement benefit can be a legitimate social policy objective that is unrelated to gender discrimination, and it followed that the objectives put forward by the INSS could, in principle, be capable of justifying a difference in treatment to the detriment of female workers.

The ECJ went on to assess the proportionality of such measures. It found that the legislation was appropriate to achieve the objectives, because it only impacted those who voluntarily intended to take early retirement in circumstances where a pension supplement would need to be paid. The Court concluded that the provisions were coherent and applied to all workers, and did not give rise to measures that went beyond what was necessary to achieve the pursued objectives—for example, it did not apply to situations where the start of an early retirement was not a deliberate decision of the worker (eg, in the event of corporate restructuring).

[4.39] *O'Rourke v Minister for Defence[45]—Workplace Relations Commission— Employment Equality Acts 1998 to 2021—defence forces—maternity leave—promotion*

The claimant was a former member of the Defences Forces, serving in the rank of Captain in the Air Corps. She alleged that she was discriminated on the ground of gender because her two absences from work due to maternity leave were treated as the equivalent of sick leave by a male officer. This led to a poor performance rating which impacted on her ability to attend training that was necessary for her to be promoted to the rank of Commander. Furthermore, as she was 'unable' to complete a fitness test due to her pregnancy, she was deemed to have failed it, which also negatively affected her eligibility to take part in the course.

When, after her maternity leave, the claimant received a 'weak' performance rating she was refused a place on an internal course which was essential to her promotion. She raised the grievance internally; it was partly upheld and her performance rating was amended to 'good'. With this performance rating she then sought to enter the course in January 2013 but the General Officer Commanding of the Air Corps was so slow in signing off on the new rating that she was not eligible until November 2014, by which time her health had deteriorated.

On 2 July 2015, the Defence Forces Medical Board recommended her retirement on medical grounds, due principally to her anxiety, as well as other medical problems.

---

45   *O'Rourke v Minister for Defence* ADJ-00007375 and DEC-E2020.

Her salary stopped in October 2015 but it took until 26 July 2016 for her retirement to be finalised on foot of judicial review proceedings initiated by her.

The claimant's internal grievance in 2013, under the Defence Forces Redress of Wrongs procedure, was the first investigation conducted by the Commandant who was appointed as Military Investigation Officer. He stated that he felt confident in his ability to conduct such an investigation but did not have any academic background in law or human resource management. In cross examination, he stated that he was not aware of specific legal concepts related to discrimination, including not being aware that pregnancy and maternity-related absences are not treated as ordinary sick leave for the purposes of a discrimination complaint. The Adjudicating Officer commented that the Commandant was a person of 'very high personal and professional integrity' and that he 'fully accepted' the Commandant's evidence. The Commandant based his finding that the claimant had not been discriminated against on the evidence of the claimant's second line supervisor. This Lieutenant Colonel assured the Commandant that he did not intend to discriminate against the claimant but that her absences had influenced his assessment of her.

A third witness, another Lieutenant Colonel, who had been the claimant's superior, brought evidence of her poor performance rating being based on other factors and not just her absences. He further noted that he was not aware of any exemption from the fitness test for pregnant women.

In finding in favour of the claimant, the Adjudication Officer noted that 'any less favourable treatment based on these types of absences [maternity leave] from the workplace is a prima facie discrimination on the ground of gender' and noted that the claimant's superiors treated her 'lengthy absences from work in 2010 and 2011 like those of a male officer who had been absent for sickness'.

When considering the procedural handbook made available to all the Defence Forces staff at the time, the Adjudication Officer remarked on the one-and-a-half pages dedicated to sexual harassment contrasted with only half a page on discrimination, without any mention of pregnancy-related discrimination at all. He concluded:

> It seems that, even though women have been serving in the Defence Forces since 1979, the possibility of sexual misconduct exercised senior commanders' minds much more than the notion that women could be disadvantaged or discriminated against because of pregnancy.

The Adjudication Officer noted that the short paragraphs were all that was available to the management and noted after cross examination that the rights of pregnant women in anti-discrimination law were, in the words of US Secretary of Defence, Donald Rumsfeld, an 'unknown unknown'.

This led the Adjudication Officer to conclude that the claimant was the victim of a major systems failure on the part of the respondent. The Adjudication Officer firmly laid the blame on the system rather than the investigators whom, he commented, were 'men of personal and professional integrity and good will who would have done right by the [claimant] if they had been appropriately instructed in what to do'. He found that, due to the 'uninformed actions' of management, the claimant was indeed discriminated against in accessing promotion.

The Adjudication Officer noted that the respondent's initial response to the claimant's grievance was too slow, nor did her subsequent performance assessment upgrade right the wrong. He noted that discriminatory actions cannot be cured without first being acknowledged, and upheld the claimant's claim on the ground of gender in relation to her lack of promotion.

However, the claimant's second complaint failed for lack of a comparator, as required under s 6(1) of the Employment Equality Acts 1998 to 2021. Her third complaint of victimisation also failed as, despite the fact that the claimant's file 'got stuck' in the system, there was no evidence that there was a 'concerted action in any way with the goal of disadvantaging the [claimant]'.

In finding in the claimant's favour for discrimination on the ground of gender in accessing promotion the Adjudication Officer ordered the respondent to: (1) undertake a 'comprehensive review of training and information materials, instructions and local practices within the Defence Forces to ensure their compatibility with the protections pregnant personnel enjoy under anti-discrimination law'; (2) roll out a training programme for all defence forces personnel with staff responsibilities to be completed by 31 December 2022; and (3) pay the claimant the maximum award of two years' salary and interest.

[4.40] *Asda Stores Ltd v Brierley*[46]*—UK Supreme Court—appeal from Court of Appeal of England and Wales—equal pay—comparators*

Asda appealed a decision of the EAT[47] and the Court of Appeal[48] that had found in favour of a group of workers on their interpretation of who an appropriate comparator was for an equal pay claim. The group of approximately 35,000 workers, predominantly women, claimed that, in the six years prior to the proceedings, they received lower pay than a valid comparator for work of equal value to the work done by that comparator. The question was whether the retail employees could use the distribution employees as comparators.

Under UK equality law, a claimant must point to a 'valid comparator' who is a real person employed by the same, or an associated, employer. Under the 'same establishment' requirement, the comparator must also be employed either at the same establishment as the claimant, or at another establishment with substantially the same terms and conditions. Should the claimant pick a comparator employed at another establishment, in order to make a 'cross-establishment comparison', the comparator must be employed on 'common terms' (not 'same' terms) as the claimant.

In the case at hand, the respondents were relying on the 'cross-establishment comparison' with employees employed at Asda's distribution depots (who were mainly men). Asda's position was that these depot employees were not employed on 'common terms'

---

[46]   *Asda Stores Ltd v Brierley* [2021] UKSC 10.
[47]   *Asda Stores Ltd v Brierley* UKEAT/0011/17/DM, see *Arthur Cox Employment Law Yearbook 2017* at [4.23].
[48]   *Asda Stores Ltd v Brierley* [2019] EWCA Civ 44, see *Arthur Cox Employment Law Yearbook 2019* at [4.32].

within the meaning of the legislation. Asda pointed to the fact that the retail and distribution locations are separate from one another and that the employees at each location have different terms and conditions of employment.

The key question on the appeal was whether the 'common terms' requirement for the purposes of equal pay legislation was satisfied. In finding for the respondents and agreeing that the depot workers were a valid comparator, the UK Supreme Court applied the following test:

(1) that the terms and conditions of employment of the comparators must be broadly the same at their establishment and the [respondents'] establishment, and

(2) that, if there are no employees of the comparator's group at the [respondents'] establishment and it is not clear on what terms they would have been employed there, the court or tribunal applies what is known as the *North*[49] hypothetical and considers whether the comparator's group would have been employed on broadly similar terms to those which they have at their own establishment if employed on the same site as the [respondents].

The Court concluded that it is:

very clear that the common terms requirement is intended to operate only within a very narrow compass where the differences in terms and conditions are wholly or mainly derived from the physical separation of the comparator's establishment.

It further concluded that the:

limited function of the threshold test is to "weed out" ... comparators who cannot be used because the differences between them and the [respondents] are based on geographical factors, and possibly also historical factors.

The Court held that the warehouse employees were valid comparators for the purposes of this claim and the appeal was dismissed.

[4.41] *Commissioner of the City of London Police v Geldart*[50]—*Court of Appeal of England and Wales—Underhill, Baker and Newey LJJ—Equality Act 2010, ss 13, 18 & 19—employment equality—sex discrimination*

In this case a female police officer claimed direct sex discrimination under s 13 of the Equality Act 2010 (the 2010 Act), indirect discrimination contrary s 19 of the 2010 Act, and pregnancy and maternity discrimination contrary to s 18 of the 2010 Act when her employer ceased paying her a 'London Allowance' (the London allowance) during maternity leave. The London allowance was payable to her under the Police Regulations 2003.[51] It was the claimant's case that she was entitled to receive the London allowance in full during her maternity leave. The respondent submitted that she was only entitled to receive the London allowance to the same extent that she was entitled to receive 'Police Occupational Maternity Pay', which she received for

---

49 *Dumfries and Galloway Council v North* [2013] ICR 993.
50 *Commissioner of the City of London Police v Geldart* [2021] EWCA Civ 611, see *Arthur Cox Employment Law Yearbook 2020* at **[4.31]** for EAT decision in *Commissioner of the City of London Police v Geldart* UKEAT/0032/19/RN.
51 Police Regulations 2003 (SI 2003/527).

18 weeks of her 41 weeks of leave. The value of her claim was £1,941.60, representing 23 weeks' of unpaid London allowance. However by initiating her claim under the Equality Act 2010, she could claim for the unpaid debt and compensation for injury to feelings caused by having the London allowance withheld. She withdrew her pregnancy and maternity discrimination claim under s 18 of the Equality Act 2010 at an early stage of the proceedings.

The claimant was successful in her direct sex discrimination claim before the employment tribunal and was awarded £4,000. The employment tribunal dismissed her indirect discrimination claim. The respondent appealed this decision to the EAT, which dismissed the appeal. In doing so, it referenced the relevant parts of the Police Regulations 2003—pay (Pt 4) and allowances (Pt 6) which it determined were clearly separate provisions. In addition, the provisions of the Police Regulations 2003 which reduced entitlement to pay did not apply to the London allowance as the London allowance was not pay. The EAT referenced the relevant part of the Police Regulations 2003 which provided that 'a member of the City of London … police force shall be paid a London allowance'. The claimant remained a member of the force throughout her maternity leave and was therefore entitled to payment of the London allowance. The EAT rejected the respondent's submission that, as the claimant had brought her claim under s 13 of the 2010 Act, and not s 18, she was required to show that a man in comparable circumstances would have been treated more favourably and held that a claimant who had been treated unfavourably on the ground of her pregnancy or maternity was a victim of sex discrimination and did not need to compare herself to a man in order to establish direct sex discrimination.

The respondent appealed to the Court of Appeal which allowed the appeal in part. It dismissed the direct sex discrimination claim and set aside the orders of the employment tribunal and the EAT. The claimant cross-appealed the employment tribunal and EAT's dismissal of the indirect discrimination claim.

The Court of Appeal agreed with the finding that the respondent had misinterpreted the Police Regulations 2003 by categorising the London allowance as pay. However, it held that the employment tribunal erred in its finding of direct discrimination. The correct approach was to focus on the reason why the claimant had not been paid the London allowance throughout her maternity leave and in its view this was because she had been absent from work and the reason for such absence was irrelevant.

The claimant's indirect discrimination claim was remitted to the employment tribunal.

[4.42] *R (On the Application of The Motherhood Plan) v Her Majesty's Treasury and Her Majesty's Revenue and Customs[52]—Court of Appeal of England and Wales—Underhill, Baker and Davies LJJ—European Convention of Human Rights, art 14—employment equality—gender*

The claimants sought to challenge the Self Employment Income Support Scheme (SEISS), which had been introduced by the respondent to make payments to

---

[52] *R (On the Application of The Motherhood Plan) v Her Majesty's Treasury and Her Majesty's Revenue and Customs* [2021] EWCA 1703 (Civ).

self-employed persons whose businesses had been negatively affected by the Covid-19 crisis. The SEISS payments were to be calculated on the basis of average trading profits of the person's business 'over the preceding three full tax years (ie 2016/17, 2017/18, 2018/19)', such that the grant would be equivalent to 80% of their average monthly income.

Judicial review proceedings were brought in the High Court by The Motherhood Plan, a registered charity, and Ms Kerry Chamberlain, a self-employed energy analyst who had taken two periods of maternity leave during the relevant tax years. The claimants alleged that using average trading profits, calculated over the three prior tax years, amounted to indirect discrimination as the SEISS disproportionately prejudiced women, who took time out in the previous three tax years for maternity reasons, as their average trading profits were likely to be less than they would otherwise have been had they not taken maternity-related leave in the relevant period.

The High Court of England and Wales dismissed the claim. The claimants appealed the decision of the High Court on three grounds, namely: (1) that the Court erred in concluding there was no discrimination against women who had not worked for pregnancy or maternity-related reasons in the relevant time period and misapplied the test under art 14 of the European Convention of Human Rights (prohibition of discrimination); (2) that the Court erred by not considering whether there was *Thlimmenos*[53] discrimination, ie, the Court failed to consider whether the respondent had failed to treat women who had taken time out of work for maternity reasons in a different manner to other persons eligible to participate in the SEISS, despite those women being in a materially different situation; and (3) that the Court erred in analysing the justifications put forward by the respondent by utilising 'an over-simplification of a multi-faceted test'.

The respondent submitted that there was no discrimination, but that even if the Court were to find discrimination, such discrimination and the measure which caused that discrimination were justified. The claimants argued that, had the High Court applied the correct approach to whether the discrimination could be justified, the respondent's defences would be unsuccessful.

The Court of Appeal found that:

> The purpose of SEISS is to compensate self-employed people for the loss of the earnings that they would have received in the current year but for the pandemic and to use past earnings as the measure of those lost hypothetical earnings. In those circumstances, the past earnings in question are not immaterial: on the contrary, they are crucial.

It held that the High Court erred in concluding that the use of average trading profits for the previous three tax years was not '*prima facie* indirect discrimination'.

The Court of Appeal did not reach a definitive conclusion on the alternate argument of *Thlimmenos* discrimination as its conclusion that there was indirect discrimination meant that the treatment must be justified 'and that issue will not be any different whatever form the discrimination took'.

---

[53] *Thlimmenos v Greece* 31 EHRR 15.

In respect of the justifications put forward by the respondent, the Court of Appeal concluded that the High Court's approach to the issue of justification was 'appropriately nuanced' and as such, it was not open to the Court of Appeal to re-determine the issue. Furthermore, the Court of Appeal noted that if it had been required to re-determine the issue, it would have reached the same conclusion as the High Court.

Although the Court of Appeal found that the terms of SEISS did constitute indirect discrimination and the High Court had erred in finding otherwise, the Court of Appeal concluded that the emergency circumstances which led to the inception of the SEISS, such as the need to implement a simple and verifiable solution at speed, justified the discrimination. The Court of Appeal dismissed the appeal.

[4.43] *Chief Constable of Devon and Cornwall Police v Town[54]—UK Employment Appeal Tribunal—appeal from employment tribunal—Equality Act 2010, ss 18, 19—discrimination on the grounds of sex/pregnancy—indirect discrimination—PCP*

The claimant was a police officer working as a response officer on the front line. When the claimant informed the respondent that she was pregnant, it carried out a risk assessment and placed her on restricted duties, which involved recommendations relating to night shifts and her working in plain clothes. However, subsequently the respondent transferred the claimant to a 'back office' role in the Crime Management Hub, a move which the employment tribunal described as one that a front line officer might regard as a 'retrograde' step in their career. The transfer was effected contrary to the claimant's wishes—she represented that it would have an adverse impact on her mental health—nor had it been recommended by the risk assessment. The transfer did have an adverse impact on the claimant's mental health and she suffered from stress, anxiety and migraines before going on maternity leave.

The claimant claimed that the transfer amounted to discrimination based on her pregnancy, contrary to s 18 of the Equality Act 2010 (the 2010 Act). She also alleged that a 'provision, criterion or practice' (a PCP) within the respondent, which dictated that a person would be considered for a role in the Crime Management Hub if they were on restricted duties for more than two weeks, amounted to indirect discrimination on the basis of sex, contrary to s 19 of the 2010 Act.

The claimant was successful before the employment tribunal. In relation to the claim under s 18, the employment tribunal held that the transfer to the Crime Management Hub did amount to pregnancy discrimination, being unfavourable treatment on the basis of the claimant's pregnancy. It also upheld the claim of indirect discrimination under s 19, finding that the PCP followed by the respondent put women at a particular disadvantage 'because it can be triggered by pregnancy in addition to other triggers like illness which could be shared between men and women'.

The respondent appealed the decision to the EAT. In terms of the claim under s 18, the EAT found that the employment tribunal had held that the treatment (being the claimant's move to the Crime Management Hub) was unfavourable as a matter of

---

[54]   *Chief Constable of Devon and Cornwall Police v Town* UKEAT/0194/19/LA.

fact. There was no appeal in relation to the question of whether it was caused by the claimant's pregnancy and as such, there was no basis for an appeal.

Regarding the claim under s 19, the EAT noted that it is not necessary that every member of a protected class be impacted for there to be a finding of indirect discrimination, it is sufficient that certain members of that class are more likely to be at a disadvantage than a comparative group. The EAT found that that was clearly the case here 'since only women can get pregnant and pregnancy is an automatic trigger for the application of the policy and women are therefore plainly disproportionately liable to be transferred'. The EAT held this was 'sufficient for the purposes of the comparative exercise'.

As such, the EAT held that the PCP followed by the respondent did amount to indirect discrimination on the basis of sex and upheld findings of the employment tribunal.

[4.44] *Cumming v British Airways plc[55]—UK Employment Appeal Tribunal— appeal from employment tribunal—employment equality—gender—parental leave policy—indirect discrimination*

The claimant worked for the respondent as part of their Eurofleet air crew. Air crew members were entitled to 10 paid rest days and 20–21 work days in a month. The respondent operated a parental leave policy in which an employee's paid rest days were reduced by one day, for every three days of unpaid parental leave days they took.

The claimant was a mother of two children under the age of 18. She took three unpaid parental leave days, and consequently her paid rest days were reduced by one day. She lodged a claim with the employment tribunal, alleging indirect discrimination on grounds of gender. She submitted that the parental leave policy unfairly disadvantaged women, in circumstances were 24.4% of the females in the Eurofleet availed of parental leave, compared to the 11.9% of the males in the Eurofleet air crew.

The employment tribunal held that there was no indirect discrimination. It found that, as the parental policy ultimately affected females and males in the same manner (ie, both genders suffered the disadvantage of having rostered paid days reduced), there was no 'particular disadvantage' to women—therefore no indirect discrimination arose.

The claimant appealed this decision to the EAT; she submitted that, as women were more likely to avail of parental leave as they were normally the primary child care givers, women were particularly affected by the parental leave policy. In response, the respondent submitted that this case had not been put before the employment tribunal, and there was insufficient evidence to support any such claim.

In relation to the claim that the arguments made to the EAT had not been submitted to the employment tribunal, the EAT held that, notwithstanding the fact that the claimant's case had not been 'put as clearly as it might be and there is no reference to what I regard as the most relevant statistic', the basic point of the claimant's case had been made.

---

[55] *Cumming v British Airways plc* UKEAT/0337/19/JOJ.

In relation to the respondent's claim that there was a lack of evidentiary support for the claimant's submission that female air crew workers in the Eurofleet crew bore the primary child care responsibilities, the EAT noted that there was no need for this evidence to be put before the Court, having regard to the statement of Lady Hale in *Essop v Home Office (UK Border Agency); Naeem v Secretary of State for Justice*[56] in which she noted that women tend to 'bear the greater responsibility for caring for the home and family than … men'.

The EAT held that the claimant had established that the employment tribunal had erred in its reasoning in relation to whether the policy resulted in a 'particular disadvantage' to women. It held that the employment tribunal had failed to properly consider the case of the claimant, and the matter was remitted to a fresh employment tribunal for proper consideration.

The respondent also cross-appealed a finding of the employment tribunal that the implementation of the parental leave policy involved a disadvantage, ie, the loss of a paid rest day. The respondent submitted that it did not automatically constitute a disadvantage as the effect of the policy was to 'deem periods of unpaid parental leave to include rest days in the usual proportion of one out of three'. The EAT allowed this appeal and this question was also remitted to the freshly constituted employment tribunal for further consideration.

[4.45] *Price v Powys County Council*[57]—*UK Employment Appeal Tribunal— appeal from employment tribunal—equality—gender—discrimination—parental leave—adoptive leave*

When the claimant queried his entitlements under the respondent's shared parental leave policy, the respondent explained to him that he would only be entitled to the equivalent of statutory maternity pay (rather than enhanced maternity pay). The claimant argued that the policy was discriminatory as employees on maternity leave and on adoption leave were entitled to pay at higher rates during their leave than those on shared parental leave.

The claimant lodged a claim of direct discrimination on the grounds of gender, relying on two comparators: a female worker on maternity pay, and a female worker on adoption pay. The employment tribunal found that the first comparator (on maternity leave) was not a valid comparator on the basis that there was a material difference between the claimant's circumstances and those of the woman on maternity leave. The employment tribunal concluded that the second comparator was also not materially the same as the claimant. The claimant appealed these findings to the EAT.

The EAT held that the employment tribunal had failed to apply other factors to the test of whether the comparators were valid; however, the EAT also held that this shortcoming

---

[56]   *Essop v Home Office (UK Border Agency); Naeem v Secretary of State for Justice* [2017] UKSC 27.
[57]   *Price v Powys County Council* UKEAT/0133/20/LA.

did not invalidate the employment tribunal's overall decision. The EAT held that the employment tribunal was correct to reject the claimant's nominated comparator of a female on adoption leave, since the circumstances of such comparator were materially different from those of a male on shared parental leave.

The EAT upheld the employment tribunal's decision that no sex discrimination had occurred in circumstances where an employer pays a man on shared parental leave less than a woman on adoption leave.

[4.46] ***De Lacey v Wechseln Ltd*[58]—*UK Employment Appeal Tribunal—appeal from employment tribunal—discrimination—pregnancy—maternity—course of discriminatory conduct***

The claimant was employed as a trainee hair stylist at the respondent's hair salon. She became pregnant in May 2015, went on maternity leave in October 2015, returned to work in August/September 2016 and resigned on 19 January 2017. She claimed she had been the subject of pregnancy, maternity and sex discrimination. She also brought a claim for constructive unfair dismissal.

Both sets of claims arose from a series of events from May to October 2015 and events arising on her return to work. The claimant was informally told that she had done very well in a competency test, only to be told after she informed her employer that she was pregnant that she had failed the test and would have to re-take it. It was agreed that the re-take of the test would be deferred until after her return from maternity leave. The claimant alleged she was given a disproportionate amount of mundane tasks in the lead up to her maternity leave, but this was not accepted by the tribunal. The tribunal did find that the claimant's boss cooled his relationship with the claimant after becoming aware she was pregnant, and had behaved in a similar way towards another pregnant trainee. After the claimant returned to work, she made a number of allegations in relation to inappropriate treatment, some of which were not accepted by the tribunal. However, the tribunal did accept an allegation that her boss had humiliated her in a daily briefing session. On 17 January 2017, the claimant asserted that the 'final straw' had occurred when she had been instructed in front of others to clean up dog faeces and had been laughed at.

The claimant asserted that the events constituted a course of discriminatory conduct which amounted to a repudiatory breach of the implied term of mutual trust and confidence. The tribunal dismissed the claimant's claims of discrimination, finding that the only two complaints that could establish a *prima facie* case of discrimination (the failure of the competency test and the cold way in which her boss had behaved towards her after he became aware of her pregnancy) were out of time. It found that the claimant had not established that there was a course of discriminatory conduct extending until January 2017, which would have brought the complaints within the time limit; nor would it be just and equitable to extend the time. However, the claimant's claim

---

58   *De Lacey v Wechseln Ltd* UKEAT/0038/20.

for constructive unfair dismissal was accepted on the basis that the claimant had been treated in ways since May 2015 which, when taken together, amounted to a breach of the implied term of trust and confidence, which the claimant was entitled to treat as a repudiatory breach of her employment contract.

On appeal before the EAT, the claimant argued that the tribunal failed to deal properly with her claim that her constructive dismissal amounted to unlawful pregnancy, maternity and sex discrimination. The claimant submitted that the tribunal, having found certain matters that were a material part of the repudiatory breach to be *prima facie* discriminatory, should have gone on to determine whether the respondent had satisfied the reverse burden of proof. The claimant asserted that if the respondent hadn't been able to do so, the discrimination claim would have been in time, because time runs for a discrimination claim arising from constructive dismissal from the date of the dismissal.

In considering this argument, the EAT found that a 'last straw' constructive dismissal may amount to unlawful discrimination if some of the matters relied on are discriminatory—the test is whether 'the discrimination thus far found sufficiently influenced the overall repudiatory breach, such that the constructive dismissal should be found to be discriminatory'. This would be a matter for a tribunal to consider based on the facts before it. The EAT found that the tribunal erred in law in failing to reach a view on whether the incidents were sex discrimination for the purposes of the discriminatory constructive dismissal claim.

The claimant also argued that the tribunal had erred in its approach to refusing to extend time to consider the discriminatory complaints. No error in law was found by the EAT on this point.

The matter was remitted to the same employment tribunal to determine whether the claimant suffered direct sex discrimination and in light of this finding, whether the discriminatory matters sufficiently influenced the overall repudiatory breach so as to render the constructive dismissal discriminatory.

[4.47] *Rooney v Leicester City Council*[59]*—UK Employment Appeal Tribunal— appeal from employment tribunal—disability discrimination—sex discrimination*

The claimant was employed as a childcare social worker by the respondent. She resigned on 29 August 2018.

The claimant brought a number of complaints to the employment tribunal, including a constructive dismissal claim and a claim for non-payment of holiday pay, overtime and expenses. A day after her first claim form was submitted, she lodged another claim form and included a claim for direct disability discrimination, harassment and victimisation, and a claim for direct sex discrimination, on the basis of the severe menopausal

---

[59]   *Rooney v Leicester City Council* EA-2020-000070-DA, EA-2021-000256-DA (previously UKEAT/ 0064/20/DA and UKEAT/0104/21/DA, respectively).

symptoms she suffered at work. The claimant cited the physical, mental and psychological effects of the menopause she suffered.

At a preliminary hearing for case management, the claimant was ordered to provide further information to the respondent setting out the full details of her disability and sex discrimination claims.

A subsequent preliminary hearing was held on 1 November 2019. The employment tribunal held that the claimant's medical conditions of anxiety, depression and menopausal symptoms did not constitute a disability for the purposes of the Equality Act 2010. The employment tribunal struck out her claim of sex discrimination, on the basis that it had no reasonable prospect of success. Furthermore, the claims of harassment and victimisation were also dismissed.

The claimant appealed the employment tribunal's finding that: (1) she was not disabled; (2) the sex discrimination claims had no reasonable prospect of success; and (3) the claims of harassment and victimisation should be dismissed.

The claimant made a further application to have her first claim form amended to include a claim relating to a protected disclosure which had come to her attention on foot of a bundle of documents provided by the respondent during the course of the proceedings. This application was refused at a preliminary hearing. This refusal was also appealed by the claimant.

In relation to the first ground, the EAT found that the tribunal had erred in law in finding that the claimant was not a disabled person. In this regard, the EAT held that the employment tribunal had failed to consider the statutory definition of what constitutes 'long term'; failed to consider the appropriate case law; and erroneously placed emphasis on conducting a balance exercise between what the claimant could do versus what she could not do.

The EAT allowed the claimant's appeal against the decision to strike out her claims of sex discrimination, finding that the employment tribunal had fallen short of the 'fundamental requirement to explain to the claimant why her complaints were struck out'.

Furthermore, the EAT found that no justifications were given by the employment tribunal as to why the harassment and victimisation claims were struck out—and as such, this ground of appeal was allowed.

Finally, the EAT held that the employment tribunal had erred in refusing the claimant's application to amend the complaint form to allow for the protected disclosure claim. It found that the employment tribunal had failed to give due consideration to the explanation for the delay, in circumstances where the claimant 'had been unaware that she had an arguable complaint until she had seen documentation provided in the tribunal bundle'.

The claimant's appeal to the EAT was successful on all four grounds, and the claim was remitted to a freshly constituted tribunal.

HARASSMENT

[4.48] *Driscoll v V & P Global Ltd[60]—UK Employment Appeal Tribunal—appeal from employment tribunal—Equality Act 2010, s 26—Directive 2006/54/EC[61]—Directive 2000/78/EC[62]—Directive 2000/43/EC[63]—constructive dismissal—harassment*

The claimant was employed as an executive assistant by the respondent, a legal recruitment consultancy, from 2 April 2019. She resigned just less than four months later, claiming that she had been subjected to harassment related to sex, race, or disability. She claimed that the harassment took the form of comments made during her employment, culminating in her constructive dismissal. The employment tribunal struck out the constructive dismissal aspect of her harassment claim, holding that, based on the EAT decision in *Timothy James Consulting Ltd v Wilton*,[64] a resignation amounting to constructive dismissal was not an act of harassment for the purpose of the Equality Act 2010. She appealed this decision to the EAT, arguing that the EAT in *Wilton* did not consider the relevant EU Directives.

The EAT observed that the provisions in the Equality Act 2010 on harassment must be construed purposively to be in accordance with the recast Equal Treatment Directive 2006/54/EC, the Equal Treatment Framework Directive 2000/78/EC, and the Race Equality Directive 2000/43/EC. The EAT concluded that the Directives proscribe harassment in relation to dismissals and that the term 'dismissal' should be construed broadly. It found that there was no principled basis to exclude constructive dismissal from the scope of the applicable Directives, as had been done in previous decisions and that *Wilton* was not correctly decided. Therefore, the EAT held that a constructive dismissal can constitute an act of unlawful harassment under the Equality Act 2010, by adopting this wide interpretation of 'dismissal'.

The EAT concluded:

> as a matter of law, where an employee (as defined by the EqA) resigns in response to repudiatory conduct which constitutes or includes unlawful harassment, his or her constructive dismissal is itself capable of constituting "unwanted conduct" and, hence, an act of harassment, contrary to sections 26 and 40 of the EqA. Whether or not it does so in the particular case will be a matter for the tribunal to determine.

The EAT allowed the claimant's appeal on this ground.

---

[60] *Driscoll v V & P Global Ltd* Appeal Nos. EA-2020-000876-LA (formerly UKEAT/009/21/LA) and EA-2020-000877-LA (formerly UKEAT/0010/21/LA).

[61] Directive 2006/54/EC on the implementation of the principle of equal opportunities and equal treatment of men and women in matters of employment and occupation.

[62] Directive 2000/78/EC establishing a general framework for equal treatment in employment and occupation.

[63] Directive 2000/43/EC implementing the principle of equal treatment between persons irrespective of racial or ethnic origin.

[64] *Timothy James Consulting Ltd v Wilton* UKEAT/0082/14/DXA & UKEAT/0204/14/DXA.

[4.49] *CPL Solutions Ltd t/a Flexsource Recruitment v Kings Oluebube[65]—Labour Court—appeal from Workplace Relations Commission—Employment Equality Acts 1998 to 2021—employment equality—discrimination on the ground of race—harassment—victimisation*

The claimant appealed the decision of the Adjudication Officer which found his complaints of racial discrimination and victimisation under the Employment Equality Acts 1998 to 2021 (the Acts) were not well founded.

The claimant was a black Nigerian national and was employed as an agency worker by the respondent, working as a warehouse operative for K&N since 14 January 2019. The claimant worked alongside other employees of the respondent. In February 2019, an employee of the respondent allegedly called the claimant a 'chimpanzee' and made monkey actions and noises in front of co-workers. On 21 May 2019, this incident occurred again. While the claimant did not report the first incident, he did report the second incident to a direct employee of K&N, who subsequently informed the respondent.

The claimant also alleged that he was subjected to victimisation following his complaint of discrimination in August 2019, when he was rostered to work the 11.00am to 8.00pm shift for two consecutive weeks, including Sundays which his manager knew were inconvenient for the claimant. The respondent stated that rostering was a matter for K&N and that the respondent had no input. Furthermore the claimant confirmed he had been treated well in the period following his harassment claims. The respondent also submitted that a high volume of annual leave requests explained the rostering. The Adjudication Officer rejected this complaint.

The respondent obtained a written statement from the claimant and conducted an investigation into both incidents. The complaint of harassment was ultimately upheld. The respondent accepted that racial harassment occurred but sought to rely on the two-limb defence set out in s 14A(2) of the Acts in that it took such steps as were reasonably practicable to: (a) prevent the person from harassing others; and (b) prevent the victim being treated differently, and where that has occurred, to reverse the effects of such different treatment.

The Court was critical of the respondent's lack of comprehensive procedures for dealing with bullying and harassment claims, including the failure of the respondent to provide the claimant with terms of reference or a timeline for the investigation and the failure to give the claimant any witness statements or the opportunity to respond to anything said by the perpetrator. The Court found that the absence of a comprehensive bullying and harassment procedure and the *ad hoc* handling of the complaint resulted in the respondent failing to satisfy the first limb of the defence and the fact that no steps were taken by the respondent to reverse the effects of the racial harassment endured by the claimant meant the respondent also failed to satisfy the second limb of the defence.

---

[65]   *CPL Solutions Ltd t/a Flexsource Recruitment v Kings Oluebube* EDA2134.

In respect of the harassment claim, the Court set aside the decision of the Adjudication Officer and found the respondent vicariously liable for the harassment of the claimant and awarded the claimant €30,000 in compensation equivalent to around 63 weeks' gross pay. The Court upheld the decision of the Adjudication Officer in respect of victimisation and found the claim not well founded as the respondent had no role in rostering K&N employees and there was no evidence from which the Court could infer that the change in roster was in response to his complaints of harassment which were concluded two months earlier.

[4.50] *Allay (UK) Ltd v Gehlen*[66]*—UK Employment Appeal Tribunal—appeal from employment tribunal—Equality Act 2010, s 109(4)—statutory defence—harassment—race discrimination—outdated training*

This was an appeal by the respondent employer of a decision by the employment tribunal; although the tribunal accepted that the reason for the dismissal of the claimant was his performance and rejected the claim of direct race discrimination, it upheld the complaint of harassment related to race. After being dismissed, the claimant raised a complaint that he had been subjected to race harassment by a fellow employee. An investigation by the employer established that the fellow employee had made the racist comments and this employee was required to attend further equality and diversity training. The ground for the respondent's appeal of the decision was that the tribunal failed to properly engage with the statutory defence under s 109(4) of the Equality Act 2010.

Under s 109(4) of the Equality Act 2010, an employer can defend a claim resulting from the otherwise unlawful discriminatory actions of an employee if it can demonstrate that all reasonable steps were taken to prevent the employee from doing 'that thing' or 'anything of that description'.

On the application of the s 109(4) defence, the EAT cited *Canniffe v East Riding of Yorkshire Council*[67] and stated that:

> *Canniffe* supports the proposition that if there is a further step that should reasonably have been taken by the employer to prevent harassment the defence will fail even if that step would not have prevented the harassment that occurred in the case under consideration.

The EAT went on find that:

> if there was a case in which excellent anti-harassment training had been provided, but nonetheless employees immediately thereafter to management's knowledge continued to engage in harassing "banter", the sole fact that the training had failed could be enough to demonstrate that further reasonable steps were required to address the ongoing harassment. However, if further steps were taken, and they appeared to have been effective, but another act of harassment occurred, the occurrence of that further act would not, of itself, establish that all reasonable steps had not been taken, so as to prevent the employer relying on the defence.

---

66   *Allay (UK) Ltd v Gehlen* UKEAT/0031/20/AT.
67   *Canniffe v East Riding of Yorkshire Council* [2000] IRLR 555.

The EAT found that in considering the steps that had been taken, and whether further reasonable steps were required, it was legitimate to consider how effective the steps that had been taken were likely to be when they were taken and, in appropriate circumstances, how effective they had proven to be in practice. The tribunal in this case was entitled to conclude that the training that had been provided to the perpetrator of the race harassment, and to a number of other employees, including two managers, who had failed to report matters to HR, had become stale and required refreshing. The EAT stated:

> In considering the reasonableness of steps that have been taken the analysis will include consideration of the extent to which the step, or steps, were likely to prevent harassment. Brief and superficial training is unlikely to have a substantial effect in preventing harassment. Such training is also unlikely to have long-lasting consequences. Thorough and forcefully presented training is more likely to be effective, and to last longer.

In confirming the decision of the tribunal that the respondent could not rely on the defence under s 109(4) of the Equality Act 2010, the EAT held that:

> While it would have been better for the Tribunal to have made more detailed findings about the policies that were in place, and the training that had been undertaken, they were entitled to conclude the training was stale and was no longer effective to prevent harassment, and that there were further reasonable steps by way of refresher training that the Respondent should have taken.

The appeal was unsuccessful.

[4.51] *MBCC Foods Ireland Ltd t/a Costa Coffee v Quilty*[68]*—Labour Court— appeal from Workplace Relations Commission—Employment Equality Acts 1998 to 2021—harassment—sexual harassment—discrimination*

The claimant worked as a barista in the respondent's coffee store. She raised a complaint against her manager in January 2020, sought a formal investigation and resigned before the investigation concluded. She filed complaints for discrimination on the grounds of gender, discrimination in conditions of employment, and sexual harassment. An Adjudication Officer upheld the complaints and awarded her compensation of €3,500. The claimant appealed the level of the award to the Labour Court.

In December 2019, the claimant's manager exchanged inappropriate messages in a group chat relating to the claimant, including a picture of himself in his boxer shorts. Shortly thereafter, the manager posted a video into the same group chat of a barista drawing male genitalia onto a coffee, indicating that this was to be practised in the store and would lead to promotion. The claimant was 19 at the time.

The claimant made complaints about her manager in January 2020, including complaints about his activities in the group chat. The area manager offered to informally investigate

---

[68]   *MBCC Foods Ireland Ltd t/a Costa Coffee v Quilty* EDA2128.

the matter and mediate between the parties, to move the claimant to another store, or alternatively to refer the matter for formal investigation. The claimant requested that a formal investigation take place. The manager was suspended. The claimant resigned in February 2020. She was contacted and asked to reconsider her resignation, but declined to do so. She indicated that she would be withdrawing the complaints. The investigation proceeded without the participation of the claimant, and the manager was ultimately demoted and transferred to a different store.

After the investigation was completed, the claimant filed her claim in the WRC. While she indicated through her representative that she would be willing to engage in an informal process, the investigation had at that stage concluded. The respondent asserted that it had dealt with the incident appropriately, they had provided up-to-date training for all managers on dignity and respect, and made a policy on harassment and bullying available to all staff. The respondent argued that the claimant delayed in her complaints, and did not engage with the processes put in place by the respondent to deal with the matter. It asserted that while the conduct was unacceptable, it was not directed at her in particular. The respondent accepted that the actions that gave rise to the claim constituted sexual harassment, but relied on the defence available to it under s 14A(2) of the Employment Equality Acts 1998 to 2021 (the Acts), and submitted that the behaviour was at the lower end of seriousness and was only complained of in the context of other, unrelated incidents.

The claimant indicated that the delay in making the complaint arose from subsequent incidents having occurred, leaving her feeling that she had been 'singled out', as well as the fact that she felt embarrassed. She asserted that she was unaware of any policies and had not received a handbook and argued that the award was not dissuasive.

The Labour Court was 'quite shocked' to note that the respondent had no clear policy on sexual harassment, describing this failure as an 'extraordinary oversight'. It found that the fact that the group chat was utilised for operational reasons would suggest an imperative to have clear social media policies in place; however, the respondent's policies did not cover the conduct of employees in work-oriented group chats. The Court found that the Adjudication Officer erred in identifying this case at the lower level of offence. The Court had regard to the manager's age, the claimant's age, the fact that he was in a position of authority, and the inappropriate content of the messages.

While the Court accepted that the steps subsequently taken by the respondent mitigated 'to some small degree the almost inexplicable inadequacies in the Respondent's protective procedures', the defence under s 14(A)(2) of the Acts was not available due to their failure to take steps in advance of the acts occurring.

The Labour Court varied the decision of the Adjudication Officer, and made orders directing the respondent to put in place appropriate policies and training and to make a payment of €20,000 to the employee (approximately equivalent to one year's remuneration).

RELIGIOUS BELIEF

[4.52]   *IX v WABE eV; MH Müller Handels GmbH v MJ*[69]*—European Court of Justice—request for preliminary ruling from Germany—Directive 2000/78,*[70] *arts 1, 2, 3 & 8—Treaty on the European Union, art 6—indirect discrimination—religious clothing—headscarves—policy of neutrality*

The applicant was a special needs carer employed by WABE, a children's day-care centre since July 2014. Wearing religious clothing was against the company's policy of neutrality (ie, employees were not allowed to wear visible signs of their political, philosophical, or religious beliefs when interacting with children). Having returned from a period of leave, the applicant refused to remove her headscarf when asked and she was subsequently suspended from work. She filed a complaint with the Hamburg Labour Court. Similarly, MH Müller (a German drugstore chain) did not allow its employees to display signs of political, philosophical, or religious belief at work, in order to protect its image of neutrality. In 2014, a female employee went to work wearing a headscarf. She initially performed work that did not require customer interaction or the removal of her headscarf. However, in July 2016 she was sent home from work for refusing to remove it. She brought a complaint before the German Federal Labour Court. The applicants made arguments in respect of discrimination on grounds of gender and religion.

The Hamburg Labour Court asked the ECJ to consider if a policy of neutrality could amount to indirect discrimination and, whether it was legitimate in circumstances where unfavourable treatment (in this case the issuing of a disciplinary warning to an employee) was connected with an employee's religion and as the prohibition in question affected primarily women. In addition, the Hamburg Labour Court wanted to know whether the German national constitutional right to freedom of religion could offer more favourable protection to employees than the right to non-discrimination could offer within the context of Directive 2000/78 itself. The German Federal Labour Court also sought clarification on the justification for a policy of neutrality and in particular whether the rule prohibiting the wearing of prominent signs of religious, political or other philosophical beliefs was permissible or whether the prohibition would only be permissible if extended to any signs of religious, political or other philosophical beliefs.

The ECJ held that if workplace guidelines prohibited the wearing of all signs of religious, political, or philosophical beliefs then the guidelines could not be considered unjustifiable and did not amount to indirect discrimination. This was, however, not applicable to settings whereby only 'conspicuous large-sized signs' were banned, which could not be justified by art 2(2)(b)(i) of Directive 2000/78 and would constitute direct discrimination on the grounds of religion or belief. It stated that no direct discrimination occurs where a policy is inconvenient to workers but does not 'establish a difference of treatment between workers based on a criterion that is inextricably linked to religion or belief'. Further, the ECJ noted that the German Constitution could

---

[69]   *IX v WABE eV; MH Müller Handels GmbH v MJ* (Joined Cases C-804/18 and C-341/19).
[70]   Directive 2000/78/EC establishing a general framework for equal treatment in employment and occupation.

be considered as more favourable in protecting individuals' right to freedom of religion given the margin of discretion awarded to Member States in determining the place of religion in society.

Finally, the ECJ held that for a policy of neutrality to be justified, there must be a 'genuine need on the part of that employer, which it is for that employer to demonstrate'.

[4.53] *Tipperary Education Training Board v Roe[71]—Labour Court—appeal from Workplace Relations Commission—Employment Equality Acts 1998 to 2021—discrimination on the ground of religion—indirect discrimination—harassment—victimisation*

The claimant was a teacher in the Central Technical Institute in Clonmel (the school), which was within the remit of the Tipperary Education and Training Board. The claimant alleged that he suffered indirect discrimination, harassment and victimisation on the grounds of religion on the basis that a May altar, which included a statue of the Blessed Virgin Mary, was erected in the school on 1 May 2015. The claimant's contention was that the statue constituted religious dogma and was offensive to him as a Humanist.

The claimant referred to a number of events preceding the incident on 1 May 2015 as constituting a 'continuum of discrimination on the grounds of religion against him'. On 1 May 2012, the claimant objected to the statue being placed in the school. As a compromise, the deputy principal directed that the May altar be moved from the main entrance to another area of the school which the claimant did not frequent. There was conflicting evidence from the witnesses as to where the May altar was located in 2013 and 2014, prior to the incident in May 2015 which gave rise to the complaint. In March 2014, Lenten ashes were inadvertently distributed during one of the claimant's classes, an incident which the claimant referred to the Equality Tribunal but which ultimately resulted in a mediated settlement being reached on 27 April 2015.

The claimant alleged that in May 2013 and May 2014, the May altar was not erected in the main entrance, which had caused the issues in 2012, an allegation which was disputed by the respondent. The claimant asserted that in May 2015, the May altar was erected in the main entrance, as it had been in May 2012. All witnesses for the respondent indicated that, to the best of their recollection, the May altar had been placed at the main entrance to the school in 2013, 2014 and then 2015. As the erection of the May altar in 2015 came just days after the mediated settlement in respect of the Lenten ashes, the claimant contended that the erection of the May altar amounted to victimisation. The claimant therefore attempted to dismantle the May altar that the caretaker had assembled. A 'tussle and heated verbal exchange' took place, with another witness ultimately intervening to diffuse the situation. The claimant alleged that the caretaker's intervention to prevent the claimant removing the statue constituted harassment. Disciplinary proceedings were commenced concerning both the caretaker and the

---

[71]   *Tipperary Education Training Board v Roe* EDA2124.

claimant. The claimant refused to participate and no finding was made against the care-taker. The claimant was then relocated to alternative teaching duties in Templemore.

Various witnesses gave evidence before the Court. A parent, who visited the school in May 2013, appeared for the claimant and gave evidence that she clearly recalled the statue being under the stairs in the school. Witnesses on behalf of the respondent gave evidence that they did not recall where the statue had been placed but recall it having been typically placed at the main entrance. Evidence was also given that a statue of Buddha was placed at the entrance to the school on one occasion to commemorate the victims of an Asian tsunami and the claimant had not objected to same.

The respondent sought to rely on the European Court of Human Rights case *Lautsi v Italy*[72] where the Court held that a passive symbol, such as crucifix on the wall, could not 'be deemed to have an influence on pupils comparable to that of didactic speech or participation in religious activities'. The claimant sought to distinguish *Lautsi v Italy* on the facts and asserted that unlike the crib, a Christmas tree or the Buddha statue, the Blessed Virgin Mary is not a passive symbol.

The Court noted that the claimant's complaint of indirect discrimination was based on the contention that the placement of the statue in May 2015 was a practice that placed him at a particular disadvantage by making him feel disrespected and inferior. The Court noted that the burden of proof in any claim of discrimination rests on the claimant. It was pivotal to the case that the claimant contended that the presence of one particular religious symbol, the statue, placed him at a disadvantage while other symbols such as the statue of Buddha and the Christmas tree did not convey a particular disadvantage to him. The Court held that the claimant failed to establish any facts from which an inference of discrimination could be drawn. The claimant also put forward an argument in relation to the historical evolution of the school in an attempt to assert that the school must be of a secular nature as a matter of law. The Court stated that such an argument was beyond the competence of the Court and therefore no finding was made.

In respect of the complaint of victimisation, the Court noted that it was focused on the placement of the May altar in 2013 and 2014. The Court considered the evidence and noted there was no animosity displayed by any of the witnesses for the respondent towards the claimant. The Court found that on the balance of probabilities, the claimant was not subject to victimisation on 1 May 2015 by the location of the May altar on that occasion.

The claimant alleged that the intervention of the caretaker to prevent the claimant removing the statue from where he had placed it on 1 May 2015 amounted to harassment within the meaning of s 14A(7) of the Employment Equality Acts 1998 to 2021. The Court specifically referred to the class of conduct required being 'unwanted' and 'related to any of the discriminatory grounds' and concluded that while the caretaker's

---

[72]   *Lautsi v Italy* [2011] ECHR 2412.

intervention was 'unwanted' by the clamant, it could not be objectively characterised as relating to the claimant's Humanism. The Court ultimately found that the claimant's allegation of harassment failed and was based on a 'mistaken understanding and application' of the relevant legislative provision.

The appeal was dismissed in full.

[4.54] *Student v Community School[73]—Workplace Relations Commission—Equal Status Acts 2000 to 2018—religious belief—school admission policy*

In September 2019, the claimant received a letter from the respondent advising her that her application to attend the respondent Community School (a post-primary school) was unsuccessful. The claimant claimed that the respondent engaged in prohibited conduct under the Equal Status Acts 2000 to 2018 (the Acts) by favouring Church of Ireland students over students of other religious faiths or of no faith.

The respondent admitted just over 200 new entrants each year and had in excess of 400 applications for those places. Whenever the applications for first year in the school exceeded the number of available places, the respondent school applied a selection process based on criteria detailed in its admission policy.

The claimant alleged she was discriminated against on the grounds of religious belief in relation to her application to the respondent for first year commencing in 2020. The respondent prioritised admission of Church of Ireland students attending a Church of Ireland national school named in the respondent's Admission Policy 2020–2021. The claimant, who was Catholic, alleged she was treated less favourably because of this policy and that this was contrary to s 7 of the Acts, which prohibits discrimination by an education establishment in relation to admission of a student to the establishment on any of the protected grounds, including religion. The claimant alleged that the respondent was a non-denominational post-primary school and so it could not avail of any exemptions under the Acts.

The claimant went through the internal appeal process between October 2019 and January 2020, without reaching a satisfactory outcome. It was alleged that the breach was continuing as the respondent continued to operate the admission policy. A claim was lodged with the WRC in March 2020.

As a preliminary point, the respondent alleged the claimant's claim was time-barred as she had been informed of its decision in September 2019.

The respondent rejected the claimant's allegation that it was a non-denominational school, and submitted that it was a designated school and multi-denominational with a 'unique ethos reflected in how it is governed'. Following a review of its admission policy in 2018, the Board of the respondent concluded that the provision made for the Church of Ireland community allowed the school to provide for certain religious values on the basis that it was not discriminatory for a post-primary school to

---

[73]   *Student v Community School* ADJ-00027446.

give preference to students of a particular religious denomination to maintain certain religious values.

A key consideration in the case related to the exceptions set out in s 7 of the Acts referring to educational establishments. Section 7 of the Acts provides that, in certain instances, when either giving priority to, or rejecting, an application on religious grounds, that conduct may be deemed non-discriminatory. Such instances include where the establishment is a school providing primary or post-primary education to students where the objective of the school is to provide education in an environment which promotes certain religious values, the school admits persons of a particular religious denomination in preference to others (s 7(3)(c)); or where the school refuses to admit a student who is not of a particular religious denomination and it is proved that the refusal is essential to maintain the ethos of the school (s 7(3)(ca)).

The Adjudication Officer noted that the exceptions under the Acts would apply if the objective of the respondent was to provide education in an environment which promoted certain religious values and the school admitted persons of a particular religious denomination in preference to others. The Adjudication Officer reviewed the respondent's admission policy and the evidence of both the claimant and the respondent on the ethos of the school, noting in particular the most current policy (2021/2022) as 'evidence of the Ethos with specific reference to what religious values it promotes and how that determines its Admission Policy based on those religious values'. The Adjudication Officer concluded that s 7(3)(c) or s 7(3)(ca) of the Acts did not apply, based on statements in the admission policy of the respondent that it does not discriminate on grounds of the religion of the student/applicant.

The claimant established, on the facts, that priority was given to Church of Ireland students from a named primary school over and above other students of different religious beliefs or no beliefs for admission to the respondent. A *prima facie* case was made out where it could be presumed that prohibited conduct had occurred in relation to the claimant and that that conduct continued. As the stated policy of the respondent was not to discriminate in its admission of students based on religion, the respondent could not rely on the exceptions under s 7 of the Acts to rebut the presumption of the prohibited conduct continuing.

No evidence was provided to the WRC that the respondent had an objective to provide education in an environment which promoted certain religious values in accordance with s 7 of the Acts, and therefore admitted persons of a particular religious denomination in preference to others.

The Adjudication Officer held that the complaint was not statute barred, as the conduct was continuing. The respondent did engage in prohibited conduct in breach of the Acts, and was ordered to:

1. cease to give pupils of Church of Ireland faith attending the named national school priority when it came to enrolment in first year;
2. amend its admission policy to ensure the prohibited conduct ended; and
3. provide a place to the claimant in second year commencing 2021–2022.

[4.55] *Page v Lord Chancellor[74]—Court of Appeal of England and Wales—Underhill & Jackson LJJ, Simler LJ—appeal from UK Employment Appeal Tribunal—employment equality—religion—victimisation*

The appellant was a magistrate. On his appointment, he signed an undertaking which acknowledged his duties to administer justice in accordance with the law and to be free from bias. He also swore a judicial oath. There were no problems with his conduct as a magistrate prior to July 2014.

In July 2014, the appellant sat as part of the panel hearing an unopposed adoption application brought by a same-sex couple. The appellant indicated his objection to the application and did not sign the order made by the Court permitting the adoption. Disciplinary proceedings were issued against him. The appellant argued that his duty was to do what was best for the child which was (in his view) being cared for by a man and a woman. The panel found the appellant guilty of judicial misconduct on the basis that 'it was wrong for him as a magistrate to make decisions on the basis of a presumption that same-sex adoption was not in the best interests of the child, rather than on the basis of the evidence before the Court'. The appellant was reprimanded and was obliged to take remedial training prior to resuming sitting. In imposing the sanction, the Lord Chief Justice stated:

> Whilst we entirely accept that you are entitled to your personal religious beliefs, such beliefs cannot influence your judgment to the extent that this conflicts with your duties as a judicial office [holder] to apply the law fairly and without prejudice.

In January 2015, the appellant gave interviews to two newspapers about the incident, where he clearly indicated that he had not changed his views and that he believed that the sanction was unjustified. He was provided with a copy of judicial guidance in relation to media engagement, and was warned that, if he failed to take account of this advice, it was likely that formal disciplinary proceedings would follow. One month later, the appellant contributed to an item on a television show, BBC Breakfast. He did not, contrary to the guidance, discuss his participation in that interview with the judicial press office in advance. In the interview, the appellant reiterated that his conduct in the 2014 case was based on what he considered to be best for the child. The report stated that the appellant 'found it hard that his religious beliefs as a Christian were seen as prejudiced'.

Disciplinary proceedings were convened arising out of the appearance on BBC Breakfast. A disciplinary panel (the Panel) upheld the findings of a conduct panel that the appellant was guilty of misconduct because the words broadcasted on BBC Breakfast had brought the magistracy into disrepute. The Panel found that the appellant's comments clearly indicated that he would be prejudiced against certain persons in the future, and considered the fact that his opinion may be genuinely and honestly held, together with the appellant's religious persuasion, wholly irrelevant. The Panel

---

[74] *Page v Lord Chancellor* [2021] EWCA Civ 254.

raised concerns about the appellant's failure to see harm in relying on information that was not before the hearing in reaching a decision, which showed a 'remarkable lack of judgment'.

The appellant was removed from the magistracy on the basis that he had breached the undertaking signed by him at the commencement of his appointment and had demonstrated a 'serious lack of sound judgement'.

The appellant appealed the decision to remove him to the employment tribunal, where that decision was upheld. The EAT also dismissed the appellant's appeal of the tribunal decision, which focused on victimisation. The appellant then appealed the EAT decision—the only issue addressed by the Court of Appeal of England and Wales was the claim that the appellant had been victimised, ie the argument that, in making the statement he made on BBC Breakfast, the appellant had engaged in a protected act, and that this was the reason that he had been dismissed.

The Court noted that the reason provided for the dismissal was that the appellant had indicated and had made statements about how he would perform his duties, which amounted to misconduct. In particular, he had made statements that indicated he had breached his judicial role and would do so again if the opportunity arose. The Court observed that it was open to the appellant to argue that this was not in fact the real reason, but he had not done so. On this basis, the Court found that the findings made by the tribunal were open to it. It found that there was no basis for interfering with the finding that the reason for the appellant's removal was not because of his complaint about earlier disciplinary proceedings against him (a potentially protected act), but rather the implication that he would not fulfil his judicial oath in future.

The Court of Appeal dismissed the appeal.

[4.56] *R (Cornerstone (North East) Adoption and Fostering Services Ltd) v Office for Standards in Education, Children's Services and Skills (Ofsted)[75]—Court of Appeal of England and Wales—Jackson, Asplin and Davies LJJ—appeal from High Court of England and Wales—Equality Act 2010—Human Rights Act 1998— religious beliefs—discrimination*

Cornerstone was an independent fostering agency which hired and supported carers for local children in need of fostering/adoption. Cornerstone only accepted heterosexual, married, evangelical Christians to act as carers. This position was said to be unlawful by Ofsted (the UK's Office for Standards in Education).

Cornerstone appealed the decision of the High Court upholding Ofsted's findings that Cornerstone's recruitment policy violated the Equality Act 2010 and the Human Rights Act 1998 (together, the Acts). In a 2019 report, Ofsted had concluded that Cornerstone's recruitment and selection process for foster-carers contravened the Acts

---

[75] *R (Cornerstone (North East) Adoption and Fostering Services Ltd) v Office for Standards in Education, Children's Services and Skills (Ofsted)* [2021] EWCA Civ 1390. See *Arthur Cox Employment Law Yearbook 2020* at **[4.40]** for the decision of the High Court of England and Wales.

by discriminating on the grounds of sexual orientation and that it contravened the Human Rights Act 1998 on the grounds of religion or belief.

In hearing the appeal the Court stated that the first port of call was to consider whether any reasons could justify the differential treatment on the grounds of sexual orientation. In this respect the Court held that the burden of proof was on Cornerstone. The Court accepted that some of Cornerstone's arguments deserved to be in its favour on the question of justification but found that they did not outweigh the impact that the measures had on the rights of persons affected by of the discriminatory criteria.

The appeal was dismissed.

[4.57] *Forstater v CGD Europe[76]—UK Employment Appeal Tribunal—Equality Act 2010, s 10—protected gender-critical beliefs—belief that sex is immutable and should not be conflated with gender identity*

CGDE is a not-for-profit think tank that focuses on international development. The claimant was a 'visiting fellow' and entered into consultancy agreements with CGDE, the last of which ended on 31 December 2018. She claimed that her relationship with CGDE came to an end because she expressed 'gender-critical' opinions. The claimant believed that sex is a material reality that should not be conflated with gender or gender identity. She engaged in debates on social media about gender identity issues, and in doing so made some remarks which some transgender people found repugnant. Some of her colleagues complained that they found her comments offensive, and her visiting fellowship was not renewed. She claimed, among other things, that her gender-critical views constituted a protected 'philosophical belief' under s 10 of the Equality Act 2010 and that she was discriminated against because of them.

The employment tribunal concluded that her beliefs did not amount to a philosophical belief that qualified for protection under the Equality Act 2010. The tribunal noted that in order for her beliefs to qualify as a protected philosophical belief under s 10, they had to satisfy the following criteria:

(i) The belief must be genuinely held.
(ii) It must be a belief and not ... an opinion or viewpoint based on the present state of information available.
(iii) It must be a belief as to a weighty and substantial aspect of human life and behaviour.
(iv) It must attain a certain level of cogency, seriousness, cohesion and importance.
(v) It must be worthy of respect in a democratic society, not be incompatible with human dignity and not conflict with the fundamental rights of others.

The tribunal accepted that the claimant's belief satisfied all but the last of the criteria. The tribunal concluded that her beliefs were 'not worthy of respect in a democratic society'.

On appeal, the EAT held that the tribunal had erred in its application of the above criteria. It confirmed that a philosophical belief will only be excluded from protection

---

[76]   *Forstater v CGD Europe* UKEAT/0105/20/JOJ.

if it is the kind of belief, the expression of which would be akin to Nazism or totalitarianism and thereby liable to be excluded from the protection of rights under the European Convention on Human Rights. The claimant's gender-critical beliefs, which were widely shared, and which did not seek to destroy the rights of transgender persons, clearly did not fall into that category. Furthermore, the tribunal had recognised that the claimant's belief that sex is immutable and binary was consistent with the law. The EAT stated that where a belief or a major tenet of it appears to be in accordance with the law of the land, then it is all the more jarring that it should be declared as one not worthy of respect in a democratic society. While her beliefs may have been offensive to some, and notwithstanding the potential to result in the harassment of transgender persons, the EAT concluded that those beliefs fell within the protection of the Convention and therefore within the Equality Act 2010.

The appeal was upheld.

REMEDIES

[4.58]   *Diskrimineringsombudsmannen v Braathens Regional Aviation AB[77]— European Court of Justice—request for a preliminary ruling from Sweden— Directive 2000/43/EC,[78] art 7 (protection of rights), art 15 (sanctions)—equal treatment regardless of racial or ethnic origin*

In accordance with their obligations under Directive 2000/43 (the Directive), Member States of the EU are required to establish means of legal protection for individuals who are discriminated against on the basis of their race or ethnic origin. Specifically, the Directive contains provisions intended to safeguard individuals' rights to equal treatment as well as provisions setting out sanctions for the breach of those rights. In this case, a request for a preliminary ruling was made by the Supreme Court of Sweden in relation to whether EU law prohibits a respondent from agreeing to compromise a complaint of discrimination without admission of liability and without an examination being conducted, or finding being made, by a competent authority in relation to the complaint.

In this case, the request for a preliminary ruling centred on the right under EU law of an individual who believed himself to have been the victim of discrimination to have an investigation conducted into, and a finding made in respect of that belief. More particularly, the referral sought clarity in relation to whether such a right exists in circumstances where the respondent to a complaint agrees to compromise the complaint through a monetary award but refuses to make any admission of liability. The respondent in this case, a regional airline, had—according to the Swedish Ombudsman responsible for combatting discrimination—singled out a passenger as being a Muslim and an Arab, and on that basis had required the passenger to undergo heightened security checks and had, as such, treated him less favourably than other passengers.

---

[77]   *Diskrimineringsombudsmannen v Braathens Regional Aviation AB* (Case C-30/19).
[78]   Directive 2000/43/EC implementing the principle of equal treatment between persons irrespective of racial or ethnic origin.

The airline agreed to compromise the passenger's complaint to the Stockholm District Court, but sought to do so without admission of liability. The District Court ordered the airline to pay damages to the passenger and did not accept the Ombudsman's finding that the complaint could not be compromised without any examination taking place as to whether discrimination had in fact occurred. The Ombudsman appealed the District Court's ruling, in relation to the Ombudsman's finding, to the Stockholm Court of Appeal. The Stockholm Court of Appeal dismissed the appeal, and the Ombudsman subsequently appealed to the Supreme Court of Sweden and requested that it make a request to the ECJ for a preliminary ruling. The Ombudsman based this appeal on the contention that in relation to a complaint in which damages are sought, compensation is not the only thing sought, and that it is inherent that either an acknowledgement by a respondent or a declaration by the national court is also required, confirming that the payment of compensation does indeed arise because discrimination has taken place.

In its referral, the Supreme Court of Sweden noted that under the provisions of national law, it was open to a respondent to agree to compromise a claim for damages made by a complainant without setting out the reasons for that compromise or to recognise that discrimination had in fact occurred. The crux of the issue referred by the Supreme Court was whether the applicable national legislation complied with the requirements of art 15 of the Directive, read in the context of art 47 of the Charter of Fundamental Rights of the European Union, which guarantees the right to an effective judicial remedy.

The ECJ noted that art 15 of the Directive obliges Member States to establish rules:

> on sanctions applicable to infringements of the national provisions adopted pursuant to that directive, and are to take all measures necessary to ensure that they are applied. Without requiring specific sanctions, that article provides that the sanctions laid down, which may include the payment of compensation to the victim, must be effective, proportionate and dissuasive.

The ECJ further noted that Swedish national law allowed for situations where a respondent's agreement to compromise a complaint could be made without admission of liability and without a finding being made by a national Court in relation to whether or not discrimination had indeed occurred. The ECJ found that the effect of this was to preclude the national Court from ruling in relation to the fact of discrimination, even though it was the grounds for the damages claimed and therefore the cornerstone of the complaint. In those circumstances, a claimant was 'unable to obtain a ruling by a civil court on the existence of that discrimination'.

The ECJ held that such a national law infringed the obligations imposed by arts 7 and 15 of the Directive when read in the light of art 47 of the Charter of Fundamental Rights of the European Union. The ECJ held that where a respondent makes no admission of liability in relation to the discrimination alleged in the context of a compromise of the complaint, a claimant must nonetheless be able to obtain a ruling or finding on whether a breach of the rights that the national law is intended to protect has in fact occurred.

As a result, the ECJ concluded that the payment of damages, even where made with the agreement of a claimant, is not sufficient to ensure effective judicial protection for a claimant who requests a finding as to whether there had been a breach of his or her right to equal treatment. The ECJ held that this is particularly the case where the claimant's interest is not economic, but rather in obtaining a finding in relation to the fact of discrimination.

[4.59]   *Anwar v The Advocate General for Scotland[79]—UK Supreme Court—Hodge, Lloyd-Jones, Briggs, Leggatt and Burrows LJJ—Treaty on European Union, art 19(1)—Charter of the Fundamental Rights of the European Union, art 47—judicial review—whether the absence of a jurisdiction to grant interim relief caused the UK to fail to provide an effective remedy for harassment suffered by the appellant on the ground of sex, race and religion—principle of effectiveness—principle of equivalence*

The UK Supreme Court considered an appeal from the Inner House of the Court of Session in Scotland concerning proceedings for judicial review. The appellant claimed compensation from the UK Government for its alleged failure to properly implement the EU Equality Directives. Specifically, she claimed that the UK had failed to provide an effective remedy for the harassment which she suffered at the hands of her former employer on the grounds of sex, race and religion by failing to enact a legislative provision to enable an employment tribunal in Scotland to grant interim relief, in this case the freezing of her employer's bank accounts pending the outcome of the tribunal proceedings in order to prevent the dissipation of the funds, which would otherwise have been available to meet her financial claim.

Under EU law, Member States are obliged to provide effective and accessible remedies for the implementation of EU-based rights (the principle of effectiveness) and in so doing must provide remedies that are equivalent to those available for comparable claims that do not involve EU law (the principle of equivalence). These requirements of EU law are based on art 19 (1) of the Treaty on European Union and on art 47 of the Charter of the Fundamental Rights of the European Union.

The UK Supreme Court noted that it is well established that in the absence of EU law governing the matter, the domestic system of each Member State must designate the courts and tribunals having jurisdiction and establish detailed procedural rules governing the safeguarding of rights derived from EU law. Member States are responsible for ensuring that those rights are effectively protected and that such rules 'must not render the exercise of those rights practically impossible or excessively difficult'.

The parties to the proceedings accepted that the principle of effectiveness requires that there be interim measures available to a claimant in an action that safeguards his/her rights under the Equality Directives. It was noted that the ECJ in *R v Secretary of State for Transport Ex p Factortame[80]* held that the effectiveness of EU law would be diminished if a national law were to prevent a court seised of a matter concerning EU law from granting interim relief to give full effect to a judgment on rights safeguarded by EU law.

---

[79]   *Anwar v The Advocate General for Scotland* [2021] UKSC 44.
[80]   *R v Secretary of State for Transport Ex p Factortame (No 2)* (Case C-213/89).

In this case, the appellant was employed by a charity. She instituted proceeding before an employment tribunal in Scotland claiming that she was subjected to harassment on the grounds of sex, race and religion contrary to s 26 of the Equality Act 2010. Her claims were upheld and she was awarded compensation in excess of £70,000. She claimed that her employer embarked on a process of closing down its operations and transferring its funds to a new charity, thereby avoiding paying the award made to her. In the course of enforcement proceedings after the decision of the employment tribunal, she secured a remedy from the Sheriff Court which prohibited the employer, or anybody acting on its behalf, from disposing of or transferring funds held by it to a third party other than in payment of any salaries or debts legally incurred. Ultimately, she recovered a sum of less than £3,000.

The employment tribunals in Scotland do not have a power to grant interim measures such as a requirement on the part of the respondent employer to provide interim security for a financial claim. Accordingly, the issues to be considered were:

1. whether the Scottish civil courts (Court of Session) or Sheriff Court have the power to grant interim relief of the type sought by the appellant pending the decision of an employment tribunal;
2. if the Scottish civil courts do have that power, whether the requirement for an appellant to institute such proceedings constitutes a breach of the EU law principles of effectiveness or effective remedy; and
3. if the answer to the first point is that the Scottish civil courts do not have such a power, does that constitute a breach of EU law?

Following an extensive assessment of Scottish law, the Supreme Court was satisfied that the answer to the first question was in the affirmative. Specifically, the Court of Session and the Sheriff Court do have the power, in certain circumstances, to grant a warrant for diligence on the dependence of an ancillary action which has been brought to provide interim security for a claim for discrimination or harassment being taken by a worker before an employment tribunal. That in turn meant that the third question did not arise.

The next question therefore was whether that ancillary jurisdiction met the requirements of EU law in terms of the principles of effectiveness and equivalence. The Supreme Court concluded that EU law does not require that an employment tribunal have the jurisdiction to grant interim remedies of the type sought by the appellant. The Supreme Court noted that the Equality Directives do not require the creation of interim measures and concluded that there is no reason why interim measures should not exist as part of the general law of a domestic legal system rather than being specified in legislation that implements the Equality Directives.

Furthermore, the Supreme Court was satisfied that the requirement to raise an ancillary action to secure interim measures did not render the appellant's exercise of his or her EU law rights practically impossible or excessively difficult.

On the principle of equivalence, the Supreme Court noted that the principle requires that a right deriving from EU law is not treated in a manner less favourable than similar domestic law claims. The Supreme Court pointed out that the correct comparator claim would be another employment-related claim before the employment tribunal based on domestic law, such as a claim for unfair dismissal. The Supreme Court noted that an employment tribunal hearing a claim for unfair dismissal cannot grant interim measures of the type to which these proceedings relate and accordingly there was no breach of the principle of equivalence.

The appellant's appeal was dismissed.

[4.60] *Wisbey v Commissioner of the City of London Police*[81]*—Court of Appeal of England and Wales—Jackson, Lewis and Simler LJJ—appeal from UK Employment Appeal Tribunal—Equality Act 2010, s 124(4) and (5)—employment equality*

The main focus of the appeal was whether the provision in the Equality Act 2010 dealing with remedies in a case of unintentional unlawful indirect discrimination is incompatible with EU law.

The claimant was an authorised firearms officer in the City of London Police. In 2017 he was removed from his role as authorised firearms officer (AFO) and from driving duties due to colour blindness, but in February 2018 he was reinstated to both of these roles. Since, as a matter of statistical fact, approx. 8% of men and only 0.25% of women suffer colour vision defects, the claimant made a claim of unlawful indirect discrimination in the employment tribunal, contending that the requirement to pass colour vision tests unlawfully discriminated against men. The employment tribunal dismissed his claim in relation to removal as AFO but upheld his claim for indirect discrimination in relation to driving duties as it was not reasonably necessary to prohibit those with colour vision defects from driving. However, the tribunal declined to make an award of compensation for injury to feelings as the indirect sex discrimination was unintentional because the respondent was not aware that the colour vision requirements would put the claimant at a particular disadvantage, as a man, nor did it intend that consequence.

He appealed to the EAT, where his claims were dismissed. The claimant then appealed to the Court of Appeal, contending that s 124(4) and (5) of the Equality Act 2010 were not compatible with EU law because they impose an additional threshold or hurdle before any consideration can be given to awarding compensation, with the result that the remedies available for this form of discrimination were neither effective nor dissuasive.

The Court noted stated that it did 'not accept that as a matter of statutory construction sections 124(4) and (5) EA 2010 restrict the right to adequate and proportionate compensation for a breach of the prohibition on indirect sex discrimination; nor that they do not have appropriate dissuasive effect'. It held that s 124(4) and (5) provide that the remedies of a declaration and a recommendation must be considered first, before an award of compensation is made. If the tribunal does decide that a declaration and a recommendation are appropriate, s 124(4) and (5) do not preclude the tribunal from also awarding compensation.

---

81   *Wisbey v Commissioner of the City of London Police* [2021] EWCA Civ 650.

The Court noted that the Equality Act 2010 makes special provision where there has been unlawful indirect discrimination but that it 'was not applied with the intention of discriminating against the complainant'. In dismissing the appeal the Court commented:

> Requiring a tribunal to first consider whether to make a declaration or a recommendation before compensation can be awarded does not inhibit or make it more difficult for a complainant to vindicate their domestic or EU rights.

The appeal was dismissed.

[4.61] *Steer v Stormsure Ltd[82]—UK Employment Appeal Tribunal—appeal from employment tribunal—Equality Act 2010—European Convention on Human Rights—Directive 2006/54/EC[83]—Employment Rights Act 1996, s 103A— victimisation—interim relief—effectiveness and equivalence*

The claimant claimed that she was subjected to sexual harassment from a fellow employee and that the respondent employer failed adequately to protect her from the harassment. She alleged that a grievance raised by her was not properly investigated. The claimant also asserted that her request to work from home so as to avoid the harassment received an unfavourable response from the respondent because of unwarranted sex-based assumptions regarding her ability to juggle work at home with her childcare responsibilities. She claimed that, when finally permitted to work from home, an instruction to install screen-shot monitoring software was an implicit attack on her integrity and an unjustified intrusion into her private life. The claimant was notified that her weekly working hours were reduced by 40%, due to her childcare responsibilities. She contended that this amounted to an express dismissal or, in the alternative, a constructive dismissal on gender grounds and victimisation for having lodged the grievance and the request to work from home. She also claimed that she was dismissed for making a protected disclosure and that this was an automatically unfair dismissal under s 103A of the Employment Rights Act 1996.

The claimant sought interim relief in relation to the whistleblowing claim (for which statutory provision for interim relief was available) and in relation to her sex discrimination and victimisation claims. When the employment tribunal refused to list the application for interim relief in relation to the discrimination and victimisation claims, because there was no statutory provision for such relief, the claimant appealed to the EAT. She claimed that an interim relief jurisdiction must be read into the Equality Act 2010 because it is required by EU law and/or by the European Convention on Human Rights (the ECHR) and/or that such a right should be granted by giving horizontal direct effect to the fundamental principles of EU law.

The claimant relied on three grounds relating to EU law. She claimed that:

1. the failure of UK domestic law to provide interim relief in discrimination and victimisation cases relating to dismissal should be remedied by the application of a

---

[82] *Steer v Stormsure Ltd* UKEAT/0216/20/AT.
[83] Directive 2006/54/EC on the implementation of the principle of equal opportunities and equal treatment of men and women in matters of employment and occupation.

conformed interpretation to the Equality Act 2010 by reading in words to the 2010 Act granting a right to claim interim relief in dismissal cases;

2. the failure to provide interim relief in cases such as this was in breach of the fundamental principles of effectiveness and/or equivalence under EU law and arts 15 and 47 of the EU Charter; and

3. the failure to grant a right to claim interim relief in discrimination and victimisation cases arising from dismissals was in breach of art 14 of the ECHR when read with arts 6 and 8 and also art 1 of Protocol 1.

The legislative background in the UK was that interim relief in dismissal cases was introduced in 1975 in relation to dismissals for trade union activity and was introduced in relation to various other specific categories of dismissal thereafter. There is, however, no interim relief provision for conventional and straightforward unfair dismissal claims or discriminatory dismissal claims. The UK statutory remedies for claims for discrimination, discriminatory dismissal and victimisation are: a declaration, compensation (which is unlimited and includes compensation for injury to feelings), and a recommendation.

In considering the various contentions made by the claimant, the EAT had to consider the Equal Treatment Directive 2006/54/EC and in particular Recital 35 thereof which obliges Member States to 'provide for effective, proportionate and dissuasive penalties for breaches of obligations under this Directive'.

The EAT noted that EU law allows Member States discretion to decide on the procedures, rules and remedies for the enforcement of rights derived under EU Directives, subject to two 'important limitations', ie, domestic law must comply with the principles of effectiveness and equivalence. Effectiveness means that the domestic law must provide an effective remedy and equivalence means that 'the procedures and remedies are no less favourable than those which apply to similar actions of a domestic nature'.

In considering the principle of effectiveness, the EAT noted that interim relief gives claimants significant benefits including early restoration of employment; swift redress; avoidance of cost; and speedy access to an effective financial remedy. The grant of interim relief also places pressure on employers to settle. However, the EAT concluded that the principle of effectiveness did not require the extension of interim relief to discrimination and victimisation cases as UK domestic law does provide an effective remedy in that a claimant, if successful at a full hearing, could be awarded the remedies of declaration and uncapped compensation and, in appropriate cases, a recommendation. Although the claimant argued that the remedy of compensation, paid many months later without the option of preserving the status quo, failed to afford remedies which were 'effective and dissuasive', the EAT found the question was not whether interim relief would improve the remedies available to claimants in discrimination and victimisation cases, but whether the current remedies satisfied the requirement of effectiveness. The EAT did not believe that the length of the delays were such that claimants were being deprived of an effective remedy. It noted that, in most cases, claimants would obtain final judgment within a year or a year-and-a-half at most and that this compared favourably with timescales for other types of civil litigation in the UK. It concluded that, as the delays were not grossly excessive, a remedy which provided full compensation for loss, including interest, although only available after a final hearing, did not infringe the effectiveness principle.

In considering whether the lack of interim relief in discrimination and victimisation cases infringed the principle of equivalence, the EAT had to identify a similar action of a domestic nature. The claimant relied on the claim for unfair dismissal for making a protected disclosure, in respect of which interim relief has been provided by statute. The EAT identified three questions to consider in this context:

1. whether claims for automatically unfair dismissal in whistleblowing cases under the Employment Rights Act 1996, s 103A are similar actions of a domestic nature as compared to the generality of discrimination and victimisation claims; if so,
2. whether the procedures, remedies and rules for the discrimination and victimisation claims are less favourable than those available in automatically unfair dismissal claims; this would depend on whether the Court considered the specific procedure/remedy sought or all the applicable procedures/remedies 'in the round'; and
3. whether the 'no most favourable treatment Proviso' (the Proviso) applies, ie, whether 'there is no breach of the equivalence requirement if the procedure and remedy rules applying to the EU based claim are no less favourable that those which apply to a similar action of a domestic nature, even if there are other similar domestic law claims which have more favourable rules relating to procedures and remedies'.

In considering the first question, the EAT found that the two sets of claims (whistleblowing and discrimination/victimisation) were comparable for the purpose of the equivalence principle.

In answer to the second question, the EAT decided that, considering all of the procedures and remedies available in discrimination/victimisation claims and those in whistleblowing dismissal claims, including interim relief, the procedures and remedies in discrimination/victimisation cases were no less favourable than those applicable in whistleblowing dismissal cases. Although 'the right to claim interim relief was a benefit', the EAT did not find that it outweighed the procedure and remedies advantages of discrimination/victimisation claims.

As the EAT concluded that the procedure remedies and rules for discrimination/victimisation claims were not less favourable than those for protected disclosure dismissal claims, that disposed of the claim based on the EU law principle of equivalence.

The EAT, in case it was wrong, went on to deal with the Proviso. The leading UK authority in respect of the Proviso is the Supreme Court decision in *Totel Ltd v Revenue and Customs Commissioners*.[84] The Proviso arises in circumstances where the search for true comparators with the EU claim discloses more than one comparable domestic claim with different levels of favourableness in procedural treatment. In *Totel*, the Supreme Court noted that on 'almost every occasion where it referred to the principle

---

[84] *Totel Ltd v Revenue and Customs Commissioners* [2018] UKSC 44; [2018] 1 WLR 4053.

of equivalence, the CJEU has added the proviso that the principle does not require the EU claim to be treated as favourably as the most favourably treated comparable domestic claim'. Accordingly, the EAT concluded that, although discrimination and victimisation claims are comparable, for equivalence purposes, with protected disclosure dismissal claims, there was no breach of the equivalence principle, as first, 'taken in the round', the procedure and remedies in discrimination and victimisation cases were no less favourable than those in protected disclosure dismissal claims. Second, the Proviso applied such that the equivalence principle was not infringed, because even if the procedures and remedies for discrimination and victimisation claims were less favourable than those in protected disclosure dismissal claims, they were not less favourable than for another similar action of a domestic nature, ie, a claim for 'ordinary' unfair dismissal, which does not have provision for interim relief.

In light of the conclusions reached, with reference to the principles of effectiveness and equivalence, the EAT did not need to consider whether a right to seek interim relief could be read into the domestic law statutory framework. Nevertheless, it proceeded to consider that question and the application of the *Marleasing*[85] principle. Following an extensive review of the case law, the EAT concluded that it would not be possible to apply a conforming interpretation in the circumstances. Even if the absence of interim relief infringed the EU principles of equivalence or the ECHR, the EAT held that the introduction, 'via an appellate ruling, of the remedy of interim relief for discrimination/victimisation cases resulting from dismissals would cross the boundary between interpretation and amendment, and would require this EAT to make decisions on matters that the Appeal Tribunal is not equipped to evaluate'.

The next question was whether the absence of interim relief for discrimination and victimisation cases constituted a violation of fundamental principles of EU law. The EAT noted that the benefit of a successful claim for breach of fundamental principles of EU law, as opposed to a claim for breach of the principles of equivalence or effectiveness, or for a violation of the ECHR, is that 'there is no need to show that a conforming interpretation is possible'. As the fundamental principles of non-discrimination and effective remedy under art 47 of the EU Charter have horizontal direct effect, they can be relied upon individuals acting against private sector employers. However, the EAT concluded that the claimant could not bring her claim under these fundamental principles as the principle of non-discrimination is recognised in domestic law by the Equality Act 2010, and domestic law also provides a remedy for sex discrimination, which satisfies the requirement of effectiveness. The EAT found the requirements of the fundamental principles were fulfilled as there was an effective remedy for discrimination and victimisation in domestic law.

On the question as to whether there was a breach of the ECHR, the EAT declared that it did not have the power to make a declaration of incompatibility. Nevertheless, the EAT went on to consider the matter and raised three questions: first, was the matter 'within

---

[85] *Marleasing SA v La Comercial Internacional de Alimentación SA* (Case C-106/89); [1990] ECR I-4135.

the ambit of substantive ECHR rights, such that Article 14 [prohibition on discrimination] can be relied on?' Second, did the claimant have the relevant status under art 14? Third, was the claimant 'in an analogous situation with those who are entitled to interim relief' for a protected disclosure dismissal claim and if so, can that differing treatment be justified?

With reference to the first question, the EAT concluded that the answer was in the affirmative. The case came within art 6 because it concerned 'access to judicial remedies for the enforcement of civil rights'.

In terms of the second question, it was not disputed that the claimant had status under art 14. The conclusion was that the status was 'other status'. Here the status of being a litigant or someone who wished to bring a claim for discriminatory dismissal and victimisation was capable of being 'other status'.

On the third question with reference to the justification of the difference in treatment between protected disclosure dismissal claimants and discriminatory dismissal and victimisation dismissal claimants, the position was that no justification was established or even put forward by the respondent. Accordingly, the claimant succeeded in demonstrating that the difference in treatment relating to interim relief, as it affected those wishing to bring a claim relating to discrimination and victimisation arising from dismissal and those wishing to bring a claim for protected disclosure dismissal was in breach of art 14 of the ECHR when read with art 6. However, the EAT did not have jurisdiction to award the only potential remedy, which was to read words into the Equality Act 2010 'in a way which reversed the effect of the breach of Article 14'.

It followed from all of the foregoing that the claimant's appeal was dismissed. Permission to appeal to the Court of Appeal on the European Convention of Human Rights point was granted.

[4.62] *Steer v Stormsure Ltd, the Secretary of State for International Trade & the Minister for Women and Equalities*[86]—*Court of Appeal of England and Wales—Bean, Warby and Laing LJJ—appeal from UK Employment Appeal Tribunal—Equality Act 2010—European Convention on Human Rights, art 14—interim relief not available under Equality Act 2010*

The appellant was employed by the respondent from 12 March 2020 until 15 July 2020. She alleged that she was subjected to sexual harassment, consisting of inappropriate conduct related to her sex, from a fellow employee, and that the respondent failed adequately to protect her from this harassment. In June 2020 she presented a grievance, which she claimed was not adequately investigated, and she asked to work from home to avoid future incidences. The appellant was granted leave to work from home but had to install work monitoring software, which she alleged infringed on her private life.

---

[86]   *Steer v Stormsure Ltd, the Secretary of State for International Trade & the Minister for Women and Equalities* [2021] EWCA Civ 887.

The appellant also alleged that, on 9 July 2020, she was told her working hours were to be reduced to 60% because she had childcare responsibilities. She contended that such a unilateral change amounted to an express dismissal, alternatively that she has been constructively dismissed and that her dismissal amounted to sex discrimination and to victimisation for protected acts (ie, issuing her grievance and requesting to work from home).

She contended that the remedies available to her included a right to seek interim relief, although no such right appears in the Equality Act 2010 (the 2010 Act). The appellant argued that the failure of domestic law to make provision for interim relief in discrimination and victimisation cases amounted to discrimination against women or 'other status', in breach of art 14 of the European Convention on Human Rights, read together with art 6, art 8, and/or art 1 of Protocol 1; the 'other status' consisting of being dismissed on discriminatory grounds compared to being dismissed for making a protected disclosure The appellant argued that this problem could be remedied by reading a right to claim interim relief into domestic legislation. Alternatively, the appellant contended that the Court of Appeal of England and Wales should declare the 2010 Act incompatible with the appellant's Convention rights in so far as it failed to make interim relief available.

The appellant presented a claim to the employment tribunal and sought interim relief, both in relation to a whistleblowing claim and to her sex discrimination/victimisation claims. The employment tribunal listed an interim relief hearing but only in relation to the whistleblowing claim and stated that the employment tribunal did not have jurisdiction to grant interim relief in the discrimination/victimisation claims. The appellant appealed this decision to the EAT on three grounds, including that the employment tribunal had erred in law in deciding that it did not have the power to grant interim relief in discrimination and victimisation claims arising out of dismissals. The EAT found that although the lack of availability of interim relief in discrimination and victimisation cases was, in principle, a breach of art 14 of the European Convention of Human Rights, it could not 'read down' the Equality Act 2010 in line with s 3 of the Human Rights Act 1998; nor did the EAT have jurisdiction to declare the Equality Act 2010 incompatible with art 14. The EAT granted permission to appeal to the Court of Appeal.

The Court of Appeal concluded that:

(a) although interim relief in the employment tribunal was available to a dismissed whistleblower but not to the appellant, this was not discrimination on the grounds of sex as, in either case, the claimant may be male or female;

(b) the status of being a litigant in a particular type of case is not discrimination on the grounds of 'other status', since being a litigant in any type of case is not a protected status;

(c) the remedies available to the appellant, taken as a whole, were not in any event less favourable to her than those available to a dismissed whistleblower; and

(d) even if they were, the difference in treatment by the legislature was justified.

Accordingly, the Court of Appeal dismissed the appeal.

SEXUAL ORIENTATION

[4.63] *Secretary of State for Justice v Plaistow*[87]*—UK Employment Appeal Tribunal—Acas Code on Discipline and Grievance—Trade Union and Labour Relations (Consolidation) Act 1992—appeal from the employment tribunal—unfair dismissal—victimisation—sexual orientation discrimination—costs—res judicata*

This case related to two appeals from the employment tribunal. The first appeal related to the employment tribunal's assessment of compensation having upheld the claimant's claim of direct sexual orientation discrimination, harassment, victimisation and unfair dismissal. The second appeal related to costs.

In relation to the first appeal, in assessing compensation, the employment tribunal had calculated compensation on a career-loss basis, and awarded a 20% uplift having regard to the respondent's non-compliance with the Acas Code on Discipline and Grievance (the Code), under s 207A of the Trade Union and Labour Relations (Consolidation) Act 1992.

The respondent appealed this award of compensation, alleging that the employment tribunal had erred in using a career-loss basis calculation, had reached a perverse decision in relation to the calculation of the claimant's base salary, and had erred in its assessment of the uplift.

In relation to the career-loss calculation, the EAT found that, in light of the expert medical evidence that the claimant suffered moderate PTSD, depression and symptoms of paranoia that would likely be life-long as a result of the discriminatory treatment he had suffered, the employment tribunal had been entitled to find that this 'was one of those rare cases where it would be appropriate to consider the Claimant's future losses on a career-long basis'. That stated, the EAT found that the employment tribunal had erred in failing to have regard to 'the more general uncertainties of life that might impact upon either the length of a person's working life or even just the length of their working day'.

In relation to the calculation of the base pay, the EAT upheld the calculation used by the employment tribunal; however, in relation to the application of the uplift, it found that the employment tribunal had failed to have regard to the totality of the award, or to demonstrate that there was proportionality between the breach of the Code and the harm suffered by the claimant. This ground of appeal was allowed.

In relation to the award of costs, the respondent alleged that the issue of *res judicata* applied. At an earlier stage of the proceedings, the claimant had made an application to strike out the respondent's response in the proceedings for unreasonable conduct in relation to its disclosure of evidence. The employment tribunal had determined that it was still possible to have a fair trial, and instead addressed the unreasonable conduct of the respondent by making an award of four days of costs against it.

---

[87] *Secretary of State for Justice v Plaistow* UKEAT/0016/20/VP, and UKEAT/0085/20/VP.

The respondent appealed the ultimate award of costs, in which the employment tribunal awarded the claimant further costs, alleging that the employment tribunal had already awarded costs based on the same or similar matters, and was therefore in contravention of the principle of *res judicata*. The EAT found that the employment tribunal had made a determination as to costs on the basis of the respondent's unreasonable conduct in relation to disclosure at an earlier stage of proceedings, and therefore it was not open to the employment tribunal to revisit this. In the absence of any agreement between the parties, the EAT remitted the matter to the employment tribunal.

The respondent's appeal was partially upheld, and was remitted to the employment tribunal for further consideration.

VICTIMISATION

[4.64] *Chief Constable of Merseryside v Knox*[88]*—UK Employment Appeal Tribunal—appeal from employment tribunal—detriment—discrimination—complaint*

The claimant was employed by the respondent as a police officer. During 2017 and 2018, he had submitted various internal grievances pertaining to matters such as sex discrimination and disability discrimination, before making a number of data access requests. In the claimant's first such request, he requested to be provided with all emails sent within the respondent between 2002 and 2017 'with a connection to me'. The respondent referred that request to its Data Access Unit, which in turn involved its Anti-Corruption Unit, which confirmed in October 2017 that it did not have the necessary software to enable it to conduct such a search. The respondent asked the claimant to provide names of email senders and recipients in order to narrow the search. The claimant objected to this request, and made three further data access requests. Notwithstanding this, the respondent emailed 14 individuals in early November 2017 requesting that they review their email accounts for emails related to the claimant. '

In January 2018, the respondent provided the claimant with the emails that had been returned following the search of the 14 individuals' email accounts over November and December 2017. The respondent apologised to the claimant for the delay in producing the data, to which the claimant objected and in respect of which he submitted an (unsuccessful) grievance in relation both to the delay itself, and the manner in which the 14 individuals had been contacted in spite of his objection to the respondent's approach. After a software update in May 2018, the respondent provided further emails to the claimant in October 2018, in response to his original data access request. The claimant submitted a complaint of victimisation to the employment tribunal.

The employment tribunal held that the claimant had indeed been victimised by the respondent, through the way in which the respondent had dealt with and responded to his original data access request. The employment tribunal was satisfied that the respondent had in fact had the capability before its software update in May 2018 to comply

---

[88]   *Chief Constable of Merseryside v Knox* UKEAT/0300/19.

more substantively than it had done with the claimant's original data access request, and that it had known this at the time. The employment tribunal further concluded that the claimant had suffered detriment as a result of the manner in which the respondent responded to the original data request, which shifted the burden of proof on to the respondent to demonstrate that the detriment he had been subjected to was not based on his grievances and data access requests. The employment tribunal held that the respondent had not discharged that burden of proof and that as such, it had victimised the claimant.

The respondent appealed the employment tribunal's decision to the EAT. In allowing the appeal, the EAT was satisfied that the employment tribunal had erred in its finding that the respondent could in fact have responded more substantively to the original data access request before the software update in May 2018. The EAT was further satisfied that the explanation for the respondent only providing further emails to the claimant in October 2018 (after the software update had enabled further and better compliance) was reasonable and acceptable. On that basis, the EAT concluded that the claimant had not in fact been subjected to detriment, and that there was insufficient evidence such as to shift the burden of proof to the respondent.

The EAT dismissed all of the claimant's victimisation claims and overturned the finding of the employment tribunal.

Chapter 5

Employment Litigation: Preliminary Issues

INTRODUCTION

[5.01]   The constitutionality of the WRC Adjudication regime was considered by the Supreme Court in *Zalewski.*

Disputes with regard to discovery in an employment context were considered by the Court of Appeal in *McCormack* and by the High Court in *Burban* and in *White.*

As usual, there are numerous cases in relation to status, whether it be employee status or worker status. See *Ward* and *Camphill Communities of Ireland* (Labour Court), *Uber BV* (UK Supreme Court) and *Lange Professional Game Match Officials Limited* and *Augustine* (Court of Appeal of England and Wales). See also *Northern Light Solutions Limited* (Upper Tribunal Tax and Chancery) and *Pimlico Plumbers and Mitchell and Nursing and Midwifery Council* (UK EAT).

The implications of a contract being illegal were considered by the High Court in *Sobhy* and by the Court of Appeal of England and Wales in *Robinson.*

Whether there is a right of appeal to the Court of Appeal following a point of law appeal to the High Court under the Employment Equality Acts 1998–2021 was considered by the Court of Appeal in *Cunningham.*

There were numerous cases on territorial jurisdiction, namely *DG* and *BU* (European Court of Justice), *A Seafarer* (WRC), *Alta* (Court of Appeal of England and Wales), *Semtech Corporation* (High Court of England and Wales) and *Clark* (UK EAT).

The adequacy of pleadings in occupational injury claim was addressed by the Court of Appeal in *Topaz Energy Group Limited.*

Privilege was addressed by the High Court of England and Wales in *Bogolyubov* and by the UK EAT in *Heart.*

Evergreen Timber Frames Limited was a case in which the UK EAT had to examine the enforceability of a severance agreement.

In the *State of Kuwait* the High Court had to consider whether, in the context of an unfair dismissal claim, sovereign immunity applied.

Limitation periods were the subject of numerous decisions. The precise calculation of a limitation period in the context of a common law claim was considered by the UK

Supreme Court in *Sedman*. The adequacy of documents filed in the context of a Labour Court Appeal was considered by that Court in *Hossain*. Time limits for Labour Court Appeals and the possible extension of time was the subject of Labour Court decisions in *Astech Entertainment Limited* and in *Donnybrook Service Station Limited*. There were also a number of cases in which the Labour Court considered whether the time limit in respect of the bringing of a claim to the WRC should be extended namely *Donegal Meat Processors, Becton Dickinson Penel* and *Forever Therapies*.

The circumstances in which a WRC complaint might be premature were considered by the Labour Court in *Ball*.

Finally, the considerations relevant to an application for judicial review against the WRC were examined by the High Court in *Erdogan*.

CONSTITUTIONALITY OF WORKPLACE RELATIONS COMMISSION ADJUDICATION REGIME

[5.02] *Zalewski v Adjudication Officer, the WRC, Ireland and the Attorney General[1]—Supreme Court—Clarke CJ, O'Donnell, McKechnie, MacMenamin, Dunne, Charleton and O'Malley JJ—Workplace Relations Act 2015—jurisdiction— administration of justice—constitutionality of the Workplace Relations Act 2015*

The appellant was employed by Buywise Discount Store Ltd as a security guard and supervisor. When dismissed for allegedly failing to follow company procedures, the appellant brought unfair dismissal and non-payment of notice claims against his former employer. The appellant attended a WRC hearing on 26 October 2016, during which the Adjudication Officer accepted written submissions and documentation. An adjournment was granted on that date due to the unavailability of a witness and when the parties returned for the resumed hearing in December 2016, the Adjudication Officer had issued a written decision on the basis of the evidence already provided. She found that the complaint of unfair dismissal was not well founded, resulting in the appellant's appeal to the Labour Court and the institution of judicial review proceeding in the civil courts. The appellant asserted that certain provisions of the Workplace Relations Act 2015 (the 2015 Act), under which his claims were to be determined, were a breach of his constitutional rights.

When the High Court ruled that the appellant did not have legal standing to pursue a constitutional challenge, he was granted leave to pursue on appeal to the Supreme Court. The Supreme Court remitted the constitutional challenge back to the High Court. The long-running case ultimately resulted in this Supreme Court decision, which held that specific aspects of the WRC's procedures were unconstitutional.

---

[1] *Zalewski v Adjudication Officer, the WRC, Ireland and the Attorney General* [2021] IESC 24. See *Arthur Cox Employment Law Yearbook 2019* at **[5.18]** for *Zalewski v Adjudication Officer* [2019] IESC 17, where the Supreme Court found that Mr Zalewski had *locus standi* to challenge the constitutionality of the Workplace Relations Act 2015 and various provisions of the Unfair Dismissals Act 1977 (as amended).

By a majority, the Supreme Court held that the exercise of powers by Adjudication Officers of the WRC was an administration of justice within the meaning of Art 37 of the Constitution. It followed that two sections of the 2015 Act were found to be incompatible with the Constitution. The Court's majority judgment was delivered by O'Donnell J. He noted the varying approaches to the definition of the administration of justice and held that a singular definitive test for determining whether a body was carrying out the administration of justice could not be established.

He commented that it was necessary to be flexible in applying the five-part test (established in *McDonald v Bord na gCon (No 2)*[2]) for determining if the administration of justice is being carried out, ie:

(i.) [A] dispute or controversy as to the existence of legal rights or a violation of the law;

(ii.) The determination or ascertainment of the rights of parties or the imposition of liabilities or the infliction of a penalty;

(iii.) The final determination (subject to appeal) of legal rights or liabilities or the imposition of penalties;

(iv.) The enforcement of those rights or liabilities or the imposition of a penalty by the court or by the executive power of the State which is called in by the court to enforce its judgment;

(v.) The making of an order by the court which is a matter of history is an order characteristic of courts in this country.

In analysing the functions of the WRC, O'Donnell J concluded that, although its adjudicative function involved the administration of justice (under Art 34 of the Constitution), the functions concerned were limited and therefore, permissible (within the scope of Art 37 of the Constitution). The Court stated that the powers of the WRC were limited, in essence:

(a) by subject matter, to the areas of employment law specifically identified in the 2015 Act;

(b) on awards of compensation, to 104 weeks' remuneration;

(c) limited enforceability, coupled with the limited capacity of the District Court to substitute compensation for redress by way of reinstatement or re-engagement;

(d) a decision of the WRC is subject to appeal, placing a limitation on the powers of the body;

(e) the WRC is subject to judicial review.

The appellant argued that s 41(13) of the 2015 Act was unconstitutional because under the 2015 Act: (a) proceedings heard before an adjudication officer cannot be in public; and (b) there is no provision for evidence to be given on oath and therefore, no penalty for giving false evidence.

In considering these arguments, the Court found there was no justification for a blanket prohibition on public hearings before an adjudication officer, stating that public hearings are the essence of the administration of justice.

---

[2]   *McDonald v Bord na gCon (No 2)* [1965] IR 217.

Secondly, the Supreme Court held that the absence of the provision for the administration of an oath or any possibility of punishment for giving false evidence is inconsistent with the Constitution, but did not go as far as declaring it unconstitutional. In doing so, the Court highlighted that the importance of evidence being given on oath lies in the power to punish for false evidence and provides an incentive for truthful testimony.

The Supreme Court concluded that, although the 2015 Act was not unconstitutional, certain aspects of the adjudication process were. See the note on the resulting Workplace Relations (Miscellaneous Provisions) Act 2021 at [5.17] below.

DISCOVERY

[5.03]   *McCormack v Health Service Executive[3]—Court of Appeal—Faherty, Binchy & Barniville JJ—appeal from High Court—Safety, Health and Welfare at Work Act 2005—discovery—personal injury proceedings*

The appellant was employed by the respondent as a psychiatric nurse at a high support residence facility (Ferndale).

The appellant brought personal injuries proceedings against the respondent alleging that:

> [F]rom 2013 onwards, the respondent began to admit patients who were unsuitable to the facilities available at Ferndale, on account of their violent and aggressive behaviour which constituted a danger to the health and safety of the staff of the unit, including the appellant, as well as other patients.

In particular, the appellant pointed to two specific incidents, which she claimed had a 'profound' effect on her, the first was where she discovered the suicide of a patient in her care and the second involved a suicide attempt by a colleague whom the appellant claimed 'was unable to cope with the difficulties being experienced by staff in Ferndale'.

The appellant claimed that the respondent was in breach of its duty of care to her, including under the Safety, Health and Welfare at Work Act 2005, as a result of which she claimed she felt 'continuously exposed to the risk of injury and does not feel safe at work' and had experienced personal injuries such as work-related stress and difficulty sleeping causing her to be certified as unfit for work on two occasions.

In the High Court, the appellant sought discovery of the following categories of documents:

(a) Any or all documentation consisting of incident report forms arising from incidents of patient violence and/or aggression at the [respondent]'s facility from 1st January 2010 to 31st December 2014;

(b) Any and all documentation consisting of incident report forms arising from the incidents pleaded in the personal injuries summons to have occurred on or about 31st December 2013 and 27th February 2014;

---

[3]   *McCormack v Health Service Executive* [2021] IECA 272.

(c) Any and all documentation consisting of assessments and/or evaluations conducted at the time of admission of patients who were admitted to the [respondent]'s facility from 1st January 2010 to 31st December 2014 together with any documentation considered in the course of any such assessments and/or evaluation;

(d) Any and all documentation arising from the monitoring or evaluation of patient behaviour by the [respondent], its servant or agents at the [respondent]'s facility from 1st January 2010 to 31st December 2014;

(e) Any and all documentation evidencing the nature or content of training or support provided to the [appellant] with regard to the management of violent or aggressive patients;

(f) Any documentation evidencing steps taken by the [respondent] to ensure the health and safety of the [appellant] in so far as violent or aggressive patients at its facility were concerned.

The respondent refused discovery of all categories except for (b) and the High Court refused to order same, holding that the categories were not relevant to the appellant's claim as she 'had not herself been injured by a violent patient' and that to make orders for discovery sought would be 'disproportionate in circumstances where it would require discovery of third party medical records, and that safety records were not relevant' to the appellant's claims.

The appellant appealed the refusal to the Court of Appeal.

The Court noted that in the intervening period, the parties had agreed to make discovery of the following category of documents:

> Documents evidencing the Admissions Policy or changes thereto for the Ferndale facility for 2012 to 2014 together with any risk assessment concerning violence or aggression during that period.

It held that this 'agreement for discovery is adequate to meet the purposes for which discovery is sought of the documents described in categories (a), (c) and (d)' as the crux of the appellant's claim in this regard centred around the change of the respondent's admissions policy in 2013 which she claimed led to a rise in violent incidents. In any event, the Court held that the categories sought at (a), (c) and (d) were not sufficiently grounded in the pleadings. It noted that the appellant had not been able to provide any specific examples of violent incidents during the time period to which her request for discovery related. The Court also refused to order discovery for categories (e) and (f), holding that 'it is difficult to see the relevance and necessity of the discovery sought in these categories in circumstances where the appellant is not making any claim that she herself was the subject of any violent or aggressive act, or even that she saw others subjected to such treatment'.

The Court noted that an appellate court should be slow to interfere with decisions reached in relation to discovery applications and referred to *Waterford Credit Union v J & E Davy*,[4] where Clarke J stated: '[W]hen a first instance court exercises a judgment of that type, it should not be overturned on appeal unless the appellate court is satisfied that the determination of the court below was outside the range of judgment calls which were open to the first instance court.'

---

[4]   *Waterford Credit Union v J & E Davy* [2020] IESC 9.

The appeal was dismissed, with the Court of Appeal finding that the trial Judge's decision was 'well within his margin of appreciation'.

[5.04]   Burban v Finesse Medical Ltd[5]—High Court—Barrett J—discovery—personal injury proceedings

This judgment concerned an application for 13 categories of discovery brought in the context of personal injury proceedings by the plaintiff against his former employer.

In the substantive proceedings, the plaintiff claimed that he had sustained an injury to his back in the course of changing a roll of paper on a machine at his employer's factory. The claim also included a claim for migraines, head pain, pained vision and adverse reaction to light.

The Court reiterated the core tests of relevance, necessity and proportionality when it comes to applications for discovery. It cited the judgment of Finlay J in *AIB Plc v Ernst & Whitney*[6] where he observed that:

> [T]he basic purpose and reason for the procedure of discovery … is to ensure as far as possible that the full facts concerning any matter in dispute before the court are capable of being presented to the court by the parties concerned, so that justice on full information, rather than on a limited or partial revelation of the facts arising in a particular action, may be done.

It noted that the factors to be taken into account when deciding an application for discovery are: (i) whether the categories sought are relevant to the matter in issue; (ii) that the discovery must be necessary for disposing of the matter fairly or for saving costs (Ord 31, r 12(5) of the Rules of the Superior Courts); and (iii) it must be proportionate.

Taking those factors into account, the Court granted 11 of the 13 categories sought, subject, in the case of certain categories, to some modifications as follows:

— Categories (1) and (2) related to medical records for a period of five years up to and including the date of the incident the subject of the proceedings, which was 20 April 2017. While the Court held that the information sought was necessary and relevant given the nature of the injuries alleged by the plaintiff and his medical history (he was the subject of an assault in 2013/2014 and treated for backache in 2016), it held that the period of five years was disproportionately long and limited the pre-injury documentation to the period from 1 January 2013 onwards;

— Category (4) sought documentation relating to applications for social welfare for a period of three years up to and including the date of the incident the subject of the proceedings and thereafter to date. The Court held that while the documents sought were relevant and necessary, to ensure proportionality it limited the timespan of this category of discovery from the date of the incident onwards.

— Category (6) sought discovery of 'all records relating to the plaintiff's use of, membership of and/or participation in all gym, sporting, leisure, hobby and/or recreational activities, facilities, venues, events and/or past-times and all correspondence and/or documentation relating thereto, for the period of one year prior

---

5   *Burban v Finesse Medical Ltd* [2021] IEHC 52.
6   *AIB Plc v Ernst & Whitney* [1993] 1 IR 375.

to 20th April 2017'. The Court noted that 'as drafted, this category would include providing details of Mr Burban's membership of his local stamp collecting club, if member he is' and it limited the category to 'all records relating to the plaintiff's use of, membership of and/or participation in all exercise and/or fitness and/or gym and/or sporting clubs, facilities or societies' during the period sought.

— Category (9) sought copies of all documentation for all kinds of insurance for the period of three years up to and including the incident and thereafter to date. The Court noted that 'as drafted this would include interactions concerning any pet insurance that Mr Burban may have purchased'. To ensure relevance, necessity and proportionality, the Court limited the category in scope to accident, health, motor and travel insurance.

The Court refused categories (10) and (12) which had sought documentation relating to the plaintiff's car usage and all travel undertaken by him as it held that these were 'fishing' attempts.

[5.05] *White v Arrabawn Co-Operative Society Ltd[7]—High Court—Simons J— discovery—personal injury—health and safety—criminal prosecution—privilege against self-incrimination*

The plaintiff alleged that he received serious burns while removing a filter from a pipeline during his employment. He brought personal injury proceedings against his employer and sought discovery of specific documents.

The defendant claimed privilege over the documents sought and alleged that as the relevant incident was the subject of a criminal prosecution by the Health and Safety Authority (the HSA), it was entitled to rely on the privilege against self-incrimination and to resist discovery without providing an explanation of how the documents were privileged.

The plaintiff was critical of the paucity of information provided by the defendant, and noted the lack of detail on the criminal charges and the interactions between the HSA and the defendant. The plaintiff was also dubious as to whether a non-natural person (such as the defendant company) could invoke the privilege against self-incrimination.

The defendant contended that the High Court could not adjudicate on the claim of privilege and it was a matter for the defendant alone to decide what documents are relevant to the defence of criminal proceedings.

The Court noted that it was required to address three potential issues:

(1) whether the categories of documents sought satisfied 'the threshold of relevance, necessity and proportionality';
(2) whether the claim that the documents were privileged should be adjudicated upon at that stage (or whether an affidavit as to documents be sworn, and the privilege issue be addressed on any later application for inspection); and
(3) if the issue of privilege was to be determined at that stage, the Court must also consider the merits of the claim of privilege in detail.

---

[7] *White v Arrabawn Co-Operative Society Ltd* [2021] IEHC 343.

The Court addressed the proposition that the defendant was entitled to refuse to make discovery of any documents which it considered may affect its defence in the criminal proceedings, and held that this ran counter to the established principle that it is impossible for the Court to permit another body decide whether or not a document will be disclosed. On that basis, the Court found that the defendant's jurisdictional objection to the High Court hearing the issue of privilege must fail. A party to proceedings was not entitled to unilaterally withhold relevant evidence from the Court.

In relation to the threshold of relevance, necessity and proportionality, the Court noted that once the threshold has been met, the burden shifts to the defendant to explain why discovery is not necessary. In this case, the defendant adopted the position that it had an absolute entitlement to assert the privilege against self-incrimination and had not made any submissions on relevance.

The Court found that all categories of documents sought by the plaintiff met the threshold of relevance, necessity and proportionality because of the manner in which the defendant had pleaded its case, ie, the defendant denied all the plaintiff's claims and 'expressly pleaded that the injured party was "entirely the author of his own misfortune" or was otherwise guilty of contributory negligence', without particularising any of its pleas.

In relation to the timing of the adjudication of the claim of privilege, the Court noted that the default position is for such an issue to be decided following a party's objection to produce documents. However, the Court has an inherent jurisdiction to abridge the process where there is a privilege plea which inevitably must succeed.

The Court noted that it was implicit in the defendant's reliance on the privilege against self-incrimination that the plaintiff would pass the discovered documents to the HSA. The Court also noted the likelihood that the HSA already had at least some of the documents sought, and certain categories would, by definition, already be available to the HSA (for example, the category of documents comprising correspondence with the HSA).

The Court found that much of the documentation sought pre-dated the accident and was not created in the context of a statutory investigation and it was at least arguable that an order requiring the defendant to disclose such documents did not breach the privilege against self-incrimination.

On the basis of the analysis of the claim of privilege, the Court found that it could not be said that the claim of privilege would inevitably succeed, and a proper assessment of the claim of privilege would require a more in-depth analysis of whether such privilege applies to non-natural persons.

The Court allowed the plaintiff's application for discovery and found that the categories of discovery met the threshold of relevance, necessity and proportionality. The claim of privilege against self-incrimination was not deemed strong enough to justify 'short-circuiting the usual procedure for asserting privilege' and the Court required the defendant to file an affidavit as to documents 'in the ordinary way', ie, the affidavit 'must state upon what grounds the objection is made, and verify the facts relied upon'.

EMPLOYEE/WORKER STATUS

[5.06] *Limerick Public Participation Network Operations Clg v Ward[8]—Labour Court—appeal from Workplace Relations Commission—Unfair Dismissals Acts 1977 to 2015—Public Participation Networks—minimum period of continuous employment*

The claimant was an independent contractor, working for the respondent as a project coordinator during 2017. At that time the respondent was an unincorporated entity and one of a number of Public Participation Networks (PPNs) established in line with the Local Government Act 2014. The respondent's funding was provided by the Department of Housing and Local Government and was administered by Limerick City and County Council (the Council). The respondent was incorporated on 9 August 2017.

The claimant contended that she worked for the respondent throughout 2017, prior to its incorporation, and that she was engaged through a third party to fulfil the same role for the respondent between August and December 2017. During that time she was liable for the remission of her taxes, did not request or receive holiday pay and submitted invoices on a monthly basis.

In December 2017, she accepted the role of project coordinator with the respondent, and was due to commence in this position on 1 January 2018. At that time the Council advised the respondent that it should not enter into any new contracts as there were issues surrounding funding. The respondent advised the Council of its existing obligations, including its binding commitment to the claimant. Although the Council was unwilling to provide the respondent with the necessary funds for the claimant's salary, the respondent maintained with the Council that it had a binding contractual obligation to the claimant. The claimant remained in her role and stated to the Court that she was assured her salary would be paid in arrears once the issue was resolved.

On 31 January 2018, the claimant was placed on a period of lay-off and on 9 February 2018, she received written notice of the termination of her employment and subsequently lodged a claim for unfair dismissal with the WRC.

The respondent argued that the claimant did not have *locus standi* to take a claim for unfair dismissal under the Unfair Dismissals Acts 1977 to 2015 (the Acts), as she had less than 12 months' continuous service. Prior to 2018 she had been engaged on a contract for services and had not been restricted from engaging in work other than for the respondent. However, her contract of employment commencing 1 January 2018 explicitly prohibited her from being employed elsewhere.

The Labour Court decided in favour of the respondent and held that the claimant did not have the requisite status under the Acts. As the claimant admitted that she fully understood the arrangement she entered into in 2017 when she agreed to work for the

---

8 *Limerick Public Participation Network Operations Clg v Ward* UDD2035.

respondent under a contract for services, the Court could not 'permit the [claimant] to resile from the arrangement she entered into … with full knowledge and understanding', therefore she did not meet the requirement of 12 months' continuous service with the respondent and the appeal was dismissed.

[5.07] *Camphill Communities of Ireland v Williams[9]—Labour Court—appeal from Workplace Relations Commission—unfair dismissal—volunteer*

The claimant was engaged by the respondent as a volunteer, in the role of long-term co-worker, since 1994. From 31 December 2018, the role of long-term co-worker ceased to exist and the respondent moved to an 'employment model'. While many of the respondent's long-term co-workers were offered the opportunity to take up roles as employees, the claimant was not given that option. No explanation was given other than a 'decision had been made'.

The claimant claimed that the nature of the relationship between her and the respondent was in fact an employment relationship and she was unfairly dismissed on 31 December 2018. In support of her claim that she was an employee, the claimant pointed to a number of features of the relationship such as: while she was not paid a salary, her accommodation and 'reasonable needs' were met by the respondent by way of a monthly allowance and she lived in accommodation provided by it; she was subject to a number of policies of the respondent such as grievance and disciplinary procedures, which 'clearly distinguish between volunteers and [long-term co-workers]'; long-term co-workers were subject to formalised supervision and control; the claimant had to undergo supervision training and meet with her manager every six weeks; and she was subject to annual appraisal reviews.

The respondent denied that the claimant was an employee. It contended that there was no contractual relationship between it and the claimant and there existed no intention to create a contract; nor was there mutuality of obligation. The respondent also pointed to the fact that it continued to operate the long-term co-worker model in the UK, where it was accepted by the tax authorities there that the model did not create any employment relationship.

The Court noted that the first issue for it to consider was whether there was a contractual relationship between the parties. It noted that it was common case that no written contract existed, but held that, taking an objective view of the intention of the parties, a contractual relationship did exist as the core elements of offer, acceptance, consideration and intention to create legal relations were present.

Considering the nature of the contract, the Court examined the definition of a 'volunteer' under the Civil Law (Miscellaneous) Act 2011 which is:

> "volunteer" means a person who does voluntary work that is authorised by a volunteer organisation and does so without expectation of payment (other than reasonable reimbursement for expenses) or other reward.

---

9   *Camphill Communities of Ireland v Williams* UDD2155.

The Court noted that although the claimant did not receive 'what would normally be considered a salary or a wage, she did receive more than reimbursement for expenses' and held that as such, she fell outside the definition of a 'volunteer'. While the respondent had submitted that the claimant could not be an employee if she did not receive a wage, the Court did not accept this, finding that the benefits the claimant received from the respondent were taxable income and fell within the definition of 'wages' under the Payment of Wages Act 1991 and 'remuneration' under the Unfair Dismissals Acts 1977 to 2015.

The Court then considered whether a mutuality of obligation existed between the parties. It noted that the contract was for the claimant to do necessary work in return for her accommodation and needs to be met by the respondent, who in turn, had to provide the claimant with the work. It also noted that evidence had been given that long-term co-workers were 'interchangeable' with employees, for whom there was mutuality of obligation, the only difference being that employees were paid a wage. In all of the circumstances, the Court held that mutuality of obligation did exist.

The Court also considered the 'integration' test, finding that the claimant was integrated into the respondent's organisation and the 'control' test, noting the claimant's evidence that: she was 'subordinate' to the Board of Directors; she was subject to policies and procedures of the respondent; she could not arrange a replacement without the respondent's approval; and she required the respondent's approval to take leave.

The Court held that the requisite tests of mutuality of obligation, integration and control were met and that an employment relationship existed.

Having found this, the Court held that the claimant had been unfairly dismissed. It held that the decision to dismiss was based on 'unsubstantiated allegations from a third party', and that the decision to terminate her employment came 'nowhere near the standard required to establish that the [claimant] was afforded fair procedure'. The Court increased the award of compensation of €40,000 given by the WRC to €60,640.

[5.08] *Uber BV v Aslam[10]—UK Supreme Court—Reed, Hodge, Kitchin, Sales, Hamblen, Leggatt and Arden LJJ—appeal from Court of Appeal of England and Wales—Employment Rights Act 1996—Working Time Regulations 1998[11]—National Minimum Wage Regulations 2015[12]—employment litigation—employee status—'worker' vs 'independent contractor'—statutory interpretation—exercise of control—working time*

The claim was brought by a group of private hire vehicle drivers based in London, who provided driving services through the respondent's app, Uber. The claimants alleged that they were 'workers' as defined under the Employment Rights Act 1996, and accordingly were entitled to the appropriate protection under employment legislation.

---

[10] *Uber BV v Aslam* [2021] UKSC 5. See *Arthur Cox Employment Law Yearbook 2019* at **[5.09]** for Court of Appeal decision.
[11] Working Time Regulations 1998 (SI 1998/1833).
[12] National Minimum Wage Regulations 2015 (SI 2015/621).

Section 230(3) of the Employment Rights Act 1996 defines a worker as an individual who works under:

(a) a contract of employment; or
(b) any other contract where they undertake 'to do or perform personally any work or services for another party to the contract whose status is not by virtue of the contract that of a client or customer of any profession or business undertaking carried on by the individual'.

The employment tribunal found that the drivers were 'workers' under s 230(3)(b) of the Employment Rights Act 1996, and rejected the respondent's submission that the drivers were independent contractors. The employment tribunal held that the claimant drivers were 'workers' while the driver:

(a) had the Uber app switched on;
(b) was within the territory in which he was authorised to work, and
(c) was able and willing to accept assignments.

The employment tribunal further held that for the purposes of the Working Time Regulations 1998 and the National Minimum Wage Regulations 2015, the drivers were 'workers' as soon as they logged onto the respondent's app.

These findings were upheld by the EAT and the Court of Appeal. The respondents appealed both findings to the UK Supreme Court.

In relation to the status of the drivers, the respondents maintained that the drivers were independent contractors. The respondents submitted that the claimants were performing the driving services under contracts with the passengers, and that the respondents were not party to these contracts. Furthermore, the respondents alleged that under a written agreement that existed between the claimants and the respondents, the respondents' role was limited to merely providing technological services to facilitate the delivery of the service, and to acting as a booking and payment collection agent.

The UK Supreme Court rejected these assertions. In determining whether there existed 'a contract whereby an individual undertakes to perform work or services for the other party' under s 230(b) of the Employments Rights Act 1996, the Court relied on *Autoclenz Ltd v Belcher*.[13] In *Autoclenz*, the UK Supreme Court held that when determining whether or not a contract is a 'worker's contract', the ordinary principles of contract interpretation do not apply, and that there may be circumstances where written agreements do not necessarily reflect the actual understanding between the parties.

The UK Supreme Court approached the question of the drivers' status as one of the statutory interpretation of s 230(3)(b), noting that the approach to statutory interpretation is 'to have regard to the purpose of a particular provision and to interpret its language, so far as possible, in the way which best gives effect to that purpose'. The UK Supreme Court found that the purpose of s 230(3)(b) is to provide employment law protection to vulnerable workers, who are 'substantively and economically' in the

---

[13] *Autoclenz Ltd v Belcher* [2011] UKSC 41.

same circumstances as employees. The UK Supreme Court, in following *Autoclenz*, looked beyond the written agreement that existed with the respondent to assess the true relationship that existed.

The UK Supreme Court upheld the finding of the employment tribunal in classifying the drivers as 'workers', noting that the following factors evidenced the considerable control the respondents exercised over the claimants:

— the respondents fixed the remuneration of the claimants;

— the respondents dictated the contractual terms under which the claimants provided the driving services;

— once logged into the app, the system was established in such a way that the drivers were restricted in accepting any requests;

— the respondents controlled the way in which the claimants delivered their driving services; and

— the respondents restricted the ability of the claimants to develop any relationship with the passengers, including the collection of the fares, the management of communication with the passengers and the processing of complaints, which was all done through the app.

In relation to the second question of when the claimants become 'workers', the respondents argued that, if the claimants were to be considered as 'workers', they could only be considered as such once they were actually driving the passengers.

The UK Supreme Court again rejected this submission. In analysing the facts of the case, the UK Supreme Court upheld the finding of the employment tribunal, that the drivers came within the definition of 'worker' as soon as they logged into the app.

The UK Supreme Court upheld the findings of the employment tribunal, and dismissed the appeal in its entirety.

[5.09] *Addison Lee v Lange*[14]*—Court of Appeal of England and Wales— Bean LJ—appeal from UK Employment Appeal Tribunal—Employment Rights Act 1996—employment status—definition of 'worker'*

A claim was taken by three drivers for the appellant, claiming that they were 'workers' under the Employment Rights Act 1996. The appellant claimed they were in fact, independent contractors as set out in their contracts. The respondent and his colleagues were allocated jobs by logging into the appellant's internal driver portal system. They were not promised a minimum number of hours of work but were told they could expect to work approximately 50 to 60 hours per week and they were subject to sanctions for refusing jobs.

The employment tribunal found that the respondent and his colleagues fell within the definition of 'worker' as set out in the Employment Rights Act 1996. The

---

[14] *Addison Lee v Lange* [2021] EWCA Civ 594. See *Arthur Cox Employment Law Yearbook 2018* at **[5.03]** for the EAT decision in *Addison Lee Ltd v Lange* UKEAT/0037/18/BA.

appellant appealed the tribunal's finding to the EAT where the appeal was dismissed on 14 November 2018. The appellant was subsequently granted permission to appeal to the Court of Appeal of England and Wales with the proviso that: 'This appeal should not be listed until after judgment is given in *Uber v Aslam* although it should then be expedited.'

Following the UK Supreme Court decision in *Uber v Aslam*,[15] the Court of Appeal set aside the appellant's original grant of permission to appeal on the basis that the subsequent decision of the UK Supreme Court meant that it had 'no reasonable prospect of success'. The UK Supreme Court found that Uber drivers were not self-employed but rather 'workers' within the meaning of the Employment Rights Act 1996. The Court also commented that it was appropriate for a court or tribunal to disregard any contractual provision that does not reflect the reality of the relationship between two parties.

[5.10]   *Commissioners for Her Majesty's Revenue and Customs v Professional Game Match Officials Ltd[16]—Court of Appeal of England and Wales—Henderson LJ, Laing LJ and Sir Patten—appeal from Upper Tribunal—mutuality of obligation— contract of employment*

The respondent's membership comprised of the English Football League, the Football Association and the Premier League (PGMOL), and its role centred around organising learning and development for top-tier football officials.

The case involved payments, derived from game fees and expenses, made by the respondent to match officials. The part-time referees, to which the appeal related, were paid match fees, travel expenses, and training attendance allowances. Match appointments were offered at the start of each week, which the referee could accept or reject, and which PGMOL could cancel. PGMOL employed a coach for each referee, provided health benefits and supplied a uniform. A Code of Practice stated that they were self-employed and that there was no guarantee that they would be offered matches. The appellant (HMRC) considered that PGMOL was liable to deduct income tax and national insurance from the payments it made to referees. HMRC asserted that the officials were incorrectly classified as independent contractors and, in light of the mutuality of obligation and control that existed between the respondent and the individual officials, the arrangements should be considered to be employment agreements.

PGMOL's argument centred on the absence of any contractual relationship between it and the 'National Group' of officials. While it accepted that certain documentation was circulated to officials before the commencement of each season, none of that documentation, whether considered as a whole or separately, amounted to an employment agreement. PGMOL submitted that the officials viewed their officiating duties as a hobby, which was managed around other, paid, employment.

HMRC argued that the documentation circulated by the respondent to the individuals, when considered in the round, constituted terms of employment and a wider employment agreement.

---

[15]   *Uber v Aslam* [2021] UKSC 5.
[16]   *Commissioners for Her Majesty's Revenue and Customs v Professional Game Match Officials Ltd* [2021] EWCA Civ 1370; see *Arthur Cox Employment Law Yearbook 2020* at **[5.10]** for decision of Upper Tribunal.

PGMOL appealed HMRC's determination that employment relationships existed between the respondent and the individuals to the First Tier Tribunal. The First Tier Tribunal allowed the appeal, on the basis that the documentation issued by PGMOL to the individuals did not give rise to employment agreements.

The First Tier Tribunal applied the test for determining employment status and concluded that: (i) the documentation contained no mutuality of obligation in terms of one party's obligation to provide work, and another party's obligation to accept it; (ii) there was no penalty for an official not officiating at a game; and (iii) the officials were so independent of the respondent (in terms of their decisions in the games that they officiated at) that they did not satisfy the employment status test.

HMRC appealed the First Tier Tribunal's conclusion to the Upper Tribunal. The Upper Tribunal established as a matter of fact that there was an overarching contract between PGMOL and the referees, and that there were match-specific, or 'individual' contracts. The question was whether these contracts amounted to contracts of employment. The Upper Tribunal upheld the finding of the First Tier Tribunal that there was insufficient mutuality of obligation in both the individual contracts and the overarching contract and therefore there were not contracts of employment between the parties

HMRC appealed the Upper Tribunal's conclusion to the Court of Appeal of England and Wales, which allowed the appeal.

The Court of Appeal considered the authorities in terms of the approach to finding a contract of employment in circumstances where there is both an overarching contract and a single engagement, ie: (i) whether the individual contracts are contracts of employment is a distinct question not resolved by the decision on the overarching contract; (ii) the fact that there is no obligation under the overarching contract to offer, or to do, work (if offered) does not decide that the single engagement cannot be a contract of employment—the nature of each contract is a distinct question; and (iii) an individual engagement can give rise to a contract of employment 'if work which has in fact been offered is in fact done for payment'.

The Court of Appeal held in relation to the documentation issued to the officials that the First Tier Tribunal had placed too much emphasis on the fact that the officials were so independent of the respondent when officiating as to fail to satisfy the employment status test. The Court of Appeal found that the First Tier Tribunal had erred as a matter of law in failing to consider the learning and development that the respondent facilitated and organised for the officials outside of the games that they officiated at, and the element of control that they placed on the officials as a result.

In addition, the Court of Appeal found that the First Tier Tribunal and the Upper Tribunal had erred in their application of the law in relation to mutuality of obligation. On the specific facts, the Court of Appeal found that there was no mutuality of obligation in the overarching contract because PGMOL was not obliged to offer, and, if offered, the referee was not obliged to accept work. However, it found that there was sufficient mutuality in the individual (match-day) contracts. It was irrelevant to the determination on mutuality of obligations that either party could terminate the contract before it was performed because, until terminated, the contract subsisted.

The Court of Appeal remitted the case to the First Tier Tribunal for consideration of whether the nature of the documentation issued by the respondent to the officials was such that it could be said that sufficient degrees of mutuality of obligation and control existed and that the documentation could on that basis be considered contracts of service, which would in turn mean that payments from the respondent to the officials would be liable for employer tax and social insurance payments.

[5.11]   *Stuart Delivery Ltd v Augustine[17]—Court of Appeal of England and Wales—Moylan, Lewis and Snowden LJJ—Employment Rights Act 1996, s 230(3)(b)— worker—obligation to personally perform services—right of substitution*

The claimant was a moped courier, who was permitted under his contractual arrangements with the respondent to accept or decline courier deliveries on an *ad hoc* basis, and/or to volunteer to work during particular slots. It being more financially rewarding to work during allocated slots, the claimant often did so on the basis that if he could not work during a slot he had previously volunteered for, he could offer the slot to other couriers on the respondent's app (although penalties were applied if a courier did not work a slot for which he/she had volunteered, and could not find a substitute cover).

When the contractual relationship between the claimant and the respondent terminated, the claimant submitted a complaint against the respondent to the employment tribunal, claiming unfair dismissal, non-payment of monies owed, as well as breaches by the respondent of its duty to pay him in lieu of his notice period and his accrued but untaken annual leave. The claimant claimed to be either an employee under an employment agreement, or a worker as defined in s 230(3)(b) of Employment Rights Act 1996 (the 1996 Act). The respondent contended that the claimant was not a worker, on the basis that he was under no obligation to perform services personally, and had a right of substitution if he could not, or did not want to, perform services during a particular slot. The respondent contended that an obligation on the claimant to personally provide services to the respondent (as opposed to being able to find substitute couriers) was a requirement in order for the claimant to be considered a worker.

The employment tribunal held that the claimant's right of substitution did not obviate the fact that he had an obligation to the respondent to personally provide services and therefore he was a 'worker' under the 1996 Act. The fact that the claimant could only appoint a substitute from the respondent's app meant that the respondent itself had control over whom he could appoint, since the respondent controlled the pool of couriers who could sign up to the app. The EAT upheld this finding.

The respondent appealed the EAT's decision to the Court of Appeal of England and Wales, arguing that the claimant's right of substitution meant that he did not have an obligation to personally provide services to the respondent.

---

[17]   *Stuart Delivery Ltd v Augustine* [2021] EWCA Civ 1514.

The Court of Appeal dismissed the respondent's appeal. The Court considered *Pimlico Plumbers Ltd v Smith*,[18] where the UK Supreme Court considered the question of when a right of substitution obviated the obligation to personally provide services. The Court of Appeal emphasised that there is no absolute rule as to when a right of substitution will obviate an obligation to personally provide services.

The Court held in this case that a right of substitution was not necessarily inconsistent with the existence of an obligation to personally provide services. The Court noted that the respondent's platform was designed so that couriers would work the slots that they had volunteered for. The Court was satisfied that a right to offer slots to other couriers, who were already engaged by the respondent, was a limited right of substitution, which was not sufficient to remove the obligation to personally perform services.

The appeal was dismissed.

[5.12] *Northern Light Solutions Ltd v Revenue and Customs[19]—Upper Tribunal Tax and Chancery—appeal from First-tier Tribunal—Income Tax (Earnings and Pensions) Act 2003—income tax—employee status*

The appellant was the service company of an individual (RL). Since 2007, RL worked for periods as a project manager for Nationwide Building Society (NBS) through the appellant intermediary service company. The appellant was incorporated in 2008 and with the exception of one period between 2012/2013, RL worked continuously for NBS. The appeal asked whether the UK 'intermediaries legislation' or 'IR 35', applied to the arrangements under which the appellant supplied the services of RL to NBS.

RL was contracted for the periods 1 February 2012 to 31 October 2012, and 22 April 2013 to 19 December 2014.

In respect of the period from 6 April 2012 to 5 April 2013, the HMRC issued a determination in the amount of £6,078 of income tax and a notice for £8,803 in respect of National Insurance Contribution (NICs). On 18 October 2017, HMRC issued further determinations and notices in respect of the periods from 6 April 2013 to 5 April 2015 in the amount of £19,613 in respect of income tax and £13,664 of NICs for the tax year 2013–14 and £14,637 of income tax and £11,728 of NICs for the tax year 2014–15.

The First-tier Tribunal held that during these periods and in accordance with the Income Tax (Earnings and Pensions) Act 2003 and its equivalent for NICs, RL would have been an employee of NBS. Section 49 of the 2003 Act sets out the conditions for income tax legislation to apply:

(a) an individual ("the worker") personally performs, or is under an obligation personally to perform, services for another person ("the client"),

(b) the services are provided not under a contract directly between the client and the worker but under arrangements involving a third party ("the intermediary"), and

---

[18] *Pimlico Plumbers Ltd v Smith* [2018] UKSC 29, [2018] ICR 1511. See *Arthur Cox Employment Law Yearbook 2018* at [5.04].

[19] *Northern Light Solutions Ltd v Revenue and Customs* [2021] UKUT 134 (TCC).

(c)   the circumstances are such that—

>   (i)   if the services were provided under a contract directly between the client and the worker, the worker would be regarded for income tax purposes as an employee of the client or the holder of an office under the client.

The appellant's grounds for appeal were, *inter alia*, that the First-tier Tribunal erred in certain respects in finding that there were elements of control exercised over RL's working day; that were was a mutuality of obligation between the parties; and that RL's right to provide a substitute was qualified.

The Upper Tribunal did not support the argument that 'there would be insufficient mutuality of obligation present in the hypothetical contracts simply because there would have been no obligation on NBS to offer work if a particular project ended before the term of the contract had expired'. The Upper Tribunal found that failure of the employer to supply any further work does not confirm that the contract is a contract for services rather than a contract of employment. It could not find any error in law on the part of the First-tier Tribunal.

In relation to RL's ability to provide a substitute, the appellant relied on *Edwards v Bairstow*,[20] submitting that there was no sufficient evidence before the First-tier Tribunal to support a finding of fact that it was impossible for RL provide a suitable substitute. The Upper Tribunal's view was that meeting notes presented to the First-tier Tribunal were sufficient evidence on which the First-tier Tribunal could base its conclusions. The notes confirmed that there were strict checks in place, that a substitute would have to be agreed between the parties and that no substitute had ever been provided.

The Upper Tribunal's view also found that NBS had a sufficient 'framework of control' in place and the First-tier Tribunal was correct to conclude that the 'intermediaries legislation' did apply. The appeal was dismissed.

[5.13]   *Smith v Pimlico Plumbers Ltd*[21]—*UK Employment Appeal Tribunal— appeal from employment tribunal—worker status—deemed employment—paid annual leave—holiday pay—unpaid leave*

The claimant worked for the respondent as a plumbing and heating engineer, ostensibly as a self-employed independent contractor from August 2005 to May 2011. Following the termination of his engagement, the claimant brought a number of employment-related complaints,[22] including a complaint seeking paid annual leave.

The initial issue was in relation to the claimant's status, and whether he had an entitlement to assert employment rights. The UK Supreme Court ultimately confirmed that the claimant was engaged as a worker, and therefore was entitled to the rights that flowed from this status, one of which was an entitlement to paid annual leave.

---

[20]   *Edwards v Bairstow* [1956] AC 14.
[21]   *Smith v Pimlico Plumbers Ltd* UKEAT/0211/19/DA, UKEAT/0003/20/DA & UKEAT/0040/20/DA.
[22]   See *Arthur Cox Employment Law Yearbook 2018* at [5.05] for the UK Supreme Court decision that Mr Smith was a 'limb (b) worker' and not a self-employed contractor in *Pimlico Plumbers Ltd & Anor v Smith* [2018] UKSC 29.

The complaint in respect of paid annual leave was remitted to the employment tribunal.

The employment tribunal dismissed the claimant's complaint in relation to paid annual leave on the preliminary basis that it was brought outside of the statutory three-month time limit.

The tribunal found that the time limit ran from the date on which the claimant took the last period of unpaid annual leave. The claimant contended that the time limit should run from the date of termination, on the basis that he was entitled to carry over unpaid leave up to that date in accordance with the European Court of Justice (ECJ) decision in *King v Sash Windows Workshop*.[23]

In *King*, the ECJ found that the employee carried over the right to be paid in lieu of annual leave up to the point of the termination of employment.

The tribunal, in applying *King*, found that the carrying over of an entitlement to a period of annual leave would only apply where the claimant had not taken annual leave at all because of the respondent's refusal to pay for it. However, the tribunal found that the claimant's own evidence in this case was that he took annual leave, but was not paid for it. It was not the claimant's case that he was deterred from taking leave because he knew that he was not going to be paid, and this was a significant distinction.

The tribunal confirmed that *King* was not concerned with leave that was taken but unpaid. Instead, that case related to accrued leave that was untaken because of the lack of payment.

The claimant appealed to the EAT, on the basis that the employment tribunal had erred in its application of *King* and consequently used the incorrect date for the purposes of determining when the statutory time limit should begin to run.

The EAT upheld the finding of the employment tribunal that *King* did not relate to those who had taken periods of annual leave that were taken but unpaid, but in fact related to leave that was not taken as a result of the failure by an employer to pay for such leave. It found that the question in *King* related to those 'who had not taken the leave at all'.

The EAT found that in identifying the right that annual leave may be carried over, the ECJ referred to 'paid annual leave rights not exercised in respect of several consecutive reference periods because his employer refused to remunerate that leave'. On that basis, the EAT found that where a worker takes unpaid leave, he cannot be said to be in a position where he has not exercised the right to paid annual leave. The right will have been at least partially exercised.

The EAT considered the statement from *King*, which was cited by the claimant and noted 'the right to annual leave and to payment on that account [are] two aspects of a single right'. On the basis of this statement, the EAT considered whether the taking of unpaid leave could amount to the taking of leave, or whether unpaid leave could never be deemed to constitute annual leave because of the lack of payment. The EAT found

---

23   *King v The Sash Window Workshop Ltd* [2017] EUECJ C-214/16.

that the ECJ statement did not find that unpaid leave cannot constitute leave, and should the ECJ have intended to create a right to carry over leave that was taken but unpaid, it would have expressed it as such.

The EAT upheld the employment tribunal's findings and its interpretation of *King* and the relevant point from which the statutory limitation period should run.

[5.14] *Alemi v Mitchell*[24]*—UK Employment Appeal Tribunal—appeal from employment tribunal—Equality Act 2010, s 83(2)—Employment Rights Act 1996, s 230—limb (b) worker—locum doctor—employee status*

The claimant's appeal to the EAT related to a decision made by the employment tribunal that, for the purposes of s 83(2) of the Equality Act 2010 (the 2010 Act), the claimant was an employee of the medical practice where he worked as a locum doctor. The respondent brought a claim against the claimant and the practice where she worked as a practice nurse. She alleged that when they worked together at the practice, the claimant had sexually harassed her and discriminated against her on grounds of sex. She argued that both her employer and the claimant were liable on the basis that the claimant was an employee or agent of her employer.

The statutory protections an individual is entitled to receive in cases where discrimination is alleged will vary based on the individual's status. In this context, the definition of employment under the 2010 Act falls to be considered. Employment is defined under s 83(2)(a) of the 2010 Act as 'employment under a contract of employment, a contract of apprenticeship or a contract personally to do work'. Under the Employment Rights Act 1996, s 230, a worker is defined as:

> an individual who has entered into, or works under
>
> (a) a contract of employment, or
> (b) any other contract, whether express or implied and (if it is express) whether oral or in writing, whereby the individual undertakes to do or perform personally any work or services for another party to the contract whose status is not by virtue of the contract that of a client or customer of any profession or business undertaking carried on by the individual [otherwise known as a 'limb (b) worker'].

The employment tribunal found that the claimant was an employee of the practice. The claimant appealed that decision to the EAT stating that the incorrect test had been applied by the tribunal leading it to disregard relevant facts and authorities. The claimant argued that a contract existed between the medical practice and his service company, and, as a result of this, he could not be considered to be an employee.

The EAT found that the tribunal had erred in law in distinguishing between an employee (under the 2010 Act) and a 'limb (b) worker'. It held that the definition under the 2010 Act was not any broader than that under the Employment Rights Act 1996 and as such, individuals in business on their own account and working personally for their clients or customers could not be considered to be employees. The appeal succeeded and the case was remitted to a fresh employment tribunal.

---

[24] *Alemi v Mitchell* [2021] IRLR 262.

[5.15] *Nursing and Midwifery Council v Somerville[25]—UK Employment Appeal Tribunal—appeal from employment tribunal—Employment Rights Act 1996, s 230—Working Time Regulations 1998, reg 2(1)[26]—employment status—mutuality of obligation—definition of a 'worker'*

The Nursing and Midwifery Council (the Council) regulates nurses and midwives in the UK. Under the Nursing and Midwifery Order 2001, its Fitness to Practise Committee (the Committee) determines allegations of impairment of fitness to practise. The claimant in this case, a barrister, acted as a panel member and chair of the Committee for two, four-year terms between 2012 and 2020.

His appointment letter stated he was not an employee of the Council but rather an independent contractor. During his tenure on the Committee, the Council was not obliged to provide him with a specified number of sitting dates, the claimant was not obliged to attend and could withdraw from dates he had accepted; however, he was obliged to provide the services personally to the Council. He also undertook a variety of other work.

The claimant brought a claim against the Council for holiday pay, on the basis that he was either an employee or a worker under the Employment Rights Act 1996 and the Working Time Regulations 1998.

The employment tribunal concluded, *inter alia*, that the respondent was not a client or customer of a profession or business carried on by the claimant and that as such, the claimant was a worker within the meaning of the Employment Rights Act 1996 and the Working Time Regulations 1998. The tribunal also found that he was not an employee.

The primary ground of appeal to the EAT was that the claimant could not be a worker within the meaning of the Employment Rights Act 1996 because mutuality in the sense of the existence of an irreducible minimum of obligation is a prerequisite to satisfying the statutory definition.

The EAT reviewed the relevant case law, including *Uber BV v Aslam*,[27] where the statutory definition of worker was described as having three elements: (1) a contract for the provision of work or services; (2) an undertaking to do the work or perform the services personally; and (3) a requirement that the person for whom the work is carried out is not a client or customer of any profession or business undertaking carried on by the individual. Legatt LJ in *Uber* stated that 'the existence and exercise of a right to refuse work is not critical, provided there is at least an obligation to do some amount of work'.

The EAT examined the test that for an individual to be considered a 'worker' he or she must have an 'irreducible minimum of obligation'. The respondent argued that as the claimant was not required to undertake any days of work on the Committee, he could not be considered a worker—he was not obliged to carry out at least the irreducible minimum amount of work. This argument was rejected by the EAT, which stated that the 'irreducible minimum' is not a prerequisite of worker status. The appeal was dismissed.

---

[25] *Nursing and Midwifery Council v Somerville* UKEAT/0258/20/RN(V).
[26] Working Time Regulations 1998 (SI 1998/1833).
[27] *Uber BV v Aslam* [2021] UKSC 5.

ILLEGAL CONTRACT

[5.16]   *Sobhy v Chief Appeals Officer*[28]*—High Court—Heslin J—judicial review— Immigration Act 2004—Employment Permits Act 2003—contract for services—lack of employment permit—maternity benefits—illegality*

The applicant, a citizen of Mauritius, was a lawful resident in the State until June 2012, when her application for a change of immigration status was refused. However, she continued to work in the State and paid PRSI contributions. In 2019, she applied for maternity benefit on the basis that she met the relevant criteria under the Social Welfare Consolidation Act 2005. The applicant was denied maternity benefit as the respondent concluded that her contract for services was illegal as she did not have a valid Garda National Immigration Bureau Card (GNIB Card) or work permit while she was working in Ireland, after her change of immigration status had been refused.

The applicant sought a number of reliefs from the High Court including an order quashing the decision of the respondent disallowing the applicant's maternity benefit and a declaration that the respondent erred in law in determining that the applicant's employment was not an insurable employment and that her contract of employment was not legal.

The primary argument advanced by the applicant was that the respondent's decision erred in law. It was submitted that an illegal contract is not void as a matter of Irish law and that the respondent should have applied the decision in *Quinn v IBRC*[29] rather than that in *FÁS v Abbot*.[30]

The respondent denied the applicant's claims. It submitted that, as the applicant did not have a valid GNIB Card or work permit, her employment and, as a result, her PRSI contributions, were not legally valid. The respondent relied on s 4 of the Immigration Act 2004 relating to the authorisation of non-nationals to be in the State and the duty of such non-nationals to apply for permissions. The respondent also relied on s 2 of the Employment Permits Act 2003, which requires a foreign national to have an employment permit in order to enter into employment in the State. The respondent further submitted that the decision in *FÁS v Abbot*, which held that a court will not enforce a contract for services if it is expressly or impliedly prohibited by statute, was the correct basis for the respondent's decision and applied to the case at hand.

The High Court held that it is not self-evident that a contract entered into in breach of the Employment Permits Act 2003 is unenforceable and invalid for the purposes of the Social Welfare Consolidation Act 2005. The Court did not accept that *FÁS* was the correct basis for the respondent's decision, noting that *FÁS* is an important decision that continues to be valid in Irish law but is no longer a comprehensive summary of the law on this point. Rather, the correct legal position is set out in *Quinn v IBRC*, as relied on

---

[28]   *Sobhy v Chief Appeals Officer* [2021] IEHC 93.
[29]   *Quinn v IBRC* [2016] 1 IR 1.
[30]   *FÁS v Abbot and Ryan* (unreported, 23 May 1995) Supreme Court, Egan J.

by the applicant, which provides a clear statement of the factors to be taken into account in determining whether a contract should be deemed unenforceable or void.

Furthermore, the High Court noted that:

> the ultimate finding in *Quinn* was a conclusion by the Supreme Court that the underlying lending contracts were enforceable, notwithstanding their illegality, starkly illustrating that it is not the position in Irish law that illegality necessarily renders a contract unenforceable or void.

The High Court held that the respondent should have balanced the competing factors as established in *Quinn* in making any determination as to the enforceability of the applicant's contract of employment and concluded that the respondent had erred in relying exclusively on *FÁS v Abbot* in coming to their decision that the applicant was not entitled to maternity benefits. The decision of the respondent was quashed.

[5.17]   *Robinson v His Highness Sheikh Khalid Bin Saqr Al-Qasimi[31]—Holroyde, Singh & Baker LJJ—Court of Appeal of England and Wales—contract of employment—defence of illegality—unfair and wrongful dismissal*

The respondent began working for the appellant in March 2007. The letter of appointment stated that she would be paid £34,000 per annum and that she would be responsible for her own tax and national insurance. In June 2009, the remuneration payable was increased to £37,000 per annum. Between 2007 and 2014 the respondent did not declare or pay any tax to Revenue on the payments made to her and the appellant only became aware of this in 2014. In 2014, the respondent asserted that the terms of the contract were that she would be paid net of tax. If this were the case, the appellant would be responsible for the unpaid tax from the years 2007 to 2014. There was also correspondence between the parties in relation to whether the respondent was an employee or was self-employed. If she was an employee, the appellant would be responsible for deducting PAYE. Some of this correspondence was relied on by the respondent as being protected disclosures. From July 2014 the appellant deducted tax equivalent amounts from the respondent's monthly salary. These were not paid to Revenue but held by the appellant in a separate account so they would be available for payment to Revenue if necessary. The dispute between the parties as to liability for the tax remained unresolved from 2014 to 2017. In March 2017, the appellant's solicitors wrote to the respondent's solicitors making it clear that if she failed to account for the tax due on the payments made to her in the past, the appellant would have to terminate her contract. Thereafter the appellant wrote to the respondent summarily dismissing her and the letter of dismissal stated that the reason for the dismissal was, among other things, the failure of the respondent to take responsibility for the tax that had been unpaid since 2007.

The respondent issued proceedings before an employment tribunal alleging, among other things, 'automatic' unfair dismissal on the ground that she had been dismissed

---

31   *Robinson v His Highness Sheikh Khalid Bin Saqr Al-Qasimi* [2021] EWCA Civ 862. See *Arthur Cox Employment Law Yearbook 2020* at **[21.07]** for decision of EAT in *Robinson v His Highness Al Qasimi* UKEAT/0106/19/RN; UKEAT/0107/19/RN; UKEAT/0136/19/RN.

for making protected disclosures, 'ordinary' unfair dismissal, wrongful dismissal and unlawful deduction of wages. She was granted interim relief in respect of the automatic unfair dismissal claim. The appellant was successful on an appeal against that interim relief and the matter was remitted to the employment tribunal for reconsideration. Ultimately the employment tribunal held that the claims of unfair dismissal, statutory particulars of employment and wrongful dismissal failed for illegality; that the respondent had not been subjected to detriment for making protected disclosures; and, on an undertaking that the amount deducted from earnings would be paid to Revenue, no order was made on the claim for unlawful deduction from wages.

The employment tribunal concluded that the respondent was not dismissed because of any protected disclosure; she was dismissed because the appellant did not want to agree that she was an employee and that PAYE applied. The employment tribunal, in respect of the 'ordinary' unfair dismissal claim concluded that two potentially fair reasons for dismissal arose. Firstly, the employee could not continue to work in the position that she held without contravention of a duty or restriction imposed by or under an enactment, namely the failure to pay tax and the appellant was at risk of participating in a fraud on Revenue if he did not deduct tax when she said that she was an employee. Secondly, the employment tribunal concluded that it was not unfair to dismiss because there was a deadlock over whether the term relating to remuneration was gross or net of tax. The tribunal, however, went on to find that there was a procedural unfairness because no meeting was held with the respondent and she was not offered an appeal. The claim for ordinary unfair dismissal would therefore have succeeded but for the defence of illegality.

On appeal to the EAT the respondent's appeal against the employment tribunal's conclusion on illegality was allowed and the claims for ordinary unfair dismissal and wrongful dismissal were remitted to the employment tribunal for consideration of the question of remedies and the interim relief granted was set aside.

The EAT held that the employment tribunal was entitled to find that when the respondent was performing the contract illegally, from 2007 to 2014, she would not have been entitled to enforce the contract. However, at the time of her dismissal, three years later, when she was not performing the contract illegally, she should not be prevented from enforcing her contractual and statutory rights.

In considering the appellant's appeal, the Court of Appeal summarised the relevant legal principles on illegality in employment law set out in *Patel v Mirza*,[32] where the UK Supreme Court stated that there are two policy reasons for the common law doctrine of illegality as a defence to a civil claim, namely that one 'should not be allowed to profit from one's own wrongdoing', and that the 'law should be coherent and not self-defeating, condoning illegality by giving with the left hand what it takes with the right hand'.

The UK Supreme Court in *Patel* stated that in considering the defence of illegality in an employment claim one has to consider: '(a) the 'underlying purpose of the prohibition which has been transgressed, (b) consider conversely any other relevant public

---

[32]   *Patel v Mirza* [2016] UKSC 42, [2017] AC 467.

policies which may be rendered ineffective or less effective by denial of the claim and (c) keeping in mind the possibility of overkill unless the law is applied with a due sense of proportionality'. This 'trio of considerations' has been referred to extensively in subsequent case law.

The Court of Appeal stated that the 'knowledge plus participation' test established in *Hall v Woolston Hall Leisure Ltd*[33] represents a necessary but not a sufficient criterion for the defence of illegality to succeed. In considering other cases on illegality, the Court of Appeal also noted that a temporal link between the illegality and the act complained of might be relevant. The Court concluded that the mere fact that one of the parties to a contract to employment has performed it illegally must be a necessary, but is not a sufficient, test for doctrine of illegality to apply. Account must be taken of matters of degree, such as the seriousness of the illegality and the proximity of the illegality to the claim; the overall assessment of proportionality should be conducted in light of the 'trio of considerations' set out in *Patel*.

Applying the foregoing, the Court dismissed the appeal. The Court held that the EAT applied the law correctly in overturning the decision of the employment tribunal. The employment tribunal could not reasonably regard the respondent's illegal performance of the contract between 2007 and 2014 as being sufficient justification for not permitting her to rely on her rights in 2017. The EAT duly conducted the proportionality exercise required by *Patel* and had regard to all of the circumstances of the case. The fact that there had been some illegal act by an employee at some point in the past may be relevant to the question of proportionality required by *Patel*, but it depends on all the circumstances, for example, the seriousness of the illegality, how far back in time it occurred, how closely it is connected with the nature of the claim being made, etc. The EAT correctly concluded that the employment tribunal could not reasonably have found, in all of the circumstances, including the respondent's illegal performance from 2007 to 2014 and what had happened between 2014 and 2017 that same was sufficient justification for not permitting her to enforce the contract in 2017.

The respondent's cross-appeal in respect of the refusal of an interim order was also dismissed.

JURISDICTION—COURT OF APPEAL

[5.18]   ***Irish Prison Service v Cunningham***[34]***—Court of Appeal—Faherty, Collins, Pilkington JJ—appeal from High Court—Employment Equality Acts 1998 to 2015—Workplace Relations Act 2015—preliminary issue—jurisdiction—right of appeal***

The claimant was employed by the respondent as a prison officer. During the course of his employment he injured his back and was unable to return to his full duties.

---

[33]   *Hall v Woolston Hall Leisure Ltd* [2001] 1 WLR 225.
[34]   *Irish Prison Service v Cunningham* [2021] IECA 19.

The respondent gave the claimant the option to take up the position of prison administrative and support officer or retire on the grounds of ill-health.

The claimant brought a claim to the WRC alleging disability discrimination under the Employment Equality Acts 1998 to 2015, arguing that the respondent failed to afford him reasonable accommodation. The WRC found in his favour, but this decision was appealed and overturned in the Labour Court. The claimant thereafter appealed the decision of the Labour Court to the High Court under s 90(1) of the Employment Equality Acts. His appeal was successful, and the High Court ordered the Labour Court to re-hear the matter.[35]

The respondent appealed the decision to the Court of Appeal. The claimant contested the appeal on a number of grounds, one ground being the lack of jurisdiction of the Court of Appeal to hear the appeal. This jurisdictional point was heard by the Court of Appeal as a preliminary issue.

The claimant argued that the Court of Appeal had no jurisdiction to hear an appeal from the High Court under the Employment Equality Acts. He submitted that s 46 of the Workplace Relations Act 2015 (the 2015 Act) governs the question of whether an appeal under the Employment Equality Acts can be heard in the Court of Appeal and the 2015 Act excludes any such appeal. He further argued that to allow such an appeal would defeat the intention of the 2015 Act to 'streamline' the process.

The respondent submitted that any exception to the right of appeal under Art 34.4.1 of the Constitution must be in 'clear and unambiguous terms' and that there was no such clear and unambiguous exception in s 90(1) of the Employment Equality Acts. The respondent further submitted that any arguments regarding the 'streamlining' of a process could not restrict the constitutional right of appeal.

The Court of Appeal held that the right to appeal a decision of the High Court to the Court of Appeal 'is available to litigants as of right', flowing from the Constitution. If the appellate jurisdiction of the Court of Appeal was to be restricted in any way, there must be a 'clear and unambiguous ouster' of the right.

The Court of Appeal held that no such ouster existed within the statutory regime applicable. The Court rejected the claimant's submission that appeal of decisions from the Labour Court to the High Court under the Employment Equality Acts were governed by s 46 of the 2015 Act.

Instead, the Court held that it was clear that any such appeal was governed by s 90(1) of the Employment Equality Acts. Section 90(1) provides: 'Where a determination is made by the Labour Court on an appeal under this Part, either of the parties may appeal to the High Court on a point of law.' There is no limitation in s 90(1) on any further appeal, the Court also noted that 'there is no plausible interpretation of that provision that would exclude an appeal' to the Court of Appeal.

---

[35]   See *Cunningham v Irish Prison Service* [2020] IEHC 282 at *Arthur Cox Employment Law Yearbook 2020* **[4.10]**.

The Court of Appeal dismissed the preliminary issue and held that the respondent was entitled to appeal the decision of the High Court. It further ordered that the appeal be heard 'without any undue delay, having regard to the novelty, complexity and importance (both to the parties and generally) of the legal issues raised by the appeal'.

TERRITORIAL JURISDICTION

[5.19] *DG and EH v SC Gruber Logistics SRL and Sindicatul Lucratorilor dim Transporturi v SC Samidani Trans SRL[36]—European Court of Justice—request for preliminary ruling from Romania—Regulation (EC) No. 593/2008,[37] arts 3 and 8—law applicable to contractual obligations—choice of law—individual employment contracts—employees who perform work in more than one Member State—'provisions that cannot be derogated from by agreement'—minimum wage*

The preliminary rulings in these joined cases related in the first case to Romanian lorry drivers employed by a Romanian-established company driving lorries regis-tered in Romania on the basis of transport licences issued in Romania but where they habitually performed their duties in Italy. Italy was where they carried out their assignments and from which they received their instructions and the place to which they returned at the end of their assignments and where most of their transport tasks were carried out. The second case related to a Romanian lorry driver employed by a Romanian company in similar circumstances but carrying out his activities exclusively in Germany, with Germany being the place from which the lorry driver carried out his tasks and from which he received his instructions and where the lorries were based. In each case, the lorry drivers issued proceedings in Romania claiming the difference between the Italian and German minimum wages respectively and the wages paid to them. In each case they were employed under a standard form contract of employment which referred to Romanian statutory provisions. The employer in each case contended that a Romanian law applied and accordingly it had no obligation to pay the Italian and German minimum wage.

In each case the Romanian Court referred questions to the European Court of Justice (ECJ) with reference to arts 3 and 8 of Regulation (EC) No. 593/2008 on the law applicable to contractual obligations (Rome 1).

Article 3 of Rome 1 sets out the general rule that the contract shall be governed by the law chosen by the parties but provides that the existence or validity of the consent of the parties as to the choice of the applicable law must be determined in accordance with arts 10, 11 and 13.

Article 8.1 of Rome 1 contains a specific rule governing employment contracts and provides that an individual employment contract should be governed by the law chosen

---

[36] *DG and EH v SC Gruber Logistics SRL and Sindicatul Lucratorilor dim Transporturi v SC Samidani Trans SRL* (Case C-152/20 and Case C-218/20).
[37] Regulation (EC) No. 593/2008 on the law applicable to contractual obligations (Rome I).

179

by the parties in accordance with art 3 but provides that such a choice of law 'may not, however, have the result of depriving the employee of the protection afforded to him by provisions that cannot be derogated from by agreement under the law that, in the absence of choice would have been applicable pursuant to paragraphs 2, 3 and 4 of this article'.

Article 8.2 provides that to the extent that the law applicable to the individual employment contract has not been chosen by the parties, the contract should be governed by the law of the country in which or, failing that, from which the employee habitually carries out his work under the contract. The country where the work is habitually carried out shall not be deemed to have changed if he is temporarily employed in another country.

Article 8.3 provides that where the law applicable cannot be determined under para 2, the contract should be governed by the law of the country where the place of business through which the employee was engaged is situated.

Article 8.4 provides that where it appears from the circumstances as a whole, that the contract is more closely connected with a country other than that indicated in paras 2 or 3, the law of that other country shall apply.

The ECJ reformulated the first and second questions asked in each of the cases such that the combined questions asked in essence:

> whether Article 8 of the Rome 1 Regulation must be interpreted as meaning that, where the law governing the individual employment contract has been chosen by the parties to that contract, and that law differs from the law applicable under to paragraphs 2, 3 or 4 of that article, whether the application of the latter law must be excluded and, if so, to what extent.

The ECJ noted that art 8.1 provides that individual employment contracts are to be governed by the law chosen by the parties in accordance with art 3 and that this choice may not deprive the employee of the protection afforded to him or her by provisions that cannot be derogated from by agreement and that would be applicable to the contract in the absence of such a choice under paras 2, 3 and 4 of art 3. If those provisions offer the employee concerned greater protection than those of the law chosen, they will override the contract while the law chosen will continue to apply to the rest of the contractual relationship.

The ECJ noted that art 8 is intended to ensure, as far as possible, compliance with the provisions protecting the employee that are laid down by the law of the State in which the employee carries out his or her professional activities. The correct application of art 8 therefore requires firstly, that the national court should identify the law that would have applied in the absence of choice and should determine, in accordance with that law, the rules that cannot be derogated from by agreement; and, secondly, that court should compare the level of protection afforded to the employee under those rules with that provided for by the law chosen by the parties. If the level of protection provided for by those rules is greater, those same rules must be applied.

The ECJ concluded that minimum wage rules of the country where the employee has habitually carried out his or her activities can in principle be classified as 'provisions that cannot be derogated from by agreement under the law that in the absence of choice, would have been applicable' within the meaning of art 8.1. Accordingly, the ECJ concluded that the answer to the first and second questions in each of the cases is that where the law governing the individual employment contract has been chosen by the parties to that contract, and that law differs from the law applicable under paras 2, 3 or 4 of art 3, the 'application of the latter law must be excluded with the exception of "provisions that cannot be derogated from by agreement" under that law' within the meaning of art 8.1 of Rome I, such provisions can, in principle, include rules on the minimum wage.

The ECJ then turned to the third question raised in each of the cases, asking in essence whether art 8 of Rome 1 must be interpreted as meaning that:

— first, the parties to an individual employment contract are to be regarded as being free to choose the law applicable to that contract even if a national provision requires the inclusion in that contract of a clause under which the contractual provisions are supplemented by national labour law and

— second, the parties to an individual employment contract are to be regarded as being free to choose the law applicable to that contract even if the contractual clause concerning that choice is drafted by the employer, with the employee merely accepting it.

On the first point, the Romanian Government submitted that in fact Romanian law does not provide for an obligation to choose Romanian law as the law applicable to the contract. On that basis the ECJ concluded that it was for the referring Court alone to assess whether that interpretation is correct. On the second limb of question, the ECJ concluded that the Rome 1 Regulation does not prohibit the use of standard clauses pre-formulated by the employer. Freedom of choice, within the meaning of art 3, can be exercised and consent is not called into question solely because that choice is made on the basis of a clause drafted and included by the employer.

Accordingly, the ECJ concluded that the answer to the third question must be interpreted as meaning that the parties to an individual employment contract are free to choose the law applicable to that contract even if the contractual provisions are supplemented by national labour law under a national provision, provided that the national provision in question does not require the parties to choose national law as the law applicable to the contract and secondly, the parties to an individual employment contract are to be regarded as being in principle, free to choose the law applicable to that contract even if the contractual clause concerning that choice is drafted by the employer, with the employee merely accepting it.

[5.20] *BU v Markt24 Gmbh*[38]*—European Court of Justice—preliminary ruling from Austria—jurisdiction—Regulation (EU) 1215/2012,*[39] *art 21—contract of employment—where can an employer be sued*

This was a request for a preliminary ruling from the Austrian courts to the ECJ regarding the interpretation of arts 7(1) and 21 of Regulation 1215/2012 (the Regulation).

---

[38]   *BU v Markt24 Gmbh* (Case C-804/19).
[39]   Regulation (EU) No. 1215/2012 on jurisdiction and the recognition and enforcement of judgments in civil and commercial matters.

BU, who was domiciled in Austria, signed a contract of employment with Markt24, a company whose registered office was in Munich, Germany, for a job as a cleaner in Munich. The contract was signed in a bakery in Salzburg, Austria.

The agreed start date was 6 September 2017—however, BU was not given any duties to perform for the duration of the contract. BU was registered for social security purposes as an employee of Markt24 with the Austrian authorities. Her employment was subsequently terminated by Markt24 on 15 December 2017.

BU brought proceedings in the Austrian courts against Markt24 for the recovery of outstanding sums owed to her. The jurisdiction of the Austrian Court to determine the matter was disputed by Markt24.

The Austrian Court referred the following five questions to the ECJ, in essence:

1. Is art 21 of the Regulation 'applicable to an employment relationship in which, although an employment contract was entered into in Austria for the performance of work in Germany, the female employee, who remained in Austria and was prepared for several months to work, did not perform any work'?

If the answer to (1) is yes:

2. Does art 21 of the Regulation preclude national rules permitting an employee to bring an action in the place they were resident at the time of the contract of employment and/or the time when the employment ended?
3. Does art 21 of the Regulation preclude national rules permitting an employee to bring an action in the place where remuneration is or was to be paid at the time of the termination?

If the answer to (2) and (3) is no:

4. Does art 21 mean that the action must be brought where the employee was prepared to carry out work or should it be brought where the contract of employment was entered into?

If the answer to question (1) is no:

5. Is art 7(1) of the Regulation applicable to the employment relationship at hand such that the action should be brought where the employee was resident at the time the employment relationship ended or where the remuneration is or was to be paid at the time of the termination?

The ECJ answered the first question by noting that the question was effectively whether or not s 5 of Chapter II of the Regulation, entitled 'Jurisdiction over individual contracts', was applicable to the employment relationship at hand. The ECJ noted that the jurisprudence of the ECJ has established that a relationship of subordination exists between an employee and an employer. This relationship of subordination was found to exist in the employment relationship in the circumstances, notwithstanding the fact that the employee, through no fault of her own, had not carried out any duties. Therefore, a 'contract of employment' existed such that s 5 of Chapter II applied.

The ECJ considered question 2 and 3 together. It noted that the purpose of the Regulation is to 'establish uniform rules of international jurisdiction', and noted that under art 4(1) and art 5(1), where an employment law dispute arises that comes within the scope of the Regulation, the rules of the Regulation take precedence over the national rules. Therefore, national rules which provide that an action can be brought where the employee was resident or was to be remunerated are not permitted, as they seek to effectively override the Regulation.

In relation to question 4, the ECJ noted that the referring Court was effectively request-ing the ECJ to determine the competent forum to hear the action. The ECJ observed that, under the Regulation, an action can be brought either:

— in the Member State where the employee is domiciled (art 21(1)(a)), or
— in the Member State where the employee habitually carried out their work, or where they last carried out their work; or where no such habitual place exists, where the business which engaged the employee was or is situated (art 21(1)(b)(i) and (ii)).

The ECJ further noted that when determining 'the place where the employee habitually carries out his work', reference should be made to the place where 'the employee in fact performs the essential part of his or her duties'. In circumstance where no work was carried out, regard must be had to the intention of the parties as to where these duties would occur. This factor 'allows a high degree of predictability of rules of jurisdic-tion to be ensured, since the place of work envisaged by the parties in the contract of employment is, in principle, easy to identify'.

The ECJ qualified this by noting that art 7(5) of the Regulation may apply in the case at hand. Article 7(5) provides that a dispute can be brought in the jurisdiction where a branch, agency or other establishment is based. In the circumstances, Markt24 did have an office in Austria. The ECJ held that it was for the referring Court to determine whether art 7(5) applied to the facts.

Finally, the ECJ did not consider the fifth question as consideration of this question was only necessary if the first question was answered in the negative.

[5.21] *A Seafarer v A Shipping Company*[40]*—Workplace Relations Commission— preliminary issue of jurisdiction—Brussels 1 Regulation (recast)*[41]

The claimant worked offshore, installing windfarms, and started working for the respondent in February 2013. The claimant worked in a variety of locations (such as the Danish, UK and Dutch sectors of the North Sea, the UK and Transit Holland sectors of the Irish Sea and the English Channel). An incident occurred on board the vessel in August 2018 which resulted in injury to the claimant. An investigation and disciplinary procedure took place and resulted in a finding of gross misconduct. The claimant was dismissed and lodged an unfair dismissal claim with the WRC. The question arose as to whether the WRC had jurisdiction to hear and determine the complaint.

---

[40] *A Seafarer v A Shipping Company* ADJ-00027736.
[41] Regulation (EU) No. 1215/2012 on jurisdiction and the recognition and enforcement of judgments in civil and commercial matters (recast).

The crux of the jurisdictional dispute was that the respondent argued that the Brussels I Regulation (recast) (the Recast Regulation) deemed Denmark or the Netherlands the appropriate jurisdiction for the claim, while the claimant argued that Ireland was the correct jurisdiction.

It was the respondent's position that the Recast Regulation applied in determining whether the WRC/Ireland had jurisdiction to hear and determine the dispute. The respondent argued that under the Recast Regulation, Ireland was not the appropriate Member State to assume jurisdiction (the claimant did not work in Ireland, his employment had no connection with Ireland, the respondent did not have a branch or establishment in Ireland nor was the respondent domiciled in an EU Member State for the purposes of Recast Regulation).

The claimant's contract of employment contained a clause which stated that it was governed by the laws and courts of Singapore. During his employment, the claimant worked on two vessels which were chartered by a Danish registered company. The respondent submitted that the claimant was effectively seconded to a vessel operated by the Danish company and worked primarily in Danish seas operating out of Danish ports and occasionally in Dutch Seas operating out of Dutch port. At no time did the claimant operate in Irish seas or out of Irish ports.

The claimant contended that the Recast Regulation was grounded on three pivotal principles of international law: freedom of choice, proximity and the protection of the weaker party. The claimant argued that he was based exclusively in Ireland for a period of 13 months prior to termination of his employment, was always paid into an Irish bank account and the contract of employment noted the claimant's 'Homeport' as Dublin.

The respondent cited an EU Commission statement which provides that: 'In disputes between the employee and the employer, the main connecting factor between the Brussels I Regulation (recast) … is the place where the employee habitually carries out his work'. The respondent referred to the High Court decision in *Goshawk Dedicated Ltd v Life Receivables Ireland Ltd*,[42] which stated that 'there can be little doubt but that the traditional common law jurisdiction has, at a minimum, been substantially eroded by the provisions of … the Brussels Regulation'. Finally, the respondent argued that art 21 of the Recast Regulation 'is categoric, in that, it is where the precise duties of employment take place'.

Considering the European Commission's *Practice Guide on the Jurisdiction and Applicable Law in International Disputes Between the Employee and the Employer*, the Adjudication Officer concluded that the Recast Regulation mandated a separate consideration of whether Ireland was the appropriate jurisdiction and, if so, what law was applicable.

The Adjudication Officer, relying on art 21 of the Recast Regulation, found that the WRC did not have jurisdiction to hear or determine the claimant's complaint. While the Recast Regulation permits employees to sue their employer where the employer is

---

[42]   *Goshawk Dedicated Ltd v Life Receivables Ireland Ltd* [2008] IEHC 90.

domiciled, the employee can also sue in the country where they habitually carry out work. The evidence indicated that the claimant mainly worked in Danish seas from a Danish port and occasionally in Dutch seas from Dutch ports. Despite having filed taxes in Ireland, being paid into an Irish bank account, having exclusive residency in Ireland for the 13 months prior to termination, and the initial training and subsequent disciplinary meeting having occurred in Ireland, the Adjudication Officer accepted the respondent's argument that the test for jurisdiction is a specific test relating to where the precise duties of employment take place and that place was Denmark or the Netherlands where the claimant habitually worked, not Ireland.

[5.22] *Alta Trading UK Ltd v Bosworth & Hurley[43]—Court of Appeal of England and Wales—Sir Vos MR, Henderson and Nugee LJJ—appeal from decision of the High Court of England and Wales—proceedings against former CEO and CFO— Swiss domicile—jurisdiction*

The first and second respondents were the CEO and CFO of the first three appellants (the Arcadia Group), which companies were involved in trading physical crude oil and oil derivatives. The appellant companies were an English company, a Swiss company, a Singaporean company and a holding company. The claim related to an alleged fraud. The appellants claimed that the respondents had diverted profits of $339,000,000 out of the Arcadia Group.

The appellants argued that the English courts had no jurisdiction in respect of the claims by reason of the Lugano Convention (Lugano II) and they contended that, under Lugano II, the claims should have been brought in the State where the appellants were domiciled, in this case Switzerland.

Article 18 of the Lugano Convention provides as follows: 'In matters relating to individual contracts of employment, jurisdiction shall be determined by this Section'; art 20 provides that: 'An employer may bring proceedings only in the courts of the State bound by this Convention in which the employee is domiciled'. Accordingly, the Court had to consider whether the claim was one relating to individual contracts of employment. If the claim did relate to individual contracts of employment, the English courts had no jurisdiction to decide the matter.

This case had a long history of litigation, yet the matter of jurisdiction was still outstanding. The Court of Appeal reviewed the decisions to date, including the reference by the UK Supreme Court to the European Court of Justice as to whether the appellants were employees for the purposes of arts 18 and 20 of the Lugano Convention. The ECJ held that an employment relationship implies the existence of a hierarchical relationship between the worker and the employer and the question as to whether such a relationship exists must, in every case, be assessed on the basis of all of the facts and circumstances characterising the relationship between the parties. The enquiry is a factual one, not determined solely on the basis of the terms of the contract. For there to be an 'individual contract of employment' there must be a relationship of subordination between the

---

[43]   *Alta Trading UK Ltd v Bosworth & Hurley* [2021] EWCA Civ 687.

company and the employee. The ECJ concluded that the respondents had an ability to influence Arcadia that was not negligible and therefore it must be concluded that there was no relationship of subordination. It followed that the English courts had jurisdiction in relation to the case because the claims did not relate to individual contracts of employment.

The UK Supreme Court was not persuaded that the ECJ had all of the evidential material necessary to reach the conclusion it reached and accordingly remitted the question to the High Court as to whether the respondents were in a relationship of subordination.

Following the remission of the case by the UK Supreme Court, the High Court concluded that the test in deciding a preliminary jurisdiction matter of this type is that the appellant must establish a good arguable case; that the court must decide, if it can, who has the better case; and where a judge cannot decide after doing his or her best who has the better of case, it is sufficient if the appellant has a plausible evidential basis for asserting jurisdiction. Applying that test and noting that the appellants bear the onus to establish jurisdiction, the High Court concluded that the respondents had a good arguable case that there was not a relationship of subordination and that the appellants had a more than negligible ability to influence the Arcadia companies.

The Court of Appeal upheld the decision of the High Court and dismissed the appeal. In so doing, the Court of Appeal noted that it doubted that the case would be a precedent for many others. Even senior managers are usually in a relationship of subordination to their employers. The respondents had an unusually free hand in running the Arcadia Group to the extent of writing their own contracts of employment. The Court of Appeal did not conclude that a senior manager or even director who is given a degree of autonomy as to how he or she does their job is outside the protection of art 18 because it would be usual for there to be a relationship of subordination.

[5.23] *Semtech Corporation v Lacuna Space Ltd, Sornin & Sforza[44]—High Court of England and Wales (Patents Court)—Purvis QC—Recast Brussels Regulation (EU) 1215/2012,[45] art 22.1—jurisdiction—whether proceedings 'relate to' contracts of employment—breach of copyright—breach of confidence—conspiracy*

The respondents were respectively the CFO and the head of Business Development in the Semtech Group. They had an undisclosed shareholding in a customer of the Semtech Group, Lacuna, to whom it was alleged they disclosed confidential information in the course of a business relationship. When the secret shareholding was discovered, they were dismissed. They were domiciled in France and they instituted wrongful dismissal proceedings in France. The Semtech Group instituted these proceedings in England. The respondents contended that the English courts had no jurisdiction because the proceedings 'relate to' their contracts of employment as a consequence of which under the Recast Brussels Regulation the courts of France, the jurisdiction of their domicile, had exclusive jurisdiction.

---

[44]   *Semtech Corporation v Lacuna Space Ltd, Sornin & Sforza* [2021] EWHC 1143 (Patents Court).
[45]   Regulation (EU) No 1215/2012 on jurisdiction and the recognition and enforcement of judgments in civil and commercial matters.

The High Court had to consider art 22.1 of the Recast Brussels Regulation, which provides that proceedings that 'relate to' contracts of employment may be brought only in the courts of the State of domicile of the employees concerned. It was undisputed that the State of domicile was France.

The Court concluded that the proceedings did relate to the contracts of employment, and therefore, it had no jurisdiction for a number of reasons. First, it found that the context of the acts complained of lay in the respondents' positions as senior employees within Semtech through which they had access to the confidential and copyright materials and the ability to provide those materials to customers such as Lacuna. Second, the essence of the case concerned their authority to deal with customers under their contracts of employment and the extent to which that authority might be vitiated by their undisclosed shareholdings in Lacuna. Third, the claimants' pleaded case put allegations of breach of those contracts at the heart of the case. Fourth, the respondents had genuine and close connections with France as lifelong citizens and residents, and their bargaining power was not as strong with Semtech as that of the employees in *Bosworth & Hurley v Arcadia Petroleum Ltd*,[46] as they had not drafted their own contracts of employment, they answered to line managers, and they clearly fell within the category of persons that art 22.1 was intended to protect.

The High Court concluded that it had no jurisdiction in this matter and dismissed the proceedings.

[5.24] *Clark v Harney Westwood & Riegels*[47]—*UK Employment Appeal Tribunal—appeal from employment tribunal—Regulation (EU) 1215/2012*[48]— *identity of employer—time limits—jurisdiction*

The claimant entered into a contract of employment with the Cayman Island firm Harney Westwood & Riegels (HWR). The contract stated that it was governed by Cayman Island law and was subject to the jurisdiction of the Cayman Island courts.

The claimant worked initially in the Hong Kong office and subsequently in the Cayman Island office of the firm. While working in both, she was given business cards stating her name and details as a partner of HWR. The claimant was paid from a bank account in the name of HWR during both periods.

Without the claimant's knowledge, an application for a temporary work permit for her to work in the Cayman Islands was made by another entity, Harvey Gill (HG), a registered partnership arising out of a merger between HWR and another firm. Work permits can only be obtained from the Cayman Islands Department of Immigration by entities at least 60% Cayman owned. The temporary (and later full) work permits that issued named HG as the claimant's employer.

---

[46]   *Bosworth & Hurley v Arcadia Petroleum Ltd* [2016] EWCA Civ 818, see also **[5.22]** for most recent decision of Court of Appeal of England and Wales in *Alta Trading UK Ltd v Bosworth & Hurley* [2021] EWCA Civ 687.
[47]   *Clark v Harney Westwood & Riegels* UKEATPA/0576/19/BA.
[48]   Regulation (EU) 1215/2012 on jurisdiction and the recognition and enforcement of judgments in civil and commercial matters (recast) (Brussels Recast).

In January 2018, the claimant was dismissed with payment in lieu of notice. The letter notifying the claimant of her termination was on HWR-headed paper. The claimant brought a claim to the employment tribunal, contending that the notice to dismiss her failed to comply with Cayman Island labour law and was ineffective in terminating her contract. However, the claimant did not lodge her claim until more than three months had passed since her termination and she failed to comply with the requirement to obtain an Early Conciliation Certificate before lodging her claim.

The employment tribunal found that, notwithstanding the terms of her contract with HWR, the claimant was in fact employed by HG. The tribunal found that it did not have territorial jurisdiction to hear the claim as the Cayman Islands was the proper forum; the claimant had failed to comply with the Early Conciliation Certificate requirements; and the claim was out of time.

The claimant appealed the decision to the EAT.

The EAT considered the principles to be applied in determining who the employer is. It acknowledged that in any situation where the corporate structure of the 'employer' comprises more than one entity, the answer might not be straightforward. The EAT identified the following principles, established in previous authorities, that are relevant to the issue of identifying whether a person, A, is employed by B or C:

a. Where the only relevant material to be considered is documentary, the question as to whether A is employed by B or C is a question of law ...

b. However, where (as is likely to be the case in most disputes) there is a mixture of documents and facts to consider, the question is a mixed question of law and fact. This will require a consideration of all the relevant evidence ...

c. Any written agreement drawn up at the inception of the relationship will be the starting point of any analysis of the question. The tribunal will need to inquire whether that agreement truly reflects the intentions of the parties ...

d. If the written agreement reflecting the true intentions of the parties points to B as the employer, then any assertion that C was the employer will require consideration of whether there was a change from B to C at any point, and if so how ... Was there, for example, a novation of the agreement resulting in C (or C and B) becoming the employer?

e. In determining whether B or C was the employer, it may be relevant to consider whether the parties seamlessly and consistently acted throughout the relationship as if the employer was B and not C, as this could amount to evidence of what was initially agreed.

To these principles, the EAT added its own consideration: 'that documents created separately from the written agreement without A's knowledge and which purport to show that B rather than C is the employer, should be viewed with caution'. It noted that the 'primacy of the written agreement, entered into by the parties, would be seriously undermined if hidden or undisclosed material could readily be regarded as evidence of a different intention than that reflected in the agreement' and stated that it would be a 'rare case where a document about which a party has no knowledge could contain persuasive evidence of the intention of that party'.

Applying those principles to the facts of the case, the EAT held that the tribunal had erred in concluding that HG was the employer. It found that the written documents clearly identified HWR as the employer and all subsequent dealings between the parties were consistent with that.

The EAT also allowed the appeal on territorial jurisdiction, finding that it flowed from the finding that as HWR was the employer, the claimant was entitled, under Brussels Recast, to issue proceedings against the partners in HWR domiciled in the UK.

However, the EAT upheld the tribunal's findings that the claim was out of time; and that and her failure to comply with the Early Conciliation Certificate requirement led the EAT to dismiss her claim for want of jurisdiction.

PLEADINGS

[5.25] *Nemeth v Topaz Energy Group Ltd[49]—Court of Appeal—Noonan, Faherty and Binchy JJ—appeal from High Court—Rules of the Superior Courts (No. 6) (Disclosure of Reports and Statements) 1998[50]—Civil Liability and Courts Act 2004—health and safety—pleadings*

The respondent succeeded in her claim before the High Court for damages against her employer in respect of an injury suffered to her right knee in the course of her employment. The appellant appealed the finding.

A particular feature of the case was the pleadings and the subsequent approach to the trial taken by the respondent. The respondent initially pleaded that her injuries arose from her being instructed to assume a squatting position for a sustained period of time. When she attempted to arise to a standing posture, she suffered a sudden injury to her right knee. The respondent's medical and engineering reports were consistent with the case pleaded, and were based on the respondent's report that she was squatting fully for a prolonged period of time and that the injury suffered arose when she was attempting to stand up from a squat. A particular publication from the European Agency for Safety and Health at Work (E-Facts 42) cited by the respondent identified risks associated with prolonged squatting.

However, on the day of the trial, CCTV footage (which had been available to the respondent for some years) demonstrated that the respondent had not in fact been squatting when she suffered the injury—rather, she squatted on her left leg but kneeled on her right knee. The duration of the event was just over one minute. The respondent proceeded with the case, and it was asserted in evidence that 'not a lot actually turns on whether it was squatting or kneeling'. The appellant strongly contested this.

---

49 *Nemeth v Topaz Energy Group Ltd* [2021] IECA 252.
50 Rules of the Superior Courts (No. 6) (Disclosure of Reports and Statements) 1998 (SI 397/1998).

The Court of Appeal noted that the trial Judge made no reference to the discrepancy between the case pleaded and the case opened at trial. It observed that this discrepancy meant that the appellant was faced with meeting a new case based on matters that had never been raised in expert reports (including failing to supply certain materials, such as a stool or a kneeling cushion). The Court found that the trial Judge had not found the appellant to be liable on the case actually pleaded. It stated that the Rules of the Superior Courts (No. 6) (Disclosure of Reports and Statements) 1998 were enacted to avoid situations like the present case, which essentially amounted to trial by ambush.

The Court of Appeal found that expert testimony from the respondent's engineer was of little value where the task was ordinary and everyday, and that his assertion that the respondent was at increased risk of the injury because of her physical characteristics was beyond his competence. Insofar as the trial Judge purported to rely on E-Facts 42, the Court of Appeal noted that this document had no application to the facts, as the respondent was not squatting for prolonged periods of time when she suffered the injury.

The Court of Appeal rejected the argument that the appellant's subsequent change in the use of the cupboard at which the respondent was kneeling/squatting could be construed as an admission of liability. It noted that to make this finding would place a defendant in an impossible position where attempting to prevent similar accidents would amount to an admission of liability.

The Court of Appeal found that there was no credible evidence to support the finding of the trial Judge and dismissed the respondent's claim, awarding High Court and Court of Appeal costs to the appellant.

PRIVILEGE

[5.26] *PJSC Tatneft v Bogolyubov[51]—High Court of England and Wales— Moulder J—no waiver of privilege arose from negative assertions in relation to legal advice—privilege—waiver of privilege*

This case concerned the well-established principle that, depending on the circumstances, a party who makes *voluntary* disclosure of privileged material, in written documentation submitted to the Court, may be obliged to make further disclosure of otherwise privileged material that relates to the same matter. The test to be applied, as set out in *PCP Capital Partners LLP v Barclays Bank Plc,[52]* is whether there is sufficient reference to the privileged material in the written documentation, and whether it has been relied on in support of the relevant party's case.

---

[51] *PJSC Tatneft v Bogolyubov* EWHC 3225 (Comm).
[52] *PCP Capital Partners LLP v Barclays Bank Plc* [2020] EWHC 1393 (Comm).

The plaintiff was a major oil producer, headquartered in Russia, and initially brought proceedings against the four named defendants in 2016, alleging that the defendants had misappropriated substantial sums owed to the plaintiff for oil that it had supplied to a refinery. The oil had been sold via a 'commission agent' (S-K), and the proceedings were initiated by the plaintiff as S-K's assignee.

A fundamental issue arose as to whether the proceedings were in fact statute barred under Russian law. This issue centred on whether S-K had actual or constructive knowledge of certain relevant facts at least three years before the proceedings were issued. The four named defendants alleged that the plaintiff did indeed have such actual or constructive knowledge, and argued that the plaintiff had made similar allegations to those made against the defendants in an arbitration claim the plaintiff had filed in 2008, and in criminal complaints made in 2008 and 2011, and that as such, S-K must have had constructive knowledge of the allegations made by the plaintiff in 2008 and 2011.

After the trial began in October 2020, the second defendant, Mr Kolomoisky, sought a declaration from the Court that the plaintiff had waived privilege in relation to certain communications between S-K and the plaintiff, and their legal advisers. Mr Kolomoisky submitted that the plaintiff had waived privilege as a result of a number of assertions made on its behalf in evidence to the Court, in which it was stated that the plaintiff had relied on privileged material in support of its case. The issue thus arose as to whether privilege could in fact be waived in respect of a negative assertion, ie, that certain matters had *not* been discussed, or that certain advice had *not* been sought or received. Mr Kolomoisky argued that the test for waiver of privilege was whether the party was placing reliance on the advice, and the reason for such reliance; importantly, Mr Kolomoisky asserted that the test applied irrespective of whether the assertion was a positive or negative one.

It was submitted on behalf of the plaintiff that the test could not be meaningfully applied to a scenario in which the party in question asserts that the specific matter was not discussed whatsoever.

Having reviewed the statements that Mr Kolomoisky argued amounted to a waiver of privilege, the Court held that certain statements did in fact result in a waiver of privilege, while others did not. The Court reaffirmed that, for there to be a waiver of privilege, the reference to the legal advice over which privilege is claimed must be sufficient; in addition, the relevant party must be seeking to rely on that reference to advance its case in relation to an issue on which the Court is being called upon to decide.

Taking the issue of negative assertions, the Court stated that the issue for the Court to determine was the purpose for which the communication was being relied upon. The Court differentiated between: (a) relying on legal advice in circumstances where the relying party had put forward a positive case in relying on the advice; and (b) in replying to an argument advanced by a counterparty, denying the argument put forward by that counterparty. The Court held that:

> When one considers the rationale for privilege, it must be correct that no waiver of privilege can occur by responding to an assertion by the other party as to the contents of an otherwise privileged communication.

In those circumstances, the Court held that there had been no waiver of privilege, on the basis that there had been no voluntary disclosure. The Court held that the reference in the communication being referred to, to discussions between lawyers, was a denial that a particular matter had been discussed. The Court stated its agreement with the rationale offered on behalf of the plaintiff, that it would be an 'odd result' if responding to an assertion that a matter was discussed, by denying that it was discussed, meant that privilege was waived.

[5.27] *Abbeyfield (Maidenhead) Society v Hart[53]—UK Employment Appeal Tribunal—appeal from employment tribunal—litigation privilege—whether privilege waived when documents voluntarily disclosed—exceptions to privilege— iniquity principle*

This judgment concerned an appeal and cross-appeal from case management orders made by the employment tribunal regarding disclosure of documents.

The claimant was employed by the respondent, a charity operating care homes and care services, from November 2011. In March 2017, the claimant was dismissed for gross misconduct, without notice, following an altercation with a gardener on or around 9 December 2016. The claimant brought claims to the employment tribunal for unfair dismissal, wrongful dismissal, discrimination on grounds of age, race, sex and/or disability, harassment and victimisation. He also made a data subject access request under the Data Protection Act 1998.

The employment tribunal ordered disclosure by the respondent of all documents and records relating to the incident at work which had led to the claimant's dismissal. It scheduled a preliminary hearing to hear any submissions the respondent wished to make in relation to documents that ought not to be disclosed on privilege or other grounds.

The respondent submitted that 78 pages containing 'communications with HR consultants consisting of requests for advice, and advice, on how to deal with the Claimant's disciplinary case and the possibility of dismissal' were covered by litigation privilege, as they were created in contemplation of litigation. The employment tribunal agreed with this assessment, but held that one of the documents was nonetheless disclosable under the 'iniquity principle', which holds that there are circumstances where certain communications, that would otherwise be privileged, must be disclosed, eg, where they contain 'legal advice sought or given with the purpose of effecting a fraud, with fraud being given a wide meaning in this context, sufficient to extend to sharp practice or engagement in something underhand in circumstances where good faith is required'. The document in question was an email from a senior officer in the respondent who acted as the appeal officer in the decision to dismiss the claimant. He had sent an email

---

[53]   *Abbeyfield (Maidenhead) Society v Hart* EA-2020-001089-JOJ.

to a HR consultant prior to the claimant's dismissal stating the claimant's 'rudeness and gross insubordination has caused major problems ... and this cannot be allowed to continue any longer. He will not therefore be returning to Nicholas House under any circumstances'.

The respondent appealed the employment tribunal's decision that the document was disclosable under the iniquity principle to the EAT. The claimant in turn cross-appealed the employment tribunal's decision that certain of the other 77 documents which the respondent had separately provided to the claimant in response to his data access request were covered by litigation privilege as it argued that in providing those documents to the claimant the respondent had waived privilege in respect of them.

The EAT noted that the 'iniquity principle' operates to disapply privilege 'when the document in question comes into existence as a step in a criminal or illegal proceeding, e.g. when a solicitor is consulted on how to do an illegal act' and that in order for the principle to be made out, 'a strong prima facie case of some fraud or illegality or some other "iniquity" must be shown'. The EAT stated that the exception should be applied strictly because there are strong reasons why the usual policy in favour of non-disclosure where litigation privilege applies is necessary, as it 'enables parties to communicate frankly with other advisers), e.g. about the strengths and weaknesses, and the risks, of their case, knowing that the communications will remain private'.

The EAT held that the email in question, when read either by itself or in the context of the chain that it formed part of, was not such to engage the iniquity principle. It held that:

> The Respondent did not seek advice on how to act unlawfully, and the consultants did not give such advice. They were advising on how to take forward a disciplinary process and on the risk of that process leading to litigation. The indication by Mr Cager that he did not wish the Claimant to return to work was the sort of frank instruction that a party may feel able to give in a privileged communication. So was the agent's response, that she had to "ensure that if my clients wish to proceed against my advice that they do so by making an informed decision".

The EAT commented that even an email in which an employer 'told its advisers that it intended to embark on an appeal process which was a sham' may not be enough to invoke the iniquity principle as, to invoke the principle, the communication needs to involve some kind of illegality, for example a request on how to act illegally.

In relation to the claimant's cross-appeal, the EAT noted that 'it is common ground that a party can waive privilege by disclosing the material in response to a SAR'; however such disclosure may not operate to waive privilege when the disclosure was made by mistake. The EAT noted that the application of these principles is 'case-specific, fact-specific and not rigid'. It noted that the point had not been pressed before the employment tribunal and the employment tribunal had not heard evidence on it and as such, allowed the appeal and remitted the matter to the employment tribunal.

SEVERANCE AGREEMENT

[5.28] *Evergreen Timber Frames Ltd v MK Harrington[54]—UK Employment Appeal Tribunal—appeal from employment tribunal—redundancy—redundancy terms—breach of contract*

The claimant was dismissed on grounds of redundancy by Evergreen. A dispute arose with regard to the redundancy settlement and in particular whether the claimant had a contractual right to have ownership of the company car previously used by him transferred to him. The transfer of the car was included in a written offer made to him. The claimant intended to accept the offer of the car but appealed, under the company's internal procedures, seeking in addition the transfer of a computer to him and the payment to him of a bonus. Following the claimant's internal appeal, the company rejected his claim for a computer and a bonus payment and decided not to transfer the ownership of the car to him.

The employment tribunal concluded that it was possible for the claimant to accept the transfer of ownership of the company car and at the same time appeal the matter so as to seek to have transferred to him the computer and seek the bonus payment.

On appeal, the EAT rejected the submission of the respondent that the description of the car as a 'gift' meant that the claimant had no contractual entitlement to it; it noted the decision in *Edwards v Skyways Ltd*[55] where the High Court rejected the employer's contention that its offer of a payment to redundant employees was unenforceable because it had been described as '*ex gratia*'. In *Edwards*, the High Court held, in that context, that the words *ex gratia* did not carry an implication that the agreement was to be of no legal effect. It concluded that a payment described in express terms as '*ex gratia*' or 'without admission of liability' could not mean that a settlement so made would be unenforceable.

Turning to the question of whether it was open to the claimant to accept the car and at the same time appeal, seeking the computer and the bonus, the EAT noted that:

> When employers and employees discuss severance arrangements, there will be numerous matters to address, reflecting the many terms and conditions found in contracts of employment and a range of statutory employment rights. An agreement might cover pay, approved leave, notice, pension contributions, the use of confidential information, benefits, incentives and, of course, any sum offered on an ex gratia basis. The negotiations of such agreements would become too complex if it were possible to reply to an offer in a form that permitted a party unilaterally to sever and then accept, some terms, while rejecting, or seeking improvement to, others.

The EAT concluded that the correct analysis was that the claimant's letter of appeal was a counter offer to improve the severance terms and could not constitute an acceptance of the terms in part, namely the offer of the car.

---

54   *Evergreen Timber Frames Ltd v MK Harrington* UKEAT/0072/20 AT.
55   *Edwards v Skyways Ltd* [1964] 1WLR 349.

Accordingly, the EAT concluded that the employment tribunal had erred in law in finding that the parties entered into a contractually binding agreement by which ownership of the car would be transferred to the claimant on termination of his employment. The case was remitted to a fresh employment tribunal for further consideration.

SOVEREIGN IMMUNITY

[5.29]   *The State of Kuwait v Nada Kanj*[56]—*High Court—Barr J—appeal from the Labour Court—Unfair Dismissals Acts 1977 to 2015—United Nations Convention on Jurisdictional Immunities of States and their Property 2004, art 11.2(a)—point of law—unfair dismissal—doctrine of sovereign immunity*

The plaintiff worked as an academic adviser at the Kuwaiti Cultural Office in Dublin until her employment was terminated in 2017. The plaintiff sought to bring a complaint under the Unfair Dismissals Acts 1977 to 2015 (the Unfair Dismissals Acts), and the respondent alleged that she was prevented from doing so by virtue of the doctrine of sovereign immunity.

The WRC found that it did not have jurisdiction to hear the complaint as the respondent embassy had claimed sovereign immunity. The plaintiff appealed to the Labour Court, where the finding was overturned and the Court found that under the United Nations Convention on Jurisdictional Immunities of States and their Property 2004, the plaintiff was entitled to bring a complaint under the Unfair Dismissals Acts and that sovereign immunity could not be invoked.

The respondent appealed the Labour Court's finding to the High Court on a point of law.

The High Court noted that the United Nations Convention on Jurisdictional Immunities of States and their Property 2004, art 11.2(a) provides an exception to sovereign immunity from jurisdiction before a court where the proceedings relate to a contract of employment. However, there are a number of limitations to the application of the exception, including where the employee is recruited to perform particular functions in the exercise of governmental authority.

There was therefore a conflict between the plaintiff and respondent at the WRC and Labour Court as to whether her role as academic adviser constituted engaging in the exercise of governmental authority on behalf of the State of Kuwait. The Labour Court found that the plaintiff's reliance on the exception was not limited by the performance of governmental authority limitation, and therefore the respondent was not entitled to rely on sovereign immunity.

In the High Court, the primary submission on behalf of the respondent was that the Labour Court had failed to provide adequate reasons as to why it had reached the conclusion that it had, and that it had applied the wrong test in holding that the plaintiff's role

---

[56]   *The State of Kuwait v Kanj* [2021] IEHC 395.

did not involve: (a) the exercise of any public powers; or (ii) governmental authority; and (iii) did not touch on the business of the State of Kuwait.

The High Court noted that where there is a conflict of evidence between the parties, it is essential that the decision maker engages with the evidence and resolves the conflict one way or the other, and that it is incumbent on the decision maker to state clearly why they are accepting certain evidence and rejecting other evidence called on behalf of the opposing party.

The High Court also pointed out that the Labour Court operates under a statutory duty that, on request, it should set out a statement 'why' it reached its determination.

The critical issue for determination was whether the plaintiff engaged in rudimentary administrative tasks which did not require decision making on the plaintiff's part, or whether the role comprised tasks related to the implementation of policy or governmental authority of the State of Kuwait. The High Court noted that there was significant evidence on behalf of both the plaintiff and the respondent on this issue.

The High Court noted that the Labour Court determination set out 'an admirable summary' of the background facts, but then gave a bald conclusion, without saying why it had reached that conclusion. The Court was entitled to come to a conclusion that it preferred one party's evidence over the other's, but it must set out the reasons why. The High Court found that the Labour Court 'gave the result, having given a summary of the evidence, but did not tie the two together by saying why the court resolved the conflict in evidence in favour of the plaintiff'.

The High Court therefore allowed the respondent's appeal on the ground that the Labour Court failed to give adequate reasons for its decision. The High Court also allowed the appeal on the ground that the Labour Court applied the wrong test in determining the application of sovereign immunity. The Labour Court mistakenly relied on a three-pronged test, whereas the relevant test in the legislation only requires that the employee be recruited to perform particular functions in the exercise of governmental authority.

The Labour Court determination was set aside and the matter was remitted to the Labour Court for a further determination in accordance with the law.

LIMITATION PERIODS FOR COMMON LAW CLAIMS

[5.30] *Matthew v Sedman*[57]—*UK Supreme Court—Hodge, Sales, Burrows, Stephens and Arden LJJ—appeal from Court of Appeal—Limitation Act 1980—employment litigation—limitation periods for common law claims*

This case concerned the calculation of the limitation period in respect of causes of action which accrue at, or on the expiry of, midnight.

The respondents claimed that part of the claim brought against them was issued outside of the six-year limitation period set out in the Limitation Act 1980.

---

[57] *Matthew v Sedman* [2021] UKSC 19.

The first and second appellants were the current trustees in a trust (the Trust). The Trust had a shareholding in Cattles plc, which subsequently acquired Welcome Financial Services Ltd. In 2007, Cattles plc published an annual report and a prospectus which were later found to contain misleading information. Trading in Cattles plc's shares was subsequently suspended and both companies issued court proceedings seeking court-sanctioned schemes of arrangement.

The resulting schemes of arrangement included provision for shareholders in each company to submit claims and the Trust had a claim in respect of each of the two companies. The rules relating to claims under the Welcome Financial Service Ltd scheme of arrangement stated that a claim form must be submitted on or prior to the 'Bar Date', which was Thursday 2 June 2011. Therefore, a valid claim under the Welcome Financial Service Ltd scheme of arrangement could be made up to midnight on Thursday 2 June 2011.

The respondents, as the former trustees of the Trust, failed to make a claim prior to midnight on Thursday 2 June 2011 and this failure led to part of the proceedings which concerned the Welcome Financial Service Ltd scheme of arrangement. Those court proceedings were brought by the appellants against the respondents seeking damages and/or equitable compensation in relation to the claims under the two schemes of arrangement. The respondents issued an application to strike out the appellants' proceedings in relation to the Welcome Financial Service Ltd scheme of arrangement claim on the basis that they had been issued out of time.

The trial Judge granted the respondents' application and the Court dismissed the appellants' appeal.

The relevant limitation period for each of the causes of action in the proceedings were set out in substantially identical terms under the Limitation Act 1980 and provided that such actions could not be brought after the expiration of six years from the date on which the cause or right of action accrued.

The issue before the UK Supreme Court was whether or not Friday 3 June 2011 should have been included in calculating the limitation period.

The appellants submitted that the cause of action accrued on 3 June 2011 and that, in accordance with long-standing authority, the day on which the cause of action accrues should not be included in the reckoning of time. They further submitted that 'the law did not recognise the metaphysical concept of a separate point in time between two days' and that the cause of action in this case only accrued at the end of 2 June 2011, ie, after midnight, so therefore it accrued on 3 June 2011.

The respondents submitted that two things had happened at exactly the same time: (i) the time for submitting a claim lapsed; and (ii) the cause of action arose. It was submitted that these two events were not consecutive but occurred simultaneously at the last moment of 2 June 2011. The respondents argued that the appellants had the whole of Friday 3 June 2011 to issue proceedings.

The Supreme Court considered the case law relied on by the appellants and found that none of the cases in question established a general position in relation to midnight deadlines. It held that there was no significant difference in whether the cause of action in the present case had accrued at the end of 2 June 2011 or at the very beginning of 3 June 2011 as, in either case, the appellants, for practical purposes, had an entire uninterrupted day on 3 June 2011 to issue proceedings.

The Court went on to state that the basis for the general rule that the day on which a cause of action accrues should not be included in the reckoning of time is that 'the law rejects a fraction of a day'. In the case before it, the Court held that it had been correctly submitted that, in a case concerning a midnight deadline, even if the cause of action accrued at the very beginning of the day following the midnight deadline, that day was an entire, uninterrupted day. To exclude that day from the reckoning of time, would result in the limitation period being six years and one full day, which would 'unduly distort the six-year limitation period laid down by Parliament and would prejudice the defendant by lengthening the statutory limitation period by a complete day'.

In dismissing the appeal, the UK Supreme Court held that any part of a day, but not a full day, arising after a cause of action accrues should not be included in the reckoning of time for the purposes of the Limitation Act 1980. As 3 June 2011 was a full day, it should be included in calculating the limitation period for issuing proceedings.

LABOUR COURT APPEALS—ADEQUACY OF DOCUMENTS

[5.31] *Parkgate Lounge Ltd t/a Abbott Lounge v Hossain[58]—Labour Court— appeal from Workplace Relations Commission—practice and procedure—Labour Court written notice of appeal—incomplete form*

The Labour Court considered as a preliminary matter whether the respondent had not complied with the requirement to provide sufficient information in its appeal of the decision of an Adjudication Officer to the extent that the appeal was an invalid appeal and accordingly whether it had jurisdiction to determine the substance of the matter.

Both parties accepted that the written notice of appeal did not contain enough information in relation to the claimant. The respondent's representative had identified on the notice the telephone number of the claimant, but the number actually provided was that of the claimant's solicitor. The respondent's representative had provided an address for the claimant, but the claimant asserted that the respondent knew that this was incorrect. No address of the claimant's representative was provided. Neither the claimant's representative nor the claimant been provided with a copy of the appeal form by the respondent. Accordingly, the first time that the claimant heard that a written notice of appeal had been submitted was when the Labour Court contacted the claimant's solicitor, believing the contact number to be that of the claimant, and notified them of a change in venue arising from pandemic-related issues.

---

[58] *Parkgate Lounge Ltd t/a Abbott Lounge v Hossain* RPA/20/17.

The respondent asserted that the discrepancy was not material, and accordingly the appeal should not be struck out arising from administrative deficiencies in respect of the written notice.

The Labour Court determined that, while absolute compliance with every aspect of the Labour Court rules is not required, there is a minimum obligation on appellants to provide the Labour Court with the information necessary to apply fair procedures in dealing with appeals. A fundamental requirement of fair procedure is that both parties are afforded an opportunity to know the case against them, and the respondent's failures had impacted this. Accordingly, the Labour Court regarded the failures as material omissions which rendered the written notice of appeal invalid. As no valid appeal was made against the decision of the WRC Adjudication Officer, the Labour Court determined that it had no jurisdiction to hear the claim and struck out the matter.

TIME LIMITS—LABOUR COURT APPEALS

[5.32]   *Aztec Entertainment Ltd v Robinson[59]—Labour Court—appeal from Workplace Relations Commission—Workplace Relations Act 2015—Labour Court appeal time limits*

Aztec Entertainment Ltd, the respondent company, appealed a decision of the WRC wherein it was found their former employee, the claimant, had been unfairly dismissed and was awarded €35,000 in compensation.

The preliminary issue dealt with was the 42-day time limit set out in the Workplace Relations Act 2015 (the 2015 Act). The appeal was received by the Labour Court a day after the time limit expired, ie, it was received on 18 March 2021 whereas 17 March 2021 was the 42nd day after the determination of the WRC. The respondent argued that exceptional circumstances applied because 17 March is a public holiday and the appeal had been sent by registered post on 16 March 2021.

Furthermore, the respondent's solicitor stated that both he and his secretary were self-isolating at home with symptoms of Covid-19. He would normally have emailed the appeal form from the office but was unable to do so and had omitted to do so before leaving the office.

In finding that the Labour Court did not have jurisdiction to hear the appeal because the case was outside the time limits, the Labour Court noted that the Labour Court rules refer to 42 days and not 42 'working days'.

The Labour Court also differentiated between the two-prong test in the 2015 Act and the one-prong test in the Residential Institutions Redress Board Act 2002. The two prongs being: (1) that exceptional circumstances existed; and (2) that those circumstances acted so as to prevent the applicant from lodging his appeal in time. The Labour Court

---

[59]   *Aztec Entertainment Ltd v Robinson* UDD2144.

commented: 'To be exceptional a circumstance need not be unique or unprecedented or very rare; but it cannot be one which is regular or routinely or normally encountered'.

The Court did not accept that exceptional circumstances existed in this case and noted that even if it were to do so, the respondent did not demonstrate that the circumstances prevented them from lodging the appeal in time.

[5.33] *Donnybrook Service Station Ltd v Murray*[60]*—Labour Court—appeal from Workplace Relations Commission—Workplace Relations Act 2015—unfair dismissal—preliminary issue—time limit for appeal—exceptional circumstances*

This was an appeal against the decision of an Adjudication Officer in a claim made by the claimant against his former employer alleging that he was unfairly dismissed. The Adjudication Officer found that the complaint was not well founded and issued a decision on 2 December 2019.

A preliminary issue before the Labour Court was whether an extension of the time limit for appeal under s 44(4) of the Workplace Relations Act 2015 was warranted in this case. Under s 44(3) of the Workplace Relations Act 2015, an appeal from the decision of an Adjudication Officer must be brought within 42 days. In this case, the last date for lodging an appeal was 12 January 2020. However, the appeal was lodged on 14 March 2020.

The claimant sought an extension of the time limit and claimed that 'exceptional circumstances' prevented him from lodging the appeal in time. He claimed that he was suffering from stress when he was dismissed and he was unable to afford legal advice at the time the decision issued. He secured a job over the Christmas period and subsequently, when he was able to consult a solicitor, he opened the envelope containing the decision of the Adjudication Officer in the presence of his solicitor. Shortly thereafter, he lodged the appeal.

The respondent submitted that the claimant was aware of the time limit on appeal and he knowingly did not open the envelope. The respondent also submitted that the bar for extension on the basis of exceptional circumstances was very high. It relied on the determination of the Labour Court in *Fitzsimons-Markey v Gaelscoil Thulach na nÓg*,[61] where the Labour Court held that a miscalculation of time or an ignorance of the law are not exceptional circumstances.

The Court agreed that the claimant's arguments did not meet the requirements of an exception on the basis that the claimant deliberately decided not to open the envelope containing the Adjudication Officer's decision. The Court noted that legal advice is not required to lodge an appeal and that the materials provided with the Adjudication Officer's decision are designed to cater to lay litigants. Even if the claimant wished to seek legal advice prior to lodging an appeal, the 42-day period was sufficient.

The Court therefore upheld the decision of the Adjudication Officer.

---

[60]   *Donnybrook Service Station Ltd v Murray* UDD217.
[61]   *Fitzsimons-Markey v Gaelscoil Thulach na nÓg* (2004) ELR 110. See *Arthur Cox Employment Law Yearbook 2016* at **[5.08]**.

TIME LIMITS—WORKPLACE RELATIONS COMMISSION COMPLAINTS

[5.34]   *Donegal Meat Processors t/a Foyle Donegal v Gillespie*[62]*—Labour Court— appeal from Workplace Relations Commission—Unfair Dismissals Acts 1977 to 2015—Minimum Notice and Terms of Employment Act 1973—statutory time limit— exceptional circumstances—summary dismissal—gross misconduct—minimum notice—unfair dismissal*

The claimant's employment was summarily terminated by the respondent for gross misconduct on 29 April 2014. The claimant appealed the termination and an appeal hearing took place on 23 May 2014. The decision to terminate the claimant's employment summarily was communicated to the claimant on 3 June 2014. The claimant filed proceedings under the Unfair Dismissals Acts 1977 to 2015 on 7 November 2014.

The Adjudication Officer found that the claimant's complaint was outside of the six-month statutory time limit for bringing a complaint.

The claimant appealed the decision to the Labour Court and alleged that the respondent was not entitled to terminate his employment summarily. As such, he was entitled to two weeks' notice under the Minimum Notice and Terms of Employment Act 1973. On the basis of the two-week notice period, to which the claimant alleged he was entitled, he claimed that the termination date should be 13 May 2014 and that his complaint was therefore within time. The claimant contended that if he was not dismissed summarily, or if the summary dismissal was not justified, his complaint would have been in time. Therefore, the claimant argued that the Court must hear the substantive case to determine whether summary dismissal was justified.

The respondent disputed the claimant's contention and noted that it is well established that the date of dismissal is the date that is communicated to the employee. The respondent noted that there was no term in the claimant's contract or the disciplinary procedure which saved the claimant's employment pending the outcome of an appeal in the circumstances.

The Court considered the claimant's position that it must examine the fairness of the dismissal in order to decide whether summary dismissal was justified. The Court did not accept that this was the proper approach and noted this was 'akin to asking the Court to exercise its jurisdiction before it determines whether or not it has jurisdiction, in the first instance'. In assessing jurisdiction, the Court found it was confined to the nature of the termination without examining the fairness of the decision. The Court noted that the claimant was not entitled to notice under his contract where his employment was terminated for gross misconduct. As such, the claimant had no entitlement to notice and his complaint was out of time.

The Court upheld the decision of the Adjudication Officer.

---

[62]   *Donegal Meat Processors t/a Foyle Donegal v Gillespie* UDD2114.

[5.35] *Becton Dickinson Penel Ltd v Goring[63]—Labour Court—appeal from Workplace Relations Commission—Unfair Dismissals Acts 1977 to 2015—dismissal— time limits*

This was an appeal to the Labour Court by the claimant under the Unfair Dismissals Acts 1977 to 2015 (the Acts).

The claimant's employment with the respondent was terminated with immediate effect on the grounds of gross misconduct. The dismissal was upheld at internal appeal and the matter was referred to the WRC.

The respondent raised a preliminary issue that the Court had no jurisdiction to hear the complaint, as the claimant's claim under the Acts was out of time and thereby statute barred.

The claim was lodged on 8 June 2018 and the claimant had been dismissed on 1 September 2017. The respondent submitted that there were no reasonable grounds upon which the Court could extend the time for the making of this complaint.

The claimant argued that the delay was caused by his trade union representative being out of the office due to illness at the time the claim should have been submitted. As his SIPTU supervisor was not made aware of this, the claim was not lodged with the WRC in time.

In finding that the claimant was out of time, the Court considered the case law on time limits and in particular noted that, as the internal appeals process had only taken two months, the claimant would still have been within the six-month time limit. The Court could not accept that the absence of a representative from a trade union as large as SIPTU 'was sufficient to explain the delay and to prevent the claim being submitted in time'. No reasonable justification was put forward for the delay and the claim was dismissed.

[5.36] *Forever Therapies Ltd v McNamee[64]—Labour Court—appeal and cross-appeal from Workplace Relations Commission—discrimination on the grounds of disability—statutory time limit—reasonable cause*

The claimant worked as an independent holistic therapist for the respondent since 2009, providing services not only to the respondent's clients but also to her own private clients. During this time the respondent operated as a sole trader but incorporated in July 2017, at which time the respondent sought to review the contracts of self-employed, part-time therapists. The claimant refused to sign the new contract and made a referral to the SCOPE section of the Department of Employment Affairs and Social Protection in respect of her employment status in September 2017.

On 17 October 2017, the respondent's representative met with the claimant and offered her the option of continuing to work for the respondent on a contract for service or

---

63   *Becton Dickinson Penel Ltd v Goring* UDD213.
64   *Forever Therapies Ltd v McNamee* EDA2132.

on a contract of service. The claimant opted to await the SCOPE decision before making any decision. The respondent ceased offering the claimant any work after 13 December 2017.

On 29 May 2018, SCOPE issued a decision that the claimant's working arrangements with the respondent and the predecessor was a contract of service.

The claimant suffered from endometriosis and epilepsy and brought claims against the respondent for discriminating against her, for failure to make reasonable accommodations and for harassment and victimisation. At the hearing, a preliminary issue regarding the statutory time limit for the bringing of the claimant's complaint was raised. The claimant submitted that the most recent discrimination by the respondent occurred at the meeting on 7 October 2017. As she did not refer her complaint to the WRC until 9 July 2018, the claimant's complaints fell outside of the six-month limitation period. The claimant was therefore required to prove reasonable cause for her delay. She submitted that she was dealing with the SCOPE referral in January 2018 and that a close relative's health also began to deteriorate in January 2018 resulting in a bereavement on 2 July 2018.

In considering this argument, the Labour Court referred to the established test from *Cementation Skanska (formerly Kvaerner Cementation) Ltd v Carroll*:[65]

> in considering if reasonable cause exists, it is for the [claimant] to show that there are reasons which both explain the delay and afford an excuse for the delay. The explanation must be reasonable, that is to say it must make sense, be agreeable to reason and not be irrational or absurd ... there must be a causal link between the circumstances cited and the delay and the [claimant] should satisfy the Court, as a matter of probability, that had those circumstances not been present he/she would have initiated the claim in time.

In this instance the Court found that the 'operative reason for the [claimant]'s delay in referring her complaint was her decision to await the outcome of her application to SCOPE'. Therefore, the claimant did not meet the threshold required of her in order to extend the statutory time period. The respondent's appeal succeeded and the decision of the Adjudication Officer was set aside.

[5.37]   *National University of Ireland Galway v Markham[66]—Labour Court—appeal from Workplace Relations Commission—European Communities (Protection of Employees on Transfer of Undertakings) Regulations 2003[67]—time limits—extension of time—reasonable cause—potential to undermine collective negotiations*

The claimant was one of a number of employees who transferred from the employment of Shannon College of Hotel Management to the respondent, by reason of a transfer of undertaking, within the meaning of the European Communities (Protection of Employees on Transfer of Undertakings) Regulations 2003 (TUPE).

---

65   *Cementation Skanska (formerly Kvaerner Cementation) Ltd v Carroll* DWT0338.
66   *National University of Ireland Galway v Markham* TUD202.
67   European Communities (Protection of Employees on Transfer of Undertakings) Regulations 2003 (SI 131/2003).

Ms Markham alleged that the respondent failed, in breach of TUPE, to apply to her the terms of a 2010 collective agreement, the Cost Recovery Plan (CRP). The CRP provided an agreed basis for implementing cost-saving measures, including potential pay restoration subject to certain growth and recovery targets being achieved. The issue of restoration had been the subject of a Labour Court recommendation dated 26 May 2015.

The Adjudication Officer declined jurisdiction to hear the complaint, filed on 22 June 2017, as it had been received outside the six-month limitation period provided for in TUPE. She refused an application to extend the period to bring the complaint.

On appeal to the Labour Court, the claimant made an application for the time period to be extended on the basis of reasonable cause. In support of that application, it was asserted that the Union had chosen to attempt to resolve the dispute with the respondent in relation to the application of the CRP through the industrial relations process, locally and with the assistance of the Conciliation Service of the WRC. The Union had taken the view that there was a risk that the process could have been jeopardised if legal proceedings had been initiated while discussions were ongoing. Accordingly, the complaint was not submitted until the negotiations had run their course.

The Labour Court did not accept that this explanation established reasonable cause for the delay in submitting the complaint. It noted that there was nothing to prevent the claimant or the Union referring a complaint within time, ie, within six months of the date they believed the claimant's entitlement under TUPE had crystallised, other than the Union's perception of the potential impact that referring such a complaint at that time might have had on the ongoing collective negotiations. The Court opined that it would have been perfectly legitimate for the claimant to have lodged her complaint within time in order to protect her position and that this could have been communicated as appropriate by the Union to the respondent.

The application to extend time was refused and the Court accordingly did not consider the substantive element of the appeal by the claimant.

PREMATURE WRC COMPLAINT

[5.38] *SNC Lavalin Engineering & Construction Ireland Ltd v Ball[68]—Labour Court—appeal from Workplace Relations Commission—employment litigation*

The claimant had been employed as the financial controller with the respondent group company for almost 17 years. In June 2017, the claimant was among the finance section that was informed that their roles were at risk of redundancy. Thereafter, she was informed that her position was to be made redundant.

In October that same year, when the payroll functions were being undertaken by employees other than the claimant, a discrepancy arose between the amounts being

---

[68]   *SNC Lavalin Engineering & Construction Ireland Ltd v Ball* UDD2119.

paid to the pensions provider on her behalf and the amount being deducted from her gross salary. This amounted to approximately €50,000 over a period of seven years.

The claimant went on certified sick leave. The respondent wrote to her setting out allegations against her arising from her apparent failure to make the aforementioned deductions and inviting her to a disciplinary hearing. The claimant sought postponement of the disciplinary hearing on two occasions. Despite the respondent's requests, the claimant never attended for a consultation with the occupational health specialist retained by the respondent.

In December 2017, the claimant submitted a WRC complaint form, to which she attached a note stating that the respondent had 'introduced an unwarranted disciplinary process, 6 weeks prior to my proposed redundancy exit date, in order to circumvent any redundancy payment'. In January 2018, after the claimant failed to appear at a disciplinary hearing, her contract of employment was terminated for gross misconduct.

The core of the respondent's submission was that the claimant was never informed that her employment would be terminated by reason of redundancy on any particular date, the reorganisation was a complex process and the claimant would have been eligible to apply for another position within the company. The claimant's proposed redundancy was overtaken by events.

The Labour Court noted that the claimant gave 'no credible explanation' for her decision to submit a complaint form to the WRC on 18 December 2017, which was two weeks before the date on which she asserted her employment terminated by reason of redundancy. The Labour Court continued, stating 'the claimant's employment was not, in fact, terminated by reason of redundancy on 31 December 2017, but was terminated for gross misconduct on 19 January 2018, the referral by the claimant of her complaint to the Commission on 18 December 2017 appears *ipso facto* to be grossly premature'.

The Labour Court concluded that the claimant had not been dismissed by reason of redundancy and her appeal to the Labour Court had failed.

JUDICIAL REVIEW OF WORKPLACE RELATIONS COMMISSION

[5.39] *Erdogan v Workplace Relations Commission and Ecomm Merchant Solutions Ltd*[69]—*High Court—Simons J—Employment Equality Act 1998—application for leave—applicant opted to judicially review a WRC decision as well as appeal it to the Labour Court—whether judicial review lies in those circumstances*

This was an application for leave to apply for judicial review. The applicant's complaint under the Employment Equality Act 1998 was dismissed by the WRC as having been made outside the six-month time limit prescribed. The applicant appealed the decision to the Labour Court and, at the same time, instituted judicial review proceedings

---

[69]   *Erdogan v Workplace Relations Commission and Ecomm Merchant Solutions Ltd* [2021] IEHC 348.

in parallel. The High Court directed that the application for leave to apply for judicial review be heard on notice. The WRC did not participate in the proceedings but the notice party, the applicant's former employer (and the respondent in the WRC complaint) defended the proceedings and opposed the application for leave, principally on the ground that the applicant's pending appeal to the Labour Court represented an adequate alternative remedy to judicial review.

The grounds advanced by the applicant were that there was a breach of the requirement 'to hear the other side' on the basis that the impugned decision of the WRC went further than the time point made before it and addressed the merits of the complaint; that the decision was unreasonable and offended 'against fundamental reason and common sense'; and that there had been a breach of the rule against bias because of remarks made by the WRC during the course of the hearing, which implied that it had predetermined the matter.

The High Court considered that the principal issue for determination was whether the statutory appeal pending before the Labour Court represented an adequate alternative remedy and noted the decision of the Supreme Court, in the employment law context, in *O'Donnell v Tipperary (South Riding) County Council*,[70] where it identified the following factors as relevant:

> The fact that the applicant has already commenced this alternative remedy and that there has been a hearing of the matter … This appeal now stands adjourned pending this judicial review. While these appeal steps are not a determinative factor, in the circumstances they are a weighty factor. Secondly, the issues which the applicant raises relate to natural justice and to fairness, which relate to the merits of the case also, which issues may be addressed and determined by the Employment Appeals Tribunal. Thirdly, the matters raised do not relate to net issues such as points of law or jurisdiction. Fourthly, the essence of the issue raised relates to evidence as to the allegedly fraudulent actions of the applicant and this may be dealt with fully by an appeal before the Employment Appeals Tribunal rather than as a review of procedures. It is manifestly a matter for an appeal process rather than a review of procedures. Fifthly, the applicant seeks reinstatement of his post … I have considered this as a factor but I do not give it a heavy weighting given that the Tribunal has the jurisdiction to hear an appeal and to reinstate and the applicant may present his full case on the appeal. Sixthly, there is a right of appeal from the Employment Appeals Tribunal to the Circuit Court, then to the High Court and, on a point of law, to this Court.

The High Court noted the relevance of those factors in the present case and in particular the inappropriateness of addressing allegations of fraud by way of judicial review procedure. The Court also observed that the appeal before the Labour Court was a *de novo* appeal. Furthermore, the procedure before the Labour Court is more formal than that at first instance and entails procedural safeguards which are not statutorily required before the WRC, including the jurisdiction to hear evidence on oath, to allow for the cross-examination of witnesses, and the right of appeal against a determination of the Labour Court on a point of law to the High Court.

---

[70]   *O'Donnell v Tipperary (South Riding) County Council* [2005] IESC 18, [2005] 2 IR 483.

The second aspect of the applicant's case was directed to the underlying merits of the WRC decision. The factual dispute between the parties could not be properly resolved in judicial review proceedings; the Labour Court was the proper forum to address this issue and 'has procedural mechanisms available to it to hear evidence on oath and to allow cross-examination'.

Furthermore, the applicant's submissions did not justify an application for judicial review. The allegations made by the applicant meant that it was 'not possible to treat the underlying merits of his claim as hermetically sealed from the time-limit point' as the applicant was seeking to rely on alleged misconduct on the part of the employer as constituting a 'misrepresentation' under s 77(6) of the Employment Equality Act 1998.

The Court noted that the position in respect of the third aspect of the applicant's case relating to bias was 'more nuanced', as:

> In principle, it is open to a party to argue that a statutory appeal does not constitute an adequate alternative remedy in circumstances where the objection made is that the decision of first-instance is tainted by bias. In particular, it can be argued that the party is entitled to a two-stage process and that a fundamental flaw at first-instance cannot be fully remedied on appeal.

However, the applicant's case was not an allegation of bias 'in the strict sense' as bias 'must be external to the decision-making process' and no external factor had been identified in the present case. There was no suggestion that the Adjudication Officer had a conflict of interest or had any prior relationship with either of the parties. The applicant argued that the bias should be '*inferred* from certain comments allegedly made by the adjudication officer during the course of the hearing'. The Court noted that it is 'only in exceptional cases that it is legitimate to establish objective bias based on statements made during the course of a hearing' and that the comments attributed to the Adjudication Officer were not exceptionable and did not support an inference of bias.

Accordingly, the Court concluded that this was not a case where a judicial review was necessary in order to rectify any deficiency in the hearing of first instance.

Turning to the question of costs, the Court noted that under Pt II of the Legal Services Regulation Act 2015, the default position is that a party who has not been 'entirely successful' in proceedings is *prima facie* entitled to costs against the unsuccessful party. However, the Court has a discretion to make a different form of costs order. Noting that applications for leave are normally made on an *ex parte* basis and that the High Court in the present case directed that the leave application be made on notice, the provisional view of Simons J was that the balance of justice required that each party bear its own costs, rather than having the costs of the *inter partes* hearing visited upon the applicant. The applicant was a personal litigant and the judicial review proceedings, 'although misconceived, were brought in good faith' and the Court considered it appropriate that some leniency should be shown to the applicant.

POINT OF LAW APPEALS

[5.40] ***Khan v General Medical Council[71]—High Court of England and Wales—Knowles J—Medical Practitioners Tribunal—fitness to practise proceedings—witness credibility—disciplinary proceedings***

The claimant was a consultant orthopaedic surgeon working for the NHS Trust. Following allegations of sexually motivated conduct towards a colleague (Miss D) in 2013, he was the subject of an internal disciplinary procedure. The claimant was dismissed from his role for gross misconduct. He was successful in bringing a claim of unfair dismissal to the employment tribunal and was reinstated. However, further allegations were made against him (by Miss A and Miss C) and the reinstatement order was revoked. In separate proceedings, he was acquitted by the Crown Court in respect of the allegations made by Miss D.

In 2019, the Medical Practitioners Tribunal in the UK considered the matter in the context of the claimant's fitness to practise. Finding all three witnesses to be credible, it decided that the claimant was unfit to practise and after almost seven years since the initial allegations were made, found that his name should be removed from the medical register.

The claimant brought an appeal to the High Court of England and Wales claiming that the Medical Practitioners Tribunal had failed to appropriately consider his good character when coming to its decision and that it had been overly reliant on a subjective assessment of the complainants' demeanour and their allegations against him, rather than on the evidence itself.

In considering the appeal, the High Court focused on the Medical Practitioners Tribunal's assessment of the evidence before it. In particular, the Court looked at whether the Medical Practitioners Tribunal had determined the credibility of the complainants based on their behaviour and the impression they made, rather than basing its assessment on the evidence as a whole.

Drawing on previous case law, the Court found that it was a requirement for the Medical Practitioners Tribunal to take good character into account 'in its assessment of credibility and propensity'. However, the Court went on to state that an inference could be made based on all of the material considered by the Medical Practitioners Tribunal including witness statements and oral evidence, that evidence of the claimant's good character had been properly taken into account as 'it would be simply unrealistic to suppose that the tribunal overlooked it'.

The claimant argued, in particular, that the Medical Practitioners Tribunal had failed to consider discrepancies in the evidence provided by Miss D; failed to consider part of the evidence; and had established facts to be true that did not reflect the evidence

---

[71] *Khan v General Medical Council* [2021] EWHC 374 (Admin).

presented to it or at least had not 'grappled with evidence which had the potential to undermine' the credibility of the complainants. The High Court agreed with the 'broad thrust' of the claimant's arguments.

The High Court referred to *R (on the application of Dutta) v General Medical Council*,[72] which stated that: 'Reliance on a witness's confident demeanour is a discredited method of judicial decision making', and accepted that there was an issue with the Medical Practitioners Tribunal's reasoning. It stated that the Medical Practitioners Tribunal's conclusions were 'preordained'. For example, having decided Miss C was a credible and truthful witness despite earlier admissions of having lied under oath before the employment tribunal, it did not consider Mr Khan's denial of the allegations she made against him. Instead, the Medical Practitioners Tribunal chose to rely on the manner in which Miss C had given her evidence.

The Court's judgment was extremely critical of the Medical Practitioners Tribunal's 'erroneous' approach to the evidence of all three complainants. It quashed the sanction of removal from the register imposed by the Medical Practitioners Tribunal and permitted the claimant's appeal.

---

[72] *R (on the application of Dutta) v General Medical Council* [2020] EWHC 1974.

Chapter 6

Employment-related Torts

INTRODUCTION

[6.01]   In *Credit Suisse*, the High Court of England and Wales considered, in the context of an application to strike out, whether an employer might have a duty to indemnify an employee in respect of losses arising consequent on performing duties on the employer's behalf.

In *Antuzis*, the High Court of England and Wales applied the law on inducement of breach of contract in circumstances where the claimants contended that the directors of their employer company had induced the company to fail to pay the minimum wage due to them.

Three decisions of the Irish Court of Appeal are noted in the context of occupational injury claims. In *O'Connor*, the approach of a trial judge to various matters arising was examined. In *Harford*, the Court of Appeal had to consider whether liability could arise in respect of nervous shock where there was no catastrophic incident but where the plaintiff realised that physical injury had been narrowly avoided. In *Chambers*, the consequences of a defective personal injury summons was considered.

In *Evans*, the circumstances in which an employer might join an employee as a third party to personal injury proceedings were considered by the High Court. In *Cunningham*, the necessity for a causal link between the employer's failures and the injuries suffered by the employee was central to the outcome. The circumstances in which the statutory duty to reimburse the Department of Social Protection arises is considered in *Fahy* and in *Condon*.

Issues connected with vicarious liability and personal injury limitation periods were considered by the Court of Appeal of England and Wales in *Blackrock Football Club Limited*. Limitation periods were also central to the asbestosis claim in *Balls*.

Finally, the considerations relevant to an application for costs in circumstances where a personal injury claim has been unsuccessful were set out by the High Court in *Ward*.

DUTY TO INDEMNIFY

[6.02] *Benyatov v Credit Suisse Securities (Europe) Ltd[1]—High Court of England and Wales—Ter Haar QC—contract of employment—implied terms—employment related torts—duty to indemnify—duty to protect from economic loss*

The claimant worked for the defendant bank, and, while travelling to Romania for work in relation to the privatisation of semi-state companies in 2006, he was arrested. He was subsequently charged with espionage and the establishment of an organised criminal group. He was convicted and sentenced to ten years' imprisonment. On appeal, his conviction was replaced with instigation of disclosure of professional secrets or non-public information, and he was given a reduced sentence of four-and-a-half years' imprisonment. As a result of his conviction, his status as an 'approved person' in the UK for undertaking and providing various financial services was withdrawn. Following his conviction, the defendant tried to assist the claimant, including making attempts to engage with the Romanian Government on an informal political basis. The defendant asserted that it had spent considerable sums of money on legal representation for the claimant, including funding proceedings before the European Court of Human Rights.

In 2015, the claimant's employment with the defendant was terminated. The claimant issued proceedings against the defendant under a number of heads, including breach of the contract of employment; and in tort, a claim that he was entitled to an indemnity in respect of, *inter alia*, lost income, lost future income and a failed property transaction arising out of his inability to work as a senior finance professional. He also claimed that he was owed a duty of care by the defendant to protect him from economic losses arising from the performance of his duties, which included a duty to intervene in Romania to demonstrate his innocence to the relevant prosecutorial and/or judicial authorities, and/or to individuals or political authorities with power to withdraw the prosecution against him.

The High Court declined to strike out the element of the claim based on the asserted implied term that the employer would indemnify the employee in respect of losses consequent on performing duties on his employer's behalf. The Court held that that the facts needed to be explored at trial before the scope and operation of any indemnity duty were determined.

The Court did however consider that the breach of contract allegation (in not providing greater support in the period after the claimant's arrest) was not sustainable. The Court stated that the whole affair was diplomatically sensitive and the respondent could not have been expected to intervene in a way which might be seen as interfering with Romanian court processes. The alleged duty was not simply that the defendant should have taken steps to defend or engage lawyers to defend him. The evidence was that the defendant did that, and continued to do that, at great expense. The allegation went further and asserted that the defendant had a duty to attempt to intervene politically in the prosecution system of a sovereign nation. The Court found that it would not be fair, just or reasonable to impose the duties contended for by the claimant and dismissed that head of claim.

---

[1]   *Benyatov v Credit Suisse Securities (Europe) Ltd* [2021] EWHC 1318 (QB).

INDUCING BREACH OF CONTRACT

[6.03] *Antuzis v DJ Houghton Catching Services Ltd*[2]*—High Court of England and Wales—Griffiths J—failure to pay minimum wage—unlawful deductions—quantum*

The claimants were Lithuanians who went to the UK and worked for the first respondent as chicken catchers on chicken farms. The farms contracted with the first respondent to provide this service. The claimants issued proceedings against the first respondent and certain directors of the first respondent relating to the failure of the first respondent to discharge their statutory rights in respect of minimum pay and in respect of the non-payment or withholding of holiday pay and in respect of certain deductions made from their pay. The claimants claimed that the second and third respondents had liability in respect of the amounts due to them by reason of the tort of inducing a breach of contract. Their claim was upheld by the High Court in 2019 where it was held that the second and third respondents were jointly and severally liable to all of the claimants for inducing breaches of contract by their employer, the company. Those breaches of contract consisted of failures to pay the claimants the minimum wage they were entitled to by law and the making of unlawful deductions.

In this case, the High Court decided the question of quantum and accepted the claimants' evidence and figures with respect to hours worked. The Court accepted the entitlement of the company to deduct rent from the wages and rejected the claimants' contention that the houses weren't fit for human habitation such that rent should not have been charged. However, the deduction for rent exceeding the statutory limits was to be repaid. Deductions in respect of 'employment fees' were recoverable by the claimants. What was described as 'arbitrary deductions' were also recoverable. Holiday pay was recoverable.

The Court accepted the claim for aggravated damages, noting that aggravated damages, unlike exemplary damages, are compensatory. In addition to the damages awarded in respect of underpayments and non-payments, the Court concluded that the claimants had an entitlement to damages to represent their mental and physical sufferings. The Court concluded that the claimants would not be fully compensated unless the cumulative effect of the treatment of them was recognised in their damages, over and above the amounts and totals of individual non-payments. Recovery of that money, even with interest, would not compensate them for the whole effect on them of their exploitation, manipulation and abuse by the respondents at the time in question. The means of inflicting this abuse was the first, second and third respondents' systematic denial of the claimants statutory rights. The Court noted that it was not compensating them for personal injury because it was not a personal injury claim. In awarding aggravated damages, the Court was recognising that the effect of non-payment and underpayment was extreme because of its total and cumulative impact on the claimants. The Court assessed the aggravated damages at 20% of the damages represented by the various money claims.

---

[2] *Antuzis v DJ Houghton Catching Services Ltd* [2021] EWHC 971 (QB). See *Arthur Cox Employment Law Yearbook 2019* at **[6.01]** for the High Court decision on liability in *Antuzis v DJ Houghton Catching Services Ltd* [2019] EWHC 843 (QB).

Turning to the question of exemplary damages, the Court noted that exemplary damages are punitive rather than compensatory. By reason of the substantial aggravated damages awarded, the Court did not think it necessary or appropriate to award exemplary damages as well. The Court noted that if it had solid evidence of the amount of profit made by the respondents from the way in which they conducted their business and if it appeared that this significantly exceeded the damages awarded against them, the Court would have considered to what extent the excess should have been taken from them by way of exemplary damages. However, as the Court had no detailed evidence of same, it concluded that it would not award exemplary damages.

PERSONAL INJURY

[6.04]   *O'Connor v Wexford County Council[3]—Court of Appeal—Noonan, Faherty and Binchy JJ—appeal from High Court—employment torts—occupational injury*

This case concerned an appeal against the decision of the High Court to dismiss the appellant's personal injuries action. At the time of the appellant's accident, he had been employed as a water inspector with the respondent for 16 years. As part of the appellant's duties, he attended the Ferns Reservoir each day to carry out various checks. The reservoir's location was somewhat sloped and in order to carry out his duties, the appellant had to access a meter room which was downhill towards one end of the reservoir.

The appellant gave evidence, that on the day of the accident, he was on his way down the embankment to the meter room when he slipped and fell. The appellant submitted that the route he had used had been shown to him when he first began the role 16 years earlier by his predecessor, Mr Keogh. Mr Keogh gave evidence that he had been shown this route some years before that by his own predecessor and he explained that, at the time when he began the role, there was a 'well-worn path' in that location, which he had used in the same way as the appellant.

The appellant's colleague, Mr Kavanagh, also gave evidence that he used this path and had in fact slipped and fallen there himself approximately eight months before the appellant's accident. In light of Mr Kavanagh's fall, the appellant had told him that he would look into having steps installed at the location. The appellant submitted that he had raised this with the respondent's engineer, who had agreed to have steps installed. However, while the engineer agreed that the installation of steps had been raised, he disputed that he had agreed to have them put in and stated that he had instead advised the appellant that he should use another route across the top of the reservoir.

The respondent submitted that the appellant should have taken the alternative, safer route across the top of the reservoir but there was a dispute among the parties as to the suitability of this route.

---

3   *O'Connor v Wexford County Council* [2021] IECA 239.

A forensic engineer gave evidence that the type of slope in question was 'unsafe and dangerous' for a workplace and that 'over time someone is inevitably going to fall in such an area'. He also stated that 'if there was any kind of inspection or risk assessment or a visit from a supervisor then it would have been obvious that this unsafe means of access was being used and that should have been addressed'.

The Court of Appeal noted several facts that were 'either agreed or never seriously disputed, were of significant relevance to the liability issue' and which had not been considered by the trial Judge, including:

(1) The appellant had received on-the-job training from his predecessor Mr Keogh who showed him the path to take to the reservoir.
(2) Three witnesses had provided 'undisputed evidence' that there was 'a well-worn path up the side of the reservoir which had been present for decades and which was there to be seen by anybody who cared to look, even on a drive through inspection'.
(3) It should have been clear to anyone carrying out a risk assessment that this path existed and it should have been specifically dealt with in any such assessment.
(4) The appellant had raised the issue of steps with the engineer.
(5) The path was obviously dangerous.
(6) There was 'no evidence to suggest that anyone had ever used the Council's proposed alternative route over a period of very many years'.

It was noted by the Court of Appeal that the trial Judge had only referred to one case in his judgment, which neither party had cited. In considering that case, the trial Judge found that reasonable care on the part of a plaintiff needed to be considered in light of 'ordinary common sense' and that, in the case before it, 'ordinary common sense' should have signalled to the appellant that using the path in question, as opposed to the alternative flat route, was reckless.

The Court of Appeal stated that, where a court intends to rely primarily on a judgment that has neither been cited nor debated by the parties, the correct approach is to ask the parties to address the court in relation to same. The parties in this case had not been given that opportunity.

The Court of Appeal found that the High Court had fallen into 'significant error' in dismissing the claim and that the trial Judge had erroneously applied legal principles. It therefore allowed the appeal and held that the majority of the responsibility for the appellant's accident lay with the respondent. However, it also found that the appellant should have appreciated the risks involved in using the path in question, particularly after Mr Kavanagh had fallen there eight months beforehand, and found the appellant liable for contributory negligence. Liability was apportioned as 75% against the respondent and 25% against the appellant.

[6.05]   *Harford v Electricity Supply Board[4]—Court of Appeal—Donnelly, Binchy and Noonan JJ—appeal from High Court—nervous shock—no catastrophic incident—narrow escape*

---

[4]   *Harford v Electricity Supply Board* [2021] IECA 112.

The central issue in this appeal was whether a person could recover damages for nervous shock in circumstances where there had been no sudden catastrophic incident but rather the respondent had realised that physical injury had been narrowly escaped and that realisation lead to psychiatric injury.

The respondent was employed by the appellant as a network technician. On Friday 12 December 2014, the respondent was tasked with repairing a public street light. This involved identifying a suitable live cable and transferring the faulty light to that alternative cable. The cable required for the light in question was a low voltage 400 volts cable, which usually had four cores.

The device which the respondent would normally have used to identify the voltage of a cable, and whether or not it was live, was not available on this particular day and the respondent was instructed to use another device, which he was unfamiliar with.

The respondent entered an excavated hole in the road to access the cable and used the device to identify the correct cable. It appeared to give the respondent a suitable signal when attached to one of the cables and so the respondent began to remove the outer protective and insulating layers from the cable. The respondent stripped the cable wrapping down until all that remained was a form of insulation called belting papers. In his evidence, the respondent confirmed that he handled the cable in this state several times without experiencing any negative effects.

The next step was for the respondent to insert test lamps to check that the cable was live. The respondent had to leave the hole to get the test lamps and, on doing so, he noticed that the cable did not look right and found that it only had three cores. This meant that the cable was in fact a medium voltage 10,000 volts cable. If the respondent had proceeded to insert the test lamps into this cable, he would have been electrocuted and suffered very serious injury or death.

Upon realising the nature of the cable in question, the respondent shut the site and reported the incident.

A few days later, the respondent began to feel overwhelmed by thoughts of what might have happened had he not realised the nature of the cable before inserting the test lamps. He attended his GP and remained off work for a period of time due to post-traumatic stress disorder and/or depression.

The High Court held that the appellant was liable for the respondent's psychiatric injury and awarded him general damages of €80,000. The High Court held that the respondent had suffered a shock by the thought of being exposed to the 10,000 volts cable and that his post-traumatic stress disorder and/or depression was brought on by this shock.

The appellant appealed against the High Court judgment on the basis that the respondent's injury was not caused by 'nervous shock' as that term is 'understood and applied in the relevant jurisprudence' and that there was no catastrophic event that led to the respondent's injury.

In its judgment, the Court of Appeal considered a wealth of case law on nervous shock from Ireland, England and Australia. It noted that the Irish Supreme Court has repeatedly stated that a 'sudden and shocking' event was a prerequisite to recovery for 'purely psychiatric injury'. The Court of Appeal stated that the respondent had not shown that he had ever actually been in danger. The Court stated that it was clear from the evidence that the medium voltage cable which the respondent had handled was insulated at all times and therefore the risk of the respondent being electrocuted had never, in fact, arisen. While the risk may have arisen had the respondent not realised the true voltage of the cable and continued with his task, this had not happened.

The Court of Appeal found that the respondent's injury was not 'shock induced' as there was no sudden horrifying event. It further stated that, in accordance with the relevant jurisprudence, a plaintiff seeking recovery for nervous shock must have suffered the nervous shock 'by reason of actual or apprehended physical injury to the plaintiff or some other person'.

The Court of Appeal held that, to find the appellant liable in this case, would result in an extension of the existing law in Ireland and would give rise to policy considerations. Accordingly, it held that a person could not recover damages for nervous shock in circumstances where there had been no sudden catastrophic incident but rather the individual had simply realised that physical injury had been narrowly escaped and that realisation led to psychiatric injury.

[6.06] *Chambers v Rathcaled Developments Ltd and SV Betong AS[5]—High Court—Barrett J—amended personal injury summons*

The plaintiff issued a personal injuries summons in February 2015 against Rathcaled Developments Ltd, in respect of a fall he sustained during the course of employment. In November 2018, the plaintiff brought an application before the Master of the High Court to join SV Betong AS as a defendant in the proceedings and to issue and serve an amended summons. The order sought was granted and the plaintiff was allowed a period of 28 days to issue and serve the amended summons on SV Betong AS.

In April 2019, the plaintiff obtained an *ex parte* order allowing a further period of five weeks to comply with the Master's Order and subsequently issued a purported concurrent personal injuries summons on SV Betong AS on 7 May 2019.

There were a number of errors with the purported concurrent summons:

1. the word 'amended' was not contained anywhere on the face of the document;
2. the proposed amended summons did not include underlining;
3. there was no indication from the document that the summons had in fact been amended; and
4. there was no indication from the document that SV Betong AS had been joined to the proceedings at a later date.

---

[5]   *Chambers v Rathcaled Developments Ltd and SV Betong AS* [2021] IEHC 458.

SV Betong AS brought an application seeking to have the concurrent personal injuries summons struck out for nullity and/or irregularity.

In its judgment, the Court noted that the defendants accepted that the errors had been innocently made. It also stated that it did not view the errors in the concurrent personal injuries summons as giving rise to 'the legal and procedural travesty for which SV Betong AS contends'.

The Court referred to Lord Denning's judgment in *Re Pritchard*[6] and noted that the following six key points could be drawn from that judgment and were of relevance to the case before it:

(1) a court should not lose sight, even in the face of the rules of court, of its ample inherent jurisdiction to correct error;

(2) a party ought not to be penalised for a technical slip, especially when its opponent has not been in the least prejudiced by that slip (and a court ought to allow any necessary amendment to put it right);

(3) a court should rightly lean in this regard towards a liberality of spirit.

(4) when an officer of the court itself makes a mistake, the consequences should not be visited on the unfortunate litigant, but should be remedied by the court itself, doubly so in the case of non-serious error;

(5) ... the historical treatment of "nullities" ... has been most confusing; often ... a proceeding has been said to be a "nullity" when it would have been more correct to say that, if the irregularity has not been waived, it will be set aside *ex debito justitiae* ("as of right", *i.e.* where a litigant is entitled to something merely on the asking for it, as opposed to its being a matter of judicial discretion/determination); and

(6) the ideal to be striven for is that an honest litigant should not be defeated by any mere technicality, any slip, any mistaken step in her/his litigation.

The Court also considered a number of Irish cases and noted:

1. In considering procedural deficiencies in court proceedings, the Irish Courts have placed an emphasis on taking a position which did not 'fetishize the technical' and which centred on what, if any, prejudice may be suffered by the other party as a result of the deficiency caused by the party who was guilty of making the error.

2. The Irish Courts have preferred to concentrate on: '(a) the particular rule(s) in play, (b) where the justice of matters lies, having particular regard to the issue of prejudice to the party not guilty of error, and (c) a proper desire to respect and enforce the law as extant/enacted whilst avoiding unyielding allegiance to technicality' than to focus too much on the concepts of irregularity and nullity.

3. Finnegan J stated in *McKenna v G(J)*[7] that 'to adopt procedure by summary summons where a plenary summons is appropriate is an irregularity and not a nullity'.

4. The six points of principle noted in *Re Pritchard* can be considered by courts adjudicating on procedural errors as helpful 'rules of thumb'.

---

6   *Re Pritchard* [1963] Ch. 502.
7   *McKenna v G(J)* [2006] IEHC 8.

Ultimately, the Court refused to strike out the concurrent summons, finding that same had been 'afflicted by irregularity' but was 'certainly not a nullity'.

[6.07] *Evans v Beacon Hospital Sandyford Ltd, Shuhaibar & Mohammed[8]—High Court—Meenan J—personal injury—medical negligence—employment-related torts—joining an employee as a third party*

The plaintiff was diagnosed with an apical right lung tumour and was operated on in the Beacon Hospital (the Hospital) on 17 June 2014. On the day following the procedure, the second defendant directed that the plaintiff's catheter be removed. When the plaintiff was unable to pass urine he underwent a further catheterisation procedure during which difficulties arose, which the plaintiff alleged caused him severe personal injuries.

The plaintiff initiated a personal injury claim, that the Hospital settled for €175,000, following a mediation in December 2019.

The Hospital issued a notice of motion seeking to have the third party joined in the proceedings. The order was made on 16 January 2020. This case concerns the notice of motion issued by the third party seeking to have that order set aside on the grounds that it was not served as soon as 'reasonably practicable'.

The relevant statutory provisions are (1) Ord 16, r 1(3) of the Rules of the Superior Courts, which provides that 'Application for leave to issue the third-party notice shall, unless otherwise ordered by the Court, be made within twenty-eight days from the time limited for delivering the defence'; and (2) s 27(1)(b) of the Civil Liability Act 1961, which provides that:

> A concurrent wrongdoer who is sued for damages or for contribution and who wishes to make a claim for contribution under this Part ...
>
> (b)   shall, if the said person is not already a party to the action, serve a third party notice upon such person as soon as is reasonably possible and, having served such notice, he shall not be entitled to claim contribution except under the third-party procedure.

The Court noted that these statutory provisions have been considered on numerous occasions by the High Court, the Court of Appeal and the Supreme Court. It is well established on foot of such authorities that whether a step is taken 'as soon as is reasonably practicable' must be considered in the context of the facts of each particular case. The Court proceeded to consider the relevant timeline and the correspondence between the solicitors for the hospital and the solicitors for the third-named party.

In respect of whether the Hospital had served the notice 'as soon as reasonably practicable', the Court noted the following points:

1.   that it is well established that legal proceedings concerning a claim for contribution or indemnity from a third party should not be initiated without a supportive report from a suitably qualified expert and that professional negligence proceedings

---

8   *Evans v Beacon Hospital Sandyford Ltd, Shuhaibar &Mohammed* [2021] IEHC 225.

should not be defended on the issue of liability without an expert report justifying the position adopted;

2. the relevant period to be considered was between October 2016 and December 2019;

3. it took until July 2018 for the Hospital to identify the doctor referred to in the personal injury summons and the relevant indemnifier;

4. while doing so, solicitors for the Hospital obtained an expert report dated 23 June 2017 from a consultant urologist identifying negligence and breach of duty on the part of the third party;

5. from correspondence between the solicitors, between September 2018 and December 2018, the solicitors for the third-named party were obtaining an expert report concerning the care given to the plaintiff by the third party. This report was not obtained until 18 November 2019;

6. meanwhile the plaintiff continued with his action and mediation was scheduled. It was clear from correspondence that the Hospital sought to involve the third party in mediation;

7. the mediation resulted in a successful resolution of the claim on 19 December 2019. Prior to this, the Hospital's solicitors were made aware of the expert evidence obtained by the plaintiff on 3 December 2019 and commenced third-party proceedings 10 days later; and

8. the third party maintained that the delay on the part of the Hospital in issuing third-party proceedings had caused the third party 'irretrievable prejudice' and in its affidavit alleged that the Hospital had 'consciously and tactically chosen not to do so in order to retain control of the litigation until settlement'.

The Court disagreed that there was any prejudice caused to the third party, and in any event this was irrelevant in line with previous authorities. In his view the correspondence did not accord with this contention—it was clear in the correspondence that the Hospital repeatedly sought the involvement of the indemnifier in any settlement.

In light of the above, the Court refused the application sought.

[6.08] *Cunningham v Rochdale Metropolitan Borough Council[9]—Court of Appeal of England and Wales—Arnold, Dingemans and Andrews LJJ—appeal from the High Court—negligence—breach of statutory duty of care—risk assessments—causation—reasonable foreseeability*

This case concerned the violent assault of an assistant head teacher at a special education school for students with emotional and behavioural difficulties run by the respondent. The appellant had suffered a fractured cheekbone and psychiatric injuries as a result of the attack, ultimately leading to his retirement from teaching.

The student who had attacked the appellant had joined the school in 2012 but, following bereavements in his family, during 2015 his behaviour deteriorated. In September 2015 he attacked the appellant for the first time and on 5 October 2015 he attacked

---

9   *Cunningham v Rochdale Metropolitan Borough Council* [2021] ECWA Civ 1717.

another student. Both of these incidents resulted in his exclusion from school for a number of days.

There was an array of supports available to the student at school, including bereavement counselling, and meetings were held throughout 2015 in relation to his behaviour and progress. On 3 November 2015, he hit the appellant without warning.

The appellant brought a claim of negligence and breach of statutory duty against the respondent, which claim was dismissed by the High Court of England and Wales. The appellant's grounds for appeal centred on the High Court's failure to consider all aspects of the appellant's case. In particular, it did not consider the respondent's breach of its duty to conduct risk assessments, its failure to follow its internal policies in conducting a restorative justice meeting between the student in question and the appellant following the first incident, and there being no return to school interview when the student returned after that assault. The appellant argued that it was this breach of duty that caused the second assault on him. The respondent rejected this argument, stating the High Court was right to find that causation could not be established.

The Court of Appeal did not agree with the decision of the High Court, finding that the respondent was in breach of its statutory duty for failing to complete the necessary risk assessments relating to the particular student in question. The Court of Appeal also found that the respondent had breached its duty by not holding a return to school interview or a restorative justice interview. The Court found that it was reasonably foreseeable 'to the school and council that Mr Cunningham might be attacked by the Pupil' and so, for the appellant to succeed in his appeal, he would need to show that, without the respondent's 'omission to act', the attack of 5 November 2015 would not have occurred.

In that regard, the appellant failed; he did not succeed in proving on the balance of probabilities that either the provision of formal risk assessments, the holding of a return to school interview, or a restorative justice interview would have prevented the attack. The Court of Appeal commented that the respondent was, even in the absence of the relevant risk assessments, aware of the particular risks faced by the appellant when dealing with this student. Similarly, the respondent had facilitated interventions to improve the student's behaviour, such that the Court found the holding of these interviews would not have prevented a further attack on the appellant.

The appeal was dismissed.

REIMBURSEMENT OF DEPARTMENT OF SOCIAL PROTECTION

[6.09] *Fahy v Padraic Fahy Tiling Contractors Ltd[10]—High Court—Twomey J—Social Welfare (Consolidation) Act 2005, s 343R—employment torts—personal injury claims—social protection reimbursement*

---

[10]   *Fahy v Padraic Fahy Tiling Contractors Ltd* [2021] IEHC 682.

This case arose from the settlement of a personal injuries claim brought by the claimant, where he alleged that he sustained an injury while carrying out work for Padraic Fahy Tiling Contractors Ltd at premises belonging to the HSE. The company was not a mark for damages and a modest settlement was reached with the HSE.

Both the claimant and the respondent asked the Court to include 'consent terms' in a court order which would have the effect of relieving the HSE from having to reimburse the Department of Social Protection for the benefits paid to the plaintiff as a result of his injuries.

The Court had previously considered a very similar issue in *Szwarc*[11] and had found that the taxpayer should not be made to subsidise insurance companies who reach private settlements with personal injuries claimants and then apply to the Court for the terms agreed between them to be inserted into a court order.

In the present case, the plaintiff and the defendant sought to distinguish the *Szwarc* decision on the following grounds:

1. The defendant here was a State body as opposed to an insurance company and the parties therefore submitted that the outcome of inserting the 'consent terms' would simply be 'one arm of the State effectively subsidising another arm of the State, and not the taxpayer subsidising an insurance company'.
2. The parties were just asking the Court to 'note' the 'consent terms' in its order as opposed to asking it to make an order in the terms of the 'consent terms'.
3. The parties submitted that if the Court needed to be satisfied that there was 'evidence' in support of the 'consent terms' sought to be included in the court order, then they could call evidence during the 'consent hearing' in respect of same.

Under s 343R of the Social Welfare (Consolidation) Act 2005, where a defendant is found responsible for personal injuries suffered by a plaintiff, and the State has compensated the plaintiff in respect of same by way of disability payments, etc, the defendant must reimburse the State in respect of the disability payments made to the plaintiff. It is also clear under s 343R(1) that 'the reimbursement of the taxpayer *takes priority* over any settlement payment to the plaintiff'.

There is one exception to the above, ie, where there is 'an order of a court' which finds that the defendant is only, for example, 10% responsible for the injury in question. In such cases, the defendant will only be obliged to reimburse the Department/taxpayer 10% of the sums paid to the plaintiff. However, the Court noted that the situation is entirely different where the parties themselves reach an agreement that the defendant is only partially liable for the injuries sustained. In such circumstances it is in the financial interests of both parties to reach such an agreement and the responsibility of the defendant has not been determined by a Court having heard tested evidence.

---

[11] *Szwarc v Hanford Commercial t/a Maldron Hotel Wexford* [2021] IEHC 474, see **[6.10]**.

With regard to the submission that the Court should only 'note' the 'consent terms' in its order, the Court found that, regardless of how one phrases it, the purpose of inserting that there was 'no loss of earnings recovered against the HSE' would 'relieve the HSE from the obligation to reimburse the Department of €42,000'.

In relation to the parties' submission that evidence could be called during the consent hearing, the Court stated that it would still be the case that any such evidence would arise from 'parties with aligned interests' as both the plaintiff and the defendant had a financial interest in convincing the Court that the 'consent terms' sought should be inserted into the court order.

Finally, the Court considered the argument put forward that the Department and the defendant 'are on the same side'. While it acknowledged that there was some 'commercial logic' to the argument being made by the defendant, the Court did 'not believe that this is a question that the HSE can decide on behalf of the Department, or indeed that this Court can decide on behalf of the Department, that it should be deprived of its reimbursement of €42,000'.

The Court concluded that:

> the previously expressed reasons in the *Szwarc* case, for not inserting "consent terms" into an order for the purposes of s 343R(2) (a "s 343R(2) Order"), continue to apply, even if the defendant is a State body, and even if the "consent terms" are simply noted in the Court Order and even if "evidence" is provided to the Court *after* the parties have settled.

The Court found there were no sufficient grounds for distinguishing this case from *Szwarc* and refused to insert 'consent terms' into the court order.

[6.10]   *Condon v Health Service Executive; Monika Szwarc v Hanford Commercial Ltd t/a Maldron Hotel Wexford[12]—High Court—Twomey J—Social Welfare Consolidation Act 2005, s 343R(2)—personal injury—settlement agreement*

This *ex tempore* judgment concerned two very similar court applications which sought to have certain terms of a settlement agreement included in an order of the Court. The settlements had arisen in the context of two unrelated personal injuries actions.

The Court's judgment considered the meaning of court 'order' in s 343R(2) of the Social Welfare Consolidation Act 2005 and the issue of whether a court order:

> should contain terms (whether as recitals or in the body of the order) which are agreed between the parties as part of settlement and therefore are in this sense "on consent" of the parties.

The Court noted that there was an alternative argument that the terms of a court order under s 343R(2) should only be those that were decided by the Court having heard the evidence put forward. The Court noted that this argument was of particular relevance in cases where the 'agreed settlement terms' which the parties sought to have included in the court order would have a 'prejudicial effect on third parties, who are not parties to

---

[12]   *Condon v Health Service Executive; Monika Szwarc v Hanford Commercial Ltd t/a Maldron Hotel Wexford* [2021] IEHC 474.

the proceedings'. It noted that, in this case, the Department of Social Protection would be prejudiced financially by the orders sought.

The Court looked at s 343R and noted that the general rule under s 343R(1) is that the:

> defendant (usually but not always an "insurance company", and so this term is used) in a personal injuries claim arising from an accident, and who pays compensation to a plaintiff, must reimburse the Minister (since the payments are made by the "Department", this term will be used) the money paid by the Department to the plaintiff in respect of illness, partial capacity, injury benefits etc paid to a plaintiff as a result of the injury.

The Court stated that to grant the applications sought and to make an order which included the settlement terms agreed between the parties, would be to deny the Department/taxpayer of the repayment to which it would otherwise be entitled.

The Court considered whether the term court 'order' contained in s 343R allowed the Court to include settlement terms agreed between the parties, as opposed to terms ordered by the Court having heard evidence, in the court order.

It stated that a very important proviso under s 343R was that before the insurance company could be discharged from repaying the Department, there had to be an order of the Court in relation to the loss of earnings aspect of the compensation in question. In the Court's view, this was to make sure that, before the insurance company is discharged from making this repayment, there has been an 'independent and neutral verification process overseen by a judge who makes a determination regarding how much of the compensation is made up of loss of earnings'.

The Court held that, if a court order were made following this process, the Department would have the security of knowing that there were grounds and evidence for why they should not be repaid.

With regard to the difference between a court order arising from a settlement and a court order arising from a court hearing, the Court noted the following:

1. Unlike in an adversarial hearing, both parties' interests are aligned in a case where the parties have settled the matter and are seeking a court order on consent of both parties.
2. In the case before it, the court order sought by the parties would financially prejudice the Department, who was not a party to the application.
3. A court order sought to reflect settlement terms agreed between the parties, is sought on the basis of submissions on either side being made after the matter has settled. It is not based on an adversarial hearing where the relevant evidence was tested.
4. In considering an application brought by a plaintiff and a defendant/insurance company to have a court order made which includes agreed settlement terms, the Court stated that it should be borne in mind that it is in the direct financial interest of the defendant/insurance company to have the agreed terms included in the court order as this enables them to avoid repaying the Department.

Ultimately, in circumstances where there was no evidence that the Department consented to the court orders sought, the Court refused to make court orders which included terms of the settlement agreements reached between the parties.

PERSONAL INJURY—LIMITATION PERIODS

[6.11] *Blackpool Football Club Ltd v DSN[13]—Court of Appeal of England and Wales—Macur LJ, Stuart-Smith LJ and Sir Richards—appeal from the High Court—limitation periods—vicarious liability*

This case concerned an allegation of sexual abuse against FR. The claimant alleged that he had been sexually abused by FR during a footballing tour to New Zealand in June 1987. The claimant was 13 years old when the alleged assault took place and issued the proceedings over 30 years later, by which time FR was deceased.

The respondent was a professional football club and, at the time of the alleged abuse, it was in a terrible financial position and did not have the funds to employ many staff. It therefore had a number of staff members who assisted the club on a voluntary basis.

As a football club, the recruitment of talented players was vital to the respondent and evidence was submitted that FR behaved as a voluntary 'scout' for the respondent. FR had his own football team for young players and it was submitted that this team was viewed as a 'feeder' team for the respondent. FR had organised several footballing tours prior to the 1987 New Zealand trip and, with the exception of a donation of £500 from the respondent, the full cost of the trip was paid for by FR. There was no evidence that the respondent had any other involvement in the footballing tour to New Zealand.

In the High Court, the trial Judge disapplied the relevant primary limitation period and found the respondent football club vicariously liable for FR's acts. The respondent sought to appeal the trial Judge's decision on various grounds and was granted leave to appeal on four grounds. Grounds 2 and 4 challenged the decision in respect of the limitation period and grounds 7 and 8 challenged the vicarious liability decision.

The Court of Appeal first considered grounds 7 and 8 and looked at the law in relation to vicarious liability, including the following two-stage test for vicarious liability set out in *Various Claimants v Catholic Child Welfare Society*:[14]

> Stage 1 is to consider the relationship between D1 and D2 to see whether it is one that is capable of giving rise to vicarious liability. Stage 2 requires examination of the connection that links the relationship between D1 and D2 and the tortious act or omission of D1.

The Court of Appeal considered whether, on the 1987 trip, FR should be treated as an employee in his role as a 'scout' and, if so, how should stage 1 apply. It concluded that the trial Judge should not have found the relationship between the respondent and FR to be 'akin to employment'. It found that FR 'had a completely free hand about *how* he did his scouting' and there was also 'no evidence of any control or direction of *what* he should do'. The Court of Appeal held that there was only an 'informal association' between FR's football team and the respondent.

---

13 *Blackpool Football Club Ltd v DSN* [2021] EWCA Civ 1352.
14 *Various Claimants v Catholic Child Welfare Society* [2012] UKSC 56, [2013] 2 AC 1.

The Court of Appeal also noted that the fact that FR ran his own business on a full-time basis and only acted as an 'unpaid volunteer' for the respondent indicated that he acted independently. It further stated that 'there was a complete absence even of a vestigial degree of control'. The Court of Appeal therefore held that the requirements of stage 1 were not met.

In referring again to *Various Claimants v Catholic Child Welfare Society*, the Court of Appeal noted that 'it must be possible to say that the employer *significantly* increased the risk of the harm by putting the employee in his or her position and requiring him to perform the assigned task'. It stated that while it could be said that FR was placed in his position as a scout by the respondent, it found that 'it stretches meaning beyond breaking point to suggest that the club required him to organise and lead the trip'. The Court further stated that the respondent had had no responsibility in relation to the boys who went on the trip; nor had it 'entrusted them to {FR's} care'.

The Court of Appeal concluded that the 'requisite close connection linking the relationship between the club and FR and the sexual abuse he inflicted upon the Claimant while in New Zealand' was missing and, accordingly, the Court allowed the appeal on grounds 7 and 8.

The Court of Appeal then turned to consider grounds 2 and 4 and the disapplication of the relevant limitation period.

The Court found that the trial Judge had 'identified the correct principles to be applied' when he decided to allow the action to proceed. It also noted that the trial Judge had 'expressly considered' the effect of the lack of records and FR's death. The Court found that the trial Judge had been entitled to reach his conclusion that there was 'no real risk of substantial (or significant) prejudice' caused by the delay in the claimant issuing proceedings and accordingly dismissed the appeal on grounds 2 and 4.

[6.12]   *Balls v Reeve*[15]—*High Court of England and Wales—Pittaway QC— Limitation Act 1980, s 33—employment-related torts—personal injury claim— Statute of Limitations*

The claimant alleged that he had been exposed to asbestos while employed as a carpenter in Mr Thurlow's construction business and that this had resulted in him contracting asbestosis and suffering significant disability.

Mr Thurlow died in November 2015 and the claimant issued his claim in October 2019 against Mr Thurlow's personal representatives. The claim related to the period between 1979 and 1984 and the respondents submitted that the claim was statute barred.

The central point of the trial was the issue of limitation, although breach of duty and causation both remained in issue.

The respondents submitted that the claimant knew he had a respiratory condition in the 1990s and, in any event, by the 2000s. In his own oral evidence, the claimant stated that he might have told Mr Thurlow that he was suffering from breathing difficulties

---

[15]   *Balls v Reeve* [2021] EWHC 751 (QB).

in 2004. Evidence was also given by Mr Thurlow's son, daughter and son-in-law that they each remembered Mr Thurlow telling them that the claimant was suffering from asbestos or asbestosis. It was submitted that if Mr Thurlow had known that the claimant was complaining of an asbestos-related injury prior to his death, then the claimant had to also have known that he was suffering from an asbestos-related injury.

The respondents also referred to a medical report from September 2017, which reported on a chest x-ray of the claimant from August 2013 showing 'mild reticulation in both lung bases suggesting interstitial pulmonary fibrosis' and the fact that the claimant had made an industrial benefits application in 2017 seeking to have 25% disability back-dated to 2015.

The respondents further submitted that if the claimant did not have actual knowledge of his condition and its cause, he had constructive knowledge, as a reasonable person would have regarded the injury as significant and caused by his exposure to asbestos.

The claimant told the Court that he had not been diagnosed with asbestosis until 2017 and argued that time did not run 'until a claimant has obtained an expert medical diagnosis'.

In relation to the application of s 33 of the Limitation Act 1980, which allows for a discretionary exclusion of the time limit for personal injuries actions or actions arising from a death, the respondents argued that the question for the Court was whether it would be 'equitable to allow the action to proceed'. They submitted that this case related to matters which occurred four decades ago, the available documentation was very limited, Mr Thurlow was now deceased and the claimant himself would be a less reliable witness given the passage of time.

The claimant argued that he had a good, arguable claim and that the delay in issuing the proceedings arose from the fact that he was only diagnosed with asbestosis in 2017.

The Court found the claimant to be a truthful and feisty witness and found that he did not have actual knowledge of the injury, caused by his exposure to asbestos while in the employment of Mr Thurlow, until he was diagnosed with asbestosis in 2017. The Court also found that the claimant did not have constructive knowledge, based on the evidence which had been put before it.

Notwithstanding these findings, the Court went on to state that if it was wrong in relation to the date of the claimant's knowledge, then it would have exercised its discretion under s 33 of the Limitation Act 1980 and allowed the claim to proceed. The Court held that it would be unjust to deny the claimant the chance to pursue a remedy. It further held that even if Mr Thurlow had had the requisite knowledge in 2004, it was unlikely that the available evidence would have differed significantly from the evidence available at the time the proceedings were issued.

With regard to the claimant's exposure to asbestos and the cause of same, the Court was referred to the claimant's evidence in relation to the work he had carried out during the relevant period and the high levels of asbestos exposure involved. On the issue of causation, the claimant relied on the expert medical evidence which stated that the claimant's 'heavy exposure to asbestos is likely to meet the Helsinki Criteria for putting him at risk of developing asbestosis and asbestos related lung disease, but would obviously be for an occupational hygienist to confirm'. It was submitted that there had been no challenge to the diagnosis of asbestosis and that, as this is a condition that only arises from asbestos exposure and the only individual who had exposed the claimant to asbestos was Mr Thurlow, causation had been made out.

The Court ultimately held that the claimant had established that Mr Thurlow was in breach of duty and that, during the course of his employment with Mr Thurlow, the claimant had been required to work frequently with asbestos and no safety measures were taken to protect him. It also held that causation had been proven by the claimant and directed that judgment be entered for the claimant.

PERSONAL INJURY—COSTS

[6.13]   *Ward v An Post[16]—High Court—Heslin J—Legal Services Regulation Act 2015, s 168(1)—costs—personal injuries proceedings—costs follow the event— discretion of the court*

These proceedings related to the award of costs following a lengthy unsuccessful personal injury action.

The plaintiff argued that, despite being wholly unsuccessful in his personal injury claim, the Court should make no order as to costs, or in the alternative, only award the defendant a portion of their costs. The plaintiff sought to rely on the discretion of the Court in respect of the distribution of costs, noting that that it is open to the Court to depart from the default position that costs follow the event.

In this regard, the plaintiff submitted that the length of the trial had been increased by the fact that he had obtained injunctive relief two years prior to the trial, and by the defendant's conduct in the proceedings generally (eg, by refusing to engage in mediation). He further submitted that a majority of employment-related litigation is characterised by a no-costs regime and that the defendant had a significant litigation advantage.

In rejecting the plaintiff's submission, the Court held that the fact that the defendant was the plaintiff's employer did not automatically make the plaintiff's proceedings an 'employment law' claim—his claim was a personal injuries action relating to alleged bullying and harassment. The Court was satisfied that the length of time the case took to ultimately get to trial or the duration of the trial itself was unrelated to any act or omission of the defendant, and the prior injunction was deemed irrelevant. The Court further noted that the defendant could not be criticised for refusing to engage in mediation, given the plaintiff's failure to substantiate his claim.

The Court stated that the plaintiff was well aware of the risks he faced should he have failed in his claim, with the Court citing correspondence exchanged between the parties

---

[16]   *Ward v An Post* [2021] IEHC 471.

evidencing the defendant's numerous efforts to make his position clear as regards the costs. The Court also observed that the defendant offered to bear its own costs if the plaintiff would withdraw proceedings and would provide a facilitator to deal with the plaintiff's grievances. This offer was rejected by the plaintiff, in the full knowledge that should he be unsuccessful in his action, he would be at risk with respect to costs.

In terms of the Court's discretion in relation to costs awards, the Court noted that any such discretion should be exercised 'having regard to the particular nature and circumstances of the case, and the conduct of the proceedings by the parties', as stated in s 168(1) of the Legal Services Regulation Act 2015. The Court noted the high threshold set in *McCaffrey & Lunney v Central Bank of Ireland*,[17] where it was held that 'there must be something exceptional about the circumstances of the case to warrant departure from the normal rule' that costs should follow the event. The Court found that the threshold to justify a departure from the normal rule had not been met and made a costs award in favour of the defendant, as the successful party, to include all reserved costs and outlay, to be adjudicated in default of agreement.

---

[17] *McCaffrey & Lunney v Central Bank of Ireland* [2017] IEHC 659.

Chapter 7

European Union Law

INTRODUCTION

[7.01]   The European Court of Justice (ECJ) considered the implications of the denial of reimbursement under insurance in respect of medical costs for an individual who had travelled to another Member State for medical treatment in *Centraal Administratie Kantoor*.

In *Commission v Poland*, the ECJ considered a new system for disciplining judges introduced by Poland which raised concerns regarding the undermining of judicial independence.

Three cases regarding the free movement of workers are noted, namely *GMA, Katoen Natie Bulk Terminals NV* and *Onofrei*.

A lawyer's freedom to provide services was considered by the ECJ in *VK*. Three posted workers decisions are considered, namely *Hungary v European Parliament and European Council, Poland v European Parliament and Council of the European Union* and *Van den Bosch Transporten BV*.

The right to remain silent and to avoid self-incrimination was considered by the ECJ in *DB*. The ECJ considered social security benefits in the following six cases: *FORMAT, Team Power Europe, A, CG, INPS,* and *K*.

In *A v Petenni*, the ECJ considered the imposition of a fine by the Audit Committee at the Patent and Registration Office of Finland on a statutory auditor who took up a position in the company at which he had carried out a statutory audit.

CROSS-BORDER HEALTH CARE

[7.02]   *Y v Centraal Administratie Kantoor[1]—European Court of Justice—request for preliminary ruling from the Netherlands—Directive 2011/24/EU[2]—Regulation 883/2004,[3] arts 20 & 24—cross-border healthcare—insured person—benefit in kind*

---

1   *Y v Centraal Administratie Kantoor* (Case C-636/19).
2   Directive 2011/24/EU on the application of patients' rights in cross-border healthcare.
3   Regulation (EC) No 883/2004 on the coordination of social security systems.

The applicant was Dutch; she lived in Belgium and was in receipt of an old-age pension from the Netherlands. Under art 24 of Regulation 883/2004, the applicant was entitled to healthcare in her Member State of residence (Belgium), paid for by the Member State which paid her pension (the Netherlands). The applicant first consulted her general practitioner in Belgium, before attending consultations in the Netherlands, and subsequently travelled to Germany for medical opinions related to a diagnosis of breast cancer. Before travelling to Germany, the applicant requested prior authorisation, but proceeded to Germany without authorisation being granted. The applicant underwent surgery in Germany, remaining as an in-patient in a German hospital for 11 days and thereafter receiving post-operative care at the German hospital.

The applicant sought to have her medical expenses arising from her treatment in Germany reimbursed on her return home to Belgium. However, the respondent declined to reimburse the applicant on the basis that it viewed the treatment she received in Germany as 'scheduled treatment' under art 20 of Regulation 883/2004, in circumstances where the treatment was availed of in neither Belgium nor the Netherlands (ie, neither the Member State in which the applicant resided, nor the Member State that paid the applicant's pension), and no prior authorisation for the treatment had been obtained.

The applicant appealed that decision in the first instance to the District Court of Amsterdam, which upheld the respondent's decision. Upon further appeal by the applicant to the Higher Social Security and Civil Service Court, two questions were referred to the ECJ as preliminary issues:

1. The referring Court requested the ECJ to confirm whether the applicant could be treated as an 'insured person' for the purposes of Directive 2011/24 (if the applicant could be so treated, the costs associated with her post-operative treatments would not be dependent on prior authorisation); and

2. If the ECJ found that the applicant could not be treated as an 'insured person', the referring Court requested the ECJ to confirm whether in light of art 56 (Freedom to Provide Services) of the Treaty of the Functioning of the European Union (the TFEU), the requirement for prior authorisation—and the resultant refusal by the respondent to reimburse the applicant's costs—contradicted the principle of free movement of services within the EU.

The ECJ considered the first question in light of the fact that the applicant was not compulsorily insured in the Netherlands, but was rather contractually insured in the Netherlands. However, the ECJ confirmed that the nature of the insurance was immaterial—the key consideration in order for a person to be considered 'insured' is whether he/she satisfies the conditions applied by the Member State responsible for providing the benefit.

Thus, the question to be answered (by the referring Court) became whether the applicant satisfied the eligibility criteria under Dutch law for the benefits in kind in question. Although reserved to the referring Court, the ECJ noted that the Dutch authorities had already acknowledged during the proceedings that there were no other conditions other than the one relating to 'prior authorisation'. On that basis, it was evident that in order to be an 'insured person', an individual must:

1. be in receipt of a pension from a Member State;
2. not be entitled to benefits in kind under the national laws of the Member State of residence (being a different Member State to the one from which the individual receives pension payments); and
3. be entitled to benefits in kind under the national laws of the Member State who pays the pension.

The ECJ was satisfied that the applicant should indeed be treated as an 'insured person', and that as such under art 7(1) of Directive 2011/24 she had grounds to expect her post-operative treatment costs would be reimbursed. The ECJ did not accept the respondent's contention that the applicant's post-operative treatment was subject to prior authorisation under art 8 of Directive 2011/24, because the Dutch legislature had not incorporated a 'prior authorisation' mechanism into its national law implementing Directive 2011/24.

However, as a result of the ECJ's conclusion in relation to the first preliminary issue, ie, the applicant could be reimbursed for her post-operative treatment, reimbursement would not extend to cover the cost of her surgeries and hospital stay, due to the distinction between 'scheduled' (Regulation 883/2004, art 20) and 'unscheduled' treatment (Regulation 883/2004, art 19). The referring Court had previously determined that the applicant's operative care and hospital costs must be treated as 'scheduled' treatment under art 20 of Regulation 883/2004, which necessitated prior authorisation (particularly in circumstances where there was a week-long period between the applicant's consultation in the Netherlands and her travelling to Germany, during which she could have returned to Belgium for treatment, which the referring Court had determined undermined any argument that the operative treatment was so urgent as to be 'unscheduled').

EFFECTIVE LEGAL PROTECTION

[7.03] *Commission v Poland[4]—European Court of Justice—application from the European Commission—Treaty on European Union, art 19(1)—Treaty on the Functioning of the European Union, art 267—judicial protection—independence—impartiality*

This was an application from the European Commission for interim measures requesting the ECJ to order Poland to suspend a new system for disciplining judges of the Supreme Court and of the ordinary courts in Poland. This system included the creation of a disciplinary chamber within the Supreme Court to adjudicate over disciplinary cases involving judges of the Supreme Court, and, on appeal judges of the ordinary courts.

---

4   *Commission v Poland* (Case C-791/19).

In its first complaint the European Commission argued that Poland had failed to fulfil its obligations under TEU, art 19(1) and TFEU, art 267 on the impartiality and independence of the disciplinary chamber, whose members were selected by the newly-revised National Council of the Judiciary (consisting of 25 members, 23 of whom were appointed by the Polish Parliament).

The ECJ upheld this complaint, as judicial independence could not be guaranteed in circumstances where the judiciary may be influenced either directly or indirectly by the Polish legislature and executive.

In relation to the first complaint, the Commission further submitted that as the definitions of conduct that would constitute a disciplinary offence by a judge of the ordinary courts included any 'obvious and gross violations of the law' and any 'error' entailing an 'obvious violation of the law', Polish legislation facilitated political control. This was 'evidenced, moreover, by the various specific cases where those provisions have been applied that have been referred to by that institution'.

The ECJ upheld this complaint, finding that such provisions 'undermine the independence of those judges and do so, what is more, at the cost of a reduction in the protection of the value of the rule of law in Poland', in breach of the second subparagraph of art 19(1) TEU.

The Commission summarised the second complaint as:

> in the light of the particular context in which the Disciplinary Chamber was created, certain characteristics of that chamber, and the process leading to the appointment of the judges called upon to sit in that chamber, that body does not meet the requirements of independence and impartiality thus required under the second subparagraph of Article 19(1) TEU.

The ECJ noted the following factors in its determination:

1. The National Council of the Judiciary was overhauled following new legislation, so that 23 out of the 25 members of the National Council of the Judiciary (responsible for selecting the Disciplinary Chamber) were appointed by the Polish legislature, or were members thereof; thereby undermining the independence of that body.
2. The newly constituted National Council of the Judiciary was established by reducing the four-year term of office of the previous members.
3. The legislative reform governing the establishment and amended composition of the National Council of the Judiciary also included the creation of the Disciplinary Chamber and a mechanism for lowering the retirement age for existing judges of the Supreme Court.
4. As a result of the premature termination of serving officers of the existing National Council of the Judiciary and the Supreme Court, numerous posts would be made vacant which would be filled by appointees nominated by the Polish legislature.

The ECJ upheld the second complaint, stating these factors 'give rise to legitimate doubts as to the independence of the [National Council of the Judiciary] and its role in an appointment process such as that resulting in the appointment of the members of the Disciplinary Chamber'.

The third complaint was summarised by the ECJ as:

> in the absence, in particular, of any criteria laid down by law to circumscribe the exercise of that power, that power could be used in order to assign a case to a specific disciplinary court and, consequently, at the very least, be perceived as a means whereby the disciplinary regime could be used for the purposes of political control of the content of judicial decisions. Furthermore, such a risk is increased in the present case by the fact that the Disciplinary Chamber is not an independent and impartial body.

In upholding this third complaint the ECJ found that the new appointment process designating the disciplinary tribunal which would hear disciplinary proceedings relating to judges of the ordinary courts who could be responsible for interpreting and applying EU law did not satisfy the second subparagraph of art 19(1) TEU 'that such cases must be examined by a tribunal "established by law"'.

The ECJ summarised the Commission's fourth complaint as consisting of two parts, ie, the Polish laws governing the ordinary courts did not ensure:

1. the hearing, 'within a reasonable time of disciplinary cases concerning judges of those courts'; or
2. the rights of defence of the accused judge'.

The ECJ upheld the third complaint in its entirety.

Finally, the ECJ upheld the complaint that the provisions of both the law on the ordinary courts and the law of the Supreme Court 'may expose a judge to disciplinary proceedings upon the adoption of a decision to submit a request for a preliminary ruling to the Court of Justice, which infringes Article 267 TFEU'.

The ECJ upheld all the complaints submitted by the Commission and found that the Republic of Poland had failed to fulfil its obligations under the second subparagraph of art 19(1) TEU.

FREE MOVEMENT OF WORKERS

[7.04] *GMA v Etat Belge[5]—European Court of Justice—request for preliminary ruling from Belgium—Treaty on the Functioning of the European Union, art 45—freedom of movement*

This was a request for a preliminary ruling on the interpretation of art 45 TFEU. The case emerged from Belgium's refusal to grant the applicant, a Greek national, a right of residence for more than three months as a jobseeker in Belgium.

The applicant initially sought a certificate of registration in Belgium as a jobseeker in order to obtain a right of residence for more than three months in October 2015.

---

5   *GMA v Etat Belge* Case C-710/19.

This application was refused and the subsequent case the applicant brought against the Belgian Immigration Office was dismissed.

The applicant then brought an appeal on a point of law before the Council of State which referred the question to the ECJ. The applicant argued that the 'reasonable period of time' that Member States are obliged to grand jobseekers from other Member States cannot be less than six months and during this time the jobseeker does not need to prove that he has a genuine chance of being engaged. The applicant also argued that the fact he got a job after the decision by the Belgian Immigration Office should have been taken into consideration.

There were two questions referred by the Council of State but the ECJ found that the answers to the first question also addressed the second question.

> Is Article 45 [TFEU] to be interpreted and applied as meaning that the host Member State is required (1) to allow jobseekers a reasonable period of time to acquaint themselves with potentially suitable employment opportunities and take the necessary steps to obtain employment, (2) to accept that the time allowed for seeking employment cannot in any circumstances be less than six months, and (3) to permit a jobseeker to stay within its territory for the whole of that period, without requiring him or her to prove that he or she has a real chance of obtaining employment?

In answering this question the ECJ noted that it could rely on all the points of interpretation in EU law when addressing a question even if the point is not referred to the ECJ in the question.

The ECJ then went on to state that the term 'worker' under art 45 TFEU has an autonomous meaning and must not be interpreted narrowly, so that a person genuinely seeking work must be classified as a 'worker'.

In response to the first part of the question, noting that the freedom of movement for workers is one of the foundations of the EU, the ECJ stated that this must be interpreted broadly. The Court continued:

> Consequently, it must be held that the host Member State is required to allow jobseekers a reasonable period of time to apprise themselves of offers of employment corresponding to their occupational qualifications and to take, where appropriate, the necessary steps in order to be engaged.

In response to the second part of the question on time, the Court noted that during the first three months an EU citizen enters a host Member State under, 'no condition other than the requirement to hold a valid identity document is to be imposed on that citizen'. The Court also noted that the 'reasonable period of time' starts to run when the EU citizen registers as a jobseeker. The Court concluded 'a period of six months from the date of registration does not appear, in principle, to be insufficient and does not call into question the effectiveness of Article 45 TFEU'.

In response to the third part of the question, the ECJ found that the Member State may require the jobseeker to provide evidence that he or she is seeking employment but 'only after the reasonable period of time has elapsed that the jobseeker is required to provide evidence not only that he or she is continuing to seek employment but also that he or she has a genuine chance of being engaged'.

[7.05] ***Katoen Natie Bulk Terminals NV v Belgische Staat and Ministerraad[6]—European Court of Justice—preliminary reference from Belgium—Treaty on the Functioning of the European Union, arts 45, 49, 56—freedom of establishment—freedom of movement of workers—freedom to provide services—dockers—port activities***

Belgian law[7] states that only recognised dockers can carry out dock work at ports in Belgium. It also stipulates the required conditions and processes an individual must complete to become a recognised docker, and provides conditions whereby a recognised docker becomes a member of the national quota of dockers.

In 2014, the European Commission informed Belgium that its laws in relation to dockers infringed upon art 49 TFEU and the freedom of establishment. The European Commission stated that Belgian law dissuaded undertakings from other Member States establishing in Belgium, as freedom to choose their own staff was restricted. In response, Belgium adopted the Royal Decree of 2016, which attempted to balance the need for improved competition in Belgian ports with the need to protect dockers. As a result, the European Commission closed its related infringement proceedings.

Katoen Natie Bulk Terminals and General Services Antwerp are two Belgian undertakings engaged in port operations in Belgium and abroad. They brought a request to the Belgian Council of State to annul the Royal Decree of 2016. They claimed the Royal Decree of 2016 restricted their freedoms when hiring dockers. On the basis of that request, the Belgian Council of State referred seven questions to the ECJ for preliminary ruling.

The questions related to the national quota of dockers, the requirements to become a recognised docker, automatic recognition, the renewal of recognition, the mobility of dockers between ports and safety certificates.

Middlegate Europe is an international road haulage company, established in Belgium. Middlegate Europe faced an administrative fine from the Belgian police for allowing unrecognised dockers to carry out dock work at Belgian ports. They brought an action against the decision in the Constitutional Court, Belgium. This was following unsuccessful challenges of the fine before the lower courts in Belgium.

Middlegate Europe argued that Belgian law in relation to dock work restricted freedoms, as guaranteed by both the Belgian Constitution and the TFEU. The Constitutional Court of Belgium, referred two questions to the ECJ for preliminary ruling. These questions predominantly related to the requirement that only recognised dockers can carry out dock work at Belgian ports, even when the work does not involve the loading and unloading of ships.

The above cases were joined by the ECJ.

---

6   *Katoen Natie Bulk Terminals NV v Belgische Staat and Ministerraad* Case C-407/19.
7   Royal Decree of July 2016 amending the Royal Decree of 5 July 2004 on the recognition of dock workers in port areas falling within the scope of the Law of 8 June 1972 organising dock work.

The ECJ found that arts 49 and 56 TFEU do not preclude Belgian law from ensuring that those engaged in dock work are recognised workers and meet a set of stipulated conditions, provided those conditions are unbiased and transparent. The ECJ found that the equal treatment of dockers, the availability of specialised labour, and safety were all reasons of public interest with the capability to justify restrictions on freedoms.

The requirements for a Belgian resident to become a recognised docker include completion of a medical assessment, tests and preparatory training. Non-resident dockers must prove they satisfy comparable conditions in another Member State. The ECJ found that arts 45, 49 and 56 TFEU do not preclude the imposition of these requirements, which are justified on grounds of safety, so long as they are imposed in a transparent and impartial manner.

Dockers recognised under the old statutory regime in Belgium are automatically included in the national quota of recognised dockers. The applicant companies argued that these dockers would be reluctant to leave the quota, negatively affecting the ability to recruit directly. The ECJ found that arts 45, 49 and 56 TFEU do not preclude national legislation continuing the recognition afforded to these dockers under the previous statutory regime.

The ECJ also considered the restrictions on dockers seeking to work in Belgian ports other than the ports where they were recognised. The ECJ found that arts 45, 49 and 56 TFEU do not preclude the attaching of conditions to the movement of dockers between ports. This restriction is justifiable in order to ensure the safe operation of each port, providing the measures are necessary and proportionate.

In relation to the need for workers carrying out logistics work to hold a safety certificate, the ECJ found that arts 45, 49 and 56 TFEU do not preclude Belgian law from imposing such a requirement, which is again justifiable in the context of safety so long as the administrative burden does not become disproportionate or unreasonable.

Middlegate Europe argued that Belgian law concerning dockers should not apply to those who are working at Belgian ports, but who are not loading or unloading ships. The ECJ found that neither art 49 nor 56 TFEU precludes Belgian law from requiring the aforementioned workers to be recognised dockers. Although this requirement may disincentivise undertakings from establishing and/or carrying out port activities in Belgium, it can be justified based on ensuring workplace safety.

However, the ECJ did find that arts 45, 49 and 56 of the TFEU preclude the following:

1. Whether or not a docker is recognised in Belgium for the purposes of the Royal Decree of 5 July 2004, as amended by the Royal Decree of 10 July 2016 is decided by an Administrative Committee comprised of members from employers' and workers' organisations (the Administrative Committee).
2. The Administrative Committee also decide whether a recognised docker will be included in the national quota of dockers, basing this decision on the need for labour. For workers not included in the national quota of dockers, their recognition only lasts for the duration of their employment contract. For each new employment, they will be required to complete a separate recognition procedure.

The ECJ acknowledged that periodic renewal of recognition ensures dockers continue to have the skills required to work safely, but currently this requirement does not apply to all. Those in the pool of dockers do not have to comply with this requirement. There are no grounds for this differing treatment.

3.   The ECJ questioned the knowledge and impartiality of the Administrative Committee and found that it was neither appropriate nor justified that the Administrative Committee was not required to abide by prescribed deadlines when making its decisions.

[7.06]   *Onofrei v Conseil de l'ordre des avocats au barreau de Paris[8]—European Court of Justice—Treaty on the Functioning of the European Union, arts 45 & 49—free movement of persons—freedom of establishment—access to the profession of lawyer—exemption from training and diploma requirements*

The Court de cassation, France referred a question to the ECJ regarding whether the French rules governing admission to the legal profession were incompatible with arts 45 and 49 of the TFEU concerning freedom of establishment and free movement of workers.

Under French law, a person must satisfy the following conditions to gain entry to the legal profession: (i) they must be a French national or a national of an EU or EEA Member State; (ii) they must hold at least a Master's degree in law or qualifications recognised as equivalent; and (iii) they must undergo theoretical and practical training provided by French regional centres and must hold a 'certificate of competence for the profession of lawyer'.

Certain categories of French civil servants, former civil servants and persons treated as civil servants are exempt from the requirements at (iii) above and the applicant in the main proceedings, an official of the EU, applied for admission to the Paris Bar under this exemption.

The applicant was refused admission under this exemption, as she had never carried out public/administrative duties in the French civil service. This refusal was confirmed by the Paris Court of Appeal, which held that the requirement to have experience with French law was necessary to 'guarantee the full, relevant and effective exercise' of litigants' rights.

The applicant appealed to the Court de cassation, which stayed the proceedings and referred the following questions to the ECJ:

1.   Does the principle that the ... [TFEU], has created its own legal system, which is integrated into the legal systems of the Member States and which their courts are bound to apply, preclude national legislation which makes the grant of an exemption from the training and diploma requirements laid down, in principle, for entry to the profession of lawyer, dependent on the requirement of sufficient knowledge, on the part of the person requesting exemption, of national law of French origin, so that similar knowledge of the law of the European Union alone is not taken into account?

---

[8]   *Onofrei v Conseil de l'ordre des avocats au barreau de Paris* (Case C-218/19).

2. Do Articles 45 and 49 TFEU preclude national legislation which restricts an exemption from the training and diploma requirements laid down, in principle, for entry to the profession of lawyer, to certain members of the civil service of the same Member State who have performed legal work in that capacity, in France, in an administration or a public service or an international organisation, and which excludes from the scope of that exemption members or former members of the European civil service who have performed legal work in that capacity, in one or more fields of the law of the European Union, within the European Commission?

The ECJ noted that in principle, the performance of work in a regulated profession (such as the legal profession) is covered by art 49 TFEU (freedom of establishment) and, insofar as the work is salaried, art 45 TFEU (free movement of workers) may also apply. However, the Court also noted that as long as no harmonisation measures have been set across the Union (which, in the case of the legal profession, they have not), Member States are entitled to set the entry requirements for that occupation.

The Court noted that a restriction on the freedom of movement can only be permissible if it is justified by an overriding reason in the public interest and is proportionate. In this regard, the Court noted that case law has held that the protection of consumers, in particular recipients of legal services provided by persons involved in the administration of justice, and, second, the proper administration of justice are objectives which feature among those which may be regarded as overriding reasons in the public interest capable of justifying restrictions on the freedom to provide services and on the free movement of workers and the freedom of establishment.

The ECJ held that the requirements that, to avail of the exemption, a person must be a member of the French civil service, having worked in France as a member of that civil service and having practised French law, were in principle capable of justification by reference to those objectives. However, it held that the requirements failed the proportionality test and went beyond what was necessary to achieve those objectives. The Court noted:

it cannot, *a priori*, be ruled out that a candidate who is a member of a civil service other than the French civil service, inter alia, the EU civil service, such as Ms Onofrei, has practised French law outside French territory in such a way as to have acquired satisfactory knowledge of it, a fortiori when, as is apparent from the order for reference, the national legislation at issue in the main proceedings does not require, for purposes of the examination of an application for exemption from the training and diploma requirements, that candidates should have knowledge of any field of national law specifically relating to the organisation of the national courts and tribunals or procedures before them.

As such, the Court held that in answer to the questions referred, arts 45 and 49 TFEU must be interpreted as:

(i) precluding national legislation which restricts an exemption from the requirements of professional training and holding a certificate of competence to exercise the profession of lawyer laid down, in principle, for entry to the profession of lawyer, to certain members of the civil service of a Member State who have performed legal work in that capacity in that Member State, in an administration or a public service or an international organisation, and which excludes from the scope of that exemption officials, members or former members of the EU civil service who have performed legal work in that capacity in an EU institution and outside French territory;

(ii) not precluding national legislation which makes such an exemption contingent on the person concerned having performed legal work in the field of national law, and excluding from the scope of that exemption officials, members or former members of the EU civil service who have performed legal work in that capacity, in one or more fields of EU law, provided that that national legislation does not exclude account from being taken of legal work involving the practice of national law.

FREEDOM TO PROVIDE SERVICES

[7.07] *VK v An Bord Pleanála[9]—European Court of Justice—reference for a preliminary ruling from Ireland—lawyers' freedom to provide services—Directive 77/249/EEC,[10] art 5—obligation for a visiting lawyer representing a client in domestic legal proceedings to work in conjunction with a lawyer who practises before the judicial authority in question*

VK represented himself in proceedings before the Irish Supreme Court. A request for a preliminary ruling was made to the ECJ where VK was represented by a lawyer, Ms O, who was established in Germany. When the case returned to the Irish Supreme Court, VK wished to engage the services of Ms O to represent him in Ireland. Ms O was not established in Ireland, however, she did claim to have practised in Ireland for several years. A further request for a preliminary ruling was made to the ECJ as to whether Irish law was compatible with EU law in so far as it required a visiting lawyer to use the services of a lawyer who practises before the judicial authority in question, including in proceedings in which a party is entitled to conduct his or her own defence.

The questions referred were, in essence:

1. Is a Member State precluded from exercising the option in art 5 of Directive 77/249/EEC, which permits a Member State to impose a requirement on a lawyer who is engaged in representing a client in legal proceedings 'to work in conjunction with a lawyer who practises before the judicial authority in question', in proceedings where the party whom the visiting lawyer wishes to represent would be entitled to self-represent?

2. If not, what factors should a national court assess in determining whether it is permissible to impose a requirement to work 'in conjunction with'?

3. In particular, would the imposition of a limited obligation to work 'in conjunction with', be a proportionate interference in the freedom of lawyers to provide services so as to be justified, in light of the public interest involved, ie, the need to protect consumers of legal services and the need to secure the proper administration of justice?

4. If so, does that position apply in all circumstances and, if not, what factors should a national court consider in deciding whether such a requirement can be imposed in a particular case?

---

9   *VK v An Bord Pleanála* (Case C-739/19).
10   Directive 77/249/EEC to facilitate the effective exercise by lawyers of freedom to provide services.

In considering the questions referred, the ECJ noted that Directive 77/249/EEC must be read in light of art 56 TFEU which prohibits any restriction on the freedom to provide services and requires the abolition of all discrimination against the person providing the service by reason of his or her nationality or the fact that he or she is established in a Member State other than that in which the service is to be provided.

The ECJ noted that any obligation imposed by national legislation which requires a lawyer from one Member State to work alongside another from the Member State in which the proceedings are based constitutes a restriction on the freedom to provide services in so far as it means that the litigant who wishes retain the services of a lawyer from a different Member State will bear additional costs to a litigant who wishes to retain the services of a lawyer established in the litigant's Member State. However such a restriction could be justified as the restriction seeks to protect the proper administration of justice and the litigant as a consumer, provided such a restriction is appropriate for achieving these objectives and only goes as far as is necessary to do so. In this case, Ms O practised in Ireland for several years, which suggested that she would be capable of representing the litigant in the same way as a domestic lawyer would be. The ECJ held that it was for the Irish Supreme Court to determine if this was the case.

The ECJ noted that the requirement for foreign-local lawyer collaboration is permitted under art 5, but not as a blanket rule and there may be circumstances in which the requirement is not justified; such circumstances fell to be determined by the national court.

The ECJ concluded:

1. Article 5 does not preclude a lawyer from being required to work 'in conjunction with' a lawyer 'who practises before the judicial authority in question' in circumstances where a litigant is entitled to self-represent.
2. The obligation for a visiting lawyer to work 'in conjunction with' a lawyer 'who practises before the judicial authority in question' is not disproportionate and is justified by the objective of the proper administration of justice.
3. However, 'a general obligation to work in conjunction with a lawyer who practises before the judicial authority in question not allowing account to be taken of the experience of the visiting lawyer would go beyond what is necessary in order to attain the objective of the proper administration of justice'.

POSTING OF WORKERS

[7.08] *Hungary v European Parliament and European Council[11]—European Court of Justice—action for annulment from Hungary—Directive 96/71/EC[12]—Directive 2018/957/EU[13]—freedom to provide services*

---

[11] *Hungary v European Parliament and European Council* Case C-620/18.
[12] Directive 96/71/EC concerning the posting of workers in the framework of the provision of services.
[13] Directive 2018/957/EU amending Directive 96/71/EC concerning the posting of workers in the framework of the provision of services.

Hungary applied to the ECJ to annul Directive 2018/957/EU (the 2018 Directive), and in the alternative, annul certain provisions of the 2018 Directive. The 2018 Directive introduced a number of amendments to Directive 96/71/EC (the Posted Workers Directive).

The aim of the Posted Workers Directive is to guarantee to workers posted to Member States the terms and conditions of employment as are laid down in that Member State by law, regulation or administrative provisions, or by collective agreements or arbitration awards which have been declared universally applicable. The 2018 Directive seeks to further enhance this protection.

The 2018 Directive amended art 3(1) of the Posted Workers Directive to expressly guarantee equality of treatment of posted workers in relation to remuneration, the conditions of workers accommodation where provided by the employer, and allowances or reimbursement of expenditure to cover travel, board and lodging expenses. Article 3 was further amended to provide that the concept of remuneration should be determined by the national law and/or practice of the host Member State and includes 'all the constituent elements of remuneration rendered mandatory by national law, regulation or administrative provision, or by collective agreements or arbitration awards which, in that Member State, have been declared universally applicable'. This concept of 'remuneration' replaced the idea of 'minimum rates of pay'.

The 2018 Directive also introduced art 3(1a) of the Posted Workers Directive which provides that where the posting of the worker exceeds 12 months, or more than 18 months if the service provider submits a motivated notification, the host Member State must guarantee equality of treatment in relation to all terms and conditions of employment as laid down in the national law of that Member State.

Hungary relied on five points in seeking to have the 2018 Directive annulled:

1. ***The choice of an incorrect legal basis for the adoption of the 2018 Directive***: Article 53(1) and art 62 TFEU were used as the legal basis for the adoption of the 2018 Directive. Hungary submitted that this was the incorrect legal basis as the 2018 Directive's principal aim is the protection of workers—it does not address the removal of obstacles to the freedom to provide services. Hungary submitted that in light of the objective of the 2018 Directive, art 153(2)(b) is the appropriate legal basis.
2. ***Disregard of art 153(5) TFEU and misuse of powers***: Hungary submitted that the 2018 Directive was contrary to art 153(5) which excludes the regulation of pay in the employment context as a competency of the EU legislature. It submitted that the amendments introduced by the 2018 Directive effectively require the application of mandatory national laws with respect to remuneration. It further submitted that the choice of the incorrect legal basis 'is a means of concealing the misuse of powers committed by the Union' in adopting the 2018 Directive.
3. ***Infringement of art 56 TFEU***: In brief, Hungary submitted that the 2018 Directive distorts competition in removing the competitive edge of certain Member States in which the level of pay is lower. Furthermore, the posting of workers is temporary in nature, and in this context the 2018 Directive goes beyond what is necessary

to protect posted workers. Finally, Hungary submitted that the 2018 Directive is contrary to art 58 TFEU in so far as it purports to apply to the transport sector.

4. ***Infringement of art 56 TFEU in that the 2018 Directive precludes the effective implementation of the freedom to provide services***: Article 1(1)(b) of the 2018 Directive states that the Posted Workers Directive cannot affect the right to strike or take collective action. Hungary alleged that this is contrary to art 56 TFEU in that it excludes the exercise of the right to strike or take collective action from the scope of art 56 TFEU.

5. ***Disregard of the Rome I Regulation***[14] ***and the principles of legal certainty and legislative clarity***: Finally, Hungary submitted that art 3(1a) contravenes the Rome I Regulation, art 3(1a) provides that where the posting is longer than 12 months, the obligations on the host Member State apply, irrespective of which law is applicable; whereas the Rome I Regulation stipulates that the applicable law is to be determined by reference to whether or not the employee is obliged to return to their country of origin after completion of work abroad, and contains no reference to length of service.

The ECJ dismissed the action in its entirety. The ECJ found that, when determining the correct legal basis for the 2018 Directive, regard must be had to the objective and content of the Posted Workers Directive. In so doing, the ECJ found that the objective of the 2018 Directive was to obtain a balance between ensuring undertakings have the opportunity to supply services within the internal market by posted workers, and ensuring these posted workers are protected. The correct legal basis had therefore been used. Furthermore, the ECJ rejected the submission that art 153 is the appropriate legal basis, as art 153 is concerned solely with the protection of workers and does not address the freedom to provide services, which is an objective of the 2018 Directive.

In rejecting the submission that the 2018 Directive is contrary to art 153(5), the ECJ found that the 2018 Directive does no more than coordinate the legislation of Member States as regards the treatment of posted workers. Furthermore, the ECJ noted that art 153(5) provides for a specific exception to the competences that the Union derives from the initial provisions of art 153; therefore, as art 153 cannot be a legal basis for the 2018 Directive, art 153(5) cannot affect the validity of the 2018 Directive. The ECJ also found that there was no misuse of power as the correct legal basis had been used for the adoption of the 2018 Directive.

In rejecting Hungary's third plea, the ECJ noted that the 2018 Directive, in enhancing the protection of posted workers, seeks to 'safeguard the freedom to provide ... services on a fair basis'. It does not nullify or distort competition. Furthermore, it does not eliminate all competition based on costs, as it does not affect any other cost components of undertakings, such as productivity or efficiency of workers. The 2018 Directive both creates a 'truly integrated and competitive internal market' and a 'genuine social convergence' through the uniform application of rules on the terms and conditions of employment. Furthermore, the ECJ found that the 2018 Directive does not go beyond what was necessary in order to achieve its objectives. In that regard, the ECJ relied on

---

[14] Regulation (EC) No 593/2008 on the law applicable to contractual obligations (Rome I).

an impact assessment conducted by the Commission on the Posted Workers Directive which found that there were substantial differences in remuneration in several host Member States between workers of undertakings established in the Member States and posted workers. The ECJ also rejected the submission that the 2018 Directive applies to the field of transport. The wording of art 3(3) states that the 2018 Directive applies to the road transport industry from the date of the application of a legislative act amending Directive 2006/22,[15] which has, as its legal basis, art 71(1) EC Treaty, which corresponds with art 91 TFEU. Therefore, the 2018 Directive does not seek to regulate the freedom to provide services in the area of transport.

The ECJ rejected the applicant's fourth plea. It found that art 1(1)(b) does not exclude industrial action from the scope of art 53. In fact, art 1(1)(b) expressly refers to these rights as existing at 'Union level' and as such the exercise of these rights must be assessed in light of EU law.

Finally, the ECJ rejected Hungary's submission that art 3(1a) of the 2018 Directive contravenes the Rome I Regulation. It found that art 3(1a) in fact constitutes a special conflict-of-law rule, under art 23 of the Rome I Regulation. Furthermore, in so far as the applicant alleged that the concept of 'remuneration' contravenes the principles of legal certainty and legislative clarity, the ECJ observed that the 2018 Directive refers to the concept of 'remuneration' as determined by national law or practice and as such, it cannot be alleged that the concept lacks certainty.

[7.09] *Poland v European Parliament and Council of the European Union*[16]*— European Court of Justice—action for annulment from Poland—Directive 96/71/EC*[17]*—Directive 2018/957/EU*[18]*—freedom to provide services*

This action was brought by Poland, which sought to annul Directive 2018/957 (the 2018 Directive) which amends certain provisions of Directive 96/71/EC (the Posted Workers Directive). The amendments introduced by the 2018 Directive seeks to ensure that the terms and conditions of employment of posted workers are as close as possible to those of workers employed in the host Member States.

Article 3(1) of the Posted Workers Directive, which provides for the equality of treatment of posted workers, was amended by the 2018 Directive to include equality in relation to remuneration, the conditions of workers accommodation where provided by the employer, and allowances or reimbursement of expenditure to cover travel, board and lodging expenses. Article 3 was further amended to provide that the concept of remuneration should be determined by the national law and/or practice of the host Member State and to include 'all the constituent elements of remuneration rendered mandatory by national law, regulation or administrative provision, or by collective

---

15 Directive 2006/22/EC on minimum conditions for the implementation of Council Regulations (EEC) No 3820/85 and (EEC) No 3821/85 concerning social legislation relating to road transport activities and repealing Council Directive 88/599/EEC.
16 *Poland v European Parliament and Council of the European Union* Case C-626/18.
17 Directive 96/71/EC concerning the posting of workers in the framework of the provision of services.
18 Directive 2018/957 amending Directive 96/71/EC concerning the posting of workers in the framework of the provision of services.

agreements or arbitration awards which, in that Member State, have been declared universally applicable'.

Furthermore, the 2018 Directive introduced art 3(1a) of the Posted Workers Directive which provides that where the posting of the worker exceeds 12 months, or more than 18 months if the service provider submits a motivated notification, the Member State must guarantee equality of treatment in relation to all terms and conditions of employment as laid down in law, regulation, administrative provision or any universally applicable collective agreements of arbitration awards.

Poland sought to annul the provisions of the 2018 Directive introducing these amendments to the Posted Workers Directive, or in the alternative annul the entire 2018 Directive.

It sought to rely on three pleas:

1. ***The choice of an incorrect legal basis for the adoption of the contested Directive***: Poland submitted that art 53(1) and art 62 TFEU were the incorrect legal basis for Directive 2018/957. It submitted that as the purpose of the 2018 Directive was to enhance the protection of posted workers, the correct legal basis was the relevant social policy provisions of the TFEU Treaty.

2. ***Infringement of art 56 TFEU***: Poland argued that the 2018 Directive restricts the freedom to provide services as provided for in art 56 TFEU. It submitted that the requirement to ensure posted workers are paid remuneration compatible with the law and practice of the host Member States and to guarantee terms and conditions comparative with law and practice if the duration of the posting exceeds 12 months, constitutes a discriminatory restriction on the freedom to provide services. It submitted that this creates an additional financial and administrative burden on service providers who employ posted workers, which ultimately removes their competitive edge in terms of cost. Furthermore, Poland submitted that art 3(1a) infringed the Rome I Regulation,[19] in requiring that obligations of the Member States be mandatory obligations if the posting exceeds 12 months, regardless of the applicable national law governing the employment relationship.

3. ***Wrongful inclusion of the road transport section within the scope of the 2018 Directive***: Finally, Poland submitted that the application of the 2018 Directive to the road transport industry under art 3(3) is incorrect as the freedom to provide services in the area of transport is to be covered by provisions of the Title of the TFEU, under art 58 TFEU.

The ECJ rejected all grounds submitted by Poland. The ECJ found that the correct legal basis for the implementation of the 2018 Directive had been used. The ultimate objective of the Posted Workers Directive was to protect the freedom to provide transnational services while ensuring both fair market conditions and the protection of workers. This objective was further pursued by the 2018 Directive which sought 'to develop the freedom to provide services on a fair basis ... since it ensures that the

---

[19]   Regulation (EC) No 593/2008 on the law applicable to contractual obligations (Rome I).

terms and conditions of employment of posted workers are as close as possible to those of workers employed by undertakings established in the host Member State'. The EU legislature was therefore entitled to rely on the same legal basis. Furthermore, the ECJ noted that circumstances had changed since the implementation of the Posted Workers Directive and the EU legislature was entitled to re-assess and redress the balance and enhance the rights of posted workers, having regard to the objective of both Directives.

The ECJ did not accept that art 56 TFEU was infringed by the 2018 Directive. The 2018 Directive seeks to ensure the full realisation of the freedom to provide services in protecting posted workers within the framework of fair competition. The entitlement of posted workers to the same terms and conditions of employment in the host Member State, including the right to equal remuneration, does not remove any competitive advantage. The 2018 Directive does not affect any other cost components, such as productivity or efficiency of the posted workers. Furthermore, the ECJ found that art 3(1a) did not infringe the Rome I Regulation, art 3(1a), in light of its nature and content, constitutes a special conflict-of-law rule, within the meaning of art 23 of the Rome I Regulation.

Finally, the Court rejected the submission that the road transport sector was wrongfully within the scope of the 2018 Directive. Article 3(3) of the 2018 Directive provides that the Directive applies to the road transport sector from the date of application of a legislative act amending Directive 2006/22/EC.[20] The legal basis for Directive 2006/22/EC is art 71(1) EC, which corresponds to art 91 TFEU. Consequently, the 2018 Directive does not seek to regulate the freedom to provide services in the road transport sector.

[7.10] *Federatie Nederlandse Vakbeweging v Van den Bosch Transporten BV[21]— European Court of Justice—request for preliminary ruling from the Netherlands— Directive 96/71/EC[22]—drivers working in international road transport—cabotage operations—collective agreements*

These proceedings arose from a preliminary reference to the ECJ from the Supreme Court of the Netherlands on the interpretation of art 56 TFEU and certain provisions of Directive 96/71/EC (the Posted Workers Directive). The preliminary reference arose in the context of Dutch proceedings concerning the application of a collective labour agreement to drivers coming from Germany and Hungary under charter contracts for international transport.

Van den Bosch Transporten, a Dutch company, concluded a number of contracts with its sister companies, Van den Bosch Transporte, a German company, and Silo-Tank, a company incorporated under the laws of Hungary. These contracts were for the international transport of goods via road and were carried out by workers coming from Germany and Hungary, who were employed by the respective German and Hungarian

---

20   Directive 2006/22/EC on minimum conditions for the implementation of Council Regulations (EEC) No 3820/85 and (EEC) No 3821/85 concerning social legislation relating to road transport activities and repealing Council Directive 88/599/EEC.
21   *Federatie Nederlandse Vakbeweging v Van den Bosch Transporten BV* Case C-815/18.
22   Directive 96/71/EC concerning the posting of workers in the framework of the provision of services.

companies. At the time of the proceedings, the charters started and ended in the Netherlands. However, most of the transport operations themselves took place outside the Netherlands.

Van den Bosche Transporten was a party to a collective labour agreement (the Goods Transport CLA). The drivers from Germany and Hungary were not afforded the terms and conditions as guaranteed under the Goods Transport CLA. On this basis, Federatie Nederlandse Vakbeweging, the Netherlands Federation of Trade Unions, issued proceedings against the three companies seeking an order that the companies comply with the Goods Transport CLA and afford these drivers the terms and conditions provided thereunder.

The proceedings were ultimately appealed to the Supreme Court of the Netherlands, which referred a number of questions to the ECJ, including:

1. Does the Posted Workers Directive apply to a worker who works as a driver in international road transport and thus carries out their work in more than one Member State?
2. If yes, what criterion should be used to determine whether such a worker is in fact posted to 'the territory of a Member State', and whether that worker 'for a limited period, carries out his [or her] work in the territory of a Member State other than the State in which he [or she] normally works' for the purposes of the Posted Workers Directive?
3. How should the term 'collective agreements ... which have been declared universally applicable', as set out in art 3(1) and (8) of the Posted Workers Directive, be interpreted?

In relation to the first question, the ECJ found that the Posted Workers Directive applies to the transnational provision of services in the road transport sector. It ruled that the Posted Workers Directive applies to any transnational provision of services, irrespective of the economic sector (with the exception of the provision of services involving merchant navy seagoing personnel, which is expressly excluded from the Posted Workers Directive under art 1(2)).

The ECJ noted that the free movement of services in the transport sector is governed by provisions in the Title of the TFEU relating to transport, under art 58(1) TFEU. However, the ECJ found that the Posted Workers Directive was of general application. Furthermore, the Posted Workers Directive is based on provisions of the EC Treaty relating to the freedom to provide services generally. Therefore, the provision of transnational services in the road transport sector involving the transport of goods is not excluded from the scope of the Posted Workers Directive.

In relation to the second question, the ECJ analysed the criteria to be used to determine whether there has been a posting of workers under the Posted Workers Directive. The ECJ noted that a worker cannot be considered to be posted to another Member State unless the performance of the work has a sufficient connection to that territory. An overall assessment of the arrangement should be conducted to determine if such a connection exists. This assessment includes analysing the nature of the activities, the degree of the connection between the activities carried out by that worker and the territory of the Member State and the proportion represented by those activities in the transport industry in that Member State. The ECJ further noted that the existence of a group affiliation between undertakings does not determine whether there is a sufficient connection between the workers performance of their work and the territory.

The ECJ then looked at drivers in the road transport sector who carry out cabatoge operations, as defined under Regulation (EC) No. 1072/2009.[23] It ruled that a driver who is employed by an undertaking established in a Member State, and who carries out cabatoge operations under a charter contract in the territory of a Member State other than the one where he habitually works, must, in principle, be regarded as a posted worker in the territory where the operations are carried out. The ECJ further held that the duration of the cabotage transport operations is irrelevant in determining if a posting under the Posted Workers Directive exists, without prejudice to the possible application of art 3(3) of the Posted Workers Directive.

Finally, in response to the third question, the ECJ held that 'collective agreements ... which have been declared universally applicable' as contained in the Posted Workers Directive, must be interpreted by reference to whether the collective agreement has been declared universally applicable under the applicable national law. These provisions also cover a collective labour agreement which has not been declared universally applicable, but compliance with which is a precondition for exemption from an essential collective labour agreement which has itself been declared universally applicable.

RIGHT TO REMAIN SILENT

[7.11] *DB v Commissione Nazionale per le Società e la Borsa*[24]*—European Court of Justice—request for preliminary ruling from Italy—Directive 2003/6/EC,*[25] *art 14(3)—Regulation (EU) No 596/2014,*[26] *art 30(1)(b—administrative sanctions of a criminal nature—right to remain silent and to avoid self-incrimination—Charter of Fundamental Rights of the European Union, arts 47 and 48—European Convention on Human Rights, art 6*

The defendant, Consob, is the Italian supervisory and enforcement body in respect of Directive 2003/6/EC (the Insider Dealing Directive) and more recently Regulation EU No 596/2014 (the Market Abuse Regulation). In reliance on Italian implementing law, Consob imposed on DB financial penalties of €200,000 and €100,000 in respect of insider trading and unlawful disclosure of inside information and also imposed on him a financial penalty of €50,000 by reason of his failure to answer questions put to him at a hearing convened by Consob. Consob also imposed a penalty of temporary loss of fit and proper person status for a period of 18 months and ordered confiscation of assets of

---

23 Regulation (EC) No 1072/2009 on common rules for access to the international road haulage market (recast).
24 *DB Commissione Nazionale per le Società e la Borsa* (Case C-481/19).
25 Directive 2003/6/EC on insider dealing and market manipulation.
26 Regulation (EU) No 596/2014 on market abuse.

equivalent value to the profit or the means applied to obtain it in respect of the insider dealing concerned. DB appealed those penalties to the Court of Appeal in Rome, which dismissed his appeal and he brought a further appeal on a point of law to the Supreme Court of Cassation in Italy. That Court referred two questions of constitutionality to the Constitutional Court of Italy, which in turn referred two questions to the ECJ for a preliminary ruling, as follows:

1. Are the relevant provisions of the Insider Dealing Directive and the Market Abuse Regulation to be interpreted 'as permitting Member States to refrain from penalising individuals who refuse to answer questions put to them by the competent authorities which might establish their liability for an offence that is punishable by administrative sanctions of a "punitive" nature'?

2. If not, are the relevant provisions of the Directive and the Regulation compatible with arts 47 and 48 of the Charter 'including in the light of the case law of the European Court of Human Rights on Article 6 of the ECHR and the constitutional traditions common to the Member States – in so far as they require sanctions to be applied even to individuals who refuse to answer questions put to them by the competent authorities and which might establish their liability for an offence that is punishable by administrative sanctions of a "punitive" nature'?

These are questions that had not been previously addressed by the Court.

The Court noted that it must take account of the rights guaranteed by art 6 of the ECHR as interpreted by the ECtHR, as the minimum threshold of protection. The ECtHR has held that even though art 6 of the ECHR does not explicitly mention the right to silence, that right is a generally recognised international standard which lies at the heart of the notion of a fair trial and accordingly, by providing an accused person with protection against improper coercion by the authorities, that right contributes to avoiding miscarriages of justice and securing the aims of art 6.

The Court noted that the protection of the right to silence is intended to ensure that, in criminal proceedings, the prosecution establishes its case without resorting to evidence obtained through coercion or oppression in defiance of the will of the accused and accordingly, the right to silence is infringed if a suspect is obliged to testify under threat of sanctions and either testifies in consequence, or is sanctioned for refusing to testify.

The Court concluded that the right to silence cannot be confined to statements of admission of wrongdoing or remarks that directly incriminate the person in question but also covers information and questions of fact which might subsequently be used in support of a prosecution and might accordingly have a bearing on conviction or sanction.

The Court noted, however, that the right to silence does not justify every failure to cooperate with competent authorities such as refusal to appear at a hearing or delaying tactics designed to postpone a hearing.

The Court acknowledged that the right to silence extends beyond a criminal prosecution and applies in administrative proceedings which may lead to the imposition of administrative sanctions of a criminal nature.

In determining whether sanctions or penalties are criminal in nature, the Court identified three criteria which must be considered. First, one must consider the legal classification of the offence under national law. Second, one must consider the intrinsic nature of the offence. Third, one must consider the degree of severity of the penalty that the person concerned is liable to incur. It is for the referring Court to assess, in light of those criteria, whether the administrative sanction at issue is criminal in nature. The Court observed, however, that some of the administrative sanctions imposed by Consob appeared to pursue a punitive purpose and present a high degree of severity such that they were liable to be regarded as criminal in nature. Moreover, and most importantly, even if the penalties imposed in this case were not criminal in nature, the right to silence must be observed in an investigation procedure conducted by an administrative authority if evidence obtained in those proceedings can be used in criminal proceedings against that person in order to establish that a criminal offence was committed.

It follows from the above that the safeguards afforded by art 47 (second paragraph) and art 48 of the Charter include the right to silence of natural persons who are 'charged' and that right includes penalties being imposed on such persons for refusing to provide the competent authority under the Insider Dealing Directive or the Market Abuse Regulation with answers which might establish their liability for an offence that is punishable by administrative sanctions of a criminal nature, or their criminal liability.

The Court distinguished its previous decisions with reference to the right to remain silent in competition enforcement proceedings by noting that it has previously held that undertakings cannot be compelled to provide answers which might involve admission of the existence of an infringement and its previous decisions in this area relate to undertakings and associations of undertakings rather than natural persons.

Turning to the second question, the Court noted that the general principle of interpretation to the effect that the wording of secondary EU legislation must be interpreted as far as possible in such a way as not to affect its validity and conformity with the primary law as a whole and in particular with the Charter. It noted, with reference to the Insider Dealing Directive, that there was nothing in the wording of the relevant provisions that precluded interpretation to the effect that respects the right to silence. Likewise, in the case of the Market Abuse Regulation, it noted that it did not require Member States to provide for the application of sanctions to natural persons who, in an investigation concerning an offence that is punishable by administrative sanctions of a criminal nature, refused to provide the competent authority with answers which might establish their liability for such an offence or their criminal liability.

Accordingly, the Court concluded that the relevant provisions of the Insider Dealing Directive and of the Market Abuse Regulation lend themselves to an interpretation which is consistent with arts 47 and 48 of the Charter in that they do not require penalties to be imposed on natural persons for refusing to provide the competent authority with answers which might establish their liability for an offence that is punishable by administrative sanctions of a criminal nature or their criminal liability.

Finally, the Court observed that Member States must exercise the discretions afforded to them by secondary EU legislation in a manner that is consistent with fundamental rights and accordingly, a competent authority cannot impose penalties on natural persons for refusing to provide that authority with answers which might establish their liability for an offence that is punishable by administrative sanctions of a criminal nature or their criminal liability.

SOCIAL SECURITY

[7.12] *FORMAT Urządzenia i Montaże Przemysłowe v Zakład Ubezpieczeń Społecznych I Oddział w Warszawie[27]—European Court of Justice—preliminary reference from Polish Supreme Court—Regulation (EEC) No 1408/71[28]—single employment contract—social security scheme—person normally employed in two Member States*

The Polish Supreme Court referred a question to the ECJ on the interpretation of art 14(2)(b) of Regulation (EEC) No 1408/71 on the application of social security schemes to employed persons, to self-employed persons and to members of their families moving within the Community (the Regulation).

UA, a Polish national, was employed by FORMAT on a fixed-term contract from 20 October 2006 to 31 December 2009. FORMAT's registered office was in Poland. During the course of his employment, UA worked in France and the UK. The Social Insurance Institution of Warsaw refused to issue a certificate confirming that UA was covered by the Polish social security system in relation to the work he carried out for FORMAT from 23 December 2007 to 31 December 2009. This was unsuccessfully appealed by UA and FORMAT to the Regional Court.

The proceedings were ultimately brought before the Polish Supreme Court, which referred the following question to the ECJ:

> Is the expression "a person normally employed in the territory of two or more Member States" used in the first sentence of Article 14(2) … to be interpreted as also applying to a person who, during the period covered by … the same contract of employment concluded with a single employer, performs work in the territory of each of at least two Member States … during directly consecutive, successive periods of several months?

The ECJ noted that in order for a worker to fall within the meaning of art 14(2), the worker must normally be employed in two or more Member States. In assessing whether a person is normally employed in two or more Member States, regard must be had to a number of factors including the duration and nature of employment as described in the contractual documents, as well as how the employment relationship is carried out in practice.

---

[27] *FORMAT Urządzenia i Montaże Przemysłowe v Zakład Ubezpieczeń Społecznych I Oddział w Warszawie* (Case C-879/19).

[28] Regulation (EEC) No 1408/71 on the application of social security schemes to employed persons, to self-employed persons and to members of their families moving within the Community.

The ECJ stated that, in analysing the fact pattern, it appeared that UA had in fact worked for 13 months in France, followed by two months in the UK, before returning to France for nearly two years. While the ECJ held that it was ultimately a matter for the referring Court to verify the facts, if this fact pattern was confirmed, UA had in fact carried out nearly all of his employment in one single Member State.

The ECJ further stated that the jurisprudence of the ECJ has established that art 14(2) does not apply to workers who normally carry out their employment in one single Member State.

In analysing the provisions of the Regulation, the ECJ stated that the purpose of the Regulation is to ensure that workers moving throughout the EU are covered by one single social security system. To that end, art 13(2)(1) of the Regulation provides that workers are covered by the social security system of the Member State in which they work. Article 14(2) provides for an exception to this general principle in establishing special rules for employees who are employed in the territory of two or more Member States. The ECJ further stated that as it is an exception, art 14(2) must be interpreted narrowly.

In interpreting art 14(2), the ECJ had regard to the provisions of art 14(1)(a) and held that an employee is regarded as working in two or more Member States for the purposes of art 14(2) provided 'the duration of the uninterrupted periods of work completed in each of those Member States does not exceed 12 months'. The ECJ held that, subject to confirmation by the referring Court of the factual pattern of the working arrangement, art 14(2) was not applicable in the case at hand.

[7.13] *Team Power Europe v Direktor na Teritorialna direktsia na Natsionalna agentsia za prihodite-Varna[29]—European Court of Justice—request for a preliminary ruling from Bulgaria—Regulation (EC) 987/2009,[30] art 14(2)—Regulation (EC) 883/2004[31]—temporary-work agency—concept of 'substantial activities, other than purely internal management activities'*

This was a request for a preliminary ruling from the Administrative Court in Bulgaria regarding the interpretation of art 14(2) of Regulation (EC) 987/2009.

Team Power Europe (Team Power) is a temporary-work agency incorporated under Bulgarian law. It provides temporary work placements for other Member States, including Germany. It entered into a contract of employment with a Bulgarian national, under which the individual carried out work in Germany under the direction and supervision of a German undertaking.

---

[29] *Team Power Europe v Direktor na Teritorialna direktsia na Natsionalna agentsia za prihodite* (Case C-784/19).
[30] Regulation (EC) 987/2009 laying down the procedure for implementing Regulation (EC) 883/2004 on the coordination of social security systems.
[31] Regulation (EC) 883/2004 on the coordination of social security systems.

The Bulgarian National Public Revenue refused to issue a certificate with respect to this individual confirming that Bulgarian legislation was applicable to the worker, on the basis that there was no direct relationship between the workers and Team Power, and the undertaking did not carry out any substantial work in Bulgaria.

This decision was appealed to the Administrative Court in Varna, which is the court of last instance on questions of social security in Bulgaria. The Court referred the following question to the ECJ:

> Is Article 14(2) of Regulation No 987/2009 ... to be interpreted as meaning that, in order for it to be possible to find that an undertaking engaged in providing temporary staff ordinarily performs its activities in the Member State in which it is established, a substantial part of its activity placing workers must be carried out for the benefit of user undertakings established in the same Member State.

The Court noted that conflict of laws rules existed so as to ensure that individuals had social security protection.

The ECJ further noted that the general position is established in Regulation (EC) 883/2004 which provides that an employed person in a Member State is subject to the legislation of that same Member State, save for certain specific situations that are provided for in arts 12 to 16 of Regulation (EC) 883/2004.

One such exception is that which deals with posted workers; it provides that a worker who is employed by an employer 'which normally carries out its activities' in a Member State, but who is posted to carry out work in another Member State, is covered by the original Member State legislation provided the duration of the work does not exceed two years.

The ECJ noted that art 14(2) of Regulation (EC) 987/2009 provides clarity on what constitutes 'normally carries out its activities', stating that the employer 'ordinarily performs substantial activities, other than purely internal management activities, in the territory of the Member State in which it is established' and that in assessing this, certain criteria must be used which are 'suited to the specific characteristics of each employer and the real nature of the activities carried out'.

The ECJ noted that Team Power assigned temporary workers for undertakings established in Member States other than in the Member State in which Team Power is established, ie Bulgaria. The ultimate question therefore was whether Team Power was performing 'substantial activities, other than purely internal management activities' in Bulgaria. Substantial activities in the circumstances of a temporary-work agency include selection, recruitment and the assignment of temporary workers, with assignment being the core function that generates turnover.

The ECJ held, therefore, that in order for it to be determined that a temporary-work agency 'normally carries out its activities' in a Member State, it must 'carry out a significant part of its activities of assigning temporary agency workers for the benefit of user undertakings established and carrying out their activities in the territory of that Member State' for local social security protection to apply.

[7.14] *A v Latvijas Republikas Veselibas Ministrija*[32]—*European Court of Justice—request for preliminary ruling from Latvia—Regulation 883/2004/EC*[33]— *Directive 2004/38/EC*[34]—*free movement—rights to access to healthcare*

The matter concerned an Italian national who resided in Latvia. After he left Italy, the applicant was no longer entitled to receive healthcare under the Italian healthcare system. He tried to register to receive healthcare under the Latvian healthcare system but his application was refused because he was not employed or self-employed in Latvia. On that basis, he was only allowed to receive healthcare benefits if he paid for them, unlike Latvian nationals in a comparable situation.

He brought an action against that decision. In the first instance, it was held by the Latvian Courts that no breach of his free movement rights had occurred because distinguishing between rights to access medical care in the circumstances could be justified by the legitimate objective of protecting public finances. It was relevant that, on acquiring permanent residence rights, the applicant would have been able to receive medical assistance. It was argued that the premiums that he had to pay to access healthcare were not disproportionate.

The referring Court decided to refer a number of questions to the ECJ, including whether it is compatible for EU citizens who exercise their free movement rights to be placed in a situation where they are no longer able to receive public healthcare services financed by a Member State.

The ECJ accepted that the medical care in question (being financed by the State without a requirement to undergo a means test) constituted 'sickness benefits' and therefore fell within the scope of Regulation 883/2004/EC.

The ECJ noted that the rights of EU citizens to exercise their free movement rights are predicated on meeting certain conditions laid down in Directive 2004/38/EC. One of those conditions is that they must have comprehensive sickness insurance cover for themselves and their family members in order not to become an unreasonable burden on the public finances of the relevant Member State.

Accordingly, while it would be unlawful interference with freedom of movement rights to deny access to sickness benefits provided by a healthcare system in its entirety, it is permissible to impose a requirement that an individual must have sickness cover so as not to become an unreasonable burden on the finances of the Member State. Any other conclusion would effectively undermine the wording of Directive 2004/38/EC and in particular art 7. An attempt to rely on the provisions of the equal treatment contained in Directive 2004/38/EC was not accepted on this basis. The ECJ concluded that imposing a requirement that the system was not free of charge was permissible.

---

[32] *A v Latvijas Republikas Veselibas Ministrija* (Case C-535/19).
[33] Regulation 883/2004/EC on the coordination of social security systems.
[34] Directive 2004/38/EC on the right of citizens of the Union and their family members to move and reside freely within the territory of the Member States.

[7.15] *CG v The Department for Communities in Northern Ireland[35]—European Court of Justice—request for preliminary ruling from Northern Ireland—Treaty on the Functioning of the European Union, art 18—non-discrimination based on nationality—social assistance*

This matter was based on the interpretation of art 18 TFEU which prohibits 'any discrimination on grounds of nationality'.

The matter arose in the context of the Agreement on the Withdrawal of the UK from the EU.

CG was a single mother of two young children; she had dual Croatian and Netherlands nationality and had resided in Northern Ireland since 2018. She declared her arrival in Northern Ireland with her partner and the father of her children, who had Netherlands nationality, in 2018. She had never carried out any economic activity in Northern Ireland and lived there with her partner until she moved to a women's refuge. She had no financial means of supporting herself or her two children.

CG was recognised as having a temporary right of residence and in June 2020 she applied to the Department for Communities in Northern Ireland (the Department) for social assistance but the Department refused, as CG had not fulfilled residence requirements.

The Appeal Tribunal of Northern Ireland referred two questions to the ECJ, but in light of the answer to the first, the ECJ concluded that there was no need to examine the second question.

The ECJ summarised the first question as:

> the referring court asks whether Article 18 TFEU must be interpreted as meaning that a national provision that excludes from social benefits Union citizens with a temporary right of residence under national law is covered by the prohibition of discrimination on grounds of nationality laid down in that article.

In answering this question the ECJ found that subsistence benefits, 'which are intended to ensure that their recipients have the minimum means of subsistence necessary to lead a life in keeping with human dignity' do come within the meaning of 'social assistance' under art 24(2) of Directive 2004/38/EC (the Directive). The ECJ therefore categorised the Universal Credit System as social assistance.

The ECJ held that the 'financial situation of each person concerned should be examined specifically, without taking account of the social benefits claimed, in order to determine whether he or she meets the condition of having sufficient resources' laid out in art 7(1)(b) of the Directive to decide whether the principle of non-discrimination in art 24(1) of the Directive can be invoked to qualify for equal treatment with the nationals of the host Member State.

---

[35] *CG v The Department for Communities in Northern Ireland* (Case C-709/20).

The ECJ answered the first question as follows:

> Article 24 of Directive 2004/38 must be interpreted as not precluding the legislation of a host Member State which excludes from social assistance economically inactive Union citizens who do not have sufficient resources and to whom that State has granted a temporary right of residence, where those benefits are guaranteed to nationals of the Member State concerned who are in the same situation.
>
> However, provided that a Union citizen resides legally, on the basis of national law, in the territory of a Member State other than that of which he or she is a national, the national authorities empowered to grant social assistance are required to check that a refusal to grant such benefits based on that legislation does not expose that citizen, and the children for which he or she is responsible, to an actual and current risk of violation of their fundamental rights, as enshrined in Articles 1, 7 and 24 of the Charter. Where that citizen does not have any resources to provide for his or her own needs and those of his or her children and is isolated, those authorities must ensure that, in the event of a refusal to grant social assistance, that citizen may nevertheless live with his or her children in dignified conditions. In the context of that examination, those authorities may take into account all means of assistance provided for by national law, from which the citizen concerned and her children are actually entitled to benefit.

[7.16] *INPS v de maternite pour les titulaires de permis unique[36]—European Court of Justice—request from preliminary ruling from Italy—Directive 2011/98/EU[37]— Charter of Fundamental Rights and Freedoms of the European Union, art 34— maternity and paternity benefits*

This ruling related to a provision in Italian law whereby there was a childbirth allowance, paid monthly, in respect of each child born or adopted, to encourage the birth rate and 'to contribute to the costs of supporting' the child.

There were certain criteria for receiving such an allowance and third-country nationals residing legally in Italy with a single work permit were refused the childbirth allowance by Italy's social security institute, INPS, on the ground that they did not have long-term resident status. The third-country nationals argued that this refusal to grant them childbirth and maternity allowance breached the terms of Directive 2011/98/EU (the Directive) and the right to social security benefits under art 34 of the Charter of Fundamental Rights (the Charter).

The Italian Constitutional Court referred the following question to the ECJ for a preliminary ruling:

> Is Article 34 of the [Charter] to be interpreted as applying to childbirth and maternity allowances under Article 3(1)(b) and (j) of Regulation [No 883/2004], referred to in Article 12(1)(e) of Directive [2011/98], and is EU law therefore to be interpreted as precluding national legislation which fails to extend the abovementioned benefits, which are already granted to foreign nationals holding a long-term resident's EU residence permit, to foreign nationals who hold a single permit under that directive?

---

36   *INPS v de maternite pour les titulaires de permis unique* (Case C-350/20).
37   Directive 2011/98/EU on a single application procedure for a single permit for third-country nationals to reside and work in the territory of a Member State and on a common set of rights for third-country workers legally residing in a Member State.

The ECJ first considered whether the question was admissible, as the facts pre-dated the implementation of the Directive and the ECJ concluded that it was admissible as 'the interpretation of EU law sought by the referring court bears a relation to the object of the dispute before it, which concerns exclusively the constitutionality of national provisions having regard to national constitutional law read in the light of EU law'.

The ECJ found that childbirth and maternity allowances did come within the scope of the Directive as they were social security benefits in that they were granted 'without any individual and discretionary assessment of personal needs, to recipients on the basis of a legally defined position' and therefore fell within its equal treatment provisions. By excluding third-country nationals, Italian legislation contravened the Directive.

The ECJ also held that the alleged purpose of the benefits, ie, to encourage birth rates, was of little importance in determining whether the benefits came within the scope of the Directive

[7.17]   *K v Raad van bestuur van het Uitvoeringsinstituut werknemersverzekeringen (Uwv)[38]—European Court of Justice—request for preliminary ruling from the Netherlands—Regulation 883/2004[39]—unemployment benefits—sick leave—transfer of residence*

The applicant (a Turkish citizen) settled in the Netherlands in 1979 and worked there until 2015. From 2005 he lived in Germany with his family, while working in the Netherlands. In May 2015, he was hired by a German employer but was placed on sick leave in August 2015, never to return to work. Having exhausted his sick pay entitlements with his employer, he received German sickness benefits from 14 October 2015 until 4 April 2016.

The applicant returned to the Netherlands in February 2016 and applied to be removed from the population register in Germany; shortly thereafter his German employer terminated his contract, to take effect on 15 February 2016. The day after his termination, he underwent surgery in Germany where he stayed for a short period. On 4 March 2016, he registered in the population register of the Netherlands.

On 22 April 2016, the applicant made an application for unemployment benefits with effect from 4 April 2016 to the Employee Insurance Schemes Implementing Body of the Netherlands, which declared that it had no power to rule on the applicant's entitlements, and a complaint was lodged by the applicant. The complaint was rejected on the basis that the applicant was not a frontier worker and Germany was the last state of employment, and therefore the competent Member State to assess such entitlements.

This decision was appealed, but the appeal was dismissed. The matter came before the referring Court, which requested the ECJ to consider whether:

— the relevant provisions of Regulation 883/2004 must be interpreted as meaning that a wholly unemployed person who has transferred his place of residence

---

[38]   *K v Raad van bestuur van het Uitvoeringsinstituut werknemersverzekeringen (Uwv)* (Case C-285/20).
[39]   Regulation (EC) No. 883/2004 on the coordination of social security systems.

while receiving unemployment (or similar) benefits before the termination of the employment relationship, was entitled to receive unemployment benefit under the legislation of the Member State in which the individual now resided; and

— whether the reasons for the transfer of residence were relevant in answering this question.

The Court found that a situation where someone is on sick leave and in receipt of sickness benefits was comparable to that of someone who pursued an activity as an employed person, and therefore came within the scope of the relevant provisions of Regulation 883/2004 provided that, in accordance with the national law of the relevant Member State, entitlement to such benefits was treated in the same way as the pursuit of an activity as an employed person. It did not find that the reasons for transfer of residence had to be taken into account in determining the answer to this question.

STATUTORY AUDITORS

[7.18] *A v Patentti-ja rekisterihallituksen tilintarkastuslautakunta[40]— European Court of Justice—request for preliminary ruling from Finland— Directive 2006/43/EC,[41] art 22a(1)(a)—statutory auditors*

This application for a preliminary ruling on the interpretation of art 22a(1)(a) of Directive 2006/43/EC arose in the context of proceedings involving A, a statutory auditor who appealed against a decision of the Audit Committee at the Patent and Registration Office Finland to impose a fine on him following his recruitment to a key management role in a company after carrying out the statutory audit at that company.

Article 22a of Directive 2006/43, entitled 'Employment by audited entities of former statutory auditors or of employees of statutory auditors or audit firms', states as follows:

> Member States shall ensure that a statutory auditor or a key audit partner who carries out a statutory audit on behalf of an audit firm does not, before a period of at least one year, or in the case of statutory audit of public-interest entities a period of at least two years, has elapsed since he or she ceased to act as a statutory auditor or key audit partner in connection with the audit engagement:
>
> (a) take up a key management position in the audited entity;
> (b) where applicable, become a member of the audit committee of the audited entity or, where such committee does not exist, of the body performing equivalent functions to an audit committee;
> (c) become a non-executive member of the administrative body or a member of the supervisory body of the audited entity.

In 2014, A acted as statutory auditor for the company, continuing until August 2018. In July 2018, A was appointed head of finance in the company, commencing employment in February 2019.

---

[40]   *A v Patentti-ja rekisterihallituksen tilintarkastuslautakunta* (Case C-950/19).
[41]   Directive 2006/43/EC on statutory audits of annual accounts and consolidated accounts.

The Finnish regulatory authority imposed a fine of €50,000 on A on the basis that he had failed to observe a two-year waiting period. A applied for a reduction in the fine on the basis that:

(i)   there had been an incorrect interpretation of the 'gravity and duration of the infringement', as 'taking up a post' in art 22a(1)(a) of Directive 2006/43 refers to a situation in which the person in question has commenced employment;

(ii)   circumstances could change before the actual commencement of employment. He argued that, given the fact that another auditor had carried out the audit for the 2018 financial year, the waiting period should run from the date of completion of the audit which the applicant had carried out for the 2017 financial year, ie 5 February 2018; and

(iii) 'the information concerning his recruitment had been notified in a transparent manner so that third parties also would understand that the situation had been carefully considered and safeguards had been put in place'.

The Finnish authority stayed the proceedings pending a response from the ECJ on the following questions:

(1)   Is Article 22a(1) of Directive [2006/43] to be interpreted as meaning that a key audit partner takes up a position of the kind referred to in that provision upon conclusion of the employment contract?

(2)   If the answer to the [first] question is in the negative: Is Article 22a(1) [of that Directive] to be interpreted as meaning that a key audit partner takes up a position of the kind referred to in this provision upon commencing employment in the position concerned?

In interpreting art 22, the Court considered the rationale for art 22, namely:

> Those rules aim, in substance, first, to ensure that statutory auditors are not involved in the internal decision-making process of audited entities and to avoid conflicts of interest, in particular by excluding the audit of entities to which those auditors are linked by an economic or financial interest, and, second, to protect them from the intervention of owners, shareholders or managers of the audit firm which employs them, in order to ensure, by preventing any interference which might influence, directly or indirectly the outcome of their audit ... it aims at preserving the confidence of third parties, such as creditors and investors, in the reliability of the audit.

The Court held that, given the significance of the perception of third parties and the independence of an auditor, the auditor must always be regarded as having a position within an audited entity within the meaning of art 22a(1)(a) of Directive 2006/43 'from the moment a contractual relationship between them is concluded, even if he or she has not yet actually taken up his or her post in that entity'.

The Court ruled that art 22a(1)(a) of Directive 2006/43 must be interpreted as meaning that a statutory auditor, such as a key audit partner appointed by an audit firm in the context of a statutory audit engagement, must be regarded as holding a key management position in an audited entity, within the meaning of that provision, as soon as he or she concludes an employment contract with the latter relating to that post, even if he or she has not yet begun to actually perform his or her duties in that post.

Chapter 8

Fixed-Term Work

INTRODUCTION

[8.01] The abuse of the use of successive fixed-term contracts was considered by the European Court of Justice (ECJ) in *EB*.

The Irish High Court addressed the concept of a 'fixed-term employee' in *Power*, in analysing whether a permanent employee of an organisation fulfilling a more senior role within the organisation on a temporary basis was 'fixed-term employee' under the Protection of Employees (Fixed-Term Work) Act 2003.

Two cases in which the ECJ was required to consider the less favourable treatment of fixed-term workers are noted, namely *KO* and *LB*. Finally, the use of successive fixed-term employment contracts as considered by the ECJ in *MV* is noted.

CONTRACT OF INDEFINITE DURATION

[8.02] *EB v Presidenza Dei Consiglio Dei Ministri[1]—European Court of Justice— request for a preliminary ruling from Italy—Directive 1999/70/EC[2]—abuse of successive fixed-term contracts*

The applicant was employed by a university as a researcher. Italian law contains specific rules applicable to fixed-term researchers, providing that fixed-term employment contracts can be concluded subject to the availability of 'the resources for planning for the purposes of carrying out research, teaching, non-curricular activities and student service activities and research'. Under Italian law, two types of contracts were in place for researchers. A 'Type A' contract could be entered into for a period of three years, renewable once for a period of two years, subject to the carrying out of an appraisal of teaching and research activities in accordance with ministerial decree. A 'Type B' contract was reserved for candidates who had been employed under the Type A contract, or who had obtained certain scientific qualifications or who had received certain grants. The Type B contract was also entered into for a period of three years and could not be extended, but the researcher concerned had the opportunity at the end of the period of

---

[1]   *EB v Presidenza Dei Consiglio Dei Ministri* (Case C-326/19).
[2]   Directive 1999/70/EC concerning the framework agreement on fixed-term work.

the contract of being appointed to a post as an associate professor (provided they had obtained appropriate scientific qualifications and subject to the conduct of an appraisal conducted in accordance with ministerial decree). An associate professor post was a contract of indefinite duration.

By separate decree, to combat job insecurity, Italian law provided for the recruitment of non-managerial staff on contracts of indefinite duration, subject to certain exceptions and conditions.

The applicant commenced employment on a Type A contract in 2012. In 2014, he obtained certain scientific qualifications. Before the end of his contract in 2015, the applicant requested a two-year extension of his fixed-term contract, which was granted.

In 2017, before the expiry of his extended contract, the applicant applied for the extension of his contract so that his fixed-term employment relationship (ie his Type A contract) would be converted into a contract of indefinite duration. This request was rejected. The University argued that the provision for recruitment of non-managerial staff on contracts of indefinite duration did not apply to university researchers hired under a fixed-term contract.

The applicant asserted that the exclusion of his contract from the rule providing for the automatic conversion of a fixed-term contract into a contract of indefinite duration was incompatible with Directive 1999/70/EC (the fixed-term work Directive). In particular, he asserted that there were no objective reasons for a researcher to be employed on a fixed-term contract for a period, particularly where this was extended, and that not allowing him to undergo the assessment envisaged in Type B contracts was discriminatory contrary to the fixed-term work Directive.

While a number of questions were referred to the ECJ, the Court found as a preliminary matter that it had to consider whether the absence of measures to penalise the abuse of fixed-term contracts such as those at issue in this case was compatible with the fixed-term work Directive.

In answering this question, the Court distinguished between the two types of contract at issue. It noted that the Type A contract allowed access to the Type B contract, allowing a university researcher to continue their academic career. It was acknowledged that the purpose of the fixed-term work Directive is to improve the quality of fixed-term work, but it also noted that clause 5 of the fixed-term work Directive clearly states that the clause is applicable solely where there are successive fixed-term employment contracts or relationships, and that a contract which is the first or the only fixed-term employment contract does not fall within the scope of clause 5. The fixed-term work Directive does not require Member States to adopt a measure requiring every first or fixed-term contract to be justified by an objective reason. The Court found that the conclusion of a Type A contract is not covered by clause 5 of the fixed-term work Directive and therefore does not fall within the scope of that provision. It would fall within the scope of that provision if it were extended, as then there would be two successive fixed-term contracts.

The Court further noted that clause 5(1) of the fixed-term work Directive sets out three measures to prevent abuse, and obliges Member States to introduce one of the measures only. The measures are rules concerning: (a) objective reasons justifying the renewal of employment contracts and relationships; (b) the maximum total duration of successive fixed-term employment contracts and relationships; and (c) the number of renewals of such contracts or relationships.

In this case, the fact that objective reasons for issuing the fixed-term contract in the first place had not been provided did not mean that the contract was unlawful, because it complied with the other two measures, ie, a maximum duration of the fixed-term contract, and only allowing one extension. No evidence was provided which suggested that these measures would be insufficient to prevent abuse of fixed-term contracts.

Examining the case law, it was noted that in certain cases the failure to provide objective reasons had led to declarations of abuse within the fixed-term work Directive. However, this case was distinguished on the basis that the person signing a Type A contract was aware at the outset of the duration of the employment relationship and that there was a limit as to how many times it could be renewed.

The Court also noted that the fact that the university has a constant need to employ university researchers did not prohibit that need from being met by having recourse to fixed-term employment contracts. It noted that the post of researcher appears to be intended as a first step in a scientist's career, with a view to subsequently moving on to other positions, such as associate professor and ultimately professor. It noted that a provision which would oblige a university to conclude a contract of indefinite duration with a researcher, irrespective of the evaluation of the results of his or her scientific activities, would not meet the above requirements.

Accordingly, the Court found that there was no breach of the fixed-term work Directive.

[8.03] *Power v Health Service Executive*[3]*—High Court—Simons J—Protection of Employees (Fixed-Term Work) Act 2003—Directive 1999/70/EC*[4]*—existing employee of organisation fulfilling more senior role within the organisation on temporary basis—contract of indefinite duration—objective justification must be provided*

The claimant was employed by the Health Service Executive (the HSE) as a permanent pensionable employee since July 1999. He was appointed as the chief financial officer of the Saolta University Healthcare Group, within the HSE, in January 2012 and occupied that role at the date of the High Court hearing. At the invitation of the HSE, he took up the role of interim group chief executive of Saolta University Healthcare Group on 5 October 2014. On 20 November 2014, the HSE wrote to the claimant confirming his appointment on a temporary basis until 31 March 2015 or until the role was filled on a permanent basis, whichever occurred sooner. He was also advised in that letter that when his temporary role as group chief executive ceased, he would revert to his 'substantive terms and conditions as a permanent employee' of the HSE.

---

[3]   *Power v Health Service Executive* [2021] IEHC 346.
[4]   Directive 1999/70/EC concerning the framework agreement on fixed-term work.

The claimant was advised in 7 May 2015 that his appointment was extended until 31 December 2016. He was subsequently advised in December 2016 that his appointment as interim group chief executive was being extended until 31 December 2017. He was advised again in January 2018 that his appointment was extended to the end of 2018.

In September 2018, the post of group chief executive for a five-year term was advertised in a competition administered by the Public Appointments Service on behalf of the HSE. The claimant was an unsuccessful candidate in that competition. The claimant resumed his position as chief financial officer of the Saolta Group in September 2019.

Therefore, this 'interim' measure remained in place for more than four years. The question which arose was whether the claimant was entitled to the protections of the Protection of Employees (Fixed-Term Work) Act 2003 (the 2003 Act). If the legislation were applicable, the claimant would, in principle, be entitled to assert a right to remain in the more senior post under a contract of indefinite duration, unless the HSE could establish that there were objective grounds justifying the use of fixed-term contracts for an aggregate duration in excess of four years.

The HSE contended that the legislation was not applicable in the case of an existing employee who fulfils a more senior role on a temporary basis, because such an employee already has the benefit of permanent employment within the organisation. Such an existing employee has a contractual entitlement, on the conclusion of the temporary appointment, to revert to their original permanent position on the terms and conditions of employment applicable to that position.

The claimant argued that he became entitled to remain in the post of group chief executive, under a contract of indefinite duration, by virtue of his having been employed in that post under successive fixed-term contracts with an aggregate duration of in excess of four years. On his analysis, the right to a contract of indefinite duration would have arisen in October or November 2018. (This was so, notwithstanding that he did not formally assert this entitlement until 14 January 2019). The claimant claimed that the objective of the legislation would be subverted if a public sector employer were permitted to utilise successive fixed-term contracts merely because a worker had permanency in respect of a lesser role within the organisation.

The Labour Court concluded that the claimant did not have *locus standi* to pursue his claim in circumstances where he was a permanent employee, employed on a contract of employment of indefinite duration. It held that the scope of the 2003 Act was confined to those employees whose relationship with their employer is co-terminous with the fixed-term contract under which they are employed. An existing employee, who reverts to their substantive grade and whose employment continues at the end of a fixed-term assignment, does not enjoy the protection of the 2003 Act. The Labour Court further held that an employee could not be both a 'permanent employee' and a 'fixed-term employee' and dismissed the claim.

On a point of law appeal to the High Court, the Court considered that the resolution of the dispute between the parties turned largely on a question of statutory interpretation, namely what is meant by the concept of a 'fixed-term employee' and that the starting point for the consideration of this question must be the domestic legislation itself, ie the

2003 Act. The concept of a 'fixed-term employee' is defined under s 2 of the 2003 Act as 'a person having a contract of employment entered into directly with an employer where the end of the contract of employment concerned is determined by an objective condition such as arriving at a specific date, completing a specific task or the occurrence of a specific event'.

The parties disagreed as to the meaning to be attributed to the phrase 'the end of the contract of employment concerned'. The HSE argued that the contract of employment was synonymous with an enduring employment relationship. It is only where the employment relationship itself will be brought to an end on the occurrence of the relevant contingency that a fixed-term contract can be said to exist. The Court did not agree with this analysis, stating:

> [O]n its ordinary and natural meaning, the definition of "fixed-term employee" merely requires that the end of the contract of employment concerned is determined by an objective condition. It does not require that this must also have the consequence that the employment relationship is brought to an end. A contract of employment may qualify as a fixed-term contract notwithstanding that the relevant employee continues in the employment of the organisation thereafter, whether by transitioning to a further contract or reverting to an earlier one.

The Court then went on to consider Directive 1999/70/EC (the fixed-term work Directive) and found that it was a matter for the domestic legislature to define the category of workers which qualify for protection. The Court noted the discretion granted to the Member States was not unlimited. The constraint upon a Member States' discretion is that they may not prescribe an overly exclusive definition. This is important because if an employee does not qualify as a fixed-term worker, then they are denied all of the benefits of the fixed-term work Directive. The HSE had contended that the fixed-term work Directive's objective was merely to promote stable employment, irrespective of the terms and conditions of that employment. This had been accepted by the Labour Court. The High Court disagreed, stating that:

> [T]he logic of the Labour Court's approach is that an employee, with a right to revert, is to be denied not only the possibility of claiming a contract of indefinite duration, they are also to be precluded from relying on the principle of non-discrimination. One consequence of this would be that an employee, who has a right to revert to their original post, would not be legally entitled to be informed about vacancies which become available within the organisation. This would mean that an employee, who might have been acting up in the more senior role for many years, would not have a legal entitlement to be notified of a recruitment process in respect of the very post which he or she has been occupying on an interim basis. This would be inconsistent with the objective of the Fixed-Term Work Directive that all workers have the same opportunity to secure permanent positions …

> Finally, the logic of the Employer's position, *reductio ad absurdum*, is that an employee could be employed in the more senior post under an infinite number of successive fixed-term contracts, provided only that the employee has the right to revert to their original, more junior post. This would be so irrespective of how great the disparity is between the two posts in respect of salary and other terms and conditions …

> Having regard to these considerations, the bright-line rule contended for on behalf of the Employer would undermine the effectiveness of the Fixed-Term Work Directive.

The Directive envisages that there be a measured assessment of whether the use of successive fixed-term employment contracts gives rise to abuse. This requires consideration not only of the aggregate duration of such contracts, but also an examination of whether their use is objectively justified ...

On the correct interpretation of the Fixed-Term Work Directive, the existence of a contractual right to revert to one's original post in an organisation, on the terms and conditions of employment applicable to that post, is no more than a *factor* to be considered in deciding whether the successive use of fixed-term contracts is objectively justified. It is not a bar to pursuing a complaint that there has been a breach, and having that claim adjudicated upon. [Emphasis in original.]

The High Court found that the Labour Court misconstrued the statutory definition of 'fixed-term employee' by interpreting a 'contract of employment' as being synonymous with an enduring employment relationship. The Labour Court erroneously decided that, in order to qualify as a 'fixed-term employee', a claimant's employment relationship must be co-terminous with the expiry of a fixed-term or fixed-purpose contract of employment.

The High Court also held that the Labour Court erred in law in its analysis of the shifting contractual relationship between the HSE and the claimant. The Labour Court appeared to have mistakenly concluded that the contract of employment remained unchanged throughout. The High Court was of the view that the employment relationship between the parties was, instead, properly characterised as involving a consecutive series of contracts of employment. This was so even before the claimant was employed as interim group chief executive. For example, a further contract of employment had been entered into between the parties in January 2012 upon the claimant's promotion to the position of chief financial officer. The existence of this contract undermined the argument that there was only ever one contract of employment between the parties.

The High Court held that the terms and conditions upon which the claimant was employed from October 2014 onwards were very different. The capacity in which he was employed, and the terms and conditions of his employment, undeniably changed upon his being appointed, on an interim basis, to the post of group chief executive. While one of the terms of the changed terms and conditions expressly provided that he would revert to his substantive, permanent position on the terms and conditions of employment applicable to that position, this did not alter the fact that, for the duration of his employment as interim group chief executive, the claimant was subject to a different set of terms and conditions under a distinct contract of employment, including higher remuneration.

The claimant's employment during the period was under five successive contracts of employment and the end of the contract of employment concerned was determined by an objective condition, ie, the arrival of a specified end date and/or the occurrence of a specific event, namely the appointment of a group chief executive on a permanent basis. The High Court acknowledged that while the label used by the parties was not necessarily conclusive of the employment relationship, it was telling that the HSE understood there to be separate contracts of employment involved.

The High Court concluded that it was clear from the correspondence between the parties that the HSE understood the claimant to be employed under successive contracts of employment. The HSE also understood that these contracts of employment would terminate, and that the claimant's employment under the terms of these contracts of employment would terminate upon his reverting to his substantive permanent position. However, the stance adopted by the HSE for the purposes of these proceedings was entirely different, claiming that there was only ever one ongoing contract of employment between the parties.

The High Court found that the classification of the dispute at the heart of this case as going to the issue *locus standi* by the Labour Court was incorrect and that while it is correct to say that only a claimant who can establish that they meet the definition of a 'fixed-term employee' is entitled to relief under the Protection of Employees (Fixed-Term Work) Act 2003, this question goes to the substantive merits of the claim and not to the procedural issue of standing. The Court stated that a claimant has the right to pursue the question of his or her employment status and the Labour Court has jurisdiction to rule on the matter. The fact that the claimant might ultimately be rejected on the merits does not mean that the claimant did not have standing to bring the matter before the Labour Court.

The High Court set aside the determination of the Labour Court and remitted it to the Labour Court for reconsideration and determination as to whether the use of successive fixed-term contracts could be objectively justified.

Finally, the High Court reiterated that this decision did not mean that an existing employee who has been acting up in a more senior role for in excess of four years is automatically entitled to remain in that post:

> This judgment goes no further than holding that where a vacant post has been filled by an individual pursuant to successive fixed-term contracts with an aggregate duration of in excess of four years, an employer cannot avoid the [2003] Act merely by dint of the fact that that individual is an *existing employee* with a right to revert to their original post. Rather, once the four-year threshold has expired, objective grounds of justification are required. The existence of a contractual right to revert to one's original post in an organisation, on the terms and conditions of employment applicable to that post, is no more than a *factor* to be considered in deciding whether the successive use of fixed-term contracts is objectively justified. It is not a bar to pursuing a complaint that there has been a breach of the [2003] Act. [Emphasis in original.]

The High Court also decided that a reference under art 267 of the Treaty on the Functioning of the European Union was unnecessary as the issue between the parties in this case fell to be resolved as a matter of domestic law.

The Court dealt with the issue of costs in a supplementary judgment,[5] where the Court made it clear that the claimant had been entirely successful in his appeal and, were the general rule in relation to costs to apply, namely that costs follow the event, then the claimant would be entitled to an order for costs as against the respondent. However, matters were complicated by the fact that the costs of these proceedings were governed

---

[5]   *Power v Health Service Executive* [2021] IEHC 454.

by Ord 105, r 7 of the Rules of the Superior Courts. This rule provides, in effect, that no costs shall be allowed in respect of a statutory appeal from a determination of the Labour Court, save by special order of the High Court.

The Court concluded that, in the very particular circumstances of the present case, it was appropriate to make a 'special order' as to costs for the purpose of Ord 105, r 7. The claimant was entitled to recover his reasonable legal costs as against the respondent. The reason for this was that the appeal raised a point of law of general public importance in respect of the scope of the Protection of Employees (Fixed-Term Work) Act 2003. The effect of the principal judgment was to correct a longstanding error on the part of the Labour Court in its interpretation of the legislation. Were the presumptive position under Ord 105, r 7, ie, that the parties to appeals from the Labour Court should bear their own costs, to apply in cases which raise points of law of general public importance, this might have the unintended consequence that appeals raising such points might not be brought before the High Court.

The second reason for making a costs order related to the litigation history between these two parties. The Court stated that the quantum of costs was to be adjudicated, ie, measured, under Pt 10 of the Legal Services Regulation Act 2015 in default of agreement between the parties. The Court placed a stay on the execution of the costs order pending the determination of the intended application for leave to appeal to the Supreme Court.

LESS FAVOURABLE TREATMENT

[8.04] *KO v Consulmarketing SpA[6]—European Court of Justice—request for preliminary ruling from Italy—Directive 1999/70/EC[7]—Framework Agreement on Fixed-term Work, clause 4—principle of non-discrimination—objective reasons justifying treatment of fixed-term workers—Directive 98/59/EC[8]—collective redundancy*

KO was recruited by Consulmarketing in January 2013 under a fixed-term employment contract which, in March 2015, was converted into a contract of indefinite duration. In January 2017, Consulmarketing initiated collective redundancy proceedings involving a number of workers, including KO, at the end of which all of the workers were dismissed. The collective redundancies transpired to be unlawful by reference to Italian law, as a consequence of which KO was entitled to a remedy. Italian law provided for different remedies depending on whether an employee was a permanent employee before or after a specific date. KO's fixed-term employment commenced before that date, but KO's contract of indefinite duration began after that date. As a consequence, the remedy of reinstatement was not available to KO.

---

[6] *KO v Consulmarketing SpA* (Case C-652/19).
[7] Directive 1999/70/EC concerning the framework agreement on fixed-term work.
[8] Directive 98/59/EC on the approximation of the laws of the Member States relating to collective redundancies.

The Italian Court referred two questions to the ECJ. They were in essence as follows:

1. Do the principles of equal treatment and non-discrimination in clause 4 of the Framework Agreement on Fixed-term Work (the Framework Agreement) preclude the Italian legal provision which provides for a dual and differentiated system of protection whereby, in the same procedure, appropriate, effective and dissuasive protection is provided to employment relationships of indefinite duration created prior to the specific date for which reinstatement is envisaged as a possible remedy, yet limited compensation only is offered in respect of fixed-term employment relationships having the same length of service as they were created prior to that date but converted into an open-ended contract after that date, which is a less effective and dissuasive form of protection?
2. Do the provisions of arts 20 and 30 of the Charter of Fundamental Rights and Directive 98/59/EC on collective redundancies preclude the arrangements in question?

The ECJ addressed the second question first. It concluded that Directive 98/59/EC on collective redundancies was not infringed by the Italian legal provision in question, in the sense that the Italian legal provision did not come within the scope of that Directive and accordingly the matter could not be considered by the ECJ.

The ECJ then went on to consider the first question, namely whether clause 4 of the Framework Agreement must be interpreted as precluding national legislation which extended a new system for the protection of permanent workers in the event of unlawful collective redundancies to workers whose fixed-term contracts entered into before the coming into force of that legislation were converted into contracts of indefinite duration after that date.

On this question the ECJ noted that it had already held that protection afforded to a worker in the event of unlawful dismissal comes under the concept of 'employment conditions' within the meaning of clause 4(1) of the Framework Agreement. It also noted that, in order to assess whether the persons concerned are engaged in the same or similar work for the purposes of the Framework Agreement, it is necessary to determine whether, in the light of a number of factors, such as the nature of the work, training requirements and working conditions, those persons can be regarded as being in a comparable situation. The ECJ concluded that it is for the referring Court to assess the facts and determine that question.

The ECJ noted that KO had been treated less favourably than her colleagues who were hired for an indefinite period before the date of entry into force of the Italian legislative provision. The ECJ noted that the fact that KO acquired a status of a permanent worker after that date did not mean that, in certain circumstances, she could not rely on the principle of non-discrimination laid down in clause 4 of the Framework Agreement. It was sufficient in that regard to find that the difference in treatment resulted from the fact that she was initially recruited on a fixed-term basis.

Accordingly, the ECJ held that it was necessary to ascertain whether there was an objective reason justifying the difference in treatment and noted that the concept of 'objective grounds' within the meaning of clause 4(1) of the Framework Agreement must be understood as not permitting a difference in treatment between fixed-term workers and permanent workers to be justified on the basis that the different treatment is provided for by a general or abstract measure such as a law or a collective agreement. The unequal treatment found to exist must be justified by the:

> presence of precise and specific factors, characterising the employment condition to which it relates, in the specific context in which it occurs and on the basis of objective and transparent criteria, in order to ensure that that unequal treatment in fact responds to a genuine need, is appropriate for the purpose of attaining the objective pursued and is necessary for that purpose.

The Italian Government submitted that the less favourable treatment of a worker in KO's situation was justified by a social policy objective encouraging employers to employ workers on a permanent basis. It argued that treating the conversion of a fixed-term contract into a contract of indefinite duration like a new recruitment was justified as the worker concerned obtained a form of stability of employment in exchange. The ECJ accepted that enhancing employment stability by promoting the conversion of fixed-term contracts into contracts of indefinite duration was a legitimate objective of social law, as it was an objective pursued by the Framework Agreement itself and that it was for the Italian Court to determine whether the measure was appropriate and necessary for the purpose of obtaining that objective. The ECJ observed that Member States enjoy broad discretion in their choice, not only to pursue a particular aim in the field of social and employment policy but also in the definition of measures capable of achieving it.

Finally, the Court noted the fact that the Italian provision reduced the level of protection for permanent workers was not of itself covered by the prohibition on discrimination set out in clause 4. As a result, differences in treatment between specific categories of permanent staff were not covered by the principle of non-discrimination established by the Framework Agreement.

Accordingly, the Court answered the first question by stating that clause 4 of the Framework Agreement must be interpreted as not precluding national legislation which extended a new system for the protection of permanent workers in the event of unlawful collective redundancies to workers whose fixed-term contracts, which were entered into before the date of entry into force of that legislation, were converted into contracts of indefinite duration after that date.

[8.05]   *Servicio Aragonés de Salud v LB[9]—European Court of Justice—request for a preliminary ruling from Spain—Directive 1999/70/EC[10]—fixed-term work—non-discrimination*

The applicant worked as a member of staff of the health service in Spain. She received an offer to be appointed as a temporary lecturer on a fixed-term contract. To allow her

---

9   *Servicio Aragonés de Salud v LB* (Case C-942/19).
10   Directive 1999/70/EC concerning the framework agreement on fixed-term work.

to perform these duties, she requested a leave of absence by reason of employment in the public sector under Spanish law. The health service refused, because the rules applicable to this leave type prohibited persons from taking such leave where the new post was to be held on the basis of a fixed-term contract.

The applicant submitted an application for another leave type, which was granted. She also appealed the decision not to grant the leave type she originally applied for, on the grounds that this decision was contrary to the principles of equality and non-discrimination contained in Directive 1999/70/EC (the fixed-term work Directive). The plaintiff was successful in her appeal. The health service appealed this decision.

The Spanish Government and the Commission submitted that the principle of non-discrimination was not applicable as the employee applied for the leave of absence while holding a permanent post.

The ECJ considered the purpose of the fixed-term work Directive and found that the principle of non-discrimination applies only to workers providing remunerated services in the context of a fixed-term employment relationship. As the applicant at the time of making the request was employed in the context of a permanent employment relationship, she could not avail of the protection of clause 4 of the fixed-term work Directive, and, as such, the ECJ had no jurisdiction in the matter.

Use of Successive Fixed-Term Contracts

[8.06] *MV ea v Organismos Topikis Aftodioikisis[11]—European Court of Justice—request for preliminary ruling from Greece—Framework agreement on fixed-term employment concluded by ETUC, UNICE and CEEP—fixed-term work—successive contracts or extended first contract*

In 2015, the applicants were employed under private law, fixed-term employment contracts in the cleaning department of the municipality of Agios Nikolaos, Greece (the Municipality). The contracts were initially for eight months but were extended and the renewed contracts ranged between 24 and 29 months. The contracts were terminated on 31 December 2017. Under Art 103(8) of the Greek Constitution, there is a prohibition on the conversion of fixed-term contracts of staff in the public sector to contracts of indefinite duration; and under Art 5 of Presidential Decree No 164/2004, successive fixed-term contracts must be in writing, and state reasons justifying their conclusion.

The applicants sought to establish that, as their contracts were successive fixed-term contracts, the contracts were in contravention of the Framework agreement. They sought to continue their employment with the Municipality on contracts of indefinite duration and a declaration that the termination was null and void.

---

[11]   *M.V. e.a. v Organismos Topikis Aftodioikisis* (Case C-760/18); ECLI:EU:C:2021:113.

The Greek Court referred three questions to the ECJ. The ECJ summarised the first question as

> to ascertain whether Clause 1 and Clause 5(2) of the framework agreement must be interpreted as meaning that the expression "successive fixed-term employment contracts" therein also covers the automatic extension of the fixed-term employment contracts of workers in the cleansing sector of local and regional authorities, which has taken place in accordance with express provisions of national law, notwithstanding the fact that the generally prescribed formal requirement that successive contracts be concluded in writing has been disregarded.

The ECJ considered the objectives and scope of the Framework. The ECJ noted that one of the objectives of the Framework is to place limits on successive recourse to fixed-term employment contracts. The ECJ stated that 'a contract which is the very first or only fixed-term employment contract does not fall within the scope'.

The contract was described as an 'automatic extension of an initial fixed-term contract, as a result of legislative measures' and it was argued that, as there were no formal conclusions in writing of one or more contracts, it was therefore not a successive contract. The ECJ said that this interpretation would 'be liable to jeopardise the object, the purpose and the effectiveness' of the Framework.

In responding to this question the ECJ concluded that the Framework covered these forms of employment contracts.

The ECJ answered the second and third questions together, which were:

(2)   Where a practice is enacted and applied for the employment of local authority cleansing department workers that is contrary to the measures, to prevent the abuse that may arise from the use of successive fixed-term employment contracts, provided for under the measure harmonising national legislation with Clause 5(1) of the framework agreement, would the obligation incumbent upon a national court to interpret national law in conformity with EU law extend to the application of a provision of national law, such as Article 8(3) of Law 2112/1920, as a pre-existing and still applicable equivalent legal measure, within the meaning of Clause 5(1) of the framework agreement, that would allow the correct legal classification of successive fixed-term employment contracts used to cover the fixed and permanent needs of local authority cleansing departments as employment contracts of indefinite duration?

(3)   If the answer to the previous question is in the affirmative, would a provision of constitutional status such as that set out in Article 103(7) and (8) of the Greek Constitution, as revised in 2001, absolutely prohibiting the public sector from converting fixed-term employment contracts, concluded when the above provision was applicable, to contracts of indefinite duration, constitute an excessive restriction upon the obligation to interpret national law in conformity with EU law, by making it impossible to apply a pre-existing equivalent and still applicable legal measure of national law within the meaning of Clause 5(1) of the framework agreement, such as Article 8(3) of Law 2112/1920, and by preventing the possibility of successive fixed-term employment contracts used to cover the fixed and permanent needs of local authority cleansing departments from being re-classified as contracts of indefinite duration following a correct classification of the lawful relationship during court proceedings, even if they cover fixed and permanent needs?

The ECJ stated that an obligation on the Member States to provide for the conversion of fixed-term employment contracts into contracts of indefinite duration arose from the Framework. However, the Member State must have laws that are effective to 'prevent and, where relevant, penalise the abuse of successive fixed-term employment contracts'. The question for the ECJ to determine was whether these measures were adequate for this purpose.

The ECJ held on these two questions that:

> where abuse of successive fixed-term employment contracts, within the meaning of that provision, has occurred, the obligation incumbent on the referring court to undertake, to the fullest extent possible, an interpretation and an application of all the relevant provisions of domestic law capable of duly penalising that abuse and of nullifying the consequences of the breach of EU law extends to an assessment of whether the provisions of earlier national legislation, which remain in force, and which permit the conversion of a succession of fixed-term contracts to one employment contract of indefinite duration, may, where appropriate, be applied for the purposes of that interpretation in conformity with EU law, even though national constitutional provisions impose an absolute prohibition, in the public sector, on such conversion.

Therefore the ECJ concluded that within the Framework Agreement 'successive fixed-term employment contracts' included the automatic extension of fixed-term contracts, which had occurred in accordance with national law, despite the fact that the successive contract were not in writing. On the second and third question, the ECJ held that national courts must interpret and apply domestic law permitting the conversion of successive fixed-term contracts to contracts of indefinite duration in conformity with EU law, regardless of national constitutional provisions that impose an absolute prohibition, in the public sector, on such conversion.

Chapter 9

Health and Safety

INTRODUCTION

[9.01] In *R*, the Court of Appeal of England and Wales considered the concept of burden of proof in criminal proceedings under the Health and Safety at Work Act 1974. Two health and safety penalisation claims are noted, namely *Supermacs* (Labour Court), and *A Worker v A Cleaning Company* (Workplace Relations Commission).

Burden of Proof

[9.02] *R v AH Ltd and Mr SJ[1]—Court of Appeal of England and Wales (Criminal Division)—Bean LJ, Cheema-Grubb J & Joseph QC—appeal from Central Criminal Court—Health and Safety at Work Act 1974, s 40—burden of proof—health and safety—reasonable practicability—leave to appeal*

The case dealt with the burden of proof in proving 'reasonable practicability' under s 40 of the UK Health and Safety at Work Act 1974 (the 1974 Act). The underlying case related to the death of a nursing home resident due to serious burns from hot water because of a defective thermostatic mixer valve and lack of staff training in resident safety. The prosecution alleged that the respondents/accused did not discharge their duty under s 33(1) of the 1974 Act, by failing to conduct the operation of the nursing home so as to ensure as far as reasonably practicable that residents were not exposed to danger.

The instant case centred around *R v Davies*,[2] in which it was held that the accused must prove, on the balance of probabilities, that it was not reasonably practicable for them to have done more to have avoided the harm.

The accused argued that *Davies* was incorrectly decided for a number of reasons, including:

1. "'[r]easonable practicability" is an element of the offence, not a defence. Parliament could have legislated for an absolute duty to ensure safety subject to a defence of reasonable practicability but did not do so';

---

1   *R v AH Ltd and Mr SJ* [2021] EWCA Crim 359.
2   *R v Davies* [2003] ICR 586.

2. the lack of distinction between offence and defence constituted a significant error in the Court's assessment of s 40 and 'its compatibility with the presumption of innocence';

3. the distinction between 'regulatory' offences and 'truly criminal' offences was arbitrary and, according to the accused, should not to be sustained; and

4. 'the modern practicalities of investigating and prosecuting health and safety cases do not render proportionate a legal burden of proof on respondent'.

The accused contended that the relevant section (s 40) should be 'read down' to impose an evidential burden only on a respondent. In so contending, the accused relied on the following:

1. Parliament was unlikely to have considered the compatibility of s 40 with the right to a fair trial;

2. section 40 was an element of the offence and there was inadequate justification for departing from the principle that the prosecution should prove this issue;

3. 'reasonable practicability' related to an objective state of affairs, and did not relate to a respondent's 'knowledge or belief in that state of affairs';

4. when the 1974 Act was enacted, adverse inferences were not available under ss 34 and 35 of the Criminal Justice and Public Order Act 1994;

5. placing the legal burden of proving reasonable practicability on the Crown would not automatically lead to it being unable to prove its case;

6. a respondent could be 'convicted and sentenced to imprisonment for up to two years despite the fact that a jury may not be sure of guilt'. The accused argued this was inconsistent with the 'golden thread' that the respondent should receive the benefit of that doubt.

Mr SJ also argued that, when the *Davies* case was decided, a custodial sentence could not be imposed in respect of an offence under the relevant sections of the 1974 Act, as they were not introduced until 2008.

The prosecution argued that the reverse burden and decision in *Davies* had been expressly approved by the House of Lords in *R v Chargot*,[3] and that this decision should not be deviated from.

The Court of Appeal found that there was nothing disproportionate in the reverse burden imposed on respondents by s 40 and held that it was bound by the earlier decisions.

The Court also noted the introduction of a maximum sentence of two years' imprisonment (which was introduced in 2008) had already occurred by the time *Chargot* was before the House of Lords, and it did not deter the House of Lords from approving the *Davies* case.

The Court ultimately felt that it was not open to a trial Judge or the Court of Appeal to hold that *Davies* was wrongly decided and permission to appeal was refused.

---

[3] *R v Chargot* [2009] 1 WLR 1.

PENALISATION

[9.03] ***Supermacs Ireland Ltd v Ryan[4]—Labour Court—appeal from Workplace Relations Commission—Safety, Health and Welfare at Work Act 2005, s 27—protected act—penalisation***

The claimant submitted that her trade union representative wrote to the HR department of the respondent to make it aware of a grievance the claimant had relating to sexual harassment. Thereafter, the claimant asserted that her hours were reduced from full time to 20 hours a week. However, under cross-examination the claimant confirmed that the hours offered to her after the letter was received by HR were in line with hours she had been offered in previous weeks.

The respondent submitted that the fluctuation was standard for the claimant's patterns of work generally. The respondent said there existed no connection between the claimant's letter and the number of hours she was offered thereafter.

In considering the application, the Labour Court noted that for a claim to succeed under s 27 of the Safety, Health and Welfare at Work Act 2005, the claimant must show that she committed a protected act; that she suffered a detriment within the meaning of s 27; and a causal connection between the protected act and the detriment.

The Court in dismissing the appeal concluded that the claimant did not establish a causal connection between the commission of a protected act and the detriment suffered.

[9.04] ***A Worker v A Cleaning Company[5]—Workplace Relations Commission—Safety, Health and Welfare at Work Acts 2005 to 2014—health and safety concerns—penalisation—reduction in hours***

The claimant was employed as a general operative with the respondent, a contract cleaning company, and worked an average of 39 hours per week from December 2017 until May 2019. On 20 May 2019, the claimant brought a number of health and safety concerns to the management of the hospital where he worked, including concerns relating to lack of training in infection control, the absence of a health and safety representative, and the absence of training on chemicals. When the claimant arrived for work the following day, he was removed from the hospital site and given a 2.5-hour assignment in an alternative location.

The claimant worked 20 hours in the week that he raised his complaint. This increased to 26.25 hours the following week, and was reduced thereafter to 17.5 hours, followed by zero hours in the week of 10 June 2019. The claimant wrote to the respondent and the hospital on 19 June 2019, outlining his health and safety concerns, but received no response.

The claimant was requested to return to work on 1 July 2019, after which point his hours were reduced. The claimant brought a claim to the WRC alleging that the reduction

---

4   *Supermacs Ireland Ltd v Ryan* HSD213.
5   *A Worker v A Cleaning Company* ADJ-00023945.

in hours constituted penalisation for having highlighted health and safety concerns, contrary to the Safety, Health and Welfare at Work Acts 2005 to 2014 (the Acts). A witness attended on behalf of the claimant and gave evidence of inadequate health and safety practices during her employment with the respondent.

The respondent did not dispute that the claimant's hours were reduced as the hospital no longer wanted the claimant working on their site and submitted that the hospital was entitled to require the removal of the claimant from their site. The respondent stated that he and the hospital managers considered the claimant's complaints and decided that his health and safety assertions were wrong.

The respondent sent the claimant various text messages seeking to meet with him, which the claimant did not respond to. The respondent claimed that the claimant's reduction in hours was as a result of his refusal to engage, and was not a punishment.

The Adjudication Officer noted that, in order to make out a complaint of penalisation, it is necessary for a claimant to establish that the detriment of which he or she complains was imposed 'for' having committed one of the acts protected by s 27(1) of the Acts. The protected act must be an operative cause, such that 'but for' the act, the claimant would not have suffered the detriment. She noted that this test requires a consideration of the motive or reasons that influenced the decision maker.

The Adjudication Officer noted that a period of six days elapsed after the claimant was removed from the hospital before the respondent sent a vague text message seeking to meet with him. The respondent failed to furnish any documentation regarding the removal of the claimant, citing reasons of client confidentiality. The Adjudication Officer noted that the respondent did not dispute that the claimant was removed from the hospital site as a result of his complaints. On that basis, she found that the claimant had established a causal link between having made his complaints known to the respondent and the hospital and his removal from site and the ensuing reduction in working hours. The Adjudication Officer upheld the claimant's claim of penalisation and awarded him compensation of €7,500.

Chapter 10

Immigration

INTRODUCTION

[10.01] The Irish High Court considered the concept of 'continuous residence' for the purposes of a citizenship application in *Jones*. Four judicial review decisions of the Irish High Court are noted relating to the right to work: a refusal to grant an employment permit to an individual who already had the right to work in the State (*Hossain*); a refusal to grant an employment visa to an applicant who had obtained a general employment permit (*Ali*); a refusal to grant permission under Decision 1/80 of the Association Council (*Dogan*); and a refusal to grant a general employment permit *(P)*.

EU Treaty rights were considered in *Abbas* by the Irish Court of Appeal. Two further judicial review proceedings are noted relating to a refusal to vary immigration permission (*Middelkamp*), and a refusal of permission to land in the State (*Wen Wei*).

CITIZENSHIP

[10.02] *Jones v Minister for Justice and Equality[1]—High Court—Barrett J—Irish Nationality and Citizenship Act 1956—judicial review—citizenship application*

The applicant, who was an Australian citizen, applied to become a naturalised Irish citizen. The Irish Nationality and Citizenship Act 1956 (the 1956 Act), provides at s 15(1) that following an application for a certificate of naturalisation, the Minister may 'in his absolute discretion' grant the application, if satisfied that the applicant 'has had a period of one year's continuous residence in the State immediately before the date of the application'.

The application for naturalisation was submitted on 1 September 2017. As such, the reckonable period under the 1956 Act for the purposes of the application was 1 September 2016 to 31 August 2017, during which period the applicant was out of the jurisdiction for 100 days (97 days on holiday and 3 days due to work commitments).

By letter dated 11 October 2018, the Minister for Justice and Equality denied the application for neutralisation on the basis that the applicant had failed to satisfy the

---

[1]   *Jones v Minister for Justice and Equality* [2019] IEHC 519.

'continuous residence' requirement of s 15(1)(c) of the 1956 Act. The Minister's conclusion was based on the applicant's absence from the jurisdiction for a period exceeding
what could be described as the 'discretionary absence period of six weeks and possibly
more in exceptional or unavoidable circumstances' that the Minister was prepared to
facilitate when considering whether an application for naturalisation under the 1956
Act. The applicant brought judicial review proceedings in respect of the Minister's
conclusion.

The Court held that the Minister, when exercising his or her function to determine
whether an applicant for naturalisation has one year's continuous residence, does not
have any discretion under the 1956 Act, ie, either an applicant has one year's continuous residence, or they do not. The Court acknowledged the level of humanity shown
by the Minister in seeking to apply a 'discretionary absence period' to take account of
'the realities of modern life in which multiple work/holiday absences may be possible
in any one year', but concluded that in doing so the Minister had 'gone beyond what is
legally permissible in this regard', because the 1956 Act did not confer any discretion
on the Minister.

The Court noted that the definition of 'continuous' in the *Concise Oxford Dictionary of
Current English* in the context of s 15(1)(c) of the 1956 Act is that, for the year prior
to the submission of a naturalisation application, an applicant must be in a position to
demonstrate a one-year period of residence in Ireland that is 'unbroken, uninterrupted,
connected throughout in space or time'.

The Court therefore stated that although it did not agree with the manner in which the
Minister reached his conclusion, the conclusion had nonetheless been correct. Turning
to the grounds of relief sought by the applicant, the Court stated that although the
applicant had asserted that the Minister had been 'overly literal' in his application of
the requirement of continuous residence under s 15(1)(c) of the 1956 Act, the Minister
had in fact been 'excessively generous', on the basis that he had sought to exercise a
discretion that he was not afforded by s 15(1)(c).

EMPLOYMENT PERMITS

[10.03]   *Hossain v Minister for Business Enterprise and Innovation[2]—
High Court—Barr J—Employment Permits Acts 2003 to 2020—judicial review—
immigration—employment permits—eligibility to apply*

The applicant was a Bangladeshi national. He had a Stamp 4 immigration permission
on the basis that he was married to an EU citizen who was exercising her EU Treaty
rights in Ireland. The marriage broke down, the applicant's wife returned to the UK and
the applicant was faced with an impending loss of permission or expiry of permission
without the possibility to renew same.

---

[2]   *Hossain v Minister for Business Enterprise and Innovation* [2021] IEHC 152.

The applicant applied for an employment permit under the Employment Permits Acts 2003 to 2020 (the Acts). His application was refused on the basis that the Minister had no jurisdiction to grant an employment permit to a person who already had a right to work in the State. The respondent relied on s 2(10)(d) of the Employment Permits Act 2003, as amended which provides as follows:

> (10) Without prejudice to the other provisions of this Act, [s 2] does not apply to a foreign national …
>
> (d) who is permitted to remain in the State by the Minister for Justice, Equality and Law Reform and who is in employment in the State pursuant to a condition of that permission that the person may be in employment in the State without an employment permit referred to in subsection (1).

The applicant submitted that the decision refusing the employment permit did not contain any reference to this section. Even if it were accepted by the Court that this was the relevant subsection on which the Minister relied, it was contended that the subsection did not preclude the Minister from granting an employment permit to the applicant. The applicant asserted that s 2 was a penal provision and the effect of s 2(10)(d) was merely that persons who had a relevant permission would not be subject to penalties if they worked without holding an employment permit. He stated that s 8 provided broad discretion to the Minister to grant employment permits and s 12 provided an exhaustive list of reasons on which the Minister could rely to refuse permit applications. It was asserted that neither s 8 nor s 12 contained any reference to a requirement that an applicant must not already be in possession of a permission to be eligible to apply, and accordingly no such eligibility requirement existed.

The applicant further submitted that the Minister appeared to be operating a blanket rule or policy against the grant or consideration of employment permits, and this was impermissible. It was submitted that the refusal letter and the review decision were irrational, unreasonable and disproportionate because they failed to take into account the fact that the applicant's immigration permission was to expire during the course of the proposed period of employment.

The respondent stated that it had not applied any fixed policy to refuse an employment permit, but the refusal was a matter of law as the respondent did not have jurisdiction to grant such permits to those who were already entitled to work, as was made clear by s 2(10)(d) of the Acts.

The Court found that while the respondent was entitled to rely on s 2(10)(d) of the Acts, his interpretation of that provision was incorrect. The Court accepted the submission that s 2 was a penal provision, and that the ordinary meaning of the words set out in that provision was that they relieved a person who held an immigration permission (such as a Stamp 4) from the obligation to obtain an employment permit while in the State. The Court was satisfied that this did not prevent the Minister from considering an application solely on the basis that the applicant already had a Stamp 4 permission. The Court was satisfied that this construction was supported by ss 8 and 12 of the Acts.

The Court did accept that there might be circumstances in which refusing a permission to apply on the basis that an individual already had a permission would be appropriate.

It cited the example of a large number of EU nationals applying for employment permits in circumstances where they already had permission to work, thereby creating an unnecessary administrative burden on the State. However, the Court stated that this did not apply in the present case as the individual's permission was, due to his change of circumstances as had been notified to the Department, at risk of imminent withdrawal or at the very least subject to expiry in the near future without the possibility of renewal.

The Court did not consider the fact that there might be a small overlap of time during which an individual would have a 'double permission' to be a significant issue. Further, it noted that there was not in principle an issue with an individual holding a permit in circumstances where they did not have permission to be in the State—it was observed that this is commonplace for applicants who apply for permits when they are overseas.

The Court granted the reliefs sought and the decision to refuse the employment permit was quashed. The application was remitted to the Deciding Officer to be considered in accordance with the terms of the Court's decision.

[10.04] *Ali v Minister for Justice[3]—High Court—Burns J—Employment Permits Act 2006—judicial review—work permit—employment visa*

The applicant, a citizen of Pakistan, worked as a chef in Pakistan and applied for a work permit from the Department of Business, Enterprise and Innovation (the Department) under the Employment Permits Act 2006 (the 2006 Act) in order to take up a position as a chef in a restaurant in Co. Wicklow.

The application was successful; a general employment permit was issued authorising the applicant to work as a chef for a two-year period commencing on 30 August 2019 in the specified restaurant, employed by the proprietor of that restaurant. The letter notifying the applicant of his successful application for a permit stated that it 'relates to employment only and it is not a residence permit'.

On this basis, the applicant applied to the Minister for an employment visa on 24 September 2019. The application was refused by communication dated 27 November 2019, on the grounds that insufficient documentation had been submitted in support of the application. The applicant appealed this decision on 11 December 2019 and submitted some further documentation with the appeal. On 25 May 2020, the Minister notified the applicant that the original decision to refuse him an employment visa had been upheld, on the basis that: 'I am not satisfied with information supplied by you concerning your personal, economic and family circumstances has been sufficient that you would observe the conditions of the visa granted.'

The applicant brought an application for judicial review of the Minister's decision; leave to apply for an order of *certiorari* of the Minister's review decision was granted by the High Court on 5 October 2020. The basis for the application for the order of *certiorari* was that the Minister had erred in fact and/or acted unreasonably and/or irrationally in refusing to grant an employment visa to the applicant.

---

3   *Ali v Minister for Justice* [2021] IEHC 494.

In considering the test to be applied by the Court in reviewing the Minister's decision, the Court concluded that the test to be applied was whether the Minister's decision was 'arbitrary, capricious or unjust', which the Court deemed equivalent to whether it flew in the face of fundamental reason and common sense. In addition, the Court added an element to the test, ie, that 'a significant amount of deference must be afforded to the decision maker'.

In his application for an order of *certiorari*, the applicant sought to rely on and to assert a constitutional right to work, in light of *NHV v Minister for Justice and Equality*,[4] as well as the fact that he had been successful in his application for a work permit issued to him. The Court did not accept this submission; it declined to accept that a citizen of Pakistan, who was resident in Pakistan, could assert a constitutional right to work in Ireland simply because he had successfully applied for a work permit (which it had transpired had not been paid for by the applicant, but rather by his prospective employer), in circumstances where such work permit was conditional on an employment visa being issued.

The Court found it to be abundantly clear that the decision being made by the Minister in relation to the application for an employment visa was very different to that made by the Department in relation to the application for a work permit under the 2006 Act. The Court further noted that the Minister has a broad discretion when exercising his or her power to grant an employment visa, and that as such, any matter which gives rise to a cause for concern for the Minister that an applicant for an employment visa would not abide with the conditions of that permission is a relevant matter for the Minister to take into consideration when determining whether to grant an employment visa.

In addition, the Court noted that the onus is on the applicant for an employment visa to include all relevant supporting documentation with their application, and that no onus is placed on the Minister to advise an applicant on their application in the context of deficiencies in the information or materials provided.

The applicant asserted that the supporting documentation submitted alongside his application for an employment visa was sufficiently detailed, and that the findings made in respect of the supporting documentation were irrational. The Court emphasised that, in exercising its judicial review function, the High Court is not an appeal court, and specifically that its role is not to determine whether it would have arrived at the same conclusion as the Minister on the basis of the materials before him or her. In addition, the Court stressed that the fact that the application for a work permit had been successful did not mean that the Minister's refusal to grant an employment visa was irrational.

The Court concluded that the decision to refuse to grant an employment visa to the applicant was one that was open to the Minister to make, on the basis of all of the evidence submitted to her by the applicant. The Court was satisfied that the lack of supporting documentation to accompany the application was a matter which quite properly could give rise to a concern on the part of the Minister, and that her concerns and

---

4   *NHV v Minister for Justice and Equality* [2017] IESC 35.

her findings did not fly in the face of fundamental reason or common sense, were not unjustified, and were matters which she was entitled to have regard to. Accordingly, the Court refused to grant the relief sought and made an order awarding the Minister's costs against the applicant.

See also *Luqman v Minister for Justice* [2021] IEHC 496 for the same findings in similar circumstances.

[10.05]   *Dogan v Minister for Justice[5]—High Court—Burns J—Employment Permits Acts 2003 to 2006—Decision 1/80 of the Association Council of 19 September 1980 on the Development of the Association—judicial review—immigration— permission to work—Turkish Association—impact of expiry of original permission*

The applicant, a Turkish national, sought orders quashing the decision of the respondent to refuse her application for permission to work and reside in Ireland under Decision 1/80 of the Association Council of 19 September 1980 on the Development of the Association (Decision 1/80).

The applicant entered the State on 29 December 2013. Her permission at that time was a student visa. The visa was granted subject to restrictions on the right to work and a requirement that she not remain in the State later than 6 November 2016. The visa was renewed up to its expiry.

The applicant was lawfully employed by the same employer from October 2014 until the expiry of her student visa in November 2016. She was granted a GNIB card, but she lost it before making her application. After her visa expired, she continued to reside in the State and work for the same employer up to January 2018. On 8 February 2019, she made an application for permission to work and reside in Ireland under Decision 1/80, on the basis that she satisfied the following conditions of art 6:

> Subject to Article 7 on free access to employment for members of his family, a Turkish worker duly registered as belonging to the labour force of a Member State ... shall be entitled in that Member State, after one year's legal employment, to the renewal of his permit to work for the same employer, if a job is available.

The respondent denied her application because at the time of the application, the individual was not in registered employment and had not had permission to remain in employment since 2016, following the expiry of her student visa.

The applicant asserted that the expiry of her student visa had no impact on her permission to work, and consequently her application, and the Employment Permits Acts 2003 to 2006 were not applicable because she was entitled to be in employment under Decision 1/80, which is a treaty within the meaning of the European Communities Acts 1972 to 2003. The respondent argued that the expiry of her student visa without renewal resulted in her no longer having permission to be in the State, and consequently she could not be considered as having satisfied the criteria of Decision 1/80.

---

[5]   *Dogan v Minister for Justice* [2021] IEHC 692.

The Court found that the applicant's right to a work permit under Decision 1/80 had already been acquired by the time her student visa expired. Having regard to the jurisprudence of the ECJ, the Court found that:

> if an entitlement to a work permit arises pursuant to Decision 1/80, then a right of residence is a corollary right. Whilst the Respondent can regulate entry into the State, once a person is lawfully within the State; has complied with the conditions of entry; and has been in lawful employment for a twelve-month period with the same employer, then an entitlement to a work permit in respect of that employment arises if a job is available.

It followed, according to the Court, that the expiry of the student visa was not material—the right to a work permit had already been acquired, and that right included a corollary right of residence. The Court found that the Employment Permits Acts 2003 to 2006 were not applicable to the applicant.

The decision of the respondent was quashed. However, the Court remitted the matter to the respondent to consider whether the permit could be issued, in circumstances where it was not clear whether a job was available from the same employer, as was required under Decision 1/80.

[10.06] *P v The Minister for Business, Enterprise and Innovation[6]— High Court—Barrett J—Employment Permits Acts 2003 to 2006—judicial review— order of certiorari—challenge to refusal of general employment permit*

The applicant was a chef and third-country national who, at the time of the case, did not hold a current immigration permission to remain in Ireland. The application for a general employment permit to allow him to take up a job as a head chef in a restaurant was made on the express basis that the respondent was being asked to exercise discretion to grant the application, notwithstanding the applicant's immigration status. The respondent refused the application, which decision the applicant sought to have reviewed. The review decision affirmed the initial refusal and the applicant commenced the within proceedings seeking an order to quash the review decision.

The applicant argued that the respondent erred in law in unlawfully fettering discretion and/or failing to recognise that a discretion to exercise under s 12(1)(i) of the Employment Permits Acts 2003 to 2006 to grant the general employment permit, notwithstanding the fact that the applicant was in Ireland without a current immigration permission. The applicant also argued that the respondent erred by failing to give any or adequate reasons as to why the discretion would not be exercised.

The Court found that the decision to refuse the permit was 'thoroughly flawed in terms of the reasoning given'. The Court stated that the respondent could not put before the Court reasons that she had failed to include in the impugned decision. On the fettering of discretion point, the Court stated that the reasoning was 'so flawed and wanting in substance' that the Court could not determine properly whether or not there had been a fettering of discretion. The Court remitted the matter for fresh consideration.

---

[6]   *P v The Minister for Business, Enterprise and Innovation* [2021] IEHC 609.

EU TREATY RIGHTS

[10.07] *Abbas v Minister For Justice And Equality[7]—Court of Appeal—Binchy, Donnelly & Noonan JJ—appeal from High Court—Directive 2004/38/EC[8]— immigration—EU Treaty rights*

The appellant Minister refused an application made by the second respondent for a residence card on the basis of the first respondent's rights as an EU citizen for him and his family members to move and reside freely within the EU under Directive 2004/38/EC (the Directive). This refusal was quashed by the High Court, and the appellant appealed that decision to the Court of Appeal.

The respondents were brothers, originally from Pakistan. The first respondent was a UK citizen who had made various payments in support of his brother over the course of a number of years. The first respondent resided in the UK from April 2004 to November 2016 before becoming a naturalized citizen of the UK. The second respondent joined his brother for a period between July 2010 and November 2011, before returning to Pakistan. He stated that during the period he was in Pakistan from November 2011 onwards, he continued to be financially dependent upon his brother. The second respondent moved from Ireland to Pakistan on a student visa in January 2014 with a view to improving his employment prospects. Throughout that period, he was lawfully resident in Ireland, while his brother remained resident in the UK, and continued to be financially supported by his brother. In November 2016, the first respondent moved from the UK to Ireland to join his brother. In May 2017, the second respondent applied to the EU Treaty Rights division of the Department of Justice for a residence card. The application was refused.

On appeal, the appellant upheld the refusal for the following reasons:

— insufficient evidence relating to dependency in Pakistan: money transfers had been made, but the Deciding Officer could not verify the authenticity of such transfers and no evidence was provided to demonstrate that, had the payment not been made, the second respondent would not have been able to support himself in Pakistan;

— insufficient evidence relating to dependency in Ireland: the Deciding Officer noted that the first respondent had helped pay for the second respondent's education, but was not satisfied that the second respondent would not have been able to support himself without that assistance; and

— evidence provided was not consistent with a dependent relationship: some evidence indicated that the respondents shared responsibility for certain outgoings (eg, lease agreement), which is not considered a dependent relationship.

The Deciding Officer stated that they had considered all information and documentation made available by the respondents in reaching this decision. The respondents applied to the High Court to review this decision.

---

[7]   *Abbas v Minister For Justice And Equality* [2021] IECA 16.
[8]   Directive 2004/38/EC on the rights of citizens of the Union and their family members to move and reside freely within the territory of the Member States.

The High Court noted that reg 5 of the European Communities (Free Movement of Persons) Regulations 2015[9] (the 2015 Regulations) implementing the Directive require a person relying on the 2015 Regulations to establish dependency on a Union citizen 'in the country from which the person has come'. The trial Judge found that Ireland was 'the country from which the person has come', because the respondent was resident in Ireland in his own right on the date when he made the application. The trial Judge was satisfied that when the application was made, there was sufficient evidence demonstrating dependency in Ireland and accordingly he found that the Minister had acted unreasonably in not accepting this information as evidence of dependency. He also queried the reasonableness of the appellant's actions in determining that the second respondent had not satisfied the requirement that he was dependent while in Pakistan, stating that in his view the second respondent 'was being asked to prove the impossible i.e. how could he prove that, if he was not in the position he found himself to be in, he would not have been able to support himself?'. The trial Judge quashed the decision of the appellant.

The Court of Appeal considered at length the meaning of the phrase 'the country from which they have come' in the context of the relevant authorities. The Court found that, in circumstances where an applicant arrives from one country to another host state prior to the EU national whose Treaty rights are being invoked, the applicant will be required to demonstrate dependence in the country from which they had come before the host state and secondly also demonstrate dependency in the host state as at the date of the application. For the purpose of these proceedings, the second respondent was required to establish dependency in two jurisdictions: in the country from which he had come (Pakistan) and then also in the host state where he had arrived prior to the first respondent joining him (Ireland). It followed, in the view of the Court of Appeal, that the appellant was correct to consider whether or not the second respondent was dependent on the first respondent in Pakistan.

In considering the appellant's decision that the second respondent had not satisfactorily demonstrated dependency on the first respondent in Pakistan, the Court noted that the outcome of the proceedings depended on whether the appellant could be found to have acted unreasonably, and that the Court should be very slow to interfere with the decisions of specialist tribunals. The Court found that, having regard to evidence made available to the appellant, the appellant's decision was neither 'unreasonable or irrational' and as such did not justify 'interference by the Court'. The appeal on this point was successful.

VARIATION OF IMMIGRATION PERMISSION

[10.08]   *Middelkamp v The Minister for Justice and Equality[10]—High Court— Barrett J—variation of immigration permission under Immigration Act 2004, s 4(7)—European Convention on Human Rights, art 8—certiorari*

---

9   European Communities (Free Movement of Persons) Regulations 2015 (SI 548/2015).
10   *Middelkamp v The Minister for Justice and Equality* [2021] IEHC 521.

This case involved an application by a Canadian national for an order of *certiorari* in respect of a decision by the Minister for Justice and Equality to refuse an application the applicant had made under s 4(7) of the Immigration Act 2004 for a variation of the visa under which she lived in Ireland.

The applicant's husband was in Ireland on a student visa for the duration of a four-year degree in dentistry, which he began in 2018. In August 2018, the applicant came to Ireland on a two-year, non-renewable visa and worked as a legal secretary in Cork while supporting her husband in his studies. Her visa was due to expire in August 2020 but, due to the Covid-19 pandemic, was automatically renewed under a series of general extensions.

In December 2019, the applicant applied under s 4(7) of the Immigration Act 2004 for a variation of her immigration permission. This application was refused, and the applicant brought judicial review proceedings on grounds of failure or refusal to consider the private and family life of the applicant and on grounds that the principles of fair procedures and natural justice were breached by the respondent in failing to provide reasons for its decision. The Court commented that the Minister's letter was 'notably limited', very brief, and 'so broad as to be meaningless'.

The Court was critical of the Minister's attempt to 'add to the reasoning that she has given in her original decision' and did not believe the Minister's belated suggestion that there were matters of international foreign policy which might be influenced by any alternative decision.

The Court considered the applicant's argument under art 8 ECHR to be relevant and, as it had been raised by her, the Court's view was that it fell to be considered by the Minister as part of her application for a variation to her permission and that she should not have had to illegally overstay her existing permission before such issues would be considered by the Minister.

The Court quashed the Minister's decision and remitted the application for fresh consideration. A costs order was also made in favour of the applicant.

PERMISSION TO LAND

[10.09]   *Wen Wei v Minister for Justice*[11]*—High Court—Burns J—Immigration Act 2004—judicial review—refusal of permission to land*

The applicant was a Malaysian national who sought permission to land and enter the State in order to undertake an English language course. She was refused permission to land, as the English course which she was intending to undertake was to be conducted online, rather than in person.

Relevant guidelines issued by the Government on 27 October 2020 relating to English language courses, stated that prospective students seeking to enter the State should

---

[11]   *Wen Wei v Minister for Justice* [2021] IEHC 161.

wait until in-person tuition had been resumed, and that failure to do so might result in students being refused leave to land. Course providers were requested to bring this restriction to the attention of prospective students.

The Court noted that this was a significant decision, having regard to the fact that under existing student guidelines, issued by the Irish National Immigration Service in 2011, non-EEA students are not permitted to enter Ireland to undertake distance learning courses. In August 2020, immigration officers were reminded of this and informed that individuals should be told 'it is not permissible for a non-EEA student to come to Ireland to undertake an online course. Individuals should not be permitted entry for this purpose and should not be registered on the basis of an online course.'

Having been refused permission to land, the applicant was served with a notice under s 4(4) of the Immigration Act 2004 (the 2004 Act), which stated that the grounds as to why she was being refused permission to land were that 'her entry into, or presence in, the State could pose a threat to national security or be contrary to public policy'. She was served with a notice under s 14 of the 2004 Act requiring her to remain at a hotel in Cork, to surrender her passport and to report to the Information Desk at Cork Airport the next morning at 11.30 am. The applicant made an urgent application seeking leave to apply by way of judicial review to quash the decision to refuse the permission to land, and to prevent the applicant's removal from the State.

The grounds of the challenge were that the s 4(4) notice failed to record the factual reasons for refusal; the respondent failed to provide reasons for the decision to refuse permission to land; the refusal on grounds of public policy was not established, having regard to the meaning of that term within the 2004 Act; or in the alternative, the notice was defective for a lack of specificity.

The Court noted that s 4(4) of the 2004 Act makes no requirement to set out written reasons—it simply states that grounds of refusal must be informed to the non-national in writing as soon as may be and that a refusal to land must be based on a ground set out in s 4(3). The Court considered that it 'is specification of one of the grounds which [s 4(4)] is referring to, rather than requiring that the reasons why a ground is established be recorded in writing'. The Court observed that this made sense in light of the nature of applications for permission to land; these applications are made orally on landing in the State and must be determined promptly by immigration officers. This is different to paper-based applications which lend themselves more readily to reasons for decisions being provided. Accordingly, the Court did not accept the argument that the grounds of refusal were required to be notified in writing under s 4(4).

The Court accepted that this did not obviate the need to give reasons for the decision to refuse permission to land. However, it noted that it was a clear that a reason was given to the applicant, namely that her course would be conducted online. The requirement to give reasons for the refusal of permission to land was met in this case through a combination of oral communication between the applicant and the detective Garda in question under the s 4(4) notice.

In considering whether it was established that the applicant's presence was contrary to public policy, the Court observed that the two relevant High Court decisions in

Ezenwaka v MJELR and *Li and Wang v Minister for Justice and Equality*[12] conflict. The Court referred to s 4(3)(j) of the 2004 Act, which provides that 'permission to land can be refused by an Immigration Officer … on the grounds that a non-national's entry into, or presence in, the State could pose a threat to national security or be contrary to public policy'. The Court considered it important that neither *Ezenwaka* nor *Li and Wang* considered the use of the word 'or' in this section. On this basis, the Court did not agree that public policy related to personal conduct only—it is noted that the subsection dealt with two different concepts:

> the first being that a non-national can be refused permission to land if her entry into or presence in the State could pose a threat to national security; and the second being that a non-national can be refused permission to land if her entry into or presence in the State is contrary to public policy.

The Court observed that the public policy at issue was the 2011 policy that students from non-EEA countries are not permitted to enter the State for the purpose of participation in an English language course if that course is being delivered online. The Court observed that this policy had been impacted by the Covid-19 pandemic, but the Covid-19 pandemic was not the basis for the public policy—the basis for the public policy was to 'regulate the admission of non-EEA students into Ireland'. The Court observed that this is a matter reserved entirely to the Minister and that EU law has no application in this realm. The Court considered that the Oireachtas must have intended to give the Minister power to refuse an individual's entry to the State for legitimate policy reasons, and accordingly found that refusing the applicant permission to land on the grounds of public policy was permitted.

The Court rejected the argument that the notice was defective due to lack of specificity, noting that the applicant had no difficulty in instituting proceedings. The application for judicial review was refused.

---

[12]   *Ezenwaka v MJELR* [2011] IEHC 328 and *Li and Wang v Minister for Justice and Equality* [2015] IEHC 638.

Chapter 11

Industrial Relations and Trade Unions

INTRODUCTION

[11.01]   In *Naisiúnta Léictreach*, the Supreme Court considered the constitutionality of the sectoral employment order regime and considered whether the electrical contractor's SEA was valid.

The relevance of the European Convention on Human Rights and in particular Article 11 to the right to form a trade union was considered by the Court of Appeal of England and Wales on three occasions. The cases are *National Union of Professional Foster Carers, R (on the application of the Independent Workers Union of Great Britain)* and *Roofoods Limited*.

Whether a declaration made by a Court of a Contracting State that industrial action is unlawful constitutes a breach of Article 11 of the European Convention of Human Rights was considered by the European Court of Human Rights in *Norwegian Confederation of Trade Unions*.

Penalisation in respect of trade union membership and activities and the possible application of Article 11 of the European Convention of Human Rights was considered by the UK EAT in *Mercer*.

The manner in which trade union disciplinary proceedings must be conducted featured in the decisions of the Court of Appeal of England and Wales and the UK EAT in *Unite the Union v. McFadden* and *Coxhill v. Unite the Union* respectively.

The possible liability of a trade union for negligence in the negotiation of a compromise agreement was the subject of the decision of the High Court of England and Wales in *Langley*.

The assessment of damages in circumstances where a union had infringed the constitutional right to earn a livelihood was considered by the Court of Appeal in *O'Connell*.

Disputes with regard to European Works Councils were the subject of the decision of the UK Central Arbitration Committee in *HSBC* and the UK EAT in *Verizon*.

Finally, the role of the Labour Court in hearing industrial relations cases on appeal from a recommendation of an Adjudication Officer was addressed by the Labour Court in *Waterford Institute of Technology*.

Sectoral Employment Orders

[11.02]   *Naisiúnta Léictreach Contraitheoir Éireann Coideachta Faoi Theorainn Ráthaoichta v The Labour Court, the Minister for Business, Enterprise and Innovation, Ireland and the Attorney General[1]—Supreme Court—Clarke CJ, O'Donnell, MacMenamin, Dunne and Charleton JJ—constitutionality of Chap 3 of Industrial Relations (Amendment) Act 2015—ultra vires*

This appeal arises from a judgment of the High Court. In the proceedings, NECI (the respondent), a company representing small and medium-sized electrical contractors, successfully applied for judicial review of a sectoral employment order (SEO) the subject of a recommendation by the Labour Court under procedures laid down in Chap 3 of Industrial Relations (Amendment) Act 2015 (the 2015 Act), and subsequently embodied in a Statutory Instrument, SI 251/2019.[2]

The effect of this SEO was to set terms and conditions for workers across the entire electrical contracting area in the State. The recommendation was made in response to applications to the Labour Court from Connect trade union, and two employers' groups, namely, the Electrical Contractors' Association (ECA), and the Association of Electrical Contractors of Ireland (AECI), which were treated as a joint applicant by the Labour Court.

The two most significant questions before the High Court were first, a challenge to the constitutionality of Chap 3 of the Industrial Relations (Amendment) Act 2015, on foot of which the Statutory Instrument was promulgated; and second, NECI's alternative case that, in making the recommendation on foot of which the statutory instrument in question was promulgated, the Labour Court had acted *ultra vires* the 2015 Act, specifically by failing to give reasons for its recommendation. NECI was successful in both of these claims. On the first issue, the High Court granted a declaration that Chap 3 of the 2015 Act violated Art 15.2.1° of the Constitution, which vests sole legislative power for the State in the Oireachtas, as the High Court held the impugned provision empowered the Labour Court to make decisions which were legislative in nature. As a matter of logic, any procedures conducted under the impugned section would also be invalid.

This was appealed to the Supreme Court, which set out five main issues for consideration:

(I)   The interpretation of certain terms contained in Chapter 3 of the 2015 Act, "Statutory Interpretation";

(II)   Whether Chapter 3 of the 2015 Act complies with Article 15.2.1° of the Constitution;

(III)   Whether the enforcement provisions contained in the 2015 Act comply with Article 6 ECHR;

---

[1]   *Naisiúnta Léictreach Contraitheoir Éireann Coideachta Faoi Theorainn Ráthaoichta v The Labour Court, The Minister for Business, Enterprise and Innovation, Ireland and the Attorney General* [2021] IESC 36. See also *Arthur Cox Employment Law Yearbook 2020* at [11.02] for the High Court decision in *Náisiúnta Leictreach Contraitheoir Éireann Cuideachta faoi Theorainn Ráthaíochta (NECI clg) v The Labour Court, the Minister for Business Enterprise and Innovation Ireland and the Attorney General* [2019] No 280 JR; [2020] IEHC 303 [2020] IEHC 342.

[2]   Sectoral Employment Order (Electrical Contracting Sector) 2019 (SI 251/2019).

(IV) The statutory *vires* issue, namely whether the Labour Court furnished adequate reasons for its recommendation; and

(V) Whether in adopting and appending the Construction Workers Pension Scheme to the recommendation, the Labour Court acted *ultra vires*.

The Court began by considering the legislative history of Chap 3, the process by which SEOs come into effect. It then took each of the five issues set out above in turn.

1. The interpretation of certain terms contained in Chap 3 of the 2015 Act, 'Statutory Interpretation'

The Supreme Court began by considering how the Labour Court interpreted and applied the words 'economic sector' in the statutory procedure. In the application, the Labour Court had to consider a question as to whether the category of workers the subject of the application should include or exclude two sub-groups, namely, electricians working in semi-state bodies, and electricians and apprentices working in maintenance work for companies. The original application to the Labour Court had included both these sub-groups. The question that subsequently arose was whether it was lawful for the Labour Court to exclude these two sub-groups of workers, who had been included in the original application.

In relation to what constitutes an 'economic sector', the Supreme Court agreed with the High Court that the Labour Court must necessarily have a discretion to define the 'economic sector', as that Court has been provided with an enhanced role under the 2015 Act, which, in contrast to the 1946 Act, is not confined to a task of 'rubber-stamping' applications. The High Court pointed out that the Labour Court must now carry out its own examination under s 14. It held that it would undermine the effectiveness of the consultation process were the limits of an economic sector to be fixed irrevocably by the terms of an application submitted, and that such a narrow view of the Labour Court's jurisdiction would have had the practical effect that interested parties would not have a meaningful opportunity to make submissions on the scope of an economic sector. The Supreme Court upheld the High Court findings on this issue.

The Court also considered the application of the term 'substantially representative' in the application. As a precondition to exercising its jurisdiction, the Labour Court must be satisfied that the applicants are 'substantially representative' of the class, type or group of employer or worker in a particular industrial area. In the High Court, the NECI submitted that how the Labour Court determined that the joint applicants were 'substantially representative' violated NECI's rights to fair procedure under the Constitution; however, the High Court rejected this submission.

The Supreme Court also accepted the High Court analysis of what 'substantially representative' meant, ie, that what was provided for was a simple statutory threshold. But, once the threshold was met, an applicant thereafter enjoyed no special status in a subsequent examination before the Labour Court. Thus, it was open to an objector, such as NECI, to raise the question of whether or not an applicant was actually substantially representative. Subject to a right on the part of an objector to make effective submissions to vindicate its rights in relation to the question of representation, there can be no constitutional objection to the terms of s 14 in itself. As a matter of fact, NECI did seek to have the question of representation raised in its pre-hearing submissions to the Labour Court, and at the hearing itself. The Supreme Court was of the view that the question as to whether the Labour Court adequately dealt with the issue was a different matter entirely, as discussed below.

2. Whether Chap 3 of the 2015 Act complies with Art 15.2.1° of the Constitution

It was on this issue that the Supreme Court's view diverged from that of the High Court. The Supreme Court held that the High Court proceeded from an incorrect premise as to the nature of the tests involved. It held that there was no impermissible delegation of legislative power in this instance. The legislation does not trespass on the function of the legislature, even though the extent of the delegation was significant:

> The power to make a recommendation which may have the force of law is nothing if not substantial. But the recommendation must take place in conformity with the statutory procedure, each step of which is laid down by the Oireachtas. The Chapter sets out both rights and duties for the protection of the parties, and for objectors. The deliberations are to take place in public. Objectors may appear and make their case. When considered closely, the statutory criteria are perhaps more subtle and nuanced than might first be thought. This analysis concludes that, in fact, the sections just analysed do set out discernible and intelligible goals; they express a set of legal principles whereby the policy of the Oireachtas is to be achieved. When analysed in context, the scope of choice is narrower than might appear at first sight. Amongst other aims, the legislation is intended to have the effect of preventing social dumping. The intent of the Oireachtas in passing the 2015 Act was that the Labour Court was to proceed with the substance of the process in which it had previously engaged, but hedged about with clear constraints and limitations which are of greater substance and consequence than might be thought. It is true that an SEO may acquire the force of law, but the Oireachtas has laid down a high level of legislative safeguard in relation to any potential SEO. For the reasons set out, therefore, I would set aside this part of the High Court judgment, together with the suspended declaration of unconstitutionality. It follows that Chapter 3 of the Act does not offend Article 15.2.1° of the Constitution.

3. Whether the enforcement provisions contained in the 2015 Act comply with art 6 ECHR

The Supreme Court agreed with the High Court, which made no findings in relation to the submissions concerning the validity of the system in the Industrial Relations (Amendment) Act 2015 for dealing with complaints of alleged breaches of an SEO, as there had been no plea in the statement of grounds to the effect that the enforcement provisions involved an unauthorised administration of justice, thereby breaching Art 34 of the Constitution. Therefore, the High Court held it was neither necessary nor appropriate to consider the submissions further. The High Court also held, and the Supreme Court agreed, that, insofar as any challenge might have been made, it should have been to the enforcement provisions to be found in the Workplace Relations Act 2015, considered in *Zalewski*.[3]

---

[3]   *Zalewski v An Adjudication Officer, the Workplace Relations Commission, Ireland, the Attorney General and Buywise Discount Stores (Notice Party)* [2021] IESC 24.

4. The statutory vires *issue, namely, whether the Labour Court furnished adequate reasons for its recommendation*

The Supreme Court then moved to the statutory *vires* issue, asking the question whether the Labour Court and the Minister complied with the provisions under Chap 3 of the Industrial Relations (Amendment) Act 2015.

The Supreme Court stated that it should not set artificially high standards as to what should be in a recommendation or report but confirmed that recommendations and reports must give adequate reasons. It stated that it is not the task of the Court to engage in a detailed description of how the Labour Court performed each step of its statutory role in this instance but that, at 'the very minimum ... in order for there to be constitutional compliance on a fair procedures basis, objectors are entitled to be dealt with in an even-handed way, by the observance of the substance of fairness in procedure, and, in particular, by a recommendation and report which set out clear reasons for the conclusions'.

The High Court found that the Labour Court report submitted to the Minister on 23 April 2019 was deficient: 'First, the report fails to record even the conclusions of the Labour Court on crucial matters, still less does the report state a rationale for those conclusions.'

The Supreme Court went on to consider the jurisprudence on the duty to give reasons and summarised the questions applicable in this case as follows:

(a) Could the parties know, in general terms, why the recommendation was made?
(b) Did the parties have enough information to consider whether they could, or should, seek to avail of judicial review?
(c) Were the reasons provided in the recommendation and report such as to allow a court hearing a decision to actually engage properly in such an appeal, or review?
(d) Could other persons or bodies concerned, or potentially affected by the matters in issue, know the reasons why the Labour Court reached its conclusions on the contents of a projected SEO, bearing in mind that it would foreseeably have the force of law, and be applicable across the electrical contracting sector?

The Court stated that the test must be an objective one:

The Labour Court was engaged in a statutory role, involving compliance with statutory duties to protect rights, where public interest required transparency. The reasons had to be sufficient, therefore, not just to satisfy the participants in the process, but also the Minister, the Oireachtas, other affected persons or bodies, and the public at large, that the Labour Court had truly engaged with the issues which were raised, so as to accord with its duties under the statute.

Having considered the recommendation and accompanying report, the Court found there was no full description of the reasons as to how or why the Labour Court had reached its conclusions. The Court was of the view that these issues were 'capable of explanation'. While the Labour Court did not have to respond to every point raised by NECI, it had before it 'a series of significant questions raised by NECI as to the criteria which it intended to employ in reaching its decision, including how it was intended to approach the issues of "economic sector" and representivity'. These questions were legitimately raised, and should have had a response, with reasons.

Therefore, in failing to provide sufficient reasoning in the report for its recommendations, the Labour Court had acted *ultra vires*.

The Court then went onto consider the Minister's role. Under s 17 of the Industrial Relations (Amendment) Act 2015, the Minister has the power to either approve, or refuse to approve, the recommendation. Also under s 17(1) of the Industrial Relations (Amendment) Act 2015, the Minister, not later than six weeks after receiving a recommendation, where he or she is satisfied, having regard to the report, that the court has complied with the provisions of Chap 3, can accept the recommendation and by order confirm its terms from such date as may be specified. Since the reasoning in the Labour Court was found to be insufficient, the Court held that the Minister could not have been satisfied that there had been statutory compliance. Therefore, it followed that the Minister, too, had acted *ultra vires*.

5. Whether in adopting and appending the Construction Workers Pension Scheme to the recommendation, the Labour Court acted ultra vires

The final issue for the Court to consider was the separate complaint made to the effect that the function of fixing the rate of pension contributions was further delegated to a third party, ie, the decision to peg the rate of pension contributions to those fixed by the trustees of the Construction Workers Pension Scheme breached the principle that a delegate cannot further delegate their function.

Under s 16(5)(f), an SEO may make provision for the requirements of a pension scheme, including a minimum daily rate of contribution to the scheme by a worker and an employer. The Labour Court took the rates of contribution which were then payable under the Construction Workers Pension Scheme, and included them in the recommended order. However, the recommendation went on to provide as follows: 'Any changes to the rates for the Construction Workers Pension Scheme should be applied to the categories of workers covered by this SEO.' The final SEO made by the Minister included this provision, which meant that any change made by the trustees of the Construction Workers Pension Scheme to their rates would automatically affect the rates payable under the impugned SEO.

The High Court held that the approach adopted under the secondary legislation was *ultra vires* the Industrial Relations (Amendment) Act 2015 which provides that the rate of any mandatory pension contribution payable will be provided for under the terms of the SEO itself. The Supreme Court observed that the 'Oireachtas has thus delegated the function of fixing the daily rate to the Minister, pursuant to a recommendation of the Labour Court'. The Supreme Court held that the Minister could not 'abdicate this function by pegging the rate to a separate rate fixed by a third party, i.e. the trustees of the Construction Workers Pension Scheme'. It stated that the terms of the SEO should be 'precise and self-contained'. The consultation process would be undermined if the rate of contribution could subsequently be changed without consulting the interested parties. In addition, it would undermine legal certainty if employer had to look beyond the SEO to determine their legal obligations. What was required, rather, was to set out a minimum daily rate of contribution to the scheme by a worker, and an employer. The recommendation did not do this. For this reason, the Court held that this section was also *ultra vires*.

The Supreme Court therefore rejected the High Court finding that Chap 3 of the Industrial Relations (Amendment) Act 2015 was 'repugnant' to Art 15.2.1° of the Constitution, but upheld the High Court findings on art 6 of the ECHR, the *vires* issue relating to adequate reasons, and the delegation of pension rates. The matter was remitted to a differently constituted Labour Court to 'prepare and furnish a recommendation giving reasons'.

RIGHT TO FORM A TRADE UNION—EUROPEAN CONVENTION ON HUMAN RIGHTS

[11.03] *National Union of Professional Foster Carers v The Certification Officer⁴—Court of Appeal of England and Wales—Underhill, Bean and Green LJJ—appeal from UK Employment Appeal Tribunal—Trade Union and Labour Relations (Consolidation) Act 1992—European Convention on Human Rights, art 11—Human Rights Act 1998, s 3—trade union registration*

This case related to the rights of foster carers to form a trade union. An association intending to represent foster carers applied to the Certification Officer to be entered on the list of trade unions maintained by the Certification Officer under the Trade Union and Labour Relations (Consolidation) Act 1992 (the 1992 Act). The Certification Officer rejected the application on the basis that foster carers were not 'workers' and accordingly the application did not comply with the requirements of the 1992 Act.

The association appealed to the EAT. It contended that foster carers should be considered to be 'workers' under the 1992 Act and also contended that the inability of foster carers to form a listed trade union would give rise to a breach of art 11, or alternatively art 14 of the ECHR (the Convention) and that it was possible for the EAT, applying the special rule of construction under s 3 of the Human Rights Act 1998, to interpret the relevant provisions so as to avoid that breach. It did not seek a declaration of incompatibility under s 4 of the 1998 Act because the EAT has no power to make such a declaration. The EAT dismissed the appeal and decided that the Certification Officer had been correct to decide that foster carers did not work under a contract and accordingly the association was not entitled to be listed as a trade union and that that state of affairs did not give rise to a breach of the Convention rights of the association or its members. The association appealed against the decision of the EAT.

Before the Court of Appeal, the association accepted, by reason of the decisions in *W v Essex County Council*⁵ and *Rowlands v City of Bradford Metropolitan District Council*,⁶

---

⁴   *National Union of Professional Foster Carers v The Certification Officer* [2021] EWCA Civ 548. See *Arthur Cox Employment Law Yearbook 2019* at [11.03] for the EAT decision in *National Union of Professional Foster Carers (NUPFC) v Certification Officer* UKEAT/0285/17/RN.

⁵   *W v Essex County Council* [1999] Fam 90.

⁶   *Rowlands v City of Bradford Metropolitan District Council* [1999] EWCA Civ 1116.

that foster carers did not provide their services under a contract and that accordingly they were not workers for the purposes of the 1992 Act. As a result, the Court of Appeal was concerned only with whether their consequent exclusion from the right to be listed under the 1992 Act would give rise to a breach of their rights under arts 11 and 14 of the Convention.

The Court of Appeal, in considering art 11, set itself the following questions:

1. Was art 11 engaged? If so;
2. Did the denial of the right to be listed constitute an interference with the art 11 rights of the association or its members? If so;
3. Was that interference justified? If not;
4. Could the definitions in the 1992 Act be 'read down' using the special interpretive of the obligation under s 3 of the 1998 Act so as to render s 2 of the 1992 Act compliant?

Article 11 of the Convention is in the following terms:

Freedom of assembly and association

1. Everyone has the right to freedom of peaceful assembly and to freedom of association with others, including the right to form and to join trade unions for the protection of his interests.
2. No restrictions shall be placed on the exercise of these rights other than such as are prescribed by law and are necessary in a democratic society.

On the first question, as to whether art 11 is engaged, the Court noted that the fundamental point which emerged from the approach of the ECtHR in *Sindicatul 'Păstorul Cel Bun' v Romania*[7] was that art 11 will be engaged as regards trade union rights, where workers are parties to 'an employment relationship' and in determining whether an employment relationship exists, the correct approach is to be found in the International Labour Organisation Convention on Freedom of Association and Protection of the Right to Organise (ILO). The ECtHR cited with approval ILO Recommendation no. 198 'concerning the employment relationship'. Specifically, para 9 of that recommendation provides that:

> the determination of the existence of [an employment relationship] should be guided primarily by the facts relating to the performance of work and remuneration of the worker, notwithstanding how the relationship is characteri[s]ed in any contrary arrangement, contractual or otherwise, that may have been agreed between the parties.

The Court of Appeal noted that there is nothing in ILO Recommendation no 198 that suggests that an employment relationship must be contractual, so as to exclude cases where the essential elements of the relationship are prescribed by law or administratively. Such a requirement would promote form over substance in a way that would be inconsistent with the decisions of the ECtHR. There are also great difficulties because Member States may differ in whether they characterise particular kinds of relationship as contractual. The Court of Appeal noted that in the case of foster carers, the fee

---

[7]   *Sindicatul 'Păstorul Cel Bun' v Romania* Application no 330/09.

paid is a reward for services provided by the foster carer to the fostering service by providing care and accommodation for the child. The Court of Appeal held that that must constitute remuneration in the relevant sense. Likewise the facts relating to the performance of the work indicated that, although the role of the foster carer has special features, those features are not inconsistent with the existence of an employment relationship. Accordingly, the Court concluded that foster carers who undertake placements should be regarded as being, during a placement, in an employment relationship with the relevant fostering service such that art 11 of the Convention is engaged.

On the second question, as to whether there was 'an interference' with the art 11 rights, the Court of Appeal concluded that refusal to list did constitute such an interference because the *de facto* position was that listing is a badge of official status from which other entitlements derive.

On the third question, as to whether the interference could be justified, the Court noted that, as the interference was 'prescribed by law', the only issue was whether it was 'necessary in a democratic society' within the meaning of art 11(2). That, in turn, depended on whether the restriction or interference pursued a legitimate aim and if so, whether same was a proportionate means of achieving that aim. The respondent contended that there were two legitimate aims, namely maintaining the distinction adopted by the legislation between those who are workers (those who work under a contract) and those who are not, and protecting the rights and wellbeing of children in foster care. Considering the first question, the Court distinguished between the aim of avoiding the risk that the grant of worker status to foster careers would damage the nature of the fostering relationship but concluded that that aim did not have the same weight where the rights sought consisted only of the right to trade union listing as distinct from individual employment rights. On the second aim, the Court concluded that it was artificial. The exclusion of foster carers from the scope of the 1992 Act was not in fact a result of any concern of the type cited, it was a result of the choice made about the definition of worker.

On the question of proportionality, the Court concluded that the aims relied on by the respondents were not capable of outweighing the significant interference with the art 11 rights.

Accordingly the Court of Appeal concluded that the exclusion of the association from the right to be listed under s 2 of the 1992 Act infringed its rights under art 11 of the Convention. The Court concluded that the term 'worker' in the 1992 Act can be read down to include foster careers, notwithstanding that they do not work under a contract.

The Court, in allowing the appeal, concluded that it should make a declaration that the definition of worker in the 1992 Act extends to persons who are parties to a foster carer arrangement with a fostering service provider.

[11.04]   *R (On the application of the Independent Workers' Union of Great Britain) v Secretary of State for Business, Energy and Industrial Strategy[8]—Court of Appeal*

---

[8]   *R (Independent Workers Union of Great Britain) v Secretary of State for BEIS* [2021] EWCA Civ 260, [2021] IRLR 363.

of England and Wales—Underhill, Bean and Phillips LJJ—appeal from High Court of England and Wales—European Convention on Human Rights, art 11—trade union recognition—freedom of association and assembly

The appellant union (the Union) had, among its membership, security guards and receptionists who worked for Cordant Security Ltd at the University of London. The Union made two applications, under the relevant UK statutory procedures for trade union recognition, to the Central Arbitration Committee (CAC) seeking recognition by Cordant and by the university for collective bargaining purposes. The CAC rejected the application regarding Cordant on the basis that there was already in force a collective agreement under which another trade union, Unison, was recognised by Cordant, the employer, as entitled to conduct collective bargaining in respect of the workers in question.

The second application was rejected on the basis that the university was not the employer. The Union sought judicial review of these decisions and the Administrative Court dismissed the claim. The Union appealed to the Court of Appeal but only with regard to the first application regarding Cordant. The Union contended that the CAC decision was unlawful because, by precluding its application for recognition, the underlying statutory provisions breached its rights under art 11 of the European Convention on Human Rights, which protects freedom of assembly and association. By the time the case came on for hearing, the university had taken back in house the work of the workers concerned and they had transferred into the employment of the university under TUPE. That in turn gave rise to a question as to whether the appeal was academic. The Court concluded that it would be excessively formulistic not to hear the appeal and accordingly the appeal in respect of the first decision was heard.

Article 11 of the European Convention on Human Rights provides as follows:

1. Everyone has the right to freedom of peaceful assembly and to freedom of association with others, including the right to form and to join trade unions for the protection of his interests.
2. No restrictions shall be placed on the exercise of these rights other than such as are prescribed by law and are necessary in a democratic society in the interests of national security or public safety, for the prevention of disorder or crime, for the protection of health or morals or for the protection of the rights and freedoms of others.

In considering whether the rejection of the application for recognition infringed art 11, the Court of Appeal considered the decision in *Demir v Turkey*,[9] where the ECtHR held:

> lawful restrictions may be imposed on the exercise of trade union rights by members of the armed forces, of the police or of the administration of the State. However, it must also be borne in mind that the exceptions set out in Article 11 are to be construed strictly; only convincing and compelling reasons can justify restrictions on such parties' freedom of association. In determining in such cases whether a "necessity"—and therefore a "pressing social need"—within the meaning of Article 11 § 2 exists, States have only a limited margin of appreciation, which goes hand in hand with rigorous European supervision embracing both the law and the decisions applying it including those given by independent courts.

---

[9]   *Demir v Turkey* [2009] IRLR 766.

The ECtHR in *Demir* then considered the evolution of its case law concerning the right of association under art 11, essentially:

1. the ECtHR has always held art 11 of the Convention 'safeguards freedom to protect the occupational interests of trade union members by the union's collective action, the conduct and development of which the Contracting States must both permit and make possible';
2. the ECtHR has always held that art 11(2) provides members of a trade union 'a right, in order to protect their interests, that the trade union should be heard'; however, 'each State [has] a free choice of the means to be used towards this end';
3. the right of association conferred by art 11 'is marked by two guiding principles', ie, the ECtHR will consider: 'the totality of the measures taken by the State concerned in order to secure trade union freedom, subject to its margin of appreciation'; and secondly, the ECtHR will not 'accept restrictions that affect the essential elements of trade union freedom, without which that freedom would become devoid of substance'. So, although Contracting States are in principle 'free to decide what measures [they wish] to take in order to ensure compliance with Article 11, [they are] under an obligation to take account of the elements regarded as essential by the Court's caselaw';
4. ECtHR case law has established the following essential elements of the right of association: 'the right to form and join a trade union ... the prohibition of closed-shop agreements ... and the right for a trade union to seek to persuade the employer to hear what it has to say on behalf of its members'. The ECtHR stated that the 'list is not finite' and will evolve according to developments in labour relations which give protection to human rights.

The ECtHR observed that its previous case law holding that the right to organise and bargain collectively do 'not constitute an inherent element of Article 11 ... should be reconsidered' as 'a failure by the Court to maintain a dynamic and evolutive approach would risk rendering it a bar to reform or improvement'. Therefore, the ECtHR concluded that the right to bargain collectively with the employer has, in principle, become one of the essential elements of the 'right to form and to join trade unions for the protection of [one's] interests' in art 11, 'it being understood that states remain free to organise their system so as, if appropriate, to grant special status to representative trade unions'.

The Court of Appeal then considered its own previous decisions namely those in *Pharmacists'Defence Association Union v Boots Management Services Ltd*[10] and *Vining v London Borough of Onesworth*[11] and endorsed the view in *Boots* that 'complaints based on the denial of a right to compel an employer to engage in collective bargaining face an uphill struggle'.

In the present case, Bean LJ noted that, before *Demir*, the ambit of essential art 11 rights as established in the ECtHR would not have included the rights which the union sought

---

[10]   *Pharmacists' Defence Association Union v Boots Management Services Ltd* [2017] EWCA Civ 66, [2017] IRLR 355.
[11]   *Vining v London Borough of Onesworth* [2017] EWCA Civ 1092.

here, namely the right of recognition for collective bargaining purposes, and observed that in *Demir* the ECtHR held that, save in very specific cases, the right to bargain collectively with the employer has become, in principle, an essential element of art 11 rights. However, Bean LJ noted that in *Demir* the ECtHR observed that the failure of domestic legislation to impose an obligation on employing authorities to enter into collective bargaining with a trade union was not at issue.

Bean LJ noted that if the trade union movement were encouraged by *Demir*, the subsequent case law of the ECtHR must have disappointed them, observing that in *Sindicatul 'Pastorul cel Bun' v Romania*,[12] the ECtHR emphasised that: 'Contracting States enjoy a wide margin of appreciation as to how trade union freedom and protection of the occupational interests of union members may be secured' and having declared that art 11 affords members the right for their trade union to be heard with view to protecting their interests, the ECtHR qualified this by adding that it 'does not guarantee them any particular treatment by the State'.

Bean LJ noted that the wide margin of appreciation afforded to Contracting States is a recurrent theme in the case law of the ECtHR; however, he pointed out that an exception to this is found in *Demir* where the ECtHR stated that only a limited margin of appreciation should be given when restrictions on art 11 rights are under consideration. Bean LJ concluded that this limit on the margin of appreciation of Contracting States appeared to be referring to particular exceptions and restrictions only, eg, those placed on members of the armed forces, the police or civil servants, 'rather than to the question of the extent of the essential rights conferred by Article 11(1)'.

The Court found that this case did not involve an exclusion of art 11 rights. Staff working for Cordant in the university workplace were free to join various other trade unions. The critical question was whether the right of freedom of association extends to the right to be represented in collective bargaining in their own independent union rather than by another one.

The Court observed that an narrow interpretation of *Demir* was confirmed in *National Union of Rail, Maritime and Transport Workers v UK*[13] and in *Unite the Union v UK*,[14] where the ECtHR 'emphasised the drastic infringement of rights involved in the *Demir* case', namely a collective agreement entered into by employers and a trade union was rendered ineffective by legislation dissolving the trade union.

Bean LJ concluded that it was appropriate to summarise the case law of the ECtHR as being to the effect that:

> to the extent that the Rules of any statutory scheme constrain access to collective bargaining for a particular trade union or its members the constraints will have to be justified by relevant and sufficient reasons, and must strike a fair balance between the competing interests at stake; but that in assessing that justification the choice made by Parliament should be given a wide margin of appreciation.

---

[12]   *Sindicatul 'Pastorul cel Bun' v Romania* [2014] IRLR 49.
[13]   *National Union of Rail, Maritime and Transport Workers v UK* [2014] IRLR 467.
[14]   *Unite the Union v UK* [2017] IRLR 438.

Applying the law to the present case, Bean LJ did not consider that there was anything in the case law of the ECtHR to indicate that the relevant UK statutory provisions refusing recognition where other unions were already recognised in respect of the workers concerned should be 'classified as a restriction which strikes at the very core of trade union activity'. The UK statutory provisions were accordingly within the wide margin of appreciation indicated by the case law of ECtHR. Accordingly, Bean LJ concluded that the Union had not established any violation of the art 11 rights of its members or of the union itself and the appeal was dismissed.

[11.05]   *The Independent Workers Union of Great Britain v The Central Arbitration Committee and Roofoods Ltd t/a Deliveroo[15]—Court of Appeal of England and Wales—Underhill, Coulson & Phillips LJJ—Trade Union and Labour Relations (Consolidation) Act 1992—European Convention on Human Rights, art 11—collective bargaining rights—workers—registration of a trade union*

This appeal concerned the collective bargaining rights of Deliveroo riders. The Independent Workers Union of Great Britain (the Union) applied to the Central Arbitration Committee (the CAC) under the compulsory recognition procedures set out in the Trade Union and Labour Relations (Consolidation) Act 1992 to be recognised by Deliveroo for collective bargaining in respect of a group of riders in its Camden & Kentish Town Food Delivery Zone. The CAC declined to accept the application on the basis that the riders were not 'workers' within the meaning of the 1992 Act because the terms under which they provided their services did not require them to do so personally but permitted the use of substitutes. The Union sought permission to challenge that decision by way of judicial review, which proceedings were dismissed in the High Court. The Union appealed.

The Union contended that the denial of registration constituted an infringement of art 11 of the European Convention on Human Rights (ECHR).

The Court observed that the appeal concerned 'the right to form and to join trade unions' referred to in the final part of art 9.1 of the ECHR. The Court noted that in *Demir v Turkey[16]* the ECtHR established that 'the right to bargain collectively with the employer has, in principle, become one of the essential elements of the "right to form and to join trade unions for the protection of [one's] interests" set forth in Article 11 of the Convention'.

Considering the art 11 ground of appeal, the Court of Appeal had to consider whether the riders were within the scope of art 11. In so doing, it noted that only workers in an employment relationship enjoy the protections arising from the closing words of art 11.1. The question whether an employment relationship exists is to be answered by reference to the criteria identified in ILO R198, rather than by reference to any definition in domestic law. Turning to ILO R198, the Court of Appeal concluded that the

---

15   *The Independent Workers Union of Great Britain v The Central Arbitration Committee and Roofoods Ltd t/a Deliveroo* [2021] EWCA Civ 952.

16   *Demir v Turkey* [2009] IRLR 766.

riders did not fall within the scope of the trade union freedom right under art 11, as the right to use a substitute deprived the riders of that status.

As the Deliveroo riders did not enjoy a right under art 11.1 which was interfered with by their being excluded from access to the compulsory recognition machinery, the question of interference did not arise in the case and the appeal was dismissed.

INDUSTRIAL ACTION—EUROPEAN CONVENTION ON HUMAN RIGHTS

[11.06] *Norwegian Confederation of Trade Unions and Norwegian Transport Workers Union v Norway[17]—European Court of Human Rights—European Convention of Human Rights, art 11—decision of Supreme Court of Norway to declare unlawful boycott on part of unions*

This case concerned the alleged violation of art 11 of the European Convention of Human Rights in relation to a decision by the Norwegian Supreme Court to declare unlawful an announced boycott by a trade union which was planned in order to pressurise a Norwegian subsidiary of a Danish company to enter into a Norwegian Collective Agreement applicable to dock workers. The applicant trade unions had entered into a Collective Framework Agreement with the largest employer organisation in Norway and the Norwegian Logistics and Freight Association in respect of a fixed-pay scheme for dock workers at major ports in Norway, including the port of Drammen. The Collective Framework Agreement, which was entered into in the 1970s, secured for Norwegian dock workers the benefits of ILO Convention No 137, including the right to permanent employment and better pay. The Collective Framework Agreement provided that, with respect to vessels sailing from a Norwegian port to a foreign port or vice versa, the unloading and loading work would be carried out by the dock workers. The Collective Framework Agreement provided for the establishment of an Administrative Office for dock work in the port of Drammen, which managed dock workers; all permanently employed dock workers in the Drammen port were employed by the Administration Office.

Holship, a wholly owned Norwegian subsidiary of a Danish freight forwarding group, established itself in Norway and was based in Drammen. It was not a member of either of the employer organisations party to the Collective Framework Agreement. Until 2013, Holship used the services of the Administration Office when it needed loading or unloading services in the port of Drammen. However, in 2013 it employed four persons in the port who, in addition to performing other tasks as employees for Holship, carried out loading and unloading operations for their employer. One of the two unions, in a letter to Holship, demanded that a collective agreement be entered into and that Holship accept the Collective Framework Agreement. Holship did not respond and thereafter the union sent a letter with a notice of boycott. The union sought an advance declaratory judgment in the Drammen City Court to the effect that the announced boycott would

---

[17] *Norwegian Confederation of Trade Unions and Norwegian Transport Workers Union v Norway* ECtHR Application No. 45487/17 (2021).

not be unlawful. The Drammen City Court ruled that the boycott would be lawful. The Norwegian High Court upheld that decision on appeal, but the Norwegian Supreme Court concluded by majority that the boycott would be unlawful.

The unions thereafter instituted proceedings against Norway under the European Convention of Human Rights (the Convention), contending that the decision to declare the boycott unlawful had violated their right of freedom of association as provided for in art 11 of the Convention.

The ECtHR noted that the aim of the boycott had been to protect rights at the heart of trade union activity, mainly the right to work and the right to stable and organised working conditions for dock workers. Boycotts and blockades are protected by a number of instruments of international law, notably ILO Convention No 87 and the European Social Charter and the EU Charter.

The ECtHR had first to consider the applicability of art 11 of the Convention and whether the announced boycott entailed the exercise of freedom of assembly and association protected by art 11.1. The Court noted that collective action, which was the subject of the domestic court judgments, was essentially a boycott, in the form of a blockade.

The ECtHR noted that it has generally held that art 11 presents trade union freedom as one form, or a special aspect, of freedom of association. The provision does not guarantee trade unions, or their members, any particular treatment by the State. The Convention safeguards freedom to protect the occupational interests of trade union members by trade union action, the conduct and development of which the Contracting State must permit and make possible. The Court noted that it had previously (*Gustafsson v Sweden*[18]) held that a blockade, creating inconvenience and damage to a business, could give rise to the application of art 11, at the suit of the business, by reason of the interference with the enjoyment of the applicant business' freedom of association, it followed that the exercise of a blockade by an applicant trade union could also give rise to the applicability of art 11. The Court observed that the ECJ had recognised, relying in part on the European Social Charter, that the right to collective action constitutes a fundamental right under EU law and that it was noteworthy that the form of collective action at issue in that case (*Laval*[19]) was also a blockade. It was undisputed that the impugned boycott was aimed at ensuring stable and safe working conditions for dock workers. Accordingly the Court found that the impugned boycott constituted a trade union action which they sought to take in order to protect, at least among other things, the occupational interests of union members in a manner capable of falling within the scope of art 11.1 of the Convention.

The Court noted that the Norwegian Supreme Court's declaratory judgment finding the intended boycott unlawful, entailed a 'restriction' on the exercise of the trade union's right under art 11.2 of the Convention. Accordingly the Court had to consider whether the restriction was prescribed by law and whether it was made in order to protect the

---

[18] *Gustafsson v Sweden* Application No. 15573/89, 25 April 1996.
[19] *Laval un Partneri* (Case C-341/05).

rights and freedoms of others. The Court concluded that the Supreme Court's judgment had an adequate legal basis, namely the Norwegian Boycott Act 1947, and also that the decision to declare the boycott unlawful was made in order to protect the 'rights and freedoms' of others, in particular the company's right to freedom of establishment guaranteed by the EEA Agreement and duly incorporated into Norwegian law.

The Court then had to consider whether the restrictions were necessary in a democratic society. In this context the Court noted that it had taken the view that art 11.1 affords members of a trade union a right, in order to protect their interests, that the trade union should be heard, but that each Contracting State has a free choice of the means to be used towards this end. The right to collective bargaining has not been interpreted as including a 'right' to a collective agreement and nor does the right to strike imply a right to prevail. What the Convention requires is that, under national law, a trade union should be enabled, in conditions not in variance with art 11, to strive for the protection of their members' interests.

The ECtHR also stated that its jurisdiction with regard to industrial action is limited to the Convention. It has no competence to assess a respondent State's compliance with the relevant standards of the ILO or the European Social Charter.

The ECtHR noted that the majority of the Norwegian Supreme Court found that the Collective Framework Agreement and its system involving priority for registered dock workers had little to do with the protection of workers and had held that the Collective Agreement demanded by the union was quite irregular and that the protection afforded to members' interests and the working and pay conditions was 'relatively indirect'. Furthermore, the Supreme Court considered the Administration Office to be a company engaged in business activities in a market to which other operators wanted access and the Supreme Court, with regard to the announced boycott, had declared that its primary effect would be to deny Holship access to the market which it wished to enter. Noting that the Supreme Court was divided in relation to these findings of fact and law, the ECtHR emphasised that it was in the first place for the domestic authorities to interpret and apply the domestic law and establish the facts on the basis of evidence before them. The Court noted, with reference to the balancing exercise undertaken by the Supreme Court, that the Supreme Court first pointed to the freedom of association established by art 101 of the Norwegian Constitution, which had to be considered, taking into account art 11 of the Convention before also pointing to the freedom of establishment under art 31 of the EEA Agreement. The ECtHR concluded that the Norwegian Supreme Court had engaged in an extensive assessment of the conflicting fundamental right to collective action enjoyed by the unions and the fundamental economic freedoms under EEA law on which the employer relied.

The ECtHR also noted that, when exercising its supervisory function, its task is not to take the place of the national courts but rather to review, in the light of the case as a whole, whether the decision they have taken under their power of appreciation is compatible with the provisions of the Convention relied on. Where the balancing exercise has been undertaken by the national authorities in conformity with the criteria laid down in the case law of the ECtHR, the Court would require strong reasons to substitute its view for that of the domestic courts. The Court concluded that sufficiently 'strong reasons' did not exist for it to substitute its views for that of the Norwegian Supreme Court in the present case. The Norwegian Supreme Court had acted within the margin of appreciation afforded to it when declaring the boycott lawful. The Court also noted that protecting the rights of others granted to them by way of EEA law might justify restrictions and rights under art 11 of the Convention. Finally, the Court noted that it is primarily for the national authorities, notably the Courts, to interpret and apply domestic law, if necessary in conformity with EU law or EEA law, the role of the ECtHR being confined to ascertaining whether the effects of such adjudication are compatible with the Convention.

The ECtHR concluded that there had been no violation of art 11 of the Convention.

PENALISATION—TRADE UNION ACTIVITIES

[11.07] *Mercer v Alternative Future Group Ltd*[20]*—UK Employment Appeal Tribunal—appeal from employment tribunal—Trade Union and Labour Relations (Consolidation) Act 1992, s 146—Human Rights Act 1998, s 3—European Convention on Human Rights, art 11—industrial relations—penalisation*

The claimant appealed the employment tribunal's dismissal of her claim that she had been suspended to prevent her from participating in trade union activities.

The claimant was employed by the respondent and was a trade union representative. The claimant, having been involved in the planning and implementation of a serious of strikes, was suspended by the respondent for abandoning her post on two occasions without permission and for engaging with the media without prior approval.

Her suspension was lifted three weeks later; however, she took a claim that contrary to s 146 of the Trade Union and Labour Relations (Consolidation) Act 1992 (the 1992 Act), she had been subjected to a detriment (being suspended) by the respondent with a view to preventing her from participating in trade union activities. Although s 146 protects workers from detriment resulting from participation in trade union activities, the scope of trade union activities has been held not to include industrial action. The claimant argued that the 'activities of an independent trade union' within the meaning of the 1992 Act included planning, organising, and participating in industrial action.

At first instance the employment tribunal dismissed her claim and decided that, under s 3 of the Human Rights Act 1998 (which provides that legislation must be compatible with the ECHR), it was not possible to give effect to s 146 of the 1992 Act, so as to include participation in industrial action, to make it compliant with art 11 of the European Convention on Human Rights (right of freedom of assembly and association). The claimant appealed the decision to the EAT.

The EAT held that the employment tribunal was correct in concluding that the detriment was an infringement of art 11. The EAT stated that: 'The right to take industrial action, and more specifically to strike, although not an "essential element" of the Article 11

---

[20]   *Mercer v Alternative Future Group Ltd* UKEAT/0196/20/JOJ.

right is "clearly protected" by it' and, following its consideration of the relevant case law, concluded that 'the ECtHR regards any restriction, however minimal, on the right to participate in a trade union-sanctioned protest or strike action as amounting to an interference with Article 11 rights.' The EAT therefore upheld this ground of the claimant's appeal.

The EAT rejected the employment tribunal finding that it was not possible under s 3 of the Human Rights Act 1998 to give effect to s 146 of the 1992 Act so as to render it compatible with the ECHR. The EAT considered the 'grain' of the legislation and held that there was nothing in the 1992 Act to exclude protection from detriment for those taking part in industrial action. The EAT upheld the interpretation of s 146 to include participation in industrial action put forward by the claimant, finding that 'that approach does not involve judicial legislation ... It is simply giving effect to what is ... a clear and unambiguous obligation under Article 11, ECHR to ensure that employees are not deterred, by the imposition of detriments, from exercising their right to participate in strike action'.

Accordingly, the appeal succeeded, and s 146 was to be read as including participation in industrial action.

TRADE UNION DISCIPLINARY PROCEEDINGS

[11.08]   *Unite The Union v McFadden[21]—Court of Appeal of England and Wales—Henderson, Singh and Laing LJJ—appeal from UK Employment Appeal Tribunal—Trade Union and Labour Relations (Consolidation) Act 1992—trade unions—breach of union rules—disciplinary processes—res judicata*

Unite (the Union) received a complaint from a female member alleging that the respondent, Mr McFadden, had slapped her bottom at an event which followed a protest march. Neither the event nor the march were organised by the Union. The Union brought disciplinary proceedings against the respondent under a particular rule in its rule book, and the Union's disciplinary panel found that the incident had occurred and constituted misconduct.

The respondent made a complaint under the Certification Officer jurisdiction established by the Trade Union and Labour Relations (Consolidation) Act 1992, which resulted in a determination that the disciplinary proceedings were null and void because the relevant union rule invoked applied only to harassment 'in the workplace'.

The Union brought a second set of disciplinary proceedings against the respondent in respect of the same incident but citing different rules from its rule book, being rules that allowed members to be charged with practising discrimination or intolerance among members on the grounds of gender and bringing discredit on the Union.

The respondent made another complaint to the Certification Officer, this time arguing that the doctrine of *res judicata* applied and that the second disciplinary proceedings were in breach of that doctrine.

---

[21]   *Unite The Union v McFadden* [2021] EWCA Civ 199, [2021] IRLR 354.

The Certification Officer rejected the claim, the EAT on appeal reversed the decision of the Certification Officer and the Union appealed to the Court of Appeal.

In the Court of Appeal, the first matter to be determined was whether the case should be heard at all because the respondent had retired in the meantime and there was no prospect of his wishing to become an officer of the Union again. The Court noted that it retains a discretion to determine an appeal in such circumstances, if it would be in the public interest. The Court concluded that it would be in the public interest because the case raised an important issue of principle which would affect not only the powers of the Union in this case, but all trade unions and their members and it may potentially affect the wider public.

The Court concluded, on the authorities, that the doctrine of *res judicata* applies where a body is given jurisdiction by statute to determine any issue which establishes the existence of a legal right; it has also been held to apply to a regulatory body established by royal charter.

On the other hand, where there are purely consensual arrangements, with no independent body entrusted with the function of adjudicating on legal rights of the parties, the doctrine of *res judicata* does not apply.

The Court stated that, as a matter of law, the rule book of a trade union is a contract between all of its members and noted with approval the decision of Elias LJ in *Christou v London Borough of Haringey*[22] which concerned the exercise of disciplinary power by an employer under a contract of employment. The Court noted Elias LJ distinguished between 'a body which is independent of the parties and is invested by law with the power to determine an issue which establishes the existence of a legal right; and other bodies which are not'. The first type of case can be regarded as being examples of 'adjudication', whereas 'it is wrong to describe the exercise of disciplinary power by the employer as a form of adjudication'. The Court found that, in this case, there was 'no independent body invested by law with jurisdiction to determine the legal rights of the parties' and therefore the doctrine of *res judicata* did not apply.

The Court went on to point out that a trade union is not free to discipline its members in a way which would give rise to oppression. This is so because a union's disciplinary process is subject to the rules of natural justice and the duty to act fairly. The Court concluded that it was not impermissible for the Union to bring the second set of disciplinary proceedings arising out of the same incident, although the Union is expected to act in a way which is fair, it is not necessarily to be criticised simply because it initially brought a charge under the wrong provision in its rules.

The Court noted the important public interest in having serious allegations, such as allegations of sexual harassment, properly dealt with. Unions should not be prevented from dealing with those allegations properly and fairly only because they made a mistake in the initial charging decision. That would not serve the interests of other union members, such as the complainant in this case, or the interests of the wider public. Accordingly, the Court allowed the appeal.

---

[22]   *Christou v London Borough of Haringey* [2013] EWCA Civ 178, [2014] QB 131.

[11.09]   *Coxhill v Unite the Union[23]—UK Employment Appeal Tribunal—appeal from employment tribunal—Trade Union and Labour Relations (Consolidation) Act 1992, ss 64 & 65—dismissal—appropriate sanction*

The claimant was a branch secretary for the respondent, Unite the Union. She claimed that she had been unjustifiably disciplined by the union contrary to s 64 of the Trade Union and Labour Relations (Consolidation) Act 1992 (the 1992 Act), as a result of the union concluding that she had used funds belonging to the union to pay for legal advice and to commence legal action against the union.

The claimant failed before the employment tribunal on the basis that her treatment was deemed to come within an exception, under s 65 of the 1992 Act, which provides that there must have been 'conduct', to which the section applies, and that 'conduct' must be the reason, or one of the reasons for disciplining the member. The employment tribunal held:

> The key consideration here was the use of union funds to sue the union, but the significance of that in this case was the use of union funds in this manner, not the fact of suing the union. We are satisfied that anyone who had used union funds in comparable circumstances, but not involving a legal challenge to a union decision, would have been treated in the same way and subject to at least the same sanctions as applied in this case.

The claimant appealed.

The EAT held that the employment tribunal had erred in determining itself that the same sanction would have been appropriate for the claimant's conduct (were she not a union branch secretary), rather than determining what the union would have done in such circumstances. The EAT stated that:

> given a fair reading, the tribunal's reasons demonstrate that it made its own assessment that the same disciplinary action would have been appropriate absent the protected component of the conduct, rather than determining whether the Union had shown it would have applied the same sanction in the hypothetical circumstances.

The appeal was allowed and the EAT remitted the matter for reconsideration by the same employment tribunal.

TRADE UNION NEGLIGENCE

[11.10]   *Langley v GMB, Koester and Trade Union Legal LLP[24]—High Court of England and Wales—Stacey J—negligence—liability of a trade union—negotiation of a compromise agreement*

The claimant was a bin man employed by Birmingham City Council (the Council), he was a GMB representative and acted as shop steward. In May 2014, the Council

---

23   *Coxhill v Unite the Union* UKEAT/0084/20/BA.
24   *Langley v GMB, Katherina Koester and Trade Union Legal LLP* [2020] EWHC 3619 (QB).

informed the union that it wished to suspend the claimant for speaking to the press without permission with reference to a matter of controversy in the community. The employer's position was that it was potential gross misconduct. There followed engagement between the union and the employer concerning the claimant's position. A union official acting on behalf of the claimant formed the view that the claimant's position in the matter was weak and that the employer had strong grounds for arguing that he had committed gross misconduct by speaking out to the press. The trade union official did not consider that his behaviour could be interpreted as either trade union activity or a whistleblowing activity, as required to gain protection under employment legislation. The Court noted that, at the relevant investigation meeting, the trade union official 'was vocal and active' in the claimant's defence and was 'as persuasive as possible'. The Court concluded that the trade union official had 'worked hard to make the case' for the claimant but both she and the claimant knew the arguments in his favour were weak.

The Court found that, after the meeting with the employer, the union official's advice was that if the matter came to a full disciplinary hearing, the claimant's conduct could be found to be gross misconduct and he could be summarily dismissed without notice pay. The union official and the claimant decided to maintain pressure on the employer in negotiating a more favourable exit package and to try to delay the disciplinary hearing for as long as possible so that the claimant could reach his 55th birthday, when he would be entitled to take his pension. The claimant was advised that the employer would not reinstate him and the best outcome would be 'some kind of termination package'. The finding of the employer's internal disciplinary investigation was that the claimant had committed gross misconduct and should be subject to disciplinary proceedings.

The disciplinary hearing was successfully delayed, and the claimant was suspended on full pay during negotiations for his exit strategy. After extensive negotiations on the claimant's behalf, the Council offered him: one year's salary, tax free; 12 weeks' notice pay; accrued holiday pay; a voluntary termination; and an agreed reference as much as possible in the claimant's favour. The union official advised him that this was a good offer and that to proceed with the disciplinary hearing was highly likely to result in his dismissal for gross misconduct, loss of notice pay and loss of future salary. The union official also explained to the claimant that any claims relating to whistleblowing or unfair dismissal would have poor prospects in the employment tribunal and that it was unlikely that the union would fund such case. Once the claimant accepted the offer in principle, it was necessary, under s 203 of the Employment Rights Act 1996, for him to take advice from a 'relevant independent adviser' on the terms and effect of the settlement agreement, especially on his rights in relation to an employment tribunal. The trade union referred the claimant to their solicitors, Trade Union Law, who advised him on the meaning and effect of the settlement terms; no advice was given as to his prospects of success in the employment tribunal if he were to take a claim. The claimant subsequently signed the compromise agreement drafted by the Council.

The following year, the claimant brought a claim of negligence in tort and contract against his trade union, the solicitor and the law firm by whom that solicitor was employed.

The claim related to the advice and representation he received from his union and the law firm following his suspension from work in May 2014 until the signing of the compromise agreement in February 2015. He claimed that the advice had been negligent and that he should have been advised to reject the offer as he maintained that he would have either retained his employment following the disciplinary hearing or, if he had been dismissed, he would have been successful in the employment tribunal. The damages claimed were the wages he would have earned if he continued as an employee earning his salary or uncapped compensation or reinstatement from the employment tribunal amounting to between STG£500,000 and STG£700,000 instead of the one year's gross pay that he received from the compromise agreement.

The union accepted that it owed a duty of care to the claimant since it had voluntarily assumed a degree of responsibility towards him by advising him and assisting in representing him. It accepted that the duty began from the moment the employer indicated that they would be suspending the claimant in May 2014 until the appointment of the solicitors in February 2015 and that the union's 'pastoral role of care and support for its member continued beyond that date'. With reference to the standard of care to be provided by the union, it was accepted 'in general terms that the duty was one of reasonable skill and care in advising and representing the claimant in internal disciplinary proceedings and in negotiations with his employer'. It was here that the parties disagreed. The union asserted it was limited to providing practical advice in the circumstances and relied on the decision in *Friend v Institution of Professional Managers and Specialists*.[25] The claimant argued that a higher standard was required and that:

> [T]he standard of the ordinary skill and care was subsumed by a quasi-legal standard of the reasonably competent trade union lay advisor and representative on legal issues and in relation to potential employment tribunal claims, the duty extended to providing formal legal advice, whether externally or internally, including a duty to apply to an Employment Tribunal for interim relief under the whistleblowing legislation.

Accordingly, the Court had to decide on the standard of care required by the trade union. The Court considered all aspects of the advice given by the trade union in terms of the settlement agreement and his prospect of success in the employment tribunal. It found that the union's advice was not conveyed in 'a bullying or oppressive way, but as a matter of fact' and noted that the union rule book gave an 'extremely wide discretion to the union as to when and whether to instruct lawyers in any particular case'. The Court noted that there was little authority on the 'precise standard of the duty of a trade union advising and acting for a member in an employment dispute with his or her employer'. It noted the test set out in *Friend*, where it was held that 'the union "must in ordinary circumstances be obliged to use ordinary skill and care" absent any specific obligations conferred by the contract of trade union membership in the rules'. In the current case, there were no specific obligations in the contract of trade union membership. The Court concluded that it was implicit in *Friend* that the standard to be imposed

---

[25]   *Friend v Institution of Professional Managers and Specialists* [1999] IRLR 173.

was the 'standard of the ordinary skill and care to be expected of a trade union, which is an organisation dedicated to protecting the rights of its members'.

The Court rejected the submission that a 'quasi-legal' duty applied as it would be 'misleading and a distortion of the nature of the role of a trade union'. The Court concluded that the union did not owe the claimant a duty to apply for interim relief because the agreed strategy was not to litigate but to negotiate, which the Court concluded was a reasonable strategy.

With reference to the solicitors, there was no dispute that the standard of care was of a 'reasonably competent employment lawyer'. The Court stated that if an error of judgment was made by the solicitors, no liability would attach unless the error was one that 'no reasonably well informed and competent member of the profession' would have made. The Court noted that when advice relates to a settlement agreement, 'the question is whether the advice is blatantly wrong', relying on the decision of the Court of Appeal in *VG v Denise Kingsmill*.[26]

In the course of the hearing, the claim against the individual solicitor fell away. The claim against the law firm, however, continued. The Court concluded that the law firm owed the claimant a duty of care 'to provide the advice of a reasonably competent employment lawyer on the matters on which they were instructed to advise and act under the scope of their retainer'. The law firm was not instructed to advise on the merits of the claim and there was, accordingly, no breach of their duties under their retainer. The advice they gave was within the scope of their retainer, ie, the meaning and effect of the compromise agreement.

The Court found that, on the facts, neither the union nor the law firm had failed in their duty to the claimant. The Court was satisfied that the claimant had sufficient time to consider the terms offered and was not pressurised or coerced into agreeing those terms. Accordingly, all of the claims were dismissed.

UNION BREACH OF RIGHT TO EARN A LIVELIHOOD

[11.11] *O'Connell v Building & Allied Trade Union, Morris, O'Shaughnessy and McNamara*[27]—*Court of Appeal—Power J—assessment of damages—breach of constitutional right to earn a livelihood*

The appellant, a block layer, operated as a sub-contractor to different builders for many years and held a C2 certificate from the Revenue Commissioners entitling him to work as a self-employed sub-contractor on building sites. For a certain period, the appellant was refused membership of the respondent trade union, BATU. The union held a monopoly position in the Limerick area where the appellant had sought to earn his livelihood. It was BATU's policy that it existed to protect workers who were in direct employment in the building trade and to limit its membership to employees of building

---

26 *VG v Denise Kingsmill* [2001] EWCA Civ 934.
27 *O'Connell v Building & Allied Trade Union, Morris, O'Shaughnessy and McNamara* [2021] IECA 265.

contractors who could provide confirmation from Revenue that they did not hold a C2 certificate. The appellant had been a member of BATU but he left Ireland and his membership lapsed. On his return to Ireland, BATU initially refused to re-admit him to the union and subsequently allowed him membership for a probationary period but at the end of that period did not grant him full membership.

The appellant instituted proceedings, claiming that BATU had conspired to prevent him from working, that he had been intimidated by its officials and that he had been black-listed as an employee. He also claimed that his constitutional right to work had been infringed. In delivering judgment on liability,[28] the High Court found that the appellant had been wrongly excluded from BATU, that BATU had perpetrated conspiracy and intimidation against him and that BATU had breached his constitutional right to earn a livelihood. The assessment of damages was held over until a later date.

The respondents appealed the judgment on liability, and the Court of Appeal[29] upheld the High Court's finding of a breach of the appellant's constitutional right to work but did not find sufficient evidence to support the findings of conspiracy and intimidation. The Court of Appeal remitted the matter to the High Court for an assessment of damages.

Thereafter, the High Court assessed general damages in the sum of €15,000 for the breach of the appellant's constitutional right to earn a livelihood and refused all other claims for damages. It is in respect of that judgment that the appellant brought this appeal.

In delivering the judgment of the Court of Appeal, Power J noted that the Court of Appeal previously held in the liability appeal that there was nothing unlawful in the union obliging employers to employ union members only, nor was there anything unlawful in employers making union membership a condition of employment. What was unlawful was the union's insistence that only members could be employed on sites in Limerick where it enjoyed a monopoly position and, at the same time, refusing membership to the appellant in circumstances where there was no evidence that he had failed to satisfy the conditions of his probation. That conduct on the part of BATU constituted interference with the appellant's constitutional right to earn a livelihood.

In considering the question of damages for breach of the constitutional right to earn a livelihood, Power J noted that it is well-settled law that, in the absence of a common law or statutory cause of action, a person may sue directly for breach of a constitutional right but liability and damages for such a breach will only arise where the common law or statute law do not provide for an adequate or effective defence or vindication of the constitutional right in question. That an action in damages for breach of a constitutional right may be invoked against the trade union was recognised by the Court of Appeal in the liability appeal on the basis that the right in question would not be appropriately

28   *O'Connell v Building & Allied Trade Union & Ors* [2014] IEHC 360.
29   *O'Connell v Building & Allied Trade Union & Ors* [2016] IECA 338, see *Arthur Cox Employment Law Yearbook 2016* at [12.05].

vindicated unless the courts were allowed to grant appropriate relief against private parties.

Power J observed that there is nothing in case law to suggest that the remedy for breach of constitutional rights is confined, in principle, to recovery only of losses that are vouched or verifiable. In assessing damages for an unjustified infringement of a constitutional right, the court has jurisdiction to award damages that are compensatory, aggravated, exemplary or punitive. The Court noted that, while the union placed considerable emphasis upon the appellant's failure to quantify his losses, it was important to note that the obligation to quantify losses arises only in the context of assessing claims for pecuniary damages.

The Court, in considering the claim for loss of earnings, noted that the burden to prove his actual loss of earnings rested on the appellant and he had failed to do so. As a consequence, the trial Judge, in considering the loss of earnings claim, did not fall into error in reaching the conclusion that the Court could not award loss of earnings.

In considering damages for loss of opportunity, the Court concluded that the trial Judge had erred in dismissing the appellant's claim for loss of opportunity. The Court held that the loss of opportunity had been established as a fact in the High Court's liability hearing and the appellant should, as a consequence, have been awarded damages in respect of that matter.

Turning to exemplary damages, the Court stated that it has been long established that a breach of constitutional rights may result in an award of exemplary damages, irrespective of whether the constitutional breach was committed by an agent of the executive or by a private entity. The Court noted that an award of exemplary damages should not be excessive but should be sufficient to punish the impugned behaviour; the court must have regard to the seriousness of the wrong and the degree of distress caused by the wrong. Accordingly, the Court concluded that the trial Judge paid insufficient attention to the seriousness of the respondent union's wrongdoing and failed to have due regard for the attack on the appellant's human dignity. The appellant was not required to identify a specific loss before the Court could award exemplary damages based on the union's conduct.

In terms of aggravated damages, the Court noted that aggravated damages, unlike exemplary damages, are a form of ordinary compensatory damages and arise by reason of the manner in which the wrong was committed and the conduct of the wrongdoer. Exemplary damages may be used to mark the court's disapproval of a defendant's conduct, but aggravated damages compensate for the manner in which a defendant either commits the wrongdoing or approaches the defence of its impugned conduct. It is open to a court to award aggravated damages even if a claim for such has not been specifically pleaded. The Court concluded that the union's behaviour did not come within the ambit of conduct that could warrant an award of aggravated damages and concluded that it would be disproportionate on the facts of the case to find that an award of both exemplary and aggravated damages was warranted.

In considering the claim for damages for distress, the Court found no error in the decision of the trial Judge to award no damages for distress.

On the question of general damages, the Court noted in particular that the right to earn a livelihood is not confined to the right to earn money. In earning a livelihood, 'an individual may advance human understanding, express creativity, safeguard mental health, contribute to community and support the common good'. The Court concluded that the trial Judge's approach to the award of general damages fell short on two fronts. He failed to have sufficient regard to the full scope of what is involved in the right to earn a livelihood. Furthermore, the omission to factor in the loss of opportunity to the overall assessment of damages was problematic. The Court concluded that the award made by the trial Judge, namely €15,000, did not reflect the magnitude of the non-pecuniary loss caused to the appellant by reason of the union's breach during the relevant period.

The appeal was allowed. The trial Judge's award of €15,000 in general damages was replaced with an award of €22,500 in general damages to reflect the established loss of opportunity. In addition, €7,500 was awarded by way of exemplary damages.

EUROPEAN WORKS COUNCIL

[11.12] *HSBC European Works Council and HSBC Continental Europe[30]— Central Arbitration Committee—Transnational Information and Consultation of Employees' Regulations 1999,[31] regs 21 and 21A—change of central management representative agent—European Works Council—Brexit*

The complaint to the Central Arbitration Committee (CAC) arose following the decision of HSBC to relocate its European Works Council (EWC) to Ireland in connection with the UK's exit from the EU. In the course of the matter, the employer referenced that the EU Commission Withdrawal Notice required UK-based EWCs to relocate and choose another representative agent within the EU before 1 January 2021 to ensure that the EWC operated in accordance with EU law. HSBC had engaged with its EWC to relocate to Ireland. It did so through a unilateral notification, as opposed to an agreement with the EWC. The EWC was notified of the change in December 2020, prior to the UK's exit from the EU. It was provided with an amended EWC Agreement reflecting the consequence of this change.

Following the UK's exit from the EU, the central representative agent for the HSBC EWC was an Irish company. The EWC argued that HSBC had breached the terms of the EWC Agreement by excluding its UK business from the scope of the EWC Agreement, preventing UK representatives from sitting on the EWC, and unilaterally amending the EWC Agreement to reflect the changes imposed by the change in location from the UK to Ireland.

These complaints were rejected by the CAC. In relation to the exclusion of UK representatives, it noted that the terms of the EWC Agreement expressly provided that

---

[30] *HSBC European Works Council and HSBC Continental Europe*, Central Arbitration Committee Case No. EWC/38/2021.
[31] European Communities (Transnational Information and Consultation of Employees Act 1996) (Amendment) Regulations 1999 (SI 386/1999).

representation was confined to EEA Member States only. A point of significance was the fact that Swiss workers had never been represented on the EWC, something that had never been challenged by the UK representatives while they were on the EWC. The CAC was satisfied that excluding UK representatives did not breach the EWC Agreement.

In relation to the amendment of the EWC Agreement, it was accepted that removing the UK business from the scope of the EWC Agreement and excluding their representatives from the EWC were matters that occurred automatically once the UK ceased to be an EU Member State; it did not require agreement from the representatives to occur. In particular, the employer submitted that the EU Commission's *Notice to Stakeholders in Respect of the Withdrawal of the United Kingdom and EU Rules on European Works Councils* dated 13 March 2019 expressly required employers to take steps to relocate UK-based EWCs to an EU Member State and that in default of such election, a relocation would happen automatically and immediately as at the withdrawal date. The employer's submission that this constituted an automatic change that did not require agreement was accepted.

[11.13] *Verizon European Works Council v Central Management of the Verizon Group[32]—UK Employment Appeal Tribunal—application arising from findings of a Central Arbitration Committee—industrial relations—obligation to consult— Transnational Information and Consultation of Employees Regulations 1999 (TICER)[33]*

The Verizon European Works Council (EWC) brought an application to the EAT seeking penalty notices to be issued by the EAT against Verizon UK Limited in respect of breaches of the Transnational Information and Consultation of Employees Regulations 1999 (the TICER Regulations) and of the Agreement made between the parties under the TICER Regulations dated 20 October 2016 (the Charter).

The breaches were found to have occurred by the Central Arbitration Committee (CAC) in a decision dated 9 October 2019. The TICER Regulations provide that failure to properly institute certain measures as required by the Regulations may result in an application to the CAC for a declaration that a breach has occurred. If the CAC does declare that a breach has occurred, an applicant may make a second application to the EAT, for the imposition of a penalty up to £100,000. The EAT may issue a written penalty notice to Central Management requiring it to pay a penalty, but this shall not apply in circumstances where the EAT is satisfied, on hearing the representations of the Central Management, that the failure resulted from a reason beyond the Central Management's control or that it has some other reasonable excuse for its failure.

At the relevant time, Verizon's global turnover was around US$139 billion and it had 5,599 employees throughout Europe. The Charter contained provisions relating to information and consultation, the structure and functioning of the EWC and a Select

---

[32] *Verizon European Works Council v Central Management of the Verizon Group* UKEAT/0053/20/DA.
[33] Transnational Information and Consultation of Employees Regulations 1999 (SI 1999/3323).

Committee elected by the EWC (consisting of five members of the EWC), the agreement that reasonable expenses necessary for the functioning of the EWC would be borne by Verizon, and applicable law and dispute resolution clauses.

On 21 December 2018, Verizon's HR director emailed the Select Committee to invite them to a meeting which ultimately took place on 10 January 2019. He did not share any details regarding the meeting but indicated the purpose was driven by Verizon's obligation to inform and consult with the EWC. At the meeting, the Select Committee was informed of a proposed reorganisation which would lead to the termination of employment of a total of 216 employees across eight jurisdictions. No representatives from the countries affected, other than those on the Select Committee, had been invited to the meeting. Less than two hours had been set aside to discuss the proposals. It was indicated at the meeting that global staff notifications regarding the proposals would not issue before 24 January 2019, and that redundancies would take effect in the period of six months commencing on that date.

The Select Committee raised concerns about Central Management's failure to properly inform the EWC about the proposed reorganisation, and pointed out the need to consult representatives from the countries impacted. Further concerns were raised by email concerning the 'tight schedule and non-involvement of EWC members who were not in the Select Committee'. On 23 January 2019, Verizon issued a press release on the reorganisation, stating that it would impact 'around 7% of its global workforce'. At the hearing before the CAC, it was accepted as a matter of fact by Verizon that they could not show that any feedback from the Select Committee was communicated to Verizon Management in time to influence its decision and that there had not been time for the EWC to prepare a formal opinion statement in accordance with the procedures of the Charter.

On 18 February 2019, the Chair of the EWC provided written confirmation of the EWC's complaints about the process. The ensuing dispute, in accordance with the Charter, was dealt with in arbitration.

The arbitrator did not reach any conclusions as to the validity of the EWC's complaints, but instead drew up a document containing guidance and recommendations to both parties. Verizon accepted the recommendations. However, the EWC did not accept the recommendations and informed Verizon that they would be making a complaint to the CAC and had appointed a legal representative in the matter to represent and advise the EWC regarding the CAC complaint. It further stated that the costs of its legal representative should be covered as per the Charter.

A dispute arose between the parties in advance of the CAC procedures regarding these costs. Verizon initially noted that a 23-page complaint had been prepared for the prior arbitration with the assistance of an advisor (who was not a legal representative). It asserted that Verizon would pay the fees of that advisor and therefore it was not reasonably necessary for Verizon to pay the EWC to receive further assistance at this stage, particularly as the CAC was not a body where lawyers were required. Verizon stated that if further assistance was required in due course, Verizon would consider any request that the EWC made at that time and that a fixed-fee quotation should be provided for prior approval in such circumstances. The EWC refuted the assertion that legal representation was not required, and provided the fixed-fee quotation requested. Verizon did not pay the fees and stated it did not consider that the EWC reasonably required legal assistance to proceed to the CAC. Notwithstanding Verizon's position, the legal representative acted for the EWC without requiring payment.

The grounds of complaint for the CAC included the inadequate consultation in relation to the proposed reorganisation, and that Verizon had refused to allow the EWC an expert of their choice and had refused to pay their expenses as required by the Charter.

On 9 October 2019, the CAC issued their decision that:

(1) Verizon had failed to comply with the required information and consultation process before making a decision on the re-organization as required ... (and in particular that they had breached the Charter by failing to inform and consult the "correct elements" of the EWC because representatives of all the affected countries were not involved);

(2) the complaint that Verizon had failed to allow the EWC an expert of their choice was not well-founded but the refusal to pay the expenses relating [to same] was a breach ... of the Charter.

The EWC sought the issue of penalty notices in respect of each of the above decisions. The EAT considered same having regard to the provisions of the TICER Regulations.

In relation to the breach of information and consultation obligations, Verizon did not put forward any reasonable excuse for these failures and there was no dispute that a penalty notice should be issued. Verizon did argue that the failures were purely procedural and that 'the gravity of the failures was slight, the period of time over which they occurred was short, [and] the reason for them was accidental and well-intentioned'.

This was not accepted by the EAT. The EAT found that the proposed reorganisation must have been in Verizon's mind well before inviting the EWC Select Committee to a meeting in December 2018. Nothing of substance was disclosed as to the reason for the meeting and, despite objections from the EWC about the lack of proper consultation, Verizon went ahead with the final decision without providing adequate opportunity for any meaningful input from the EWC (and in particular representatives of all the affected countries). The EAT found that this did not seem to be 'remotely consistent' with the spirit of the TICER Regulations or the Charter. The EAT stated that the timing of the meetings indicated an element of paying 'lip service' to Verizon's obligations, but no more. It found that this was a significant failure of compliance by a very substantial undertaking, albeit relating to one redundancy exercise involving 216 employees out of a much larger workforce. Having regard to mitigating arguments made by Verizon and the fact that the maximum penalty was £100,000, the EAT imposed a penalty of £35,000.

Verizon argued that no penalty notice could be issued in respect of the refusal to pay the legal representatives' fees, as they had a reasonable excuse for refusing to pay same, ie Verizon were relying on their understanding of the legal position as set out in a previous decision of the CAC in *Emerson Electric Europe*.[34] This was not accepted by the EAT as a matter of fact. The objections raised were that a detailed document had already been prepared and that Verizon was not willing to commit in advance to an estimated fixed fee of £15,000 plus VAT. Regarding the first point, the EAT found that it was not reasonable to 'suggest that pre-proceedings should be started by using a document which had been prepared for a different (albeit closely related) purpose or that there was no need for the expert who was going to assist with the CAC proceedings to be involved from the outset'. As to the second point, it was Verizon who introduced the idea of a fixed-fee quotation. The EAT agreed with the CAC, who found that Verizon's suggestion meant that either the individual members of the EWC or their chosen experts were required to take an unfair financial risk in bringing CAC proceedings. The EAT found that this was not a reasonable approach, particularly coming from a such a substantial organisation which had access to, and would have used, legal assistance in the CAC proceedings. However, mitigating points made on behalf of Verizon were accepted by the EAT (ie, that Verizon did mention the possibility of paying the CAC reference fees at a later stage, and that the EWC did not suffer any prejudice as their legal advisor worked free of charge and subsequently charged substantially less than the sum estimated, which Verizon paid promptly following the CAC decision). Having regard to those points, the EAT imposed a penalty of £5,000 upon Verizon.

INDUSTRIAL RELATIONS ACTS—THE ROLE OF THE LABOUR COURT

[11.14]   *Waterford Institute Of Technology v A Worker[35]—Labour Court—appeal from recommendation from Workplace Relations Commission—Industrial Relations Act 1969, s 13(9)—jurisdiction of the courts in industrial relations cases*

The claimant appealed a recommendation of an Adjudication Officer in a dispute relating to a grievance brought by the claimant where the respondent sought to query the attendance of the claimant at her place of employment on a particular date.

An issue arose at hearing when TUI, on behalf of the claimant, asserted the claimant's data protection rights set out on the cover of the claimant's submission. The Court advised the claimant that it could not agree to be bound by same. The Court had concerns as to whether the parties understood the role and jurisdiction of the Court in industrial relations cases, as opposed to employment rights cases, and took the opportunity to clarify the issue.

The Court drew the parties' attention to the role of the Court under the Industrial Relations Act 1946, which is to try to resolve a dispute between an employer and a

---

34 Emerson Electric Europe, CAC decision of January 2016; available at *https://assets.publishing.service. gov.uk/government/uploads/system/uploads/attachment_data/file/850838/Decision.pdf* [last accessed 11 February 2022].
35 *Waterford Institute of Technology v A Worker* LCR22385.

worker; the requirements under the Industrial Relations Act 1946 in respect of representation at the hearing; and the requirement to have such hearings in private.

The Court stated that in industrial relations disputes, the Court is a court of last resort and issues should come before the Court only when all internal procedures have been exhausted. It pointed out that, in previous decisions relating to issues arising from disciplinary procedures, it has sent the parties back to complete the procedures before considering any issues arising from same.

The Court noted that an employer can ask a worker to account for their whereabouts during working hours and, if unhappy with the response, can investigate further, including by way of the disciplinary procedures. Any procedural issues that arise should normally form the basis for an appeal, as distinct from a grievance.

The Court noted that in industrial relations cases, issues such as damages, compensation for stress or anxiety, and apologies are not remedies 'within the gift of the Court'. The remedies available to the Court in cases of this type are to uphold or overturn or vary the recommendation of the Adjudication Officer.

The Court also dealt with an application made by the union that it recuse itself by refusing to do so on the basis that the Court could not accept that the fact that a party to a hearing did not like the facts as laid out by the Court could form a reason for the Court to recuse itself. Likewise, the Court could not allow a threat of industrial action by the union official, by reason of its refusal to recuse itself, to influence its decision on the recusal application.

In dealing with the dispute before it, the Court concluded that the informal resolution path set out in the Adjudication Officer's recommendation should be followed and upheld the decision of the Adjudication Officer.

Chapter 12

Injunctions

INTRODUCTION

[12.01] The circumstances in which injunctions will be granted to employers by reason of breach of confidence on the part of a former employee were considered by the High Court in *Microstrain* and by the High Court of England and Wales in *Zoll*.

In a number of cases, employees sought the intervention of the Court by way of injunction in ongoing disciplinary proceedings. The jurisdiction of the Irish High Court was invoked in this context in *Lally* and in *Keogh*. The intervention of the High Court of England and Wales was sought in *Rayner* and in *SMO*.

In *O'Donovan*, the Court of Appeal considered whether an injunction should be granted so as to restrain a probationary dismissal. In *Delaney*, the High Court considered whether a dismissal of an employee by reference to the employee's failure to obtain security clearance from a third party should be injuncted. In *Mason*, the test to be applied in considering whether an injunction should be granted to restrain a dismissal was considered at some length by the High Court. In *Avsar*, the High Court of England and Wales considered whether an injunction should be granted so as to restrain a probationary dismissal.

Finally, six UK cases in which injunctions were sought to restrain post termination competition on the part of employees are noted. They are *C Wzrd*, the *Delivery Group*, *Source Bioscience*, *Gemini Europe*, *Quilter* and *APEX Resources*.

Breach of Confidence

[12.02] ***Microstrain Ltd t/a Cubicm3 v Delany, McFadden, Brennan, Piorunkiewicz, McGovern, Gavin & Resolute Engineering Group[1]—High Court—Allen J—interlocutory motion—breach of contract of employment—confidential information—competitor—imaging order—search order***

This case concerned allegations that six former employees of the plaintiff had obtained and taken confidential information from the plaintiff during their employment in breach

---

1   *Microstrain Ltd t/a Cubicm3 v Delany, McFadden, Brennan, Piorunkiewicz, McGovern, Gavin & Resolute Engineering Group* [2021] IEHC 136.

of their contractual and common law duties. It was alleged that those employees used this information to set up the seventh defendant, Resolute Engineering Group, in competition with the plaintiff.

On motion *ex parte* on behalf of the plaintiff in the High Court in November 2020, the plaintiff successfully obtained various orders against the defendants, namely regarding the delivery up of all devices in the defendants' possession or control which contained information or which previously contained information which might have been deleted in relation to the plaintiff's business and restraining those defendants from deleting, interfering with or taking any other steps to destroy any such material on any such devices. An imaging order was also ordered in respect of the plaintiff's data on certain devices to be delivered up by the defendants. The defendants made numerous admissions in their replying affidavits and submitted to all bar one of the reliefs sought by the plaintiff. The relief contested by the defendants at the interlocutory motion was a search order sought by the plaintiff against the defendants in respect of the imaged data, namely to search to establish what information of the plaintiff was on the defendants' devices, what use was made by the defendants of such information, how the competing business was established and how the first six defendants had commenced working for it while still employed by the plaintiff. The plaintiff contended that the granting of such an order now would save an unspecified amount of time in the proceedings.

Allen J declined to grant the search order sought by the plaintiff. He noted that the purpose of an imaging or search order is to preserve evidence to ensure that it is not altered, destroyed or hidden.[2] However, imaging was not capable of separating information which was and was not relevant to the proceedings and could, by consequence, contain irrelevant and personal information. Therefore, any search of the imaged documents would need to be justified as a separate exercise in the context of the discovery exercise, ie the defendants would have to make discovery and then the plaintiff would have to justify a search of the imaged data. To make such an order would pre-empt the discovery process. Further, such justification was not present at this time, particularly in light of the fact that the defendants had already made considerable admissions in the proceedings (and the discovery required may as a consequence be limited) and the additional costs such a search may entail.

The remaining issue before the Court on the interlocutory motion was the defendants' contention that the plaintiff should not be awarded the costs of the interim application but rather the defendants should be awarded the costs of the interlocutory motion on the grounds that the plaintiff did not on the interim application make full disclosure (and in consequence the orders to which they have submitted on the interlocutory application would not have been granted on the interim application if the Court had been appraised of the full facts) and that the evidence on which the application was grounded was hearsay as the conduct to which they admitted (eg copying confidential information) was done prior to the commencement of employment of Mr Elliot who swore the affidavit grounding the application.

---

[2]   *Anton Piller KG v Manufacturing Processes Ltd* [1976] Ch 55.

The plaintiff was obliged on *ex parte* application to make a full and frank disclosure of all facts which it was material for the Court to know. The defendants alleged that the plaintiff failed to disclose to its forensic IT consultant certain essential information and also on seven occasions the Court was either actively or by omission misled by the plaintiff. Following careful consideration, Allen J did not find any substance to any of these allegations.

In respect to the plaintiff's reliance on hearsay, Allen J found that a technical omission by the plaintiff to give a means of knowledge for hearsay in the grounding affidavit was not such as would justify disallowing the costs of the grounding affidavit, still less the entire costs of the interim and interlocutory injunctions.

Allen J made an order for the payment of costs of the interim application and the interlocutory application against certain of the defendants (the first three defendants who were labelled the 'executives' by the plaintiff) and reserved to the trial Judge the plaintiff's costs of both applications against certain others (who were labelled the 'employees' by the plaintiff). The plaintiff's application for an order for a substantial payment on account of the costs of the interim application and motion, and the defendants' application for a stay on execution for the order of costs were refused by Allen J.

[12.03] *Zoll Medical UK Ltd v Treilcock*[3]—*High Court of England and Wales— Ellenbogen J—application for interim relief—breach of contract—equitable duties—post-termination restrictions—whistleblowing—confidential information*

The applicant was the UK branch of a large international business, headquartered in the US, which marketed, sold and maintained medical resuscitation devices and accessories. The respondent was a senior employee of the applicant until his dismissal on 29 October 2020. This case concerned the applicant's application for interim relief in the form of a preservation and delivery up order and an information order.

The applicant alleged that the respondent had breached both his contract and his equitable duties to the applicant when he emailed confidential information to both his personal email address and to an email address within a newly incorporated company. The respondent had incorporated this company during his employment, without the applicant's knowledge, in breach of his contract. It was also alleged that the respondent had used a USB device connected to his company laptop to access confidential information both during his employment and following his termination. The respondent had wiped his company laptop before returning it to the applicant and the applicant submitted that the true extent of the information retained by the respondent was not yet fully known.

The applicant submitted that the respondent had taken data including financial information, know-how, commercial terms with suppliers, customer information and details relating to other employees. In response, the respondent argued that he had retained company information for the purposes of supporting whistleblowing claims he had made against his former employer. The applicant contended that the respondent was

---

[3]   *Zoll Medical UK Ltd v Treilcock* [2020] EWHC 3798 (QB), [2020] 12 WLUK 192.

not entitled to rely on his purported whistleblowing claims to justify the retention of company information and that he was required instead to rely on the court's disclosure processes for such purposes.

The High Court applied the three-stage test from *American v Cyanamid v Ethicon Ltd*,[4] and determined that there was a serious issue to be tried, remarking that there was strong *prima facie* evidence that the respondent breached his contractual and equitable duties both during his employment and post-termination. The Court concluded that, as the information taken by the respondent that the applicant was aware of, may only be the 'tip of a much larger iceberg of wrongdoing', and it was not clear whether the respondent could pay any such damages if awarded at trial, damages would not be an adequate remedy. In respect of the third stage, the Court held that the balance of convenience lay in favour of granting the orders sought by the applicant as the respondent was in possession of 'confidential information in the class of trade secrets and the like which would cause serious damage to the [applicant's] business interests, were they to be disclosed to a third party'.

The Court determined that the orders sought by the applicant were proportionate and, given the mandatory nature of the relief sought, it was satisfied that granting the orders was the conclusion that involved the least risk of injustice if it turned out to be wrong.

Disciplinary Proceedings

[12.04]   *Lally v Board of Management of Rosmini Community School*[5]*—High Court—Butler J—teacher—pandemic—falsified school rolls—injunction*

The plaintiff was a teacher in the defendant secondary school. The defendant took issue with the plaintiff's management of 'blended learning' during the pandemic and initiated formal disciplinary proceedings on the basis that she had allegedly cancelled 67 classes without notice, and falsified school rolls. The defendant prepared a report on the plaintiff's activities based on an audit of the online teaching platforms used by the plaintiff and a disciplinary process was initiated against her.

The plaintiff argued that she had technical difficulties and had not marked rolls for classes that had not taken place and that the audit carried out by the school was of Google Meet only, and did not take account of other platforms such as Google Docs, Google Sheets, Google Drive, Google Forms, Google Slides and Gmail. She sought an interlocutory injunction to restrain the disciplinary process. She argued that the report furnished to the school board of management for consideration had not been carried out in accordance with departmental guidelines and contained findings of fact by the principal. A second, edited, comprehensive report was prepared by the principal, where he removed statements of fact. However, she alleged that the school board of management could not be objective and were biased, and called into question whether fair procedures had been applied.

---

4   *American v Cyanamid v Ethicon Ltd* [1975] AC 396.
5   *Lally v Board of Management of Rosmini Community School* [2021] IEHC 633.

The Court granted the injunction to restrain the disciplinary process pending determination of the legal proceedings. The Court noted that the obligation on the principal to act fairly in preparing the report would not be as simple as giving the plaintiff a right of reply; the facts set out in the report 'must be both ascertained and presented fairly'. While the Court acknowledged that the school might wish to progress disciplinary proceedings, such desire was outweighed by the possible damage to the plaintiff's reputation and record, which was unblemished. If the plaintiff succeeded in establishing that the board of management was biased, then any conclusion reached by it adverse to her would be legally unsustainable. Accordingly, the Court held the 'balance of justice in this case would appear to favour the determination of the litigation whilst the status quo was maintained and before the disciplinary process is allowed to proceed' and the injunction was granted.

[12.05]   *Keogh v A V Pound & Co Ltd[6]—High Court—Allen J—interlocutory relief—restraining a suspension and the continuation of an investigation—costs— whether the substantive motion was rendered moot by the actions of the respondent*

The plaintiff was employed by the defendant as a shipping coordinator. He became involved in a personal relationship with his direct line manager in January 2021. The defendant's company policy on personal relationships provided the following: 'Due to the nature of these relationships, the Company requires that you inform the Group HR Manager if you are involved in a relationship with another employee of the Company.'

The line manager ultimately reported the relationship to her manager in late February 2021. The company group HR manager conducted five investigation meetings into the matter, and on 9 March 2021, the plaintiff was suspended, pending the outcome of the investigation into his alleged failure to disclose his personal relationship with his manager.

The plaintiff applied for an interlocutory injunction restraining the continuing suspension and investigation. The defendant lifted the suspension and discontinued the investigation before such time as the substantive motion was heard.

This judgment related to costs, with both sides submitting that the other party should pay the costs. The plaintiff submitted that the lifting of the suspension and discontinuation of the investigation were precipitated by the motion—as such, the substantive action had become moot by the defendant's response to the motion. The defendant contested this, arguing that the lifting of the suspension and discontinuation of the investigation would have happened in any case, and that the application was 'unnecessary and premature'.

The High Court noted the plaintiff's submission that the subject matter of the proceedings had been rendered moot was too simplistic, noting that the lawfulness of the suspension and investigation was still hotly contested between the parties. In this regard, the Court noted that the plaintiff had delivered his statement of claim, long after the suspension was lifted, claiming, among other reliefs, a declaration that his

---

[6]   *Keogh v A V Pound & Co Ltd* [2021] IEHC 640.

purported suspension was unlawful, damages for breach of contract and exemplary damages for reputational damage. The defendant strongly refuted this, and maintained the lawfulness of the suspension and investigation.

In relation to the question of mootness, the High Court pointed to the following two relevant principles as contained in *Lofinkakin v Minister for Justice*:[7]

    (i) a case, or an issue within a case can be described as moot when a decision thereon can have no practical impact or effect on the resolution of some live controversy between the parties and such controversy arises out of or is part of some tangible and concrete dispute then existing;

    (ii) therefore, where a legal dispute has ceased to exist, or where the issue has materially lost its character as a lis, or where the essential foundation of the action has disappeared, there will no longer be in existence any discord or conflict capable of being justiciably determined.

The High Court determined that the substantive issue was unresolved in this case, as the lawfulness of the suspension and investigation was very much still at issue.

It noted that it is well established that the question of costs of interlocutory relief is far more nuanced than simply considering whether the motion would ultimately have succeeded or not, and requires consideration of the practical necessity for the relief, as well as the legal and factual issues presented by the motion and action.

The High Court observed that the defendant's submission that, had the plaintiff permitted the investigation to continue, his suspension would ultimately have been lifted and the investigation would have been carried out in accordance with fair procedures, was speculative in nature. The Court did not accept that because the suspension had been lifted, it ultimately followed that it would have been lifted if the plaintiff had allowed it run its course.

The Court held that the lifting of the suspension and cessation of the investigation did not render the proceedings moot. Irrespective of the outcome of the interlocutory motion, the question of the lawfulness of the investigation and suspension would have had to go to full trial for resolution. The High Court held that the 'justice of the case requires that whichever of the [plaintiff] or the respondent ultimately prevails on that issue should have the costs of the interlocutory motion', and ordered that the costs of both parties be costs in the cause.

[12.06] *Rayner v Barnet Enfield and Haringey Mental Health Trust*[8]*—High Court of England and Wales—Murray J—interlocutory relief—disciplinary procedure*

Mr Rayner was successful in obtaining an interim injunction restraining his employer from proceeding with disciplinary proceedings, pending the full hearing of the matter.

In this case, the applicant sought to continue the injunction restraining his employer from continuing with his disciplinary hearing in order to await the outcome of the

---

7   *Lofinkakin v Minister for Justice* [2013] 4 I.R. 274.

8   *Rayner v Barnet Enfield and Haringey Mental Health Trust* [2021] EWHC 1263.

determination by the relevant regulatory body (the United Kingdom Council for Psychotherapy (the UKCP)), as to whether the conduct that was the subject of the disciplinary hearing breached the UKCP's Code of Ethics and Professional Practice.

In rejecting the application, the Court concluded that there was no bar to the respondent holding its disciplinary hearing prior to the determination by the UKCP, and the initial interim order was discharged. In coming to that conclusion, the Court noted that there was no contractual basis to stop the respondent holding a disciplinary hearing prior to a determination by an adjudication panel under the UKCP complaints process.

The Court further noted that:

> It is arguable that it is an implied term of the employment contract of a medical professional that he or she will adhere to the standards of professional conduct of his or her professional body, to the extent that they are relevant to his or her employment. It does not, however, in my view follow from this that the employer will, in deciding whether the employee has adhered to professional boundaries and/or observed standards of professional conduct, defer to or otherwise be bound by the professional body's determination as to whether the employee has so adhered and/or observed.

It was also found that the applicant had failed to establish any properly arguable legal basis for his assertion that the respondent was "'bound' to defer to the decision of the UKCP on the question of whether his conduct breached safe professional boundaries and therefore was bound to await the outcome of the UKCP's own proceedings'.

In applying the standard test for injunctions as set out in *American Cyanamid Co v Ethicon Ltd*[9] the Court held that there was no serious issue to be tried, nor would it be just and convenient for the Court to continue the initial interim injunctive relief.

[12.07] *SMO v Hywel Dda University Health Board*[10]—*High Court of England and Wales—Linden J—contract of employment—disciplinary procedure—duty of mutual trust and confidence—breach of contract—injunction*

The claimant was a consultant surgeon employed by the respondent Health Board. His colleagues complained about his conduct to the effect that he had behaved in an intimidating and aggressive manner. The Health Board instituted disciplinary proceedings under the disciplinary procedures in place for consultants employed in Wales. There was a multi-stage procedure and the claimant was suspended. Ultimately, there was an investigation into two matters, firstly that the claimant's standard of behaviour including team working and relationships was unacceptable; and secondly that the claimant had failed to display the required standards for clinical decision-making and practice.

The investigation outcome was that the first charge was sufficiently established, but the second was not. The first charge was then to be further addressed at the next stage of the process, which could ultimately have resulted in dismissal or a final written warning following a hearing in front of an enquiry panel and a report to the medical director which would be followed by a further disciplinary hearing. Meanwhile, however,

---

[9] *American Cyanamid Co v Ethicon Ltd* [1975] AC 396 (HL).
[10] *SMO v Hywel Dda University Health Board* [2020] EWHC 727 (QB), [2021] IRLR 273.

the Health Board embarked on a parallel investigation to determine whether there had been a serious breakdown in working relationships, being a process which was entirely outside of the relevant disciplinary proceedings and was done in what the employer claimed to be the exercise of its entitlement to enquire into the matter.

The claimant issued proceedings in the High Court, alleging that the second, parallel investigation was breach of the express and implied terms of his contract and seeking an injunction to restrain the Health Board from proceeding with the second working-relationships investigation. The High Court held that the second working-relationships investigation was an impermissible breach of contract because its subject matter fell to be investigated under the relevant disciplinary procedures and the Health Board could not avoid employees' safeguards included in the disciplinary procedures by embarking on the parallel procedure. That finding was reached by reference to the specific features of the relevant disciplinary procedure. The High Court also found that the parallel working-relationships investigation was, on the facts, a breach of the implied duty of mutual trust and confidence. The High Court concluded that an injunction should be granted to prevent the working-relationships investigation other than in the course of the ongoing disciplinary proceedings.

In reaching its conclusion, the High Court had to consider the Health Board's argument to the effect that the working-relationships investigation could result in dismissal, not on the grounds of conduct, but on the grounds of some other substantial reason. In considering that contention, the Court reviewed the decision of the Court of Appeal in *Perkin v St George's Health Care NHS Trust*.[11] In that case, the Court of Appeal, in upholding the decision of the EAT, found the dismissal was fair and noted that a break-down of confidence between an employer and one of its senior executives for which the latter was responsible and which actually or potentially damages the operations of the employer's organisation (or rendered it impossible for senior executives to work together as a team) is capable of being some other substantial reason and therefore could result in an employer fairly dismissing the employee whom the employer deems responsible. The Court of Appeal considered that the classification of the reason for the dismissal, whether as conduct or as some other substantial reason, did not matter, as, on either basis, there was a permissible reason for the dismissal.

The High Court also considered the decision of the EAT in *Ezsias v North Glamorgan NHS Trust (No 2)*, where the employment tribunal found that the reason for the dismissal was the breakdown in working relationships between the claimant and his colleagues and therefore some other substantial reason and accordingly, the disciplinary proce-dures did not apply. The EAT did not interfere with this conclusion. It was found as a fact that the sole reason for the dismissal was the fact of the breakdown in working relationships rather than because an allegation of misconduct against the claimant had been upheld and therefore there was no breach of the requirement that the disciplinary procedures be invoked. In refusing permission to appeal in *Ezsias*, Mummery LJ in the

---

[11]   *Perkin v St George's Health Care NHS Trust* [2006] ICR 617.

Court of Appeal stated that 'it would obviously be wrong ... for an employer in the case to which the contractual disciplinary procedure applied to seek to sidestep it by categorising allegations of personal professional misconduct as some other substantial reason, or ... as breaches of the implied duty of trust and confidence.' He noted that this was not what had happened in this case and approved the observation of Elias LJ in *Perkin* that employment tribunals 'must be alert to the possibility that an employer will seek to evade the disciplinary procedures by describing the reason for dismissal as a breakdown in a relationship'.

In *SMO*, the Court concluded, however, that the fact that the conduct or performance of an employee may lead to dysfunctional working relationships, does not necessarily mean that the employer's reason for its response to the situation is the conduct or performance of the employee. What it does mean is a matter for evidence.

On the implied duty of mutual trust and confidence, the Court of Appeal referred to the distinction drawn in *IBM UK Holdings Ltd v Dalgleish*[12] between cases where the employer is exercising an expressed or implied discretionary power, and cases where the concern is simply with the conduct of the employer. In the first category, the discretion is required to be exercised in accordance with the duty of mutual trust and confidence, but the test is as to the rationality of the employer's exercise of its contractual discretion. In the second category, the test is whether the employer has, without reasonable and proper cause, conducted itself in a manner calculated or likely to destroy or seriously damage the relationship of confidence and trust between employer and employee.

The test for whether there has been a breach is objective, but the court will take into account the employer's subjective reasons for the actions complained of. A breach of mutual trust and confidence is a repudiatory breach and this is an indication of the degree of seriousness of the employer's conduct which must be established by the claimant. The Court concluded that the working-relationships investigation here fell into the second category. It was not the exercise of a discretionary power which was expressly or impliedly conferred on the employer by the contract of employment. The Health Board simply decided on a particular course of action. The Court concluded that it was a breach of the implied duty of mutual trust and confidence for the Health Board to embark on the working-relationship investigation in the circumstances in which it did so.

The Court also noted that, with the two procedures continuing in parallel, the claimant was 'on Morton's fork', ie, contesting the disciplinary proceedings could be taken as evidence that the working relationships have irretrievably broken down; on the other hand, admitting that the relationships have broken down and apologising would confirm the case against him under the disciplinary proceedings.

For the reasons set out above the Court granted the injunction to restrain the continuation of the working-relationships investigation.

---

12   *IBM UK Holdings Ltd v Dalgleish* [2018] IRLR 4.

Dismissal

[12.08] *O'Donovan v Over-C Technology Ltd and Over-C Ltd[13]—Court of Appeal—Costello J—appeal from the High Court[14]—injunction—dismissal*

The respondent was employed as the Chief Financial Officer of Over-C Technologies Ltd (Over-C). His contract of employment provided that his employment was subject to an initial six-month probationary period, during which his performance would be assessed by Over-C and, if satisfactory, his employment would continue.

The respondent commenced in August 2019 and in January 2020 (before the end of his probationary period) he was dismissed on the grounds of poor performance. The respondent issued High Court proceedings seeking to restrain his dismissal. He argued that he had been dismissed for misconduct, not poor performance, and as such the termination had been effected in breach of the terms of his contract. He argued that his contract included an implied term that any disciplinary procedures would be carried out in accordance with natural and constitutional justice and that this term had been breached in the manner in which he was dismissed.

The High Court did not accept that the respondent had been dismissed on the grounds of misconduct. However, it nevertheless found the respondent had established a strong case that his dismissal was not lawful. It held that the obligation to afford an employee fair procedures in relation to his or her termination during their probationary period may apply to dismissals for poor performance as well as for misconduct, and flowing from that held that the respondent had established a strong case that he had an implied contractual right to fair procedures in the assessment of his performance during his probationary period which was breached by the manner in which he was dismissed. The High Court granted an order preventing Over-C from dismissing the respondent pending trial of his action and ordering it to pay his salary for a period of six months from the end of January 2020 (when he had been dismissed).

Over-C appealed to the Court of Appeal, which agreed with the High Court's finding that the respondent had not established a strong case that his dismissal was for misconduct. However, it did not concur that the right to fair procedures also applies in relation to dismissals on the grounds of poor performance during an employee's probationary period as it held that to imply a right to fair procedures in such a case 'would negate the whole purpose of a probation period'.

The Court of Appeal held that during an employee's probationary period 'both parties are—and must be—free to terminate the contract of employment for no reason, or simply because one party forms the view that the intended employment is, for whatever reason, not something with which they wish to continue'. If an employer has a contractual right to dismiss on notice without giving any reason, a court cannot imply a term that the dismissal may only take place if fair procedures have been afforded. The Court

---

13 *O'Donovan v Over-C Technology Ltd and Over-C Ltd* [2021] IECA 37.
14 See *Arthur Cox Employment Law Yearbook 2020* at **[12.05]** for the High Court decisions in *O'Donovan v Over-C Technology Ltd and Over-C Ltd* [2020] IEHC 291; [2020] IEHC 327.

noted that the exception to this is where an employee is dismissed for misconduct, in such a case fair procedures must be followed and the principles of natural justice apply.

The Court acknowledged that there may be overlap between conduct amounting to 'poor performance' and conduct amounting to 'misconduct' at times, however in the context of this case it held that an allegation that an employer is of the view that an employee has not 'discharged his duties' is not sufficient to introduce an element of 'misconduct' to warrant the implication of the right to fair procedures in a dismissal on those grounds.

Having reaffirmed the common law position that probationary dismissals (other than on the grounds of misconduct) do not attract a right to fair procedures, the Court held that the trial Judge:

> did not adequately address the implications of his finding that Mr. O'Donovan had failed to establish a strong case that he had been dismissed on grounds of misconduct when the trial judge proceeded nonetheless to hold that he had established a strong case that he was entitled to fair procedures in respect of his dismissal ... [and] erred when he held that Mr. O'Donovan had a strong case that he was entitled to fair procedures in relation to the assessment of his performance.

The Court held that the respondent's argument that dismissal on grounds other than misconduct attracts a right to fair procedures 'fell very far short from establishing that he had made out a strong case in this regard'. As such, the Court held that the High Court had erred in holding that the respondent had satisfied the test for injunctive relief set down in *Maha Lingham v Health Service Executive*,[15] ie, that he had a strong case likely to succeed in trial.

In addition and separately, the Court found that the High Court should not have granted the injunction as it erred in holding that damages were not an adequate remedy. Noting that the High Court had acknowledged the respondent's claim was one for wrongful dismissal, the Court of Appeal held that 'by definition, damages are an adequate remedy within the meaning of the jurisprudence in those circumstances and, accordingly, no injunction ought to have been granted'.

The Court allowed the appeal, vacated the order of the High Court and made an order for costs against the applicant in respect of the appeal and the High Court hearing.

[12.09] *Delaney v Aer Lingus (Ireland) Ltd*[16]*—High Court—Allen J— injunctions—dismissal—garda vetting—mandatory qualifications*

The plaintiff was employed by Aer Lingus as a cabin crew member based at Dublin airport. He was required to hold an airside access card, which is a security pass issued by daa plc that allows holders to access restricted areas of the airport. The process for the issue of any one of these cards requires garda vetting. The defendant instructed its employees (including the plaintiff) to complete garda vetting checks as required for the purpose of obtaining and retaining the security pass. The defendant had no control over

---

[15] *Maha Lingham v Health Service Executive* [2005] IESC 89.
[16] *Delaney v Aer Lingus (Ireland) Ltd* [2021] IEHC 72.

the process, which was conducted by a third party that was not a party to the action (daa plc).

The plaintiff did not renew his security pass. It expired on 10 December 2019 and he was placed on special unpaid leave. It later became apparent that the pass could not be renewed by reason of the fact that daa plc refused to renew the pass, as the plaintiff had previously been found in possession of a small quantity of cannabis and MDMA at a music festival and had a pending prosecution for possession of drugs.

The plaintiff was called to a meeting. He was represented at this meeting by his solicitor. He was informed that, without a security pass, he could not work as a cabin crew member. Following the meeting, the plaintiff was dismissed and informed that his contract was terminated due to frustration of contract and that he would be paid his salary in lieu of notice.

The plaintiff sought injunctive relief restraining the defendant from taking any steps for the purpose of effecting or implementing the purported dismissal, and directing the defendant to pay his salary pending the trial of action. The matter was adjourned, first for a short period of time and then generally due to court closures arising from public health restrictions. The plaintiff's dismissal was effected. At the hearing of the application, the Court was informed that the plaintiff had secured alternative employment.

The plaintiff argued that the contract was not frustrated, and that he was not in breach of a fundamental term of the contract. The plaintiff did not accept that holding a security pass was a requirement of the contract. He asserted that the defendant, as the plaintiff's employer, had overall responsibility to ensure that the plaintiff was able to carry out his duties for remuneration, and that it should have re-deployed him, as opposed to dismissing him or placing him on unpaid leave. He asserted that the defendant did not seek to determine whether the offence alleged against him in the course of the vetting process was serious; or whether he had a defence to it; or whether he intended to challenge the vetting process. The plaintiff stated that the defendant did not allow his solicitor time to engage with daa plc prior to dismissing the plaintiff.

Regarding the frustration of contract argument, the Court noted that the defendant did not take the position that the expiry of the security pass had legally frustrated the contract—the reason provided for the dismissal was that the plaintiff did not have a security pass.

The Court considered that the plaintiff's argument that holding a security pass was not a requirement of the contract was not a strong one—without the pass, crew could not perform their duties.

In response to the re-deployment argument, the Court noted that this was inconsistent with the plaintiff's argument that he should not have been placed on unpaid leave, noting that 'if [the Plaintiff's] contract of employment did not provide that he could be placed on unpaid leave, neither did it provide that the Plaintiff was obliged to redeploy him'.

The Court accepted that any appeals to fairness in relation to dismissal were in the wrong forum and were not a matter to be considered by the High Court—the fairness of a dismissal is a matter for the Workplace Relations Commission.

The Court did not accept that Aer Lingus, as a third party, was obliged to deal with daa plc, nor to persuade daa plc to issue the plaintiff with a security pass. It noted that the plaintiff did not attempt to identify any legal obligation on the part of Aer Lingus to engage with daa plc or provide more time for the plaintiff's solicitor to engage with daa plc. The Court stated that if the plaintiff's case was that his employer failed to do something that it was bound by contract to do but behaved unreasonably, he was in the wrong forum.

The Court found that the plaintiff fell well short of the standard required to obtain injunctive relief. While the Court accepted that fair procedures and natural justice must be observed when considering an allegation of misconduct that reflected on the employee's good name or reputation, the Court found that the plaintiff had failed to establish that he had a strong case that he was likely to succeed in his argument that he was dismissed by reason of misconduct. While the plaintiff had asserted that he was dismissed by reason of the allegation against him which had resulted in the vetting disclosure (possession of drugs), the respondent was consistent in its position that it did not take this into account.

It followed from this finding that potential reputational damage would not tip the balance of convenience in favour of granting relief—the plaintiff was not dismissed due to misconduct—he was dismissed because he failed to continue to hold a security pass. The application was refused.

[12.10] *Mason v ILTB Ltd t/a Gillen Markets and Dermot Browne[17]—High Court—Butler J—interlocutory injunction—dismissal—unfair procedures*

The plaintiff was employed as the managing director and company secretary of the defendant since January 2016. The defendant was a private company, involved in the provision of wealth management and investment advisory services to its clients, which is a regulated entity under the Central Bank Act 2010. Relations between the parties were already strained when a meeting took place between the plaintiff and the majority shareholder during which the majority shareholder accused the plaintiff of fraud in relation to a bonus payment made to himself. It was disputed as to whether the plaintiff was summarily dismissed. Thereafter a board resolution was passed to set up an investigation into the payment. At the same time that the board resolution was passed, the High Court granted an interim injunction restraining the defendant from taking steps to terminate the plaintiff's employment, as a result of which the defendant did not take any steps to appoint an external investigator or to suspend the plaintiff. The interim order made by Allen J restrained the defendant from giving effect to or implementing the purported dismissal of the plantiff, from publishing or disseminating the

---

[17]   *Mason v ILTB Ltd t/a Gillen Markets and Dermot Browne* [2021] IEHC 477.

allegations of misconduct (there was a suggestion that the Central Bank and the gardaí would be notified) and from passing any board resolutions concerning the plaintiff.

This interlocutory application sought to restrain the defendant from proceeding to dismiss the plaintiff. The defendant disputed the factual basis of the plaintiff's claim. The defendant placed heavy emphasis on the fact that the plaintiff had not been either dismissed or suspended and, consequently, contended that the intervention of the Court in the disciplinary or investigative process was premature. Finally, the defendant argued that the circumstances which led to this point were largely irrelevant when what was now being proposed was a 'gold standard' investigation to be carried out by an independent lawyer with employment law and industrial relations experience.

The parties were agreed that, because the plaintiff was seeking mandatory relief to enforce the contract of employment pending the determination of the proceedings, the threshold standard was not the ordinary interlocutory injunction standard of 'a fair question to be tried' but, rather, the higher 'strong case' standard. The Court was satisfied that, on the basis of the evidence before the Court at the interlocutory stage and allowing that the disputed facts of the plaintiff's case may have to be taken at their height, the plaintiff exceeded by some margin the fair question to be tried threshold and raised a case which was not only stateable but which had a real prospect of success. The Court observed that a solicitor's letter sent on behalf of the defendant stated that the bonus payment to the plaintiff was 'improper, irregular, unauthorised and unlawful' and found that: 'It is difficult to construe this letter other than as meaning the respondent company was proposing to go through the formality of an investigation in order to support a decision which it had already reached'. The Court found the 'strong case' standard was also met when the board of the defendant suspended the plaintiff at a meeting without notifying him that such a step was being considered.

The defendant argued that a finding that the plaintiff had a strong case might not, in the particular circumstances, be sufficient to justify the Court finding the plaintiff had passed the initial threshold. It argued that because it had a real and serious concern as to the legitimacy of the bonus payment, as the plaintiff's employer it must be allowed to investigate that concern and, depending on the outcome of the investigation, to take appropriate action. The Court was not convinced by this argument and stated that the defendant had clearly 'made up its mind' that the bonus payment was improper and therefore the 'proposed investigation, no matter how professionally it might be carried out, is merely window dressing'.

On the balance of justice, the Court stated that:

> the adequacy of damages for either party in the event that an injunction is granted, or refused, contrary to their interests and they subsequently prevail at trial, is a significant factor in the assessment of the balance of justice, but not a factor to be considered as a stand-alone criterion before the balance of justice is considered more generally. The factors which are relevant and the weight to be attached to those factors will vary from case to case, bearing in mind always that the remedy is intended to be flexible.

The High Court granted an interlocutory injunction restraining the defendant employer from taking any steps to terminate the applicant's employment, pending the full hearing of the case. The Court indicated that it would not allow the employer to proceed with a proposed 'gold standard investigation' into the alleged misconduct for the reasons set out above. The Court also indicated that it would make an order requiring the first defendant to facilitate the plaintiff's return to work, stating that, as an unsuspended employee, the plaintiff was entitled to attend at his workplace and to carry out his duties.

In a later judgment,[18] the Court dealt with the issue of costs arising from the interlocutory injunction application, and the form the order of the Court should take.

In relation to the issue of costs, the plaintiff submitted that, as he had been successful in obtaining interlocutory relief, he should be awarded the costs associated with the action, in relying on the rule that costs followed the event.

The defendant's submissions focused on the proposition that costs should follow the event unless the court is satisfied that that is not possible in circumstances of an interlocutory injunction to make a determination on who should be liable as to costs. The defendant argued that, as the substantive issue had not yet been resolved at the trial of action, the issue of costs should be reserved or made in the cause. In so doing, the defendant pointed to a number of factual points that were in dispute between the parties, including whether the plaintiff's payment to himself of €14,000 constituted gross misconduct.

The Court rejected the defendant's submission that the Court was unable to justly make a cost determination where there was a significant factual disagreement between the parties, noting that to follow that logic would mean that the costs of any injunction application would always have to be reserved to the substantive trial. In the case at hand, the plaintiff had met the threshold of a 'strong case', and the factual disagreements, which the defendant pointed to, were not central to the legal or factual aspects of the case.

That stated, the Court ultimately decided that, in the circumstances, the order for costs should be stayed 'pending the outcome of the substantive action both because of the ongoing working relationship between the parties and the fact of ongoing litigation, or perhaps more accurately because of both of those matters in conjunction with each other'.

In relation to the form the court order should take, the plaintiff requested a wide range of orders, including an order restraining the defendants from giving effect to a board resolution and from suspending him. The defendant submitted that the orders should relate solely to the impugned process in dispute. The Court ultimately made a number of orders, including restraining the defendant from proceeding with any investigation, from giving effect to the board resolution and from taking any steps in relation to the termination of the plaintiff's employment arising from matters set out in a solicitor's letter.

---

18   *Mason v ILTB Ltd t/a Gillen Markets and Dermot Browne* [2021] IEHC 539.

[12.11]   *Avsar v Wilson James Ltd*[19]—High Court of England and Wales— Eady J—suspension and termination of employment—injunction—duty of mutual trust and confidence—trade union activity

The claimant was employed in October 2020 by the respondent, which provided security services to third parties. Shortly after he commenced employment, the employer wrote to the claimant, inviting him to a probation review meeting to discuss his future employment on the basis that his conduct during the probationary period had 'not reached the required standards'. The respondent went on to assert that, in his previous employment as a security officer at a university, he had engaged in trade union activities with a union, who 'believe that outsourcing is antiquated and discriminatory', with a view to compelling the university to take him and his colleagues into in-house employment; this action was ongoing in the employment tribunal. As the respondent was a provider of security services to its clients, it asserted that there was 'a conflict of interest between [the claimant's] opinion and work with the union' and the respondent. He was warned that the outcome of the meeting might be dismissal and he was suspended thereafter.

The claimant sought an injunction in the County Court to require the respondent to end his suspension and to restrain the respondent from further disciplinary proceedings against him. He contended that the respondent had acted unlawfully by seeking to terminate his employment which constituted an unlawful act of victimisation on the grounds of the ongoing employment tribunal proceedings against his previous employer; or detriment relating to his trade union activities arising from his previous employment. The County Court dismissed the application, holding that there was no serious issue to be tried; there was no real prospect that the claimant would obtain a final injunction; and damages would be an adequate remedy.

The claimant applied for permission to appeal to the High Court, where Eady J, in deciding whether to grant permission to apply, considered the findings of the County Court.

The High Court noted that the County Court was required to apply the three-stage test laid down in *American Cyanamid*,[20] namely whether there is a serious issue to be tried, whether damages would be an adequate remedy, and whether the balance of convenience is in favour of granting the injunction.

With reference to the first test, Eady J noted that this was a claim for breach of contract, ie, breach of the implied term of mutual trust and confidence, which she described as 'the irreducible and necessary bedrock of an employment relationship'. She concluded that the claimant had established that there was a serious issue to be tried as to whether the respondent had acted in breach or, anticipatory breach, of the implied term of trust and confidence, having, without reasonable and proper cause, suspended him and by inviting him to a hearing to discuss the matters set out in the letter. Eady J cited,

---

[19]   *Avsar v Wilson James Ltd* [2020] EWHC 3412, [2021] IRLR 300.
[20]   *American Cyanamid Co v Ethicon Ltd* [1975] AC 396.

with approval, the decision of the Court of Appeal in *Mezey v South West London and Saint George's Mental Health Trust*,[21] where Sedley LJ observed that suspension is not a purely natural act, 'it changes the status quo from work to no work, and it inevitably casts a shadow over the employee's competence'. The High Court therefore overturned the finding of the County Court on this issue.

Turning to the adequacy of damages in relation to the invitation to the probation hearing, the High Court noted that, should the respondent terminate the employment of the claimant, he had a potential cause of action in an employment tribunal for non-pecuniary losses he might have suffered, such as injury to feelings. Accordingly, the High Court upheld the finding in the County Court and concluded that a case had not been made out by the claimant as to the inadequacy of damages.

Finally, turning to the balance of convenience, Eady J noted that, although the contract of employment is one of personal service, this does not mean that a court will not grant injunctive relief to restrain a breach of contract in circumstances where trust and confidence remain intact. Eady J concluded that, had she taken the view that damages were not an adequate remedy, she would have found that the balance of convenience favoured the grant of an injunction on the grounds that the basis for the invitation to the probation meeting was 'inextricably linked with the Claimant's trade union activities'.

The application was dismissed by reason of the High Court's findings with regard to the adequacy of damages.

Non-compete

[12.12] *C Wzrd Ltd v Kortan*[22]—**High Court of England and Wales—Simon Barker QC—springboard injunction**

This was an interim application by C Wzrd Ltd for an injunction against Mr Kortan, a former director and the company (D2), set up by Mr Kortan, with the intention of trading in competition with the applicant.

C Wzrd Ltd was formed to provide an online platform for market analysis of cryptocurrencies. It was a wholly owned subsidiary of the Wzrd Group Ltd, the second applicant, which had three shareholders, who were also the directors. There was no formal agreement between Mr Kortan (one of the directors) and the applicants, whether as a director, employee or shareholder. Mr Kortan was under no contractual restraints as to future business activity. A few months into trading, relationships broke down and Mr Kortan downloaded a copy of the applicants' database of members and contacts, he formed a rival entity (D2) with a view to trading in competition with the applicants. He made online postings encouraging the applicants' members to seek subscription refunds and otherwise disparaging the applicants.

---

21   *Mezey v South West London and Saint George's Mental Health Trust* [2007] EWCA Civ 106.
22   *C Wzrd Ltd v Kortan* [2020] EWHC 1360 (Ch).

In March 2020, the applicants issued proceedings against Mr Kortan for breach of statutory and fiduciary duty as a director, infringement of trade mark, and passing off. They also issued an application for interim injunctive relief. They sought to: (i) prevent Mr Kortan from being engaged by, or assisting D2 in its development; and (ii) prevent Mr Kortan acting in competition with the applicants, soliciting their customers, prospective customers or employees, and/or interfering with the supply of goods and/or services to the applicants. At a hearing of the interim application, the respondents gave undertakings, as a holding measure, in or substantially in, the form of the injunctive relief sought, pending an effective hearing of the application. The applicants submitted that a six-month 'springboard' injunction was appropriate.

The Court held that the applicants were entitled to injunctive relief against Mr Kortan, it noted that the objective of a springboard injunction was to 'neutralise the timing advantage which the ex-employee seeks to gain and protect the employer from unfair competition'. The Court added:

> It is commonplace for courts to impose interim or springboard injunctions on errant directors who seek to set up competing businesses while in office and/or utilising misappropriated information or other property. The precise terms will vary according to the circumstances, including any particular agreement(s) between the company and the director, and the appropriate enforcement of the director's statutory duties ... The aim of any interim injunctive relief is to be confined restoration of the status quo ante.

In finding for the applicants, the Court noted that Mr Kortan's behaviour (both the acknowledged and the alleged behaviour) and his resignation as a director engaged the springboard principle. The Court was persuaded by the fact that there was a strong likelihood of the applicants succeeding at trial in establishing liability for breach of fiduciary duty.

However, the Court noted the lack of a restraint of trade clause and the broad scope of the injunction application (in particular the element of attempting to prevent interference with supply of goods and service to the applicants). The Court observed that there was no evidence to suggest Mr Kortan had interfered in any way at any time. It also found that:

> Similarly, with regard to enticement of its employees, the evidence was that the [applicants] had no employees. The injunction sought to restrain soliciting any prospective customer, defined as anyone with whom the [applicants] might have dealt: that was an impossibly wide and uncertain definition.

The Court underlined the importance when making an injunction application, of ensuring that the injunction request accurately reflects the circumstances of the case and advised against inclusion of 'boilerplate' language. It was found that the first part of the injunction application was too broad as it excluded Mr Kortan from any and all involvement with D2, irrespective of D2's business.

In terms of the duration of any limitation, the Court noted that, although the applicants were 'entitled to fair, just and proportionate protection for the purpose of restoring what had wrongfully, or arguably wrongfully, been taken or undermined', they 'bore the burden of spelling out the precise nature and period of the defendants' unfair and unjust competitive advantage and their own unfair and unjust competitive disadvantage'.

The Court held that the six-month period they sought was excessive and that the appropriate period was three months.

The Court therefore granted a more limited injunction than that sought by the applicants.

[12.13] *The Delivery Group Ltd and Postal Choices Ltd v Yeo[23]—High Court of England and Wales—Saini J—interim injunction—post-termination non-compete*

This case related to an application for an interim injunction against the respondent, a former employee of the second applicant, who joined a competitor in the parcel delivery industry. The application related to covenants on non-dealing with restricted customers and confidentiality.

The Court noted that, where an interim injunction would give the applicant all, or most, of the relief sought by way final injunction—as by the time of the trial any final injunction would have expired—there must be an assessment of the claim's merits. It is not sufficient for an applicant in those circumstances to satisfy only the 'serious issue' to be tried test.

The Court therefore applied the *American Cyanamid*[24] principles involving a three-stage examination of whether there is a serious issue to be tried, the adequacy of damages and the balance of convenience.

In considering the non-dealing covenant, the Court held that there was no issue about the meaning of the non-dealing covenant and the main issue related to the legitimate business interests of the former employer and the width of the covenant.

The Court was satisfied that the applicants had a legitimate business interest to protect, ie, the confidential information to which the respondent had access, client connections and workforce stability. The Court noted that client connections have long been held to be protected by way of post-termination restraints. The Court observed that the narrower and more specialist the market, the more likely it is that a non-dealing covenant will be upheld. Furthermore, the upholding of non-dealing covenants is influenced by the obvious difficulties in policing confidentiality clauses. The Court concluded that the non-dealing clause, which was limited to customers of the applicants within a limited retrospective period and with whom the respondent had dealt personally, was justifiable by the confidential information allegedly possessed by the respondent as well as by the client contact he had in a specialist marketplace.

The Court rejected the contention that the 12-month duration of the non-dealing covenant was too long, noting that the length of the covenant is an example of an issue which is unsuitable for determination at the interim stage.

Furthermore, the Court rejected the respondent's contention that the consideration was inadequate (the covenant had been introduced during the course of the employment in return for mutual longer notice periods).

---

23   *The Delivery Group Ltd and Postal Choices Ltd v Yeo* [2021] EWHC 1834 (QB).
24   *American v Cyanamid v Ethicon Ltd* [1975] AC 396.

The covenants were not too wide to be enforceable and, on examining the merits in more detail, the covenants had been demonstrated to be limited, justified and reasonable.

Finally, with reference to the non-dealing covenants, the Court noted that damages would be very difficult to quantify, it had taken years for the applicants to build their reputation and market-leading position, the respondent had no independent resources and would be unable to meet any damages claim; often in employee competition cases damages are not an adequate remedy.

The Court found that the applicants had a case on the non-dealing covenants that was likely to succeed at trial, the balance of convenience clearly lay in favour of the granting of the injunction because the greater risk of injustice lay in not restraining the respondent.

On the confidentiality injunction, the Court considered that there was not a serious issue to be tried. The pleaded case was not sufficiently strong. There was no more than an 'inference' that the respondent had used the applicant's confidential information and the Court noted that the sworn statements presented to it were speculative. The Court concluded that that was not a sound basis on which to obtain injunctive relief. There was no arguable case that the respondent had breached or intended to breach obligations of confidentiality and, accordingly, the injunction was refused.

Ancillary orders had been sought, including an order for delivery up and an order for disclosure by affidavit.

The Court concluded that there was no evidence to indicate that the respondent had confidential information and, accordingly, no basis for an order as to delivery up.

Likewise, with reference to the order for disclosure by affidavit, the Court concluded that this was not an exceptional case where an affidavit requiring the respondent to provide a list of information was justified. The relief was not necessary to enable the applicants to plead their case and would put the onus on the respondent to disprove wrongdoing rather than on the applicant to prove its case.

[12.14]   *Source Bioscience UK Ltd v Wheatcroft*[25]—*High Court of England and Wales—Farbey J—interim injunction—post-termination non-compete*

The applicants sought various interim injunctions against the respondents. The applicants formed part of a group of companies that provided laboratory services to a range of clients in the pharmaceutical industry, including the NHS and private health care providers. Within the core business of the first applicant was infectious disease testing, including Covid-19 testing. The first respondent was a former employee and the second respondent was another life sciences company planning to enter into the market for Covid-19 testing.

The second respondent was willing to give the undertaking sought by the applicants, as a consequence of which, the matter did not proceed against the second respondent.

---

[25]   *Source Bioscience UK Ltd v Wheatcroft* [2021] EWHC 2909 (QB).

In relation to the first respondent, the applicants sought prohibitions of the disclosure of confidential information, the solicitation of customers and the offering of employment to the applicants' employees, as well as orders relating to the preservation of evidence and restraints on inducing breach of contract. The first respondent was willing to give certain undertakings, and so the proceedings continued in relation to two restrictions, namely, a restriction for three months after the termination date on being 'involved in any capacity with any business concern which is or intends to be in competition with any Restricted Business' and a restraint for the same three-month period on being 'involved with the provision of goods or services to or otherwise have any business dealings with any Restricted Customer in the course of any business concern which is in competition with any Restricted Business'.

The first respondent began working for the first applicant in 2014 in a middle-management capacity. The contract of employment included a number of post-termination restrictions including those referred to above. He was subsequently promoted on a number of occasions but the original contract of employment was not replaced. He resigned in May 2021 and in June 2021 his former employer, the first applicant learned that he was going to work for the second respondent. In communications thereafter, the first respondent contended that his new employer was not intending to establish a Covid-19 testing business in the UK and was not a competitor of the applicants.

The Court noted that there was also significant email evidence that the first respondent may not only have accepted a job from the second respondent, but was also instrumental in recruiting to the second respondent a number of other employees from the first applicant. The Court rejected the contention that the relationship between the first respondent and the second respondent was not a real or compelling threat to the applicants.

The Court stated that the *American Cyanamid*[26] principles are to be applied in employee restrictive covenant cases. It noted that the 'serious issue to be tried' test is a low bar for employer applicants. They must show that the claim is not frivolous or vexatious and that the restrictive covenant is not 'obviously bad'. The starting point is that the 'contracting parties should ordinarily be held to their bargain'. The Court noted that the covenants in contracts of employment are generally valid if contractually enforceable and reasonable, with the reasonableness be to be determined on the facts as they stood at the time the contract was entered into. The reasonableness test requires a balancing exercise between the legitimate interests of the employer and the rights of the former employee.

The Court rejected the contention that there was no serious issue to be tried as the covenants did not survive the first respondent's first promotion and held that the existing contract of employment remained in force. The Court concluded that there was a serious issue to be tried as to the effect of the covenants and whether or not they bound the first respondent.

---

[26] *American v Cyanamid v Ethicon Ltd* [1975] AC 396.

On the adequacy of damages question, it was noted that, if the applicants' confidential information was disclosed to a competitor, they would lose their competitive advantage and the competitor would gain an unfair advantage by benefiting from the applicants' wide and well-established expertise in the industry. Quantifying the harm that would be caused to the applicants' competitive advantage would be difficult. On the other hand, the loss which might be suffered by the first respondent until the expiry date would be quantifiable as a loss of income and would be adequately addressed by the applicants' undertakings as to damages. The Court concluded that the disputed provisions were limited in scope and limited in time and gave proper protection to the applicants in circumstances where there was *prima facie* evidence that the first respondent had infringed his obligations.

The Court granted the orders sought on the basis that it was just and convenient to do so.

[12.15]   *Gemini Europe Ltd v Sawyer*[27]—*High Court of England and Wales—Ellenbogen J—interim injunction—non-compete—direct competitor—delay in seeking injunctive relief*

This was an application for an interim injunction to prohibit the respondent from contravening a non-compete clause which, the applicant asserted, formed part of the respondent's contract of employment.

The applicant company was part of a group of companies operating in the cryptocurrency market, in facilitating customers to buy, sell and store crypto assets. The respondent was appointed by the applicant as MD, Europe in November 2019. In July 2020, he gave the applicant his three months' notice, and notified the applicant of his intention to take up employment with a direct competitor of the applicant. He was subsequently placed on garden leave before taking up employment with the competitor.

It was not the applicant's submission that the respondent would deliberately use the confidential information he had access to during his employment with the applicant—rather, the applicant argued, the respondent had become privy to a substantial amount of confidential information, and 'the risk of his unwitting, or inadvertent use' of the information was such that the enforcement of the non-compete was warranted.

The High Court began by noting the well-established legal principles of granting interim relief, as set out in *American Cyanamid Co v Ethicon*[28]—namely, the court must consider if there was a serious case to be tried, whether damages would be an adequate remedy and whether the balance of convenience lay in favour of granting the interim relief.

Having regard to the above, there were four substantive issues for the High Court to determine:

1.   Did the non-compete clause as contained in the contract of employment apply?

---

[27]   *Gemini Europe Ltd v Sawyer* [2020] EWHC 3377 (QB).
[28]   *American Cyanamide Co v Ethicon* [1975] 1 All ER 504.

2.   Was the non-compete wider than necessary to protect the confidential information of the applicant?
3.   If the non-compete was enforceable, was an injunction necessary and appropriate to protect the confidential information of the applicant? and
4.   Had the applicant delayed in making the application such that it was disentitled to relief?

The High Court addressed the issue of delay at the outset. The respondent alleged that the applicant had inappropriately delayed in seeking injunctive relief only when the respondent was due to commence employment with the competitor, as opposed to seeking relief upon being informed of the respondent's intention to commence employment with the competitor. The High Court rejected this submission and found that there was no unreasonable delay on the part of the applicant. It noted that:

> The fact that an application can be brought on the basis of an anticipatory breach of contract, does not mean that it ought to be brought at that stage, or that any failure to do so is unreasonable.

In relation to whether the non-compete contained in the contract of employment applied, the High Court observed that the respondent had in fact entered into three separate employment agreements—a contract of employment directly with the applicant; thereafter a contract with a professional employer organisation under which the applicant was identified as the client; and, finally, a second contract of employment directly with applicant when the contract with the professional employer organisation terminated. The second agreement with the respondent contained identical terms to the first agreement. In assessing the factual circumstances, the High Court found that the contract with the professional employer organisation was 'no more than a vehicle for payment'. It therefore was up to the High Court to determine the enforceability of the non-compete as contained in the two agreements directly with the applicant.

The High Court analysed the non-compete clause and determined that it was enforceable, save for a subsection of the clause that related to future financial interests. The High Court severed the impugned subsection and held that there was nothing unreasonable about the nine-month restriction period.

In relation to the question as to whether the respondent was in fact exposed to confidential information such that an injunction was necessary and appropriate, the High Court held that it was likely that the applicant would establish at the trial of action that the respondent had had access to a significant body of confidential information which the applicant was entitled to protect.

The High Court ultimately determined that the applicant's case in relation to the substantive points at issue was stronger than the respondent's case, and as such, it would likely succeed in obtaining the injunction sought.

The Court determined that damages would not be an adequate remedy in the circumstances, and held that the balance of convenience 'favours the continuation of the interim injunction pending a speedy trial'.

[12.16] ***Quilter Private Client Advisers Ltd v Falconer & Continuum (Financial Services) LLP[29]—High Court of England and Wales—Calver J—claim for damages—post-termination non-compete and confidentiality obligations— constructive dismissal—inducement of breach of contract***

The applicant was a financial advisory business and financial intermediary. The first respondent was a chartered financial planner specialising in high net worth individuals and business owners. She took up employment with the applicant in January 2019. In July 2019, the first respondent gave notice of resignation to the applicant and was put on garden leave for two weeks such that her employment ended on 19 July 2019. The first respondent was engaged by the second respondent with effect 24 July 2019. The second respondent was also a financial advisory business and competed with the applicant for the same type of clients.

The first respondent had been hired by the applicant to take over the clients of a retiring employee. By the time the first respondent left the employment of the applicant she had met 40 of 181 of her clients and 120 of the clients had been transferred to her.

The first respondent's contract of employment with the applicant included post-termination restrictions, including a nine-month non-competition covenant, a 12-month non-solicitation covenant and a 12-month no-dealing covenant. For the purpose of the non-solicitation and no-dealing covenants the term 'customer' was defined as meaning a customer of the applicant with whom the respondent was materially concerned or had material personal contact at any time during the 18-month period prior to termination. For the purpose of the non-competition covenant the first respondent was precluded for a nine-month period from being employed or engaged in, or assisting or being interested in, any undertaking which provided services. Services were defined as services with which the first respondent was materially concerned at any time during the 12 months prior to termination and, in particular but not limited to, the business of the provision of life, pension and investment services and financial advisory and planning services.

The first respondent became unhappy in her role with the applicant after a short period. She complained about lack of administrative support, the nature of her objectives and the products which she was required to sell. She conceded in evidence that, in May 2019, she began scanning onto her personal laptop large quantities of the applicant's client documentation. There was no evidence to suggest that the second respondent's representatives, who at that time were engaging with the first respondent with a view to securing her services, were aware that the first respondent was scanning that documentation.

On 4 July 2019, the first respondent gave two weeks' notice of resignation to the applicant. She did not give any reason for resigning. Her employment with the applicant ended on 19 July 2019. On receipt of the letter of resignation from the first respondent, the applicant wrote to her on 12 July 2019, placing her on garden leave and setting out

---

[29] *Quilter Private Client Advisers Ltd v Falconer & Continuum (Financial Services) LLP* [2020] EWHC 3294 (QB).

her obligations and restrictions while on garden leave. They also reminded her of her obligations under her contract of employment in respect of the restrictive covenants.

It emerged in evidence that by late July or early August the applicant was aware that the first respondent had commenced work with the second respondent. The applicant did not seek injunctive relief until four-and-half months later and it did not write to either of the respondents objecting to the first respondent working for the second respondent.

In September 2019, the second respondent's competency training manager completed a competency assessment of the first respondent and stated in her report that the first respondent was working from her existing client bank, namely clients transferred with her from the applicant.

Eventually, in October 2019, the applicant sent letters before action to each of the respondents. In the case of the first respondent, it alleged infringement of the restrictive covenants and disclosure of confidential information and demanded undertakings. In the letter to the second respondent it noted that its employment of the first respondent was in breach of ongoing restrictions set out in her contract and requiring an undertaking that they would not facilitate her in a breach of her post-termination obligations. The second respondent responded seeking copies of enclosures that had been omitted and the applicant failed to respond at all to that letter and failed to take the urgent action it had threatened.

On 10 December 2019, the applicant issued proceedings and applied for an interim injunction, delivery up of documents and an early trial. The Court granted an expedited trial of the claim limited to the issues of liability and injunctive relief only, against certain undertakings provided by the respondents including undertakings to deliver up documents.

At the trial, the applicant claimed against the first respondent breach of the non-competition, non-solicitation and non-dealing covenants and inappropriate removal and use and disclosure of confidential information and breach of express and implied terms of the contract of employment. Against the second respondent, the applicant claimed inducement of breach of contract and facilitation of the misuse of confidential information by enabling the first respondent to upload confidential information onto its systems. Against the respondents jointly, the applicant claimed an unlawful means conspiracy.

The first respondent claimed that she had been constructively dismissed by the applicant, as a consequence of which she had no ongoing contractual obligations to the applicant. She also claimed that the restrictive covenants were void and unenforceable. The second respondent denied that it had induced a breach of contract.

The Court concluded that the first respondent was not constructively dismissed; the matters of which the first respondent complained were not, objectively considered, likely to seriously undermine the necessary trust and confidence in the employment relationship.

Turning to the assessment of the contractual obligations of the first respondent, the respondents submitted that the first respondent's duty of fidelity did not include a duty not to conceal her own wrongdoing and not to mislead the applicant about her future employment plans. The Court rejected this argument, holding that the duty of fidelity includes a duty of honesty.

The respondents also admitted that the contract contained an implied term that the first respondent would not act without reasonable and proper cause so as to destroy or damage the applicant's trust and confidence in her. The Court concluded that the scanning by the first respondent of the applicant's documents onto her personal laptop was a breach of her duty of fidelity as well as a breach of the duty of trust and confidence owed to the applicant, as was her use of that confidential information for her own purposes.

Turning to the validity or otherwise of the restrictive covenants, the Court noted that in respect of each covenant there were three questions to be answered as follows:

(1) Have the former employers shown on the evidence that they have legitimate business interests requiring protection in relation to the employee's employment?

(2) What does the covenant mean when properly construed?

(3) The covenant must be shown by the employer to be no wider than is reasonably necessary for the protection of his legitimate business interests. Reasonable necessity is to be assumed from the perspective of reasonable persons in the position of the parties as at the date of the contract ... The covenantee must show that the covenant is both reasonable in the interests of the contracting parties and reasonable in the interests of the public ... for any covenant in restraint of trade to be treated as reasonable in the interests of the parties "it must afford *no more than* adequate protection to the benefit of the party in whose favour it is imposed". [Emphasis in original.]

The Court went on to note that, even if a covenant is held to be reasonable, the Court would use its discretion to decide its reasonableness as at the time of the trial, in granting injunctive relief.

Turning to the first question, the Court concluded that there was no doubt that the applicant had legitimate business interests which required protection, namely the special trade connections.

On the second question, the Court noted that it must construe the contract in accordance with the ordinary principles of contractual construction and in a sensible and rational way. The Court also concluded that if, in construing the contract, there is an element of ambiguity such that there were two possible constructions, one of which would lead to a conclusion that it was an unreasonable restraint of trade and unlawful and the other leading to the opposite result, 'the court should uphold the covenant on the basis that the parties are to be deemed to have intended their bargain to be lawful and not to offend against the public interest'.

The Court concluded that the applicant had failed to show that the non-competition covenant was no wider than reasonably necessary for the protection of its legitimate business interests. The Court also noted, most importantly, that the length of the notice period in the contract of employment 'can be an indication of the unreasonableness regarding the duration of the restraint'. The restrictions applied irrespective of the length of time that the first respondent had been employed by the applicant. During the probation period her employment could be terminated by two weeks' notice. It was unreasonable for her to be prevented from being employed by a competitor for nine months when she might be in the employment of the applicant for only two weeks.

The applicant also failed to demonstrate that a restriction in respect of non-clients was necessary as part of the non-compete covenant. The Court concluded that the legitimate business interest of the applicant could be protected by a non-dealing covenant relating to its customers and that non-competition covenants for employees such as the first respondent were not industry standard. Neither the first respondent's previous employer nor her subsequent employer had such covenants. The applicant also failed to address the first respondent's contention that the applicant had regulatory obligations to act in the best interests of its clients and that non-competition and non-dealing clauses acted as a fetter on a client's ability to instruct an advisor of their choice. The Court concluded that the non-competition covenant was an unlawful restraint of trade and void.

Turning to the non-solicitation and non-dealing covenants, the Court observed that the clauses would prevent the first respondent from soliciting or dealing with customers who had been in place with the applicant 18 months prior to the termination of her employment. The clients might no longer be clients, or might have been clients with whom the applicant had personal contact on just one occasion during that period. The Court concluded that a backstop of 18 months together with a period of restraint of 12 months was excessive for a junior employee such as the first respondent.

The Court also concluded that the post-termination impact of the confidentially clause was likewise an unreasonable restraint of trade and unenforceable, noting that it defined information as including information which the applicant itself considered to be confidential, a definition that was potentially without limit.

Accordingly, the Court found that the restrictive covenants were unenforceable.

The applicant's case against the second respondent was essentially that the second respondent had induced the first respondent to act in breach of her contractual obligations to the applicant and that the second respondent, in breach of its own equitable obligation of confidence, knowingly received the confidential documents of the applicant and misused them or permitted the first respondent to misuse them.

The Court dismissed the claim of inducement of breach of contract. It found that there were three elements in that tort, namely there must be contract, there must be a breach of the contract and the conduct of the respondent must have been such as to procure or induce that breach. The Court noted that, to be liable for the tort of inducing a breach of contract the respondent has to know that it was inducing a breach of contract in question. The knowledge of the second respondent that the first respondent was employed by the applicant when she attended her induction course with the second respondent was not the same as knowledge that by so doing she was in breach of contract. There could be no liability in respect of any inducement of breach of the restrictive covenants because the covenants were all found to be invalid and unenforceable.

The Court rejected the claim of equitable duty of confidence owed to the applicant because it found that the second respondent did not know that the first respondent had uploaded confidential documents belonging to the applicant onto the second respondent's IT system and it did not know that the first respondent was using confidential information from the applicant's documents to complete and populate the second respondent's client database.

The Court dismissed the claim against the second respondent.

[12.17]   *APEX Resources Ltd v MacDougall, Caval Ltd*[30]—*Outer House Court of Session—Lady Wolffe—post-termination—non-compete—application for an interdict—injunction*

The applicant and respondent (Caval) were each involved in the business of recruitment consultancy, specialising in the construction sector. The other respondents were former employees of the applicant, having resigned variously in December 2020 and January 2021. Shortly after their resignation they joined Caval, a recruitment company, established elsewhere in the UK, which was at that time establishing itself in Glasgow. The former employees had each signed employment contracts, including various restrictive covenants precluding them from competing with or soliciting clients of the applicant for a specified period of time in a specified geographical area (the UK).

Interim interdicts/injunctions had been obtained on an *ex parte* basis restraining the former employees from breaching their restrictive covenants and restraining them and Caval from breach of confidence.

On the recall hearing (equivalent to an application for an interlocutory injunction) certain undertakings were offered and accepted but there was a challenge to the non-compete clause and the non-compete interim order.

The Court noted in particular the decision of the High Court of England and Wales in *Quilter v Falconer & Continuum*[31] where Calver J held restrictive covenants to be unenforceable and wider than was reasonably necessary. In that case, Calver J set out three questions, derived from the authorities, namely:

(1)   Have the former employers ... shown on the evidence that they have legitimate business interests requiring protection in relation to the employee's employment?

(2)   What does the covenant mean when properly construed?   .

(3)   The covenant must be shown by the employer to be no wider than is reasonably necessary for the protection of his legitimate business interests. Reasonable necessity is to assumed from the perspective of reasonable persons in the position of the parties as at the date of the contract ... for any covenant in restraint of trade to be treated as reasonable in the interest of the parties "it must afford no more than adequate protection to the benefit of the party in whose favour it is imposed".

The Court noted that it was accepted that the applicant had a reasonable interest to protect and that there was no real dispute among the parties as to the interpretation of the non-compete clause. The dispute related as to whether the non-compete was too

---

30   *APEX Resources Ltd v MacDougall, Caval Ltd* [2021] CSOH 40.
31   *Quilter v Falconer & Continuum* [2020] EWHC 3294, see **[12.16]**.

wide or whether it was no wider than reasonably necessary for the protection of the legitimate business interests of the applicant.

The Court observed that that question was highly sensitive to the facts and that different considerations may apply in industries where establishing a client relationship requires compliance with onerous regulatory requirements, such as the financial services industry. In such cases the regulatory context can make it difficult for an existing customer to transfer its business, whereas in businesses which operate in areas without such regulation, clients may more regularly leave one service provider for another. Also of relevance is the nature of the business interests which the employer seeks to protect. The Court noted that there is much greater ease of movement by clients from one recruitment agency to another. In this case, the restrictive covenants were specific to particular clients with which the respondents had engagement in their APEX employment. That was a factor which distinguished the outcome in *Quilter*, which involved the financial sector. The Court concluded that the applicant had advanced a case sufficient to establish that the non-compete clause could be regarded as reasonably necessary, notwithstanding the existence of a parallel non-solicit covenant.

The Court was satisfied that the applicant had put forward a sufficient case on a compelling and reasoned basis for the six-month duration of the non-compete. The applicant satisfied the Court that it had legitimate business interests that merited protection, namely the strength and continuity of its relationships with its clients and candidates, and the integrity and stability of its workforce. The Court noted that the value of the business of the applicant resided in personal relationships built up over time with clients and candidates, in contrast with other kinds of business, such as supplying goods, where the personal relationship might be secondary to the goods supplied.

The Court concluded that the applicant had established and presented a *prima facie* case that the non-compete clause was no more than was reasonably necessary to protect its legitimate business interests.

Turing to the balance of convenience, the Court was satisfied that it continued to favour the applicant. It noted that the balance of convenience will favour the protection of an existing business against a new one. While Caval was an existing recruitment consultant elsewhere in the UK, it was only establishing itself in Scotland in January 2021.

The Court was also satisfied that it was not enough for the respondents to contend that the applicant's remedy lay in a claim for damages, because proof of loss in these cases is difficult to establish.

Accordingly, the orders sought by the applicant were made.

Chapter 13

Insolvency

INTRODUCTION

[13.01] In *Watson*, the Court of Appeal of England and Wales considered whether the employment tribunal constituted a 'court' for the purposes of making a determination as to the liability under the Third Parties (Rights against Insurers) Act 2010.

Rights against Insurer

[13.02] *Irwell Insurance Company Ltd v Watson[1]—Court of Appeal of England and Wales—Bean, Flaux and Males LJJ—appeal from UK Employment Appeal Tribunal—Third Parties (Rights against Insurers) Act 2010—insolvency—assignment of statutory rights*

The claimant was employed by Hemingway Design Ltd (Hemingway) and when dismissed, brought claims against Hemingway in the UK employment tribunal for unfair dismissal and disability discrimination. Shortly after the claims were brought, Hemingway entered a creditors' voluntary liquidation and was dissolved.

Hemingway had a policy of insurance with Irwell Insurance Company Ltd (Irwell), which covered claims by employees in employment tribunal proceedings. Following Hemingway's liquidation, the claimant joined Irwell as third respondent to the employment tribunal claims, arguing that Hemingway's liability had transferred to Irwell upon Hemingway's liquidation, in accordance with the Third Parties (Rights against Insurers) Act 2010 (the 2010 Act). Irwell resisted liability arguing that the question as to whether it should provide cover was a matter of interpretation and construction of the insurance contract and that this was not a matter falling within the jurisdiction of the employment tribunal.

The 2010 Act allows a third party to recover directly from an insurer in the event of an insured's insolvency by providing that the third party can bring a single action against the insured and the insurer. Section 2(6) of the 2010 Act provides that where a 'court' makes a declaration as to liability, it may give the appropriate judgment against the insurer.

---

[1]   *Irwell Insurance Company Ltd v Watson* [2021] EWCA Civ 67.

The tribunal held that determination of liability under the 2010 Act was not something that it could decide, noting that the issue had nothing to do with an employment contract; that there was no contractual nexus between the claimant and Irwell; and that the issues between the claimant and Irwell did not arise out of any employment relationship. The tribunal reserved judgment and stayed the proceedings pending determination in the ordinary courts of whether Irwell was liable to the claimant under the 2010 Act.

The claimant appealed this to the EAT. The EAT held that an employment tribunal does fall within the words 'the court' in s 2(6) of the 2010 Act and as such, the tribunal does have jurisdiction to make a declaration as to an insurer's liability under s 2(2)(a) of that Act.

This decision was appealed to the Court of Appeal. The Court noted that the authorities on whether a tribunal is a 'court' for the purpose of statute indicated that this would depend on context. The Court held that it was plain that the 'principal mischief at which the 2010 Act was aimed' was the need for a third party to have to issue two sets of proceedings in order to make a successful claim against the insurer of an insolvent tortfeasor and that if Irwell's construction of the word 'court' was correct, the 'one-stop shop' created by the 2010 Act for claimants would not be available to claimants raising causes of action within the exclusive jurisdiction of the employment tribunals (such as unfair dismissal).

The Court considered but did not accept the reasons put forward as to why employment tribunals should not be deemed as 'courts', including that such tribunals do not have an inherent jurisdiction to grant declarations and that they lack enforcement powers. The Court rejected the argument that Parliament could not have intended employment tribunals to deal with questions of insurance law, finding that such tribunals regularly have to deal with difficult questions of law across a variety of topics, not confined to what would be regarded as mainstream employment law.

Accordingly the Court held that an employment tribunal is a 'court' within the meaning of s 2(6) of the 2010 Act and dismissed the appeal.

Chapter 14

Judicial Review

INTRODUCTION

[14.01]   The Supreme Court in *Kelly* had to consider the implications for a decision to dismiss a civil servant of the participation of a Minister, who had a prior involvement in the matter, at the Cabinet meeting at which the decision to dismiss was made.

The dismissal of a hospital consultant under the common contract was considered by the High Court in *O'Sullivan*. The availability of discovery in judicial review proceedings was considered by the High Court in *NK*. The manner in which a probationary Garda might be dismissed was considered by the High Court in *Murphy* and again in *Fahy*. In *Ahmed*, the Court of Appeal reviewed the decision of the Medical Council to impose a sanction of 'advice' on a registered medical practitioner.

The approach of the Court to a dispute relating to a public service promotion was considered by the High Court in *Robinson*. The public service sick pay scheme was considered by the High Court in *Delaney*. Finally, two decisions of the High Court relating to time limits for judicial review proceedings are noted: they are *Murphy* and *Roche*.

BIAS

[14.02]   *Kelly v Minister for Agriculture[1]—Supreme Court—Dunne, O'Donnell, McKechnie, MacMenamin and Charleton JJ—appeal from Court of Appeal—judicial review—determination by the Cabinet of Ireland to dismiss the applicant from the position of harbour master at Killybegs Fishery Harbour Centre—objective bias*

The applicant applied to judicially review a determination by the Cabinet of Ireland to dismiss him from the position of harbour master at Killybegs Fishery Harbour Centre with effect from 30 September 2009. The High Court (Hedigan J) refused the application and the Court of Appeal upheld the decision of the High Court. Leave was given to appeal to the Supreme Court.

The decision to dismiss was preceded by an investigation, an appeal to the Civil Service Appeal Board and ultimately the Cabinet. The applicant contended that the

---

[1]   *Kelly v Minister for Agriculture* [2021] IESC 23.

investigation into his conduct was tainted by bias, with specific reference to a meeting concerning the applicant that took place in 2004 between a Minister (who was also the local TD), the Assistant Secretary General of the Department of the Marine and Natural Resources (the Department) and the investigating officer. The applicant contended that what took place at that meeting tainted the disciplinary process which followed and which culminated in his dismissal.

In addition, the applicant contended that the fact that the same Minister who had made the complaints in the meeting in 2004, participated in a Cabinet meeting in 2009 which decided that the applicant should be dismissed from his civil service position resulted in the decision being tainted by bias.

The respondents contended that there was not sufficient evidence of bias in the procedures adopted and that the evidential and legal test for establishing bias was not met. They contended that the Minister's participation in the Cabinet decision could not cause a legal apprehension of bias.

The Court of Appeal had concluded that the first involvement of the Minister in 2004 took place after the decision to initiate a review into the applicant's conduct, and that the Minister's meeting derived from conduct during the disciplinary process (and not prior or extraneous to it). They also found that, even if there had been grounds for a finding of either form of bias, any flaw was rectified by the hearing before the Civil Service Appeal Board, where the applicant had been afforded the opportunity to present his case and to call witnesses.

The Court of Appeal held that the decision of the Cabinet, at which the Minister in question was present, was governed by constitutional and legal protection where, as a matter of necessity, the Cabinet was involved in a simple binary process to either act on or reject the opinion of the Civil Service Appeal Board.

In granting leave to appeal to the Supreme Court, the Supreme Court considered that the case raised issues of law of general public importance relating to the test for bias, its application in the case and the involvement of the Minister at the meeting with the investigating officer (in 2004) and subsequently the meeting of the Cabinet (2009).

The background to the case was as follows: the applicant had been appointed to the established civil service position of harbour master at the Killybegs Fishery Harbour Centre in 1996. An issue arose as to whether the applicant, by providing pilotage services to vessels using the harbour through a company of which he was a director and a 1% shareholder, infringed legal obligations binding on him by reason of the office held by him. In August 2004, an anonymous complaint was received by the Department to the effect that, while acting as harbour master, the applicant had been engaged in commercial pilotage for a number of years. The Department decided to investigate on foot of the complaint, and the personnel officer of the Department was appointed to carry out the investigation (September 2004). The applicant was formally notified of the decision to carry out the investigation (October 2004) and pending completion of the investigation he was suspended with immediate effect under s 13 of the Civil Service Regulation Act 1956.

Separately, in October 2004, a local TD and Minister made a complaint to the Assistant Secretary General of the Department regarding several concerns relating to harbour management at Killybegs, with specific reference to the applicant having employed his brother-in-law in the harbour, allegedly without following due process, and that the applicant was switching off the CCTV system there. The Minister attended a meeting thereafter with officials from the Department, at which the Minister outlined a wider range of complaints in relation to the applicant. The fact that the Minister made these complaints was not made known to the applicant at the time. The meeting in question was attended by the personnel officer of the Department, who had been appointed to investigate the earlier anonymous complaint.

Thereafter, the personnel officer carried out an investigation and interviewed the applicant with regard to a wide range of matters, extending beyond the initial complaints with reference to pilotage. Eventually, the personnel officer produced provisional conclusions and findings which he had arrived at on the balance of probabilities. He found that the preponderance of the allegations had been shown to be true, although some were not substantiated. The applicant was asked to furnish a response in accordance with the terms of the relevant departmental circular. The applicant sought a number of extensions of time and sought additional documentation, including certain un-redacted statements of witnesses. The personnel officer offered to provide un-redacted statements, but only if the applicant gave a written undertaking that they would be used solely for the defence of his position in the disciplinary process and not for the purpose of defending himself in respect of criminal charges apparently pending before the Circuit Court. As the applicant declined to give such an undertaking, he was refused the un-redacted statements and he contended that this was evidence of bias. The applicant submitted evidence and corroborating material to the investigating officer, and submitted documentation which he claimed showed that the Department had been aware of his pilotage activities and had acquiesced in them.

Thereafter, the investigating officer conducted further investigations and furnished to the applicant a revised statement of allegations having regard to additional information he had received. The investigating officer enclosed the underlying documents, invited the applicant to respond and advised the applicant of his entitlement to meet with the investigating officer. The applicant was informed that he was at risk of dismissal from the civil service and that the investigating officer proposed to recommend same to the Minister.

There were various delays and eventually the investigating officer disclosed the outcome of his investigation in February 2007. In August 2007, the applicant was furnished with the un-redacted witness statements on an unconditional basis. In September 2008, a final report, recommending the applicant's dismissal, was issued. The applicant appealed to the Appeal Board. The Appeal Board sat in January, February and March 2009. The Appeal Board heard from two witnesses called by the applicant. During the hearing before the Appeal Board a chronology of events was produced by the Department to which the applicant objected. The Appeal Board disregarded the chronology.

In July 2009, the applicant was notified of the decision of the Appeal Board. The Appeal Board was satisfied that the investigating officer had considered the relevant evidence fairly and carefully, and conducted a thorough investigation. It rejected the applicant's complaints about being prevented from making his case. The Appeal Board concluded that the applicant was a director and 1% shareholder in the private company providing pilotage services. The Appeal Board found that the company was paid for commercial pilotage work at Killybegs Harbour but that the applicant had received no payment from the company. The Appeal Board did not accept that the applicant would not derive any benefit from his pilotage work, noting that the company was paid for the work carried out by him and whether he drew an income or not from the company was a matter within his own discretion.

The Appeal Board concluded that the applicant was aware that there was a serious conflict of interest and he had sought to deal with the matter in an ambiguous fashion in correspondence and downplay his role as a commercial pilot. The Appeal Board did not disturb the recommendation of dismissal in respect of this matter. The Appeal Board also upheld the investigating officer's findings concerning other matters which they were satisfied amounted to misconduct inappropriate to his official position and warranting disciplinary action. On these, the Appeal Board disagreed with the investigating officer's recommendation as to the appropriate sanction, concluding that the grounds were not sufficiently serious to justify dismissal.

In July 2009, the applicant was informed that the Department intended to recommend to the Cabinet his dismissal from his post as harbour master and he was invited to submit representations within 14 days to be included in the papers sent to Cabinet. The applicant duly did so and his submissions were included along with the letter of suspension and the opinion of the Appeal Board in the papers that went to Cabinet.

On 30 September 2009, the Cabinet met. The local TD and Minister was present and among the issues considered was whether to dismiss the applicant. The Cabinet decided to dismiss the applicant in accordance with s 5 of the Civil Service Regulation Act 1956 and the applicant was so advised in October 2009.

In March 2010, the applicant applied for and was granted leave to seek a judicial review by way of certiorari to quash the Cabinet decision to dismiss him. In so doing, the applicant made specific reference to the 2004 meeting between the Minister and the investigating officer, and the participation of the Minister in 2009 in the decision to dismiss the applicant.

The applicant contended that the investigation and the Cabinet decision were affected by actual bias and objective bias. In support of this contention, the applicant relied on the fact that the involvement of the Minister and the Minister's meeting with the investigating officer were made known to him only in the course of the pre-trial discovery process.

Dunne J, (with whom McKechnie J agreed) in addressing the actual bias argument, noted the following:

> [F]irst of all ... actual bias is rarely found to exist and therefore an allegation of actual bias is rarely likely to succeed ... Secondly, in order to establish actual bias, it is necessary to show that the decision-maker reached his or her decision, having been influenced by some

existing relationship, interest, or attitude, without which the decision would have been different. Thirdly, the relevant issue said to have influenced the decision-maker is one that must be
shown to have predated the decision-making process and be external to the process.

In considering whether the investigative process was affected by actual bias, Dunne J
noted that it was not suggested that the investigating officer had any pre-existing relationship with or attitude towards the applicant which might have influenced his decision
on foot of the investigation. The Court noted that, by the time the investigating officer's
meeting with the Minister took place, a decision had already been taken to initiate an
investigation into the applicant and his conduct as harbour master, as a result of the
complaints made by unanimous letter. Dunne J could see no reason why the Minister,
as the local TD, would not be entitled to bring complaints that she had in relation to
the applicant to the attention of the relevant Department and its officials. Dunne J saw
this as part of the legitimate work of a TD and the fact that one was a Minister did not
take away from this entitlement. Dunne J also noted that the matters complained of by
the Minister did not form part of the subsequent investigation. Accordingly, Dunne J
concluded that the meeting between the Minister and the investigating officer was not
relevant.

Dunne J stated that the fact that the Minister's involvement was included in the chronology presented to the Appeal Board, to which the applicant objected and which was
ultimately withdrawn, was confirmation of the fact that the Minister's involvement was
not concealed.

Dunne J went on to consider the assertion that certain decisions made by the investigating officer in the course of the investigation were indicative of actual bias, on the basis
that the investigating officer could not have avoided being influenced by the Minister.
Dunne J concluded that it is clear from the case law that in 'considering the question
of actual bias, decisions made or taken in the course of an investigation or proceedings
cannot, of themselves, give rise an inference of bias'. Dunne J stated that 'bias must
arise from a factor outside the process impugned'.

Dunne J concluded as follows on the question of actual bias:

> [I]t would be necessary to prove that the decision-maker was deliberately setting out to hold
> against a particular party, irrespective of the evidence. Mr. Kelly has not proved that [the
> investigating officer] reached his conclusions irrespective of the evidence. On the facts of this
> case, there is simply no evidence to support the contention that [the investigating officer] was
> so influenced by the meeting with the Minister that he deliberately found against Mr. Kelly
> in relation to some of the complaints made, with the consequences in relation to the sanctions
> recommended. I therefore would reject the contention that there was actual bias on the part
> of [the investigating officer].

Having reached that conclusion, Dunne J found it unnecessary to consider whether the
conduct of the appeal by the Appeal Board could have rectified any flaw in the process.

On the question of objective bias associated with the Minister's meeting with the investigating officer, and her participation in the Cabinet meeting at which the decision was
made on foot of the recommendation made by the investigating officer, Dunne J cited

with approval the judgment of Denham J in *Bula Mines Ltd v Tara Mines Ltd (No 6)*[2] where she stated the following:

> [I]t is well established that the test to be applied is objective, it is whether a reasonable person in the circumstances would have a reasonable apprehension that the applicants would not have a fair hearing from an impartial judge on the issues. The test does not invoke the apprehension of the judge or judges. Nor does it invoke the apprehension of any party. It is an objective test—it invokes the apprehension of the reasonable person.

Dunne J noted that the case law established that 'a finding of objective bias against one member of a body, when that body has the responsibility of making a decision, will taint the decision of the body overall'. Dunne J also noted that the case law established that 'an allegation of objective bias by reason of matters which occurred many years earlier, and which are long forgotten, will not give rise to a reasonable apprehension of bias on the part of a decision-maker'. Dunne J concluded, with reference to the Minister's meeting with the investigating officer, that it would not give rise to a reasonable apprehension in the mind of a reasonable observer acquainted with all the relevant facts that the investigation would not be impartial.

Turning to the decision of the Cabinet to dismiss the applicant, Dunne J noted that the High Court and the Court of Appeal had rejected the applicant's arguments in this regard. Dunne J distinguished between executive and adjudicative decision-making at Cabinet level. Dunne J concluded that she could not see any difficulty in a Minister expressing a view, strong or otherwise, in relation to a particular issue, and then making a decision thereon. Dunne J noted the range of material that was put before the Cabinet and noted 'the function of the Cabinet was to decide whether or not to dismiss Mr Kelly, and that their function was not to act, as it were, as some form of appeal body from the decision of the Appeal Board'.

Dunne J concluded:

> It is, in my view, impossible to conceive of a situation in which the hypothetical, reasonable observer, aware of the relevant facts, would not have had a reasonable apprehension of bias, by reason of the involvement of the Minister in the ultimate decision to dismiss Mr Kelly.

Dunne J pointed to the fact that, at the commencement of the process, the Minister had contacted the Department and had outlined 'a range of serious concerns' relating to the management of the Harbour. The Minister then met with the investigating officer and 'expressed trenchant views in relation to Mr Kelly which went far beyond any concerns that might have existed in relation to Mr Kelly's conduct as Harbour Master'.

Although the Minister had no further involvement in the investigative process, she did participate in the Cabinet meeting where the decision to dismiss Mr Kelly was taken. Dunne J found that:

> If a similar situation had arisen in any other area of public administration, I have no doubt that there would be no hesitation in saying that the decision taken was one which was tainted by objective bias. The fact that this decision was taken by the government does not, in my

---

[2]   *Bula v Tara Mines Ltd (No 6)* [2000] 4 IR 412.

view, mean that the decision is immune from being tainted by objective bias ... It should have been apparent to the Minister that it was inappropriate for her to participate in the Cabinet decision leading to the dismissal of Mr Kelly, given her previous interest and involvement in the matters at issue, and thus she should not have participated in the meeting. I, therefore, disagree with the conclusion of the Court of Appeal that, "*the reasonable observer could have no reasonable apprehension that the decision taken in relation to the appellant was not taken following a fair hearing by an impartial decision maker, the government*".

Accordingly, Dunne J allowed the appeal.

O'Donnell J agreed that the decision of the Cabinet to dismiss the applicant must be quashed but did so for different reasons. He attributed greater significance to the events surrounding the Minister's meeting with the investigating officer and less significance to the Minister's participation at the Cabinet meeting, while considering that both matters were relevant to the decision. O'Donnell J agreed that there was no question of actual bias in the case. The legal issue was the question of objective bias.

O'Donnell J concluded that weight must be given to the meeting between the Minister and the investigating officer by reason of the fact that the meeting was set up at all, that it is unlikely that such a meeting would have been afforded to a member of the public, that the normal function of civil servants is to accept direction from Ministers, that no official note of the meeting was kept and that shortly after the meeting the applicant was informed for the first time of the fact of the investigation, and suspended from duty.

On the point as to whether, in order to establish objective bias, the matters apprehended must be extraneous to the decision-making process, O'Donnell J stated:

> Bias must be extraneous to the correctness of the decision sought to be impugned. But this reasoning does not, in my view, go the distance of contending that bias must also be extraneous to the process leading to the decision.

O'Donnell J concluded that the bias alleged here was extraneous to the investigation and the decision.

On the Minister's engagement with the investigating officer, O'Donnell J found that, although the 'events in 2004 were unusual and unsatisfactory', a reasonable bystander would probably conclude that it was implausible that a single meeting five years preceding a long and thorough investigation, the findings of which were not challenged and had been carefully reviewed by the Appeal Panel, could influence the findings in the report presented to the Cabinet.

On the Minister's participation in the Cabinet meeting, O'Donnell J distinguished between the position of a judge and that of a member of the Cabinet. He noted that although, a judge would be disqualified for expressing strong views or for having a pecuniary or other interest in the subject matter he or she is deciding on, holders of public office need only publicly declare their interest in the matter before making their decision.

However, O'Donnell J noted the special features of this case in the following terms:

> In this case, however, the Minister was also an active participant in the investigation, made a complaint in relation to it, was present at the outset of it, was one of the first people to meet

the investigator and expressed strong views to the investigator, and then participated in the final decision ... I consider that the reasonable bystander would not, at a minimum, be able to be confident that the procedure was not affected by the twin involvements of the Minister as a complainant/informant at the outset of the process, and as a decision-maker at its conclusion. In the unusual circumstances of this case, I consider that a reasonable bystander would have a reasonable apprehension that the process which should have involved an inquiry (and appellate review) in accordance with fair procedures, and a government decision, was affected by the ministerial involvement at each stage. It follows that I agree that, in the particular and unusual circumstances of this case, the decision to dismiss Mr Kelly to be quashed.

O'Donnell J allowed the appeal and went on to express a preliminary view that: 'It would be permissible to remit the matter to the Cabinet to permit it to make a decision on the report, in the light of the factual matters set out in the judgment of Dunne J.'

MacMenamin J agreed that the decision to dismiss the applicant should be quashed on the basis of the fact that the Minister attended the Cabinet meeting. He accepted the reasoning of Dunne J. However, he differed with reference to the Minister's involvement at the beginning of the process 'bearing in mind that [the investigating officer] was not only an investigator, but also had an adjudicative role whose views were binding on the Appeal Board'.

MacMenamin J found on the facts that 'the evidence establishes that to an objective observer, the investigator, whose findings were to have binding effect, embarked on the investigation with this range of quite damning criticisms in his mind' being the criticisms noted by the investigating officer in his note of his meeting with the Minister. MacMenamin J concluded that: '[T]o my mind, the objective observer, possessed now of the relevant facts, would have to draw the inference that, seized of information from an authoritative and influential source, [the investigating officer] was going to carry out a process involving adjudication regarding a person who was difficult' and who had had many criticisms levelled against him by the Minister.

MacMenamin J noted that the investigating officer's adjudicatory role is provided for in clause 3 of Circular 1/1992. The Appeal Board did not decide to hold a *de novo* hearing. Its jurisdiction to review was limited to the grounds specified in the Circular. MacMenamin J noted that the investigating officer's role went beyond mere fact finding, it included an adjudicative function. The investigating officer recommended sanctions to the Department, who adopted them; the role of the Appeal Board was circumscribed and it was debarred from conducting a *de novo* review of the applicant's conduct. MacMenamin J concluded the fact that the investigating officer found some allegations made by the Minister not proved was extraneous to the central question of whether there was objective bias. MacMenamin J concluded that the same test must be applied throughout the process and that, applying the law on objective bias to the meeting with the investigating officer, it was appropriate to conclude that objective bias arose by reason of that meeting.

MacMenamin J also noted that at no point during his own part of the investigatory/adjudicatory process did the investigating officer make known to the applicant that he had had a meeting with the Minister in which the Minister had cast aspersions on the applicant's character.

MacMenamin J concluded as follows:

> The entire process leading to the applicant's dismissal by the Cabinet was tainted by objective bias, applying a cumulative test to both the initiation and conclusion, of the process. It is necessary to bear in mind throughout, that the test for objective bias is, itself, an objective one … It is not what we judges think, but rather the inference which an objective observer would draw as to the process, seen in its entirety. In my view, the order to be made must encompass the entire disciplinary process from the outset.

MacMenamin therefore allowed the appeal.

Finally, with reference to submissions by the applicant relating to the Cabinet meeting, Charleton J noted the provision for Cabinet confidentiality at Art 28.4.3 of the Constitution, which states: 'The confidentiality of discussions at meetings of the Government shall be respected in all circumstances save only where the High Court determines that disclosure should be made in respect of a particular matter.' Charleton J pointed out that 'governmental authority is collective' and that there was no evidence as to whether or not the Minister voted in this matter; nor was there any evidence that the Minister had influenced the collective decision to dismiss Mr Kelly. Charleton J therefore concluded that 'the appeal from the Court of Appeal should be dismissed and the order of the High Court affirmed dismissing Mr Kelly's application to overturn the procedure leading to his dismissal on the grounds of apparent bias'.

CONSULTANTS CONTRACTS

[14.03] *O'Sullivan v Health Service Executive[3]—High Court—Barr J—judicial review—consultant contract 1998—administrative leave—delay—recommendation for dismissal—natural justice—prematurity—bias*

In September 2018 the applicant, a consultant gynaecologist employed in the respondent's hospital in Kilkenny (the hospital), directed his registrar to carry out a procedure whereby medical devices were inserted into the vaginas of five patients. This was done as part of what the applicant contended was a 'feasibility study'. None of the five patients had been informed that a feasibility study was going to be carried out; none of the patients had consented to the insertion of the device; and none of the patients were aware at the time that the procedure had been carried out on them. The applicant had not sought or obtained any clearance from the hospital's ethics committee to carry out the feasibility study and the applicant had sourced the devices otherwise than through the normal HSE procurement panels, having purchased the equipment himself. None of the data obtained was entered onto the patient's charts and some of the data was stored on the applicant's mobile phone and subsequently deleted.

The matter came to light because some of the nursing staff were concerned that there was an infection control risk with the procedure, and a microbiologist employed by the hospital advised that there was a risk of transmission infection from one patient to

---

3   *O'Sullivan v Health Service Executive* [2021] IEHC 282.

the other and it was decided that testing for infection in the patients would be advisable. There followed open disclosure meetings with each of the patients, conducted by the hospital clinical director. Full disclosure was made to them and they were greatly shocked and upset by the disclosures.

There followed a number of reviews of what had occurred, including a Systems Analysis Review (SAR). On receipt of the SAR Report (May 2019), the clinical director of the National Women's and Infants Health Programme was requested to give his views (June 2019) on the matter. He concluded that while none of the patients had suffered physical harm, several had suffered psychological injury and that the significant issue was not harm, but wrong to the patient. He noted that the applicant appeared not to have demonstrated insight or remorse for his actions. He expressed significant reservations about the applicant's continued involvement in clinical practice until these issues were fully resolved.

The chief executive of the respondent thereafter commenced the process leading to the placing of the applicant on administrative leave. The applicant was invited to make representations with regard to the possibility that he be placed on administrative leave and duly did so. On 6 August 2019, the chief executive advised the applicant that a decision had been made to place him on administrative leave.

In September 2019, the applicant met with the chief executive. In the course of that meeting, he stated that it had been an error of judgment on his part not to have had obtained both the consent of the five patients prior to undertaking the procedures, and the prior approval of the hospital ethics committee. Thereafter the chief executive decided to obtain an expert opinion from a consultant obstetrician and gynaecologist practising in Northern Ireland. The resulting expert report did not exonerate the applicant completely, but was supportive of his position and concluded that the applicant 'made an error of judgment, and was wrong in deciding to undertake this observational study as described without informed consent and ethical approval'. The expert went on to state that the applicant was not guilty of 'professional misconduct' concluding that his 'overall conduct has fallen below—but not seriously below—the standard of conduct expected among doctors. Further, I consider that, on the evidence presented, Prof. O'Sullivan does not pose an immediate and/or serious risk to the safety, health and welfare of patients'.

The expert report was sent to the applicant on 6 December 2019 but, by reason of an IT issue in the applicant's solicitor's office, it was not seen by them. On 23 December 2019, the chief executive wrote to the applicant advising him that he considered him guilty of serious misconduct and informed him that he proposed to recommend his removal from his position as a consultant gynaecologist employed by the respondent. He invited the applicant to make representations by a set date. This period was subsequently extended and submissions were made by reference to the expert report. Thereafter, on 31 January 2020, the chief executive again advised the applicant that he had decided to propose his removal from his employment and under the consultant contract he would notify the Minister for Health with a view to having a committee established to consider his proposal that the applicant should be dismissed.

On 24 February 2020, the applicant secured leave from the High Court to bring judicial review proceedings challenging a number of aspects of the procedures that had been adopted and secured a stay in respect of any further processes.

In the judicial review proceedings the applicant challenged the following:

1. The decision of the chief executive to place him on administrative leave, claiming that it was irrational by reason of the fact that it was made 10 months after the events complained of, during which period there had been no complaint or concern raised about his suitability to treat patients.

2. The decision made by the chief executive on 23 December 2019 to make a recommendation that the applicant be dismissed, contending that the decision was fatally flawed due to the fact that he did not have the opportunity to comment on the expert report; and the decision made by the chief executive in January 2020 that he would make a recommendation that the applicant should be dismissed, because the decision flew in the face of the expert opinion commissioned by the chief executive. The applicant contended that, as the chief executive was not medically qualified or qualified in the area of medical ethics, his decision to ignore that opinion was irrational and ought to be struck down.

3. The entire investigatory process, on the basis that it had been tainted by bias due to the fact that the applicant had been an outspoken critic of management of the hospital and of the respondent generally over a long period of time.

The Court upheld the respondent's contention that the challenge to the decision to place the applicant on administrative leave was out of time. The applicant allowed the three-month period for the judicial review to lapse, and did nothing to challenge the administrative leave decision until February 2020. The applicant did not satisfy the Court that there was 'good and sufficient reason' why he had not brought his challenge to the decision placing him on administrative leave within the three-month period after the making of that decision; and neither did he persuade the Court that the reasons why he did not bring the application until February 2020 were 'due to circumstances beyond his control'. Accordingly the Court rejected the challenge to the decision to place him on administrative leave. The Court did note that it was, and continued to be, open to the applicant to request the chief executive to reconsider the issue of his continuation on administrative leave, including in reliance on the expert report. If the chief executive were to continue the administrative leave thereafter, the applicant could challenge that standalone decision by way of judicial review.

The respondent contended that the applicant's application with reference to the decisions of the chief executive of December 2019 and January 2020 to recommend his dismissal could not succeed because they were premature. Under the consultant contract, the chief executive had three options in the context of disciplinary processes: he could decide that the alleged misconduct was either not proven or was trivial, in which case that would be the end of the matter; he could find that there was misconduct, in respect of which a warning would suffice; or he could recommend the dismissal of the applicant, which recommendation would have to be put before a committee appointed by the Minister. The Ministerial Committee had not been established by reason of the stay obtained by the applicant in February 2020.

The Court was satisfied that the appropriate principles to apply when considering the issue of prematurity were laid down by the Supreme Court in *Rowland v An Post*,[4] and held:

> In essence, that case provides that even where there can be shown to have been an error in the procedure, which procedure is still ongoing, the court will not necessarily intervene to stop the procedure, unless it is satisfied that any such error, or adverse consequence for the affected party, cannot be satisfactorily addressed by the necessary steps being taken at a later stage in the disciplinary, or investigatory procedure.

The Court was not satisfied that there had been any substantive grounds of complaint raised by the applicant concerning the procedure so far. However, even if it could be shown that there was some error or unfairness, the Court concluded that it should accede to the respondent's application to refuse the relief at this stage on the grounds that it would be premature for the Court to intervene. The applicant would be able to raise his concerns before the statutory committee in due course. The process was ongoing and, on that basis alone, the Court refused the relief sought.

The Court went on to consider whether, apart from the prematurity ground, any of the submissions made by the applicant with reference to the expert report should be upheld. The Court concluded that the decisions of the chief executive made in December and again in January should not be struck down on the grounds that the applicant had not had an opportunity to make submissions on the expert report.

The Court held that the fact that the applicant had not seen the report prior to the chief executive decision in January, by reason of a computer failing in the applicant's solicitor's office, did not vitiate the decision of the chief executive. As the report was 'largely in favour' of the applicant, it was reasonable for the chief executive to assume the applicant had no further submissions on it. Furthermore, when the true position became known to the chief executive, he extended the time and considered the submissions made thereafter before making his decision of January 2020, which, the Court concluded meant that there was no 'effective denial of [the applicant's] rights to fair procedures'.

The Court dealt with the challenge to the chief executive's decision not to accept the conclusions contained in the expert report, grounded on the chief executive's lack of medical or medical ethics qualifications and held that decision makers are 'free to depart from advice that they have been given, as long as they provide clear and cogent reasons why they are departing from that advice'. The Court noted that it is the chief executive 'alone who must make the requisite decision under Appendix IV of the [consultant's] Contract and under the statute'.

The Court noted that, in reaching his decision, the chief executive was entitled to have regard to all of the matters that were before him, including the preliminary assessments carried out by the hospital, the SAR Report and the clinical director's report. It found

---

4   *Rowland v An Post* [2017] 1 IR 355.

that the chief executive was entitled to weigh them in the balance, along with the expert report and stated that:

> merely because the CEO is a man who has no medical training and had very little experience of running a national health service at the time, that he was therefore bound to follow the opinion furnished by the independent expert ... when he had before him a considerable body of evidence, which in any reasonable analysis, has to be seen as being supportive of the decision that he ultimately reached.

The Court considered and rejected the applicant's submissions with regard to bias and was not satisfied that the applicant's complaints relating to leaks to the media during the process could be attributed to the respondent, its servants or agents.

Finally, the applicant contended that due to his persistent criticisms of the respondent, the chief executive was biased against him in the manner in which he carried out the investigation and in particular by his failure to act in accordance with the opinion set out in the expert report. The Court was not satisfied that there was any substance to this allegation; nor was there evidence that the chief executive had acted in a way that was unfair, unjust or biased.

The Court refused all of the reliefs sought by the applicant and lifted the stay on the further progression of the matter to the Ministerial Committee.

Subsequently, in a ruling on costs delivered on 20 May 2021[5] Barr J considered the respondent's application for the costs of the proceedings to date and the applicant's application for a stay on the substantive orders and on the costs.

The Court noted that the principles governing the award of costs generally are set out in Ord 99 RSC and ss 168 and 169 of the Legal Services Regulation Act 2015, as explained in the *Chubb Europe Group*[6] and *Higgins*[7] cases. In summary, the respondent is entitled to an order for its costs unless there are circumstances which would justify the Court departing from the general rule that costs follow the event.

Barr J stated that the fact that the Court made certain *obiter dicta* statements in relation to the possibility of the applicant making a further request to the respondent's CEO to review the decision to place him on administrative leave did not constitute a valid reason to depart from the general rule. Furthermore the fact that the Court had to resolve an argument based on different legal authorities did not convert the action into public interest litigation because courts resolve those disputes all the time. Accordingly the Court held that the litigation could not be seen as coming within the general exception known as public interest litigation. There were no points of law of exceptional public importance or exceptional constitutional importance involved, nor was there any novel issue in the case. Accordingly the Court ruled that the cost of the proceedings be awarded to the respondent.

---

5   *O'Sullivan v HSE* [2021] IEHC 365.
6   *Chubb European Group SE v The Health Insurance Authority* [2020] IECA 183.
7   *Higgins v Irish Aviation Authority* [2020] IECA 277.

With reference to the application for a stay on the investigation, the Court concluded that it was better for all concerned that the stay on the investigation should be lifted so as to enable the matter to be brought to a conclusion which was in the best interests of the applicant, the respondent and the general public.

The Court acceded to the applicant's application for a stay on the order for costs for a period of 28 days and if a notice of appeal was lodged within that time, the stay would continue until the final determination of the matter before the Court of Appeal.

DISCOVERY IN JUDICIAL REVIEW PROCEEDINGS

[14.04] *NK and AR v Minister for Justice[8]—High Court—Burns J—judicial review—discovery—provision of supporting documentation related to decision*

In the substantive proceedings in this case, the applicants sought an order of *certiorari* in respect of a decision by the respondent to refuse the second applicant's application for a permanent residence card and to revoke his current residence card. A ground upon which the applicants sought to challenge that decision was that the respondent relied on undisclosed information provided by the Garda National Immigration Bureau (GNIB) and the Hungarian authorities. The matter before the Court was an application by the applicants for discovery in their judicial review application.

In the context of the substantive application, the respondent pleaded that she had arrived at the impugned decision 'having due regard to all of the facts, information, circumstances and documentary evidence and that she did not rely on undisclosed and unparticularised information'. The respondent asserted that she had notified the applicants, prior to the decisions being made, that the GNIB had provided information to her that indicated that the first applicant had been living and working in Hungary since 2012. This was relevant to her decision, as the application for a permanent residence card was made under the European Communities (Free Movement of Persons) Regulations 2015.[9] The applicants sought discovery of all documents relating to communications between the Hungarian authorities and the GNIB relating to the first applicant.

In an affidavit submitted by the respondent, it was averred that 'the Respondent ... did not have any information beyond that which was communicated to the Applicant: namely that the EU citizen had been living and working in Hungary since 2012'. The Court found that the affidavit submitted was:

> categorical that the information from the Hungarian authorities was to the effect that the First Applicant was living and working in Hungary since 2012; that this information was given to the Applicants; and that the Respondent had no further additional information from the Hungarian authorities regarding the First Respondent which was considered by her when making the initial decision or the review decision.

---

8   *NK and AR v Minister for Justice* [2021] IEHC 161.
9   European Communities (Free Movement of Persons) Regulations 2015 (SI 548/2015).

The applicants argued that the affidavit failed to fully deal with the issues and that they were entitled to satisfy themselves that the documentation that the Minister referred to represented all the information provided to her, and that the Minister had a duty to make appropriate disclosure to the High Court of all relevant material before her when she made the decision.

The Court considered the authorities on the matter, quoting extensively from *Marques v Minister for Justice and Equality*[10] and *McAvoy v An Garda Síochána Ombudsman Commission*[11] and stated that 'discovery in judicial review proceedings "ought to be the exception rather than the rule"'. The Court referred to McDermott J's approach to discovery in judicial review proceedings in *McAvoy*, clarifying when discovery will be appropriate and found that this application was, in effect, an attempt to go behind the affidavit to verify whether the averments were correct without establishing any basis as to why the averments may be incorrect. The Court observed that there was 'no basis' for any suspicion that there was other information before the respondent when making her decision and that the application for discovery was 'merely speculation on the part of the Applicant making this a classic fishing expedition'.

The Court refused to make an order for the discovery sought, and made an order for the respondent's costs in respect of the discovery motion against the applicant.

DISMISSAL OF GARDA ON PROBATION

[14.05] *Murphy v The Commissioner of An Garda Síochána*[12]*—High Court—Barrett J—Garda Síochána (Admissions and Appointments) Regulations 2013*[13]*—fair procedures—proposal to dismiss probationer garda*

The applicant was a probationer garda, which under the garda 'Code of Professional Practice' is a person who has been attested with garda powers but is still undergoing training.

Arising from actions in the early hours of New Year's Day 2019, the applicant was charged with a public order offence under the Road Traffic Acts. While the prosecution of that charge was pending, by letter dated 17 December 2019, the Garda Commissioner notified the applicant that he proposed, under reg 12 of the Garda Síochána (Admissions and Appointments) Regulations 2013, to dispense with the applicant's services as a member of An Garda Síochána (the Notice). The Notice stated that allegations regarding the applicant's behaviour on the night in question had been brought to the attention of the Commissioner. It went on to state: 'The behaviour displayed by you [the applicant] on 1st January 2019 does not represent behaviour that is consistent with that expected of a member of An Garda Síochána. Furthermore, it does not attribute to your suitability and ability to serve as an efficient and effective

---

10 *Marques v Minister for Justice and Equality* [2017] IEHC 597.
11 *McAvoy v An Garda Síochána Ombudsman Commission* [2015] IEHC 203.
12 *Murphy v The Commissioner of An Garda Síochána* [2021] IEHC 354.
13 Garda Síochána (Admissions and Appointments) Regulations 2013 (SI 470/2013).

member of An Garda Síochána.' It stated that, accordingly, the Commissioner had 'to consider and decide whether you are likely to become an efficient and well-conducted member of the Garda Síochána in accordance with Regulation 12(8)'. The Notice gave the applicant 28 days to make submissions concerning the allegations.

The applicant engaged solicitors who wrote to the Commissioner seeking copies of any materials on which the Commissioner intended to rely in making his decision, as no such materials had been provided with the Notice. No reply was forthcoming and the applicant issued High Court judicial review proceedings, challenging the Commissioner's decision to issue the Notice.

In the first instance, the Court examined whether the Commissioner's decision to issue the Notice was a reviewable decision and found that it was. The Court found that the failure by the Commissioner to furnish the applicant with the material that the Commissioner intended to rely on in making his decision, including a 'suitability file' which contained a number of favourable reports in respect of the applicant, was an inherent procedural flaw in the Commissioner's approach and meant that the applicant was not in a position to make informed submissions. The Court held that if the applicant were to make informed submissions: 'he needed (and was entitled as a matter of procedural fairness) to see what material was intended to be relied upon by the Commissioner in reaching his decision to do that.'

The Court also found that requiring the applicant to make submissions might compromise any defence that he intended to make in the parallel criminal proceedings pending against him under the Road Traffic Acts.

In August 2020, after the applicant had been granted leave to bring his judicial review proceedings, the Commissioner issued a fresh notice under reg 12(9) to the applicant, this time enclosing the materials on which he intended to rely in making his decision and giving the applicant 28 days to respond. The applicant's solicitors challenged this in correspondence, claiming that it was in breach of the order of the Court granting leave, which directed that 'there be a stay on the determination the subject of these proceedings pending the outcome of the proceedings herein' and in correspondence, the Chief State Solicitor's Office subsequently withdrew this second process.

The Court noted that while the issuance of this second notice did not breach the terms of the Court's order (which prohibited a determination being made in these matters but did not prevent the continuance of any process leading thereto), it was 'notable' that:

> the Commissioner was willing to provide the materials that ought to have accompanied the notice of 17th December 2019. Indeed the provision of the said materials could be argued to involve an implicit acceptance that the provision of such material was appropriate and necessary.

The principal reliefs sought by the applicant were:

(i)   an order quashing 'the determination of the respondent to dispense with the applicant's services as a probationary member of An Garda Síochána'; and

(ii) an injunction and an order of prohibition preventing the Commissioner from dismissing the applicant.

While the Court held that (i) could not be granted as there had been no such determination, and the threshold for (ii) had not been met (indeed noting that it was 'difficult to conceive of circumstances in which a court would so interfere with the internal operation of An Garda Síochána' so as to grant those reliefs), it proposed a 'hybrid' order quashing the decision to issue the Notice in December 2019. As this was a relief which had not been sought or discussed at the hearing, the Court scheduled a brief further hearing to allow the parties to make submissions on this proposed order. In relation to costs, the Court noted that as the applicant had won his application 'he would seem to have a fairly unanswerable case to be awarded his costs', however the Court stated that should either side take a different view it would schedule a brief hearing on the matter.

In a separate judgment,[14] the High Court addressed the allocation of costs of the judicial review proceedings after the application for judicial review was dismissed.

There were two issues for the High Court to consider:

1. 'whether the general rule, namely that the successful party is entitled to its costs, is displaced because much of the costs are attributable to a procedural issue upon which the respondents were unsuccessful'; and
2. 'the approach to be taken in respect of the costs of a notice party employer in judicial review proceedings in the context of social welfare legislation'.

In addressing the first issue the Court referred to *Chubb European SE v Health Service Executive*[15] and stated that:

> where a party has prevailed in the proceedings but has not been successful on an identifiable issue or issues which have materially increased the costs of the case, that party may obtain his costs but may suffer two deductions: one in respect of his own costs in presenting that issue, and the other requiring him to set-off the costs of his opponent in meeting that issue against such costs as are ordered in his favour.

The Court found that the parties in the present case should each bear their own costs, as there was a procedural issue that took up much of the hearing, which would have had a material impact on the costs. The Court noted that, had the respondents not raised 'this fruitless procedural objection', then the matter would have been dealt with in much less time and would have significantly reduced the costs.

In addressing the second question, the Court noted that the notice party sought their costs and that the judicial review proceedings were of detriment to the notice party. Referring to *Usk and District Residents Association Ltd v Environmental Protection Agency*,[16] the Court noted: 'the entitlement to costs is limited by reference to the extent of the interest of the notice party in the proceedings, and by consideration of whether it is reasonable for the notice party to participate'.

---

[14]   *Murphy v Chief Appeals Officer (Social Welfare Appeals Office) Minister for Employment Affairs and Social Protection* [2021] IEHC 711.
[15]   *Chubb European SE v Health Service Executive* [2020] IECA 183.
[16]   *Usk and District Residents Association Ltd v Environmental Protection Agency* [2007] IEHC 30.

In considering the notice party's role, the Court found that the notice party's partici-pation was not sufficient to justify costs in its favour and noted that the notice party 'largely duplicated' the participation of the respondents.

In response to the applicant's cross-application for costs, the Court noted there was no reasonable basis for such an application.

No order for costs was made.

[14.06]   *Fahy v The Commissioner of An Garda Síochána[17]—High Court— Barrett J—Garda Síochána (Admissions and Appointments) Regulations 2013[18]— fair procedures—proposal to dismiss a probationer garda*

The applicant was a probationer garda, which the court noted is 'a fully attested member of An Garda Síochána and so not a trainee Garda ... and who might colloquially, but not in a legal sense, be described as being at a training stage of their careers'.

In a letter dated 25 July 2019 (the Notice), the Garda Commissioner notified the applicant that he proposed, under to reg 12(8) of the Garda Síochána (Admissions and Appointments) Regulations 2013 (the 2013 Regulations), to dispense with the applicant's services as a member of An Garda Síochána. The Notice stated that the applicant's suitability with regard to her performance had been brought to the atten-tion of the Commissioner. The applicant had, on six separate occasions, failed to meet the minimum standard required for the Phase II Fitness Assessment. The Notice stated:

> You cannot now complete your training or attain the BA in Applied Policing. These are seri-ous matters and I have to consider and decide whether you are likely to become an efficient and effective member of An Garda Síochána in accordance with Regulation 12(8) of the Garda Síochána (Admissions and Appointments) Regulations 2013. Before doing so I hereby give you an opportunity in accordance with Regulation 12(9) of the Regulations of advancing to me on or before the 22 of August 2019 (28 days from [the] date of this notification) any submission you wish to make concerning the allegation(s).

The applicant then made various submissions to the Commissioner. However, in a letter dated 7 February 2020, the Commissioner notified the applicant of his decision to dispense with her services.

In the first instance, the Court considered whether the decision of the Commissioner was in accordance with basic fair procedures, the Court held that the decision was not made in a vacuum. It noted that the applicant was engaged in a process commenced by the Notice and was involved in the interventions which followed her failure to pass the required fitness test.

The Court observed that the applicant was afforded the opportunity to make submis-sions following the issuing of the Notice. Although the submissions she made did not alter the outcome, that did not mean that her submissions did not have the possibility

---

[17]   *Fahy v The Commissioner of An Garda Síochána* [2021] IEHC 440.
[18]   Garda Síochána (Admissions and Appointments) Regulations 2013 (SI 470/2013).

to alter the outcome. The Court further observed that the decision of the Commissioner pointed to an 'earnest consideration of the submissions', which demonstrated that the outcome was not 'pre-ordained'.

However, the Court noted that the applicant's original two-year probationary period was extended on four occasions—twice before the Notice was issued and twice after that Notice issued. In each case, the extension was effected under reg 12(4) of the 2013 Regulations. In both its interim and supplementary judgments, the Court considered whether the extensions of the applicant's probationary period were done in accordance with the 2013 Regulations. The question which arose was whether the extensions effected after the Notice issued should have been carried out under reg 12(4) or reg 12(10).

The Court held that following the issuance of the Notice, the Commissioner erred in law in proceeding under reg 12(4) to extend the applicant's probationary period as the circumstances in this instance were specifically set out in reg 12(10) and therefore he should have proceeded on that basis. The Court held that the extensions granted after July 2019 were unlawful as they were not for the purpose provided for under reg 12(4) but 'were solely for the purpose for which the power under regulation 12(10) is granted to the Commissioner'.

The Court therefore held that, as the Commissioner was not acting lawfully in respect of the extensions that were carried out after the Notice issued, no valid extension of the probationary period had taken place and that the applicant was no longer on probation when the decision was taken to discontinue her employment.

The Court made the following orders in favour of the applicant: (i) an order of *certiorari* quashing the Commissioner's decision to dispense with the applicant's services; (ii) a declaration that the Commissioner misapplied or misconstrued the relevant provisions of the 2013 Regulations; and (iii) a declaration that the Commissioner did not act lawfully when he purported to extend the applicant's probationary period under reg 12(4) and that, as such, she was no longer a probationary garda at the time of her purported dismissal.

MEDICAL COUNCIL

[14.07] ***Ahmed v The Fitness to Practise Committee of the Medical Council, the Medical Council and (by Order) the Minister for Justice and Equality, Ireland and the Attorney General[19]—Court of Appeal—Donnelly J, Faherty and Ní Raifeartaigh JJ concurring—Regulated Professions (Health and Social Care) (Amendment) Act 2020—European Convention on Human Rights—whether the absence of a right of appeal in respect of a sanction imposed by the Medical Council is unconstitutional— whether the decision of the Committee and the Council was ultra vires***

---

[19]   *Ahmed v The Fitness to Practise Committee of the Medical Council, the Medical Council and (by Order) the Minister for Justice and Equality, Ireland and the Attorney General* [2021] IECA 214.

The applicant, a registered medical practitioner, was the subject of nine allegations which were referred to the Medical Council, part of one of which led to a finding by the Fitness to Practise Committee of poor professional performance by the applicant. The Medical Council, on considering that finding, imposed a sanction of 'advice' on the applicant but did not impose conditions on his registration.

At the time, a doctor on whom such a sanction was imposed without conditions did not have a statutory entitlement to appeal to the High Court against the finding and sanction.

The applicant was employed as a registrar in medical oncology in a regional hospital. The allegation on which the finding of poor professional performance was made was that on a particular date and in respect of a particular patient the applicant failed to request certain medical tests.

The Committee found that that specific allegation was proven and established beyond reasonable doubt and that it amounted to poor professional performance. It did so by reference to the evidence of an expert witness called by the CEO of the Council.

The applicant challenged, by way of judicial review, the findings and report of the Committee and the decision of the Council to impose the sanction. As there was no way to appeal against the imposition of a sanction of 'advice', the applicant also challenged the constitutional validity of ss 71 and 75 of the Medical Practitioners' Act 2007 and the compatibility of those provisions with the European Convention on Human Rights.

The High Court concluded that there was no basis for the granting of any of the reliefs sought and dismissed the proceedings. The High Court found that the finding made by the Committee was neither irrational nor unreasonable and there was clearly evidence before the Committee on which it could reach the decision it did. In refusing the application for a declaration of repugnancy to the Constitution, the Court followed the earlier decision of the High Court in *Akpekpe v Medical Council*.[20] Likewise, the Court refused the application for a declaration for incompatibility under s 5 of the European Convention on Human Rights Act 2003.

The Court of Appeal had to consider whether the appellant was out of time for bringing the judicial review; whether there was any basis for granting any of the reliefs sought in connection with the findings of the Committee and the decision of the Council; whether the absence of a right of appeal infringed the Constitution; and whether same is compatible with art 6 of the Convention.

The right of appeal to the High Court was, after the commencement of the proceedings, modified by the Regulated Professions (Health and Social Care) (Amendment) Act 2020, which now permits an appeal to the High Court where sanctions of advice, admonishment or censure alone are imposed by the Medical Council. The 2020 Act did not have retrospective effect to enable the applicant in this case to appeal.

---

[20] *Akpekpe v Medical Council* [2014] 3 IR 420.

On the time point, the Court concluded that the time did not begin to run until the decision of the Council to impose the sanction. The application for judicial review was accordingly made within the period provided for in Ord 84, r 21.

In terms of the application to quash the finding of the Committee and the decision of the Council, the Court noted that the notice of appeal focused on irrationality and unreasonableness by reference to a claimed lack of evidence to sustain the Committee's finding. The Court was satisfied that leave to appeal had not been sought to challenge the decisions of the Committee and the Council on broad constitutional or Convention grounds.

The Court stated that it was clear that the burden of proof was on the applicant to prove his or her case in judicial review and accordingly the onus was on the applicant to establish irrationality or unreasonableness. The Court considered that the essence of the claim was that the decision of the Committee ought to be quashed because there was no evidence to support its findings or, alternatively, that there was so little evidence that the principle of proportionality required it to be quashed. The Court noted that in *Sweeney v Fahy*,[21] the Supreme Court had identified that there are significant limitations on the extent to which it is appropriate for the Superior Courts to exercise the judicial review jurisdiction arising out of allegations that the evidence before a lower court or other decision maker was insufficient to justify the conclusions reached, rather than insufficient to establish that the decision maker had any lawful capability to make the relevant decision in the first place. The Supreme Court noted that, save in extreme cases, absence of sufficient evidence as to the merits would only render the decision incorrect and therefore not amenable to judicial review, which is concerned with the lawfulness rather than the correctness of the decision sought to be challenged. At a minimum, there must be a fundamental error to support the proposition that the decision is not merely incorrect but is unlawful.

The Court concluded that the absence of a statutory right of appeal did not affect the role of the Court in judicial review and did not require the Court to broaden the scope of the review such that it would become an appeal. Following an exhaustive review of the evidence before the Committee, the Court was satisfied that the trial Judge did not err in rejecting the contention that there was no evidence to support the finding of poor professional practise. The Court was satisfied that there was evidence before the Committee to support that finding.

On the question of proportionality, the Court noted that, in the context of the judicial review test of reasonableness, the question might be whether the decision is a proportionate one in the context of the protection of constitutional rights. The applicant raised the constitutional right to work, the right to a good name and the right of access to the courts and raised them in the context of the lack of an appeal afforded to him by reason of the sanction imposed on him. The Court noted that the case as pleaded as to proportionality by reference to the decisions of the Committee and Council was lacking in detail. The applicant had claimed that the finding and the sanction were each disproportionate, but the Court noted that the sanction itself could not be disproportionate

---

[21]   *Sweeney v Fahy* [2014] IESC 50.

because it was the lowest level of sanction available to the Council. The Court was satisfied that there was nothing inherently disproportionate in a finding of poor professional performance based on a single incident or in such a finding where the sanction would not impact on the doctor's registration.

It followed from the foregoing that the appeal against the refusal to grant *certiorari* of the decision to find the applicant guilty of poor professional performance was rejected.

Turning to the constitutional point, the Court noted that the applicant had contended that the absence of a right of appeal to the High Court was a violation of his constitutional rights on the basis that it was an error to focus on the sanction (minor in nature) rather than on the finding (serious in nature). He contended that a finding of poor professional performance is a serious finding which might have devastating consequences for a doctor. The Court was critical of the pleadings, by reason of the fact that the pleadings did not identify the article of the Constitution on which the appellant sought to rely; claims regarding the right to work, the right to a good name, and equality were not mentioned in the pleadings. The Court concluded, however, that there was a sufficient plea before the High Court for the Court to proceed to adjudication on the issue of the failure to provide him with a right of appeal.

The Court characterised the essential question as being whether the denial of right of appeal from a disciplinary body is itself a violation of the right of access to the courts. The applicant had accepted that there is no right of appeal in every circumstance in disciplinary proceedings. The Court noted that there was no authority in support of the proposition advanced by the applicant. The Court, having reviewed the authorities, found that none of them supported any general proposition that every finding of a disciplinary body must be followed by a full right of appeal to the courts. What is guaranteed is access to the courts for the purpose of protecting rights. The judicial review mechanism was available to, and was availed of, by the applicant. That provided him with access to the courts to ensure that the process under which the decision-making Committee reached its finding of facts was carried out in a manner that respected the constitutional rights of the applicant and that the decision arrived at was rational. The applicant's right of access to the court had been exercised by him. Judicial review was sufficient protection. The Court concluded that the applicant had a fair hearing before an independent and impartial body in which his rights were fully respected. Thereafter, he had the right to challenge before the courts.

The Court accepted that the right to work may be engaged by the finding of poor professional performance even where a sanction imposed has not affected the applicant's registration as a doctor. The Court, however, did not accept that this meant that the State must provide a right of appeal to the High Court in every case where State action has caused an effect on working life. What the State must do is provide the machinery which protects and vindicates that right and the State had discharged its obligation by setting up the statutory mechanisms under which the Committee and the Council operated. The absence of a right of appeal is not a failure to vindicate the right to work because that right is protected by the provision of a fair mechanism for the determination of the allegations, together with the access to judicial review by which the fairness of the disciplinary hearing can be challenged.

The Court reached the same conclusion with regard to the right to a good name. The Court was satisfied that the publication of the fact that a sanction had been imposed on a doctor did not violate his right to his good name or reputation.

Finally, the Court referred to the change in the law effected by the 2020 Act which provided for a right of appeal where the sanction imposed was merely advice. The Court was satisfied that the mere fact that the legislation had been amended, and the fact that the Minister or other members of the Oireachtas expressed certain views as to why they were doing so, was not persuasive as to the correct interpretation of the Constitution.

The Court concluded that the absence of a right of appeal to the High Court was not a denial of the constitutional right of access to the courts and did not amount to a failure to vindicate the applicant's good name and reputation or his right to work under Art 40.3 of the Constitution.

Turning to the claim under art 6 of the Convention, the Court noted that art 6 provides that 'everyone is entitled to a fair and public hearing within a reasonable time by an independent and impartial tribunal established by law'.

The Court noted that art 6 does not provide for a right of access to a court, nor does it provide for a right of appeal arising out of a finding by an independent and impartial tribunal. The Court concluded that there was a fair and impartial hearing concerning the finding of poor professional performance sufficient to satisfy the applicant's art 6 rights. The sanction was imposed on foot of the finding. The sanction did not involve an infringement of his right to continue to practise his profession. The jurisprudence of the European Court of Human Rights on art 6 did not support the appellant's contention that his rights thereunder had been breached. Accordingly, the appeal by reference to the Convention was also dismissed.

In summary, the Court concluded that there was sufficient evidence before the Committee for it to reach a factually sustainable conclusion that the specific allegation against the appellant was proven and this amounted to poor professional performance. That decision was rational, reasonable and proportionate. The sanction was also proportionate. The relevant statutory provisions were not repugnant to the Constitution on the ground that the appellant was not afforded a right to appeal and same did not infringe art 6.1 of the Convention.

PUBLIC SERVICE PROMOTION

[14.08] *Robinson v The Minister for Defence, the Attorney General and Ireland[22]—High Court—O'Regan J—judicial review*

The applicant sought judicial review of a decision by a General Officer Commanding of the Air Corps (a GOC), not to permit the applicant to take part in a competition for promotion to a senior post.

---

22   *Robinson v The Minister for Defence, the Attorney General and Ireland* [2021] IEHC 672.

The applicant, a sergeant in the Air Corps, sought to take part in a competition for promotion to Company Sergeant. An administrative circular set out the requirements to be eligible to interview for this post as having 'successfully completed a Senior NCO Course approved by the General Staff' or having 'reached a satisfactory standard of training as certified by the corps director concerned'.

The applicant's commanding officer (the CO) declined to recommend his application as the applicant had not completed a Senior NCO Course and the GOC 'would not certify any other level of training'.

The applicant and two other individuals subsequently wrote to the GOC, requesting confirmation that they had reached the satisfactory level of training to apply for the post. That letter was submitted to the GOC by the applicant's CO, together with a cover note from the CO setting out his opinion that the applicant should not be permitted to enter the competition as 'the completion of a senior NCO course was an essential requirement for promotion to the rank of flight sergeant'.

By letter dated 26 September, the GOC issued his decision. He declined to admit the applicant to the competition, stating:

> They have NOT completed a Senior NCO Course, nor have they been certified as having reached a satisfactory standard of training. It is my policy, that apart from those instances where the exigencies of the service require it, all personnel should complete the Senior NCO Course prior to promotion to senior NCO rank.

The applicant issued judicial review proceedings. He argued that the GOC had adopted a 'fixed and inflexible policy and unlawfully fettered his discretion' in the application of the admission criteria which amounted to 'an error of law, and was therefore irrational and/or unreasonable'. He further claimed that the GOC's decision was in breach of fair procedures, as he had failed to consider the level of training the applicant had actually undertaken, and that the GCO had taken into account irrelevant considerations, namely the contents of the CO's cover letter. The applicant also asserted that the promotion competition gave rise to a legitimate expectation that his 'extensive training and experience' would be considered in line with the criteria set out in the administrative circular and that this legitimate expectation was breached when the GOC determined that the applicant was not eligible to compete as he had not undertaken the NCO Course.

The Court held that the GCO had not applied a 'fixed and inflexible policy' so as to unlawfully fetter his discretion. It noted that the applicant had incorrectly recorded the GCO's decision in his Statement of Grounds 'by failing to make any reference whatsoever to the actual policy identified' and that, as such, it was not possible to make any determination on whether the policy was 'fixed and inflexible' or not. Further, the Court noted that the applicant had not made any representation to the GCO that his standard of training might 'equate or closely mirror' the requisite Senior NCO Course.

The Court held that there was no evidence to suggest that the GCO was influenced by irrelevant considerations, namely the CO's cover letter, in making his decision. It also held that the applicant had not discharged the burden of establishing that his level of training was not taken into account, noting that the GCO's decision referred to the applicant's 'high level of training' and 'specialist skill set'.

Finally, while the Court accepted that the concept of legitimate expectation could apply to procedures, it held that the applicant 'has not discharged the burden of establishing that there was in fact any breach of legitimate expectation in respect of procedures'.

The application was dismissed.

PUBLIC SERVICE SICK PAY

[14.09] *Delaney v Irish Prison Service, the Minister for Justice and Equality, Ireland and the Attorney General*[23]*—High Court—Hyland J—workplace accident— entitlement to sick pay—certiorari*

The applicant was a prison officer. He was instructed to transport a prisoner to court in August 2019. When the applicant went to the prisoner's cell, the prisoner became violent. The applicant was bitten and head-butted by the prisoner and sustained injuries to his arm and shoulder which required surgery.

In October 2019, the applicant requested that the incident be treated as an occupational injury under the respondent's occupational injury or disease policy. This policy (combined with relevant circulars) states that leave from work arising from occupational injury or disease suffered by an officer, which is not caused by his/her own negligence, will not be combined with periods of absence due to ordinary illness in terms of sick pay.

The respondent issued the applicant with a decision refusing this application on 31 October 2019, and informing the applicant that the prison governor had been unable to provide the requisite recommendation due to inconclusive evidence. The respondent appealed this decision internally, providing supporting documentation on the incident, but the appeal was refused in December 2019, as, again, there was no governor recommendation. The impact of these decisions was that the applicant was not entitled to be paid while on sick leave arising from the incident.

The applicant applied to the High Court for an order of *certiorari* quashing the decision of the respondent to refuse to treat his absence from work as an occupational injury.

The High Court observed that the applicant had not been provided with reasons for the refusal. The applicant raised the fact that he was only told in April 2020 that the reason for the decision was because the governor could not be satisfied there was no negligence on his part during the cell incident. The respondent argued that the applicant must have known that 'inconclusive evidence' meant there was insufficient evidence to determine whether the respondent had been negligent. The Court held that reasons 'must be given at the time of the decision and not at a later date' and quashed the decisions of October 2019 and December 2019. The matter was remitted to the Irish Prison Service.

---

23   *Delaney v Irish Prison Service, the Minister for Justice and Equality, Ireland and the Attorney General* [2021] IEHC 702.

TIME LIMITS

[14.10]   *Murphy v Chief Appeals Officer (Social Welfare Appeals Office), Minister for Employment Affairs and Social Protection[24]—High Court—Simons J—Social Welfare Consolidation Act 2005—preliminary point—contract of service or contract for services*

The applicant in this matter was a tour guide with the notice party Córas Iompair Éireann (CIE) and the underlying dispute was whether she had been engaged in 'insurable employment' for the purpose of the social welfare legislation.

The applicant made a reference to the Department of Employment and Social Protection for a decision on whether her employment was insurable employment.

In March 2019, the deciding officer found that her employment was insurable under the Social Welfare Consolidation Act 2005. CIE appealed and the applicant objected to its appeal on the grounds that it was invalid as it was brought in the name of CIE Tours International, a separate entity to Córas Iompair Éireann, the applicant's employer.

The appeals officer made a decision on 3 July 2019 rejecting her submission that the appeal was invalid. Although there was a lack of consensus as to whether judicial review was the appropriate remedy in the circumstances, the Court was satisfied that this decision was amenable to judicial review and, therefore, the judicial review proceedings were not premature, as had been asserted by the respondent.

The next matter related to the date of the application for judicial review, which was made one month outside of the three-month time period allowed under RSC, Ord 84. The Court allowed an extension for the following reasons:

— The Court has discretion in the legislative context where the statutory scheme is such that it impacts on persons who may be vulnerable and have little formal education. The Court proceeded to call the system of appeals 'labyrinthine' and noted that it would be 'unduly harsh' to shut out the matter for not complying with the time limit where the time limit was not obvious.

— The Court noted that although the applicant in this case was a qualified barrister, '[t]he appeals officer had, in effect, determined the validity of the appeal as a preliminary issue in advance of the oral hearing into the underlying merits of the appeal. Yet the letter … does not explain what remedies are available against that determination. Still less does the letter explain that there is any time-limit prescribed.' The submission by the respondent that judicial review proceedings were premature compounded the issue.

After considering the above preliminary points, the Court considered the merits of the case. The applicant submitted that the appeal has been taken in the name of what she

---

[24]   *Murphy v Chief Appeals Officer (Social Welfare Appeals Office), Minister for Employment Affairs and Social Protection* [2021] IEHC 455.

described as an 'alien' company, namely CIE International Tours Inc. However, the Court noted that the applicant had, herself, in her submissions, been loose in her description of her employer and could not therefore 'approbate and reprobate' the respondent. The Court stated that it was 'unreal' for the applicant to suddenly insist that a much greater level of precision apply. The application for judicial review therefore failed on its merits.

The proceedings were dismissed.

In a separate judgment,[25] the High Court addressed the allocation of costs of the judicial review proceedings after the application for judicial review was dismissed.

There were two issues for the High Court to consider:

1. 'whether the general rule, namely that the successful party is entitled to its costs, is displaced because much of the costs are attributable to a procedural issue upon which the respondents were unsuccessful' and
2. 'the approach to be taken in respect of the costs of a notice party employer in judicial review proceedings in the context of social welfare legislation'.

In addressing the first issue the Court referred to *Chubb European SE v Health Service Executive*[26] and stated that:

> where a party has prevailed in the proceedings but has not been successful on an identifiable issue or issues which have materially increased the costs of the case, that party may obtain his costs but may suffer two deductions: one in respect of his own costs in presenting that issue, and the other requiring him to set-off the costs of his opponent in meeting that issue against such costs as are ordered in his favour.

The Court found that the parties in the present case should each bear their own costs, as there was a procedural issue that took up much of the hearing, which would have had a material impact on the costs. The Court noted that, had the respondents not raised 'this fruitless procedural objection', then the matter would have been dealt with in much less time and would have significantly reduced the costs.

In addressing the second question, the Court noted that the notice party sought their costs and that the judicial review proceedings were of detriment to the notice party. Referring to *Usk and District Residents Association Ltd v Environmental Protection Agency*,[27] the Court noted: 'the entitlement to costs is limited by reference to the extent of the interest of the notice party in the proceedings, and by consideration of whether it is reasonable for the notice party to participate.'

In considering the notice party's role, the Court found that the notice party's participation was not sufficient to justify costs in its favour and noted that the notice party 'largely duplicated' the participation of the respondents.

---

25 *Murphy v Chief Appeals Officer (Social Welfare Appeals Office) Minister for Employment Affairs and Social Protection* [2021] IEHC 711.
26 *Chubb European SE v Health Service Executive* [2020] IECA 183.
27 *Usk and District Residents Association Ltd v Environmental Protection Agency* [2007] IEHC 30.

In response to the applicant's cross-application for costs, the Court noted there was no reasonable basis for such an application.

No order for costs was made.

[14.11]   *Roche v Teaching Council of Ireland[28]—High Court—Hyland J—RSC, Ord 84, r 21—judicial review—extension of time for leave to bring proceedings—circumstances justifying an extension*

The applicant sought leave to challenge the Teaching Council's refusal to register her as a qualified teacher at post-primary level. The refusal was communicated to the applicant by letter dated 4 June 2019.

Solicitors for the applicant wrote to the Teaching Council on 18 June 2019 stating that the applicant intended to challenge this decision. However, judicial review proceedings were not commenced until 27 July 2020, some 13 months after the decision was communicated.

The applicant sought an extension of the time for bringing the proceedings, under RSC Ord 84, r 21(3). She pointed to four factors in support of her application for an extension: (i) it was necessary for her to await the outcome of a data access request she had made of the respondent; (ii) various incidences of ill health; (iii) the non-availability of counsel over the summer vacation in 2019; and (iv) the 'lockdown' measures that took effect from March 2020 in response to the Covid-19 pandemic.

The High Court refused the application for leave to issue judicial review proceedings, which was brought 13 months after the applicant was notified of the relevant decision, 'well outside' the three-month time limit under Ord 84, r 21.

The Court held that the documents requested by the applicant under her data access request were not necessary to commence her application for judicial review—the correct approach would have been to commence proceedings within the time limit, and then any additional relevant documentation that was obtained could have been introduced by way of a supplementary affidavit.

With regard to the applicant's health, the Court noted that the health conditions pointed to by the applicant did not relate to the time between her being notified of the relevant decision and the commencement of proceedings, so could not be relied upon to excuse the delay.

In relation to factor (iii), the Court noted that, contrary to the applicant's averment that she understood that there is 'a convention in legal practice not to issue new instructions during the months of August and September, and to pause litigation until the new legal term resumes in October', there is no such convention, there are always counsel available during that period, and there are judges available to hear applications for leave to apply for judicial review. In any event, the Court noted that this vacation period only represented one small portion of the overall delay.

---

[28]   *Roche v Teaching Council of Ireland* [2021] IEHC 712.

Lastly, in relation to factor (iv), the Court noted that the disruption due to the Covid-19 measures only commenced in March 2020, at which point the applicant's proceedings were already 'hopelessly out of time'. In any event, the High Court continued to sit during that period and judges were available to hear urgent applications. The Court observed that there was no evidence that the applicant's solicitor made any effort to initiate proceedings during that time and 'tellingly' the pleadings and affidavits were not in fact finalised until 23 July 2020. It also noted that the High Court had refused to grant an extension of time on the basis of Covid-19 restrictions in *H v Director of Public Prosecutions*[29] and *Director of Public Prosecutions v Tyndall*.[30]

In all of the circumstances, the Court held that none of the four factors advanced by the applicant represented 'good and sufficient' reason for an extension of time and the application for leave was refused.

---

[29]   *H v Director of Public Prosecutions* [2021] IEHC 215.
[30]   *Director of Public Prosecutions v Tyndall* [2021] IEHC 283.

Chapter 15

Legislation

INTRODUCTION

[15.01] This chapter covers a selection of Acts from 2021, including the Gender Pay Gap (Information) Act 2021 which introduced new requirements related to Gender Pay Gap reporting, as well as the Workplace Relations (Miscellaneous Provisions) Act 2021 which was introduced on foot of the Supreme Court decision in *Zalewski* and brought about fundamental changes to the way in which the Workplace Relations Commission operates. It also includes 2021 Statutory Instruments of note, including those establishing the new Codes of Practice on workplace bullying and on an employee's right to disconnect.

ACTS

Family Leave and Miscellaneous Provisions Act 2021 (No 4 of 2021)

[15.02] Parent's leave was introduced by the Parent's Leave and Benefit Act 2019 (the 2019 Act). A welcome addition to the various types of family leave already available to employees in Ireland, the 2019 Act provided that 'relevant parents', were entitled to two weeks' paid leave in respect of any child adopted by, or born to them on or after 1 November 2019. Parent's leave had to be taken within 52 weeks of the child's birth or placement with their adoptive family. Parent's benefit is paid (subject to eligibility) at a rate of €245 per week by the Department of Social Protection. Within the first 10 months of the scheme's introduction, some 10,000 eligible parents availed of parent's benefit making it an extremely popular benefit with employees.

In Summer 2020, as the Covid-19 pandemic took hold and its impact on society and on parents began to be assessed, there were calls for increased support for working parents. However, while changes to parent's leave were put forward in response, it is worth noting that prior to the enactment of the 2019 Act, the Government had committed to increasing parent's leave incrementally up to seven weeks by 2021.[1]

---

[1] First 5—A Whole Government Strategy for Babies, Young Children and their Families 2019–2028, available at: *https://first5.gov.ie/userfiles/pdf/5223_4966_DCYA_EarlyYears_INTERACTIVE_Booklet_280x215_v1.pdf#view=fit* [last accessed 11 February 2022].

As part of Budget 2021, it was announced that:

— parent's leave and benefit would increase from two to five weeks; and

— the time frame within which parent's leave must be taken would be extended from one to two years from the child's birth or placement with their adoptive family.

[15.03]   These changes are now effective under the Family Leave and Miscellaneous Provisions Act 2021 (the 2021 Act). Employers and parents alike should note that the changes apply retrospectively—parents who have taken two weeks' parent's leave prior to the enactment of the 2021 Act, will now have an entitlement to an additional three weeks. The five weeks of parent's leave may be taken either together or as separate weeks. The Covid-19 pandemic, coupled with the increased entitlement will encourage more employees to avail of the scheme. It must be noted that the legislation does not place an obligation on employers to pay employees or to top up payments while availing of the leave, this is a matter for employers to decide upon; the legislation provides a state benefit for the duration of the leave, hence the references to it being a 'paid leave'.

[15.04]   Separately, the deadline for the transposition of the EU Directive on Work-Life Balance[2] is 2 August 2022. This Directive contains proposals to ensure greater flexibility for parents and family carers in relation to leave and an improved work-life balance. In recognition of this, the 2021 Act also includes a mechanism for its review in 12 months' time to include budgetary analysis on the potential for the further extension of parent's leave to nine weeks and the need to increase the rate of payment during the period.

Adoptive Leave

[15.05]   Prior to the enactment of the 2021 Act, adoptive leave was available to a female employee adopting a child or a sole male adopting employee. An adopting father, other than a sole male adopter, was only entitled to adoptive leave where the adopting mother died. Further, a male same-sex couple could not avail of the leave.

In a further effort to provide for gender equality within the family and the workforce, the 2021 Act amends the Adoptive Leave Acts 1995 and 2005 (the Acts) to enable any couple that jointly adopts a child to choose which of them will take adoptive leave. Under the Acts, an eligible employee may avail of 24 weeks of state paid adoptive leave from the date the child is placed in his/her care and can take up to 16 additional weeks' unpaid adoptive leave provided he/she has given their employer four weeks' notice in writing of their intention to take the leave.

---

[2]   Directive (EU) 2019/1158 on work-life balance for parents and carers and repealing Council Directive 2010/18/EU.

Employers are advised to update their existing family leave polices to reflect the changes introduced by the 2021 Act.

[15.06] *Gender Pay Gap (Information) Act 2021*

The much-anticipated Gender Pay Gap Information Act 2021 (the Act) was signed into law by the President on 13 July 2021.

The Act amends the Employment Equality Acts 1998 to 2015 to require the Minister for Children, Equality, Disability, Integration and Youth to make regulations requiring certain employers to publish information relating to the gender pay gap in their organisations. Employers will also be required to publish the measures taken by them to eliminate or reduce the gender pay gap.

On publication of the Bill, the Government stated that its aim is to provide transparency on the gender pay gaps that exist in organisations. The Government believes that firms which can report a low or non-existent pay gap will be at an advantage in recruiting future employees and that mandatory reporting will incentivise employers to take measures to address the issue insofar as they can.

[15.07] Previously, no gender pay gap reporting obligations existed for Irish employers. However, the principle of equal pay for equal work has been enshrined in law for a long time. It formed part of the original constitutional architecture of the EU at the time of the adoption of the Treaty of Rome in 1957 and an equivalent provision is now contained in art 157 of the Treaty on the Functioning of the European Union. The principle of equal pay for men and women, originally in the Equal Pay Directive 75/117/EEC enacted in 1975, is now contained in the Recast Directive 2006/54/EC on the implementation of the principle of equal opportunities and equal treatment of men and women in matters of employment and occupation.

Furthermore, the European Commission recently introduced a proposal for a directive to strengthen the application of the principle of equal pay for equal work or work of equal value between men and women through pay transparency and enforcement mechanisms, which, if adopted, will introduce wide-ranging reforms in the area of equal pay across the EU, far beyond the measures proposed in relation to gender pay gap reporting contained in the Act.

Measures that Must Be Contained in the Regulations

[15.08] The Gender Pay Gap Information Act 2021 requires the Minister for Children, Equality, Disability, Integration and Youth (the Minister), as soon as reasonably practicable after the commencement of the legislation, to make regulations requiring employers to publish information relating to the pay of their employees for the purpose of showing whether there are differences in such pay referable to gender and, if so, the size of such differences.

The information, which must be published by employers under the regulations, includes the following:

— the difference between both the mean and the median hourly pay of male and female employees;

— the difference between both the mean and the median bonus pay of male and female employees;

— the difference between both the mean and the median hourly pay of part-time male and female employees;

— the percentage of male and female employees who received bonuses and benefits in kind.

The mean, commonly known as the average, is calculated when one adds up the wages of all employees and divides this figure by the number of employees. The median is the figure that falls at the midpoint of a range when all employees' wages are considered from smallest to largest. The median is typically considered to be a more representative figure as the mean can be skewed by a handful of highly-paid employees.

[15.09] In addition, employers will be required to publish, concurrently with the above gender pay gap information, the reasons for such differences and the measures (if any) taken or proposed to be taken by the employer to eliminate or reduce such differences.

The regulations will only apply to employers with 250 or more employees in the first two years after their introduction. In the third year, the requirements will also apply to employers with 150 or more employees. Thereafter, the requirements will apply to employers with 50 or more employees. The regulations will not apply to employers with fewer than 50 employees.

The Minister has indicated that a central website onto which employers will be required to upload their information will be established.

Measures that May Be Contained in the Regulations

[15.10] In addition to the above requirements that must be contained in the regulations, the Act provides that the regulations may, but are not required to, prescribe the following:

— the class of employer, employee and pay to which the regulations apply;

— how the number of employees and pay is to be calculated; and

— the form and manner in which information is to be published, along with the frequency of publication (which will not be required more than once per year).

The regulations may require the publication of the difference between both the mean and the median hourly pay of temporary male and female employees, the percentage of employees in each of the four (lower, lower middle, middle and upper) quartile pay bands who are male and female or the publication of information by reference to job classifications.

[15.11]   The regulations may also provide that, where the employer does not have access to the information it is required to publish but another person does have access to that information, the other person must give the information, or access thereto, to the employer to allow it to comply with its obligations under the regulations.

The regulations may require that employers ensure that personal data undergoes pseudonymisation on or before publication.

[15.12]   Although the Act provides that the regulations may require the publication of the above information and actions, the Minister confirmed, as the Act had been passed by the Oireachtas, that the regulations will in fact require the publication of this information and actions, unless an issue arises at drafting stage. Therefore, it was to afford some flexibility to the drafters of the detailed regulations that the word 'may' and not 'shall' is used in these provisions of the Act.

Enforcement of Gender Pay Gap Reporting Measures

[15.13]   An employee who claims that his/her employer has failed to comply with the requirement to publish gender pay gap information may make a complaint to the WRC. The WRC will investigate the complaint if it is satisfied that there is a *prime facie* case warranting investigation. If the WRC upholds the complaint, it may order the employer to take a specified course of action to comply with its gender pay gap reporting obligations. This is the only remedy that may be ordered. There is no provision for the payment of compensation to the employee or for a fine to be imposed.

[15.14]   The Act also provides that where the Irish Human Rights and Equality Commission is satisfied that it has reasonable grounds for believing that an employer has failed to comply with the requirement to publish gender pay gap information, as provided for in the regulations, it may apply to the Circuit Court or the High Court for an order requiring the employer to comply. An employer that fails to comply with a Circuit Court or High Court order, will be in contempt of that Court.

The Irish Human Rights and Equality Commission may itself carry out, or invite a particular undertaking, group of undertakings or the undertakings making up a particular industry or sector, to carry out an equality review or prepare and implement an equality action plan. It will be for the Irish Human Rights and Equality Commission to decide whether to exercise these powers following a request by the Minister.

Conclusion

[15.15]   While the enactment of this legislation is welcome, the requirement that the Minister makes regulations to provide for gender pay gap reporting means that the detail of the proposals is not yet known. The regulations will prescribe the form which publication of gender pay gap information must take and the manner in which compliance with the obligations contained in the Act will be achieved. The Minister has confirmed that it is his intention that the regulations, giving effect to the proposals contained in the Act, will be published and in force by the end of 2021. He stated that the 'direct way in which the employer will be expected to report and engage on an annual basis will be set out clearly within the regulations'. Clarity on what precisely is expected of employers in this regard is eagerly awaited.

[15.16]   The passing of the Act may mean that the legislation will apply to employers (at least those with 250 or more employees) from 2022 onwards, unless the Government decides to give employers more time to prepare.

Workplace Relations (Miscellaneous Provisions) Act 2021

[15.17]   On 22 July 2021, the President signed the Workplace Relations (Miscellaneous Provisions) Act 2021 (the Act) into law. The purpose of the Act is to amend the Workplace Relations Act 2015 to address the concerns raised by the Supreme Court in *Zalweski v An Adjudication Officer*[3] about the manner in which the WRC operates.

Some of the key features of the Act are:

1.   the eligibility for appointment of adjudication officers and the revocation by Government in certain circumstances of such appointments;
2.   the administration of oaths or affirmations by adjudication officers, the summoning of witnesses to give evidence/produce documents, the conduct of proceedings in public by the WRC and for the publication of decisions by the WRC;
3.   the requirement that applications in relation to the enforcement of decisions of adjudication officers shall be made on notice; and
4.   the requirement that chairman, deputy chairman and ordinary members of the Labour Court shall be independent in the performance of their functions.

Details in relation to each of these matters are set out below.

Amendments to the Workplace Relations Act 2015

[15.18]   Section 7(1) of the Act extends the exclusion of certain offences from the punishments currently contained in this section (which provides for the following punishments: on summary conviction, to a class A fine or imprisonment for a term not

---

[3]   *Zalewski v An Adjudication Officer, the Workplace Relations Commission, Ireland, the Attorney General and Buywise Discount Stores (Notice Party)* [2021] IESC 24, see **[5.02]**.

exceeding six months or both; or on conviction on indictment, to a fine not exceeding €50,000 or imprisonment for a term not exceeding three years or both) to:

1. Section 41(12) which provides that where a person to whom a notice has been given fails or refuses to comply with the notice, or refuses to give evidence in proceedings to which the notice relates or fails or refuses to produce any document to which the notice relates is guilty of an offence and the punishment for this offence is a class E fine.

2. Section 41(12A)(b) which creates the following new offence: a person who gives a statement material in the proceedings while lawfully sworn as a witness that is false and that he or she knows to be false is guilty of offence and the punishment for this offence is on summary conviction, to a class B fine or to imprisonment for a term not exceeding 12 months, or both, or on conviction on indictment, to a fine not exceeding €100,000 or imprisonment for a term not exceeding 10 years, or both.

3. Section 51, which is excluded from this provision under the Act and which provides that it is offence for a person to fail to comply with an order directing an employer to pay compensation to an employee and which provides for a punishment on summary conviction, to a class A fine or imprisonment for a term not exceeding six months or both. No punishment on indictment is provided for in relation to this offence.

[15.19]   Section 40(1) provides that the Minister may appoint: (a) such and so many of the members of the staff of the Commission, and (b) such and so many other persons, as he or she considers appropriate to be an adjudication officer or adjudication officers for the purposes of the Act. This remains unchanged. The Act contains a new s 40(1A), which provides that adjudication officers will not be eligible for appointment in the following circumstances (contained in a new s 40(6)(d) (i)–(iv)), if the adjudication officer concerned:

(i)   is convicted on indictment of an offence;

(ii)   is convicted of an offence involving fraud or dishonesty;

(iii)   has a declaration made against him or her under s 819 of the Companies Act 2014 (declaration restricting director of insolvent company in being appointed or acting as director); or

(iv)   is subject to, or is deemed to be subject to, a disqualification order as a director.

[15.20]   Section 40(5) is amended to provide that the appointment of adjudication officers (appointed under the Act) will cease:

(1)   if the Government (formerly the Minister) revokes the appointment in accordance with this section;

(2)   in the case of a person appointed to be an adjudication officer who is a member of the staff of the Commission, or (this 'or' has been newly added, but seems to be a drafting error), if the person concerned ceases to be a member of the staff of the Commission; or

(3)   in the case of an appointment that is for a fixed period, on the expiry of that period; or

(4) under the new subsection (d) which provides if the adjudication officer

    (i) is convicted on indictment of an offence,

    (ii) is convicted of an offence involving fraud or dishonesty,

    (iii) has a declaration made against him or her under s 819 of the Companies Act 2014 (restriction order), or

    (iv) is subject to, or is deemed to be subject to, a disqualification order within the meaning of Chap 4 of Pt 14 of the Companies Act 2014.

[15.21]   Section 40(6), which relates to the cessation of the appointment of adjudication officers who were formally rights commissioners/equality officers, etc, is amended in the same way as s 40(5) above.

Section 40(7) on the revocation of such appointments is extensively amended. The new s 40(7) provides a new detailed process which must be followed in this regard. Section 40(7)(a) provides that the Government rather than the Minister will revoke the appointment if it is satisfied that one or more of the following grounds apply, namely that an adjudication officer:

    (i) has become incapable through ill-health of performing his or her functions;

    (ii) has engaged in serious misconduct;

    (iii) has failed without reasonable cause, in the opinion of the Government, to perform his or her functions for a continuous period of at least 3 months beginning not earlier than 6 months before the date of the giving of the notice under paragraph (c);

    (vi) has contravened to a material extent a provision of the Ethics in Public Office Acts 1995 and 2001 that, by virtue of a regulation under section 3 of the Ethics in Public Office Act 1995, applies to him or her.

[15.22]   Section 40(c) provides that where the Government proposes to revoke the appointment of an adjudication officer, they shall give notice in writing to the adjudication officer concerned of the proposal. Section 40(d) provides that the notice shall include a statement:

    (i) of the reasons for the proposed revocation of appointment,

    (ii) that the adjudication officer may, within a period of 30 working days from the giving of the notice or such longer period as the Government may, having regard to the requirements of natural justice, specify in the notice, make representations to the Government in such form and manner as may be specified by the Government, as to why the adjudication officer should not have his or her appointment revoked, and

    (iii) that where no representations are received within the period referred to in subparagraph (ii) or the period specified in the notice, as the case may be, the Government shall, without further notice to the adjudication officer, proceed with the revocation of the appointment of the adjudication officer in accordance with this subsection.

Section 40(e) provides that, in considering whether to revoke the appointment of an adjudication officer, the Government shall take into account:

    (i) any representations made by the adjudication officer … and

    (ii) any other matter the Government considers relevant for the purpose of their decision.

Section 40(f) provides that where, having taken into account the matters referred to above, the Government decides to revoke the appointment of an adjudication officer, the Government shall give notice in writing to the adjudication officer of the decision and the reasons for that decision.

[15.23] The Act contains a new s 41(12A) which provides for the administration of oaths/affirmations by the adjudication officer and that the giving of false statements under oath/affirmation is an offence punishable by:

(a) An adjudication officer may require a person giving evidence in proceedings under this section to give such evidence on oath or affirmation and, for that purpose, cause to be administered an oath or affirmation to such person.

(b) A person who, in or for the purpose of proceedings under this section, gives a statement material in the proceedings while lawfully sworn as a witness that is false and that he or she knows to be false shall be guilty of an offence and shall be liable—

   (i) on summary conviction, to a class B fine or to imprisonment for a term not exceeding 12 months, or both, or

   (ii) on conviction on indictment, to a fine not exceeding €100,000 or imprisonment for a term not exceeding 10 years, or both.

[15.24] Section 41(13) is amended to provide that proceedings will be conducted in public:

unless the adjudication officer, of his or her own motion or upon the application by or on behalf of a party to the proceedings, determines that, due to the existence of special circumstances, the proceedings (or part thereof) should be conducted otherwise than in public.

[15.25] Section 41(14) is amended and provides that every decision of an adjudication officer shall be published on the internet in such form and in such manner as the Commission considers appropriate. However, it provides that an adjudication officer 'may determine that, due to the existence of special circumstances, information that would identify the parties in relation to whom the decision was made should not be published by the Commission'.

Section 43(1) provides for the making of a District Court order directing an employer to carry out the decision of an adjudication officer. It currently provides that 'the District Court shall ... without hearing the employer or any evidence ... make an order'. This provision will be amended to delete 'the employer or' and instead introduce a new s 43(6) which provides that applications to the District Court in this regard shall be made on notice to the employer concerned.

Amendments to the Industrial Relations Act 1946

[15.26] The Act also contains amendments to the Industrial Relations Act 1946 (the 1946 Act).

Section 10, which deals with the establishment of the Labour Court is amended to include a new s 10(13) which states that: 'The chairman and the ordinary members shall be independent in the performance of their functions.'

Section 21, which deals with the power of the Court to summon witnesses, is amended by extending the powers to the following additional Acts: the Redundancy Payments Act 1967; the Protection of Employees (Employers' Insolvency) Act 1984; or any investigation under the Employment Equality Act 1998.

The Act also inserts a new s 21(3A) into the 1946 Act which replicates the amendment to the 2015 Act that the giving of false statements under oath/affirmation is an offence punishable on summary conviction, to a class B fine or to imprisonment for a term not exceeding 12 months, or both, or on conviction on indictment, to a fine not exceeding €100,000 or imprisonment for a term not exceeding 10 years, or both.

Amendments to the Redundancy Payments Act 1967

[15.27]   39 of the Redundancy Payments Act 1967 is amended to provide for the holding of hearings in public and publication of decisions, including party names, as provided for in the amendment to the 2015 Act, unless there are special circumstances to deviate from this practice.

Amendments to the Industrial Relations Act 1969

[15.28]   Section 4 of the Industrial Relations Act 1969 is amended to provide that: 'A deputy chairman shall be independent in the performance of his or her functions.'

Amendments to the Unfair Dismissals Act 1977

[15.29]   Section 8 of the Unfair Dismissals Act 1977 is amended to provide for proceedings to be heard in public and the giving of false statements under oath/ affirmation is an offence punishable on summary conviction, to a class B fine or to imprisonment for a term not exceeding 12 months, or both, or on conviction on indict- ment, to a fine not exceeding €100,000 or imprisonment for a term not exceeding 10 years, or both.

Amendments to the Protection of Employees (Employers' Insolvency) Act 1984

[15.30]   Section 9 of the Protection of Employees (Employers' Insolvency) Act 1984 is amended to provide for the giving of oaths/affirmations and the related offence for false statements so given. A new s 9(AB) is introduced which allows for witnesses to be summoned to give evidence and produce documents. It states that a person so summoned shall be entitled to the same immunities and privileges as those to which he or she would be entitled if he or she were a witness in proceedings before the High Court. Further it provides that a person who fails to comply with the notice or refuses to give evidence/produce documents, shall be guilty of an offence and shall be liable, on summary conviction, to a class E fine. It includes provisions in relation to the hearing being conducted in public and the publication of decisions. Again, this replicates amendments to the 2015 Act detailed above. Finally, the new s 9(4E) provides that: 'The Minister may, by regulations, make provision in relation to any matter relating to the presentation of, the referral of, or the hearing of a complaint under this section that he or she considers appropriate.'

Amendments to the Employment Equality Act 1998 and the Equal Status Act 2000

[15.31]   Section 79 of the Employment Equality Act 1998 and s 25 of the Equal Status Act 2000 are amended to provide that hearings will be held in public and for the administration of oaths/affirmations and the accompanying offence in relation to false statements.

Review of the Amendments and Report to the Dáil

[15.32]   Finally, the Act provides that the Minister shall, not later than 12 months after s 13 comes into operation, commence a review of the operation of the amendments contained in the Act and not later than 12 months after the commencement of the said review, make a report to each House of the Oireachtas of the findings made on the review and of the conclusions drawn from the findings.

[15.33]   *Companies (Rescue Process for Small and Micro Companies) Act 2021*

On 22 July 2021, the Companies (Rescue Process for Small and Micro Companies) Act 2021 (the Act) was signed into law by the President.

[15.34]   The Company Law Review Group's *Report Advising on a Legal Structure for the Rescue of Small Companies* was published on 22 October 2020. The Review Group identified that the examinership process, under Pt 10 of the Companies Act 2014, was prohibitively costly for small companies due to the central role of the courts in the process. In that context, the Act provides for an alternative to examinership, the Small Company Administrative Rescue Process (SCARP), which will allow small and micro companies to restructure their debts within 70 days. The amendments are provided for by the insertion of Pt 10A after s 558 of the Companies Act 2014.

Eligibility

[15.35]   The process is only available to small and micro companies (as defined under ss 280A and 280D of the Companies Act 2014 respectively). The company must also be insolvent (ie, unable to, or will likely be unable to, pay its debts as they fall due).

SCARP

[15.36]   The eligible company furnishes a 'process advisor' (who must be a qualified liquidator) with a sworn statement of affairs of the company. The process advisor is then required to determine the company's reasonable prospect of survival based on this statement. They take certain factors into account including the availability of funding, the cost structure, whether the business plans are based on objective and independent advice, the wider economic situation, the market in which the company operates, the expertise, brand and historic success of the company, the place of the company if it is part of a structure, whether a secured creditor has interest in trading receivership, and any other matters considered relevant.

The process advisor then prepares a report similar to the independent expert's report in the examinership process, setting out whether there is a reasonable prospect of survival and the funding required to allow the company to continue to trade.

Within seven days of receipt of the process advisor's report, the board of directors of the company must pass a resolution to appoint the process advisor to implement the rescue plan. The process advisor must notify creditors within two working days of their appointment and request submissions in respect of their claims.

Within 49 days of appointment, the process advisor must:

1.   prepare a rescue plan; and
2.   hold meetings of the creditors and members to approve the rescue plan.

Rescue Plan

[15.37]   The rescue plan should: specify each class of members and creditors and specify those whose interests will not be impaired by the plan: provide equal treatment for each claim of a particular class (unless agreed otherwise); include necessary changes in management and necessary changes in the constitution; and provide for its implementation. A company director will be guilty of a category 3 offence if he or she fails to implement any provision of the rescue plan in the time that the process advisor states.

[15.38]   As part of the rescue plan, the process advisor shall consider whether, in order to survive, the company must repudiate certain contracts. Regard should be had to whether repudiation would be more advantageous for the relevant person than a winding up of the company or receivership, the burden placed on the company in case of non-repudiation and whether a rescue plan can be prepared without repudiation. The court must be satisfied that repudiation is necessary for the company's survival to repudiate the contract. Notice by the process advisor to the relevant person shall be given, with detailed explanations as to the reasons and the consequences, and rights linked to this repudiation

Power of the Court to Stay Proceedings or Restrain Further Proceedings

[15.39] Unlike examinership, SCARP does not afford a company an automatic period of protection from its creditors. However, if the company, the directors, or the process advisor make an application to the relevant court, it can stay all proceedings and restrain further proceedings against the company for a specified period. These include the winding up of the company, the appointment of a receiver and the repossession of goods. The court can also order that no attachment, sequestration, distress or execution shall be put in force without the consent of the advisor, that no action to realise a security (except with consent) is to be made, that no examiner be appointed and that no order for relief under s 212 goes ahead.

Powers of the Process Advisor

[15.40] The process advisor enjoys any powers with which a statutory auditor has been conferred under the Companies Act 2014. They have the power to convene and preside over meetings, the right to take notice of and attendance at meetings and the power to take certain acts where they have become aware of any act being taken in relation to the income, assets and liabilities of the company which is to the detriment of the company.

Production of Documents and Evidence

[15.41] It is the duty of officers and agents of the company to provide the advisor with books and documents of any company which are in their power and attend before and give assistance to the process adviser when required.

Meetings of Members and Creditors

[15.42] Seven days' notice must be given prior to this meeting. Modifications can be suggested but must be approved by the process advisor. The plan will be deemed to be accepted by a meeting of members or creditors or of a class of members or creditors when 60% in number and value of the claims represented at the meeting have voted in favour of the resolution for the rescue plan.

The plan is binding on the company, directors, members and creditors where it is accepted by at least one class of creditors whose claims would be impaired by implementation of the rescue plan and if in the next 21 days of the notice of approval no objection has been filed (see below). Within 48 hours of approval, the court and registrar should be provided with notice of the approval. Notice shall be given to employees, revenue commissioners and any creditor or member whose claim would be impaired if the rescue plan was implemented.

Objections

[15.43]   There are prescribed grounds on which an objection can be made. It should be sent to the relevant court and to the process advisor within 21 days of the filing of the notice of approval. The objection will be heard in court. The onus is on the process adviser to show that the objection should not be upheld.

STATUTORY INSTRUMENTS

[15.44]   *SI 674/2020—Industrial Relations Act 1990 (Code of Practice for Employers and Employees on the Prevention and Resolution of Bullying at Work) Order 2020*

The Industrial Relations Act 1990 (Code of Practice for Employers and Employees on the Prevention and Resolution of Bullying at Work) Order 2020 (the Code) was jointly published by the Health and Safety Authority (HSA) and the Workplace Relations Commission (WRC).

The Code is effective from 23 December 2020. It replaces the two previous codes that had established employers' obligations in relation to workplace bullying (namely, the 'Code of Practice for Employers and Employees on the Prevention and Resolution of Bullying at Work' issued by the HSA in 2007; and the 'Code of Practice Detailing Procedures for Addressing Bullying in the Workplace' issued by the then Labour Relations Commission in 2002).

Now, employers' and employees' obligations in relation to the prevention and resolution of workplace bullying under both health and safety legislation and workplace relations legislation are contained in the Code.

The Code stresses that 'bullying' and 'harassment' remain two distinct concepts and the Code solely addresses the question of workplace bullying. That stated, the Code notes that an employer can have one policy document containing its policy and procedures in relation to both bullying and harassment. Key aspects of the Code are set out below.

Definition of 'Bullying at Work'

[15.45]   The Code retains the definition of bullying as contained in previous codes. Bullying is defined as:

> repeated inappropriate behaviour, direct or indirect, whether verbal, physical or otherwise, conducted by one or more persons against another or others, at the place of work and/or in the course of employment, which could be reasonably regarded as undermining the individual's right to dignity at work.

Therefore, in order to be considered as workplace bullying, the conduct must be:

— repeated;

— inappropriate;

— workplace connected, ie, at the place of work and/or in the course of employment; and

— 'reasonably regarded as undermining the individual's right to dignity at work'.

The Code elaborates on these elements. It describes bullying in terms of 'seriously negative targeted behaviours', and this behaviour must 'undermine their esteem and standing in a harmful, sustained way'. It further states that the behaviour must be 'clearly wrong, undermining and humiliating'. Moreover, in determining if the conduct is bullying, the '"reasonableness" of behaviours over time must be considered'.

[15.46]   The Code must be read in light of *Ruffley v Board of Management of St Anne's School*,[4] a decision of the Irish Supreme Court which addressed the various components of the definition of workplace bullying. In *Ruffley*, O'Donnell J noted that, in order to be considered workplace bullying,

> conduct must be repeated, not merely consist of a number of incidents; it must be inappropriate, not merely wrong; and it is not enough that it be inappropriate and even offensive: it must be capable of being reasonably regarded as undermining the individual's right to dignity at work.

[15.47]   Furthermore, in addressing whether the behaviour constitutes 'repeated' behaviour for the purposes of workplace bullying, O'Donnell J stated that: 'What must be repeated is inappropriate behaviour undermining the personal dignity of the individual.' On the question of 'inappropriate' behaviour, he noted that this test 'looks to the question of propriety in human relations, rather than legality'. Furthermore, O'Donnell J stressed that 'dignity at work' is a distinct component of workplace bullying which 'identifies the interests sought to be protected by the law, and just as importantly limits the claims which may be made to those which can be described as outrageous, unacceptable, and exceeding all bounds tolerated by decent society'.

[15.48]   It is evident from both the Code and the *Ruffley* case that it is not sufficient for the behaviour to merely be repeated and inappropriate. The inappropriate nature

---

4   *Ruffley v Board of Management of St Anne's School* [2017] IESC 33, see *Arthur Cox Employment Law Yearbook 2017* at **[6.04]**.

of the alleged behaviour must meet a certain minimum threshold if it is to constitute bullying.

Interestingly, the Code also provides clarity on what is not bullying. It notes that while disrespectful behaviour, conflicts and relationship breakdowns are not ideal in the workplace, they do not automatically reach the 'adequate level of destructiveness' to be considered bullying.

[15.49]   The Code provides a non-exhaustive list of what is not bullying, which includes:

— strongly expressing differences of opinion;

— offering constructive feedback, guidance, or advice about work-related behaviour, which is not of itself welcome; and

— ordinary performance management.

Management of Bullying

[15.50]   A fundamental aspect of managing bullying in the workplace is the prevention of its occurrence in the first instance. In that regard, both employers and employees have obligations in establishing a positive environment that is free from bullying, intimidation and ongoing negative behaviour.

Employer's Role

[15.51]   The Code identifies three key aspects to an employer's role in effectively managing workplace bullying, namely:

— to act reasonably to prevent workplace bullying patterns developing and to resolve complaints, which includes assessing the complaint, recording actions and putting in place a suitable response based on each case arising;

— to prepare a Safety Statement under s 20 of the Safety, Health and Welfare at Work Act 2005 (the 2005 Act); and

— to develop a proper workplace anti-bullying policy, in consultation with employees.

Employee Obligations

[15.52]   Employees have an obligation to 'create a co-operative relational climate' and to relate in 'clear, civil and respectful ways to everybody in the workplace'. They also have statutory obligations under s 13 of the 2005 Act, which require employees, for example:

— to comply with the relevant statutory provisions and take reasonable care to protect their own safety, health and welfare and that of any other person who might be affected by their acts or omissions;

— to cooperate with their employer to enable their employer comply with its statutory obligations; and

— to not engage in any improper conduct that is likely to endanger their own safety, health and welfare at work or that of anyone else.

Organisational Culture

[15.53]   The Code also identifies another key factor in the prevention of workplace bullying—namely the role of the organisational culture. The Code identifies a number of essential elements required for the creation of a positive organisational culture. These include good leadership, proper communication and staff training, and the resolution of complaints in a supportive, effective and fair manner.

Resolving Bullying at Work

[15.54]   A key of focus of the Code is the resolution of bullying in the workplace through informal means. The Code notes that a prompt and informal problem-solving approach can offer the best method for addressing allegations of bullying effectively, especially where the individuals involved will continue to work together.

To that end, the Code introduces the concept of an 'initial informal process' and a 'secondary informal process'. The concept of a 'secondary informal process' is entirely new and accordingly introduces what might be termed a three-stage process of resolution—an initial informal process, a secondary informal process, and a formal process.

Initial Informal Process

[15.55]   The initial informal process seeks to resolve an allegation of bullying informally by agreement between the individuals, through an informal discussion with the appropriate manager.

Regard must be had to the principles of natural justice and fair procedure when implementing all stages of the resolution process, including the initial informal stage. For example, the Code notes that in instances of smaller organisations, it may not be appropriate for the person managing the organisation in question to play a role at this initial informal stage as they may be required at a later appeal or judgement. In those circumstances, it may be necessary to use an independent professional body to mediate or otherwise resolve the complaint. Employers are advised to give due consideration to the option of mediation, as it can be a quick and effective mechanism to resolve workplace complaints.

Secondary Informal Process

[15.56]   The secondary informal process can be invoked if the initial informal process is unsuccessful or unsuitable in light of the nature of the complaint. Key steps in the secondary informal process include:

— the nomination by the employer of a separate individual to deal with the particular complaint on behalf of the organisation. This person must be someone in authority within the organisation who has appropriate training and experience;

— the nominated individual establishes the facts, the context and the next course of action (albeit still in an informal manner);

— concrete examples of bullying behaviour are put before the person complained against, who is given the opportunity to respond;

— a course of action is agreed to progress the issue to resolution; and

— steps to stop bullying and to monitor the progress of resolution are implemented. A proposal for a long-term course of action should ideally be signed and dated by both parties.

Formal Process

[15.57]   The Code recommends that management explore and, if appropriate exhaust, all informal avenues of resolution before initiating a formal process. Management should consider the circumstances of the complaint and make a reasonable evidence-based decision to invoke the formal process.

The formal resolution process includes two steps—a formal complaint and a formal investigation. The Code outlines the process organisations should follow when instigating a formal investigation. Any investigation should be conducted in line with terms of reference, which establish an indicative timeline for completion.

Individuals who have the appropriate training and experience should conduct the investigation, be they a nominated member of management or an independent third party. Of note, there is no obligation in the Code to consult on the identity of the internal or external person as investigator.

[15.58]   It should be noted that there is some ambiguity in the Code in relation to the function of the investigation. The stated objective of the investigation 'is to ascertain whether, on the balance of probabilities, the behaviours complained of occurred, it having already been established that the behaviours come within the description of workplace bullying'. However, the Code goes on to state that the test to be established is 'whether the complaint is valid' and whether the accused employee 'has a case to answer'. There appears to be ambiguity between ascertaining 'whether … the behaviours complained of occurred' and whether the employee 'has a case to answer'. This apparent distinction is akin to the distinction between the establishment, as a matter of fact, of what occurred and the establishment of a *prima facie* case.

Communication of Outcome

[15.59]   The Code notes that the effective communication of any outcome is critical to the resolution process. Communication must be done in a sensitive and fair manner. All parties directly involved in the complaint are entitled to know if the complaint was upheld in whole or in part, and the reasons for any such decision. However, specific details regarding any disciplinary action being taken against any particular party on foot of the process are confidential. Other parties are not entitled to receive this information as part of the communication of the outcome.

Principles of Fair Procedure and Natural Justice

[15.60] The Code enshrines the principles of fair procedure and natural justice in the formal process, by expressly providing for the following:

— **right to representation**: the Code provides that 'A work colleague or employee/trade union representation (provided the person has representation in line with the principles of natural justice and fair procedure) may accompany the [claimant] and the person complained of, if so desired'. It is notable that no provision is made for parties to be accompanied by lawyers; and

— **right of appeal**: the Code provides that both parties have the right of appeal within the formal process, this right appearing as a pre-disciplinary right of appeal in the case of a respondent where the investigation upholds the complaints. Furthermore, it should be noted that any such appeal is not an appeal on the merits or a de novo hearing. The Code states that any such appeal 'should focus on the conduct of the investigation in terms of fair process and adherence to procedure. It should be noted that an appeal is not a re-hearing of original issues'. Therefore, any appeal must relate to process and procedure grounds.

[15.61] The Code notes that the 'outcome of the appeal shall be final insofar as the employer duties under health and safety legislation is required'. However, surprisingly, the Code does not address what will happen if an appeal is upheld. Presumably, in such circumstances, the appeal outcome might be that the matter should be re-investigated. Accordingly, it follows that in those circumstances the outcome of the appeal is not 'final' insofar as the employer is concerned.

Malicious Complaints

[15.62] The Code also addresses the making of a malicious complaint, being 'an allegation being made without foundation, and with malicious intent, where a person knowingly or without regard to whether it is true or not, accuses another person of allegedly bullying them'. Such complaints can have significant consequences in terms of reputational damage to the accused, and may result in disciplinary action being brought against any employee making such complaints.

Requirement To Keep Records

[15.63] The Code emphasises the requirement of employers to keep and maintain records of complaints and investigations in line with the GDPR and the Data Protection Act 2018. The Code outlines the obligations of an employer at each stage:

1. **Initial informal stage**: a written record of the matter should be kept, including any determination that the alleged behaviour does not constitute bullying.
2. **Secondary informal stage**: the nominated individual should keep nominal records of all stages of the process, including the complaint raised, the initial meeting, outcomes reached and actions agreed. The purpose of these nominal records is to evidence an organisational response to a complaint made and an attempt at its resolution.

3. **Formal process**: a written record should be kept of all stages of the formal process, which includes statements of all parties, including witnesses, any decisions made and any preventative, protective or remedial action taken. Furthermore, any decision to escalate a complaint to the formal process should also be recorded.
4. **Workplace policy**: in developing and implementing workplace policies, employers should keep a record of any consultation with employees and any training provided to employees.

Employers are advised to be mindful of their obligations under data protection legislation in relation to the sharing and retention of any of such records.

Role of the HSA and the WRC

[15.64]   The Code elaborates on the role of both the Health and Safety Authority (the HSA) and the WRC in relation to the processing of complaints and the prevention of bullying in the workplace.

The HSA, operating under the statutory powers of the 2005 Act, has the ultimate aim of protecting employees through overseeing the employer duty to provide a safe workplace and system of work. One aspect of this is through its operation of the Workplace Contact Unit (the WCU). Employees who consider themselves to be bullied can submit a complaint to the WCU about the way in which their employer handled their complaint, or seek further information in relation to their treatment. The HSA can ultimately assess the employer's processing of the complaint to determine if their actions were adequate. In circumstances where it determines that an employer has failed to act reasonably in relation to a complaint of bullying, the HSA can issue enforcement action ranging from verbal advice to an Improvement Notice. The Code clarifies that the HSA has no role in relation to disciplinary action or in relation to conflict resolution between parties to a bullying complaint.

[15.65]   The objective of the WRC, as noted by the Code, is 'to achieve harmonious working relations between employers and employees'. It offers a range of services that may assist in the resolution of workplace bullying, such as individual and collective workplace mediation and an overall review of workplace relations generally. Furthermore, under s 13 of the Industrial Relations Act 1969, a matter can be referred to the WRC for adjudication, after internal processes have been exhausted. Any such referral for adjudication relates to the conduct of an investigation on grounds of fair process and procedure.

Key Considerations for Employers

[15.66]

— Employers' obligations under the Code apply irrespective of whether employees are based at a fixed location, at home or are mobile. Furthermore, the Code expressly provides that bullying can occur through digital or cyber means. Therefore, employers still have obligations to prevent workplace bullying, even in circumstances where the majority of their workforce might not be physically present in the workplace.

— Employers are advised to review and update their anti-bullying policies to bring them in line with the Code.

— It is also recommended that employers take pro-active steps to promote a positive workplace culture. This includes effectively developing and promoting their anti-bullying policies, training staff appropriately on these policies and ensuring all complaints are dealt with respectfully, sensitively and in complete confidence.

— Employers are further advised to attempt to effectively resolve complaints though informal mechanisms, if possible. Employers should take steps to ensure complaints of bullying are fully and effectively resolved on a long-term basis. This can be achieved through, for example, ongoing monitoring, team building exercises or specific anti-bullying awareness programmes.

Failure to adhere to the Code is admissible in evidence in any criminal proceedings under the 2005 Act. Furthermore, the Code is admissible in any proceedings before a court, the WRC or the Labour Court, in accordance with the Industrial Relations Act 1990.

[15.67] *SI 159/2021—Workplace Relations Act 2015 (WRC Code of Practice on the Right to Disconnect) Order 2021*

The three key elements contained in the WRC Code of Practice on the Right to Disconnect (the Code) are:

(a) the right of an employee to not routinely perform work outside normal working hours;

(b) the right to not be penalised for refusing to attend to work matters outside of normal working hours; and

(c) the duty to respect another person's right to disconnect (eg, by not routinely emailing or calling outside normal working hours).

An employer's failure to adhere to the principles of the Code will not be an offence in and of itself, but the Code will be admissible in evidence.

Failure to adhere to the Code could result in increased awards of compensation both in the civil courts for matters such as personal injury complaints caused by bullying and/or stress; and in respect of complaints based on statutory rights such as working time, unfair dismissal (including constructive dismissal) and health and safety at work.

Pre-existing Obligations Referred to in the Code

[15.68] The Code is effectively grounded in pre-existing legislative obligations including:

— **Working time**: The Code reiterates obligations arising from the Organisation of Working Time Act 1997, including a maximum 48-hour average working week, employees' entitlements to daily and weekly rest breaks, employers' obligations to maintain records of hours worked, and employees' duties to cooperate with any such mechanism to record working time.

— **Health and safety**: An employer has a duty to provide a safe place of work under the Safety, Health and Welfare at Work Acts 2005, which the Code links with the obligation to ensure employees do not work hours in excess of those set out in the Organisation of Working Time Act 1997.

— **Terms of employment**: The Code reiterates an employer's requirement to notify employees of any terms and conditions related to hours of work, including hours of work within a normal working day and normal working week.

Employer's Obligations set out in the Code	Suggested Action
Provide detailed information to employees on working time and inform employees of what their normal working hours are reasonably expected to be.	Ensure existing contracts accurately reflect obligations in relation to working time.
Ensure employees take rest periods.	Where an employee's work is based on a set timetable/roster, set breaks should be included (ie, 15 minutes after 4.5 hours, 30 minutes after 6 hours). Where working time is more flexible, specify an employee's entitlements in relation to rest breaks in a Right to Disconnect Policy. Notify the employee that he/she is expected to take breaks and identify a contact person in the event that the employee experiences issues.
Ensure the workplace is safe, having particular regard to an employer's obligation under s 8(2)(b) of the Safety Health and Welfare at Work Act 2005, ie, to manage work activities in order to prevent conduct/behaviour that poses a risk to employee safety, health or welfare at work.	Adhere to working time requirements. Implement a Right to Disconnect Policy as outlined below. Require that an employee notifies the employer of any potential hazards in relation to disconnecting/working time.
Not to penalise an employee for complying with the provisions of the Safety Health and Welfare at Work Act 2005, or exercising a right or performing a duty under that Act.	Ensure managers, line managers and supervisors are made aware of an employee's working time entitlements and right to disconnect. Clearly outline parameters for communications outside of working time in the Right to Disconnect Policy.

In addition to employer's obligations, the Code also refers to certain existing employee obligations such as managing their own working time, taking reasonable care to ensure their safety at work, cooperating with mechanisms to record working time and considering others' right to disconnect by not routinely emailing/calling outside normal working hours.

The Right to Disconnect Policy—What to Include

[15.69] *Working Time*

— The policy should stipulate that employees are not expected to respond to work emails or messages outside of working hours or during annual leave, other than occasional legitimate situations where it is necessary to do so. Examples given are to fill in at short notice for a sick colleague, where unforeseen circumstances arise, or where business reasons require contact outside of normal working hours.

— Include an acknowledgment, if applicable, that business needs may require out-of-hours working, based on an employee's role and as agreed in his/her employment contract.

— Provide clear guidance on disconnecting where work is conducted across global time zones and the expectation for responding to digital communications.

— Consider those with diverse requirements where normal working hours may be flexible, eg those with caring responsibilities. Where an employee chooses to work outside normal hours, the right to maintain work-life balance boundaries cannot be compromised.

[15.70] *Communications*

— Tone and urgency of communications out of hours should be proportionate.

— Consider the use of email footers/pop-ups to remind employees/customers that there is no requirement to reply out of hours, and a response should not be expected.

— Senders should stipulate that a response is not expected, or ideally, use the delay send function.

— Emergency communications should be an exception, not the norm.

[15.71] *Manager's Role*

— Managers must demonstrate commitment to the policy through being active role models. Senior management should openly articulate support for the policy and implement appropriate actions.

— Training should reinforce appropriate behaviours around a right to disconnect and open communication with employees should be encouraged.

— Managers should take action where reluctance to disconnect is due to an employee's increased workload, performance or organisational culture.

— Goals and deliverables must be delivered in normal working hours, other than in exceptional circumstances.

[15.72] *Culture*

— Include the right to disconnect as part of the employee on-boarding process and in an employee's employment contract.

— The Code suggests, where possible, that organisations establish a monitoring committee or assign responsibility to a member of HR to oversee the implementation of the policy.

— Review the effectiveness of the policy annually.

[15.73] *Raising Concerns*

— Where occasional contact outside of normal working hours becomes the norm, this should be addressed. Examples of a failure to respect an employee's right to disconnect include:
 — regular contact outside of normal working hours;
 — an expectation to work through lunch/breaks;
 — penalisation for unavailability outside normal working hours; and
 — favourable treatment for those who are connected out of hours.

— The Code suggests an informal approach to addressing issues in the first instance, ie the employee seeks to resolve the issue potentially with the help of HR/a manager. If this fails, the company's grievance procedure may be initiated.

[15.74] Although many of the principles of the Code are enshrined in existing legislation, employers are now be expected to set out parameters to ensure that those existing obligations are adhered to, and to protect an employee's right to disconnect. Failure to do so will carry the risk of an increase in employee-initiated litigation as well as a potential increase in awards of compensation.

Brexit

[15.75] *SI 634/2020 Withdrawal of the United Kingdom from the European Union (Consequential Provisions) Act 2020 (Part 1) (Commencement) Order 2020*

This Order provides that Pt 1 of the Withdrawal of the United Kingdom from the European Union (Consequential Provisions) Act 2020 shall come into operation on 17 December 2020.

Part 1 of the Act deals with preliminary and general matters such as citation, construction and commencement. It also provides for expenses in the administration of the Act to be paid out of monies provided by the Oireachtas. Part 1 concludes by repealing certain provisions of the Withdrawal of the United Kingdom from the European Union (Consequential Provisions) Act 2019.

[15.76] *SI 669/2020 Withdrawal of the United Kingdom from the European Union (Consequential Provisions) Act 2020 (Part 12) (Commencement) Order 2020*

This Order commences Pt 12 of the Withdrawal of the United Kingdom from the European Union (Consequential Provision) Act 2020 which amends certain provisions of the Protection of Employees (Employers' Insolvency) Act 1984. The Order brings this part into force with effect from 23 December 2020.

[15.77] *SI 680/2020 Withdrawal of the United Kingdom from the European Union (Consequential Provisions) Act 2020 (Part 5) (Commencement) Order 2020*

Part 5 of the Withdrawal of the United Kingdom from the European Union (Consequential Provisions) Act 2020 amends certain definitions under s 10 of the Employment Permits Act 2006. This Order brings Pt 5 into effect from 11.00 pm on 31 December 2020.

[15.78] *SI 693/2020 Withdrawal of the United Kingdom from the European Union (Consequential Provisions) Act 2020 (Parts 17, 18, 19 and 20) (Commencement) Order 2020*

This Order brings into operation Pts 17, 18, 19 and 20 in relation to immigration, international protection, and recognition of certain divorces, legal separations and marriage annulments and amendment of the Defamation Act 2009 respectively. These parts came into operation on 31 December 2020 at 11.00 pm.

[15.79] *SI 717/2020 Occupational Pension Schemes (United Kingdom Members) Regulations 2020*

These Regulations introduce a concept of a 'UK member' in the context of occupational pension schemes. A UK member is an external member of a scheme who remains entitled to any benefit under that scheme in respect of a period of service in the UK. The Regulations retain protections afforded to UK members under the Pensions Act 1990 post-Brexit.

Regulation 3 amends references to members in the Pensions Act 1990 to include UK members, except in Pts X and XII of the Pensions Act 1990.

[15.80] *SI 728/2020 European Union (Withdrawal Agreement) (Citizens' Rights) Regulations 2020*

These Regulations make provisions in relation to residence documents. The Regulations provide for the application of the European Communities (Free Movement of Persons) Regulations 2015 (SI 548/2015) to UK nationals and their family members to whom Pt 2 of the Withdrawal Agreement applies, and make provision for the issue of residence documents to such persons.

[15.81] *SI 729/2020 Immigration Act 2004 (Visas) (Amendment) (No. 2) Order 2020*

This Order amends arts 2 and 3 of the Immigration Act 2004 (Visas) Order 2014. In particular, it provides definitions such as 'United Kingdom national' and 'family members' relevant to the European Union (Withdrawal Agreement) (Citizens' Rights) Regulations 2020.

The Order also inserts a provision under which non-nationals who are family members of a UK national and holders of a residence document issued in accordance with art 18(4) of the Agreement on the Withdrawal of the United Kingdom of Great Britain and Northern Ireland from the European Union and the European Atomic Energy Community are included in classes of members who are not required to be in possession of a valid Irish visa when landing in the State.

[15.82]   *SI 730/2020 Protection of Employees (Employers' Insolvency) Act 1984 (Transfer of Personal Data) Regulations 2020*

These Regulations facilitate the exchange of certain information post-Brexit in order to process applications made to the Insolvency Payments Schemes by employees in insurable employment in Ireland whose employer is in a state of insolvency under the laws of the UK. The Regulations provide for exchange of information between the Minister for Enterprise, Trade and Employment and a relevant officer appointed in connection with the insolvency of an employer in the UK.

Data Privacy

[15.83]   *SI 297/2021 European Union (Enforcement of Data Subjects' Rights on Transfer of Personal Data Outside the European Union) Regulations 2021*

This instrument amended the Data Protection Act 2018 by inserting a judicial remedy for individuals whose data has been transferred outside of the EU without following the applicable safeguards. The judicial remedy allows for the enforcement of third-party beneficiary rights conferred under binding corporate rules and data protection clauses approved by the Commission, as well as standard contractual clauses previously brought forward by the Commission (under Directive 95/46/EC) or authorised by a supervisory authority in accordance with art 46(3)(a) of the General Data Protection Regulation.

[15.84]   *SI 334/2021 Data Sharing and Governance Act 2019 (Commencement of Certain Provisions) Order 2021*

This Order provided 7 July 2021 as the day on which the Data Sharing and Governance Act 2019 (other than s 6(2)–(3)) came into operation.

The Order provided 31 March 2022 as the day on which s 6(2)–(3) of the Data Sharing and Governance Act 2019 came into operation.

Employment Permits

[15.85]   *SI 286/2021 Employment Permits (Amendment) Regulations 2021*

The Employment Permits (Amendment) Regulations 2021 were commenced on 14 June 2021. These Regulations amend the Employment Permits Regulations 2017[5] to provide for the following:

— the addition of Dietician to Sch 3 (employments in respect of which there is a shortage in respect of qualifications, experience or skills which are required for the proper functioning of the economy);

---

[5]   Employment Permits Regulations 2017 (SI 95/2017).

— the removal of the following from Sch 4 (employments in respect of which an employment permit shall not be granted):

— physiotherapist,
— occupational therapist,
— speech and language therapist,
— social worker, and
— nursing auxiliaries and assistants (health care assistant);

— to set the minimum annual remuneration applicable for the grant of applications for healthcare assistant,

— to insert qualification requirements for healthcare assistant; and

— to update Sch 2, Pt B (regulatory bodies or government Minister from which or whom a copy of the registration or recognition of qualifications is required).

[15.86]   *SI 559/2021 Employment Permits (Amendment) (No 2) Regulations 2021*

These Regulations amend the Employment Permits Regulations 2017 (SI 95/2017) (the 2017 Regulations).

These Regulations make the following amendments:

— increase the quotas of general employment permits for meat processor operatives, meat boners and horticulture operatives;

— remove the quota of general employment permits for heavy goods vehicle drivers;

— introduce a new quota of general employment permits for work riders;

— introduce new quotas of general employment permits, and new application requirements, for catering and bar managers, hotel and accommodation managers, restaurant and catering establishments managers and publicans and managers of licensed premises;

— introduce a new quota for dairy farm assistants and remove certain restrictions in relation to employment permits for such employment;

— add social workers to Schedule 3 to the 2017 Regulations; and

— remove dispensing opticians, electricians, masons, roofers, roof tilers and slaters, plumbers and heating and ventilating engineers, carpenters and joiners, floorers and wall tilers, painters and decorators, and construction and building trades supervisors from Schedule 4 to the 2017 Regulations.

Gender Balance

[15.87]   *SI 93/2021 Statistics (Gender Balance in Business Survey) Order 2021*

This Order, made under s 25(1) of the Statistics Act 1993 and the Statistics (Delegation of Ministerial Functions) (No 2) Order 2020 (SI No 263 of 2020), requires certain undertakings to provide general information relating to each member of their senior executive team, and their board of directors.

The Order applies to any undertaking employing 250 or more persons and is classified for statistical purposes under sections B, C, D, E, F, G, H, I, J, K, L, M, N, R or S of NACE Rev. 2 set out in Annex I to Regulation (EC) No 1893/2006, as amended by Regulation (EC) No 295/2008, Regulation (EU) No 70/2012 and Regulation (EU) 2019/1243.

Undertakings meeting this criteria are required to provide information once only for the purposes of the survey on Gender Balance in Business.

For each senior executive team member of the undertaking on 1 January 2021, information relating to the name, job title, gender, number of years they have been a member of the team and the number of years they have been employed by the undertaking must be provided.

For each member of the board of directors of the undertaking on 1 January 2021, information relating to the name, job title, gender, whether he or she is an executive or non-executive member of the board and the number of years he or she has held the position referred to must be provided.

Undertakings are also required to provide information on the time taken to complete the questionnaire or provide the information as requested.

Immigration

[15.88]   *SI 262/2020—Immigration Act 2004 (Visas) (Amendment) (No 2) Order 2020*

This Order extended the applicability of art 3(d) of the Immigration Act 2004 (Visas) Order 2014[6] from 10 July 2020 to 31 October 2021.

[15.89]   *SI 287/2021 Immigration Act 2004 (Visas) (Amendment) (No 2) Order 2021*

This Order came into operation on 16 June 2021 and amends Sch 1 of the Immigration Act 2004 (Visas) Order 2014 (SI 473/2014) by the insertion of:

  (i) 'Argentina' after 'Antigua and Barbuda',
 (ii) 'Bolivia' after 'Belize',
(iii) 'Brazil' after 'Botswana',
 (iv) 'Chile' after 'Canada',
  (v) 'Guyana' after 'Guatemala',
 (vi) 'Paraguay' after 'Panama',
(vii) 'South Africa' after 'Solomon Islands', and
(viii) 'Uruguay' after 'United States of America.'

The Order provides that nationals of the above countries are not required to be in possession of a valid Irish visa when landing in the State.

---

6   Immigration Act 2004 (Visas) Order 2014 (SI 473/2014).

Additionally, the Order amends Sch 5 of the Immigration Act 2004 (Visas) Order 2014 (SI 473/2014) by the deletion of 'Argentina', 'Bolivia', 'Brazil', 'Chile', 'Columbia', 'Ecuador', 'Guyana', 'Paraguay', 'Peru', 'South Africa', 'Suriname' and 'Uruguay'. The Order provides that nationals of these countries are not required to be in possession of a valid Irish transit visa when arriving at a port in the State for purposes of passing through the port in order to travel to another State.

The Order has the effect of reversing the Immigration Act 2004 (Visas)(Amendment) Order 2021 (SI 23/2021).

[15.90] *SI 403/2021 Immigration Act 2004 (Registration Certificate Fee) (Amendment) Regulations 2021*

The Immigration Act 2004 (Registration Certificate Fee) (Amendment) Regulations 2021 came into effect on 29 July 2021 and amend the Immigration Act 2004 (Registration Certificate Fee) Regulations 2012 (SI No 444 of 2012).

They amend reg 4 of the 2012 Regulations to provide that persons who hold a residence document or permanent residence document issued in accordance with art 18(4) of the Agreement on the Withdrawal of the United Kingdom of Great Britain and Northern Ireland from the European Union and the European Atomic Energy Community are exempt from paying a fee for obtaining the residence document.

They also provide that the registration fee is waived in respect of persons who hold a residence card issued under reg 7(5)(a) of the European Communities (Free Movement of Persons) Regulations 2015 (SI No 548 of 2015), or a permanent residence card issued under reg 15(3) of the 2015 Regulations.

[15.91] *SI 538/2021 Immigration Act 2004 (Visas) (Amendment) (No 3) Order 2021*

The Order further amends the Immigration Act 2004 (Visas) Order 2014.

It reinstates the Short-Stay Visa Waiver Programme, with effect from 31 October 2021, to extend the Programme until 31 October 2026.

The Order adds Colombia, Indonesia, Kosovo, Peru, Philippines, Republic of North Macedonia and Vietnam to the list of states or territorial entities in Schedule 3 of the 2014 Order whose nationals may be covered by the Programme.

Industrial Relations

[15.92] *SI 608/2020 Employment Regulation (Amendment) Order (Contract Cleaning Joint Labour Committee) 2020*

This Order fixes the statutory minimum rates of remuneration and other conditions of employment for workers employed in the Contract Cleaning Industry, providing cleaning and janitorial services in, or on the exterior of establishments including hospitals, offices, shops, stores, factories, apartment buildings, hotels, airports and similar establishments.

Joint Labour Committee for the Early Years' Service

[15.93] *SI 292/2021 Early Years' Service Joint Labour Committee Establishment Order 2021*

The Early Years' Service Joint Labour Committee Establishment Order 2021 came into operation on 1 July 2021. This Order gives effect to the recommendation of the Labour Court for the establishment of a Joint Labour Committee for the Early Years' Service sector.

The Schedule to the Order sets out the scope of the sector to include:

— services providing service to children who have not attained the age of six years and who are not attending a recognised school; and

— services which cater for children under the age of 15 years enrolled in a school providing primary or post-primary education and which provides a range of activities that are developmental, educational and recreational in manner outside of school hours and the primary purpose of which is to care for children where their parents are unavailable, and the basis for access to which service is made publicly known to the parents and guardians of the children but excluding services solely providing activities relating to the arts, youth work, competitive or recreational sport, tuition and religious teaching.

[15.94] The Schedule to the Order provides that the Order is not designed to include the care of children by a relative, the exclusive care of children of the same family in that person's home or does not include the care of one or more children undertaken by a relative of the child or children or a person taking care of not more than six children, of which not more than three are pre-school children, of different families (other than the person's own such children) at the same time in that person's home.

The Schedule to the Order also sets out the scope of the workers in the sector to include workers who are wholly or mainly in direct contact with children and who are involved in the education and/or care of children, and managerial and supervisory workers.

National Minimum Wage

[15.95] *SI 517/2021 National Minimum Wage Order 2021*

The National Minimum Wage Order 2021 comes into effect on 1 January 2022.

This order was made on the basis of a recommendation dated 13 July 2021, from the Low Pay Commission under s 10C(1) of the National Minimum Wage Act 2000 (inserted by s 7 of the National Minimum Wage (Low Pay Commission) Act 2015). This Order sets the national minimum hourly rate of pay from 1 January 2022 at €10.50, and the board and lodging rates as follows:

1. Lodgings: €24.81 per week, or €3.55 per day; and
2. Board: €0.94 per hour worked.

Organisation of Working Time

[15.96] *SI 585/2020 European Union (Workers on Board Seagoing Fishing Vessels) (Organisation of Working Time) (Share Fishermen) Regulations 2020*

These Regulations implement art 21 of Directive 2003/88/EC in relation to certain aspects of organisation of working time as they relate to share fishermen working aboard Irish-registered seagoing fishing vessels. In particular, these Regulations set out the maximum hours of work and minimum hours of rest for share fishermen working on board such seagoing fishing vessels, along with requirements to maintain records of hours of work and rest for each fisherman. They also set out enforcement powers for authorised officers as well as offences and penalties for non-compliance.

Pensions

[15.97] *SI 87/2021 Occupational Pension Schemes (Revaluation) Regulations 2021*

This Regulation, made under ss 5 and 33 of the Pensions Act 1990 (as amended by s 23 of the Social Welfare and Pensions Act 2012), provides for a minus 0.3% revaluation of preserved benefits for 2020.

[15.98] *SI 128/2021 European Union (Occupational Pension Schemes) Regulations 2021*

The purpose of this statutory instrument is to amend the Pensions Act 1990 (ie, to transpose requirements of Directive (EU) 2016/2341 (IORPs) (recast)). Parts of the Directive were already transposed into Irish law, but some requirements of the Directive not already provided for in Irish law, are now transposed by these Regulations.

Different from the 1990 Act, these Regulations provide for a number of new require-ments in relation to governance. These new requirements include management standards in schemes, safekeeping of assets, the provision of clear and relevant information to members, the removal of obstacles to cross-border provision of pension services and the facilitation of cross-border transfer of schemes. In addition, the Regulations include provisions that aim to enhance the powers of the Pensions Authority. The aim of grant-ing enhanced powers is for effective supervision of occupational pensions, and also to provide for exchanges, disclosures or transmission of information.

[15.99] *SI 308/2021 Service Pay and Pensions Act 2017 (Section 19(4)) Order 2021*

Section 19 of the Public Service Pay and Pensions Act 2017 purports to restore the pay of the public servants whose pay was reduced in accordance with the Financial Emergency Measures in the Public Interest (No 2) Act 2009. The 2021 Order provides that from 1 July 2021, the annualised amount of the basic salary of a public servant to whom the Order applies stands at the amount at which it stood immediately before the enactment of s 2 of the Financial Emergency Measures in the Public Interest (No 2) Act 2009.

[15.100] *SI 632/2020—Public Service Pay and Pensions Act 2017 (Section 27(3)) Order 2020*

This Order provides for the annualised amount of the public service pension of a person to whom ss 25 and 26 of the Public Service Pay and Pensions Act 2017 does not apply. The Order also provides for full restoration of public service pension.

Protection of Young Persons

[15.101] *SI 250/2021 Protection of Young Persons (Employment) (Exclusion of Workers in the Fishing and Shipping Sectors) Regulations 2021*

These Regulations provide that an employer in the fishing or shipping sectors may employ a young person in either of those sectors on terms other than those specified in s 6(1)(a) of the Protection of Young Persons (Employment) Act 1996 provided that: any young person so employed is allowed equivalent compensatory rest time within a reasonable period, and, in the case of an employer in the fishing sector, such terms are in accordance with the requirements of reg 5(2) of the European Union (International Labour Organisation Work in Fishing Convention) (Minimum Age) Regulations 2020.

These Regulations revoke the Protection of Young Persons (Employment) (Exclusion of Workers in the Fishing and Shipping Sectors) Regulations 2014.

Regulated Professions (Health and Social Care)

[15.102] *SI 54/2021 Regulated Professions (Health and Social Care) (Amendment) Act 2020 (Commencement of Certain Provisions) Order 2021*

This Order provides for 10 February 2021 to be the commencement date of certain sections of the Regulated Professions (Health and Social Care) (Amendment) Act 2020, which amend the provisions under the Medical Practitioners Act 2007 relating to the registration on the Supervised Division of the Medical Council's Register.

[15.103] *SI 259/2021 Social Workers Registration Board Approved Qualifications Bye-Law 2021*

This Bye-law stipulates the minimum qualifications awarded in the State which are approved by the Social Workers Registration Board. These qualifications are the standard of proficiency required for registration with the Social Workers Registration Board in the State.

[15.104] *SI 409/2021 Regulated Professions (Health and Social Care) (Amendment) Act 2020 (Commencement) (No 3) Order 2021*

The Regulated Professions (Health and Social Care) (Amendment) Act 2020 (Commencement) (No 3) Order 2021 came into effect on 1 August 2021.

This Order appointed 1 August 2021 as the day on which certain provisions of the Regulated Professions (Health and Social Care) (Amendment) Act 2020 came into operation. The sections being commenced amend the Nurses and Midwives Act 2011 mainly in relation to registration and fitness to practise. The Order also commenced sections which amend the Pharmacy Act 2007 in relation to membership of disciplinary committees and in relation to reports by authorised officers.

[15.105] *SI 464/2021 Public Service Pay and Pensions Act 2017 (Section 42) (Payments to General Practitioners and Pharmacists for the Administration of Vaccines against Covid-19) (No 2) Regulations 2021*

These Regulations came into operation on 1 August 2021 and will cease to have effect on 1 January 2022. The Regulations provide for payments to be made to general practitioners and pharmacists for the administration of vaccines against Covid-19 to people either in a HSE-run mass vaccination clinic or in a location other than such a clinic, on behalf of the HSE.

Safety, Health and Welfare at Work

[15.106] *SI 528/2021 Safety, Health and Welfare at Work (Construction) (Amendment) Regulations 2021*

The Safety, Health and Welfare at Work (Construction) (Amendment) Regulations 2021 came into effect on 15 October 2021.

The purpose of these Regulations is to amend the Safety, Health and Welfare at Work (Construction) Regulations 2013 to gradually bring to an end the extended validity of safety awareness registration cards provided for by the introduction of the Safety, Health and Welfare at Work (Construction) (Amendment) Regulations 2020 (SI 102/2020).

[15.107] *SI 591/2021 European Union (Minimum Safety and Health Requirements for Improved Medical Treatment on Board Vessels) Regulations 2021*

These Regulations came into operation on 20 November 2021 and transposed Directive 92/29/EEC, as amended by Directive 2019/1834/EU on minimum safety and health requirements for improved medical treatment on board vessels. The Regulations apply to all vessels, except warships, non-commercial pleasure craft, inland waterway craft, and tugs operating in harbour areas. The Regulations provide that an owner of a vessel must ensure that there are sufficient medical supplies and equipment on board and that there are up-to-date medical guides available. The Regulations also provide minimum requirements for lifeboats and life-rafts, sick bays, and antidotes when carrying dangerous substances on board, and details on training requirements.

[15.108] *SI 610/2021 Safety, Health and Welfare at Work (General Application) (Amendment) Regulations 2021*

These Regulations amend the Safety, Health and Welfare at Work (General Application) Regulations 2007 (SI 299/2007) and became effective on 20 November 2021.

The Regulations revise Schedule 2 in relation to Personal Protective Equipment, and transpose the provisions of Directive 2019/1832/EU.

[15.109] *SI 619/2021 Safety, Health and Welfare at Work (General Application) (Amendment) (No 2) Regulations 2021*

These Regulations amend the Safety, Health and Welfare at Work (General Application) Regulations 2007 to 2021, introducing specific PPE requirements for operators of all-terrain vehicles (ATVs) when used as part of work practices. These Regulations become effective on 20 November 2023.

Sectoral Employment Order—Construction

[15.110] *SI 598/2021 Sectoral Employment Order (Construction Sector) 2021*

This Order comes into operation on 1 February 2022 and confirms the terms of the recommendation from the Labour Court under s 15 of the Industrial Relations (Amendment) Act 2015. The Order provides for statutory minimum pay, pension and sick pay entitlements for craft persons, construction operatives and apprentices employed in the construction sector.

Social Welfare (Consolidated Claims, Payments and Control)

[15.111] *SI 160/2021 Social Welfare (Consolidated Claims, Payments and Control) (Amendment) (No 9) (Covid-19 Pandemic Unemployment Payment—Entitlement to Increase for Qualified Adult) Regulations 2021*

These Regulations provide that where a person is in receipt of a social welfare payment which includes an increase for a qualified adult and the qualified adult concerned has an entitlement to Covid-19 pandemic unemployment payment in their own right, the increase for the qualified adult remains payable.

[15.112] *SI 161/2021 Social Welfare (Consolidated Claims, Payments and Control) (Amendment) (No 11) (Emergency Measures in the Public Interest-Jobseeker's Benefit) Regulations 2021*

These Regulations amend s 62(4) of the Social Welfare Consolidation Act 2005 by waiving the rule that jobseeker's benefit is paid only from the fourth day of unemployment until 30 June 2021.

[15.113] *SI 162/2021 Social Welfare (Consolidated Claims, Payments and Control) (Amendment) (No 12) (Emergency Measures in the Public Interest-Jobseeker's Allowance) Regulations 2021*

These Regulations amend s 141(2) of the Social Welfare Consolidation Act 2005 by suspending the rule that jobseeker's allowance is paid only from the fourth day of unemployment until 30 June 2021.

[15.114] *SI 234/2021 Social Welfare (Consolidated Contributions And Insurability) (Amendment) (No 1) (Reckonable Income) Regulations 2021*

The Regulations aim to provide clarification in relation to the voluntary contribution charge payable by previously employed social insurance contributors. For these purposes, all income is inclusive of income from any pension payable as a result of employment, when assessing the amount of the reckonable income of such contributors.

Training and Qualifications

[15.115] *SI 442/2021 European Union (Recognition of Professional Qualifications In Inland Navigation) Regulations 2021*

The European Union (Recognition of Professional Qualifications in Inland Navigation) Regulations 2021 come into effect on 17 January 2022.

They give effect to the derogation set out in art 39(3) of Directive (EU) 2017/2397, as amended, on the recognition of professional qualifications in inland navigation. The Regulations provide for the recognition by the State of certificates of qualification and service record books, held by crew in the field of inland navigation, which are recognised as being valid on all EU inland waterways, including inland waterways in the State. The Regulations also make provision for cooperating with other Member States regarding suspension of such certificates and the recording of navigation time and journeys for holders of service record books.

[15.116] *SI 454/2021 European Union (Training, Certification and Watchkeeping for Seafarers) (Amendment) Regulations 2021*

These Regulations amend the European Union (Training, Certification and Watchkeeping for Seafarers) Regulations 2014 (SI 242/2014) to give effect to amendments introduced by Directive (EU) 2019/1159 including updated minimum requirements for training and qualifications of seafarers on ships subject to the IGF and Polar Codes, as well as masters, officers, ratings and other personnel on passenger ships. The Regulations also provide for revised requirements on the mutual recognition of seafarers' certificates issued by Member States.

[15.117] *SI 491/2021 Radiographers Registration Board Approved Qualifications and Divisions of the Register (Amendment) Bye-Law 2021*

This Bye-law was made by the Radiographers Registration Board in exercise of its powers under s 31 of the Health and Social Care Professional Act 2005 as amended. It became effective on 28 September 2021 and amends the Radiographers Registration Board Approved Qualifications and Divisions of the Register Bye-law 2021 (SI 375/2021).

This Bye-law identifies the qualifications awarded in the State which are approved by the Radiographers Registration Board as attesting to the standard of proficiency required for registration in the Radiographers Division of the register established by the Radiographers Registration Board. It also identifies the conditions for registration in the Radiographers Division of that register.

Workplace Relations (Miscellaneous Provisions) Act 2021

[15.118] *SI 397/2021 Workplace Relations (Miscellaneous Provisions) Act 2021 (Commencement) Order 2021*

This Order provided 29 July 2021 as the day on which the Workplace Relations (Miscellaneous Provisions) Act 2021 came into operation.

Worker Participation (State Enterprises) Act 1988

[15.119] *SI 484/2021 Worker Participation (State Enterprises) Act 1988 (Section 9) Order 2021*

This Order provides that every employee of Aer Rianta International cpt and daa International Ltd shall, for the purposes of the Worker Participation (State Enterprises) Acts 1977 to 2001, be regarded as an employee of daa plc.

Chapter 16

Part-Time Work

INTRODUCTION

[16.01] Whether a part-time worker, who works fewer hours on any shift than their full-time comparators should be entitled to the work breaks associated with the longer hours was considered by the UK EAT in *Forth Valley*.

Less Favourable Treatment

[16.02] *Forth Valley Health Board v Campbell[1]—UK Employment Appeal Tribunal—appeal from employment tribunal—Part-Time Workers (Prevention of Less Favourable Treatment) Regulations 2000,[2] reg 5—part-time employee—less favourable treatment*

The claimant, a part-time employee of the respondent, brought a claim under the Part-Time Workers (Prevention of Less Favourable Treatment) Regulations 2000 (the Regulations) claiming that the fact that he did not receive a paid 15-minute break during certain shifts amounted to less favourable treatment on the basis of his part-time status, contrary to reg 5(2)(a), which prohibits less favourable treatment than a comparable full-time worker, 'on the ground that the worker is a part-time worker'.

The employment tribunal held that this claim did amount to less favourable treatment on the ground of the claimant's part-time status, contrary to reg 5(2)(a) and awarded him £965 in compensation. The respondent appealed this decision to the EAT.

The EAT noted the facts agreed between the parties, ie, the entitlement to a paid, 15-minute break arose when an employee worked a shift of six hours or more. The claimant, as a part-time employee, only worked six-hour shifts at weekends and when he worked these shifts, he received a paid 15-minute break. He did not receive this paid break when he worked on weekdays, as on those days he worked shorter, four-hour shifts. The claimant's chosen comparator was a full-time employee, who worked eight-hour shifts and so always received a 15-minute break.

---

[1]   *Forth Valley Health Board v Campbell* [2021] UKEAT/0003/21/2708.
[2]   Part-Time Workers (Prevention of Less Favourable Treatment) Regulations 2000 (SI 2000/1551).

The EAT noted that at first instance, the tribunal had rejected the respondent's assertion that the reason the claimant was not afforded the paid break when he worked a four-hour shift was because of the length of the shift, not because of his status as a part-time worker. The tribunal had found this argument 'circular and not well founded', stating that it undermined the purpose of the Regulations, as 'a part-time worker by definition was going to work less [sic] hours than a full time comparator'. As such, the tribunal held that the 'sole reason' the claimant was not afforded the break was because of his part-time status.

The EAT held that the tribunal 'fell into error by conflating the two different issues of total hours worked on the one hand and shift length on the other'. Although it noted the tribunal was correct to say that a part-time employee will, necessarily, work less hours than a full-time employee, it held that 'it is hard to see how the Tribunal was able to reach the conclusion that the week-day shift pattern worked by the Claimant was in any way related to his part-time status. Nothing in its findings in fact or in the agreed facts justified such an inference.' It also noted *McMenemy v Capita Business Services Ltd*,[3] in which the Court had held that for reg 5(2)(a) to be breached, the workers' part time status must be the *sole* reason for the less favourable treatment.

The EAT concluded 'having regard to the facts as agreed and found by the Tribunal, there was no basis in law on which the Tribunal could properly have come to the view that the difference in treatment between the Claimant and his full time comparator was "on the ground" that he was a part-time worker, far less that his part-time status was the sole ground for such difference in treatment (per *McMenemy*)'. Accordingly it allowed the appeal and dismissed the claim.

---

[3]   *McMenemy v Capita Business Services Ltd* [2007] IRLR 400.

Chapter 17

Partnership

INTRODUCTION

[17.01]   The High Court of England and Wales considered the exercise of a discretionary power by a law firm under a partnership agreement in *Tribe*.

Partnership Agreement

[17.02]   *Tribe v Elborne Mitchell LLP[1]—High Court of England and Wales—Karet J—partnership—exercise of a discretion under a partnership agreement*

The claimant, a retired solicitor, instituted proceedings against his former firm. The claimant had been a partner in the firm and its predecessor for more than 25 years. The claimant claimed that he was not awarded a fair profit share in the last two years of his partnership. The partnership was governed by a Members' Agreement (the Agreement).

The Agreement provided that the profits for each year should be divided on the basis that each equity partner would receive a fixed share. If there was a profit, a discretionary fund would be created comprising of up to 40% of the total distributable profit. That discretionary fund was to be allocated by a resolution of the partnership on the recommendation of the senior partner who was to have substantial regard for financial performance. The partners then received an equal share of anything that remained.

The claimant claimed that in respect of the years in question, the senior partner's recommendation and the decision of the partnership did not abide by the constraints on the exercise of a discretionary power set out by the Supreme Court in *Braganza v BP Shipping Ltd*.[2] There was also a dispute as to the correct construction of the Agreement.

In approaching the construction of the Agreement, the Court, bearing in mind the Supreme Court decision in *Wood v Capita Insurance Services*,[3] proceeded on the basis

---

[1]   *Tribe v Elborne Mitchell LLP* [2021] EWHC 1863 (Ch).
[2]   *Braganza v BP Shipping Ltd* [2015] UKSC 17.
[3]   *Wood v Capita Insurance Services* [2017] UKSC 24.

that where there are rival meanings, the Court can give weight to the implications of rival constructions by reaching a view as to which construction is more consistent with business common sense.

Turning to the exercise of the discretion, the Court concluded that where in any contract, one party is permitted to exercise a discretion in making an assessment or choosing from a range of options, taking into account the interest of both parties, there is an implied term. The precise formulation of that term has been variously expressed. In essence, it is that the relevant party will not exercise its discretion in an arbitrary, capricious or irrational manner. Such a term is extremely difficult although not impossible to exclude.

The Court noted that the Court of Appeal in *Re Charterhouse Capital Ltd*,[4] which concerned a special resolution to amend the articles of association of a company, set out, by reference to previous caselaw, the principles that apply in such a situation as follows:

(1) The limitations on the exercise of the power ... arise because ... the manner of their exercise is constrained by the purpose of the power and because the framers of the power of a majority to bind a minority will not, in the absence of clear words, have intended the power to be completely without limitation. These principles may be characterised ... as implied terms ...

(2) A power to amend will be validly exercised if it is exercised in good faith in the interests of the company ...

(3) It is for the shareholders, and not the court, to say whether an alteration of the articles is for the benefit of the company but it will not be for the benefit of the company if no reasonable person would consider it to be such ...

(4) The view of shareholders acting in good faith that a proposed alteration of the articles is for the benefit of the company, and which cannot be said to be a view which no reasonable person could hold, is not impugned by the fact that one or more of the shareholders was actually acting under some mistake of fact or lack of knowledge or understanding ... the court will not investigate the quality of the subjective views of such shareholders.

(5) The mere fact that the amendment adversely affects, and even if it is intended adversely to affect, one or more minority shareholders and benefit others does not, of itself, invalidate the amendment if the amendment is made in good faith in the interests of the company ...

(6) A power to amend will also be validly exercised, even though the amendment is not for the benefit of the company because it relates to a matter in which the company as an entity has no interest but rather is only for the benefit of shareholders as such or some of them, provided that the amendment does not amount to oppression of a minority or is otherwise unjust or is outside the scope of the power ...

(7) The burden is on the person impugning the validity of the amendment of the articles to satisfy the court that there are grounds for doing so.

---

4   *Re Charterhouse Capital Ltd* [2015] EWCA Civ. 536.

The parties were agreed that those principles applied to the relevant decisions of the firm. They also agreed that in the context of an LLP, a decision-making power must be exercised in good faith and in what the member considers to be the best interests of the LLP.

The Court concluded that the senior partner must exercise good faith in making the recommendations and must not take into account irrelevant matters or ignore relevant ones. The recommendation should be reasonable in the circumstances. It is a broad discretion, because it is a recommendation to the partners, not a final decision, and because it is about matters on which the partners may have a range of opinions. Partners can discuss the recommendations and their concerns with the others, and they must agree that the recommendations of the senior partner meet the tests in *Re Charterhouse*. The decision should be reasonable in the circumstances of allocating the discretionary fund.

Applying the principles above, the Court found the recommendations of the senior partner to be reasonable and the partners' resolution following those recommendations to be valid. The claim was dismissed

Chapter 18

Pensions

BUDGET 2022

[18.01] Budget 2022 was announced on 12 October 2021. The budget did not make any changes to private pensions. There was no change to the state pension age (currently 66). The state pension will be increased from €248 to €253. The living alone allowance will be increased by €3 to €22.

DIRECTIVE (EU) 2016/2341[1] (IORP II DIRECTIVE)

IORP II Directive transposed into Irish law

[18.02] The IORP II Directive was transposed into Irish law by way of the European Union (Occupational Pension Schemes) Regulations, 2021[2] (the 2021 Regulations). The 2021 Regulations were signed into law by the Minister for Social Protection on 22 April 2021.

The Minister indicated that, in keeping with the Government's Roadmap for Pensions Reform, the requirements of the IORP II Directive will apply to all funded occupational pension schemes and trust RACs, including small schemes (albeit with a five-year lead in for one-member arrangements)—'pay-as-you-go' unfunded public sector arrangements are excluded from the scope of the 2021 Regulations (as the IORP II Directive does not apply to them).

The 2021 Regulations introduce increased governance, investment and disclosure requirements for trustees of pension schemes and significantly increased oversight and intervention powers for the Pensions Authority. The 2021 Regulations also remove some obstacles to cross-border provision of pension services and the facilitation of cross-border transfer of schemes. The 2021 Regulations apply to most funded arrangements immediately with an obligation to provide a compliance statement (in a form to be prescribed by the Pensions Authority) by 31 January in each year regarding compliance

---

[1]   Directive (EU) 2016/2341 on the activities and supervision of institutions for occupational retirement provision.

[2]   European Union (Occupational Pension Schemes) Regulations 2021 (SI 128/2021).

in the previous year. The first such statement is to be provided by 31 January 2022 for compliance in 2021.

Key highlights include the following:

— Trustee requirements: knowledge, experience, fitness and probity. Minimum of two compliant trustees by 31 December 2021.

— Effective governance system including written policies on risk management, internal audit, actuarial functions and outsourcing.

— Requirement to have internal control system.

— Key function holders to be appointed: risk management, internal audit and actuarial by 31 January 2022.

— Current one-member arrangements not required to comply for five years (ie, April 2026). New ones to comply immediately.

— Requirement to issue pension benefit statement to members (including deferred members) annually from 2022.

— Increased Pensions Authority powers: compliance statement and notification requirements for outsourcing arrangements.

— Trustees must conduct own risk assessment every three years: first such statement due by April 2024.

— Whistleblowing obligations: key function holders (and depositary where appointed) have whistleblowing obligations.

Pensions Authority IORP II Draft Code of Practice

On 22 July 2021 the Pensions Authority (the Authority) published a draft code of practice for trustees of occupational pension schemes and trust Retirement Annuity Contracts (RACs) (the Code). The draft Code sets out the Authority's expectations for the conduct and practice of trustees of pension schemes. It is stated as not intending to 'prescribe how to comply with every requirement under legislation' but is to provide further explanation of how to comply with specific requirements that have been introduced by the 2021 Regulations. The Code was open for public consultation up to 16 September and the final Code is due to be published in the week commencing 15 November 2021.

The Authority has indicated that the format of the Annual Compliance Statement (ACS) form will be published in the week of 15 November 2021, with trustees expected to prepare the 2021 ACS before 31 January 2022. Trustees will not be required to submit the 2021 ACS to the Authority in 2022, although the Authority may request sight of the 2021 ACS from trustees as part of its ongoing supervisory activity. Trustees will be required to submit the 2022 ACS by the end of February 2023. Further details will be provided by the Authority on how to make the 2022 ACS submission during the course of 2022. The ACS must be certified for accuracy and completed by at least two trustees (or in the case of a corporate trustee by at least two directors).

The Authority has indicated that it will publish specific guidance in relation to the application of IORP II to master trusts in December 2021, and to small self-administered schemes and single member schemes in October 2021.

LEGISLATION

Social Welfare Act 2020

[18.03]   The Social Welfare Act 2020 was enacted on 22 December 2020 and, among other things, repeals s 7 of the Social Welfare and Pensions Act 2011. The effect of this is to cancel the increase in the state pension age to 67 (previously due to take effect from 1 January 2021) and the further increase to age 68 (previously due to take effect from 1 January 2028).

This change will affect scheme rules that were previously amended to take into account the planned increase in State pension age. Any such rules will require to be reviewed once the Government decides what action to take with regard to increasing state pension age in light of the Report of the Pensions Commission, which is investigating this issue.

Occupational Pension Schemes (Revaluation) Regulations 2021

[18.04]   The Occupational Pension Schemes (Revaluation) Regulations 2021[3] were enacted on 22 February 2021 and prescribe a revaluation factor of negative 0.3% in respect of the revaluation of preserved benefits under s 33 of the Pensions Act 1990 (as amended) for the year 2020.

Criminal Justice (Money Laundering and Terrorist Financing) (Amendment) Act 2021

[18.05]   With effect from 29 January 2019, all occupational pension schemes established under trust were required to (among other things) take 'all reasonable steps' to gather and hold certain information on the pension scheme's beneficial owners and set up a beneficial ownership register. This requirement has now been revoked for Revenue Commissioner approved schemes. The effect of commencement of relevant sections of the Criminal Justice (Money Laundering and Terrorist Financing) (Amendment) Act 2021, along with the coming into operation of the European Union (Anti-Money Laundering: Beneficial Ownership of Trusts) Regulations 2021,[4] means that, with effect from 24 April 2021, occupational pension schemes (where established as an approved scheme under Pt 30 of the Taxes Consolidation Act 1997), among other arrangements

---

3   Occupational Pension Schemes (Revaluation) Regulations 2021 (SI 87/2021).
4   European Union (Anti-Money Laundering: Beneficial Ownership of Trusts) Regulations 2021 (SI 194/2021).

(including approved retirement funds), are excluded from the requirement to establish and maintain a beneficial ownership register. It also means that they are not included in the new requirement to file a return of beneficial ownership information to the State's central register of beneficial ownership established for trusts. (*NB*—the exemption applies to the scheme trust but where there is a corporate trustee the requirement to disclose the beneficial owners of that corporate trustee remains.).

The Sustainable Finance Disclosure Regulation[5]

[18.06] The Sustainable Finance Disclosure Regulation (the SFDR) was published in January 2020 and took effect on 10 March 2021. Its aim is to lay down harmonised rules on transparency with regard to the integration of 'sustainability' risks, the consideration of adverse sustainability impacts, the provision of sustainability-related information, and to support the European Union's goals in relation to climate, sustainability and the environment. The SFDR will apply to all financial market participants which term includes pension funds.

Certain obligations (involving high-level, principles-based disclosure requirements) came into effect on 10 March 2022. These are due to be supplemented by more detailed requirements due to enter into force from 1 July 2022.

The broad impact is that trustees are required to take environmental, social and governance factors (with related disclosures) into account in the context of the requirements under both SFDR and IORP II (and to a related degree under the Shareholders' Rights Directive[6] (SRD)).

This is an area where practice will no doubt develop both in Statement of Investment Policy Principles (SIPPs) and investment management agreements and reporting.

EUROPEAN LEGISLATION

EMIR (European Market Infrastructure Regulation)

[18.07] EMIR Regulation 648/2012[7] as amended by EMIR Refit Regulation 2019/834[8] (together the Regulation) was published in the *Official Journal* on 28 May 2019 and came into force on 17 June 2019. Under the Regulation, certain pension arrangements (which are deemed to be financial counterparties under the Regulation) are required to clear certain over the counter (OTC) derivative contracts including interest rate,

---

5   Regulation (EU) 2019/2088 on sustainability-related disclosures in the financial services sector.
6   Directive (EU) 2017/828 amending Directive 2007/36/EC as regards the encouragement of long-term shareholder engagement.
7   Regulation (EU) 648/2012 on OTC derivatives, central counterparties and trade repositories.
8   Regulation (EU) 2019/834 amending Regulation (EU) 648/2012 as regards the clearing obligation, the suspension of the clearing obligation, the reporting requirements, the risk-mitigation techniques for OTC derivative contracts not cleared by a central counterparty, the registration and supervision of trade repositories and the requirements for trade repositories.

foreign exchange, equity, credit and commodity derivatives via a central counterparty. Pension arrangements had originally been granted an exemption in respect of these clearing obligations until 18 June 2021.

The Commission Delegated Regulation (EU) 2021/962[9] was recently published in the *Official Journal* and this regulation has further extended the central clearing exemption for pension arrangements by a further year until 18 June 2022.

PENSIONS AUTHORITY

Defined Benefit Engagement Programme Findings Report

[18.08]   The Pensions Authority (the Authority) met with selected defined benefit scheme trustees as part of the engagement programme in order to examine governance practices, with a particular focus on the management of scheme risks. It also examined how well schemes were equipped to meet the imminent IORP II enhanced governance and risk management requirements.

In the Defined Benefit Engagement Programme Findings Report (the Report), published in December 2020, the Authority found that while many trustee boards demonstrated a strong performance, it expressed concern that in a number of cases there was 'incompleteness of risks identified, poor identification of controls, failure to implement controls, and a general lack of risk awareness'.

The Report focuses on six key areas—risk identification/mitigation; employer covenant; management of outsourced services; conflicts of interest; independence/challenge (ie, independence of trustee thought process and trustee challenge of scheme advisers); and member communication—and provides an important insight for trustees on the views, approach and expectations of the Authority in each of these areas.

The Authority noted in the Report that, in future, trustees will be asked to prepare and examine a much wider range of financial and actuarial data than they currently do and that trustees should focus on what might happen in the future; not just on what has happened to date. The Authority recommended that, in order to achieve this, many trustees will need to improve board understanding in the areas of risk quantification, risk management, risk interdependencies and scenario-planning tools. The Report's appendix sets out the types of information likely to be sought by the Authority as part of its future engagement with the trustees of defined benefit schemes.

In the conclusion of the Report, the Authority reminded readers that the level of supervisory attention given by the Authority to a defined benefit scheme will 'depend on the likelihood of the scheme meeting the benefit obligations set out in the scheme rules' and that schemes will be categorised on this basis. Schemes will be notified in due course to which category they have been assigned.

---

9   Regulation (EU) 2021/962 extending the transitional period referred to in art 89(1), first subparagraph, of Regulation (EU) 648/2012.

Report on master trust engagement

Between January and September 2020, the Authority undertook an engagement programme with a number of defined contribution master trusts and the firms responsible for establishing master trust arrangements. The report containing the Authority's findings was published in November 2020.

The main findings of the Authority included:

(a) *Governance*: Very few master trusts had independent trustees; rather they consisted of employees of the founder. In some instances, it was evident that the trustee boards had little autonomy in decision-making, as all major decisions required prior consultation with or approval of the founder.

(b) *Appointment of service providers*: In appointing service providers many trustee boards were required to consult with or seek approval from the founder demonstrating a lack of independence in relation to the trustee board; and the Authority saw little evidence of the criteria or scenarios trustees would consider before changing a service provider demonstrating a lack of quality control.

(c) *Investment*: In many cases the investment objectives set by trustees of master trusts were inadequate with no clear performance target levels and while some master trusts have incorporated environmental, social and governance (ESG) factors into investment decisions, the majority had given little consideration to this matter.

(d) *Charges for members and employers*: The Authority was disappointed at the lack of transparency around master trust charges and especially found it difficult to identify all investment charges.

(e) *Risk management, internal audit and internal controls*: Although IORP II has not yet been implemented in Ireland, the Authority is of the view that the requirements of IORP II in relation to these matters are well known; yet, in most cases, there was little evidence of a robust system of risk management or effective internal audit functions being implemented.

(f) *Member/employer communications*: Most master trusts provided useful communications to members through a number of channels. However, there was little evidence of written policies for member engagement which the Authority would expect to see.

The report is a useful signpost to some of the material issues that employers and trustees need to fully consider in the context of evaluating the merits of any proposal to join or migrate to a master trust arrangement.

Pensions Authority Conviction of Company Director

On 26 July 2021, a director of Total Facades Ltd was convicted in Waterford District Court for failing to remit employee pension contributions to the trustee of the Construction Workers Pension Scheme (CWPS) within the statutory timeframe under s 58A(1) of the Pensions Act 1990, as amended. Total Facades Ltd had deducted pension contributions from the wages and salaries of its employees between April and August 2018 for remittance to the trustee of CWPS but had failed to remit the contributions within the statutory timeframe. A significant portion of the employee contributions due to the scheme were repaid prior to sentencing and the director was fined €1,000 for the failure.

REVENUE UPDATE

Revenue Update to Pensions Manual, Chapter 2

[18.09]   Chapter 2 of the Revenue Pensions Manual (Membership of Occupational Pension Schemes) was amended in September 2021 to require that pension administrators should notify Revenue via MyEnquiries (or by email for Transport Layer Security (TLS) enabled administrators) where an employee is temporarily absent or is seconded for a period exceeding five years and who remains as a member of an occupational pension scheme.

Revenue Update to Pensions Manual, Chapter 23

[18.10]   On 29 June 2021, Revenue updated Chapter 23 of the Pensions Manual to provide updated guidance for non-resident owners of Approved Retirement Funds (ARFs), vested Personal Retirement Savings Accounts (PRSAs) or Approved Minimum Retirement Funds (AMRFs).

Among the updates, Revenue included a link to the new Refund of Taxes Paid on ARF Distributions Claim form which is to be completed by non-resident claimants seeking a repayment of Irish tax on an Irish pension as well as additional information for refund claims made by non-resident claimants with unit linked ARF funds. The additional information includes further detail and worked examples in relation to the application of double taxation agreements to distributions from ARFs, vested PRSAs and AMRFs.

CASE LAW

Irish Case Law

[18.11]   *O'Connell v The Financial Services and the Pensions Ombudsman*[10]*—High Court—O'Connor J—improper cancellation of life assurance policies*

The High Court dismissed the appeal against the Financial Services and the Pensions Ombudsman's (FSPO) decision to partially uphold Mr O'Connell's complaint that his life assurance policies had been incorrectly cancelled. The Court restated the

---

10   *O'Connell v The Financial Services and the Pensions Ombudsman* [2020] IEHC 559.

test for such appeals as set out by Finnegan J in *Ulster Bank v Financial Services Ombudsman*:[11]

(1) The burden of proof is on the appellant.
(2) The onus of proof is the civil standard.
(3) The court should not consider complaints about process or merits in isolation, but rather should consider the adjudicative process as a whole.
(4) The onus is on the appellant to show that the decision reached was vitiated by a serious and significant error or a series of such errors.
(5) The court will adopt a deferential stance having regard to the degree of expertise and specialist knowledge of the Ombudsman.

O'Connor J noted that Mr O'Connell had 'singularly failed to persuade this Court of any serious and significant error made by the Ombudsman' and that 'cherry picking or isolating an apparent error is not sufficient'. The case highlights the high threshold that must be overcome by individual claimants in order to set aside a decision of the FSPO.

[18.12] *Utmost Paneurope DAC v FSPO and W*[12]—*High Court—Simons J— insurance claim—inability to work due to disability—whether medical condition covered by insurance*

The claimant made a claim to her insurer on the basis of her inability to work due to disability, caused by two conditions, fibromyalgia and rheumatoid arthritis. In making her claim, she argued that her disability was predominantly due to the rheumatoid arthritis which was covered by her income policy with Utmost Paneurope DAC (UPE), the fibromyalgia was not. This was rejected by UPE as it was the claimant's fibromyalgia which predominantly impacted her ability to work.

The FSPO upheld the complaint, concluding that UPE had placed too great an emphasis on quantifying the level of impact the two medical conditions had on the claimant's ability to work. It found that this was unreasonable and unfair to the claimant and directed UPE to retrospectively admit the claim and make future payments to the claimant.

UPE appealed the FSPO's decision to the High Court. In his judgment, Simons J considered two main issues:

(a) whether the FSPO had made a significant error in law; and
(b) whether the remedy directed by the FSPO was valid.

Ultimately, the Court concluded that the FSPO erred in determining UPE was unreasonable. The FSPO placed too great an emphasis on UPE's decision to decline cover without measuring that conduct against both the Consumer Protection Code and the terms of the policy, which expressly permitted UPE to verify a claim's validity before deciding whether to admit that claim.

In doing so, the High Court made it clear that, although the FSPO has a hybrid jurisdiction, the two elements are not entirely independent of each other and there is necessarily some degree of overlap. The High Court indicated that the FSPO is

---

[11] *Ulster Bank v Financial Services Ombudsman* [2006] IEHC 323.
[12] *Utmost Paneurope DAC v FSPO and W* [2020] IEHC 538.

not free to ignore the plain terms of a contract when making a decision based on the conduct and/or reasonableness of an insurance provider. The High Court overturned the FSPO's decision and directed it to reconsider the complaint.

UK Case Law

[18.13]   *Britvic Plc v Britvic Pensions Ltd and Simon Richard Mohun*[13]—*Court of Appeal of England and Wales—Sir Vos MR, Coulson and Nugee LJJ—interpretation of words in pension plan—retail price index*

The Court of Appeal of England and Wales unanimously overturned the High Court ruling,[14] adding to the long line of case law on judicial interpretation of documents, and reflecting the courts' reluctance to resort to corrective construction when dealing with unambiguous language. The case revolved around the 'beguilingly simple' issue as to the correct interpretation of the words 'any other rate' contained in Rule C.10(2) of the Britvic Pension Plan. This rule provided that members' and executives' pensions would increase in line with the retail price index, subject to a cap of 5% 'or any other rate decided by the Principal Employer'.

The High Court found that Rule C.10(2) created a two-stage mechanism whereby the trustees would apply the retail price index by default and then, the employer could exercise its discretion to apply a higher, but not lower, rate instead. According to the High Court, to read 'any other rate' as 'any other rate, higher or lower' would be 'excessively literal' and the Court therefore favoured an interpretation which would give 'reasonable and practical effect to the scheme' and which was more consistent with 'business common sense'. The High Court supported this interpretation, arguing that the drafter would have intended to comply with s 51(3) of the Pensions Act 1995, which requires increases of at least the 'relevant percentage'. The High Court also relied on elements of documentary evidence including the outline benefit summary which guaranteed rate increases equivalent to predecessor plans to new members.

The Court of Appeal conceded that the interpretation of the High Court was more in line with the contextual and legislative background. However, recalling the approach provided by Lord Hodge in *Barnardo's v Buckinghamshire*[15] for interpreting pension scheme deeds, the Court of Appeal was bound to start by analysing the language used and attribute less weight to the factual matrix.

After reflecting on the case law on interpretation (*Investors Compensation Scheme Ltd v West Bromwich Building Society*;[16] *Chartbrook Ltd v Persimmon Homes Ltd*;[17]

---

13   *Britvic Plc v Britvic Pensions Ltd and Simon Richard Mohun* [2021] EWCA Civ 867.
14   *Britvic Plc v Britvic Pensions Ltd and Simon Richard Mohun* [2020] EWHC 118 (Ch).
15   *Barnardo's v Buckinghamshire* [2018] UKSC 55.
16   *Investors Compensation Scheme Ltd v West Bromwich Building Society* [1998] 1 WLR 896.
17   *Chartbrook Ltd v Persimmon Homes Ltd* [2009] 1 AC 1101.

Rainy Sky SA v Kookmin Bank;[18] *Arnold v Britton;*[19] *Wood v Capita Insurance Services Ltd*[20]), the Court of Appeal concluded that because 'any other rate' in its natural and ordinary meaning means 'any other rate, higher or lower', it must be interpreted as such. While it was recognised that the drafter may have made an error in the wording of the rule, the Court was not satisfied that an 'obvious mistake on the face of the document' was made, nor that there was a clear cure to the mistake, so as to justify a corrective construction.

[18.14] *Punter Southall Governance Services Ltd v Jonathan Hazlett (as a representative defendant)*[21] *(Axminster Carpets)—High Court of England and Wales—Morgan J—occupational pension scheme—unclaimed benefits—forfeiture provisions—trustees' discretion*

The Axminster Carpets case revolved around a number of legal issues in the Axminster Carpets Group Retirement Benefits Plan (the Plan). This case primarily related to the validity of forfeiture provisions and trustees' discretion with regard to unclaimed benefits. Forfeiture provisions are often included in occupational pension schemes, stating that a member loses their right to benefits if they do not claim the benefits after a certain period of time (typically six years).

The Plan was established in 1961 and came to be governed by a definitive trust deed and rules in 1992 (the 1992 Deed). The 1992 Deed contained a clause which gave the trustee the ability to apply unclaimed monies for other purposes. As the clause did not contain clear and explicit wording to the effect that a member's right to benefits would be forfeited if unclaimed after a specified period of time it was held that the clause did not constitute an effective forfeiture provision.

A further deed was drafted in 2001 (the 2001 Deed) which contained explicit language to the effect that benefits would be forfeited if unclaimed. In contrast to the 1992 Deed, it was held that the explicit reference to forfeiture rendered this provision an effective forfeiture provision.

Interestingly, the High Court of England and Wales found that a forfeiture provision does not necessarily contravene a scheme's amendment power (to the extent that it contains a restriction on diminishing accrued benefits) as it does not always act to diminish the benefits to be provided to members. As the forfeiture only operated in circumstances where a member failed to make a claim, it could not be said that benefits were diminished but rather there was merely a risk of same.

The Court further offered guidance on the extent of a trustee's discretion to use unpaid monies. It outlined that a trustee must first ensure that members are not underpaid as members are often not at fault for a failure to claim monies. However, the Court noted that other factors such as administrative difficulties in paying arrears or previous

---

[18] *Rainy Sky SA v Kookmin Bank* [2011] UKSC 50.
[19] *Arnold v Britton* [2015] UKSC 36.
[20] *Wood v Capita Insurance Services Ltd* [2017] UKSC 24.
[21] *Punter Southall Governance Services Ltd v Jonathan Hazlett (as a representative defendant)* [2021] EWHC 1652 (Ch) (*Axminster Carpets*).

underpayment due to an error of a previous trustee may be considered when using monies for purposes other than paying members.

The Court also offered guidance on the limitation period for claiming arrears. It stated that there is no limitation period for a member to claim arrears or compensation for a breach of trust caused by a current trustee. In circumstances where such arrears or breach of trust arise as a result of the actions of a previous trustee, members have a period of six years from the breach in which to pursue a claim against the previous trustee. The Court considered that a claim for arrears does not include interest but the court may award such interest at its discretion while claims for breach may include interest.

This case underlines the importance of clear drafting when including a forfeiture clause in a trust deed. Further, the case provides useful guidance to trustees as regards their discretion in dealing with unpaid monies as well as the options available to members in pursuing claims for unpaid benefits and breaches of trust against current and former trustees.

[18.15]   *Iggesund Paperboard (Workington) Ltd, Iggesund (UK) Pensions Ltd v Messenger[22]—High Court of England and Wales—Chief Master Marsh—pension increase rule amended—retail price index—lack of flexibility—rectification of pension deed*

This case concerned a pension increase rule which, prior to the scheme being amended, had facilitated the use of an index other than the retail price index (RPI) to be applied to pension increases. The amended version of the trust deed and rules omitted the former flexibility (by omitting the words 'or such other index as the actuary advises to be appropriate') thus hardwiring RPI as the basis for increases to pensions in payment.

The High Court noted that there are:

> two common situations in which rectification of pension deeds is sought. The first is where the employer and trustees intended to make a particular change but the change was incorrectly reduced to writing. The second is where the employer and trustee did not intend to make the amendments, so that they did not address their minds at all to the relevant words.

The present case was deemed to fall into the second category in that the words were omitted and their omission was not spotted.

The case highlights the detailed gathering of evidence which is required in a claim for rectification. The Court noted on a detailed review of the documentation relating to the drafting of the amended deed and rules as well as evidence from the individuals involved in drafting same that 'there was an error which was carried through from the beginning of the drafting process'. The Court noted that this occurred notwithstanding the full review of the documents by specialist advisers. The Court described the case as 'the clearest possible case for rectification of a pension deed based on an

---

[22]   *Iggesund Paperboard (Workington) Ltd, Iggesund (UK) Pensions Ltd v Messenger* [2021] EWHC 627 (Ch).

omission that was not noted by any of the persons involved'. It concluded that 'the short point is that there is no good reason to make any other order than an absolute order for rectification in the circumstances of this case where what has been uncovered is clearly an unintended error'.

[18.16] *Burns v Burns[23]—High Court of England and Wales—Master Teverson—Civil Procedure Rules, Pt 24—self-invested pension plan—dishonest assistance*

The claimant, Mr Burns, made a claim of dishonest assistance against three members of a limited liability partnership (the Part 24 defendants) in the High Court of England and Wales and applied for summary judgment in line with Pt 24 of the Civil Procedure Rules.

The claimant held a personal pension worth £293,782 with a wealth management company until he was induced by his cousin, Mr Keith Burns, to transfer the balance into a self-invested pension plan managed by Castle Trust. Castle Trust transferred 80% of this sum to Capitis Fora LLP, the members of which were the Part 24 defendants. The funds were invested by Capitis Fora in property development without adequate security and were lost.

Although the claimant denied having read a brochure detailing the structure of the pension plan and the activities of Capitis Fora, he invited the Court to assume in the Part 24 defendants' favour that it had been available to him. The Court allowed the claimant to rely on the brochure as evidence of dishonest assistance by the Part 24 defendants, despite his denial of having read it. The Court accepted that the brochure implied that any money transferred to Capitis Fora as part of a pension plan would be invested in a portfolio of real property and not property development, and that adequate security would be obtained.

A claim of dishonest assistance requires proof that a trust or fiduciary relationship has been breached, that the breach has been assisted by the defendant and that the defendant has acted dishonestly. On the evidence of the brochure, the Court was satisfied that the investment of the funds in property development without adequate security represented a breach of trust and that the Part 24 defendants assisted in that breach.

In their defence, the Part 24 defendants argued that they had not acted dishonestly because they carried out due diligence in advance of investing the funds in the property development. The Court applied the test for dishonesty, as laid out in *Ivey v Genting Casinos (UK) Ltd*,[24] ie, 'whether the Defendant's conduct was honest or dishonest according to the standards of ordinary decent people'. It was determined that the Part 24 defendants had acted dishonestly because they were aware that their use of the money diverged from the commitments made in the brochure and they 'ought to have known that the use ... made of the Claimant's pension monies was improper'.

The Court found that, since the Part 24 defendants clearly took an unauthorised risk with the claimant's money, they did not have a realistic prospect of defending the claim

---

23   *Burns v Burns* [2021] EWHC 75 (Ch).
24   *Ivey v Genting Casinos (UK) Ltd* [2018] AC 391.

of dishonest assistance at trial. This satisfied the requirement for summary judgment, and the Court granted such a judgment against the Part 24 defendants for dishonest assistance in breach of trust.

[18.17]   *Lloyds Banking Group Pensions Trustees Ltd v Lloyds Bank Plc[25]—High Court of England and Wales—Morgan J—equalisation of benefits payable to male and female members with equivalent age, service and earnings histories*

The High Court of England and Wales had previously established that trustees of pension schemes have a duty to equalise benefits payable to male and female members with equivalent age, service and earnings histories. At issue in this decision was the implication of that finding for historic cases in which members who had transferred out of a scheme had received a cash equivalent transfer payment which was lower than they were entitled to because it was unequalised.

The Court found that a member transferring out of a scheme was entitled to a cash equivalent transfer payment of their accrued benefits, calculated to account for equalisation. Accordingly, the trustee who paid the member less than this amount because they did not equalise benefits did not fulfil their obligation to the member.

Transfers made in the period 1990–1997

In their defence, the defendants argued that, in relation to transfers made in this period, they were discharged from their duty to provide additional benefits by s 99 of the Pension Schemes Act 1993. Section 99 states that when trustees 'have done what is needed to carry out what the member requires', they are discharged from their obligation to provide benefits related to the cash equivalent. The defendants argued that what 'needed to be done' in the relevant case was to pay the member the sum which the trustee had calculated as the cash equivalent of the benefits accrued.

The Court judged that what 'needed to be done' was in fact to pay the member the sum to which they were entitled, accounting for equalisation, as this was what the member required under law. Trustees were not discharged from their duty to provide additional benefits, and so members who received payments lower than they ought to have may demand that the trustee perform the outstanding duty.

Transfers made in the period after 1997

The defendants argued that following amendments to the Pension Schemes Act 1993 and the introduction of the Occupational Pensions Schemes Regulations 1996,[26] they were discharged from their duty to provide additional benefits on transfers made in this period. Their argument was that statements issued to members based on erroneous calculations were nonetheless valid statements of entitlement under the law, as amended.

---

[25]   *Lloyds Banking Group Pensions Trustees Ltd v Lloyds Bank Plc* [2020] EWHC 3135 (Ch).
[26]   Occupational Pension Schemes (Scheme Administration) Regulations 1996 (SI 1996/1715).

The Court rejected this argument on the grounds that reg 9(5) of the 1996 Regulations, which provides for the increase or reduction of an erroneously calculated cash equivalent transfer payment, applies until the payment is made, so the trustee breaches their obligation at the time of payment. Furthermore, the Court found that the legislative intent behind reg 9(5) was that trustees be liable to be ordered to belatedly perform the obligation even after the payment had been made.

The Court also judged that claims by members in accordance with these findings were not time barred under the rules of the pension scheme or any statute of limitations.

[18.18] *Cobb Europe Ltd v Down*[27]—*High Court of England and Wales— rectification of resolution contrary to common interest of the employer and trustees*

Cobb Europe Ltd and the trustees of the Cobb Pension Scheme applied for relief from the High Court of England and Wales in relation to changes in the rate of pension increases. The claimants also sought approval of a settlement reached with members of the pension scheme in relation to the equalisation of retirement ages for male and female members.

The Court approved the settlement regarding changes to the normal retirement age of female members following the ruling of the European Court of Justice in *Barber v Guardian Royal Exchange Assurance Group*,[28] on the grounds that it was of benefit to all represented parties. Regarding the uncompromised issues, the Court heard detailed evidence of the factual and legal background of the claim for relief.

At a meeting of the trustees in November 1993, it was agreed that pensions for full members would be increased by 5% per annum. Following the receipt of a draft valuation report from the scheme actuary, the trustees decided in September 1999 that pension increases would be restricted to Limited Price Indexation, the lower of RPI or 5%. The employer consented to this decision and the change was announced to members of the scheme. In 2001, a resolution was adopted which, read literally, reversed the 1999 decision and restored the 5% per annum increase. It was not the intention of the signatories to effect this reversal and subsequently benefits continued to be paid in line with the 1999 decision.

The claimants asked the Court to order that the 2001 resolution be rectified so that it did not alter the standing of the 1999 decision to restrict pension increases to LPI. The claimants, citing *Re Charles A Blatchford and Son Ltd Group Pension Scheme*,[29] argued that the test which should be applied was whether the resolution conflicted with a common interest of the employer and trustees which persisted up to the execution of the resolution.

The Court agreed and found that the employers and trustees did in fact have such a continuing common interest with which the resolution conflicted. Accordingly, the Court ordered that the 2001 resolution be rectified as requested.

---

[27] *Cobb Europe Ltd v Down* [2020] EWHC 3552 (Ch).
[28] *Barber v Guardian Royal Exchange Assurance Group* (Case C-262/88).
[29] *Re Charles A. Blatchford and Son Ltd Group Pension Scheme* [2019] EWHC 2743 (Ch).

[18.19] *London Fire Commissioner v Sargeant*[30]—*UK Employment Appeal Tribunal—Employment Equality Act 2010—firefighters—pension scheme—age discrimination—less favourable treatment*

This case followed the Court of Appeal's decision in *Lord Chancellor v McCloud and Secretary of State for the Home Department v Sargeant*[31] that the transitional provisions in judges' and firefighters' pension schemes were discriminatory on grounds of age.

Sections 61 and 62 of the Employment Equality Act 2010 (the 2010 Act) provide that an occupational pension scheme must be taken to include a non-discrimination rule. It provides trustees or managers of a scheme with a power to pass a resolution making non-discriminatory alterations to a scheme where they would not usually have the power to do so.

In June 2016, an employment tribunal held that the claimant firefighters, who alleged age discrimination, were not barred from bringing claims of less favourable treatment on the grounds of age by virtue of the defence in the 2010 Act. Schedule 22 of the 2010 Act provides for a statutory defence to a claim for discrimination including where a person is required to do anything under a 'requirement of an enactment'. The various fire and rescue authorities appealed that decision.

The fire and rescue authorities argued that, as they were merely implementing the rules of the pension scheme, they could not be liable for age discrimination as their actions were required under the 'enactment' governing the scheme. The respondents argued that the discriminatory provisions were overridden by s 61 of the 2010 Act so that the fire and rescue authorities were no longer required to apply discriminatory rules, therefore the defence contained in Schedule 22 was not applicable.

The EAT found that any scheme provision (even one contained in legislation) which required action to be taken that led to unlawful discrimination was overridden by the non-discrimination rule contained in the rules of the scheme. The claimant authorities could therefore not rely on the statutory defence that they were required to act as they did by an enactment. Their appeal was dismissed.

[18.20] *Adams v Options SIPP UK LLP (formerly Carey Pensions UK LLP) and the Financial Conduct Authority*[32]—*Court of Appeal of England and Wales—Newey, Rose and Andrews LJJ—self-invested personal pension provider liability—unregulated 'introducer'*

This case is an appeal from the High Court concerning the potential liability of an execution-only self-invested personal pension provider to an investor, Mr Adams, who sustained substantial losses by investing in a personal pension vehicle provided by them, on the advice of a financial advisor, who was an unregulated 'introducer'.

---

30   *London Fire Commissioner v Sargeant* UKEAT/0137/17/LA.
31   *Lord Chancellor v McCloud and Secretary of State for the Home Department v Sargeant* [2018] EWCA Civ 2844, see *Arthur Cox Employment Law Yearbook 2019* at **[4.05]**.
32   *Adams v Options SIPP UK LLP (formerly Carey Pensions UK LLP) and the Financial Conduct Authority* [2021] EWCA Civ 474. See *Arthur Cox Employment Law Yearbook 2020* at **[16.23]** for decision of the High Court of England and Wales.

The Court of Appeal found in favour of Mr Adams and concluded that the financial adviser had advised on investments by encouraging Mr Adams to invest in storage pods, which were higher risk than his existing investment, by transferring his pension into a Carey SIPP. It further found that Mr Adams was entitled to the return of his funds as well as compensation. The Court of Appeal rejected the High Court decision regarding enforcement of the agreement between Mr Adams and Carey Pensions and declined to exercise its discretion under s 28 of the Financial Services and Markets Act 2000 (the 2000 Act) to uphold the agreement. The Court held that while consumers can, to an extent, be expected to bear responsibility for their own decisions, there is a need for regulation 'to safeguard consumers from their own folly'. It further held that while SIPP providers were not barred from accepting introductions from unregulated sources, s 27 of the 2000 Act was designed to throw risks associated with doing so onto providers.

This case illustrates that if a person praises an unregulated investment, which would need to be acquired by means of a particular vehicle, then the law may, depending on the circumstances, treat him as advising that the vehicle should be adopted.

This Court of Appeal judgment has the potential to have significant implications in the UK for 'execution-only' SIPP providers and others in the regulated sector who accept clients brought to them by financial advisors who are unregulated 'introducers'. If the unregulated introducer oversteps the mark and undertakes unauthorised regulated activities, the authorised entity may face a claim by the consumer to unwind the transaction and return the funds under s 27 of the 2000 Act.

[18.21]   *Mrs E v Teachers' Pensions Scheme[33]—UK Pensions Ombudsman—overpayment of pension—recovery—change of position defence*

On the 22 June 2021, the UK Pensions Ombudsman in his determination of a complaint by Mrs E against Teachers' Pensions, upheld Mrs E's complaint in part, agreeing with the Adjudicator's opinion.

Mrs E's complaint related to the fact that Teachers' Pensions was attempting to recover an overpayment of £13,506.15 from her. This overpayment arose because Teachers' Pensions originally calculated Mrs E's retirement benefits using an incorrect pensionable service record.

Mrs E was a deferred member of the Teachers' Pension Scheme (the Scheme), with two periods of pensionable service. Following the first period of employment from November 1975 to February 1980, Mrs E received a full refund of her pension contributions from the Scheme. However, Teachers' Pensions failed to subsequently update her record, and as a result, her records indicated she still had pensionable service from 1975 to 1980. Mrs E later returned to employment from February 1983 to August 2008. From 2004 onwards, Mrs E received annual estimates of retirement benefits

---

[33]   *Mrs E v Teachers' Pensions Scheme* CAS-30002-K6Z8.

(EORBs), which provided a breakdown of her estimated benefits from the Scheme and the State pension, in addition to details of her pensionable service in years and days. Following an internal review of its membership records in April 2014, Teachers' Pensions discovered that Mrs E's pensionable service was incorrect and logged a note stating that her record needed to be updated. However, no further action was taken. Shortly afterwards, Mrs E reached normal retirement age and Teachers' Pensions provided her with a retirement benefit statement dated September 2014 (2014 benefit statement), detailing the tax-free lump sum and annual income she was expected to receive. However, in December 2018, Mrs E's pension was reduced and in response to Mrs E's query, Teachers' Pensions admitted that it had made an error in its initial calculation of her retirement benefits in 2014. As a result, Teachers' Pensions sought to recover the overpayment of £13,506.15, but offered to pay Mrs E £500 for the distress and inconvenience caused.

The Ombudsman directed that Teachers' Pensions reduce the amount of overpayment it was seeking to recover to £5,667.51 and to contact Mrs E to discuss an affordable repayment plan. He further directed that Teachers' Pensions pay Mrs E £1,000 in recognition of the serious distress and inconvenience she suffered, with the option for her to have the fee offset against the recovery of the overpayment. As part of the Ombudsman's determination, he noted the irreversible payments that the member had made, the conduct of the pension scheme, and the communication with the member. He further noted that the test of good faith in a change of position was a subjective one and that Mrs E did receive and spend the overpayment in good faith and therefore satisfied the good faith and change of position defences. The Ombudsman found that it was not enough for Teachers' Pensions to show that Mrs E was sent documents which contained incorrect information, Teachers' Pensions must also show that Mrs E had spotted the error and appreciated its implications which, the Ombudsman found, she had not.

European Union Case Law

[18.22] *United Biscuits (Pension Trustees) Ltd v Revenue and Customs Commissioners*[34]*—European Court of Justice—Directive 2006/112/EC*[35]*—whether pension fund management services are exempt from VAT*

United Biscuits unsuccessfully applied for a VAT reimbursement from the United Kingdom tax authority for pension fund management services it provided to its employees. The High Court rejected an action taken by United Biscuits, and the decision was appealed. The Court of Appeal referred the case to the European Court of Justice for a

---

[34] *United Biscuits (Pension Trustees) Ltd v Revenue and Customs Commissioners* (Case C-235/19).
[35] Directive 2006/112/EC on the common system of value added tax.

preliminary ruling on whether EU law provides for pension fund management services to be exempt from VAT.

Article 135(1) of Directive 2006/112/EC (the Directive) provides that Member States shall exempt 'insurance and reinsurance transactions' from VAT. The Court identified the crucial issue to be whether pension fund management services were included within the concept of insurance transactions, as referred to in the Directive.

The Court, citing settled case law and general understanding, found that the essence of an insurance transaction includes the provision of indemnity from risk, which is absent from the management of pension funds. This characteristic of insurance transactions was also held to be the justification for the exemption in the Directive, since the technical difficulty in determining the correct amount of VAT to be levied derives from the coverage of risk. Furthermore, within the Directive, a distinction is drawn between insurance and other operations, with the 'management of group pension funds' included among such other operations.

The Court rejected the submission of the applicant that this distinction is undermined by annexes to the Directive in which pension fund management services are referred to as a 'class of insurance' on the grounds that the wording giving rise to this ambiguity was present only in the Danish and English-language versions of the Directive and not in most of the versions.

For these reasons, the Court determined that it was the intent of the EU legislature that pension fund management services not be regarded as insurance transactions. The Court judged that pension fund management services, which do not provide any indemnity from risk, are not covered by the VAT exemption for insurance transactions in EU law.

[18.23]   *SC v Zaklad Ubezpieczen Spoleczynch I Oddizal w Warszawi[36]—European Court of Justice—request for preliminary ruling from Poland—Regulation (EC) No 883/2004[37]—worker who has been employed in two Member States—minimum period required by national law for acquisition of entitlement to retirement pension—account taken of contribution period completed under legislation of another Member State*

This was a request for a preliminary ruling from the Supreme Court in Poland concerning the interpretation of art 52(1)(b) of Regulation (EC) No 883/2004 on the co-ordination of social security systems. The request was made in proceedings concerning the determination of the amount of the pro rata retirement pension to be paid by the Pensions Authority in Poland.

Regulation (EEC) No 1408/71, which since has been repealed, considered the period of insurance or residence under which an employed person or self-employed person was subject for the acquisition, retention or recovery of the right to benefits. That Regulation was effectively reproduced by Regulation (EC) No 883/2004. The ECJ noted

---

[36]   *SC v Zaklad Ubezpieczen Spoleczynch I Oddizal w Warszawi* (Case C-866/19).
[37]   Regulation (EC) No 883/2004 on the co-ordination of social security systems.

therefore that previous determinations in relation to Regulation (EEC) No 1408/71 remained relevant to Regulation (EC) No 883/2004. Article 52(b) of Regulation (EC) No 883/2004 provides that the competent Member State institution shall calculate the amount of benefit which is due to the individual by calculating a theoretical amount, which includes non-contributory periods of employment and subsequently an actual amount (ie a pro-rata benefit).

The ECJ noted that the provisions of Regulation (EC) No 883/2004 do not set up a common scheme of social security law but have the sole objective of ensuring coordination between the various national schemes which continue to exist. The Regulations further one of the basic principles governing EU law, which is to ensure that the exercise of the right to freedom of movement does not have the effect of depriving workers of social security advantages to which they would have been entitled if they had spent their entire working life in just one Member State.

Accordingly, the Court found that the theoretical amount of the benefit must be calculated as if the insured person had worked exclusively in the Member State concerned (ie, including periods in other Member States) but the actual amount of the benefit is to be determined by the competent institution excluding insurance periods completed in another Member State. This was, in effect, an application of the principle of apportionment to ensure that each competent institution is required to pay only that part of the benefit relating to the relevant periods completed under the legislation it applies.

Chapter 19

Redundancy

INTRODUCTION

[19.01] In the context of a claim for statutory redundancy, the relevance and implications of an offer of alternative employment were considered by the Labour Court in *Summeridge* and in *Cosy Tots*. A similar question was considered by the UK EAT in *Stevenson*.

The implications of failure to comply with an employer's collective redundancy obligations were considered in the UK in *Palmer* (High Court of England and Wales) and in *Carillion* (UK EAT).

REDUNDANCY PAYMENTS ACT 1967

Alternative Employment/Location

[19.02] ***Summeridge Ltd v Byrne[1]—Labour Court—appeal from the Workplace Relations Commission—Redundancy Payments Acts 1967 to 2014—lay-off—redundancy***

Summeridge Ltd appealed the decision of the WRC given under the Redundancy Payments Act 1967, which held that the claim by the claimant for redundancy under the 1967 Act was well-founded.

The claimant had worked for respondent as a bartender since January 2015 in The Elms, which was previously known as The Area Bar and Restaurant at Liffey Valley prior to a transfer of undertaking in 2017.

On 27 December 2018, the claimant received a letter from the respondent stating that the premises would be temporarily closed from 31 December 2018 for four months, with the potential of an extension to that period, and that he would be placed on temporary lay-off for the period. The respondent emailed the claimant on 28 January 2019

---

[1] *Summeridge Ltd v Byrne* RPD211.

offering him a position on his existing terms and conditions from 4 February 2018, with an amendment to his normal place of work, which would now be the Harbour Master Bar until The Elms reopened.

The claimant declined the position as he believed that the additional expenses he would incur commuting to and from work, for parking or occasional public transport coupled with the length of the commute, in comparison to his work at The Elms, was not economical in relation to the money he would be earning. The Harbour Master Bar was 12.6 km away from his home, whereas The Elms had been in walking distance or a short car journey with free parking. The claimant also noted he was aware that The Elms premises was up for letting, which appeared to contradict what was set out in the initial communication from the respondent about the lay-off being temporary. The claimant informed the respondent that he would be applying for redundancy on the basis that he understood his role at The Elms was no longer available.

Over the next couple of months, the claimant and the respondent engaged in email correspondence in relation to the proposed transfer and the claimant's notice of redundancy. The respondent renewed the offer of re-deployment, stating that the position was not being made redundant and served a counter-notice on the claimant. The respondent blamed the delay of the re-opening of The Elms on an inability to get an insurance quote and a sewage leak. The respondent also offered €500 to the claimant plus a One-for-All voucher to the value of €500 to cover the additional costs he might incur for the commute and parking. The claimant maintained that, due to the low income he was receiving, this offer was not sufficient to cover his expenses on an ongoing basis.

The Labour Court considered two main issues:

1. the suitability of the offer of alternative employment made by the respondent to the claimant; and
2. whether the refusal of the claimant to accept the offer of a position in an alternative location was unreasonable.

The Court accepted that the respondent had at all times acted in a *bona fide* manner in attempting to retain the claimant and offering him alternative employment and found that in the circumstances it was reasonable that the respondent believed that the business would re-open at some point.

However, upon considering the evidence of the claimant in relation to: (i) the additional costs he would incur by commuting and for parking; (ii) the extra travel time that would be involved; and (iii) the lack of public transport when he was working a late shift, the Court held that the change of location was 'of such magnitude' that the claimant's refusal to accept the position offered by the respondent in the Harbour Master Bar was not unreasonable. The Court further accepted that there was no position available to him at his established place of work in The Elms, which remained closed at the time of this decision.

In upholding the decision of the WRC, the Court found that the claimant was entitled to the claimed statutory redundancy payment.

[19.03] *Cosy Tots & Co Ltd v Conn*[2]*—Labour Court—appeal of decision of the Workplace Relations Commission—Redundancy Payments Acts 1967 to 2014—suitable alternative employment*

This was an appeal by the respondent employer, of a decision of the WRC in which the claimant's complaint under the Redundancy Payments Acts 1967 to 2014 was upheld.

The claimant was a cook at the respondent employer. A decision was made to close the premises in which the claimant was working and a number of meetings between the respondent and the claimant took place. The respondent wrote to the claimant to offer her a position in one of their other creches. The claimant did not consider this alternative to be suitable for her. The claimant sought to be made redundant, in accordance with the Acts. The respondent believed that in offering an alternative position with the same terms and conditions, they had met their obligations under the Acts. The claimant was successful before the WRC and the respondent appealed this decision.

The respondent argued that it had offered the claimant suitable alternative employment in one of their other creches, located in Barrow St, Dublin 2 and that the claimant had failed to even consider same:

(i) the new location was only 5 km further from her home, making her journey to work 21 minutes as opposed to 11 minutes by car, the claimant maintained it was not a reasonable alternative, as she was concerned about collecting her granddaughter from school;

(ii) the claimant did not engage with the respondent regarding the offer to consider alternative working hours to facilitate her in caring for her granddaughter;

(iii) the claimant mistakenly believed that the new premises was fitted with a smaller kitchen and a reduced ventilation system and raised health concerns; and

(iv) although the respondent offered to discuss all reasonable options before a conclusion was reached, it was clear that the claimant did not wish to engage and had made up her mind that she was only willing to accept redundancy.

The respondent referenced s 15(2) of the Redundancy Payments Act 2014, which provides that redundancy payments are not an entitlement if the employer has offered suitable employment to the employee and if the employee has unreasonably refused the offer. It was the respondent's position that there was an offer of suitable employment in this case, which was unreasonably refused.

In finding that the Barrow St offer was not suitable alternative employment, the Court focused not on the physical distance between the two locations, but on how long it would take to get to the Barrow St location via public transport (as car parking would be difficult to find at Barrow St). The Court held that:

> As the offer made to the [claimant] was not one of suitable employment, it follows that the [claimant] was made redundant and is entitled to a payment under the Act. It is not necessary

---

2   *Cosy Tots & Co Ltd v Conn* RPD219.

for the Court to consider other arguments put forward for the [claimant] in support of her decision to refuse the offer.

The appeal was dismissed.

[19.04]   *Stevenson, Leeke and Steward v Mid Essex Hospital Services NHS Trust[3]— UK Employment Appeal Tribunal—appeal from employment tribunal—redundancy—suitable alternative work—entitlement to redundancy pay*

This was an appeal of the employment tribunal's rejection of the claimants' claim that they were entitled to redundancy payment.

The claimants had been employed in the role of Head of HR with the respondent. They were all made redundant following a restructuring within the respondent's organisation, and they each refused the offer of alternative employment in the role of Senior HR Lead. The respondent denied the claimants the redundancy payment on the basis that they had refused the offer of suitable alternative employment.

The claimants brought proceedings to the employment tribunal seeking to recover the redundancy payments. The employment tribunal dismissed their claim. It found that in circumstances where the grade, pay, location and hours were similar to that of the previous roles, the position of Senior HR Lead was suitable alternative work. The claimants had therefore unreasonably refused an offer of suitable alternative employment, and as such, were not entitled to a redundancy payment.

In an appeal to the EAT, the claimants argued, among other points, that the tribunal had erred in law in failing to have proper regard to the content of the job description and the degree and autonomy of the proposed role, as against the previous role, when considering the suitability of the alternative work. The respondent submitted that any appeal to the EAT was an appeal of a point of law only—and the EAT should not 'subject the reasons of the employment tribunal to unrealistically detailed scrutiny'.

The EAT upheld the claimants' appeal. It held that an assessment of the suitability of an alternative role 'will always require a careful comparison of the alternative employment with the employee's former employment'. In the circumstances, the employment tribunal had failed to have regard to the practical differences between the claimants' previous roles as Head of HR and the allegedly suitable alternative role as Senior HR Lead.

The issue of suitability of the alternative employment and the reasonableness of the claimants' behaviour in refusing the offer were remitted to the employment tribunal.

---

[3]   *Stevenson, Leeke and Steward v Mid Essex Hospital Services NHS Trust* EA-2019-000834-RN (previously UK EAT/0334/19/RN).

Collective Redundancy

[19.05]   *R (on the application of Palmer) v Northern Derbyshire Magistrates' Court[4]—High Court of England and Wales—Andrews LJ and Linden J—Trade Union and Labour Relations (Consolidation) Act 1992, ss 193 & 194—judicial review proceedings—collective redundancies—failure to notify Secretary of State— criminal proceedings*

This case related to judicial review proceedings arising from a criminal prosecution brought against the claimants as a director and an administrator of the company, for the failure of the company to give notice to the Secretary of State of proposed collective redundancies in accordance with the Trade Union and Labour Relations (Consolidation) Act 1992.

The company was incorporated in England and traded as a retailer in the north of England as well as in Scotland. The company was issued with a statutory demand of £1.2 million, as a result of which it was placed into administration. As part of the administration process, steps were taken to cease operations in the Scottish warehouse. The Court found that the decision to make 84 employees redundant was made on 8 January, when the closure of the warehouse became apparent. On 14 January 2015, the employees were informed by letter that they were at risk of redundancy. They were given 15 minutes to read the 'at risk' letter, before being handed another letter, notifying them that no alternatives to redundancy had been identified and they were dismissed, with effect from that day. Criminal proceedings were issued against the claimants in the English courts for the failure to give appropriate notice of collective redundancies to the Secretary of State.

Section 193 of the 1992 Act sets out an employer's obligation to notify the Secretary of State in writing of certain redundancies. It provides that where an employer is proposing to dismiss 100 or more employees, the employer should notify the Secretary of State in writing of the proposal before giving notice to terminate and at least 45 days before the first dismissal takes effect. This timing is reduced to at least 30 days, where the proposal relates to 20 or more employees.

Section 194 of the 1992 Act provides that it is an offence for an employer to fail to provide notice in accordance with s 193, and any such offence is liable on summary conviction to a fine. Section 194(3) provides that where an offence is committed by a body corporate and it is proven to 'have been committed with the consent or connivance of, or to be attributable to neglect on the part of, any director, manager, secretary or other similar officer of the body corporate, or any person purporting to act in any such capacity', then any such person will also be guilty of an offence.

---

4   *R (on the application of Palmer) v Northern Derbyshire Magistrates' Court* [2021] EWHC 3013 (Admin).

The criminal proceedings were challenged by the claimants by way of judicial review on two main grounds—the 'jurisdictional issue' and the 'officer issue'.

In relation to the jurisdictional point, the Court noted that the central issue was 'whether the offence with which [the claimants] has been charged is one that could only have been prosecuted in Scotland'. The Court considered a number of facts, including the fact that the failure to notify the Secretary of State took place in England and a significant measure of activities constituting the offence occurred in England and concluded that the English courts had jurisdiction to hear the proceedings.

In relation to the 'officer issue', one of the claimants, the administrator, challenged the criminal proceedings on the basis that an administrator is not a 'director, manager, secretary or other similar officer' of the company, as provided under s 194(3) of the 1992 Act. The Court assessed the role of an administrator, noting that the function of the administrator is to ultimately try to rescue the company as a going concern. The Court stated that, having regard to the role of the administrator and the language of s 194(3), 'the focus is upon any individual acting in a sufficiently senior managerial capacity who could be regarded as bearing some responsibility, in practical terms, for the corporate body's failure to give the requisite notice to the Secretary of State'. Therefore, s 194(3) extended to an administrator.

The High Court dismissed both grounds of challenge.

[19.06] *Carillion Services Ltd (in compulsory liquidation) v Benson[5]—UK Employment Appeal Tribunal—appeal from employment tribunal—Trade Union and Labour Relations (Consolidation) Act 1992, s 188—liquidation—collective redundancy—consultation period—mitigation*

Prior to entering liquidation in 2018, Carillion Services Ltd was part of the Carillion plc group (the claimant in this case) employing close to 18,000 people in the UK in business and construction services. The financial difficulties faced by the claimant were not in dispute before the employment tribunal with both sides agreeing that the claimant ran into financial difficulty in July 2017, a position that continued to worsen until it entered liquidation on 15 January 2018.

Despite dismissing more than 20 employees by reason of redundancy within a 90-day period, amounting to a collective redundancy, the claimant did not enter into any form of consultation with its employees prior to dismissing them. The respondents argued that this was a failure to comply with the requirements of the UK's collective redundancy legislation (specifically s 188 of the Trade Union and Labour Relations (Consolidation) Act 1992) to 'consult with representatives about proposals to dismiss as redundant 20 or more employees at an establishment within a period of 90 days or less'.

Rather than contest the facts, the claimant admitted it had not carried out any kind of consultation process. Instead, when the respondents in this case issued claims against it, it relied on an exemption under s 188(7) of the 1992 Act, arguing that

---

[5]   *Carillion Services Ltd (in compulsory liquidation) v Benson* EA-2021-000269-BA.

'special circumstances' existed such that it was exempt from the requirement to consult with its employees before implementing a collective redundancy.

The issue was brought before the employment tribunal, where the claimant argued that during January 2018:

> a decision from lenders that further financial support was now entirely contingent on Government guarantees; confirmation from Government that such support would not be forthcoming; and the subsequent majority decision of the banks on Sunday 14 January 2018 to withdraw financial support ... [this] sudden and unexpected turn of events was disastrous for the Group and clearly constituted a special circumstance.

As a result, 'it was inevitable and unavoidable that the Group's employees (with some limited exceptions) would ultimately be dismissed'.

The tribunal considered whether or not the circumstances upon which the claimant relied were special and if so, whether it was reasonably practicable for the claimant to comply with its consultation obligations under the 1992 Act.

While a 'sudden disaster' may amount to a special circumstance, the tribunal found that the gradual decline of the claimant's business from July 2017, would not. Relying on the decision of the Court of Appeal in *Clarks of Hove Ltd v Bakers' Union*,[6] the tribunal concluded that the duty to consult was triggered and that special circumstances did not exist such that it was not reasonably practicable for the claimant to comply with that duty.

The EAT summed up the claimant's arguments as alleging that the tribunal had failed to fully consider the context in which the claimant entered into liquidation and had limited its attention to the causes of the company's insolvency. Fundamentally disagreeing with the claimant's interpretation of the tribunal's judgment, the EAT rejected the appeal.

It found that the tribunal had considered each factor put forward by the claimant as amounting to a special circumstance. The fact that each factor had not been repeated at each part of its judgment was not indicative that it had borne each aspect in mind in coming to its conclusion that there were no special circumstances, as envisaged by the *Clarks* decision. The EAT rejected the contention that, given the compulsory nature of the liquidation, the claimant was unable to avoid dismissing its employees and so, a special circumstance arose whereby it was not reasonably practicable to engage in consultation in respect of 'ways of avoiding dismissals'. The EAT noted out that the matters identified for consultation under the 1992 Act (avoiding dismissal altogether, reducing the number of dismissals and mitigating the consequences of dismissal) comprised a non-exhaustive list and that even when dismissal is unavoidable there is value in consultation with employees.

---

6   *Clarks of Hove Ltd v Bakers' Union* [1978] 1 WLR 1207.

Chapter 20

Taxation

INTRODUCTION

[20.01] In this chapter we discuss the various changes to the Irish tax regime that affect employers and employees, including changes relating to the Universal Social Charge, employer-provided benefits, flat-rate expenses, share incentive schemes and pensions.

We also note relevant employment tax cases from 2021, including a case on the taxation of payments made under a compromise agreement, employment status cases, and cases involving the denial of a tax credit in circumstances where employment tax liabilities are not discharged in full. A case on the calculation of ex gratia redundancy payments as well as cases related to employer provided benefits are also noted. Finally cases relating to the taxation of pension entitlements are also addressed.

UNIVERSAL SOCIAL CHARGE

[20.02] Revenue issued *eBrief 017/21* on 3 February 2021, which confirmed that the Tax and Duty Manual (TDM) Part 18D-00-01 in relation to Universal Social Charge (USC) has been updated to reflect changes arising from the Finance Act 2020. The updated Manual indicates that:

— The reduced rate of USC for medical card holders will be extended for a further year (extended until 2021). In the case of an individual whose total income in the year does not exceed €60,000 and is either: (i) aged 70 or over; or (ii) holds a full medical card, the 2% rate applies to all income over €12,012.

— The USC rate threshold will increase in line with increases to the National Minimum Wage that have applied in 2020 and 2021. The standard rates of USC for 2021 are:

   (i)   0.5% on the first €12,012 (0.5% on the first €12,012 for 2020);

   (ii)   2% on the next €8,675 (2% on the next €8,472 for 2020);

   (iii) 4.5% on the next €49,357 (4.5% on the next €49,560 for 2020); and

   (iv) 8% on the balance (8% on the balance for 2020).

DETERMINATION OF EMPLOYED OR SELF-EMPLOYED STATUS

[20.03] On 26 August 2021, Revenue issued *The Employers' Guide to PAYE (eBrief 162/21)* confirming that TDM Part 42-04-35A (*The Employers' Guide to PAYE*) has been updated. The updates include refreshed guidance in relation to the criteria used to determine if an individual is an employee or self-employed. This reflects the new *Code of Practice for Determining the Employment or Self-employment Status of Individuals* published in July 2021. The overriding consideration or test remains whether the person performing the work does so 'as a person in business on their own account'. The criteria used to determine if an individual is an employee now also includes whether the employee: (i) is entitled to sick pay; (ii) is obliged to perform work on a regular basis that the employer is obliged to offer them (this is known as 'mutuality of obligation'); and (iii) has their tax deducted from their wages through the PAYE system. The criteria used to determine if an individual is self-employed now includes if the employee: (i) is not obliged to take on specific work offered to them; and (ii) is registered for self-assessment tax returns or VAT.

OUT-OF-COURT SETTLEMENTS—EXEMPTION FROM INCOME TAX

[20.04] On 19 May 2021, Revenue issued *eBrief 107/21*, which confirmed that TDM Part 07-01-27 (*Exemption from Income Tax in respect of certain payments made under Employment Law*) has been updated to include additional guidance on out-of-court settlements. A payment made under such an agreement qualifies for an income tax exemption where all of the following conditions are met:

— the agreement in settlement of a claim is evidenced in writing;

— the original statement of claim by the employee is evidenced in writing;

— the agreement is not between connected persons as defined in s 10 of the Taxes Consolidation Act 1997 (TCA 1997) (eg employer and relative, employer and director);

— the claim would have been a *bona fide* claim under a 'relevant Act' had it been made to a 'relevant authority' (eg, sufficient grounds for the claim; claim is within the scope of one of the relevant Acts; claim made within specified time limits, etc);

— the claim is likely to have been the subject of a recommendation, decision or determination by a relevant authority that a payment be made to the person making the claim; and

— the payment does not exceed the maximum amount which could have been awarded under relevant legislation by the Rights Commissioner, Director of the Equality Tribunal, Employment Appeals Tribunal, Workplace Relations Commission or Labour Court as appropriate.

The Manual now contains updated guidance on the format and contents of the employee's statement of claim. The statement of claim must be evidenced in writing and though the exact format and details to be included will vary depending on the facts and circumstances of each individual case, it would be expected to include information such as the nature of the claim, the nature of the relationship between the parties involved or a high-level summary of the allegations and the impact of same. The guidance clarifies that an employee does not have to engage an external advisor to prepare the documentation on his/her behalf and that there is also no requirement for the statement of claim to have been formally submitted to any authority dealing with employment disputes provided all other conditions set out above are met.

PAYE EXCLUSION ORDERS

[20.05]   Revenue issued *eBrief 140/21*, in relation to Employment Exclusion Orders, on 16 July 2021. Section 985, TCA 1997 places a statutory obligation on employers to deduct tax at source under the PAYE system from emoluments. A PAYE Exclusion Order issued by Revenue to an employer (or other person paying emoluments), under s 984, TCA 1997, relieves that employer (or other person) from that obligation. A number of updates were made to TDM Part 42-04-01 (*PAYE Exclusion Orders*). In particular, detail has been provided regarding bonuses paid where a PAYE Exclusion Order is in place. The statutory basis of assessment for employment income is the actual amount of income received in the year of assessment, ie the 'receipts basis'. However, in the case of income where a PAYE Exclusion Order is in place, the Manual confirms that such income continues to be assessed on the 'earned basis'. The tax treatment of bonuses paid where a PAYE Exclusion Order is in place, either when the bonus is paid, or during the period the bonus was earned, will differ as outlined below:

— When a bonus is earned before the PAYE Exclusion Order was in place, but paid when the order is in place, PAYE should apply.

— When a bonus is earned during the period that a PAYE Exclusion Order is in place but paid after the PAYE Exclusion Order ceases, PAYE is not due in respect of the bonus income. The payment should be included in the payroll submission for that period in the gross pay amount, but excluded from the taxable pay figure.

— When the bonus payment relates to a period, only a portion of which is covered by a PAYE Exclusion Order, the employer is relieved from the obligation to operate PAYE on the portion of the bonus payment in respect of this period. However, the employer is required to operate PAYE on the bonus payment earned in respect of the period not covered by the exclusion order.

Examples of these circumstances and an outline of the process which employers should apply in such cases are set out in the updated TDM.

The updated Manual also confirms that Revenue concessions regarding PAYE Exclusion Orders issued due to the unprecedented circumstances and the restrictions on travel as a consequence of Covid-19 ceased on 31 December 2020 and normal rules apply from that date. In all cases where an employee/employer availed of a concession afforded by Revenue, records of facts and circumstances should be maintained outlining the circumstances and such records should be available to Revenue on request.

TRANSBORDER WORKERS RELIEF

[20.06]   On 6 August 2021, Revenue issued *eBrief 157/21*, which confirmed that TDM Part 34-00-06 (*Transborder Workers Relief*) has been updated. Transborder Workers Relief is aimed at Irish resident individuals who commute daily or weekly to a place of work outside of Ireland and who pay foreign tax in relation to this foreign employment. The effect of the relief when applicable is that Irish tax only arises where the individual concerned has income other than foreign employment income. The changes to the Manual include confirmations that the relief is not available to proprietary directors or income which is subject to the remittance basis of taxation as well as details of how the relief is to be claimed and the new fields required to be completed in the income tax return when the relief is availed of.

The updated Manual also contains new guidance on 'incidental duties'. One of the conditions for relief is that the duties of the qualifying employment must be exercised wholly outside of Ireland in a country with which Ireland has a tax treaty. The guidance clarifies that Revenue is prepared to regard duties performed in Ireland which are 'merely incidental' to the performance of the duties outside of Ireland as effectively performed outside of Ireland for the purposes of the relief. When determining whether duties are merely incidental, it is not enough to just look at the number of days that they were exercised but instead it is necessary to examine the precise nature of the duties performed, which must be subservient or ancillary in nature in order to qualify. The guidance lists administrative duties such as arranging meetings or business travel or giving employee feedback as examples of incidental duties. In contrast, a director attending a board meeting in Ireland even when all other duties are in substance performed abroad cannot be regarded as incidental duties, as attendance of board meetings is considered to be part and parcel of a director's core duties. Attendance at other committee meetings would also be considered the performance of substantive duties.

The updated guidance also notes that the concession allowing employees required to work from home in Ireland due to Covid-19 to continue to claim the relief when all the other conditions are satisfied applies through the 2021 tax year.

EMPLOYER-PROVIDED BENEFITS—NEW SUITE OF TAX AND DUTY MANUALS

[20.07]   On 30 July 2021, Revenue issued *eBrief 148/21*, in relation to a new suite of Tax and Duty Manuals regarding employer-provided benefits. This briefing noted that, following a comprehensive review of Revenue's guidance material on employer-provided benefits, it was decided to produce a consolidated suite of TDMs. New material has been added where appropriate, and existing material has been refreshed as required.

TDM Part 05-01-01 provides an index and details the structure for the consolidated Manuals as follows:

Chapter 1	Part 05-01-01a	Introduction to the taxation and valuation of employer-provided benefits
Chapter 2	Part 05-01-01b	Employer-provided vehicles
Chapter 3	Part 05-01-01c	The provision of free or subsidised accommodation
Chapter 4	Part 05-01-01d	The provision of preferential loans
Chapter 5	Part 05-01-01e	The small benefit exemption
Chapter 6	Part 05-01-01f	The provision of travel passes
Chapter 7	Part 05-01-01g	The provision of bikes and safety equipment ('cycle to work scheme')
Chapter 8	Part 05-01-01h	The provision of security assets or services
Chapter 9	Part 05-01-01i	The provision of work-related equipment and supplies
Chapter 10	Part 05-01-01j	The provision of staff awards
Chapter 11	Part 05-01-01k	Salary sacrifice arrangements
Chapter 12	Part 05-01-01l	The provision of miscellaneous benefits
Chapter 13	Part 05-01-01m	The provision of third-party benefits

FLAT-RATE SCHEDULE EXPENSES

[20.08]   On 18 January 2021, Revenue issued *eBrief 006/21* in relation to flat-rate expenses. Flat-rate expenses are those which cover the cost of equipment an employee needs for work (for example, tools, uniforms, stationery etc), provided that an employee incurs these costs in the performance of his/her duties and that the costs relate directly to the nature of his/her employment. This eBrief confirmed that the list of flat-rate schedule expenses in the TDM Part 05-02-01 is no longer relevant. However, the list of the current flat-rate expenses is available on the Revenue website.

RELIEF FOR CONTRIBUTIONS TO PERMANENT HEALTH BENEFIT SCHEMES AND TAX TREATMENT OF BENEFITS RECEIVED UNDER PERMANENT HEALTH BENEFIT SCHEMES

[20.09]   On 27 January 2021, Revenue issued eBrief 011/21, which stated that TDM Part 15-01-10 (*Relief for Contributions to Permanent Health Benefit Schemes and Tax Treatment of Benefits Received under Permanent Health Benefit Schemes*) has been updated to clarify the difference between 'Permanent Health Benefit Schemes' and 'Employee Protection Insurance'. Permanent Health Benefit Scheme generally refers to a Revenue-approved insurance policy taken out by an individual which is intended to provide a source of income in the event of the individual being unable to carry on his/her occupation due to an accident or sickness. An individual is entitled to claim income tax relief on the premiums he or she pays in respect of a Revenue-approved Permanent

Health Benefit policy, to the extent that the premiums do not exceed 10% of his or her total income in the relevant tax year. Payments received under such a scheme are treated as emoluments subject to PAYE. Employee Protection Insurance, on the other hand, is a policy taken out by employers to insure themselves against the possibility that they have to continue to pay all or part of an employee's salary while he/she is out sick from work due to illness or injury. The contract is between the insurance company and the employer such that the employer is the policyholder and the employee does not benefit from the proceeds of the policy directly. The TDM confirms that Employee Protection Insurance is not a Permanent Health Benefit policy and claims on such policies will result in the employee being paid through payroll by the employer. Such payments are subject to PAYE. The employer can claim a deduction under s 81, TCA 1997 for policy costs incurred.

PAYMENTS ON TERMINATION OF AN OFFICE OR EMPLOYMENT, OR REMOVAL FROM AN OFFICE OR EMPLOYMENT

[20.10]   On 9 July 2021, Revenue issued *eBrief 136/21*, which confirmed that TDM Part 05-05-19 (*Payments on Termination of an Office or Employment or Removal from an Office or Employment*) has been updated to provide additional clarification regarding the tax treatment of 'fire and re-hire' scenarios. The Manual states that a redundancy will generally not be regarded as taking place where there is a 'fire and re-hire' agreement in place at the time of the termination, or there is otherwise an expectation or understanding by either party that an offer of re-hire would be made at some point in the future (irrespective of the terms of such an offer or the length of time between the fire and the re-hire).

RECOUPMENT OF OVERPAYMENTS OF SALARY BY AN EMPLOYER FROM AN EMPLOYEE

[20.11]   On 8 April 2021, Revenue issued *eBrief 080/21*, regarding updates to the TDM Part 42-04-70 (*Recoupment of Overpayments of Salary by an Employer from an Employee*) as follows:

— updated examples for recoupment of 'in-year' and 'out of year' salary overpayments have been provided. Where the overpayment is being recouped by means of a deduction from emoluments in the current year, the gross amount of the overpayment is deducted from gross pay (that is before the deduction of income tax, PRSI and USC). On the other hand, where the overpayment is being recouped by means of a deduction from emoluments paid in a later year, the gross amount of the overpayment is deducted from the net pay; and

— updates effective from 1 January 2019 concerning real-time PAYE data have been incorporated.

On 2 June 2021, Revenue issued a related briefing (*eBrief 112/21*) which confirmed that additional content had been added to paragraph 6 of the TDM regarding the payment of emoluments following the death of an employee.

ELECTRONIC EMPLOYER'S SHARE AWARDS RETURN

[20.12]   Section 8 of the Finance Act 2020 introduced mandatory electronic reporting of certain share-based remuneration. This includes restricted stock units, restricted shares, convertible shares, forfeitable shares, discounted shares, growth shares and any other award with cash-equivalent of shares. Revenue *eBrief 123/21*, which issued on 23 June 2021, confirmed that the Electronic Employer's Share Awards return (Form ESA) 2020 was available for download from the Revenue website to facilitate such electronic reporting. Instructions and explanatory notes for customers and agents on the completion and filing are included in the form with further information being available in s 3.3 of Chapter 15 (*Share Scheme Reporting*) of the Revenue Share Schemes Manual.

The new electronic return will apply for the tax year 2020 onwards. A filing deadline of 31 August 2021 initially applied for the 2020 return, however, Revenue confirmed in *eBrief 163/21*, issued on 31 August 2021, that the filing date for the 2020 return had been further extended to 14 September 2021, in recognition of the fact that this is the first year for filing the new Form ESA. Note that for subsequent years, the reporting date of 31 March following the relevant tax year will apply.

Revenue issued *eBrief 120/21* on 20 June 2021; it confirms that a number of chapters of the Share Schemes Manual have been updated to include references to the reporting obligations on the Form ESA. In addition, two new chapters have been added to the Share Schemes Manual relating to: (i) Growth Shares (Chapter 13); and (ii) Cash Settled-Awards (Chapter 14).

Both growth shares and cash-settled awards allow employers to reward and incentivise their employees without diluting equity.

Growth shares are a special class of ordinary shares that have a low or nil value until a certain target is reached by the business, eg, the target may refer to company performance, an individual employee's performance, leaver provisions etc. The new chapter confirms that an employer must operate payroll taxes (income tax, PRSI and USC but not employer PRSI) when awarding these shares based on either: (i) the market value (if the shares awarded are free shares); or (ii) the discount value (if the shares awarded are discounted shares). However, if the shares have a nil value at the date of the award, then no tax arises. Details of such awards must be reported on the Form ESA.

Cash-settled awards refer to cash payments based on the value of the shares in a company offered to employees under some employee benefit plans. The method of calculating the cash amount varies depending on the scheme. The payment may equal the value of the underlying shares on a particular date, or any increase in their value over a set period of time. Examples of such awards include Stock Appreciation Rights (SARs), phantom shares and cash-settled Restricted Stock Units (RSUs). The new chapter provides that where such awards are paid as cash amounts, employers must operate payroll taxes as normal including employer's PRSI on the cash payment. The payment should not be reported under the '*Share Based Remuneration*' field of the relevant payroll submission, however details of cash-settled share awards should be included on the Form ESA.

SHARE AWARDS

[20.13]   Revenue issued *eBrief 121/21* on 20 June 2021 regarding Approved Profit Sharing Schemes (APSS). An APSS provides a mechanism whereby a company may appropriate shares to its employees and the employee is, subject to certain conditions, exempt from the income tax charge on the share appropriation (though USC and PRSI remain chargeable). The eBrief confirms that updates have been made to Chapter 10 of the Share Schemes Manual which deals with APSS. Companies which have schemes which are no longer active should notify Revenue so that the inactive schemes can be de-registered. APSS instruments submitted to Revenue for approval must be governed by Irish law. Trustees of an APSS are required, in relation to any year of assessment, to make an annual return of information on Form ESS1 and the Manual confirms that a nil ESS1 return must be filed where no activity has taken place for an approved scheme during a year of assessment. The Manual confirms that the filing deadline for the 2019 ESS1 was extended from 31 March 2020 to 31 October 2020. It provides new details on the treatment that will apply where a scheme participant is accidentally omitted from an appropriation of shares and the tax treatment of a distribution in specie from a demerged company where shares have been appropriated to participants of an APSS and the release date for those shares has not been reached.

On 27 January 2021, Revenue issued *eBrief 012/21* dealing with restricted shares. Restricted shares under s 128D, TCA 1997 are shares acquired by an employee/director of a company where there is restriction of at least one year in that individual's ability to transfer, assign, pledge or otherwise dispose of those shares. The benefit of such restricted shares, if they satisfy the conditions under s 128D, TCA 1997, is a reduction in the income tax charge from between 10% and 60%, depending on the period of the restriction. One of the qualifying conditions is that the restricted shares must be held in a trust established by the employer or held under such other arrangements as the Revenue Commissioners may allow. This eBrief confirmed that Chapter 8 of the Share Schemes Manual has been updated to confirm that queries regarding arrangements other than restricted shares under s 128D being held under a trust established by an employer should be sent to the Employee Share Scheme Section of Revenue via MyEnquiries or at *shareschemesection@revenue.ie*.

A save as you earn (SAYE) scheme is a tax efficient employee share option which is linked to a formal savings contract between employee participants and a qualifying third party financial institution. At the end of the savings period employees use the amount saved to exercise the options and fund the acquisition of the underlying shares. Given that a 'qualifying financial institution' refers to banks licenced in the EU, to clarify the post-Brexit position, Revenue *eBrief 013/21*, which was issued on 27 January 2021, confirmed that a 'qualifying savings institution' for SAYE schemes also includes a financial institution prescribed by the Minister for Finance. Barclays Bank UK PLC and Yorkshire Building Society have been prescribed as such and therefore have retained their qualifying savings institutions status for the purposes of SAYE schemes.[1]

---

[1]   See Taxes Consolidation Act 1997 (Section 519C(1)) (Prescribed Persons) Order 2020 (SI 357/2020).

PENSIONS

[20.14]   On 23 March 2021, Revenue issued *eBrief 059/21*, in relation to VAT & Employees' Pension Fund. The TDM on VAT & Employees' Pension Fund was updated to provide further clarification on the circumstances where an employer can claim deductibility for costs incurred in relation to an employee pension fund. The new Manual provides that a taxable person (the employer) is entitled to VAT deductibility in respect of costs incurred in the setting up, on-going management, administration, and management of the assets of a pension scheme where certain conditions are met.

To be entitled to deductibility, an employer must meet certain conditions:

— the costs of the input transaction must form part of the employer's general costs and must be, as such, components of the price of the taxable goods or services it supplies;

— the costs incurred must be invoiced to and paid by the employer and not passed on to the pension fund; and

— the existence and extent of the right to deduction is determined in light of the direct and immediate link with the employer's economic and taxable activity.

The Manual also includes new sections on circumstances where: (i) the pension trustee must contract with a third part service provider directly; (ii) the pension fund reimburses costs incurred by the employer; and (iii) the employer reimburses costs incurred by the pension fund.

On 28 May 2021, Revenue issued *eBrief 110/21*, in relation to the Pensions Manual (Chapter 17), which deals with overseas employers, overseas employees and employees seconded from overseas. Chapter 17 of the Pensions Manual has been updated following the enactment of the relevant parts of the Withdrawal of the United Kingdom from the European Union (Consequential Provisions) Act 2020.

The amendments maintain the *status quo* position following the withdrawal of the United Kingdom from the European Union for reliefs including:

— relief for contributions to UK pension schemes; and

— relief for migrant workers who wish to continue to contribute to a pre-existing 'overseas pensions plan' in another EU Member State or the United Kingdom.

On 10 September 2021, Revenue issued *eBrief 172/21*, which confirmed certain updates to Chapter 2 of the TDM on Membership of Occupational Pension Schemes. The updates are contained in paragraph 4. The update states that pension administrators should notify Revenue via MyEnquiries (or by e-mail, for Transport Layer Security (TLS) enabled administrators) where an employee who is temporarily absent or is seconded for a period exceeding five years remains as a member of an occupational pension scheme.

EMPLOYMENT TAX CASES

Taxation of Payments made under Compromise Agreement

[20.15] *Tax Appeal[2]—Appeal Commissioners—TCA 1997, ss 112, 123, 201, 192A & 6613—termination—compromise agreement—tax entire payment as income tax—apportionment—chose in action—capital gains tax*

This was an appeal against a Revenue decision to tax a payment under a compromise agreement entirely to income tax. An employee of a firm alleged that, through a series of events, he was subject to victimisation, defamation and injury to his professional reputation by the treatment of him by his employer. Following engagement with the firm's solicitors and the taxpayer's counsel, a compromise agreement was reached, which provided for a payment be made in the gross amount of €180,000 and the termination of the employment.

Revenue, had taken the position that the entire amount was subject to income tax under s 123, TCA 1997 as a payment received on the retirement or removal from an office or employment. The taxpayer, while acknowledging that a portion of the payment would be subject to income tax, brought this appeal against Revenue's position to tax the entire amount on the basis that he believed a significant portion of the payment was exempt, based on the following provisions:

— s 201(2)(a)(i)(II), TCA 1997 as a payment received 'on account of injury to or disability of the holder of an office or employment';

— s 192A, TCA 1997 as a payment made under relevant employment legislation providing for the protection of employees; or

— s 613(1)(c), TCA 1997 as 'compensation or damages for any wrong or injury suffered by an individual in his or her person or in his or her profession'.

In consideration of the s 123, TCA 1997 assertion by the taxpayer, it was found that Revenue's submission that the payment was 'in consideration or in consequence of, or otherwise in connection with, the termination of the holding of an office or employment' could only be true of €55,000. This was based on the taxpayer's agent's calculations of salary entitlements (which included four months' salary and holiday pay and days in lieu). It was found that although there was no apportionment expressed in the contract there was no evidence to suggest that the taxpayer was entitled to anything else above this €55,000.

In relation to the remainder of the payment, the Tax Appeal Commissioner (TAC) noted that the underlying principle in the interpretation of contractual documents is to discern the intention of the contracting parties. Having considered the clauses of the compromise agreement, the TAC disagreed with the appellant that any of the legislative provisions above were applicable. However, the TAC found that it was clear from the

---

[2]   115TACD2021.

drafting of the agreement (despite there not being an express apportionment) that the remaining €125,000 was paid to stop the appellant from taking proceedings against the company in relation to his defamation allegation. As such, s 123 could have no application to this element of the payment and, notwithstanding that the taxpayer agreed to resign, the remaining €125,000 was made in consideration of settling his 'claims' against the firm and assessable to tax under a different charging provision.

The TAC determined that the taxpayer would have a right of action to sue the firm and that this right could be correctly characterised as a chose in action. The TAC, referring to *Zim Properties v Procter*,[3] was of the view that a chose in action should be deemed an asset for the purposes of capital gains. In reference to s 532, TCA 1997 which defines an asset as 'All forms of property shall be assets for the purposes of the Capital Gains Tax code whether situate in the State or not'; and under s 535(2)(a)(iii) a capital sum is 'received in return for forfeiture or surrender of a right or for refraining from exercising a right', the remaining €125,000 was determined to be subject to capital gains tax.

The TAC apportioned the claim to employment-related severance, which was subject to income tax, and a right of action, which they viewed as a chose in action and subject to CGT.

Determination of Employed versus Self-employed Status

[20.16]   The categorisation of a worker as an employee versus self-employed continues to be a highly litigated area. Particular focus was placed in the below cases on 'mutuality of obligations' as a criteria to determine employment status with the courts emphasising that it is not in and of itself determinative of the matter and consideration should be given to other indicia.

[20.17]   *Tax Appeal[4]—Appeal Commissioners—self-employed/employee status—TCA 1997, s 112—contracts of service/contracts for service—mutuality of obligations*

This was an unsuccessful appeal made by the taxpayer in respect of Revenue's decision to tax dentists, doctors and a dental hygienist as employees under Schedule E, TCA 1997 rather than self-employed workers under Schedule D, TCA 1997. The appellant, who owned the clinic and engaged the workers, argued that each of the practitioners was hired as an independent contractor working under a contract for service rather than a contract of service.

The appellant's main submissions were that there was no mutuality of obligation so as to constitute a contract of service and the relevant legal tests to determine whether the practitioners were self-employed or employees supported the view that they were independent contractors. Revenue submitted that there was the requisite contractual

---

3   *Zim Properties v Procter* [1985] STC 90.
4   117TACD2021.

relationship that contained mutuality of obligations and those same legal tests to determine the employment status of the practitioners supported their view that they were in fact employees.

The TAC determined with respect to the mutuality of obligation requirement necessary for a contract of service to exist that, although the contracts on face value appeared to exclude this, it was in fact present in each of the contractual relationships. The TAC pointed to the fact that in the case of a dentist, they could opt not to accept every particular patient or could cancel a specific appointment but this did not mean that the dentists were relieved of the obligation to work the remainder of their contracted hours in a given day or week, nor did it relieve them of work-related obligations in relation to a given patient for the remainder of a course of treatment. It was further found that the right to cancel an appointment was qualified by the requirement to provide advance notification to the appellant and/or to schedule the appointment for a time when the dentist was available to perform the work. In the case of the dental hygienist and the doctors, the appellant pointed to the clause in those contracts requiring substitution of service where the practitioner was unavailable (at the expense of the practitioner) to honour or keep an appointment as evidence that there was no mutuality of obligation and it was incumbent on the practitioners to look after their own appointments. However, the TAC, on the facts, found that in practice substitution by use of a locum, for example, was never done and the reception of the clinic would instead arrange/rearrange appointments that would suit the practitioner.

Despite its finding on mutuality of obligation, the TAC noted that its presence is not in and of itself a sole deciding factor in the determination of employment status. Instead, the correct legal analysis is to also consider each of the following tests: (i) control; (ii) integration; (iii) the opportunity to profit; (iv) the bargaining power of the parties; (v) substitution and personal service; and (vi) the categorisation of employment status by the parties. Having engaged in a detailed consideration of each of the tests to the facts at hand, the TAC concluded that the workers were engaged under contracts of employment and reiterated that despite the contracts expressly categorising the relationship as one between independent contractors, the reality of the relationship (whether express or implied) is the determining factor.

[20.18]   *Tax Appeal[5]—Appeal Commissioners—PAYE—contractor/employee—TCA 1997, s 472—employee tax credits*

This was a successful appeal by a taxpayer for PAYE credits in circumstances where she was initially engaged as a self-employed physiotherapist in a physiotherapy practice but subsequently during the year became an employee of that practice.

The practice, following an audit by Revenue, was instructed to regularise staff members' contracts where Revenue were of the view they were employees of the practice rather than contractors. Before this audit, the taxpayer was a self-employed person for the purpose of taxation however following this audit, she was issued with a contract in

---

[5]   121TACD2021.

September 2018. The contract was headed with 'Terms of Employment', referred to the taxpayer as a 'part-time employee' and set out the name of the employer, the address of employment, the job description, duties and leave entitlements. The TAC noted that the only possible reference to a self-employed status was that the taxpayer was to invoice the practice every month. When the taxpayer requested copies of her payslips and to be paid as an employee under the contract, her employment was terminated. The taxpayer complained to Revenue about the lack of PRSI contributions and payslips by the practice. Revenue rejected the complaint and also refused to allow employee tax credits for the period of four months between September and the time she was terminated on the basis that she had not paid PAYE. In doing so, Revenue accepted a letter from the practice stating that the taxpayer was self-employed together with timesheets she submitted to her employer (that the practice claimed were invoices) as evidence that the taxpayer was self-employed and did not carry out any further investigation.

The TAC found that the taxpayer was an employee, based on the clear terms of the contract of employment and the reality of the situation and did not accept the veracity of the letter. The TAC found that the invoices were in reality just time-sheets setting out the amount of hours worked and patients seen without mention of any rate. The Commissioner also voiced concern with Revenue's approach to investigating the complaint, relying on the letter from the employer rather than engaging with the employee about her working pattern (especially considering that the taxpayer's employment status was formalised following the Revenue's own audit).

[20.19] *Phillips v Commissioners for Her Majesty's Revenue and Customs[6]— First-tier Tribunal—employment status—contract for services versus contract of services*

This case involved a determination of an individual's employment status. The First-tier Tribunal carried out a detailed analysis of the nature of the engagement between the appellant and an entity (C&G) in determining that the appellant was self-employed. C&G was an insurance broker providing niche bespoke insurance products which engaged the appellant in developing a new medical malpractice product due to his experience and contacts in the field. This included an analysis of the intention of the parties in negotiating the engagement terms, the remuneration structure, the degree of control and direction that C&G exercised over the appellant's activities, the degree of financial risk that the appellant was at in respect of his engagement with C&G, and the benefits that he was entitled to. In support of the conclusion that the appellant was performing his activities as a person in business on his own account, the First-tier Tribunal noted the fact that he was remunerated on the basis of commissions generated by C&G and had received advance payments on account of future expected commissions. His freedom to decide which insurers and clients to approach, and the fact that he had negotiated the retention of IP rights in an insurance product that he had worked on were also relevant considerations.

---

6   *Phillips v Commissioners for Her Majesty's Revenue and Customs* [2021] UKFTT 91.

See also the decision of the Court of Appeal of England and Wales in *Commissioners for Her Majesty's Revenue and Customs v Professional Game Match Officials Ltd*[7] at [**5.10**].

Denial of Credit in Respect of Tax Deducted from Emoluments of Certain Directors—s 997A, TCA 1997

[20.20]   Several cases before the TAC concerned the applicability of s 997A, TCA 1997. This section applies to directors or employees who have a material interest (being the ability either alone or with connected persons to control at least 15% of the ordinary share capital) in the company that pays emoluments to that director or employee. Its purpose is to deny such directors and employees a credit for tax deducted from their remuneration until such tax has been remitted to the Collector General.

[20.21]   *Tax Appeal*[8]*—Appeal Commissioners—TCA 1997, s 997A—credit— directors with material interest—denial of deduction—time limits to raise assessment—full and true disclosure*

The appellants were directors and held a 72% and 19% shareholding, respectively, in a company which was put into liquidation. The company had paid the appellants their salary for the year in question and operated employment taxes on this but, due to financial difficulties, did not discharge its employer's tax liability in full. The appellants completed their self-assessment forms and sought a credit for the employment tax deducted. Revenue, under s 997A, TCA 1997, denied the appellant a credit for the income tax deducted from the appellants. The TAC considered two issues: (i) whether s 997A, TCA 1997 applied; and (ii) whether the amended assessments by Revenue were made out of time.

The TAC held that s 997A applied as the appellants had a material interest in a company which had failed to discharge its tax liabilities. However, although the section was the appropriate remedy in respect of denying credits for unpaid tax, it can be only be invoked in circumstances where an amendment is made within the time frame permitted for making enquiries in relation to amending an assessment. An amendment outside of that time limit is only permitted where the return did not contain a full and true disclosure of all material facts necessary for the making of an assessment. The TAC found that the relevant returns did contain a full and true disclosure of all material facts necessary for the making of an assessment. In circumstances where an amendment is made outside of the four-year time limit prescribed by the legislation, the onus is on the Revenue to prove that it had reasonable grounds to believe that the returns were completed in a fraudulent or negligent manner and that the taxpayer should be afforded the opportunity to appeal such a conclusion. As such the appeal was allowed as Revenue was out of time to engage s 997A.

---

[7]   *Commissioners for Her Majesty's Revenue and Customs v Professional Game Match Officials Ltd* [2021] EWCA 1370; see *Arthur Cox Employment Law Yearbook 2020* at [**5.10**] for decision of Upper Tribunal.
[8]   18TACD2021.

[20.22] *Tax Appeal⁹—Appeal Commissioners—TCA 1997, s 997A—credit—directors with material interest—denial of deduction—discretion*

The appellant was a proprietary director and 99% shareholder of the company which had entered voluntary liquidation in September 2012 and had outstanding employer's tax liability of approximately €53,000. The appellant had filed income tax returns and claimed credits for the full amount of tax deducted by the company in 2010 and 2011. Revenue withdrew the credit and raised as assessment for the income tax owed as a result of the withdrawal in 2013. The appellant appealed this assessment.

The TAC denied the appeal reasoning that the wording of s 997A, TCA 1997 is unambiguous and does not contain any discretion to depart from the section based on the reasons why the employment tax liability was not discharged by the company. There was no dispute that the appellant was a director of the company holding a material interest nor that the company did not discharge its employer tax liabilities in full for the period in question, therefore s 997A applied. The effect of the section is to secure the payment of taxes from the emoluments derived from such individuals.

[20.23] *Tax Appeal¹⁰—Appeal Commissioners—TCA 1997, s 997A—credit—directors with material interest—denial of credit—examinership—scheme of arrangement*

The appellant was a 95% shareholder and director of the company who was in receipt of a salary from the company on which PAYE was operated. The company fell into financial difficulty and could not discharge all of its debts, including the amounts owed to the Revenue Commissioners. As a result, the company went through examinership and availed of a reduction in its debt under a court-approved scheme of arrangement resulting in less PAYE being paid than originally due. The scheme document provided that the discharge of the debt as outlined in the proposals was to be in full and final settlement of all claims and entitlements of each creditor to which a payment was made. Revenue subsequently raised an assessment under s 997A, TCA 1997 against the appellant withdrawing his income tax credit as the company's employment tax liabilities had not been discharged in full.

The appellant appealed, arguing that proposals approved by the court precluded the respondent from levying income tax on his income that related to the PAYE debts written down in the examinership. The appellant argued that, after accepting the proposals in the scheme of arrangement, the respondent could not then seek to resurrect this debt through the use of s 997A, TCA 1997 and doing so was contrary the terms of those proposals. The TAC agreed with the appellant and held that Revenue was not entitled to raise the assessment, which had the effect of defeating the court-approved proposals. Therefore, there was no need to explore s 997A, TCA 1997 further and the assessment was held to be incorrect.

---

9   37TACD2021.
10   51TACD2021.

Calculation of Ex Gratia Redundancy Payment

[20.24] *Tax Appeal[11]—Appeal Commissioners—TCA 1997, s 123—taxation of ex gratia payments—termination of employment—redundancy—calculation of tax-free pension lump sum—SCSB—double taxation*

This was an appeal regarding the calculation of the tax-free portion of a redundancy payment. The amount of a termination payment that can be received tax-free can be calculated by either applying the: (i) basic exemption; (ii) increased exemption; or (iii) standard capital superannuation benefit (SCSB), whichever calculation yields the best results for the taxpayer. When using the increased exemption or SCSB method, the present value of the taxpayer's tax-free pension lump sum must be deducted unless the entitlement is waived. The appellant argued that a previous deduction of a tax-free pension lump sum that was made when calculating his increased exemption on a previous redundancy should not be included in the current SCSB calculation of the tax owed on his current redundancy. The appellant had transferred his previous pension into a subsequent pension scheme and Revenue treated this as one pension and calculated his entitlement to an overall tax-free lump sum on retirement and used this figure (ie, it included a tax-free lump sum from the previous pension and the current pension) when calculating the tax-free portion of the subsequent redundancy payment. The appellant argued this amounted to double taxation.

The TAC disagreed and held the legislation requires the deduction to reflect the present value of the tax-free pension lump sum and the fact that a similar calculation was made in the past does not alter this obligation. The TAC rejected the appellant's argument that the fact that the quantum of a statutory tax exemption had been limited on two separate occasions by the same statutory provision had the result that he had been taxed twice on the same sum. Rather, the legislative scheme requires a deduction to be made to reflect the present value of a tax-free lump sum when calculating the extent or value of the tax exemption to which a taxpayer is entitled on a termination of employment.

Replacement Share Options

[20.25] *Vermilion Holdings Ltd v Commissioners for Her Majesty's Revenue and Customs[12]—Inner House of the Court of Session—options—by reasons of employment—replacement options*

The Inner House of the Court of Session held that replacement share options issued to a director fell outside s 471 of the Income Tax (Earnings and Pensions) Act 2003 (which charges employment related securities to PAYE and national insurance contributions)

---

[11]   65TACD2021.
[12]   *Vermilion Holdings Ltd v Commissioners for Her Majesty's Revenue and Customs* [2021] CSIH 45 (TCC).

because they were not made available by reason of his employment. The original option was granted in lieu of fees for advisory services rendered to Vermillion Holdings Ltd by the now director through his consultancy company (prior to him being director). HMRC accepted that the original option was not 'employment-related'. As part of a refinancing, that option was released for the grant of a less favourable replacement option and at the same time he was appointed director. The Inner House of the Court of Session held that the replacement option was not, as a matter of fact, granted by reason of employment as there was no 'real link' between the director's employment and the right or opportunity to acquire the replacement option. The replacement option had less favourable terms than the original and therefore was not a right or opportunity but merely a diminution of existing rights. Furthermore, the director would have been offered the replacement regardless of the new directorship. The substance of the transaction was rather one of compromise and exchange and not connected to the directorship.

Provision of Living Accommodation—Better Performance Test

[20.26] *Tax Appeal[13]—Appeal Commissioners—TCA 1997, ss 118 & 120—living accommodation—BIK—'better performance test'—body corporate—charitable trust*

The appellant was employed by a charitable trust and, as part of this employment, he was provided with accommodation for the duration of his employment. The accommodation was a residential property occupied by the appellant and one other person and was outside the grounds of the charity. The appeal concerned the determination made by Revenue that the provision of living accommodation was chargeable to income tax as a benefit-in-kind (BIK) under s 118, TCA 1997.

The provision of rent-free accommodation by an employer is generally a taxable BIK under s 118, TCA 1997. However, the appellant argued that he fell within the exception to the charge set out in s 118(3), TCA 1997, which states that a taxable benefit will not arise where an employee (but not a director) is required by the terms of their employment to live in accommodation provided by the employer in part of the employer's business premises so that the employee can properly perform his or her duties. This is known as the 'better performance test'. In addition, either of the following conditions must also apply:

— the accommodation is provided in accordance with a practice which has commonly prevailed in trades of the class in question and as respects employees of the class in question; or

— it is necessary, in the particular class of trade, for employees of the class in question to live on the premises.

---

[13]   16TACD2021.

In dismissing the appeal, the TAC agreed with Revenue's position that the 'better performance test' was not satisfied as, while it may have be desirable for the appellant and the employer that the appellant live close to his place of employment, they did not see it as a necessary requirement for his duties to live in the accommodation. The TAC also noted that s 118 only applies to benefits made by 'bodies corporate' and that in this regard it was necessary to consider whether a charity comes within the terms of the section. Having analysed the relevant legislation, in particular s 120, TCA 1997 which applies s 118, TCA 1997 to 'unincorporated societies, public bodies and other bodies' and the definition of a charitable trust under the Charities Act 2009, the TAC ultimately determined that a charitable trust came within s 120, TCA 1997 and therefore fell within the concept of body corporate for the purposes of s 118 TCA.

Income Tax on Travel and Subsistence Expenses

[20.27] *Tax Appeal[14]—Appeal Commissioners—TCA 1997, ss 81(2), 112, 114, 117 & 118—travel and subsistence expenses—wholly and exclusively for purpose of trade—foreign expenses—wholly, exclusively and necessarily in performance of duties of office or employment*

This was an appeal concerning payments by the appellant (a company) and an assessment of PAYE/PRSI/USC of €12,266 between 2013 and 2015. The core issue to determine was whether or not expenses paid to directors, as a result of travel expenses incurred by them when meeting suppliers and travelling abroad on promotion/business development activities on behalf of the company, are subject to income tax through PAYE.

In reaching its conclusions, the TAC found that both parties had relied on the incorrect legal basis for their arguments. The parties focused on s 81(2), TCA 1997 and whether the expenses were incurred wholly and exclusively for the purposes of the trade. However, the subject matter of the dispute was whether the expenses were subject to income tax through PAYE and not whether the expenses were deductible expenses for the company. Section 81(2), TCA 1997 is only prescriptive in respect of computing the amount of the profits or gains to be charged to tax under Case I or II of Schedule D and it does address the PAYE tax consequences that might arise on expenses that are deemed to be non-deductible. Instead, the relevant potential charge to PAYE tax for the expenses arises under ss 112, 114, 117 and 118, TCA 1997. Whether or not the payment of the expenses by the company to the directors was subject to PAYE depended on whether these were expenses, that were incurred 'wholly, exclusively and necessarily in the performance of the duties of the office or employment' under s 114, TCA 1997. Applying this test to each category of expense in question, ultimately, the TAC reduced the amount of the disallowed expenses thereby reducing the assessment against the appellant.

---

[14] 32TACD2021.

[20.28] *Tax Appeal*[15]*—Appeal Commissioners—TCA 1997, ss 112, 114, 117, 118, 929, 983, 985A & 990—director—travel and subsistence—Income Tax (Employments) (Consolidated) Regulations 2001*[16]*—normal place of work— deductibility—necessarily incurred*

This was an appeal against Revenue's findings that certain expense payments made by a company to the appellant were not incurred 'wholly, exclusively and necessarily' in the performance of his employment duties as prescribed by s 114, TCA 1997. The appellant was a Projects Engineer and was an employee and director paid by the company for providing his services to another agency company, who in turn provided a pharma company with project engineer services using the appellant. Under the arrangements, the company invoiced the agency company based on the appellant's timesheets, approved by the pharma company and the agency. In turn, the agency company invoiced the pharma company. The travel expenses related to the trip to and from the appellant's home and the pharma company site and the subsistence in the large related to overnight subsistence.

Section 114 sets out the test for deductibility:

> Where the holder of an office or employment of profit is *necessarily* obliged to incur and defray out of the emoluments of the office or employment of profit expenses of travelling in the performance of the duties of that office or employment, *or* otherwise to expend money wholly, exclusively and necessarily in the performance of those duties, there may be deducted from the emoluments to be assessed the expenses so necessarily incurred and defrayed. [Emphasis added.]

With respect to the first limb of this test, Revenue argued that the appellant was not entitled to claim 100% of the travel and subsistence expenditure representing the 'home to work' element by virtue of the fact the appellant's 'normal place of work' was in fact the pharma company's site; Revenue cited well-established case law to this effect particularly *Ricketts v Colquhoun.*[17] The TAC noted that though the cases cited did not rest easily with modern day employee work practices such as the use of technology, remote hubs and working from home, he was bound by them. However, the TAC was of the view that the pharma company site could not, on the facts, be considered the appellant's 'normal place of work' given that he was not an employee of the pharma company; his work there was of a transient nature; he had no fixed desk there; and he spent considerable amounts of time abroad. Furthermore under the contractual arrangement, his employer company was entitled to bill the agency company/pharma company for the time spent by the appellant travelling to and from his home to the sites required by the pharma company. The travel time was an integral part of the contract. The company could not charge the agency company/pharma company for the travel time unless travel time was incurred. This meant that, in executing the contract, the appellant could not perform his employment contract unless he incurred the travelling costs and related subsistence associated with the contract his company had with the agency

---

[15]   113TACD2021.
[16]   Income Tax (Employments) (Consolidated) Regulations 2001 (SI 559/2001).
[17]   *Ricketts v Colquhoun* 10 TC 118.

company/pharma company. As such, the TAC found that the appellant could not fulfil his employment contract 'without incurring the particular outlay' of travelling to the sites and, the expense was 'necessarily' incurred for s 114, TCA 1997 purposes and was deductible.[18]

[20.29] *Smallman & Sons Ltd v Commissioners for Her Majesty's Revenue and Customs[19]—First-tier Tribunal—employer provided cars—agency agreement—BIK*

The First-tier Tribunal held that cars made available to company directors, under an undocumented agency arrangement by which the directors met all costs on arm's length terms, were made available to the directors by reason of their employment and therefore a taxable benefit for the directors. The First-tier Tribunal dismissed the company and directors' appeals against assessments to national insurance contribution and income tax. The cars were chosen by the directors but acquired in the name of the company, by lease purchase, in order to benefit from favourable finance rates available to the company. The First-tier Tribunal disagreed with the appellants' argument that the directors were essentially making the cars available to themselves and, as the cars were not made available by the company they were not made available 'by reason of employment'. The First-tier Tribunal determined that there was no evidence that the leasing company accepted that the company was contracting as agent for the directors or would have recourse to the directors in case of default.

Deductibility of Employee Expenses

[20.30] *Kunjur v Commissioners for Her Majesty's Revenue and Customs[20]— First-tier Tribunal (Tax)— Income Tax Employment and Pensions Act 2005, s 336—income tax—employment income—whether expenditure on accommodation for trainee maxillofacial surgeon wholly, exclusively and necessarily for purpose of employment*

This case involved a determination on whether a taxpayer's accommodation costs were wholly, exclusively and necessarily incurred in the performance of his employment duties and whether he was obliged to incur the expenses as a holder of that employment.[21]

The taxpayer, a qualified dental surgeon, accepted the only available position on a four-year course to train as a maxillofacial surgeon at a hospital in London with expected periods at Kings College. He rented modest accommodation nearby and claimed a deduction for the cost of this accommodation against his employment income while on the course. He had tried commuting from Southampton but found this left him too

---

18   In doing so the TAC cited *Ricketts in H F Kelly (Inspector of Taxes) v Commandant Owen Quinn* [1961] IR 488.

19   *Smallman & Sons Ltd v Commissioners for Her Majesty's Revenue and Customs* [2021] UKFTT 300 (TC).

20   *Kunjur v Commissioners for Her Majesty's Revenue and Customs* [2021] UKFTT 362 (TC).

21   As provided for by s 336 of the Income Tax Employment and Pensions Act 2005.

tired to discharge his obligations as a doctor safely. He submitted that his on-call duties required him to be able to treat patients within 30 minutes of a call. Additionally, as he was always informally on call in respect of the maxillofacial patients, he was always at work while in his rented accommodation.

HMRC denied the claims, arguing that his employment contract did not require him to rent premises close to the hospital, that he did not work from home, and that he did not incur the expenses in the performance of his duties. HMRC therefore asserted that he was not obliged to incur the expenses as a holder of employment and that they were not incurred wholly, exclusively, and necessarily for the purposes of the employment.

The First-tier Tribunal partially allowed the claim noting that all three aspects of the deductibility test would need to be satisfied in relation to each portion of the expense namely:

(1) The expenses were incurred, under his contract as a doctor.

    (a) On this point, it found that the taxpayer's obligations to place the interests of his patients above his own were obligations of his employment as a doctor.

    (b) He had to live within 30 minutes of the hospital when on call, and the First-tier Tribunal agreed that it was unreasonable to expect him to move his family, or to use undergraduate hospital accommodation.

    (c) The First-tier Tribunal found that he was obliged to incur the accommodation expenditure as the holder of an employment.

(2) Wholly, exclusively and necessarily.

    (d) The First-tier Tribunal found the taxpayer did not obtain any private benefit from the accommodation at weekends (when the doctor returned home, unless on call), and when the doctor was formally on call and actually in attendance at the hospital (or when on the phone with, or at, the hospital on informal call).

    (e) However, the First-tier Tribunal found the taxpayer did not need to be close to the hospital on the nights where he undertook research and prepared articles as required by his employment and as such obtained a private benefit from the use of the accommodation during this time.

(3) In the performance of his duties.

    (f) The First-tier Tribunal found that when the taxpayer was informally on call and gave advice over the telephone from the accommodation, the accommodation and telephone was used in the performance of the duties for the duration of the calls. When he was formally on call and was present at the hospital the accommodation was not being used in the performance of the employment.

    (g) The First-tier Tribunal noted that being present at the accommodation waiting for a call was not part of the performance of his duties.

The First-tier Tribunal therefore limited the relief to time spent on the phone with the hospital giving advice from the accommodation while on informal and formal on-call duty, as only this proportion satisfied all three elements of the test as outlined above and requested the parties to agree the proportion.

Pensions

[20.31]   *Tax Appeal[22]—Appeal Commissioners—TCA 1997, s 483—pension—gift of pension entitlement to Minister for Finance—relief for certain gifts*

This was an appeal against assessments to income tax in respect of the appellant's claim for relief for gifts made to the State under s 483, TCA 1997. The appellant was a TD and argued that the act of foregoing his entitlement to his ministerial pension constituted a 'gift of money made to the Minister for Finance for use for any purpose for or towards the cost of which public moneys are provided' and therefore he was entitled to claim relief under s 483, TCA 1997 against his other income in respect of the years under appeal. The TAC held, in relation to the s 483, TCA 1997 claim, that s 483, TCA 1997 necessitates an actual gift of money. However, by foregoing his ministerial pension, the appellant merely disposed of his right to a future pension stream as opposed to having made a contemporaneous 'gift of money'. As such, the appellant could not have made a 'gift of money' as he was not in possession of the 'money' at the time of the gift and therefore was not entitled to relief under s 483, TCA 1997. The TAC further held that though a pension is a chargeable emolument for the purposes of s 112, TCA 1997, as the appellant chose to forego his pension entitlement, he was not in receipt of the pension foregone nor had he any legal claim to it. Given this, he could not be assessed to tax under Schedule E on the element of pension foregone as no pension was 'payable' to him.

[20.32]   *Tax Appeal[23]—Appeal Commissioners—TCA 1997, s 531A—Directive 2008/94/EC[24]—pension entitlement—liability to USC—relevant emolument—Social Welfare Acts—legitimate expectation—estoppel*

This was an unsuccessful appeal by a taxpayer regarding pension entitlements which were assessed by Revenue as being emoluments and therefore subject to USC. The taxpayer was an employee of a company which became insolvent and his pension fund also became insolvent. A case was submitted to the ECJ, which ruled in favour of the taxpayer with respect to the argument that the State had failed to accurately transpose Directive 2008/94/EC for the protection of employees in the event of company insolvency. The ECJ ruled in favour of the taxpayer and accordingly he was paid his pension entitlements from the scheme from the Central Fund of the Exchequer, which the Department of Social Protection then administered on behalf of the State.

The appellant argued that he has been incorrectly assessed to USC in relation to these payments as social welfare, and similar type payments payable under the Social Welfare Acts are excluded from the definition of 'relevant emoluments' on which USC is chargeable by virtue of s 531(AM)(a)(I), TCA 1997. The TAC determined these were not social welfare or similar payments drawn from money granted to the Department of Social Protection but were payments made under s 48B of the Pension Act 1990 drawn

---

[22]   11TACD2021.
[23]   109TACD2021.
[24]   Directive 2008/94/EC on the protection of employees in the event of the insolvency of their employer.

from the public Revenue of the State. Therefore, the payments did not qualify as being exempt from USC. There were also arguments around the interpretation of Revenue guidance, which the appellant submitted had essentially given him a legitimate expectation that a USC charge would not be applicable. Whereas the Commissioner had sympathy for this argument stating that at best the guidance was imprecise, he reiterated that the TAC does not have the jurisdiction to consider or determine arguments grounded in legitimate expectation or estoppel because such points fall outside of its statutory jurisdiction.

[20.33] *Tax Appeal[25]—Appeal Commissioners—pension—additional voluntary contribution—entitlement to a deduction—jurisdiction of TAC*

This was an appeal against a refusal by Revenue to grant tax relief to the appellant in respect of a once-off additional voluntary pension contribution (AVC) made in 2017 in respect of the tax year ended December 2016. The appellant had commenced employment with the employer in 2017 and soon after made the AVC payment to the pension fund of his employer. Prior to 2017, the appellant had been self-employed and was not in receipt of Schedule E employment income. Before submitting his income tax return for 2016, the appellant contacted Revenue and enquired regarding the relief available for the AVC payment and regarding the fact that the Form 11 ROS return only allowed him to enter the payment in the 'RAC/PRSA/QOPP relief claimed in 2016' box. The appellant submitted that he was informed that 'the making of the contribution was the key issue in terms of receiving the tax credit for 2016 and to include the payment in the box that would accept it'. The appellant submitted that at 'no point did the official cast any doubt on the eligibility of the payment for tax credit'.

He therefore submitted his 2016 income tax return and claimed a deduction in this return against his 2016 Schedule D-Case I Income. The appellant submitted that as a result of seeking and obtaining clarification regarding the validity of this relief claim from the respondent's customer service section, prior to the return deadline, he decided not to make any additional PRSA contribution that would have been deductible against his Schedule D-Case I income for 2016.

A number of weeks later, Revenue informed the appellant that it would not allow a tax deduction for the AVC payment. There was various further correspondence and ultimately the appellant's pension deduction claim was disallowed by Revenue and was appealed to the TAC.

The TAC agreed with Revenue that contributions to occupational pension schemes can only be relieved by reference to net relevant emoluments from the occupation in a relevant period and that there is an absence of discretion in s 774(7a), TCA 1997 which only provides for relief as an expense of employment income under Schedule E. The TAC held that, as the appellant had no Schedule E income in 2016, he was not entitled to claim relief in that year in respect of the AVC made in 2017 to his employer's pension scheme. The TAC also noted that, insofar as the appellant sought to set aside

---

[25]   07TACD2021.

the refusal of the repayment claim based on an alleged unfairness, such grounds of appeal do not fall within the jurisdiction of the TAC and thus did not fall to be determined as part of the appeal.

Taxation on Receipts Basis

[20.34]   *Tax Appeal[26]—Appeal Commissioners—TCA 1997, s 112—taxation additional pay—receipts basis—earning basis*

This is an unsuccessful appeal by the appellant, a post primary teacher, against a refusal by Revenue to treat additional pay awarded to the appellant in 2019, but relating to earnings in the years 2013 through to 2019, as taxable in the years 2013 through to 2019. The TAC denied the appeal as by virtue of s 112, TCA 1997, the payment had to be taxed in 2019, the year of receipt.

---

[26]   99TACD2021.

Chapter 21

Transfer of Undertaking

INTRODUCTION

[21.01] The Labour Court in *Bidvest* considered whether in fact an economic entity existed which was capable of being transferred. The implications for employee rights of multiple transferees was considered by the UK EAT in *McTear Contracts Limited*. The obligation to inform and consult was considered by the Labour Court in *Kenmare Brewhouse* and by the UK EAT in *Lewis*.

Transfer?

[21.02] *Bidvest Noonan (ROI) Ltd v Lynch[1]—Labour Court—appeal from the Workplace Relations Commission—European Communities (Protection of Employees on Transfer of Undertakings) Regulations 2003[2]—agency provided workers to an employer—no economic entity existed capable of being transferred—no transfer had occurred under the TUPE Regulations*

The Labour Court upheld the decision of the WRC, which found that, as there was no entity capable of being transferred, no transfer of undertakings had occurred under the European Communities (Protection of Employees on Transfer of Undertakings) Regulations 2003 (TUPE).

The claimant commenced work with the respondent in September 2014 and her last day working for the respondent was 24 August 2017. The claimant alleged that either she was transferred to another organisation, in which case the respondent had not complied with the requirements of regs 4 and 8 of TUPE, or she was made redundant. The respondent asserted that the claimant and her colleagues were transferred by operation of TUPE to a named company.

In 2004, the respondent was approached by its client, University Hospital Kerry (part of the HSE), and was asked to recruit a number of health care assistants (HCAs), which were then to be placed with the client. While the recruitment process was run by the

---

[1] *Bidvest Noonan (ROI) Ltd v Lynch* TUD203.
[2] European Communities (Protection of Employees on Transfer of Undertakings) Regulations 2003 (SI 131/2003).

respondent, the HSE had a member of staff on the interview board. A total of 14 staff, all at HCA grade, were recruited in this manner. The staff were paid through the respondent's payroll and issues relating to annual leave and sick leave were dealt with by Mr O'Connor, a manager with the respondent. In practice, a member of the nursing staff from the hospital contacted Mr O'Connor requesting a HCA who would then report to the nurse. The nurse would assign tasks and hours to the HCA.

In August 2017, the HSE sent an email to all HSE staff outlining the New Multi-Supplier framework for the provision of short-term temporary and locum agency staff, including HCAs, from 1 September 2017. The respondent was not made aware of this development at the time and attempted on a number of occasions to clarify with the hospital how this would impact on their HCAs. Eventually, the operations manager at the hospital informed the respondent that the hospital was legally obliged to use an alternative provider from 1 September 2017.

Several exchanges of correspondence between the claimant and the respondent culminated in a letter dated 21 September 2017 from the respondent, advising her that as the client, University Hospital Kerry, had transferred its business, the claimant would be processed as a leaver from the respondent and would be given her P45 in due course. She was also requested to return her HSE ID badge.

The Court had to determine whether there was a transfer within the meaning of TUPE. For a transfer to occur, there must be a transfer of an economic entity. The Court then considered what constituted an economic entity. In this case, the workforce consisted of 14 HCAs assigned to University Hospital Kerry. They were all the same grade and had no management structure. They were not a cohesive group and were individually assigned; they had no operating method nor 'any scope to influence the organisation of their work'. The Court determined that no autonomous entity existed within the respondent; rather there was an arrangement akin to an agency arrangement whereby the respondent provided HCA staff to University Hospital Kerry. On the basis that no entity capable of being transferred existed, the Court was satisfied that no transfer as defined by TUPE occurred and the appeal failed.

Multiple Transferees

[21.03] *McTear Contracts Ltd v Bennett, Mitie Property Services UK Ltd and Amey Services Ltd[3]—UK Employment Appeal Tribunal—appeal from employment tribunal—Transfer of Undertakings (Protection of Employment) Regulations 2006[4]—transfer of undertakings—service change provision—transfer to multiple transferees*

For a number of years up to 2017, Amey undertook the replacement of kitchens within the social housing stock of North Lanarkshire Council under a contract. From around

---

3   *McTear Contracts Ltd v Bennett, Mitie Property Services UK Ltd and Amey Services Ltd* UKEATS/0023/19/SS.

4   Transfer of Undertakings (Protection of Employment) Regulations 2006 (SI 2006/246).

March 2017, the Amey employees working on the contract were divided into two teams, working independently. The teams were not allocated to a geographical area within the local authority boundary and both teams worked across the whole of the local authority area.

The local authority re-tendered the kitchen installation contract and did so in two lots, one being the northern part of the territory and the other being the southern part of the territory. Amey's HR team produced a spreadsheet identifying the locations at which work had been undertaken during the final period of the Amey contract. The spreadsheet sought to identify the number of the jobs each of the two teams had worked on in each of the areas corresponding to the two lots under the new contract. As result of this approach, Amey concluded that one team broadly corresponded with lot one and another team broadly corresponded with lot two. Neither of the successful tenderers took on the contracts of employment of the claimants, but Amey maintained that the claimants' contracts had transferred to the relevant new contractor.

The employment tribunal concluded that there was a service provision change and the employees in each of the two relevant teams transferred to the relevant contractor and that liability for each affected employee could transfer to only one of other of the transferees. However, between the date of the employment tribunal decision and the hearing in the UK EAT, the ECJ issued its judgment in *ISS Facility Services NV v Govaerts*,[5] as a result of which an additional ground of appeal was raised with reference to the decision in *Govaerts*.

The EAT found that, as a result of the decision in *Govaerts*, the conclusions of the tribunal were open to doubt and that the principle in *Govaerts* should apply equally to the UK indigenous service provision change regime. The EAT noted that:

> there is no reason in principle why an employee may not, following such a transfer, hold two or more contracts of employment with different employers at the same time, provided that the work attributable to each contract is clearly separate from the work on the other(s) and is identifiably as such. The division, on geographical lines, of work previously carried out under a single contract into two new contracts is, in principal, [sic] a situation where there could properly be found to be different employers on different jobs.

The EAT found that, given the 'fact sensitive nature of the enquiry' necessitated under *Govaerts*, the case should be remitted to the same employment tribunal, which would have to consider the application of the decision in *Govaerts* to each of the claimants individually.

Obligation to Inform and Consult/Dismissal

[21.04] *Kenmare Brewhouse Ltd t/a McCarthy's Bar and Restaurant v O'Leary*[6]— *Labour Court—appeal from Workplace Relations Commission—European*

---

5   *ISS Facility Services NV v Govaerts* [2020] ICR 1115; (Case C-344/18).
6   *Kenmare Brewhouse Ltd t/a McCarthy's Bar and Restaurant v O'Leary* TUD207.

Communities (Protection of Employees on Transfer of Undertakings) Regulations 2003[7]—failure to inform and consult—failure to comply with statutory requirement to place on temporary lay-off

The Labour Court overturned a decision of the WRC and found that there was a breach of the European Communities (Protection of Employees on Transfer of Undertakings) Regulations 2003 (TUPE), and the claimant was effectively dismissed.

The claimant was employed by Ruskin Concept Ltd from May 2008. On 20 December 2018, her employment was transferred to the respondent. When the premises were being sold, Ruskin Concept had written to all staff and advised them that TUPE applied and that the respondent would be taking on all staff. After the transfer, the respondent placed the claimant on temporary redundancy with immediate effect. The claimant claimed that the respondent did not comply with the requirements of TUPE and that she was dismissed.

When the claimant sought to progress her redundancy application, the respondent stated that she had been advised that she was on temporary redundancy due to renovations and that when they were completed, she could return to work. The claimant stated that she had been advised by one of the directors of the company that she was being made redundant and that she should approach Social Welfare. She alleged that neither the respondent nor her previous employer complied with the requirements of TUPE, including reg 4 on terms and conditions of employment and reg 8 on the provision of information and measures that would impact on the claimant. She alleged that she was effectively dismissed with effect from the 20 December 2018 and started a new job in April 2019.

The respondent claimed that when it took over the business on 20 December 2018, it closed the business to carry out renovations and to relaunch it as a restaurant and a bar. The respondent did not dispute that a transfer had occurred and stated that it was their intention to offer all the existing staff a job in the renovated business. The respondent asserted that when they said temporarily redundant, they actually meant short-term lay-off. On 1 March 2019, the respondent wrote to all employees that had transferred, informing them that they were on a short lay-off, explaining the future of the business, and asking that they let the respondent know whether they would be taking up employment with them.

The Court stated that it was clear that very little interaction took place between either the transferor or the transferee with the claimant, as evidenced by the lack of written documentation relating to the transfer and what the respondent claimed was a temporary lay-off. The Court noted that reg 4 sets out that all rights and obligations arising from a contract shall transfer, including the right to be paid, and to be informed if there are issues that will impact on an employee's employment status. The Court found that the respondent failed to comply with its obligations set out in reg 4. Regulation 8

---

[7]   European Communities (Protection of Employees on Transfer of Undertakings) Regulations 2003 (SI 131/2003).

requires that employees are provided with information in advance of the transfer, and the Court did not accept that the respondent only decided on the day of the transfer that it was going to close the business temporarily to renovate it as a pub and restaurant. The respondent's failure to engage with the claimant relating to the impact of the temporary closure on her employment was found to be the most serious of the breaches under reg 8; however, the Court also noted the respondent's failure to convey the legal, economic and social implications of the transfer.

The Court concluded that the claimant was entitled to consider herself dismissed with effect from 20 December 2018. In respect of the breach of reg 4, the Court awarded her compensation of €600. The Court ordered the respondent to pay four weeks' remuneration in compensation, ie the maximum amount of compensation which can be awarded, for the breach of reg 8. The Court also determined that the claimant was unfairly dismissed and awarded the claimant compensation in the sum of €2,688 (16 weeks average salary), bringing the total sum awarded to the claimant to €3,960.

[21.05] *Lewis v Dow Silicones UK Ltd[8]—UK Employment Appeal Tribunal— Shanks J—appeal from employment tribunal—Transfer of Undertakings (Protection of Employment) Regulations 2006,[9] reg 4(9)—transfer of undertakings—unfair dismissal—fundamental breach of contract—substantial changes to working arrangements—employee's detriment*

The claimant worked at the Combined Heat and Power Plant in South Wales as one of ten operations technicians. He started in June 1999 and was initially employed by Npower. The respondent, Dow Silicones UK Ltd, bought the plant in 2013 but the staff were outsourced to Engie Renewals Ltd, who became the claimant's employer. In 2017, the respondent decided to 'insource' the staff; this involved them transferring from Engie to the respondent under the Transfer of Undertakings (Protection of Employment) Regulations 2006 (TUPE Regulations) on 1 March 2018. The respondent intended to make changes to the working arrangements at the plant. The claimant was not happy with these changes and he resigned on 5 March 2018 claiming unfair dismissal. He alleged that the respondent was acting in fundamental breach of his contract of employment and that his resignation gave rise to a constructive dismissal and/or that he could rely on reg 4(9) of TUPE which provides:

> where a relevant transfer involves or would involve a substantial change in working conditions to the material detriment of a person whose contract of employment is or would be transferred under paragraph (1), such an employee may treat the contract of employment as having been terminated, and the employee shall be treated for any purpose as having been dismissed by the employer.

There was no individual written contract of employment relating to the claimant but it was common ground that the Npower collective agreement for graded staff dated May 2012 was incorporated into his contract.

---

8   *Lewis v Dow Silicones UK Ltd* UKEAT/0155/20/LA.
9   Transfer of Undertakings (Protection of Employment) Regulations 2006 (SI 2006/246).

There was no dispute that the respondent was going to introduce changes in the way the operations technicians worked at the plant. The main change was to the standby/callout arrangements. Although the employment tribunal found that employees were not forced to provide standby cover if circumstances prevented this because of, for example, sickness or childcare difficulties, the system was subject to monitoring, and failure to provide cover when required could result in disciplinary action or affect performance-related pay. In addition, the respondent wished to change the operations technicians' responsibilities in relation to safety. This was to involve training over a period of six months and important new responsibilities.

The employment tribunal decided that there had been no dismissal on either basis and that his claim therefore failed. The claimant appealed on the grounds that that decision was perverse.

On appeal, the claimant stated that the employment tribunal erred in failing to find that there was a fundamental breach of contract and that the transfer would involve substantial changes to his material detriment for the purposes of reg 4(9) of the TUPE Regulations having regard to the proposed changes in relation to: (a) standby/callout duties; (b) holiday entitlement; (c) the elimination (or reduction) of the shift and unsocial hours allowance; and (d) the introduction of new safety responsibilities.

The EAT accepted the employment tribunal's finding that the respondent intended to honour the claimant's existing entitlements, once they had been established to their satisfaction. Accordingly, the EAT concentrated only on the proposed changes in relation to standby/callout duties and safety responsibilities.

The EAT agreed with the employment tribunal which found that these changes were ones that could properly be made by the claimant's employer within the express terms of his existing contract as found in the Npower collective agreement and rejected the appeal based on fundamental breach of contract and constructive dismissal.

However, the EAT went onto consider reg 4(9). The employment tribunal found that the new standby/callout arrangements did not involve a substantial change to the claimant's working conditions to his material detriment because: (a) the respondent had a contractual right to introduce the new system and the claimant 'owed' the hours; and (b) the claimant already worked additional hours for Engie by way of cover. The EAT disagreed with the employment tribunal's findings in this regard. It stated that:

> The fact that an employer is contractually entitled to introduce a change in working conditions does not mean it is not a change. And the fact that [the claimant] may have provided many hours of cover by way of wholly voluntary overtime when asked under the previous arrangements cannot mean that effectively having to provide cover when rostered and called upon does not represent a change which is of its nature substantial ... Plainly [the claimant] considered the change detrimental to him and I cannot see any basis for saying that his position is not reasonable.

The EAT found that this was a substantial change to the claimant's material detriment and held that the employment tribunal's finding to the contrary was 'perverse'. The EAT reached a similar conclusion in relation to the safety responsibilities.

Accordingly, the EAT allowed the appeal in relation to the employment tribunal's finding on reg 4(9) of the TUPE Regulations and substituted a decision that, by reason of the changes to his working conditions in relation to standby/callout duties and safety, the claimant was entitled to treat his contract of employment as terminated and be considered as having been dismissed by the respondent. It remitted the complaint of unfair dismissal based on reg 4(9) to a freshly constituted employment tribunal for determination.

Chapter 22

Unfair Dismissal

INTRODUCTION

[22.01] *AA Euro Recruitment* (Labour Court) is a rare example of where agency worker status or otherwise becomes a central point in an unfair dismissal claim.

Simoes (UK EAT) is an example of dismissal by reason of the employee asserting his/her statutory rights.

The UK EAT had to consider the defence of Capability in *TWI Ltd*.

The correct approach to the assessment of Compensation was considered by the Labour Court in *CityJet*.

As always, there were a great many cases where Conduct was the defence relied on by the employer. The conduct concerned included sexual harassment (*AK*, High Court), disqualification from driving (*Folman*, Labour Court), refusal to carry out instructions, (*Connemara Marble*, Labour Court), sexual assault (*a Beverage Company*, Labour Court), hostile and aggressive behaviour towards a customer (*Q-Park*, Labour Court), unauthorised absence (*Sectec Employment*, Labour Court), failure to report an incident (*Donegal Meat Processors*, Labour Court), possession by an employee of the Revenue Commissioners of contraband cigarettes (*Keane*, Labour Court), lack of trust (*McAllisteir*, Labour Court), assault (*Smurfit Kappa*, Labour Court), receipt of a top-up payment (*DPP Law Ltd*, Court of Appeal of England and Wales), the employee placing a covert security camera in his office (*Northbay*, UK EAT), improper authorisation of an expense (*Thompson*, UK EAT) and the attendance of a public servant at a political rally (*London Burough of Hammersmith and Fulham*, UK EAT).

Likewise, a great many Constructive Dismissal claims are noted. In most cases, the claims were not successful for various reasons. They included failure to follow grievance procedures (*Gallivan* and *Cope Ltd*, Labour Court), the expiry of a fixed term contract (*Horeau*, Labour Court) and failure to exhaust internal appeals (*Get Fresh Vending*, Labour Court). Cases in which a constructive dismissal claims succeeded were *Monaghan* (Labour Court), *Ure* (UK EAT) and *Flatman* and *Hall* (UK EAT). The possibility that the grievance procedure might survive the repudiation of a contract was considered by the UK EAT in *Gordon*.

The Labour Court had to consider whether there was in fact a dismissal of the claimant by the respondent in *Boyle Sports* and in *The Blue Door*. *Bus Atha Cliath* (Labour Court) is an example of a case where the employer succeeded in the defence that the claimant could not continue to be employed without contravention of a statutory duty.

In *Trackwork*, the UK EAT considered a case where the claimant claimed that they had been dismissed by reason of discharge by them of their health and safety obligations.

In *McCormack*, the Labour Court set out the obligations of an employer who seeks to rely on the defence of Incapacity.

Two UK cases address the Other Substantial Grounds defence, namely *L v K* (Sottish Court of Session) where a teacher was found to be in possession of a computer containing indecent images of children and *Phoenix Product Development Limited* where the claimant was the inventor of a company product and the company founder and where there was an irreparable breakdown between in relations between the claimant and the Board.

The Redundancy defence to an unfair dismissals claim featured in *Dublin Tech Summit* (Labour Court) and in *Conolin* (Labour Court) and in *Barratt* (Court of Appeal of England and Wales).

The remedies of Reinstatement and Reengagement feature in *PGA European Tour* (Court of Appeal of England and Wales), *Oppermann* (Labour Court) *and Community Integrated Care* (UK EAT).

AGENCY WORKERS

[22.02] *AA Euro Recruitment Ireland Ltd v Cotter[1]—Labour Court—appeal from Workplace Relations Commission—Unfair Dismissals Acts 1977 to 2015—unfair dismissal—agency employees—deemed employee*

The claimant had been placed as a security guard on a client of the respondent's site. During the claimant's placement, an incident occurred which led to the client advising the respondent that the claimant's placement was to come to an end. An investigation was carried out into the incident and the claimant was suspended pending the outcome. The claimant was subsequently placed on lay off and submitted that no alternative position was offered to him, despite the respondent advertising for same.

---

[1]   *AA Euro Recruitment Ireland Ltd v Cotter* UDD2112.

The respondent raised two preliminary issues before the Labour Court:

1. The respondent submitted that it was an employment agency and the claimant had registered with the respondent as an agency worker. The respondent argued that, in accordance with s 13 of the Unfair Dismissals (Amendment) Act 1993, the respondent was not the claimant's employer and that responsibility for the claimant's dismissal lay with the client and not with the respondent.
2. The respondent also argued that the claimant had named the wrong respondent entity in his WRC complaint.

Neither of these issues had been raised before the Adjudication Officer.

With regard to the second issue, the Court found that the error in the Adjudication Officer's decision with regard to the incorrect title of the respondent could be remedied by the Labour Court in its determination.

With regard to the jurisdictional issue, the Court agreed that the respondent was an employment agency but stated that in order to determine whether the claimant himself was an agency worker for the purposes of the Unfair Dismissals Act 1977 to 2015, the relationship between the claimant and the respondent and the relationship between the claimant and the client had to be considered closely. It stated that this 'question will depend on the level of control each had on the complainant and his work'.

The following matters influenced the Court in making its determination:

1. There was no evidence that the claimant had 'registered as an agency worker', as submitted by the respondent. The claimant told the Court that he had responded to an online advertisement, which made no reference to the respondent being an employment agency or to the job being for an agency. He also submitted that he had never been told that he was an agency worker and the Court noted that the contract of employment made no reference to this either.
2. The Court considered the question of direction and supervision but was provided with conflicting evidence by the parties. The claimant submitted that he was provided with his weekly roster by the respondent, he reported to the respondent's managers, if any security issues arose he reported same to the respondent and the respondent's name was on his uniform.
3. The Court considered it 'significant that both of the respondent's managers who gave evidence to the Court had little or no contact with the [claimant] by virtue of their roles. And those named by the complainant as having such control over his working times and conditions were not present to contradict such evidence'.
4. The Court also considered the terms of the commercial contract between the respondent and the client and determined that it was the responsibility of the respondent to direct and supervise the claimant. The Court also noted that no evidence had been put forward by the respondent to contradict this.

The Court found that in this particular case it was hard to come to any conclusion other than that the claimant was employed directly by the respondent and, in reality, was not an agency worker. It also decided that the claimant had *locus standi* to maintain his claim against the respondent and held that the respondent's appeal on this issue had failed.

ASSERTING STATUTORY RIGHTS

[22.03]   Simoes v De Sede UK Ltd[2]—UK Employment Appeal Tribunal—appeal from employment tribunal—Employment Rights Act 1996, s 104(1)—Working Time Regulations 1998,[3] reg 11—unfair dismissal—dismissal for asserting infringement of statutory rights

The claimant was employed as a sales assistant by the respondent for just under two months, from 29 June to 17 August 2018.

In July 2018, the claimant was asked to work for 14 days in a row to cover the holiday leave of her manager. The claimant took issue with the request and after consulting with ACAS, alleged to the respondent that it would constitute a breach of reg 11 the Working Time Regulations 1998. The responded refused to make alternative arrangements and the claimant did work the requested days. However when her manager returned from holidays the claimant was informed that her employment was being terminated and she was dismissed.

The claimant brought a claim to the employment tribunal, asserting that her dismissal contravened s 104 of the Employment Rights Act 1996. Section 104(1) provides that a dismissal is unlawful if the reason for the dismissal is that the employee 'alleged that the employer had infringed a right of his which is a relevant statutory right'. Section 104(2) goes on to provide that: 'It is immaterial ... whether or not the employee has the right, or (b) whether or not the right has been infringed; but ... the claim to the right and that it has been infringed must be made in good faith'.

The claimant was unsuccessful before the employment tribunal, which analysed the relevant case law and held that 'in order to engage the protection of section 104, it seems that a Claimant must complain about a breach of statutory right which has already taken place i.e. it must be a historic breach'. The tribunal held that as such, s 104 did not apply in this instance.

The EAT held that while this was a correct analysis of the law, it was incorrect on the facts to find that the breach complained of was not historic. The EAT held that the breach of the Working Time Regulations 1998 had 'crystalised' when the claimant was instructed to work the hours in question, not when the hours were actually worked. The EAT held:

> It was not a case of "If you ask me to do that then it will be a breach of my rights" as the instruction had already been given: she had been asked and the instruction was repeated after her concerns had been raised. It is the instruction which was alleged to breach the Claimant's working time rights. She did not have to wait until she had completed the rota that she had asserted in good faith infringed her rights.

The EAT allowed the appeal and held that the claimant was unfairly dismissed contrary to s 104.

---

2   *Alda Simoes v De Sede UK Ltd* UKEAT/0153/20/RN.
3   Working Time Regulations 1998 (SI 1998/1833).

CAPABILITY

[22.04] *Fallahi v TWI Ltd[4]—UK Employment Appeal Tribunal—appeal from employment tribunal—written warning—challenge—re-evaluate—capability dismissal*

The EAT confirmed that where a claimant in an unfair dismissal claim requests the tribunal to revisit the basis for an earlier written warning, the tribunal should only do so where the warning was 'manifestly inappropriate'. This is the first time that the EAT confirmed this principle in the context of a capability dismissal, it being a well-recognised principle in misconduct dismissals before UK tribunals.

The respondent had identified concerns with the claimant's performance, which had initially been managed through an informal objective-setting process to run over a 12-month period. However, before the expiry of the 12-month period, the respondent, having decided that the claimant had demonstrated insufficient improvement, convened a formal capability hearing, following which a final written warning was issued to the claimant, including further objectives for improvement and a three-month review period for implementation of same.

Two months into the review period, having formed the view that insufficient improvements had been demonstrated by the claimant, the respondent dismissed him on capability grounds.

At first instance before the employment tribunal, the claimant argued that the respondent's decision to proceed straight to a final written warning was not justified. The claimant sought to examine the respondent's motivations for proceeding to a final written warning. The employment tribunal did not accept the claimant's line of argument, or his request, holding that a re-evaluation of a prior written warning should only be allowed in circumstances where that earlier warning was 'manifestly inappropriate'. The employment tribunal was satisfied that this was not the case here, since the claimant's performance issues were well documented and long-standing. The employment tribunal also pointed to the fact that the respondent's capability procedure contained a provision allowing stages to be abridged.

The claimant appealed the employment tribunal's decision. However, the EAT agreed with the conclusion reached at first instance and declined to allow the claimant's appeal.

COMPENSATION

[22.05] *Cityjet v Gil[5]—Labour Court—appeal from Workplace Relations Commission—Unfair Dismissals Acts 1977 to 2015—unfair dismissal—mitigation of loss—compensation*

---

4   *Fallahi v TWI Ltd* EA-2019-000110-JOJ.
5   *Cityjet v Gil* UDD215.

This was a joint appeal against the decision of an Adjudication Officer at first instance in a claim made by the claimant against his former employer, City Jet, where he alleged that he was unfairly dismissed. The Adjudication Officer held that the complaint was well founded and awarded the claimant €6,000 in compensation.

The respondent did not dispute that the claimant was dismissed from his employment and had made an offer to him in full and final settlement of his appeal under the Unfair Dismissals Acts 1977 to 2015 as amended (the Acts). The respondent's position was that, should the claimant reject the offer, then the respondent would not be defending its appeal before the Court.

As the respondent accepted that the dismissal of the claimant was unfair, then the only issue before the Court was the appropriate quantum of compensation.

The Court interpreted s 7(2)(c) of the Acts, which provides that in examining the financial loss, the Court must have regard to the measures adopted by the claimant to mitigate his loss. The legislation does not allow the Court to award compensation in an amount that goes beyond the financial loss attributable to the dismissal. The Court sought specific details on the losses incurred and the efforts made to mitigate those losses. While details were provided to the Court on the financial loss suffered by the claimant, no details were provided to substantiate those losses and no details were given on the claimant's efforts to mitigate the losses.

The Court therefore reduced the award to €1,792.92, ie, four weeks' pay.

CONDUCT

[22.06]   *AK v United Parcel Service*[6]*—High Court—Hyland J—appeal from Labour Court—bullying and harassment—failure to raise a question of law*

This case involved a point of law appeal from a decision of the Labour Court upholding an appeal from a decision of the WRC that a dismissal for gross misconduct was unfair. The High Court found that the Labour Court was correct in holding that the dismissal was within the range of reasonable responses open to the employer and dismissed the appeal.

On 26 September 2016, Mr A, a colleague of the appellant, made a complaint of sexual harassment against her. Mr A complained that on 29 June 2016 the appellant approached him and asked him out. The appellant stated that she did not ask him out but told him he was driving her mad with his mixed messages and she wished he would make up his mind. He replied that he already had a girlfriend, to which the appellant said he did not. Mr A further complained of a situation on 23 September 2016 where the appellant approached him at his desk and asked could he not be nice to her for two minutes. He replied by saying he was busy with work and the appellant continued to stay at his desk staring at him for a few minutes and then left.

---

[6]   *AK v United Parcel Service* [2021] IEHC 543. See *Arthur Cox Employment Law Yearbook 2020* at **[19.12]** for the Labour Court decision in *United Parcel Service CSTC Ireland Ltd v Kiss* UDD2018.

On 16 November 2016, the respondent upheld the two complaints but did not recommend disciplinary action. The appellant appealed the outcome of the investigation and sent an email to the investigators and asked them to encourage Mr A to enter into mediation, or she would make her own complaint against him. On 13 December 2016, the outcome of the appellant's appeal was given, where the complaint regarding the appellant approaching Mr A and invading his personal space was upheld. Another complaint regarding Facebook pictures was overturned. The appellant and Mr A were advised to enter into mediation, however Mr A refused. The appellant then made a complaint of sexual harassment and bullying against Mr A, *inter alia* because he refused to enter into mediation with the appellant.

In March 2017, a decision on the appellant's complaint found there was no basis for the complaint and that the appellant had made the complaint maliciously. She complained about the process, and, in April 2017, a disciplinary outcome concluded that the appellant's complaint was not made maliciously. In May 2017, her grievance was rejected. After this, the appellant sent a detailed email to Mr R, a colleague and friend of Mr A, in respect of the sexual harassment complaint and subsequent events and then sent a detailed email to Mr A.

After this, Mr A made a further complaint of harassment and bullying by the appellant. The appellant was placed on paid suspension pending an investigation into the allegations. Thereafter an investigation was conducted and the respondent upheld Mr A's complaint and found that the action of sending both emails was inappropriate and unwelcomed by both parties and that the content of both emails was totally inappropriate and neither email should have been sent. It recommended the matter be sent to a disciplinary officer to consider whether the application of the respondent's disciplinary procedure was appropriate. A disciplinary meeting was held, and a decision was made terminating the appellant's employment for bullying and harassment which was found to constitute gross misconduct. She appealed this decision but the appeal was rejected, the decision noting that the appellant did not dispute she had breached confidentiality, had sent emails of a highly inappropriate nature, and that the appellant had given no indication that she would not continue with the behaviour were she to remain with the respondent. Accordingly, it was concluded there was no reason to overturn the original decision.

The WRC upheld her complaint of unfair dismissal and awarded her €37,500 in compensation. It concluded that the respondent's actions in terminating the appellant's employment were not within the range of reasonable responses, although it found that the emails sent to Mr A and Mr R were inappropriate and were not justified. The respondent appealed against that decision to the Labour Court. The Labour Court upheld the appeal, overturning the WRC decision.

In relation to the content of the emails sent to Mr A and his colleague, while the High Court noted that it did not believe the appellant intended to cause hurt or upset by these emails and believed at the relevant time that she was justified in sending them in a misguided attempt to clear the air, the High Court stated that a consideration of the content was necessary to give context to its ultimate decision to uphold the conclusion of the Labour Court.

In the email to Mr R, Mr A's friend, the appellant stated that Mr A narrowly ruined her career, that he lied without conscience, that he had a habit of lying, that he lied deliberately and consciously to her, that he was trying to ruin her life, that he nearly bullied her to death, that he was a coward, that he made false accusations and that he was abusive. In the email to Mr A, she said he had put her through an absolute nightmare, she was scared he would attack her, that he was shameless, arrogant and manipulative, that he was not a healthy individual, that sometimes she thought he was pure evil, that he lied without conscience and that if she wanted to take revenge on him for ruining her life she would have done that a long time ago.

As this appeal to the High Court was on a point of law, the Court was limited to considering whether the Labour Court made an error of law. The grounds of appeal were as follows:

  i. The behaviour of the appellant, which was the reason given for her dismissal, did not constitute bullying and harassment;
  ii. The outcome of the sexual harassment complaint filed against the appellant by Mr A was wrong and the respondent's handling of the situation directly led to her dismissal;
  iii. The appellant was victimised by reason of the various processes carried out by the respondent in the course of the various investigations into complaints made by Mr A and complaints made by the appellant.

The respondent argued that the appeal should be dismissed exclusively on procedural grounds as it was not lodged within time, no extension of time has been sought, and the appellant has failed to identify the point of law on which her appeal is made. The respondent also argued that the decision of the Labour Court was substantively correct, that the behaviour of the appellant was such that it was within a range of reasonable responses to dismiss her and that there was no unfairness to the appellant. The Court rejected the respondent's arguments that the appeal should be dismissed on procedural grounds, including that the appellant was not legally represented.

The victimisation ground of appeal was rejected as it had not been put before the Labour Court and could not be introduced as a new ground of appeal before the High Court.

The Court found, that the appellant was in essence claiming that the Labour Court erred in failing to explain how her behaviour constituted bullying and harassment, and that her conduct did not in fact meet the test of bullying and harassment.

The Court found that the appellant had failed to raise any question of law that goes to the legality of the decision of the Labour Court. Therefore, her appeal must fail without any consideration of the substance of the decision of the Labour Court. However, because she not represented, the Court went on to explain why: (a) the respondent was correct in concluding that the behaviour was bullying and harassment and warranted dismissal; and (b) the Labour Court was correct in concluding that the dismissal was reasonable having regard to the conduct of the appellant.

The Court referred to the definition of bullying and harassment set out in the decision of the Supreme Court in *Ruffley v The Board of Management of St Anne's National School*:[7]

---

[7]   *Ruffley v The Board of Management of St Anne's National School* [2017] IESC 33.

At each point the statutory drafter has chosen a term at a markedly elevated point in the register: conduct must be repeated, not merely consist of a number of incidents; it must be inappropriate, not merely wrong; and it is not enough that it be inappropriate and even offensive: it must be capable of being reasonably regarded as undermining the individual's right to dignity at work.

The High Court stated that the emails of May and June 2017 undoubtedly constituted deeply inappropriate behaviour. The first was indirect in the sense that the email was sent to a friend of Mr A; the second was direct in that the email was sent to Mr A himself. There was a dispute between the parties as to whether the appellant had been told she was free to send an email to Mr A's friend or whether she had been told she should not do so. In the circumstances, the Labour Court held it was 'highly improbable that the managers in question would have given the "explicit permission" alleged by the [appellant]'.

The High Court stated that it was bound by those findings of fact but added that even if the appellant had been told that she was free to send an email, the email that she actually sent was utterly inappropriate and harmful and therefore any agreement for her to contact Mr A's friend could not sanction the contents of that email. The Court stated that it was inconceivable that any employer could treat the sending of these emails as anything but conduct of a most serious kind. From the objective point of view of the recipient, the Court was satisfied that the emails could reasonably be regarded as undermining the recipient's right to dignity at work.

Moreover, the Court found that the behaviour of the appellant was repeated since, although only two emails had been sent, they were part of a pattern of behaviour, starting with the behaviour that gave rise to the finding of sexual harassment, the making of the complaint of sexual harassment against Mr A, the decision to take that complaint because he would not engage in mediation, and the failure by the appellant to accept that she needed to move on from the events of 2016.

In relation to the issue that was in fact before the Labour Court, ie whether the dismissal was reasonable having regard to the appellant's conduct, the Court was satisfied that the Labour Court was entirely correct in its decision. The High Court could see no basis for any error of law in the Labour Court's decision that the employer had acted reasonably in dismissing the appellant on the basis of her conduct. It held that the decision to dismiss the appellant was clearly well within the bounds of a reasonable response open to the respondent. The Court rejected the appeal and upheld the decision of the Labour Court.

[22.07] *Bus Éireann v Folman*[8]*—Labour Court—appeal from Workplace Relations Commission—unfair dismissal—fair procedures—whether reinstatement an appropriate remedy*

The Labour Court considered whether reinstatement was an appropriate remedy in circumstances where the claimant had contributed to his own dismissal.

---

8   *Bus Éireann v Folman* UDD2152.

The claimant was employed by the respondent as a driver. There were a number of issues with his performance and he received a final written warning. The claimant was subsequently disqualified from driving, arising from which the respondent 'felt it had no option' but to dismiss him.

The WRC held that the claimant was unfairly dismissed and ordered reinstatement. The respondent appealed this finding to the Labour Court; it conceded that the dismissal was procedurally unfair but that reinstatement was not an appropriate remedy as the relationship of trust and confidence between the parties had irretrievably broken down. The respondent also argued that the claimant had contributed to his own dismissal, which it said ought to be taken into account in any award of compensation.

The Labour Court upheld the appeal. It noted that '[r]e-instatement is generally granted where the employee is found not to have contributed to the dismissal' and found that in this case, there were 'ongoing issues with the manner in which the [claimant] was conducting himself while carrying out his job' and 'trust issues that would make his return to the workplace unworkable' such that neither reinstatement nor re-engagement were appropriate remedies. Taking into account the circumstances and the loss being claimed, the Court ordered compensation of €5,000.

[22.08] *Connemara Marble Industries Ltd v Murphy[9]—Labour Court—appeal from Workplace Relations Commission—Unfair Dismissal Acts 1977 to 2015— unfair dismissal—reasonableness of decision to dismiss—fair procedures—failure to mitigate loss*

The claimant had worked in the family business since the age of 13, in the roles of sales assistant, tour guide and jewellery designer, and was employed from 1 January 2011 until 21 February 2017.

Following her father's death in August 2015, the claimant inherited a one-sixth interest in the business. The other five-sixths were held by her five siblings, two of whom were also directors and managed the day-to-day running of the business.

Difficulties arose between the claimant and her siblings from December 2015. In November 2016 the claimant was warned of disciplinary action if she continued to refuse instructions from the company directors. On 18 November, there was a serious incident on the company premises involving the claimant and certain other of her siblings which resulted in the Gardaí being called, a planned tour bus being cancelled and the business closed for the rest of the day. Arising from this incident the claimant was placed on suspension pending an investigation into allegedly engaging in activities detrimental to the company.

The claimant subsequently claimed that her employment had been terminated on 18 November 2016 (when she was placed on suspension). In February 2017 the respondent wrote to the claimant noting the claimant's position, enclosing her P45 and seeking return of company property.

---

[9]   *Connemara Marble Industries Ltd v Murphy* UD/18/134.

The claimant had submitted a claim of constructive dismissal under the Unfair Dismissal Acts 1977 to 2015 on 12 December 2016, however in April 2017 the claimant submitted a subsequent claim of unfair dismissal and the claim of constructive dismissal was withdrawn. The claimant also brought claims under the Protected Disclosures Act 2014 and the Minimum Notice and Terms of Employment Act 1973.

When the matter came before the WRC, the Adjudication Officer held that the claimant was unfairly dismissed and awarded her €30,000 in compensation. This decision was appealed to the Labour Court.

The Court noted that it was 'deeply regrettable' that this case involving family members falling out over a business which they inherited equally, and which was founded by their father, was not resolved by more amicable means. The Court noted that the fact of dismissal was not in dispute, therefore the onus was on the respondent to show that it was justified.

The Court noted that the respondent contended the dismissal was justified on grounds of the claimant's gross misconduct. It noted that it was clear that the claimant, as a shareholder, had concerns regarding how the company accounting was conducted and was of the view that the directors were misappropriating the company funds, despite the accountant's assurance that the director's remuneration details were in order. This gave rise to a breakdown in trust and confidence. The Court found that, while it had been presented with conflicting evidence, there was a consistency in the evidence given regarding the events of 18 November 2016, which was clearly very disruptive of business. The Court was of the view that the claimant contributed to that disruption and was satisfied that these actions by the claimant could be regarded as sufficiently grave to justify dismissal, as they impacted on the business and reputational interests of the respondent.

However, while the Court accepted that such conduct was sufficiently serious as to warrant dismissal, it held that the question before it was whether or not it was reasonable to dismiss the claimant in the circumstances.

The Court found that, based on the evidence given, it was satisfied that there were valid grounds for the suspension of the claimant following the events of 18 November 2016. However, it noted that the respondent had informed the claimant that it intended to carry out an investigation into those events; no such investigation was undertaken and the claimant was dismissed without consideration of any mitigating factors. As such, the Court held that the respondent's actions in dismissing the claimant were not founded on reasonable grounds. The Court also found that the respondent did not give due regard to the claimant's right to natural justice as normal disciplinary procedures were not adhered to, ie there was no investigation of the events leading to the dismissal; there were no disciplinary hearings; and the claimant was dismissed without notice and without an opportunity to appeal. Therefore, the Court held that the dismissal was also contrary to the provisions of the Code of Practice on Grievance and Disciplinary Procedure.[10]

---

[10]   Code of Practice on Grievance and Disciplinary Procedure (SI 146/2000).

Having regard to all the circumstances, the Court found that the decision to dismiss the claimant was tainted with procedural unfairness and accordingly, the claimant was unfairly dismissed.

The Court refused to order reinstatement, as requested by the claimant, as it found that despite the imperfect procedural manner in which the dismissal had been conducted, there were substantial grounds justifying the dismissal; the claimant had contributed fully to her dismissal and the relationship of trust and confidence had broken down. In ordering compensation, the Court noted that the claimant had made little effort to mitigate her loss and ordered the respondent to pay the claimant compensation in the amount of €25,000.

[22.09] *A Beverage Company v A Worker[11]—Labour Court—appeal from Workplace Relations Commission—Unfair Dismissals Acts 1977 to 2015—conduct— allegation of sexual assault*

This was an appeal by the claimant against a decision of an Adjudication Officer under the Unfair Dismissals Acts 1977 to 2015. Following a request from the respondent, the Court, in accordance with the provisions of s 44(7) of the Workplace Relations Act 2015, decided to conduct the proceedings otherwise than in public because of the existence of special circumstances and, as a consequence, to anonymise this decision.

The agreed facts were that the respondent organised a Christmas party where the claimant and other staff members were invited. The respondent hosted the event and negotiated discounted hotel rooms for staff members who may have wanted to stay the night. The following February, a staff member made a complaint to the respondent that she had been sexually assaulted by the claimant in a hotel room following the event.

The respondent met with the claimant to inform him of the complaint made against him and to inform him that the respondent was considering suspending him pending a full investigation. Three days later, the claimant was informed that he was suspended with pay.

In accordance with the respondent's disciplinary policy, an investigation was undertaken and a single finding was made to the effect that, on the balance of probabilities, the claimant sexually assaulted the complainant in her hotel room after the respondent's Christmas party. A disciplinary hearing took place thereafter and the decision was made to dismiss the claimant. The claimant was unsuccessful in both of his subsequent appeals.

In commenting on the claimant's behaviour, the Labour Court noted 'the complaint received by the respondent has never been engaged with by the [claimant] in that he has never denied or otherwise challenged the complaint originally received by the respondent'.

---

[11]   *A Beverage Company v A Worker* UDD2132.

The Labour Court considered the claimant's argument that the event originally complained of happened outside the workplace. As part of these considerations the Labour Court noted that the claimant would not have been in the hotel room with this staff member 'other than as a result of their employment with the respondent'. The Labour Court further noted that the shift roster of the original complainant was altered by the respondent to allow her attend the Christmas party and that the room where the alleged assault took place was a room to which a negotiated staff discount applied. Given all this evidence, the Court concluded:

> that the event was sufficiently connected with the employment as to mean that, for the purposes of the Act, it occurred in the course of employment to the degree that the disciplinary policy of the respondent could reasonably be applied in order to address the complaint made to the respondent by the original Complainant. In addition, it is the Court's judgment that the alleged event in question had the potential to impact on employee relations in the workplace, to cause reputational and/or other damage to the respondent and/or to risk bringing the respondent's name into ill repute (for example by reports in the press) and to cause the employer to genuinely lose trust and confidence in the [claimant].

The claimant raised no issue regarding the disciplinary process but argued that the investigation relied upon was flawed. The respondent engaged a practising barrister to conduct the investigation. The claimant submitted that the investigation failed to observe the requirements of natural justice and fair procedures. In dismissing this claim the Labour Court commented:

> In all of the circumstances, and noting that the [claimant] was on full notice of the allegations made against him and was afforded full opportunity to provide the investigator with his account of the alleged events and failed to do so, the Court is unable to conclude other than that the independent investigation reached a finding which was not inconsistent with the information available.

The Court concluded that the investigation 'was not flawed to the degree that its findings could not fairly be relied upon' and that the claimant was not unfairly dismissed.

[22.10] *Q-Park Ireland Ltd v Fitzpatrick*[12]*—Labour Court—appeal from Workplace Relations Commission—altercation with customer—reputational risk—CCTV footage*

The claimant was employed by the respondent as a parking host from November 2013 to August 2018. In June 2018, a written complaint was received from a customer that the claimant had acted in a hostile and aggressive manner towards the customer by slamming his hands on the customer's bonnet, and had both verbally and physically assaulted the claimant. On receipt of the complaint, the claimant's actions were verified by reference to CCTV footage, and the claimant was also filmed smoking a cigarette immediately following the incident, contrary to the law and to the respondent's policy.

---

[12]   *Q-Park Ireland Ltd v Fitzpatrick* UDD2135.

An internal investigation was commenced by one of the respondent's business managers, following conversations with the customer. The claimant was represented during the investigation; the respondent submitted that all evidence and allegations were put to him and that his previously blemish-free record was taken into account. During the investigation, the claimant confirmed that he had neglected to report the altercation with the customer to the respondent, and displayed a flippant attitude when asked about the smoking issue, admitting to regularly smoking on the respondent's premises, including during interactions with customers. The investigator concluded that the claimant had shouted at, and used abusive language towards the customer, and that he had admitted to breaking the law by smoking on the respondent's premises. The investigator found that the claimant's actions towards the customer posed a reputational risk to the company, and the claimant was invited to attend a disciplinary hearing. The claimant was informed that the allegations against him could be considered to be gross misconduct and could result in dismissal.

Another business manager conducted the disciplinary hearing, and concluded that the claimant's version of the incident with the customer did not align with the CCTV footage. In addition, the business manager concluded that the claimant had received a copy of the respondent's disciplinary procedure, which included its policy in relation to smoking on company premises. The business manager agreed with the investigator's finding that the claimant's actions posed a reputational risk to the company. The business manager further determined that the employment relationship had been undermined by the claimant's actions, and summarily dismissed the claimant.

The claimant submitted an internal appeal against the decision to dismiss, which was heard by the respondent's managing director, who ultimately upheld that decision.

The claimant submitted a complaint of unfair dismissal against the respondent to the WRC, where the respondent contended that the claimant's dismissal was not unfair since it had arisen from his own conduct. The respondent further contended that smoking amounted to an act of gross misconduct under the respondent's disciplinary policy and that the claimant had destroyed the relationship of trust with the respondent, such that a reasonable employer faced with the same set of circumstances would have reached the same conclusion as the respondent.

The claimant submitted that, prior to his dismissal, he had a blemish-free employment record with the respondent, and that Google reviews of the respondent had been very complimentary of the claimant. The claimant submitted that he had secured additional revenue for the respondent by offering its services to small businesses, and had worked late and during times when he was not rostered in order to familiarise himself with a new IT system and to ensure that his colleagues were also familiar with it. The claimant submitted that the initial investigation was flawed in several respects, and rejected the respondent's assertion that his attitude towards the smoking incident had been flippant. In relation to the incident with the customer, the claimant submitted that by acting as he had done, he was seeking to protect himself from a car that continued to approach, and beep in a threatening manner, while the claimant was assisting other customers. In the circumstances, the claimant contended that the decision to dismiss had been disproportionate.

An Adjudication Officer decided that the claimant had indeed been unfairly dismissed, and ordered the respondent to pay him €18,000 by way of compensation. The respondent appealed the Adjudication Officer's decision to the Labour Court.

The Court reaffirmed the position that, in complaints of unfair dismissal where misconduct is stated as the basis for dismissal, the test is that applied in *British Leyland UK Ltd v Swift*,[13] which was confirmed in Ireland in *Foley v Post Office*.[14] The test set by Denning LJ in *British Leyland* is:

> If no reasonable employer would have dismissed him, then the dismissal was unfair. But if a reasonable employer might have dismissed him, then the dismissal was fair.

As such, the test to be applied by the Court was whether the decision to dismiss fell within the 'band of reasonableness'.

Interestingly, the Court noted that the 'band of reasonableness' test is often misinterpreted to mean that the Court need only be concerned with the procedures followed by an employer in effecting a dismissal, which it noted would be an illogical interpretation. The Court stressed that if the basis for the instigation of those procedures does not stand up to an assessment of reasonableness, that factor cannot be ignored by the Court.

The Court held that, in placing his hands on the customer's bonnet, in circumstances where the customer's car was moving in his direction, the claimant had responded perfectly normally and explicably to a perceived danger. The Court concluded that what followed, ie an exchange of words between the claimant and the customer and gesticulations from the claimant towards the customer, could not be unexpected and could not be considered a reasonable basis for a decision to dismiss.

In relation to the smoking incident, the Court acknowledged that employers are required to uphold the law, and that smoking in a confined area is a breach of the law and that in many such instances, the Court would not interfere with an employer's right to dismiss. However, the Court noted that in this case, the breach of law had only come to the respondent's attention as a result of the CCTV footage after the incident with the customer, which the Court held could only have been a 'frustrating and distressing' one. Moreover, the Court noted that the Adjudication Officer had confirmed that he did not know whether the claimant would have been dismissed had the only matter at issue been the smoking issue, but that the incident with the customer was the main issue in any event. The Court stated that it did not wish to be seen to excuse a breach of the law, which the claimant had sought to justify by reference to a lack of previous admonishment for the same behaviour. However, it was satisfied that a lesser penalty would have been handed down by the respondent had it viewed the incident with the customer as a 'frightening and distressing' one, rather than a dismissible one.

In all of the circumstances, the Court upheld the decision of the Adjudication Officer and concurred with the level of compensation awarded to the claimant by the Adjudication Officer.

---

[13] *British Leyland UK Ltd v Swift* (1981) IRLR 91.
[14] *Foley v Post Office* (2000) ICR 1283.

[22.11]   *Seetec Employment And Skills Ireland DAC v Redmond[15]—Labour Court—appeal from Workplace Relations Commission—absenteeism—gross misconduct—fair procedures*

The claimant had been employed by the respondent company as an employment advisor. He was dismissed on 17 June 2019 due to unauthorised absences over a 12-month period, constituting gross misconduct. The claimant had been absent for 25 days in total, in excess of those permitted under his employer's sickness and absence policy.

The WRC held that the respondent had made a reasonable decision, concluding that the process of dismissing the claimant was fair and that his complaint of unfair dismissal was not well founded. The claimant appealed the decision to the Labour Court.

The respondent had issued the claimant with four final written warnings before he was dismissed. He had previously been dismissed in 2018, that decision being over-turned on appeal. He was reinstated and transferred to a suitable alternative premises and a final written warning was put in place for an extended 12-month period. The claimant argued before the Labour Court that the disciplinary processes against him in relation to his absenteeism had been flawed and resulted in a pre-determined outcome by way of a final written warning. He argued that the respondent had failed to follow its own policies and to afford him fair procedures. He submitted that no investigation took place prior to a hearing, following which the decision to dismiss him was taken. The claimant argued that the allegations against him were not provided to him in advance of the hearing, nor was he informed of the identity of his accuser. He submitted in fact, that his accuser had been his line manager and that it was she who had conducted the disciplinary hearing, as well as each of his 'return to work interviews' following his successful appeal against a previous dismissal and subsequent transfer to a new work location.

The Court commented that there was no dispute as to the facts of the claimant's absences from work and that each of the final written warnings he received was a response to his infringement of the relevant workplace policy. The Court noted the claimant's awareness at all times of the respondent's concern in respect of his repeated absenteeism and his significant contribution to the decision ultimately to dismiss him. It rejected the claimant's argument that he had not been aware of the identity of his accuser, stating he had not faced an accuser in 'any accepted sense of the word'. However, the Court did find that the respondent had issued overlapping final writ-ten warnings for the same issue without 'any foundation of coherence' and that the 'repeated issuance of final stage penalties' had created uncertainty 'as regards the significance of the disciplinary penalties invoked'.

The appeal was upheld and the claimant was awarded €5,400, taking into account his financial loss, the contribution to his dismissal and his efforts to mitigate his loss.

---

[15]   *Seetec Employment And Skills Ireland DAC v Redmond* UDD2122.

[22.12] *Donegal Meat Processors v Nicell*[16]*—Labour Court—appeal from Workplace Relations Commission—unfair dismissal—reasonableness—gross misconduct*

The claimant had been employed by the respondent company and worked in its boning hall. He was dismissed on 20 August 2018 for failure to report an incident in which he was involved, in contravention of the respondent's policies for operating in a safety-critical environment. The respondent found that he had deliberately ignored its health and safety guidelines and as such had endangered himself and others.

It was accepted by both sides that an incident occurred in the boning hall where the claimant worked on 27 July 2018 and that his co-worker was injured by a knife as a result. The incident was not reported by either the claimant or his colleague at the time it occurred, as was required by the respondent's policy. The respondent also required that any employees involved in workplace incidents would be tested for alcohol and drug use. Management was made aware that the incident occurred through a message on social media on 28 July 2018, but was unaware of the claimant's involvement until he made a statement on 1 August 2018.

The claimant appealed the respondent's decision to dismiss him but this decision was upheld owing to his failure to follow 'fundamental policies and procedures'. Following that, he initiated a claim before the WRC where it was held that the claimant's case for unfair dismissal was well founded and the respondent appealed the decision to the Labour Court.

There were no procedural points for argument before the Court and the claimant did not dispute the fact that he had acted in breach of the respondent's policies and injured his colleague with a knife. The investigator and both the disciplinary and appeal decision makers gave evidence on the respondent's behalf, submitting that the claimant had received comprehensive knife training, was aware of the safety-critical nature of the environment in which he worked and of his responsibility to report the incident immediately. The Court's attention was also drawn to the fact that there was no value to conducting a drug and alcohol test unless conducted immediately following the incident. The respondent highlighted that failure to follow safety-critical procedures amounted to gross misconduct under its disciplinary policy. Further, the respondent argued that the claimant had not raised any arguments in mitigation and that its trust and confidence in him were gone.

The claimant countered that he had co-operated fully with the investigation, that the first aider who had attended to the incident on 27 July was in a better position to report upon it, and that the sanction imposed upon him had been grossly disproportionate.

Noting the safety-critical nature of the working environment, the Court looked to the respondent's policies. It commented that they were clear and unambiguous and held that the respondent had acted 'within the range of responses which could be expected of a reasonable employer in the circumstances'. Dismissal was not disproportionate or unfair and the appeal was upheld.

---

[16]   *Donegal Meat Processors v Nicell* UDD2139.

[22.13]   *Revenue Commissioners v Keane*[17]—*Labour Court—appeal from Workplace Relations Commission—Unfair Dismissals Acts 1977 to 2015—unfair dismissal—fair procedure*

The claimant was employed by the respondent from 2007 until his dismissal in 2018. The Special Compliance Branch of the respondent, engaging in an undercover operation, responded to a social media post advertising contraband cigarettes for sale and arrangements were made for the cigarettes to be delivered. The cigarettes were subsequently delivered by the claimant on 5 January 2018 and were seized by officers of the respondent. The claimant submitted that his girlfriend had bought the cigarettes during a trip to Poland and, on their return, she had offered them for sale on social media. The claimant admitted that he was aware that his girlfriend's actions were illegal but he still agreed to assist her.

Upon being informed of the incident, the personnel officer of the respondent invoked the disciplinary process. He initiated an investigation and appointed himself as the investigator, he then called the claimant to what was referred to as an investigation meeting on 17 January 2018. In his report, he found that: the claimant's actions constituted serious misconduct; the claimant compromised his position with Revenue Commissioners; the claimant contravened the standards expected as outlined in the Revenue Code of Ethics; his behaviour could damage Revenue's reputation and bring the organisation into disrepute; and that, as the claimant had been employed by the Revenue for over a decade, the claimant 'knew or ought to have known that his actions conflicted with his duties' and could warrant dismissal. Two days later, the claimant was dismissed by the personnel officer. The claimant appealed the decision to the Disciplinary Appeals Board, but it was upheld.

In challenging the dismissal, the claimant contended that he was not advised that the meeting on 17 January was a disciplinary meeting, nor was he aware that the sanction of dismissal was being considered. The claimant also alleged that no investigation had occurred, as was required by the Civil Service Disciplinary Code (the Disciplinary Code). The claimant also submitted that the Disciplinary Appeals Board deprived him of the right to legal representation by rejecting his request for an adjournment due to his trade union advising him two weeks before the hearing that they were not in a position to represent him.

The respondent submitted that the Disciplinary Code provides that wherever 'the facts are not complex and where the suspected misconduct is not serious, the fact-finding exercise may take place as part of the disciplinary hearing'. The respondent outlined that it was part of the claimant's role to confront non-compliance with Revenue rules and that the claimant was subject to both the Civil Service Code of Standards and Behaviour and the Revenue Code of Ethics. The respondent noted that the sale of

---

[17]   *Revenue Commissioners v Keane* UDD2125.

contraband cigarettes was also contrary to both the Finance Acts and Revenue rules which were part of what the claimant was employed to safeguard.

The Court accepted the respondent's position that its role in society necessitated it dealing with the claimant's actions as 'serious and very significant'. However, the Court also noted that the respondent was obliged to ensure that the disciplinary procedure adhered to the principles of natural justice and fair procedures.

The Court found that the personnel officer's report made it clear that he considered himself to be carrying out an investigation under the Disciplinary Code and it was therefore an 'inescapable conclusion' that the personnel officer was both the person who purported to conduct the investigation and the decision maker who decided to dismiss the claimant. The Court noted that the purported investigation encompassed the essential characteristics of a disciplinary hearing, which had the potential to result in the claimant's dismissal. The Court could not find anything in the Disciplinary Code which supported the procedural path invoked by the respondent.

The Court concluded that the respondent had not adhered to the process as set out in the Disciplinary Code and that, if the actions that the personnel officer took constituted both an investigation and the disciplinary process, his assumption of both of those functions was unfair. The Court noted particularly that the Disciplinary Code clearly required a 'clear investigative phase where the alleged misconduct at issue is of a serious nature' and neither party disputed the seriousness of the claimant's conduct. Additionally, the Court noted that the Disciplinary Code allowed the relevant manager to submit a counter statement to the Appeals Board and that this had been made by the personnel officer It found that the counter statement went far beyond providing the Board with relevant documentation and 'amounted to a full and comprehensive rebuttal of all elements of the appellant's appeal'.

The Court ultimately overturned the decision of the Adjudication Officer and found that the claimant's dismissal was unfair. The respondent's failure to clearly delineate the roles of investigation, disciplinary and appeal amounted to a flawed process in dealing with the allegations against the claimant. In determining the appropriate level of compensation, the Court had regard to the claimant's failure to mitigate his loss and that he contributed 100% to his own dismissal and determined that the amount of compensation which would be just and equitable was nil.

[22.14] *McAllister v Organic Lens Manufacturing[18]—Labour Court—appeal from Workplace Relations Commission—Unfair Dismissals Acts 1977 to 2015—unfair dismissal—conduct—reinstatement*

The claimant was employed by the respondent from 1997 to 2019. From November 2015 to March 2016, the claimant was absent from work on various periods of sick leave.

---

[18] *McAllister v Organic Lens Manufacturing* UDD2137.

In February 2016, the respondent transferred the claimant to a new role, about which the claimant raised concerns, contending that his new role was having a negative impact on his health. While the respondent addressed the claimant's concerns, the claimant was redeployed temporarily to another role.

In January 2017, an occupational health physician engaged by the respondent concluded that the claimant was fit to return to work in the role to which he had been transferred in February 2016. The claimant disputed that conclusion and an agreement was reached by the claimant and the respondent which, for reasons that were disputed, was not implemented. The claimant went on sick leave in March 2017. In April 2017, the claimant submitted grievances against two of the respondent's managers, which were not upheld and against which the claimant unsuccessfully appealed internally. The claimant remained on sick leave until he was dismissed by the respondent in June 2019.

In May 2019, the claimant had indicated to the respondent that he was fit to return to work. The respondent advised that it was not in a position to confirm a date on which the claimant could return to work. The claimant attended the respondent's premises and spoke with the general manager, who subsequently wrote to the claimant's union representative to request a meeting in relation to the claimant. A meeting never took place and the general manager informed the claimant that he was being dismissed. The claimant sought an appeal against the decision to dismiss, which was not acceded to.

The claimant submitted a complaint against the respondent under the Unfair Dismissals Acts 1977 to 2015, and the WRC found that the claimant's complaint was well-founded and awarded him €16,200 in compensation, finding that he had been 20% responsible for his dismissal. The claimant appealed to the Labour Court, seeking reinstatement.

Before the Labour Court, the respondent argued that the claimant was dismissed because the respondent did not trust him to behave in a professional manner in his dealings with the respondent, which it contended went to the root of the contract of employment. On that basis, the respondent argued that reinstatement was an inappropriate remedy in circumstances where a fundamental breakdown in the employment relationship had occurred. Alternatively, the respondent argued that, if the Court were to find in favour of the claimant, it should also find that the claimant contributed wholly to his dismissal such that he had no entitlement to redress. The respondent also noted that the claimant's efforts to mitigate his loss were insufficient. Moreover, the respondent pointed to the numerous supports it had provided to the claimant, including numerous consultations with medical professionals but that, despite this, the claimant had refused reasonable requests to return to work. In addition, the respondent noted that it had attended, and paid for, external mediation with the claimant in relation to his grievances, and had created a role for him while his grievances were investigated.

Ultimately, the respondent contended that the claimant had acted so unreasonably in his dealings with the respondent that the only reasonable option for the respondent was to dismiss him.

The claimant did not accept that it was not possible to repair the employment relation-ship between the parties, and argued that he had been targeted for raising grievances, following which the respondent had focused on terminating his employment through redundancy, mutual agreement, and eventually dismissal. The claimant pointed to the absence of any disciplinary process being followed, and to the respondent's refusal to offer him a right of appeal against his dismissal.

The Court observed that the key facts were not disputed by the parties, ie that after an extended period, the respondent concluded that the claimant had acted unreasonably, had consumed too much management time and should be dismissed as a result. The Court stressed that before reaching a decision to dismiss, an employer must comply with fair procedures; and that the right to be heard is a fundamental one.

The Court agreed with the decision of the WRC that the respondent's decision to dismiss the claimant without any disciplinary process being followed, without any charge being put to him, without giving him the opportunity to respond to the charge, or to appeal it meant that, the dismissal must be held to have been unfair. The Court stated that it 'could not possibly condone as "reasonable" an action that breaches the [claimant's] rights in such a stark manner, notwithstanding any views of the Respondent regarding the [claimant's] behaviour'.

In relation to the remedy of reinstatement requested by the claimant, the Court noted that there is good reason why such remedy is deployed only very infrequently, as it:

> is to be expected in most cases that dismissal itself indicates a breakdown in the employee/employer relationship and it is not the role of the Court to inflict hardship on both parties by requiring them to restore a relationship which is often long past any possibility of restoration.

Ultimately, the Court was not satisfied that ordering reinstatement was in the interests of either the claimant or the respondent. It therefore turned its attention to compensation, noting that it did not accept the position put forward by both parties that the other party was exclusively responsible for the breakdown in the employment relationship.

The Court varied the decision of the WRC by awarding an additional €4,800 to the claimant by way of compensation, taking the total compensation awarded to the claimant for his unfair dismissal to €21,000.

[22.15] *Smurfit Kappa Ireland v Folan*[19]*—Labour Court—appeal from Workplace Relations Commission—Unfair Dismissals Acts 1977 to 2015—Industrial Relations Act 1990 (Code of Practice on Grievance and Disciplinary Procedures) (Declaration) Order 2000—dismissal for gross misconduct—lack of procedural fairness—distinction between investigation and disciplinary process—contribution to own dismissal*

---

[19] *Smurfit Kappa Ireland v Folan* UDD2156.

The claimant was dismissed for gross misconduct following an incident with a colleague in which the claimant struck the colleague across the face with an iron bar. Following an investigation and disciplinary process, the claimant was dismissed. The claimant brought an unfair dismissal claim, seeking reinstatement. The WRC found that the claimant had not been unfairly dismissed within the meaning of the Unfair Dismissals Acts 1977 to 2015.

The Labour Court noted that under Industrial Relations Act 1990 (Code of Practice on Grievance and Disciplinary Procedures) (Declaration) Order 2000,[20] there must be a clear distinction between an investigation and the disciplinary stage of the process. It found that this distinction had been blurred in the circumstances of this case, as the investigator had wholly over-stepped his role in making a finding of gross misconduct. The distinction was further blurred by a re-construction of the incident, which was staged during the disciplinary process.

Furthermore, the claimant was denied his right to natural justice in being deprived of the opportunity to argue his case before he was dismissed. The Labour Court accepted the claimant's submission that a written exchange did not in fact meet this threshold.

In light of the above, the Labour Court found the 'process through which it was determined that the [claimant] should be dismissed is fatally flawed and there could be no doubt that the dismissal does not meet the tests for fairness'.

The Labour Court refused to make an order for reinstatement in circumstances where the claimant himself admitted to striking a colleague in the face causing injury. Furthermore, despite finding that the dismissal had been unfair, the Labour Court found that the claimant had fully contributed to his own dismissal and, as such, no compensation was awarded.

The Labour Court overturned the decision of the WRC and allowed the appeal.

[22.16] *DPP Law Ltd v Greenberg[21]—Court of Appeal of England and Wales (Civil Division)—Lewison, Popplewell & Lewis LJJ—appeal from EAT—dismissal—gross misconduct*

The appellant had been employed by the respondent legal aid firm as a criminal defence solicitor since 2004, and was dismissed by the respondent in 2017 for gross misconduct arising from his accepting £150 from the father of a client as a 'top up' payment.

The employment tribunal determined that the respondent genuinely believed that the appellant had committed gross misconduct, on the basis that the payment of £150 constituted a 'top up' of fees due to the respondent from the Legal Aid Authority, which was forbidden by the terms of the legal aid contract between the respondent and the

---

20 Industrial Relations Act 1990 (Code of Practice on Grievance and Disciplinary Procedures) (Declaration) Order 2000 (SI 146/2000).
21 *DPP Law Ltd v Greenberg* [2021] EWCA Civ 672.

Legal Aid Authority. The employment tribunal dismissed the appellant's claim and deemed his dismissal to have been fair.

The appellant appealed the employment tribunal's decision to the EAT, which found in his favour and overturned the decision of the employment tribunal on the basis that it deemed the evidence against the appellant to have been 'essentially circumstantial and inferential', and further, that the employment tribunal had not engaged in any meaningful evaluation of the reasons for the respondent's decision to dismiss such that it had not been sufficiently 'rooted in findings of fact'.

The respondent appealed the EAT's decision to the Court of Appeal, which held that the EAT had approached its examination of the employment tribunal's rationale incorrectly. The Court of Appeal then laid out guidelines for appellate tribunals or courts in reviewing the reasons given by employment tribunals:

1. It is incumbent on the EAT to analyse the decision of the employment tribunal fairly and in the round, without focusing on phrases in isolation and without being 'hypercritical' of, or hypersensitive to, individual passages.
2. The employment tribunal is not obliged to identify every one of the factors relied on in reaching its conclusions of fact in relation to a decision to dismiss. The Court of Appeal noted that to expect this would be to place an 'intolerable burden' on the fact finder.
3. On the basis of the approach as outlined above, it is not acceptable for an appellate court to conclude that a failure by the employment tribunal to expressly refer to evidence means that such evidence either did not exist or was not considered by it in reaching its decision, ie, 'What is out of sight in the language of the decision is not to be presumed to be non-existent or out of mind'.

The Court of Appeal concluded that it had been the EAT, not the employment tribunal, which had acted in error, and that the EAT's conclusions had not been based on a fair and rounded interpretation of the employment tribunal's decision. The Court of Appeal concluded that the EAT's failure to take account of findings that had been made by the employment tribunal, simply because they were not expressly contained in the employment tribunal's decision, had been erroneous. The Court of Appeal overturned the EAT conclusion that the employment tribunal had fallen victim to a 'substitution mindset' when it concluded that the appellant had indeed been fairly dismissed. In doing so, it effectively held that the appellant had not been unfairly dismissed.

[22.17] *Northbay Pelagic Ltd v Anderson[22]—UK Employment Appeal Tribunal—appeal from employment tribunal—unfair dismissal—misconduct—covert recording*

The claimant was a director, shareholder, and employee at Northbay Pelagic Ltd. During the course of his employment, his relationship with another of the respondent's directors broke down. The claimant was suspended in March 2016 and was dismissed shortly thereafter on grounds of misconduct. His misconduct comprised a number of acts, one of which was the allegation that he had placed a covert security

---

[22] *Northbay Pelagic Ltd v Anderson* UKEATS/0029/18/JW.

camera in his office after he had been suspended. His office was intended for his personal use only. However, the claimant believed that someone had entered his office and accessed his computer as he had found his keyboard and a USB key lying on the floor. He installed the camera with a very limited view and no evidence was found to suggest that any other employees were ultimately recorded by it.

The claimant brought a claim for unfair dismissal. The UK employment tribunal upheld the claimant's claim and awarded him compensation, highlighting issues with the investigation of allegations against the claimant. The respondent was of the opinion that the claimant had broken the law when he installed a covert camera without its permission. The employment tribunal rejected this argument, along with four other misconduct reasons put forward by the respondent as cause for dismissal. The employment tribunal held that the decision to dismiss was outside the band of reasonable responses open to the respondent. The respondent appealed to the UK EAT.

The EAT considered the claimant's role not only as an employee but also as a director and a shareholder of the company and that he was likely to have other commercial and personal interests. In the circumstances where his relationship with the respondent had broken down and the fact that his computer was likely to contain confidential information, the EAT held that the respondent ought to have conducted a balancing exercise between its right of privacy and the claimant's desire to protect his confidential information. The EAT held that the decision to dismiss was outside the band of reasonable responses and that the decision of the employment tribunal had been the correct one.

[22.18] *Brown v Veolia ES (UK) Ltd[23]—UK Employment Appeal Tribunal—appeal from the employment tribunal—Trade Union & Labour Relations (Consolidation) Act 1992, s 207A—unfair dismissal—wrongful dismissal—remedy—uplift*

The claimant was employed as business development manager by the respondent at the time of her dismissal, which arose following an investigation and disciplinary process.

She brought a claim of unfair dismissal and wrongful dismissal to the employment tribunal. She also sought an uplift for alleged breaches of the ACAS Code of Practice (the Code) under s 207A of the Trade Union & Labour Relations (Consolidation) Act 1992.

The employment tribunal dismissed her claim of unfair dismissal, finding that there were reasonable grounds for her dismissal and, while the investigatory and dismissal process was a 'catalogue of ineptitude and misjudgement', the employment tribunal was 'just persuaded that the respondent was acting within the band of reasonable responses in treating it as sufficient in the circumstances'. However, her claim of wrongful dismissal was upheld, as her conduct did not constitute 'gross misconduct' as defined in the respondent's policy. Finally, the employment tribunal awarded an uplift of 5% on the award of damages in relation to the wrongful dismissal.

---

[23]   *Brown v Veolia ES (UK) Ltd* UKEAT/0041/20/JOJ.

The claimant appealed these findings to the EAT on a number grounds. The first ground of appeal related to the employment tribunal's finding as to the reason for dismissal. The EAT dismissed this ground, finding that the tribunal had expressly held that the principal reason for her dismissal was conduct.

The claimant appealed against the employment tribunal's finding that her dismissal was fair, submitting that the tribunal had 'set the bar too low' in relation to fairness. Furthermore, she submitted that the employment tribunal had failed to have regard to the fact that the respondent had breached the Code in considering the fairness of her dismissal—breaches of the Code had only been considered when determining the issue of the uplift.

The EAT overturned the conclusion of the employment tribunal in relation to the fairness of her dismissal, noting 'that this is one of those rare cases where, with respect, the [tribunal]'s conclusion on the reasonableness of the Respondent's investigation and disciplinary process cannot stand'. The EAT also held that the Code should have been considered when having regard to the fairness of her dismissal. The employment tribunal's findings as to the fairness of her dismissal were set aside and remitted to the employment tribunal.

The claimant also appealed the decision in relation to the ACAS uplift, submitting that the employment tribunal's uplift of 5% was 'perverse in light of the findings concerning the extent of the breaches and the size and resources of the Respondent'. The EAT held that the employment tribunal had erred in failing have regard to the breaches of the Code when considering the uplift application as they related to the claim of wrongful dismissal. Furthermore, the employment tribunal had failed to have regard to the fact that uplift applications in wrongful dismissals were penal in nature. The uplift application was also remitted to the employment tribunal for re-consideration.

[22.19] *Thompson v Informatica Software Ltd*[24]*—UK Employment Appeal Tribunal—unfair dismissal—gross misconduct—client entertainment—breach of policy*

The claimant was employed by the respondent as Vice President of the UK and Ireland. He authorised the payment for a trip to Pebble Beach Golf Club in California for a customer from the public sector and the respondent's sales manager. When management discovered that the claimant had authorised it, the claimant was dismissed for gross misconduct arising from his entertainment of a public sector customer in breach of the respondent's compliance policy, anti-corruption policy, code of business conduct and global travel and expenses policy.

The claimant submitted a complaint to the employment tribunal in the first instance, which was dismissed, and subsequently appealed that decision to the EAT.

The grounds on which the claimant based his appeal were: (i) interpretation of the anti-corruption policy; and (ii) the question of whether the claimant had acted in 'wilful disregard' of that policy.

---

[24] *Thompson v Informatica Software Ltd* EA-2020-000463-00.

On the first point, the claimant submitted to the EAT that the employment tribunal had erred in its interpretation of the respondent's anti-corruption policy because: (a) the customer was not a 'Foreign Official' as defined in the policy; and (b) because only 'corrupt' payments came within the scope of the policy (it having been accepted at all times by the respondent that the claimant had not set out with the intention to breach the anti-corruption policy).

In relation to that ground, the EAT was satisfied that to take such a literal interpretation of the policy was incorrect. The EAT noted that employer policies do not require strict interpretation in the same way that a contract or piece of legislation might; it stated that the appropriate question was whether a reasonable employer could have reached the same interpretation as the respondent. On that basis, the EAT was satisfied that the spirit of the policy was that employees should exercise caution and approach the legal or human resources departments (as was expressly recommended in the policy) in the event of doubt as to a potential breach.

On the second point, the EAT expressed the view that 'wilful disregard' and 'deliberate breach' were not one and the same thing. The respondent was satisfied that the claimant had not been dismissed due to an intentional authorisation of inappropriate expenditure or an intentional breach of the respondent's anti-corruption policy. The more important issue was that the claimant had authorised the expense even after the indicative cost was relayed to him and despite him feeling uncomfortable about it. The claimant confirmed that he had not considered the respondent's anti-corruption policy before approving the expense (a document he was required to confirm that he had read and understood every three months); he had neither devoted sufficient attention to the matter nor consulted either of the human resources or legal departments; and that in hindsight, he should have withdrawn his authorisation of the trip.

In relation to that ground, the EAT found that it was appropriate to afford 'wilful disregard' its normal meaning, as such the employment tribunal had been entitled to conclude that the respondent had acted reasonably when determining that the claimant had been in wilful disregard of the anti-corruption policy. The claimant's appeal was dismissed.

[22.20] *London Borough of Hammersmith and Fulham v Keable[25]—UK Employment Appeal Tribunal—appeal from employment tribunal—dismissal—reinstatement*

The claimant was employed as a public protection and safety officer by the respondent. He attended a rally outside the UK House of Parliament where he was filmed making a number of comments while in conversation with another individual, including making references to anti-Semitism, Zionism, Nazism and the Holocaust. The conversation was filmed and shared widely on social media, including by a member of parliament. The claimant was identified as an employee of the respondent council on social media.

---

[25] *London Borough of Hammersmith and Fulham v Keable* EA-2019-000733-DA (previously UKEAT/0333/019DA) and EA-2020-000129-DA (previously UKEAT/0134/20/DA).

Following the sharing of the video on social media, the Labour leader of the respondent council emailed the respondent, requesting that they investigate the matter and take appropriate action. An investigation was carried out, the outcome of which was that a disciplinary process should be carried out.

A disciplinary process was carried out, following which the claimant was dismissed. He appealed his dismissal, citing the failure of the respondent to consider lesser sanctions, and emphasising his length of service and unblemished disciplinary record. The dismissal was upheld on appeal.

The claimant brought an unfair dismissals claim to the employment tribunal. The employment tribunal found that the reason he had been dismissed was that he 'had made statements which were considered to be offensive and which they considered had brought the Respondent into disrepute'. The employment tribunal concluded that the investigation 'came within the broad band of reasonable investigations'. However, it found that the dismissal was unfair, both in relation to the procedure and in substance.

In relation to the procedural unfairness, the employment tribunal noted that the statements the claimant had made, which were relied upon in the disciplinary decision letter as the basis for the dismissal, were different statements to those which the claimant had been advised were at issue. As such, the claimant had been deprived of the opportunity to state his case at the disciplinary hearing. In relation to the substantive unfairness, the employment tribunal noted the respondent had acted unreasonably in deciding to dismiss the claimant and failed to have regard to the following factors: the claimant did not himself publish the comments; the comments were not found by the respondent to be discriminatory, anti-Semitic or racist; and the comments were not alleged to be unlawful, criminal or libellous.

Additionally, the employment tribunal held that the claimant should have been asked to comment on the possibility of his heeding a warning as a less severe available sanction. Having considered this, the employment tribunal held that the decision to dismiss was well outside the band of reasonable responses. A separate hearing took place to deal with appropriate remedies, at which the employment tribunal ordered the reinstatement of the claimant.

The respondent appealed both the finding of unfair dismissal and the order of reinstatement, on four grounds:

1. the employment tribunal had misdirected itself by making its own determination as to what response fell within 'the range of reasonable responses';
2. the employment tribunal had misdirected itself by relying upon *Smith v Trafford Housing*[26] without first bringing the authority to the attention of the parties;
3. in relation to the remedy of reinstatement, the employment tribunal had misdirected itself in concluding that 'it was plain that the Council had not lost trust and confidence in the Claimant'; and

---

26 *Smith v Trafford Housing* [2013] IRLR 86.

4. the employment tribunal had misdirected itself in failing 'to explain why it remained practicable to reinstate given the appellate guidance suggesting that such a remedy would be exceptional in such circumstances'.

The EAT upheld the finding of employment tribunal and held that it was entitled to make that judgment based on the facts. It found that in finding that dismissal fell within the range of reasonable responses, the employment tribunal had not substituted its own determination. It further held that the employment tribunal had correctly found the procedures to be flawed, and noted that the allegations had not been put to the claimant and therefore the investigation was unreasonable; and that the decision maker had insufficient evidence to support his assertion that the average person would find the statement to be offensive. Furthermore, the respondent should have provided the claimant with the opportunity to comment on whether a warning was appropriate, and whether the claimant would heed such a warning, and that the failure to do so was unreasonable.

On the second ground of appeal, the EAT held that, while it would have been preferable for the employment tribunal to bring this authority to the attention of the parties in advance and give them an opportunity to provide written submissions, a failure to do so did not amount to an error of law.

The EAT dealt with the third and fourth grounds of appeal together. It held that the order for the claimant to be reinstated was reasonable in the circumstances, based on the facts that the claimant had made concessions regarding how he would behave in the future; he remained on good terms with his colleagues; none of his colleagues had raised complaints against him; and the respondent had conceded that the claimant was good at his job. The claimant's length of service and previously unblemished disciplinary record were also considered to be relevant.

The EAT upheld the decision of the employment tribunal and dismissed the appeal.

CONSTRUCTIVE DISMISSAL

[22.21] *Griffith J Roberts Ltd v Sedleckas*[27]—*Labour Court—appeal from Workplace Relations Commission—Unfair Dismissals Acts 1977 to 2015*

This was an appeal by the claimant of the decision of an Adjudication Officer that he was not unfairly dismissed by the respondent. The claimant worked for the respondent as a hydraulic fitter/general operative since October 2006. At times, when work was scarce, the respondent asked its staff to do other jobs such as painting, unpacking deliveries, cleaning and servicing directors' cars.

On 19 April 2019, when the claimant was asked to clean a director's car, he declined and left the premises. The parties disputed the fact of dismissal. While the claimant alleged that he was dismissed, it was the respondent's position that the claimant voluntarily resigned and requested his P45.

---

[27] *Griffith J Roberts Ltd v Sedleckas* UD2033.

The claimant contended that, on 19 April 2019, he came to work as usual but it was a quiet day and no major jobs were scheduled for him. He was approached by his manager with a request to service and clean his car. The claimant alleged that it made him feel humiliated, as cleaning the director's cars was not part of his duties. He claimed that the respondent told him that if he was not going to clean the car, he should not come into work the following day. The claimant gave evidence that he panicked and asked for redundancy and his P45 and then consulted his union.

On the advice of his union, the claimant attended work the next working day. He informed the respondent that he was attending work because he did not want them to accuse him of leaving the job voluntarily. The respondent asked the claimant, if he would clean the car when asked to do it again, but the claimant refused. Notably, however, the claimant confirmed to the Labour Court that, in the past eight years of his employment, he had performed various jobs, including cleaning directors' cars, and that he had not objected to it previously.

A director of the respondent gave evidence that assigning jobs such as cleaning cars was the norm when things were quiet. On 19 April 2019, the claimant had refused to complete the task assigned to him and asked for his P45. The next day he again refused to comply with the request to clean cars and headed into the office to collect his P45. The Labour Court observed that, as the dismissal was in dispute, the onus was on the claimant to establish that a dismissal in line with s 1 of the Unfair Dismissals Act 1977 had, in fact, occurred.

The Labour Court noted that the claimant had refused to perform a task which had been a part of his duties in the past. He offered no explanation for his refusal and walked out of the workplace of his own volition and proceeded to request his P45. The Court noted that, while the respondent had not enquired into the reason for the claimant leaving his job and had not persuaded him to stay on, these actions did not amount to a dismissal. The Court upheld the Adjudication Officer's decision that the claimant had not been dismissed by the respondent.

[22.22] *Gallivan v St Marks SNS[28]—Labour Court—appeal from Workplace Relations Commission—constructive dismissal—whether dismissal occurred—failure to follow grievance procedures*

This case involved an appeal by the claimant to the Labour Court against an Adjudication Officer's decision that she had not been constructively dismissed by the respondent.

The claimant was employed by the respondent as a special needs assistant. She resigned from her employment on 28 January 2019 and in her resignation letter she stated that she was resigning so that she could take up a position as a part-time school secretary on 4 February 2019. The fact of dismissal was in dispute.

It was the claimant's case that a series of events had occurred from 2014 which involved the making of comments, actions and innuendo from certain members of

---

28   *Gallivan v St Marks SNS* UDD2034.

staff, including the principal, which were directed at her and related to her family and private life and suggested dishonesty on her part. In addition, the environment towards her was extremely hostile.

It was the case of the respondent that no dismissal occurred in January 2019; the claimant had voluntarily resigned from her employment. Further, the claimant had never raised a grievance under the school's grievance and disciplinary procedures. The respondent rejected the allegations made by the claimant regarding its treatment of her in their entirety.

Four of the school staff gave evidence, each of whom the claimant alleged had made the offending statements/comments directed towards her. All of the witnesses denied the allegations.

The Labour Court noted the existence of 'comprehensive grievance procedures' which were available to the claimant and the fact that she had obtained legal advice in 2018 which of itself satisfied the Labour Court that the claimant had the means and opportunity to be aware of the existence and detail of the grievance procedures available to her.

Having regard to the evidence of both parties, the Labour Court was satisfied that the claimant had failed to establish that any behaviour of the respondent could reasonably be interpreted as having entitled the claimant to terminate her employment in a manner that could be found to amount to constructive dismissal. The claimant's appeal therefore was dismissed by the Labour Court.

[22.23]   *Akina Dada Wa Africa v Horeau*[29]—*Labour Court—appeal from Workplace Relations Commission—Unfair Dismissals Acts 1977 to 2015—Maternity Protection Acts 1994 and 2004—unfair dismissal—constructive dismissal*

The claimant commenced employment with the respondent in January 2015, under a fixed-term contract stated to expire on 31 December 2016. On the date on which the fixed-term contract was due to expire, the claimant was on maternity leave.

The claimant never returned to work following the commencement of her maternity leave in 2016, and in October 2017, resigned from her employment and claimed to have been constructively dismissed by the respondent. In making her claim, the claimant asserted that her fixed-term contract was deemed to have been extended as a result of her maternity leave to the date on which she alleged that she was constructively dismissed. The respondent's position was that the claimant ceased to be an employee on the date of her resignation, and that it could not be said that there had been a constructive dismissal.

The claimant contended that the respondent had maintained the claimant in employment until the end of her maternity leave in June 2017 in order that she could

---

[29]   *Akina Dada Wa Africa v Horeau* UDD216.

'enjoy the benefits of maternity leave'. In this regard, the claimant argued that, as the respondent did not offer enhanced maternity pay to its employees and the claimant's right to state maternity benefit was unaffected by whether or not her employment continued throughout the relevant period. The claimant further contended that the respondent's communications with her, following the date on which her fixed-term contract was stated to expire, suggested that the respondent continued to regard her as an employee, and that in effect, her employment had been extended. By way of example, the claimant noted that the respondent acknowledged the claimant's intention, communicated in March 2017 (three months after the fixed-term contract was stated to expire), to take 16 weeks' additional maternity leave. Moreover, in May 2017, the claimant, through her representative, communicated her intention to return from maternity leave in June 2017 and no reply was issued by the respondent denying the claimant had any right to do so. The claimant further submitted that when her maternity leave ended in June 2017, she expected to return to work and was never advised or informed to the contrary by the respondent. As such, the claimant argued that her contract of employment should be deemed to have continued by mutual agreement, such that she therefore remained an employee of the respondent at the time of her purported resignation in October 2017.

In response, the respondent argued that where there may be a practice in some organisations of renewing fixed-term contracts of employment that expire during maternity leave, such a practice is not universal and is a precautionary practice adopted to mitigate against the risk of being in breach of the Pregnant Workers Directive.[30] Moreover, the respondent argued that the facilitation by it of the claimant's request for additional maternity leave represented the discharge of a statutory duty or, if not the discharge of a statutory duty, then the discharge of what the respondent misunderstood to be a statutory duty. In any event, the respondent asserted that neither circumstance could operate in practice to extend the fixed term of the contract of employment, which expired on 31 December 2016.

In evidence, the claimant pointed to the Form P45 issued to her following her purported resignation, in which the respondent had stated that her final date of employment was 18 June 2017.

The Court stressed that, in order for the claimant to enjoy the protections of the Unfair Dismissals Acts 1977 to 2015 as amended, a contract of employment must be in force at the date of the purported dismissal, and that this was a key dispute between the parties.

The Court noted that, on a literal interpretation of s 10(2) of the Maternity Protection Acts 1994 and 2004, the fact that an employee may be on maternity leave on the stated date of expiry of a fixed-term contract of employment does not affect the expiry of that contract. The Court noted that this position was consistent with the ruling in *Melgar v Ayuntamiento de Los Barrios*,[31] which itself was based on the application of the

---

[30] Directive 92/85/EEC on the introduction of measures to encourage improvements in the safety and health at work of pregnant workers and workers who have recently given birth or are breastfeeding.

[31] *Melgar v Ayuntamiento de Los Barrios* (Case C-438/99), [2001] ECR 1-6915.

Pregnant Workers Directive. In an Irish context, the Court pointed to *McBrierty v NUI Galway*,[32] where it was held that the non-renewal of a fixed-term contract, in circumstances where the employee is on maternity leave, cannot be regarded as a dismissal within the meaning of the Pregnant Workers Directive.

The Court further noted that both parties had drawn its attention to *Assisco Assembly Ltd v Corcoran*,[33] where it was highlighted that in cases where pregnancy-related dismissals arise, the burden of establishing that there was no discrimination lies with the employer. The Court stressed that as a matter of law, the claimant's maternity leave had no impact on the expiry of her fixed-term contract on 31 December 2016, but that the Court was required to consider what had transpired subsequent to that date, in order to conclude whether the contract was deemed to have been extended by the parties.

The Court concluded that the respondent had clearly not sought to extend the employment relationship beyond 31 December 2016. The Court accepted that the respondent was mistaken in law in continuing to interact with the claimant as if she remained an employee following that date, and up to the end of her maternity leave. However, the Court placed importance on the fact that the respondent did cease to interact with the claimant after the expiry of her maternity leave in June 2017, and also on the fact that the date listed by the respondent on the Form P45 issued to the claimant tallied with the expiry of her maternity leave (although the date was incorrect by a small number of days). The Court was satisfied that, although the respondent had misapplied the law, the claimant's contract of employment was not intended to be, and as such was not, continued beyond the stated expiry date.

Thereafter, the Court concluded that since the claimant's purported resignation occurred after the expiry of her maternity leave, she was not employed by the respondent on the date on which she purported to resign. The Court stressed that a dismissal, constructive or otherwise, can only occur in circumstances where there is an employment relationship in being. Where there is no such relationship, which the Court held was the case here, the Court held that neither the Workplace Relations Commission nor the Labour Court has jurisdiction to hear a complaint submitted under the Unfair Dismissals Acts 1977 to 2015 as amended.

[22.24] *Conor Mc Laughlin Mc Morrow & Mc Laughlin Solicitors v Monaghan*[34]*—Labour Court—appeal from Workplace Relations Commission— constructive dismissal—contract test—unilateral amendment*

The claimant was employed as a solicitor working in a practice from November 2008. The respondent became the claimant's employer in November 2018 by virtue of the

---

[32]   *McBrierty v NUI Galway* EDA 091.
[33]   *Assisco Assembly Ltd v Corcoran* EED033/2003.
[34]   *Conor Mc Laughlin Mc Morrow & Mc Laughlin Solicitors v Monaghan* UDD2110.

transfer of an undertaking under the European Communities (Protection of Employees on Transfer of Undertakings) Regulations 2003.[35]

Following the transfer, the respondent purported to make unilateral changes to the claimant's terms and conditions of employment. The changes included a removal of the claimant's prior service, reduction in annual leave entitlement from 20 to 12 days, the inclusion of a six-month probationary period, change to the location clause and increase to the duration of restrictive covenants from six to 12 months.

The respondent also failed to discharge the fees for the claimant's practising certificate. The claimant received notifications from the Law Society outlining that payment had not been made. The claimant notified the respondent but received no response to her emails. Ultimately, the claimant did receive her practising certificate.

The claimant advised the Court that the respondent told a client that nobody with the claimant's name worked in that practice, and did not include the claimant's details on the practice's website. The respondent claimed that the conversation with the client was a genuine misunderstanding as he thought the client was looking for another solicitor in a different practice, and the website details were not included as the claimant had not provided them in the correct format.

The claimant filed a formal grievance and the respondent met with her in that regard. At the meeting, the respondent offered the claimant a severance package, which the claimant declined. The claimant sought to arrange a further grievance meeting with the respondent, however, there was confusion in relation to scheduling and ultimately a further meeting did not take place. The claimant then resigned from her employment.

The respondent alleged that the claimant should have appealed the outcome of the grievance if she was dissatisfied at any point. The respondent also contended that he had advised the claimant in their meeting that he was no longer going to pursue the contractual changes. However, the respondent accepted that the meeting notes that he had submitted to the Court did not reflect that contention.

The Court examined the test applicable to constructive dismissal and noted that the 'contract test' provides that where an employer's conduct constitutes a repudiatory breach that goes to the root of the contract, or which shows that the employer no longer intends to be bound by an essential term of the contract, then the employee is entitled to treat himself as discharged from employment. The Court also noted a second test, the reasonableness test, which relates to whether an employer conducted affairs so unreasonably that the employee could not be expected to put up with it any longer.

The Court found that the unilateral changes to the claimant's contract constituted a significant breach of the employment contract and as such, the respondent was guilty of conduct such as to entitle the claimant to terminate her employment. The Court observed that the claimant had been unsuccessful in seeking to resolve her grievance through the grievance procedure.

---

[35] European Communities (Protection of Employees on Transfer of Undertakings) Regulations 2003 (SI 131/2003).

The Court upheld the finding of the Adjudicating Officer that the claimant was constructively dismissed and awarded her €5,641.80 by way of compensation (reducing the sum from €13,300, which had been awarded by the WRC).

[22.25] Cope Ltd t/a Cope Galway v Bell[36]—Labour Court—constructive dismissal—failure to use established internal procedures

The claimant commenced employment with the respondent in March 2013. Her employment terminated 30 October 2018, after the claimant tendered her resignation with two weeks' notice on 17 October 2018. She alleged that she was constructively dismissed, which the respondent denied.

The claimant alleged that an incident took place on 17 September 2018 during which a colleague was verbally abusive towards her. She subsequently wrote to her HR manager to make him aware of the incident. She was informed of the grievance procedure but she felt discouraged from making a formal complaint.

She then went on stress leave for considerable periods of time between the occurrence of the alleged event and the date of her letter of resignation and, while she acknowledged that the respondent did discuss the employee assistance policy with her, she submitted that the respondent's behaviour was so unreasonable and had undermined the contract of employment to such a degree as to mean that she was entitled to consider herself constructively dismissed.

The Labour Court noted the reasonable level of engagement by the respondent with the claimant following her initial complaint and during the short period of time she attended for work prior to her resignation. The Court also noted that the claimant had had the confidence to communicate with senior management about issues during this time.

The Court stated that, having regard to all of the circumstances and in particular the short period of time which was available to the respondent to deal with the issues raised, it was not satisfied that the claimant had met the high bar required to establish a complaint of constructive dismissal. The Court found that the claimant terminated her employment without having sought to resolve her grievances through the established internal procedures. This meant her subsequent decision to resign could not be regarded as a reasonable response to the situation. The Labour Court rejected the claimant's complaint of constructive dismissal and, in so doing, set aside the decision of the WRC to award her €8,400 in compensation, instead finding that the claimant was not unfairly dismissed.

[22.26] Get Fresh Vending Ltd v Walshe[37]—Labour Court—appeal from Workplace Relations Commission—constructive unfair dismissal—sufficiently proximate events

---

36 *Cope Ltd t/a Cope Galway v Bell* UDD2145.
37 *Get Fresh Vending Ltd v Walshe* UDD2412.

This was an appeal to the Labour Court by the claimant against the decision of an Adjudication Officer. The claimant commenced employment with the respondent in the position of catering assistant in a school on 28 April 2014, until her resignation on 10 September 2018. On 25 May 2018, there was an 'inappropriate verbal exchange' between the claimant and a colleague in relation to the colleague allegedly having used the claimant's hair net without her consent. This exchange occurred potentially within the earshot of pupils. The claimant's colleague reported the exchange to the principal of the school, who in turn reported it to the respondent. A disciplinary procedure was initiated against the claimant, culminating in her being issued with a final written warning, which would remain on her record for a period of six months. Although she had the opportunity to do so, the claimant did not appeal the issuing of the warning, but took issue instead with the way the process had been conducted and requested that the final written warning be retracted.

On 10 September 2018, the claimant resigned; she informed the Court that she decided to resign due to the respondent's 'attitude and unreasonable behaviour'. The Court noted that the claimant's submissions referred to several incidents in 2017 and 2018, which were unconnected to the events giving rise to her resignation, and were not sufficiently proximate to her decision to resign to be considered in the context of a claim for constructive dismissal.

In making its decision, the Court noted that an applicant in a constructive unfair dismissal case must establish that the decision to resign was reasonable because of the employer's alleged unreasonable conduct and/or breach of contract and that an employee must exhaust all internal procedures available to him/her before resigning. In this case, as the claimant had not availed of her internal right of appeal, she had not exhausted the internal procedures available to her before deciding to resign. The Court concluded that the claimant's appeal failed and there was 'nothing inherently unfair in the procedures followed by the Respondent' in relation to the matter.

[22.27] *Chemcem Scotland Ltd v Ure[38]—UK Employment Appeal Tribunal—appeal employment tribunal—constructive dismissal—was a failure to return to work at the end of maternity leave an acceptance of the employer's breach of contract?*

This was an unusual case which very much turned on its own facts. It concerned a civil engineering company as the respondent employer and the claimant employee who was also the daughter of the majority shareholder of the employer. The claimant went on maternity leave and did not return, she then lodged a claim with the employment tribunal and asserted that she had been constructively dismissed. The claimant argued that the respondent had committed a variety of breaches of contract which had transgressed the obligation of mutual trust and confidence between them and she submitted that, in these circumstances, she was entitled to regard these acts as repudiatory. The claimant asserted that she had accepted the repudiation and had been unfairly dismissed.

---

[38]   *Chemcem Scotland Ltd v Ure* UKEAT/0036/19/SS.

The respondent's actions included varying her pay without warning, switching her to a different payroll, failing to pay her statutory maternity pay on time, failing to answer her queries about her pay entitlement and misleading her as to the true position. The situation was complicated by the fact that these breaches were committed by the claimant's father, the majority shareholder, who had left the claimant's mother and formed a relationship with another member of staff. As a consequence, any dialogue between the claimant and her father during maternity leave was difficult and the relationship between them was very fraught.

The UK employment tribunal held that although the claimant had stated in evidence that she did not return to work after her maternity leave because her statutory maternity pay had been discontinued in a circumstance where the respondent had been entitled to discontinue her payments, there were a variety of other factors that justified her decision not to return to work. Those factors were repudiatory in character and, as a consequence, the claimant was entitled to refuse to return to work and to treat the employer's conduct as constructive dismissal.

The employment tribunal further held that her failure to return to work constituted a communication of her decision not to return to work, even though nothing was said to the employer.

The respondent appealed, arguing that the claimant had failed to communicate her acceptance of its repudiatory acts and, in the absence of such a communication, there could not as a matter of law be a termination of contract.

The appeal was dismissed and the EAT held: (1) that the employment tribunal was correct to treat the various repudiatory acts as a sufficient ground for the claimant's decision to rescind the contract and claim constructive dismissal; and (2) while in normal circumstances, the claimant's failure to return to work might not carry the implication that she had accepted her employer's breaches, in this case 'it plainly could'. It was a matter for the tribunal as a finder of fact to judge whether her non-appearance amounted to an acceptance of the repudiatory acts. The employer had not challenged the factual basis of the employment tribunal's conclusions, which were that the claimant had not returned to work because of her father's treatment of her. Her father knew that, if she returned to work, his new partner would come under the claimant's management and he did not want that to happen. Further, when the claimant did not return, her employer did not get in contact with her to ask why not. The particular circumstances demonstrated the true position and there was no need for an express communication by the claimant of acceptance of the repudiatory acts.

[22.28]   *Hall v London Lions Basketball Club UK Ltd[39]—UK Employment Appeal Tribunal—appeal from employment tribunal—Employment Rights Act 1996, s 1—unfair dismissal—constructive dismissal—fixed-term contract*

The claimant was employed as a professional basketball player by the respondent, on a fixed-term contract that was due to expire at the end of the 2017/18 basketball

---

[39]   *Hall v London Lions Basketball Club* UK Ltd UKEAT/0273/19/OO.

season. The contract provided for certain circumstances in which the respondent could terminate the claimant's contract before the end of the season.

The respondent advised the claimant that it proposed to reduce his salary under the contract by 10%. The claimant informed the respondent that he would be unable to accept such a reduction. Thereafter, the respondent ceased paying any part of the claimant's salary. As a result, the claimant resigned from his employment and brought a claim to the UK employment tribunal alleging that the respondent had made an unlawful deduction from his wages, that he had been constructively dismissed, that the respondent had breached s 1 of the Employment Rights Act 1996 and that the respondent had not paid him in lieu of accrued but untaken annual leave.

The employment tribunal found in favour of the claimant in respect of each element of his claim and concluded that the respondent had breached the contract of employment and that the claimant had therefore been constructively wrongly dismissed. However, in calculating damages, the tribunal only awarded an amount equivalent to 14 days' salary, rather than the salary that would have been payable had the contract run until the expiry of the season. The rationale for this was that the contract allowed the claimant to serve 14 days' notice of his intention to terminate his contract of employment in circumstances where the respondent committed a serious breach of same. With regard to the claimant's claim for non-payment of accrued but untaken annual leave, the employment tribunal pro-rated the claimant's weekly salary when calculating the amount it deemed to be owed to him, concluding that since he worked approximately 20 hours each week, he was a part-time employee.

The claimant appealed the employment tribunal's decision to the EAT. The appeal centred on two issues:

1. The claimant had a right to terminate his contract of employment, on 14 days' notice, in the event of the respondent committing a serious breach of same. Did that right limit his common law right to damages for the respondent's subsequent breach?
2. Should weekly salary be pro rated for part-time employees when calculating annual leave?

Taking the first issue, the EAT confirmed that at its core, the fundamental purpose of damages was to leave a claimant in the position he/she would otherwise have been in had the other party complied in full with its obligations under the contract.

The EAT noted that the respondent did not have an equivalent right to that of the claimant to terminate the contract on 14 days' notice. In fact, the EAT concluded that there was no provision in the contract that operated to allow the respondent to terminate same prior to the end of the 2017/18 season.

The EAT concluded that since the employment tribunal had found that the claimant had been constructively wrongly dismissed by reason of the respondent performing a repudiatory breach of the contract which the claimant accepted by resigning, it should have approached the question of damages 'in the ordinary way', without examining whether the claimant's right to terminate the contract on 14 days' notice, in the event of a serious breach by the respondent, meant that his right to claim damages was limited as a consequence to 14 days. As such, the EAT held that damages should be assessed from the date on which the claimant was constructively wrongly dismissed to the date on which the 2017/18 season ended.

In relation to the second issue (the pro rata treatment of payment for accrued annual leave), the EAT concluded that there was no basis for applying pro rata treatment to the claimant's pay in lieu of annual leave, since pro rata treatment for part-time employees was already part of the applicable regulations (the Working Time Regulations 1998)[40]. As such, the EAT clarified that the correct method of calculating payment in lieu of accrued but untaken annual leave was to take the number of weeks of accrued but untaken annual leave as at the date of termination of employment, and multiply it by the claimant's normal weekly salary.

[22.29]   *Gordon v J&D Pierce (Contracts) Ltd[41]—UK Employment Appeal Tribunal—appeal from employment tribunal—constructive dismissal—implied obligation of trust and confidence*

The claimant entered into a contract of employment with the respondent, J&D Pierce. He brought a claim to the employment tribunal arguing that he had been constructively dismissed as the implied obligation of trust and confidence had been breached by the respondents.

The employment tribunal found that the respondent had not breached the implied obligation of trust and confidence, and as such there was no right of resignation. The employment tribunal further held that even if there had been a breach of contract such that the claimant could resign, he could not succeed in his action as he had affirmed the contract of employment by engaging with the grievance procedure. The employment tribunal held that through his engagement in the grievance process, he had forfeited his right to rely on the breach of the implied obligation of trust and confidence.

The claimant appealed the decision to the EAT.

The claimant argued that the employment tribunal had erred in law in failing to apply the full test relating to the implied obligation of trust and confidence as established in *Malik v BCCI*.[42] Specifically, the claimant argued that the employment tribunal referred to conduct that was likely to 'destroy' the implied obligation of trust and confidence rather than conduct that would 'destroy or seriously damage' that relationship.

The EAT rejected the claimant's argument in relation to breach of trust and confidence. It found that the employment tribunal had correctly applied the full test of 'destroy or seriously damage', notwithstanding the fact that, in its judgment, the tribunal had abbreviated the test to 'destroy'. Further, in assessing the breakdown of the employment relationship, the EAT found that the degree to which the claimant and respondent

---

[40]   Working Time Regulations 1998 (SI 1998/1833).
[41]   *Gordon v J&D Pierce (Contracts) Ltd* UKEATS/0010/20/SS.
[42]   *Malik v BCCI* [1997] IRLR 462.

had contributed to the situation must be considered. The EAT ultimately held that no right of resignation arose, and as such, the claimant was not entitled to claim constructive dismissal.

In relation to the affirmation of the contract, the EAT held that the employment tribunal erred in law in finding that the claimant had affirmed his contract of employment by engaging in the grievance procedure. The EAT found that where an employee believes that the contract of employment has come to an end due to a breach of the implied obligation of trust and confidence, it does not follow that the parties intend that the clauses dealing with the resolution of disputes have come to end. The EAT held that grievance procedures and appeal mechanisms under contracts can be treated as severable and continue to exist independently, even where the remainder of the contract is treated as terminated. The EAT concluded that the employee did not affirm the contract of employment by engaging in a grievance process and dismissed the appeal.

[22.30] *Flatman v Essex County Council*[43]*—UK Employment Appeal Tribunal— appeal from employment tribunal—breach of contract*

The claimant was employed as a school assistant by an Essex County Council school, where she cared for a disabled pupil. Part of her duties required some heavy lifting, for which she had requested manual handling training. This training was never arranged. Ultimately the claimant suffered back problems and went on sick leave. The principal of the school informed her that on her return she would not have to do the lifting, and that the manual handling training was being organised. The claimant did not return to school despite these assurances; she resigned and claimed constructive dismissal. The employment tribunal rejected her claim. It found that while the employer was in breach of the Manual Handling Operations Regulations 1992, there was still no fundamental breach of contract as the communication from the principal demonstrated that the employer appreciated the problem and was taking steps to address it. The claimant appealed this decision to the EAT.

In allowing the appeal, the EAT held that the tribunal at first instance had incorrectly looked only at events at the time of the claimant's resignation. The EAT held that the employment tribunal should instead have considered whether there had already been a breach of contract at any time since the commencement of her work with that disabled pupil. The EAT held that if there had been a prior fundamental breach, that breach could not be subsequently rectified by the employer to avoid a constructive dismissal, ie once the claimant had gone on sick leave, the subsequent communication by the principal to provide training could not 'cure' the breach. The employee's claim for constructive dismissal can be upheld only if the employee does not affirm the contract and waive the breach (eg, by waiting too long to resign).

In this particular case, the EAT held that an implied term had been breached by the respondent either: (a) on the respondent's failure to provide the manual handling

---

43   *Flatman v Essex County Council* UKEAT/0097/20.

training; or (b) when the claimant went on sick leave. The EAT held that both these instances amounted to a fundamental breach of the implied term, and that after such a breach, the respondent could not cure or 'remedy' the breach by subsequent action. The appeal was upheld.

DISMISSAL?

[22.31]   *Boylesports Unlimited Company v Markey[44]—Labour Court—appeal from Workplace Relations Commission—unfair dismissal*

The claimant worked as an IT Helpdesk Administrator with the respondent, until 28 November 2017, when he allegedly resigned from his employment. The claimant alleged that he was unfairly dismissed by the respondent and was coerced to resign on the day.

In addition to his normal working hours, the claimant also worked on-call and received additional remuneration for the on-call work. On 28 November 2017, the claimant's manager raised two issues in relation to his claims for on-call work. The first issue related to an on-call claim of €100 for which the manager accepted the claimant's explanation but informed him of the procedure to be followed. The second issue concerned a claim raised by the claimant for on-call texts. The claimant's manager told him that it was not permissible to claim for texts while on-call. It transpired that the claimant had raised claims in relation to 28 such texts and he offered to reimburse the respondent in relation to the corresponding payments of €560. He acknowledged that it had been a mistake on his part.

The claimant alleged that his manager left the meeting to confer with the chief technical officer and shortly thereafter he returned to say that he wanted the claimant gone as he had breached their trust. The manager told the claimant that 'it is not looking good for you' and proceeded to give him two options: either the manager would initiate an investigation to look into the matter or the claimant could resign and he would be offered a month's pay. The claimant rang his wife and opted to resign. He claimed that the manager asked him to email his resignation but then changed his decision and asked the claimant to print the resignation. The manager then went on to dictate the start of the resignation and directed the claimant to leave the respondent's premises.

The respondent denied these allegations and submitted that the manager had only informed the claimant about investigating the overpayment issue and the claimant had offered to resign instead.

The manager called to the claimant's home to collect IT equipment when the claimant told him that he had consulted his family and decided that he had not made the right decision and wanted information in relation to the investigation. The claimant alleged that the manager assured him that he had made the right decision and, given his

---

44   *Boylesports Unlimited Company v Markey* UDD214.

experience, he would not have any trouble finding another job. The respondent stated that they had acted reasonably in relation to the enquiry into the claimant's on-call claims and that he was not asked to resign. On this basis, the respondent submitted that the claimant was not dismissed by the respondent.

The claimant submitted that he was not afforded an opportunity to seek advice from an appropriate person and he panicked when he was told that the chief technical officer wanted him gone from the business. It was submitted that the manager and HR should have given him an opportunity to withdraw his resignation and have the overpayment issue fairly investigated. The claimant had also offered to repay the amount overpaid to the respondent.

The Labour Court noted that the claimant did not have any previous experience in employment as this was his first job. The Court held that it expected employees in managerial roles to have a reasonable degree of expertise while handling workplace issues. On this basis, it held that it was not unreasonable for the claimant to believe that he was coerced into resigning. These circumstances were exacerbated by the fact that the claimant was not permitted to withdraw his resignation and participate in an investigation and as such, he was unfairly dismissed.

The Court took into consideration the fact that the claimant had contributed to the circumstances and had not made any attempts to mitigate his loss. Accordingly, the Court ordered compensation of €5,750 by way of loss of earnings.

[22.32] **_The Blue Door v Fitzgerald_**[45]**—_Labour Court—appeal from Workplace Relations Commission—unfair dismissal—mitigation of loss_**

The claimant worked as a chef for the respondent from February 2018 to August 2019. The claimant was on certified sick leave from April 2019. The parties met to discuss the ongoing situation on 1 August 2019 and the claimant sent further medical certificates to the respondent on 6 August 2019. On 7 August, the respondent issued the claimant with his P45 and payment for holiday time as well as an 'ex gratia' payment. The covering letter described the termination 'as agreed'.

The WRC found that the claimant had been unfairly dismissed and awarded a sum equal to four weeks' pay by way of compensation. The claimant appealed to the Labour Court on grounds that the quantum was an insufficient recognition of his loss.

The respondent argued that the claimant had resigned and that there had been no unfair dismissal. After learning that the claimant would be unavailable for work for some time, the respondent explained the difficulties this would cause and the claimant said the respondent 'should do what was best for the business but he asked the Respondent to wait until after the bank holiday as this would be an extra day for him'. The respondent understood this to mean that the claimant did not require his job to be held open and, after the bank holiday on 6 August 2019, sent the claimant his holiday and bank holiday pay, plus an ex gratia payment of €200 in goodwill.

---

45   *The Blue Door v Fitzgerald* UDD2126.

The claimant argued that there had been no such agreement, and that the agreement referred to by the respondent was that he would continue to send medical certificates. In finding for the claimant, the Labour Court found that the documentary evidence showed that the respondent sent a dismissal letter on 7 August 2019, which crossed in the post with the claimant's medical certificate, and did nothing to clarify the claimant's position subsequently. The claimant had no chance to exercise his rights under natural justice prior to this dismissal, which, in itself made the dismissal unfair.

In assessing the appropriate level of damages, the Labour Court found that the claimant fell short of the required mitigation of loss by submitting only one job application per month and held that:

> This falls well short of the standard requirement that a dismissed employee should devote part of every single normal working day to finding alternative employment in order to mitigate their losses.

The Court awarded €8,000 in compensation for unfair dismissal.

FRUSTRATION

[22.33]   *Bus Atha Cliath-Dublin Bus v Irabor*[46]—*Labour Court—appeal from Workplace Relations Commission—Unfair Dismissals Act 1977 to 2015, s 6(4)(4)— unfair dismissal—frustration of contract*

This was an appeal to the Labour Court of a decision of the WRC that the claimant's complaint of unfair dismissal was not well founded. The claimant was employed by the respondent as a bus driver. On 17 November 2014, he was involved in a fatal collision while driving a bus. He was subsequently convicted of careless driving causing death, and received a four-year driving ban with effect from 1 January 2019.

The claimant appealed his conviction and informed the respondent that an appeal had been lodged. The appeal did not suspend his driving ban, which remained in effect from 1 January 2019.

On 14 March 2019, the respondent wrote to the claimant informing him that his contract of employment was frustrated as a result of his driving ban—and as such, he was dismissed. The claimant, through his trade union representatives, sought to appeal this decision; the respondent refused to hear this appeal, noting that as his contract was frustrated, it was not a matter for the Disciplinary Appeals Board to hear.

The claimant brought an unfair dismissal claim to the WRC, submitting that he had not been afforded fair procedures. The respondent submitted that his contract of employment had concluded due to frustration caused by his driving ban. The WRC ultimately found that the complaint of unfair dismissal was not well founded. This was appealed to the Labour Court.

---

[46]   *Bus Atha Cliath-Dublin Bus v Irabor* UDD2168.

The Labour Court found that the dismissal fell within s 6(4)(d) of the Unfair Dismissals Act 1977 to 2015 (the Acts), which provides that a dismissal is not an unfair dismissal if it results wholly or mainly from 'the employee being unable to work or continue to work in the position which he held without contravention (by him or by his employer) of a duty or restriction imposed by or under any statute'. In the circumstances, the claimant could not drive without breaching a court-imposed driving ban.

The Labour Court held that the case fell within s 6(4)(d) of the Acts, and as such was not an unfair dismissal.

HEALTH & SAFETY

[22.34] ***Sinclair v Trackwork Ltd[47]—UK Employment Appeal Tribunal—appeal from employment tribunal—Employment Rights Act 1996, s 100(1)(a)—unfair dismissal—health and safety—penalisation***

The claimant was employed by the respondent and was tasked with implementing new health and safety measures. The respondent did not inform the claimant's colleagues that he would be implementing such measures, and his colleagues filed complaints about the claimant's behaviour. The claimant was dismissed because of the 'upset' and 'friction' that his activities had caused.

The claimant alleged that the dismissal was automatically unfair as the principal reason for dismissal was that he carried out health and safety activities (which had been designated to him). The employment tribunal dismissed the claimant's complaint, finding that the reason for dismissal was the demoralisation of the workforce by the way in which the claimant carried out his actions. The claimant appealed to the EAT.

The EAT allowed the claimant's appeal and found that the claimant's activities did not exceed his mandate and were not 'malicious, untruthful or irrelevant to the task in hand'. As such, the manner in which the tasks were carried out was not separable from the activities themselves.

The EAT found that it would undermine the protection of s 100(1)(a) of the Employment Rights Act 1996 (automatic unfair dismissal where the reason for dismissal was the employee's carrying out of health and safety related duties as designated by the employer) if the employer could rely on upset caused by the health and safety activity as being unrelated to the activity itself.

The EAT found that the protection afforded to those carrying out health and safety activities under s 100 of the Employment Rights Act 1996 was broad. The way that the designated activities were carried out would not remove the protection.

The EAT went on to find that where an employee's conduct was 'wholly unreasonable, malicious or irrelevant to the task in hand' when carrying out the designated activities,

---

47 *Sinclair v Trackwork Ltd* UKEAT/0129/20/OO(V).

that could result in the removal of the protection of s 100. However, the EAT found that the claimant's conduct did not fall into that category—he was 'diligently carrying out his duties', which caused tension within the workforce. Although the tension and upset among the workforce led to the claimant's dismissal, that upset resulted from the respondent's failure to notify employees of the claimant's mandate and not from any malice on the part of the claimant.

The appeal was upheld and the matter was remitted to the employment tribunal to consider the remedy.

INCAPACITY

[22.35] *Ashford Castle Hotel v McCormack[48]—Labour Court—appeal from Workplace Relations Commission—Unfair Dismissals Acts 1977 to 2015—unfair dismissal—capability*

The claimant was employed by the respondent hotel, initially as a doorman from 2003 to 2011, and subsequently as a concierge, until he was dismissed in October 2017 on the ground of his inability to perform the duties for which he had been employed. The claimant submitted a complaint of unfair dismissal to the WRC, which an Adjudication Officer rejected.

Ownership of the hotel changed in 2014, and the claimant went out on sick leave in November 2014, having raised a number of concerns with the defendant which had gone, to his mind, unanswered. The claimant did not return to work between that date and the date of his dismissal in October 2017.

During the period between November 2014 and October 2017, the claimant submitted medical certificates and was referred by the respondent for occupational health assessments on five occasions. On the last occasion, two months before the claimant was dismissed, the occupational health physician advised that: 'Given the profound sense of grievance reported and his protracted absence and ongoing symptoms, I do not believe a return to work would be successful at this time and this is not likely to change in the medium term i.e. 3–6 months at least'.

The claimant raised multiple grievances with the respondent after going on sick leave in November 2014. On two occasions, in February 2015 and May 2015 respectively, the claimant's solicitor informed the respondent that the claimant wished to invoke the respondent's grievance procedure. The claimant was invited to a meeting to discuss his grievances, but failed to attend. Subsequently the claimant sought a formal meeting with the respondent to discuss what he contended to be his 'prolonged mistreatment and harassment'. Two meetings took place on 7 October 2015 and 12 October 2015, and the outcome of the respondent's investigation into the claimant's grievances was issued to the claimant on 22 October 2015. A request was received from the claimant's

---

[48]   *Ashford Castle Hotel v McCormack* UDD2115.

solicitor for an extension to the deadline for submitting an appeal against the grievance outcome, which was acceded to; however, no appeal was submitted.

In early 2016, correspondence was exchanged in relation to the claimant's staff accommodation. Subsequently, in September 2016, the claimant submitted an allegation of bullying against an employee of the respondent. On 21 November 2016, the claimant wrote to a senior employee of the respondent seeking a meeting to discuss grievances with the respondent. A meeting took place on 7 December 2016, and on 10 January 2017 the senior employee of the respondent who had had the meeting with the claimant issued his report containing his findings in relation to the 48 grievances raised by the claimant during the meeting. In that report, the claimant was advised of the deadline for making an appeal, as well as the individual to whom any appeal should be addressed. Having submitted an appeal, the claimant failed to attend the meeting scheduled to hear the appeal.

The respondent submitted that following the fifth occupational health assessment in August 2017, the respondent wrote to the claimant on 18 and 27 August 2017, and met with him on 13 September 2017 to discuss 'his position within the organisation and possible return to work'. The following day, the respondent wrote to the claimant again, inviting him to make submissions in relation to how the respondent could facilitate his return to work. However, the claimant did not make any submissions. Thereafter, by letter dated 4 October 2017, the respondent dismissed the claimant on the basis that he was incapable of performing the duties of his employment. The letter of dismissal contained a right of appeal, and an associated timeframe within which any appeal was required to be made. The claimant appealed the respondent's decision to dismiss him, was invited to an appeal meeting on 25 October 2017, but failed to attend the appeal meeting.

The respondent submitted that a dismissal effected due to an incapability to perform the work for which an individual was employed is not an unfair dismissal within the meaning of the Unfair Dismissals Acts 1977 to 2015, as amended. In particular, the respondent relied on matters identified by Lardner J in *Bolger v Showerings (Ireland) Ltd*,[49] ie, that the employee's ill health must be the reason for the dismissal, and the employee must be given reasonable notice that the prospect of his/her being dismissed, as a result of his/her incapability to perform his/her duties, is being considered. The respondent contended that it had met the test in the present case.

The claimant asserted that his sick leave was occasioned by his work environment, and that this continued absence from the workplace was the result of the respondent's failure to address the issues with his work environment that he had raised, and due to the fact that the respondent had not processed his grievances in a fair or impartial manner. In relation to the timeline of events leading up to his dismissal, the claimant submitted that he did in fact respond to the respondent's letter dated 14 September 2017 inviting him to make submissions in relation to how it could facilitate his return to work. Further, the claimant pointed to an email he sent to the respondent on

---

[49]   *Bolger v Showerings (Ireland) Ltd* [1990] ELR 184.

21 September 2017, advising it that he had submitted a complaint to the WRC and requesting the respondent to be 'patient' and allow his complaints to be ventilated before the WRC (in this regard, the Court noted that the claimant did not in fact submit a complaint to the WRC until 2 April 2018). The claimant submitted that ill health was the reason he was unable to attend the appeal meeting in relation to the respondent's decision to dismiss him.

The Court identified that the substantive issue before it was whether the claimant's dismissal was occasioned 'wholly or mainly from his capability to perform the work he was employed to do, in circumstances where he was absent from work due to ill health from November 2014'. The Court referred to the requirements in relation to capability arising from ill health stated in *Bolger*:

> For the employer to show that the dismissal was fair, he must show that:
> (1)   It was the ill-health which was the reason for his dismissal;
> (2)   That this was the substantial reason;
> (3)   That the employee received fair notice that the question of his dismissal for incapacity was being considered; and
> (4)   That the employee was afforded an opportunity of being heard.

The Court considered that the respondent had, over a period of almost three years, had the claimant assessed by an occupational health physician on five occasions, and that on each occasion he had been deemed unfit to return to work. The Court also noted that no reason other than the claimant's absence had been put forward by either party as a motivating factor in the claimant's dismissal. The Court further noted that having received the medical report in respect of the fifth and final occupational health assessment in August 2017, the respondent met with the claimant and invited him to make submissions in relation to facilitating a return to work, and that by that time, the claimant was aware that the prospect of his being dismissed by reason of his incapability was being considered. In observing that the only evidence of any proposal put forward by the claimant was to pause the process pending the adjudication of a complaint to the WRC (which was not submitted until 2 April 2018), the Court concluded that, when effecting the claimant's dismissal, the respondent believed him to be incapable of performing the work for which he had been employed, due to his ill health. On that basis, the Court concluded that the dismissal was fair, and accordingly upheld the decision of the Adjudication Officer.

OTHER SUBSTANTIAL GROUNDS

[22.36]   *L v K⁵⁰—Scottish Court of Session—appeal from decision of UK Employment Appeal Tribunal—some other substantial reason—possession of a computer containing indecent images of children*

---

50   *L v K* [2021] CSIH 35. See *Arthur Cox Employment Law Yearbook 2020* at [19.22] for decision of the UK EAT in *K v L* UKEATS/0014/18/JW.

This is an appeal from a decision of the UK EAT. Police Scotland officers attended at the home of the respondent, a teacher, to carry out enquiries relating to an IP address linked to online indecent images. They removed a number of computers and thereafter the respondent was charged with possession of a computer containing indecent images of children. His son, who lived with him, was similarly charged. Ultimately no criminal proceedings were brought against either of them and the police retained possession of the computers. The respondent informed the headmaster of the school where he was employed of what had happened and the headmaster sought advice from the local education authority, the employer. The employer made enquiries of the prosecution authority and was sent a redacted summary of the evidence obtained. That was not sent to the headmaster and did not play any part in the subsequent procedures.

The respondent attended an investigatory hearing arranged by the employer. He could not recall where he had purchased the computer. His son had access to it. After he was charged, he was told that a report would be sent to the prosecuting authority, which thereafter sent him a letter stating that he was not being prosecuted but the right to prosecute him was reserved. His son received a similar communication. When asked by the employer whether a computer with indecent child images had been in his possession within his household, the respondent responded in the affirmative. Disciplinary proceedings were instituted. At an investigatory hearing, the respondent accepted that the computer contained indecent images of children. Thereafter there was a disciplinary hearing at which the respondent again confirmed that he had a computer in his home which contained indecent images of children. He did not know how they came to be there. His son and his son's friends had access to the computer. He could not say why there had not been a prosecution. The issue of reputational risk to the employer was raised but there was no significant discussion of it.

At the conclusion of the hearing, the view of the decision maker was that it could not be concluded that the respondent downloaded the images, but it could not be confirmed that he had not been involved. This gave rise to safeguarding concerns and to reputational risk. Reputational risk arose in part if the teacher was prosecuted in the future and it became known that in the meantime the employer had taken no action. A formal risk assessment came to the conclusion that the respondent posed an unacceptable risk to children. A letter of dismissal was issued. The respondent did not exercise his right to an internal appeal against that decision, but made a claim of unfair dismissal.

At the employment tribunal, the employer defended the proceedings on the basis that the dismissal was for some other substantial reason of a kind justifying dismissal, as distinct from misconduct. That reason was that, as a consequence of the circumstances, the teacher was deemed to present an unacceptable risk to children; there was a potential for reputational risk to the employer; and there was a breakdown in the trust and confidence which the employer is required to have in the respondent.

The employment tribunal concluded that the test for some other substantial reason of a kind justifying dismissal was met. It was then for the tribunal to decide whether the employer had acted reasonably in dismissing for that reason, the test being an objective one. It noted that the respondent knew he was at risk of dismissal; he was aware of the charges and the potential consequences of the disciplinary proceedings and it was reasonable for the employer to have legitimate concerns as to his continuing employment and to conclude that there was a risk that the respondent was involved in downloading the images. There was an unacceptable risk to children if he returned to work and it was reasonable to conclude that there was a risk of reputational damage and that there had been a breakdown in trust and confidence. The some other substantial reason was reflected in the letter calling the respondent to the disciplinary hearing. The focus was not on whether the respondent was guilty. The tribunal held that the decision, while a difficult one, fell within the band of reasonable responses and accordingly the unfair dismissal claim was dismissed.

On appeal, the UK EAT noted that the letter of invitation to the disciplinary hearing was based on misconduct and gave no notice that reputational damage was a potential ground of dismissal. It concluded that the lack of notice of same rendered the dismissal unfair. Furthermore the understanding of the EAT was that the dismissal was on the grounds of misconduct and it concluded that, given that the guilt of the respondent could not be established, the alleged misconduct should not have been taken into account. The respondent could not be dismissed because he might have committed the offence. The only standard of proof was the civil one, mainly the balance of probability. Furthermore, the evidence was insufficient to support dismissal on the ground of reputational damage. In any event the spectre of reputational damage had abated with the decision not to prosecute and accordingly the approach adopted was unreasonable and not compliant with the statutory requirements.

On appeal from the EAT, the Court of Session concluded that the EAT had proceeded on the erroneous basis that the reason for dismissal was conduct related, namely the downloading of indecent images of children by the respondent. This in turn led to the view that the employer and the tribunal had to be satisfied that there was a proper basis for believing that the respondent was probably guilty. However, as the employment tribunal made clear, the respondent was dismissed for 'some other substantial reason'. It was the view of the Court of Session that once the employment tribunal determined that the some other substantial reason was genuine and substantial, leaving aside the lack of notice, the only remaining question was whether the employer acted reasonably or unreasonably in treating it as a sufficient reason for dismissing the employee. On the facts as established, the employer was entitled to proceed on the basis that the respondent might be prosecuted in the future and that his involvement in the existence of the images could not be excluded. As an education authority, the employer was conscious of its statutory responsibility for protecting children entrusted to it. The Court of Session noted that it was clear that the employer decided that it could no longer place the necessary trust and confidence in the respondent, not because it was satisfied that he was guilty, but because there was a real possibility that he was an offender.

In summary, the employer was not prepared to take the risk that the respondent was not responsible for the images. There was an additional concern as to reputational risk. The Court noted that the decision facing the employer was a difficult one. Notwithstanding their child protection responsibilities, another education board might be prepared to take the risk which the employer here considered to be unacceptable. The Court noted that the fact that it might be a reasonable response not to dismiss did not mean that this employer's decision to dismiss was unreasonable. The Court found that the employment tribunal applied the correct test to the findings of fact, and concluded that the EAT not only erred in the reason for dismissal, but it also wrongly interfered with a decision which was open to the employment tribunal and was free of legal error.

With reference to the other basis on which the EAT upheld the appeal, ie, the absence of any mention of reputational risk in the letter requiring the respondent to attend a disciplinary hearing, the Court concluded that the some other substantial reason test can be failed if there is a procedural unfairness which renders the decision to dismiss unreasonable. This is primarily a matter for the employment tribunal whose decision should be respected unless it is tainted by an error in law or is itself beyond the bounds of reasonableness, in other words is perverse. Although reputational risk was not called out in the letter, it was discussed at the hearing. The Court concluded that reputational risk was self-evident from the letter and did not require detailed elaboration, not least since it was ancillary to the child protection issues which were set out in the letter.

The Court concluded that it was unable to identify any flaw in the analysis and reasoning of the employment tribunal on the point made with reference to the letter.

The appeal was upheld and the decision of the employment tribunal that the claim of unfair dismissal be dismissed was restored.

[22.37] *Moore v Phoenix Product Development Ltd[51]—UK Employment Appeal Tribunal—unfair dismissal—some other substantial reason—irreparable breakdown in relations*

The claimant was an inventor of a water efficient toilet which was manufactured and marketed by the respondent, of which he was a founder. He was the chief executive of the respondent until 2017 when he was replaced in that role although he remained on as an employee and a director. Following a series of incidents, the remaining members of the board lost confidence in him and he was dismissed without a right of appeal. The claimant claimed that the dismissal was procedurally and substantively unfair.

The employment tribunal rejected his claims. It found that he was dismissed for some other substantial reason, ie, there was an irreparable breakdown in relations and therefore the dismissal was not unfair. The claimant appealed on a number of grounds.

The EAT dismissed the appeal. It was satisfied that the employment tribunal had not erred. The employment tribunal had considered the main allegations as to unfairness; it was not obliged to address every evidential point raised. The employment tribunal was entitled to conclude that, had the claimant exercised his right to appeal the respondent's decision, the appeal would not have succeeded. The EAT held that, although an appeal is usually a part of fair procedures, it will not invariably be so and the employment tribunal had a statutory obligation to take all the circumstances into account.

---

[51]   *Moore v Phoenix Product Development Ltd* UKEAT/0070/20/OO.

REDUNDANCY

[22.38]   ***Dublin Tech Summit F5 Digital Media Communications Ltd v Lundy*[52]—
*Labour Court—appeal from Workplace Relations Commission—Unfair Dismissals
Acts 1977 to 2015—redundancy—fair procedures***

The claimant was employed by the respondent as marketing and communications manager from March 2017.

Following a meeting in July 2019 between the managing director and the business owner, it was decided that costs would have to be reduced and that there would have to be a reduction in the numbers of staff employed. This led to the claimant's role and another role involved in direct client relationship management being assessed for elimination.

The managing director met with the claimant and that other member of staff and discussed their skills and abilities. The claimant was not advised prior to or at the meetings that the purpose of the meetings was to make a decision as regards which role to eliminate; nor was she advised that the meetings could lead to the loss of her employment through redundancy; nor was the claimant invited to make suggestions as to alternatives to the termination of her employment.

Based on those conversations, it was decided to retain the other staff member's role and the claimant was informed that her role would be made redundant. The claimant brought a claim to the WRC alleging that she had been unfairly dismissed. She claimed that a personal hostility between her and the new managing director influenced the decision to make her redundant. The claimant asserted that a request she had made for a salary increase in 2019 was received badly by the respondent and influenced its decision to select her for redundancy.

The WRC held that the respondent had not shown that it had selected the claimant for redundancy by reference to objective criteria and found that she had been unfairly dismissed. The WRC awarded compensation of €16,000.

The respondent appealed this decision to the Labour Court, submitting that it had conducted a fair and transparent process leading to the termination of the claimant's employment by reason of redundancy.

The Court accepted that the respondent was entitled to restructure its business and to reduce its workforce having regard to operational requirements and financial considerations. It further noted that it was common case between the parties that the role of the claimant was made redundant. However, the Court stated it could not accept that the selection process followed by the respondent was fair or transparent in circumstances where neither employee was made aware that their role was being considered for redundancy. The Court held that the absence of knowledge on the part of the claimant

---

[52]   *Dublin Tech Summit F5 Digital Media Communications Ltd v Lundy* UDD219.

deprived her of an opportunity to properly address the matters under consideration in the selection process or to make proposals regarding her future role in the company.

In those circumstances, the Court concluded that the procedures followed by the respondent in deciding which of the two roles under consideration would be selected for redundancy were so lacking in transparency and fairness that it could not accept that the claimant was dismissed through redundancy. Nor could the respondent demonstrate a fair process of decision-making leading to the dismissal of the claimant, as against another employee, arising from the redundancy of the claimant's role. As such, the respondent had failed to discharge the burden resting upon it to establish that the dismissal of the claimant was fair.

The Court varied the decision of the WRC by reducing the amount of compensation awarded by it to €7,750, being the amount which the Court considered just and equitable in all of the circumstances.

[22.39] *Tanneron Ltd v Conolin*[53]—*Labour Court—appeal from Workplace Relations Commission—unfair dismissal—redundancy selection criteria were not impersonal and objective*

The Labour Court overturned a WRC decision and found that a pharma and biotech consultant was unfairly dismissed on the basis of a redundancy selection process that failed to meet the impersonal and objective test required and awarded €23,000 in compensation.

The claimant was employed by the respondent from 2008 to July 2018, as a principal consultant, offering advice on quality control to pharma and biotech clients. The respondent submitted that the decision to make the claimant redundant arose because it had accrued heavy losses and was kept afloat by cash injections from its French parent company. In 2018, the firm's headcount fell from 22 to 12, as it sought to survive. It pointed out that the claimant was already paid just over €26,000 in statutory entitlements.

According to the claimant, the selection criteria were drawn up in such a way as to disadvantage him. Alternatives to redundancy were not considered, as is required in such situations. The respondent stuck rigidly to the original selection criteria. The small size of the organisation meant that the respondent was already aware of who had the least advantageous performance figures. A review of sales and income as applied over a longer period could have produced a different outcome. The claimant also questioned why payments were made to senior managers at the time job cuts were being implemented.

The Court stated that the first issue for it to determine was whether there was a genuine redundancy situation, and that redundancy was the main reason for dismissal. It was the

---

[53]   *Tanneron Ltd v Conolin* UDD2151.

contention of the claimant that he was dismissed for perceived poor performance and that this dismissal was 'dressed up' as a redundancy. However, the employer was intent upon achieving staff reductions, numbers were decreased and there was no evidence that the claimant was replaced. The Court stated that a company which was suffering losses, and which required an injection of funds from a parent company in order to continue in business, as was the case of the respondent, was an enterprise that needed to make radical changes to its financial circumstances.

The Court stated that the burden of proof rests with the employer to show that alternatives to redundancy were considered and that there were good reasons why any such alternatives were not chosen. Failure to meet this burden of proof leads to the possibility that employees may have been dismissed unfairly contrary to the Unfair Dismissals Acts. To that extent, the Court accepted the evidence of the respondent that it had considered alternatives.

The claimant argued that the requirement for consultation prior to redundancy was not met and that the respondent decided on selection criteria and refused to deviate from that criteria. The Court stated that there is an onus on a party when seeking to rely on an argument that a consultation process was inadequate, to show that they put forward alternatives to what was proposed if they argue that any such proposal was flawed. The Court was satisfied that the claimant had failed to come up with appropriate alternatives and had not made out a case on this point.

The claimant argued that he was disadvantaged by the criteria used for selection for redundancy as he had been deprived of the opportunity to effect sales and to generate fee income in the 12-month period prior to the termination of his employment, ie, the period used to apply the criteria for such selection. Again, the Court dismissed this argument, as no evidence was forthcoming. The claimant argued that if the review of sales and fee income had been over a longer period, he would not have been selected for redundancy. Although this may have been true, the Court stated that 'any time frame chosen for review is arbitrary and open to challenge but if the criteria meet the necessary requirements and if the application of the criteria is impersonal and objective, then, it can be expected, unless there are other relevant factors, that a redundancy accords with the legislative requirements'.

The Court stated that the most important issue raised by the claimant was whether the selection criteria were fair or whether, by being based on performance, they were simply a cloak used to weed out a perceived under performer. The Court stated that it had to 'apply extra scrutiny to criteria based on performance' to ensure that no one individual 'was targeted for dismissal due to their performance or perceived performance in order to circumvent their rights under the Unfair Dismissals Act'. In particular, the Court was concerned that, in a relatively small organisation, it was 'possible for an employer to identify easily, in advance of setting criteria, who might be performing and who may not'. The Court noted evidence about the claimant's non-availability to take on work at one time and his non-use of the Resource Planner as well as allusions to the claimant establishing his own business. The Court had to decide if any of these issues were considered by the respondent when setting out the criteria that led to the claimant being selected for redundancy.

Given the size of the organisation and the relatively small number of employees, the Court considered it to be likely that the management team who set out the criteria for redundancy was aware of which employees were likely to be affected once criteria regarding sales and fee income were set. Therefore, the Court held that the criteria were applied in the knowledge that the claimant would be among those to be made redundant.

The Court held that knowledge of who was 'likely to be deemed redundant once criteria were applied may not be, in and of itself, a reason to determine automatically that the criteria were subjective and/or personal'. However, the Court stated that criteria based on performance must be 'impersonal and objective' and must be applied 'fairly and uniformly'.

The Court was not satisfied that the respondent had met the burden of proof that the redundancy was impersonal; nor was it satisfied that, on the balance of probabilities the claimant 'was not singled out to be let go because he was deemed to be a poor performer'; finally it was not satisfied that 'the criteria applied were not applied with that end in mind'. The Court did not find it credible that a management team in these circumstance would not keep a close eye on sales and income and the 'fact that the respondent stated otherwise raised issues of credibility' which led the Court to find that the more credible explanation was that the claimant 'was identified as a poor performer and criteria for selection for redundancy were chosen, in part at least, with a view to ceasing his employment'. Therefore, the Court found that there was an unfair dismissal.

The Court held that neither reinstatement or re-engagement were feasible and that the claimant's attempts to find alternative employment fell 'well short' of what was required. However, he did mitigate his losses through his own business, and money was paid to the claimant at the time of his dismissal in respect of his purported redundancy. The Court awarded €23,000 in compensation to the claimant, in addition to what was paid to him when he was dismissed.

[22.40] *Gwynedd Council v Barratt[54]—Court of Appeal of England and Wales— Bean, Nugee and Asplin LJJ—unfair dismissal—redundancy—right of appeal*

The claimants were employed as teachers by the respondent, but were dismissed in August 2017 when the school in which they taught closed. A new school then opened at the same location and the teachers who had been employed at the 'old' school were informed that they would need to submit applications for posts at the 'new' school. The claimants' applications for posts in the 'new' school were not successful and they were made redundant as a result. The claimants lodged complaints with the employment tribunal asserting that their dismissal had been unfair because, *inter alia*, neither had been offered the right to appeal their dismissal from the 'old' school.

---

[54]   *Gwynedd Council v Barratt* [2021] EWCA Civ 1322. See *Arthur Cox Employment Law Yearbook 2020* at **[19.33]** for the UK EAT decision in *Gwynedd Council v Barratt* [2020] 6 WLUK 61.

The employment tribunal concluded that the claimants' redundancies had been genuine, but that the manner in which they had been effected was unfair. In so finding, the employment tribunal noted that the respondent had not consulted adequately or meaningfully with the cohort of affected employees, and that employees who were unsuccessful in applications for posts at the 'new' school were not given the opportunity to appeal against their dismissal from the 'old' school.

The respondent appealed the employment tribunal's decision to the EAT, which dismissed the appeal and upheld the employment tribunal's decision. The respondent then appealed the EAT's conclusion to the Court of Appeal of England and Wales.

In dismissing the respondent's appeal, the Court of Appeal held that 'the absence of an appeal is not fatal to the employer's defence'. The Court of Appeal further stated that 'it would be wrong to find a dismissal unfair only because of the failure to provide the employee with an appeal hearing'. The Court was satisfied that the employment tribunal had not deemed the dismissal unfair solely because the claimants had not been afforded a right of appeal, and noted with approval that the employment tribunal had correctly assessed the matter, including whether the respondent's decision to dismiss the claimants came with the range of reasonable responses available to it in the circumstances. The Court of Appeal emphasised that the employment tribunal had not based its decision that the dismissals had been unfair on the lack of appeal alone, but also on the fact that the respondent had not consulted properly with the affected cohort of employees.

RE-ENGAGEMENT

[22.41]   *Kelly v PGA European Tour*[55]*—Court of Appeal of England and Wales—Underhill & Lewis LJJ, Laing LJ—appeal from UK Employment Appeal Tribunal—unfair dismissal—order for re-engagement—loss of trust and confidence—practicability test*

This was an appeal of a decision of the EAT regarding an order of the employment tribunal to re-engage an employee.

The claimant had been employed since 2015 as group marketing director for the PGA European Tour. Before this, he had been employed as the marketing director of the PGA European Tour since 1989. In 2015, the newly appointed chairman met with the claimant on two occasions and requested that the claimant consider retirement. The claimant covertly recorded these meetings, a fact which came to light after the claimant was dismissed by way of letter in October 2015.

---

[55]   *Kelly v PGA European Tour* [2021] EWCA Civ 559. See *Arthur Cox Employment Law Yearbook 2020* at **[19.36]** for the EAT decision in *Kelly v PGA European Tour* UKEAT/0285/18/DA.

The claimant brought an unfair dismissal claim to the employment tribunal, alleging that he had been unfairly dismissed and discriminated against on grounds of age. The respondent conceded that he had been unfairly dismissed by reason of an unfair procedure. The employment tribunal held that he had not been dismissed by reason of his age. It also made an order that the claimant be re-engaged in the role of commercial director, China, a position which had been vacant at the time.

The respondent appealed against the order for re-engagement to the EAT, which ultimately set the order aside. The EAT held that re-engagement was not practicable where the employer genuinely believed that the employee was not capable of performing the role, or where there was a breakdown of trust and confidence in the employee-employer relationship. In the circumstances, the respondent had formed a view that the claimant did not have the capabilities to carry out a senior leadership position, and furthermore, the respondent had lost all trust in the claimant arising from the fact that he had secretly recorded the meetings he had with the chairman.

The EAT also held that the employment tribunal had erred in ordering the re-engagement of the claimant to the position of commercial director, China—a role which required the ability to communicate in Mandarin, which the claimant did not possess. The EAT remitted the question of whether any compensation should be reduced to the employment tribunal, in circumstances where the claimant might have been fairly dismissed.

The claimant appealed the decision of the EAT to the Court of Appeal.

The Court of Appeal held that, when considering the making of an order for re-engagement, the employment tribunal is required to consider if it is practicable, having regard to the circumstances. The Court stated that, when deciding what is practicable where trust and confidence have broken down, the question is 'whether the employer had a genuine, and rational, belief that the employee had engaged in conduct which had broken the relationship of trust and confidence between the employer and the employee'.

The Court of Appeal rejected the claimant's argument that, in making an order for re-engagement, the employment tribunal should have considered any vacancies which the respondent had filled prior to the remedies hearing. The Court of Appeal held that when considering the making of an order of re-engagement, the employment tribunal was only obliged to consider whether there was 'comparable or suitable employment available at the date of the remedies hearing'.

The Court of Appeal refused to overturn the EAT's finding that the employment tribunal had erred in ordering that the respondent re-engage the claimant in the position of commercial director, China. The Court of Appeal held that, in circumstances where the ability to speak, write and read Mandarin was an essential requirement for the role, and where the claimant did not possess this skill, it was impracticable for the respondent to re-engage the claimant in such a role.

The Court of Appeal also rejected the claimant's submission that the EAT had erred in not remitting the matter to the employment tribunal for consideration of the practicality of the respondent re-engaging the claimant. There were no other roles in which the claimant could be re-engaged, and as noted above, it was not practicable to re-engage the claimant in the position of commercial director, China.

Finally, the Court of Appeal rejected the claimant's argument that the EAT erred in remitting the question of whether the compensation should be reduced, in circumstances where the claimant might have been fairly dismissed. The Court of Appeal held the employment tribunal had failed to 'consider that evidence to determine if it could assess the chances of a fair dismissal being undertaken at some stage in order to establish the loss that the claimant had suffered'. The Court of Appeal upheld the EAT's decision to remit this question to the employment tribunal.

The appeal was dismissed in its entirety. Underhill LJ agreed with the findings of the Court but added that lack of trust and confidence 'must have a reasonable basis' and that 'while that is an objective question it must be judged from the perspective of the particular employer: that reflects a proper recognition that an employment relationship has got to work in human terms'.

REINSTATEMENT

[22.42]   *MPSTOR Ltd v Oppermann*[56]*—Labour Court—appeal from Workplace Relations Commission—reinstatement*

The claimant was employed from 2006 to 2018, when his contract of employment was terminated. The respondent appealed against the WRC determination that MPSTOR Ltd was the employer of the claimant at all relevant times, while the claimant appealed on the basis that if the respondent was the correct employer of the claimant, the proper redress ought to have been reinstatement.

It was the respondent's submission that the claimant was always employed by MPSTOR Ltd and that there was no difference between MPSTOR and MPSTOR Ltd. The share acquisition by Sanmina (who became the parent of MPSTOR Ltd) did not change the employment status of employees, who, in the respondent's view remained employees of MPSTOR Ltd. The claimant was employed as vice president of MPSTOR Ltd for two-and-a-half years prior to his dismissal. The parent company oversaw the workings of the subsidiary (MPSTOR Ltd), but the claimant was paid through the MPSTOR Ltd payroll, and continued to carry out the same tasks (on slightly better terms and conditions) as he had pre-acquisition.

In response, the claimant argued that his contract was signed by Human Resources for Sanmina. The claimant's contract was opened to the Court, and it was noted that it did not define who the employer was, although the contract referred to the employer and to the company, it did not define either. It was the claimant's position that the Court should

---

56   *MPSTOR Ltd v Oppermann* UDD2133.

apply the *contra proferentem* rule and interpret the contract against the respondent. The contract stated that the claimant was employed as vice president of MPSTOR. It was the claimant's submission that MPSTOR was a brand and was different to MPSTOR Ltd. The contract also referred to the company's bonus plan—a reference to Sanmina Corporation Bonus plan. There was also a reference to Sanmina policies. The letter of dismissal that the claimant received was on Sanmina Ireland headed paper and referred to the claimant as VP MPSTOR (not VP MPSTOR Ltd) and was signed by an employee of Sanmina.

The Labour Court held that the Unfair Dismissals Act 1977 to 2015 defines the employer as the person with whom the employee has a contract of employment.

The Court found that there was no evidence provided to support the contention that MPSTOR and MPSTOR LTD were not the same entity. The Court accepted the respondent's submission that it was a distinction without a difference and applied this when reading the contract. It found that the contract of employment was with MPSTOR LTD as MPSTOR LTD returns to Revenue listed the claimant as an employee and there was no change in his employment status during the share acquisition, apart from a new contract with enhanced terms.

The Court in considering the appropriate remedy, found that damages were more appropriate than reinstatement on the basis that the respondent had expressed total opposition on a number of grounds to reinstatement. The Court noted that:

> a thread running through the caselaw is the Court must consider the needs of the employer as well as the needs of the employee. The caselaw also highlights the importance of hearing both parties on this issue notwithstanding the fact that the Court has full discretion on the form of redress ... it shall award. Other factors identified by the caselaw that need to be considered are ... the position that the employee held within the company ie if they were in a senior position, the reluctance to compel an employer to continue a relationship, whether mutual trust still exists, and whether the remedy will do justice between the parties.

Having heard submissions from the claimant, it was not clear whether the claimant 'would actually take up the position if the Court ordered reinstatement'. The Court therefore held that compensation was an appropriate remedy in the circumstances and ordered the respondent to pay €262,260 in compensation to the claimant.

[22.43] ***Dafiaghor-Olomu v Community Integrated Care and Cornerstone Community Care[57]—UK Employment Appeal Tribunal—appeal from employment tribunal—Transfer of Undertakings (Protection of Employment) Regulations 2006[58]—re-employment***

This case involved a decision of the Aberdeen employment tribunal, which refused an order of re-employment by the first respondent, a charity providing residential care to

---

[57] *Dafiaghor-Olomu v Community Integrated Care and Cornerstone Community Care* UKEATS/0001/17/JW.
[58] Transfer of Undertakings (Protection of Employment) Regulations 2006 (SI 2006/246).

vulnerable people. Instead, its decision was to make a financial award to compensate the claimant for an unfair dismissal. She appealed against that decision.

The claimant was a Nigerian national with a work visa for the UK. She had worked as a manager at Sunnyside, one of the residential homes operated by the first respondent. By the date of the appeal hearing, operation of this facility had transferred to the first respondent under the Transfer of Undertakings (Protection of Employment) Regulations 2006 (TUPE) and the first respondent no longer operated in Scotland.

The EAT commented that the claimant's immigration status was a 'complicating factor' in this case as her work permission was revoked as a consequence of her unfair dismissal, therefore, re-engagement with her former employer was a more appealing resolution than compensation.

The employment tribunal found that placing the claimant back into employment with the first respondent was not practicable for a number of reasons, ie, the first respondent no longer operated in Scotland, the claimant did not have a valid work visa, and the manager role was no longer in place at the first respondent.

In her appeal, the claimant argued that the employment tribunal's decision was flawed in that re-engagement was impractical as the claimant was based in Aberdeen, and due to the absence of consideration of her submissions to it that she would consider posts that were located elsewhere within the UK.

The claimant argued that, having 'actively sought the primary remedy of re-employment without placing any express restrictions upon where she would be prepared to accept such re-employment', meant the issue of re-employment outside the north-east of Scotland was obvious and that, given the large organisations run by both respondents, should naturally have been considered by the employment tribunal. Failure to do so before concluding that re-engagement was impracticable was a 'material error of law'.

The EAT concluded that 'the claimant sought re-employment without placing any express limitation on geographical location'; however, the employment tribunal had based its original decision on an assumption that the claimant's personal circumstances did not favour re-employment elsewhere in the UK. The EAT commented that the 'claimant could not have known that her assumed personal circumstances weighed with the tribunal as they did' and that if the employment tribunal had asked the claimant rather than making an assumption, evidence to the contrary would likely have been provided to it. The EAT remitted the case to the employment tribunal for reconsideration.

The claimant also challenged the employment tribunal's finding that the claimant was dismissed prior to the transfer under TUPE and was not in the workforce that transferred to the first respondent and also its consideration of an irrelevant factor, being the removal of the role of manager from its operations.

The EAT found that where a change in ownership takes place 'then the risk of a dismissed employee of the former employer bringing a claim against the new owner of the employing undertaking can be regulated by contract'. However, it stated that in the case of a change of service provider, 'there is generally no contractual relationship between the former provider and the new provider'. As a result, only the application of TUPE can permit liability for employees to pass to the new provider. In this case, there was no change in the ownership of the service and as such, the first respondent was not a 'successor employer' and the appeal on this ground failed.

Chapter 23

Wages

INTRODUCTION

[23.01] Three cases related to the unlawful deduction from wages are noted: *Balans* (Labour Court), *Grzebalski* (Labour Court) and *Langton* (UK EAT). The UK EAT considered the issue of suspension without pay pending the completion of a workplace investigation in *Agbeze*.

Furthermore, there are three cases dealing with the UK national minimum wage: *Tomlinson-Blake* (UK Supreme Court), *Opalkova* (UK EAT) and *Augustine* (UK EAT).

Payment of Wages Act 1991

Deductions/Reductions

[23.02] *Tesco Ireland Ltd v Balans[1]—Labour Court—Payment of Wages Act 1991—unlawful deduction—properly payable—computational error*

The claimant, a warehouse operative in the respondent's distribution centre, was initially employed in 2012 on a part-time contract covering the night shift three days per week. He was offered a full-time role in 2013 and his employment contract recorded a basic rate of pay at €9.69. This contract also provided for a premium payment of 20% in respect of unsocial hours and a further premium of 20% in respect of 'hours worked between Saturday and Sunday'.

The parties entered into a new contract in June 2015, which provided for a basic rate of pay at €11.87 per hour; however, the respondent contended that this was an error in that the basic rate was calculated to incorrectly incorporate the 20% premium for unsocial hours, which the claimant had received under the 2013 contract. The express written terms of this new contract were not upheld by the respondent as the employee was paid €10.29 per hour, rather than the €11.87 per hour rate that was expressly included in the contract.

---

[1]   *Tesco Ireland Ltd v Balans* PWD2114.

The claimant made a complaint under the respondent's internal grievance procedure in October 2016. That complaint was dismissed in March 2017, as was the subsequent appeal in May 2017. In August 2017, the claimant made the following complaints to the WRC:

1. a breach of the Payment of Wages Act 1991 (the 1991 Act) relating to an alleged impermissible deduction of wages;
2. an entitlement to a premium for 'hours worked between Saturday and Sunday' and the meaning of this phrase in the claimant's contract of employment;
3. an order for compensation in relation to an unresolved grievance; and
4. an application for an extension of time within which to make a claim for compensation.

The WRC found that the basic rate of €11.87 as set out in the 2015 contract, despite being accepted as an erroneous figure, should still be the rate payable to the claimant. The WRC held that the fact that the respondent paid the claimant €10.29 per hour as opposed to €11.87 was an unlawful deduction under the 1991 Act, and recommended that the respondent pay the claimant redress of €1,000 under the Industrial Relations Act 1969 for the manner in which its grievance process was operated.

The WRC further held that there was no reasonable cause to justify an extension of the six-month period for the purposes of lodging a claim with the WRC and that the claimant's claim that 'hours worked between Saturday and Sunday' included the hours from 00:00 to 06:00 on Saturday was not well founded. Both parties appealed to the Labour Court.

The Labour Court noted that the enforcement of a contract under common law is not a matter for the Labour Court. In order to ground a claim under the 1991 Act, the wages concerned must be 'properly payable'. The Labour Court disagreed with the WRC regarding the claimant's rate of pay, and found that no unlawful deduction had been made, as the rate of pay specified in the claimant's contract of employment arose as a result of a computational error and was not properly payable.

The Labour Court concurred with the WRC on the extension of time issue. It found that the respondent's grievance practice was procedurally sound and overturned the €1,000 award made by the WRC. With regard to the 'hours worked between Saturday and Sunday', the Labour Court found that, while the wording could be expressed more clearly, the premium was not payable for hours worked from 00:00 to 06:00 on Saturday.

The claimant appealed to the High Court, claiming that the Labour Court had purported to rectify the contract and exercise a jurisdiction it did not enjoy. The claimant argued that the terms of the contract were clear and there was nothing computational about deliberately paying someone less than is specified in a contract of employment.

The respondent argued that there was no indication that the claimant understood that he was to get a wage increase upon signing the 2015 contract and pointed out that the claimant did not make any complaint regarding his wages from June 2015 to October 2016. The respondent argued that the Labour Court had made a finding of fact that there was an error in the figure set out in the contract, a conclusion to which it was entitled to arrive. The respondent stressed that if it was to be bound by this error, there could be 'far-reaching implications' for the respondent in terms of other employees' wages.

The High Court found that central to the Labour Court's analysis was the concept of wages 'properly payable' and the circumstances in which any deficiency in respect of such payment arose as a result of an error of computation. The High Court found that the Labour Court appeared to confuse these two central issues:

> where the difficulty arises is that the Labour Court, rather than making the necessary assessment of wages properly payable under the 1991 Act proceeded to perhaps unwittingly conflate that issue with the separate issue of whether there had been a deduction and whether that deduction came within the exception governed by s. 5(6).

The High Court held that in conflating these issues, the Labour Court fell into error in failing to appropriately assess the wages properly payable to the claimant within the meaning of the 1991 Act. The High Court accepted the claimant's argument that any error made in the drafting of the contract was not to be equated with a deficiency or non-payment attributable to a computational error. The High Court also found that the Labour Court had erred in law by assuming or inferring that the apparent acceptance by the claimant of payment of the lesser sum automatically meant that this was the sum which he was liable to be paid. The High Court held that the proper and full resolution of this issue required more extensive factual and legal analysis by the Labour Court, but was also clear that this did not mean that the final result had to be different.

On the question of the premium payment, the High Court held that there was adequate evidence before the Labour Court for it to determine that the phrase 'hours worked between Saturday and Sunday' did not include hours worked from 00:00 to 06:00 on Saturday, and that the Labour Court was entitled to come to that conclusion.

On the extension of time point, the High Court found that the claimant had not claimed he was lulled into a false sense of security by engaging in the internal grievance procedure, and that he had not claimed that he had relied on a representation that the respondent would not rely on the relevant time limits. The High Court was again satisfied that there was adequate evidence available to the Labour Court to allow it to conclude as it did.

The High Court allowed the claimant's appeal on the first ground (the payment of wages claim) and remitted the matter to the Labour Court for further consideration, without expressing a view either way in relation to the substantive question.

In light of the High Court's judgment, the question before the Labour Court was the amount 'properly payable' to the claimant in the period between 15 February 2017 and 14 August 2017, ie, the reckonable period for the purposes of the claimant's WRC claim. In doing so, the Labour Court stressed that it was not permitted to treat the difference between the amount provided for in the claimant's contract of employment and the amount actually paid to the claimant, as a computational error within the meaning of s 5(6) of the 1991 Act.

The Labour Court considered the definition of 'wages' in s 1 of the 1991 Act and took the view that if the Oireachtas had intended the terms of a contract to be the only factors to be taken into account when deciding what is 'properly payable' to an employee, then that would have been reflected in the definition. However, the Court noted that the definition covers all factors pertaining to the employment, and indeed takes account of the contract 'or otherwise'—and not, simply, what is provided for by a mistake in the contract.

The Labour Court stated that it was satisfied that the amounts 'properly payable' to an employee must be determined by all of the circumstances pertaining to the employment. In that context, the Labour Court noted that a 2009 collective agreement provided for a rate of pay to be applied to all members of the cohort of employees to which the claimant belonged.

The Labour Court accepted that it does not have jurisdiction to correct or amend a contract, and that a referral to the Circuit Court would be required in order to so amend or correct. That said, the Labour Court also noted that the issue before it was to determine the amount 'properly payable' to the claimant under the 1991 Act.

The Labour Court was of the view that an employer would struggle—in the absence of good and objective reasons—to assert a right under the 1991 Act to pay an employee less than the rate of pay agreed in a collective agreement, in circumstances where such agreement was accepted as being applicable. On the same basis, the Labour Court's view was that an employer could not be compelled by the 1991 Act to pay an employee more than the rate of pay agreed as being applicable to the cohort of employees to which an employee belonged, unless there were clear and objective reasons to do so.

As noted above, the Labour Court was satisfied that it was required to take account of factors outside of the contract of employment in order to determine what was 'properly payable' to the claimant. In that regard, the Labour Court held that it could not ignore the fact of the collective agreement. Furthermore, the Labour Court noted that the claimant's contract of employment provided that the collective agreement applied to his employment by the respondent, and that the claimant had benefitted from the terms of the collective agreement, in that the hourly rate of pay actually paid to him, when premiums provided for under the collective agreement were included, exceeded the rate of pay set out in his contract of employment. Accordingly, the Labour Court determined that the respondent had not breached the terms of the 1991 Act—upholding the respondent's appeal to the Labour Court and overturning the decision of the WRC.

[23.03]   *Tesco Ireland Ltd v Grzebalski[2]—Labour Court—appeal from Workplace Relations Commission—Payment of Wages Act 1991, s 7(1)—sick pay—Sick Pay Scheme*

The claimant was employed by the respondent as a warehouse operative. The respondent operated a Sick Pay Scheme which applied to employees who had passed probation and provided for sick pay for a maximum of eight weeks in any sick leave year (1 January to 31 December), subject to the production of medical certificates and compliance with the respondent's notification procedures.

---

[2]   *Tesco Ireland Ltd v Grzebalski* PWD211.

The claimant was absent on certified sick leave from 6 December 2018 until the end of December 2018 and received sick pay during this period. The respondent wrote to the claimant on 18 January 2019 and notified him that further absence could lead to disciplinary action and his suspension or removal from the respondent's Sick Pay Scheme.

The claimant was on a further period of certified sick leave in February and March 2019 and was not paid during that period. The claimant brought a complaint under the Payment of Wages Act 1991, seeking eight weeks' pay in accordance with the respondent's Sick Pay Scheme.

The respondent submitted that the claimant was notified that further absence could result in his removal from the Sick Pay Scheme, and its decision to not pay the claimant in respect of the absence in February 2019 was reasonable.

The Court found that the respondent did not inform the claimant that it had decided to remove him from the Sick Pay Scheme. Therefore, the claimant was entitled to benefit from the Scheme and to receive payment for up to eight weeks of absence, subject to compliance with the notification procedures. The Court ordered that the respondent pay the claimant eight weeks' gross pay less statutory deductions.

[23.04] *Amdocs Systems Group Ltd v Langton*[3]*—UK Employment Appeal Tribunal—appeal from employment tribunal—unauthorised deductions from wages*

The claimant was employed by the respondent from 2003. On commencement of his employment he was provided with a letter of offer, a contract and a benefits summary. Included therein were the terms of a long-term sickness scheme covered by the respondent's insurer. Also set out was the level of income protection payments (IPP) payable under the scheme, including reference to an 'escalator'. The income protection payments under the scheme were set to increase by 5% every year after the first year of sickness absence.

In 2009, the claimant was diagnosed with a long-term illness and began to receive the IPP. However, his payments were not escalated by 5% each year and, when he queried this with his employer, he was informed that the escalator had ceased in 2008 as it had been removed from the respondent's insurance policy.

The claimant brought a claim against the respondent in the employment tribunal for unauthorised deductions from his wages. The tribunal upheld his claim, stating that he was contractually entitled to the escalator. The respondent appealed to the EAT, on the basis that the correct interpretation of the long-term sickness scheme documentation was that its obligation was limited to pay only the amount of IPP covered by its insurance policy.

The EAT reviewed all of the documentation that had been provided to the claimant on commencement of his employment. It found that although there was an express reference in the documentation to the respondent's insurer, it did not limit an employee's entitlement to whatever benefit was covered by insurance. The EAT noted that if that had been the case, steps should have been taken by the respondent to bring this to the

---

[3]   *Amdocs Systems Group Ltd v Langton* EA-2019-001237-AT.

claimant's attention. It went on to note that the claimant had never been provided with a copy of the insurance policy, despite reference to the long-term sickness scheme being governed by the rules of same. The appeal was unsuccessful, and the claimant was awarded the annual escalation in payments he had not received during his period of sick leave. The EAT stated that: 'To be effective, the limitation of the employer's exposure must be unambiguously and expressly communicated to the employee, so that there can be no doubt about it.'

[23.05] *Agbeze v Barnet Enfielf and Haringey Mental Health NHS Trust[4]—UK Employment Appeal Tribunal—appeal from employment tribunal—zero-hours worker—suspension—suspension without pay—investigation*

The claimant was employed by the respondent as a 'bank' (ie, a reserve) healthcare assistant. The claimant was employed under a zero-hours contract of employment—the respondent was not obliged to offer him any work, and he was not obliged to accept any work offered to him. The contract of employment also provided that the claimant would be remunerated according to the specific duties he performed when providing services to the respondent.

During a period of suspension lasting several months, to allow for an investigation to take place into an allegation of misconduct by the claimant, the claimant was treated as being ineligible to be offered any work. Arising from this, the claimant made a claim of unlawful deduction from his wages, arguing that it was an implied term of his contract of employment that he was entitled to be paid his average earnings during his suspension, as long as there was work available that he would otherwise be in a position to undertake. The employment tribunal rejected the claimant's claim.

The claimant appealed the employment tribunal's decision to the EAT. The EAT noted that the claimant's contract of employment with the respondent only provided for an express obligation on the part of the respondent to pay the claimant for periods where work was specifically offered and accepted, and that this case did not involve a permanent employee. In addition, the EAT noted that while there was no express term in the contract of employment confirming that the claimant would be unpaid if ever suspended, this did not strengthen the claimant's claim, since other provisions in the contract of employment confirmed that the claimant had no right to remuneration from the respondent unless he had actually provided services to it.

National Minimum Wage

Sleep-in Shifts

[23.06] *Royal Mencap Society v Tomlinson-Blake[5]—UK Supreme Court—Kerr, Wilson, Carnwath & Kitchin LJJ, Arden LJ—appeal from Court of Appeal of*

---

4   *Agbeze v Barnet Enfielf and Haringey Mental Health NHS Trust* UKEAT/0232/20/VP.
5   *Royal Mencap Society v Tomlinson-Blake* [2021] UKSC 8, for Court of Appeal decision, see *Arthur Cox Employment Law Yearbook 2018* at **[23.07]**.

England and Wales—National Minimum Wage Act 1998—National Minimum Wage Regulations 1999,[6] regs 3, 4, 15 & 21—National Minimum Wage Regulations 2015,[7] regs 21, 24–28, 30 & 32—care worker—sleep-in shift—wages

This case concerned how the working hours of carers working 'sleep-in' shifts were to be calculated for the purpose of UK National Minimum Wage (NMW) legislation.

The first claimant was a care support worker employed to provide 24-hour care to vulnerable adults in their home. The claimant's day work was salaried work for the purpose of NMW legislation, however her sleep-in shifts were counted as 'time work' within the meaning of the relevant Regulations. During the sleep-in shifts, the claimant was permitted to sleep but had to 'keep a listening ear out' and be available for work should it arise. The Court noted that the claimant actually had to work during her night shifts infrequently: she had given evidence that she had only been required to work six times in a period of 16 months. The claimant was paid £29.05 for each sleep-in shift, comprising an allowance of £22.35 plus one hour's pay of £6.70 'in recognition of "the reasonable expectation" of the amount of work she would have to do during her sleep-in shift'. If any additional time was worked during the sleep-in shift, it was paid at normal rates of pay. The claimant claimed that she was entitled to be paid the NMW for each hour of her sleep-in shift.

The second claimant worked at a residential care home as an on-call night-care assistant. He was provided with free accommodation and a payment of £50 per week (which rose to £90 per week). The claimant was required to be in his accommodation and 'on call' from 10 pm–7 am each night. He was allowed to sleep during those hours, but could be called upon at any time for assistance (although the Court noted that in practice he was very rarely called upon). The claimant was dismissed and brought a claim for arrears of pay, claiming that he should have been paid the NMW for all of the night-time hours that he was required to be 'on call'.

The first claimant was successful before the employment tribunal, the EAT and the Court of Appeal. The second claimant was unsuccessful before the employment tribunal and his appeals to the EAT and the Court of Appeal were dismissed. On further appeal, both cases were heard together by the UK Supreme Court.

The Supreme Court found for the employer in both cases, holding that under the relevant Regulations, only the hours when a worker on a sleep-in shift is 'actually awake for the purposes of working' must be counted for the purpose of that worker's NMW entitlements.

In reaching this conclusion, the Court examined the relevant legislative provisions in detail. The National Minimum Wage Act 1998 sets a minimum hourly rate of remuneration. The National Minimum Wage Regulations 1999 (the 1999 Regulations) and the National

---

[6]   National Minimum Wage Regulations 1999 (SI 1999/584).
[7]   National Minimum Wage Regulations 2015 (SI 2015/6221).

Minimum Wage Regulations 2015 (the 2015 Regulations) set out provisions with regard to time when a worker is to be 'deemed' as working and so entitled to the NMW.

Regulation 32 of the 2015 Regulations (which revoked and replaced similar provisions in the 1999 Regulations) provides as follows:

(1) Time work includes hours when a worker is available, and required to be available, at or near a place of work for the purposes of working unless the worker is at home.

(2) In paragraph (1), hours when a worker is "available" only includes hours when the worker is awake for the purposes of working, even if a worker by arrangement sleeps at or near a place of work and the employer provides suitable facilities for sleeping.

The Court interpreted the provisions in light of the recommendations of the Low Pay Commission, which the Court noted, had recommended that 'sleep-in workers should receive an allowance and not the NMW unless they were awake for the purposes of working'. The Court held:

In my judgment, applying the approach explained above, the special rule for sleep-in workers ... is quite clear. The basic proposition is that they are not doing time work for the purposes of the NMW if they are not awake. However, the regulations go further than that and state that not only are they not doing time work if they are asleep: they are also not doing time work unless they are awake for the purposes of working.

The Court went on to hold:

If the employer has given the worker the hours in question as time to sleep and the only requirement on the worker is to respond to emergency calls, the worker's time in those hours is not included in the NMW calculation for time work unless the worker actually answers an emergency call. In that event the time he spends answering the call is included.

In so holding, the Court agreed with the Court of Appeal in overruling previous UK case law in *Burrow Down Support Services Ltd v Rossiter*[8] and *British Nursing Association v Inland Revenue*,[9] which had held that workers performing night shifts were actually working (as opposed to merely being available for work) during times when they were expected to be asleep and when the calls they were expected to answer were infrequent, and so fell outside reg 32(2) and were entitled to be paid NMW. The Court also over-ruled *Scottbridge Construction Ltd v Wright*,[10] in which the Court had followed *British Nursing* and held that a night watchman was 'working' when he was on-call on a sleep-in shift, notwithstanding that the times when he was not able to sleep on his shift were very rare.

---

8   *Burrow Down Support Services Ltd v Rossiter* [2008] ICR 1172.
9   *British Nursing Association v Inland Revenue* [2002] EWCA Civ 494; [2003] ICR 19.
10 *Scottbridge Construction Ltd v Wright* [2003] IRLR 21.

Induction Training

[23.07] *Opalkova v Acquire Care Ltd[11]—UK Employment Appeal Tribunal—National Minimum Wage Regulations 2015,[12] reg 33—whether induction training is 'work'*

The claimant worked for the respondent in providing home-based care. The claimant argued that she was entitled to be paid the minimum wage in respect of her time spent attending induction training.

The employment tribunal referenced reg 33 of the National Minimum Wage Regulations 2015 and concluded that, as the claimant was not employed by the respondent at the time she was undergoing the induction training (in that she would not be allowed to carry out normal duties during that training period and therefore was not employed by the respondent), she had no entitlement to minimum wage and dismissed the claim, the claimant appealed to the EAT.

The EAT allowed the appeal and held that the tribunal at first instance had erred in its failure to consider: (a) whether the claimant had entered into a contract with the respondent at the relevant time; and, if she had, (b) whether her attendance at induction training could be considered 'work'. Having considered the legislation, the EAT held that 'the concept of work, for the purposes of these regulations, is not necessarily or always to be confined to the carrying out of the primary duties for the purpose of which the contract is formed'. The EAT held that whether training can be considered work depends on the circumstances of each case, eg, whether the training is compulsory, and who provides the training; it concluded that the claimant should have received the minimum wage for the induction training.

Reductions

[23.08] *Augustine v Data Cars Ltd[13]—UK Employment Appeal Tribunal—appeal from employment tribunal—National Minimum Wage Act 1998*

The claimant had worked for the respondent as a driver for eight months in 2016 and claimed that he had not been paid the national minimum wage, was owed holiday pay, and had been wrongfully dismissed. The issue of holiday pay had been dealt with by consent at a preliminary hearing.

The employment tribunal found in the claimant's favour in relation to the claim for minimum wage and awarded him £574.73. The claimant appealed this decision.

---

[11] Opalkova v Acquire Care Ltd UKEAT/0209/20/RN.
[12] National Minimum Wage Regulations 2015 (SI 2015/6221).
[13] *Augustine v Data Cars Ltd* EA-2020-000383-A.

The EAT identified six grounds of appeal and considered them as follows.

First, the claimant argued that the tribunal was wrong by not treating payments made by the claimant for the use of a rented van as reductions when calculating the amount of remuneration for the purposes of the national minimum wage.

In considering this argument the EAT noted that: 'The test that Parliament has determined appropriate in the context of a national minimum wage calculation is whether the expenditure is in connection with the employment.' The EAT concluded that the tribunal erred in not considering this test, and found that the vehicle rental expenditure was allowable as a deduction when calculating national minimum wage.

Second, the claimant did not agree with the tribunal's findings that payments in relation to his uniform did not fall to be deducted for the purpose of national minimum wage calculation.

In using the same test set out for ground 1, the EAT again concluded that the tribunal had erred and that the payments relating to the uniform should have been deductible for the purpose of the national minimum wage legislation.

Third, the claimant argued that the tribunal had failed by not making a declaration that the holiday pay complaint was well founded, even though this had been dealt with by consent in a preliminary hearing.

In rejecting this ground the EAT found that there was no proper basis for the tribunal to revisit a consent order to add a declaration.

Fourth, the claimant argued that the tribunal should have made an award for consequential loss and in particular with the claimant being unable to complete the Knowledge (an in depth study of street routes and place of interest that taxi drivers in London must complete to obtain a licence to operate a black cab). The claimant submitted that he would have passed this test swiftly, if the respondent had paid him properly.

This came down to matters of fact provided to the tribunal and the EAT concluded the tribunal had 'proceeded on an erroneous factual basis'. The EAT allowed the appeal and remitted the matter to the tribunal for fresh consideration.

Fifth, the claimant said that there had been different sums for a week's pay provided by the respondent in the preliminary hearing and the respondent should have been estopped from changing its position on this.

In dismissing this ground the EAT noted that 'the earlier judgment was made by consent and there was no adjudication or finding on the previous occasion as to the correct calculation of a week's pay'. Therefore the EAT rejected this ground of appeal.

Sixth, the final ground was based on burden of proof namely: (a) the tribunal failed to consider the burden of proof in the National Minimum Wage Act 1998 which puts the burden of proof on the employer; (b) the respondent did not produce records and the tribunal should not have relied on the oral evidence in this regard; and (c) the liaison manager who appeared on behalf of the respondent was not a credible witness.

In considering this point the EAT noted that:

> It does not follow, even if a witness may be considered by the tribunal to lack credibility, or for there to be concerns about their credibility, in relation to one matter, that a tribunal is therefore bound to disbelieve or discount their credibility in relation to another matter.

This final ground of appeal was also rejected.

Chapter 24

Whistleblowing

INTRODUCTION

[24.01] Whether a disclosure satisfied the conditions so as to cause it to be a protected disclosure featured in *Rosderra Irish Meats* (Supreme Court), *Northside Security Services* (Labour Court), *Fingal County Council* (Labour Court) and *Twist DX Limited* (UK EAT).

Whether the person making the disclosure suffered detriment by reason thereof arose in five decisions of the UK EAT namely *Dobbi, Watson, Purnell, Martin* and *Aston*.

Dismissal by reason of the making of protected disclosure was the subject of *Guelph International Bank* and *Secure Care UK* (both UK EAT).

The circumstances in which treatment of a whistleblower might give rise to an infringement of art 10 of the European Convention on Human Rights were considered by the European Court of Human Rights in cases involving *Liechtenstein* and *Luxembourg*.

PROTECTED DISCLOSURE/RELEVANT WRONGDOING?

[24.02] *Baranya v Rosderra Irish Meats Group Ltd[1]—Supreme Court—O'Donnell, MacMenamin and Woulfe JJ—Protected Disclosures Act 2014—leave to 'leapfrog' appeal—meaning of term 'protected disclosure' and distinction between protected disclosure and grievance*

The applicant sought leave to 'leapfrog' appeal against the judgment and order of the High Court to dismiss an appeal on a point of law against the determination made by the Labour Court insofar as that Court found that the applicant had not made a protected disclosure and therefore his claim, a protected disclosure unfair dismissal claim, must fail. The Labour Court determination was a result of an appeal against a decision of an Adjudication Officer which in turn had followed Circuit Court proceedings seeking interim relief. The net point was whether a communication made by the

---

[1] *Baranya v Rosderra Irish Meats Group Ltd* [2021] IESCDET 72. See *Arthur Cox Employment Law Yearbook 2020* at **[21.03]** for the High Court decision in *Baranya v Rosderra Irish Meats Group Ltd* [2020] IEHC 56.

559

claimant to his employer in the course of his employment was a protected disclosure under s 5 of the Protected Disclosures Act 2014.

The claimant, on the commencement of his second period of employment with his employer, advised that he did not wish to engage in a particular task, namely the 'scoring' of a high volume of carcasses per day in the employer's meat plant. The claimant contended that he advised his supervisor that he did not wish to do the scoring as it caused him a lot of pain and he asked to move to another role. The claimant contended that the communication constituted a protected disclosure and that the same disclosure was made to two other individuals, namely the Health & Safety manager and the HR manager. The respondent employer disputed the claim that he made a protected disclosure and submitted that his employment was terminated by the act of walking off the line, which it contended constituted gross misconduct. After his dismissal, the claimant made a complaint of unfair dismissal and he sought interim relief from the Circuit Court under s 11 and Sch 1 of the Protected Disclosures Act 2014. The application to the Circuit Court was successful and he was re-instated to his employment by order of the Circuit Court. The order was revoked by the Circuit Court thereafter on procedural grounds and the application for interim relief was re-heard. Ultimately the Circuit Court held that the communication made was a protected disclosure but accepted the respondent's contention that the dismissal was not wholly or mainly as a result of the protected disclosure. Thereafter, the WRC rejected the complaint that the dismissal resulted wholly or mainly from having made a protected disclosure. The WRC distinguished between a protected disclosure and a grievance and found that the communication was a grievance and not a protected disclosure.

On appeal, the Labour Court concluded that the disclosure was in fact a grievance as to a health and safety issue and should have been dealt with under the grievance procedures and was not a protected disclosure. The Labour Court concluded that the communication related to the fact that the claimant wished to change roles as he was in pain and did not disclose any wrongdoing on the part of the respondent. The decision of the WRC was upheld.

The applicant appealed the Labour Court decision on a point of law to the High Court. The essential ground of appeal was that there was an error of law by the Labour Court in reading into s 5 of the 2014 Act, a requirement that a protected disclosure must state an allegation of relevant wrongdoing on the part of the employer and that the Labour Court erred in determining that the claimant's communication was a grievance rather than a protected disclosure. The High Court dismissed the appeal and concluded that the claimant had failed to establish any error on the part of the Labour Court. The High Court concluded that some information in the relevant communication must attribute some act or omission on the part of the respondent that the claimant might reasonably believe tends to show one or more of the relevant wrongdoings. In the absence of any asserted act or omission, the concept of relevant information is not fulfilled; that the disclosure was made to the Health & Safety manager did not change the foregoing.

In his application for leave to appeal to the Supreme Court, the claimant contended that the decision of the High Court involved a matter of general public importance as to what type of communication could qualify as a protected disclosure.

The Supreme Court considered that a matter of general public importance had arisen regarding the application and the interpretation of the Protected Disclosures Act 2014, that these issues may arise in future proceedings, and that it would be in the public interest to obtain clarity. The Supreme Court noted that the High Court referred to the fact that the parties agreed that there was no Irish jurisprudence dealing with the interpretation of the 2014 Act and that there appeared to be a difference of opinion between the Circuit Court, the Labour Court, and the High Court as to whether the communication in question was, or was capable of being, a protected disclosure. Furthermore, the decision of the High Court is stated by the Workplace Relations Act 2015 to be 'final and conclusive', but the Supreme Court had already held a similar limitation on an appeal to the Court of Appeal was subject to the 'leapfrog' available to the Supreme Court under Art 34.5.4° of the Constitution. Accordingly, unless the Supreme Court permitted such an appeal, no appeal would lie from the decision of the High Court. The Supreme Court was satisfied that the threshold of exceptional circumstances had been met where no appeal lay from the decision of the High Court to the Court of Appeal. The application was granted.

[24.03] *Northside Security Services Company Limited By Guarantee v Dunne*[2]— *Labour Court—appeal from Workplace Relations Commission—Protected Disclosures Act 2014—relevant wrongdoing*

The claimant security officer alleged he was penalised for having made a protected disclosure wherein he reported that an employee of the company (Company X), which provided facility management to the respondent, was using the CCTV for 'nefarious activities'. The claimant alleged that he was in fear of the employee in question and that the respondent did 'nothing to protect him'. He therefore maintained that he was penalised for making a protected disclosure. The claimant did not want to move locations as he believed that this would indicate that he was somehow at fault.

The respondent reported this issue to Company X and the matter was dealt with internally. On the day the Company X employee was suspended, the claimant was moved to a different building for his safety but returned to work in his usual building for the following shift. The claimant went on sick leave soon after.

The respondent argued that this was not a protected disclosure as defined under the s 5 of the Protected Disclosures Act 2014 (the 2014 Act). The Labour Court noted that its jurisdiction in these matters under the 2014 Act was set out in s 12(1), wherein there is protection afforded to employees who make a protected disclosure. The Court considered the definition of protected disclosure in the 2014 Act as well as the definitions of 'security service' and the 'primary functions of a security officer' as defined in the Employment Regulation Order (Security Industry Joint Labour Committee) 2017.[3]

The Labour Court was satisfied that, on a plain reading of the 2014 Act and the definition of security officer, monitoring a CCTV system is a primary function of a security

---

2   *Northside Security Services Company Limited By Guarantee v Dunne* PDD211.
3   Employment Regulation Order (Security Industry Joint Labour Committee) 2017 (SI 231/2017).

officer and this includes the reporting of wrongdoing. Under s 5(5) of the 2014 Act: 'A matter is not a relevant wrongdoing if it is a matter which it is the function of the worker or the worker's employer to detect, investigate or prosecute and does not consist of or involve an act or omission on the part of the employer.' Therefore, the Labour Court concluded that the allegation at the centre of this claim was within the remit of a security officer function and therefore the allegation was 'not a relevant wrongdoing, as it is the function of the worker or the worker's employer to detect, investigate or prosecute'.

The Labour Court added that 'nefarious deeds perpetrated by a third party without the [r]espondent's knowledge or within its control, could not be matters related to an alleged act or omission by the employer'.

The Court concluded that the wrongdoing reported was not a protected disclosure within the meaning of the 2014 Act and the Court was therefore not required to consider whether penalisation had occurred.

The claimant's appeal failed and the decision of the Adjudication Officer was affirmed.

[24.04] *Fingal County Council v Nolan[4]—Labour Court—appeal from Workplace Relations Commission—Protected Disclosures Act 2014—protected disclosure— health and safety issue*

This was an appeal from the WRC, where the Adjudication Officer dismissed the claimant's complaint against the respondent made under the Protected Disclosures Act 2014. The claimant started working with the respondent in 1979 as a cleri-cal officer and in 2013 was successful in a competition for an Acting Grade 7 post. In 2017/2018, while in this role, the claimant was subjected to harassment and intimidation from service users both at, and outside of, his place of work.

This included an incident where he was followed on the M50 motorway; another where he was shown a picture of the road he lived on and told the colour of his front door; and another where he was verbally abused at his gym.

Following the claimant's report, his line manager asked whether he wanted to report the incidents to the Gardaí but the claimant did not want to do so. There were further incidents of threats and harassment, with one culminating in a service user being barred from the respondent's building.

The claimant went on sick leave in September 2018 and, after five weeks, he attended the respondent's doctor following a request. Thereafter, the claimant was invited to a meeting where he was advised he was being transferred back to his substantive grade.

The claimant's argument was that he had made a protected disclosure and, by no longer being in a Grade 7 role which included a housing allowance, had been penalised.

The respondent argued that a protected disclosure had not been made and that these were health and safety issues which were unfortunately a hazard of the position the claimant held and the department he was working in.

---

4   *Fingal County Council v Nolan* PDD214.

The Labour Court noted that although a concern is a health and safety issue, this does not automatically exclude it from the protection of the 2014 Act; however, s 5(5) of the 2014 Act 'does provide that a matter is not a relevant wrongdoing if it is the function of the respondent to investigate the wrongdoing'.

The Labour Court, in rejecting the appeal, found that the respondent did investigate the wrongdoing that threatened the health and safety of the claimant and that the issues reported did fall within s 5(5) of the 2014 Act, as such the respondent was required to investigate and so this was not a relevant wrongdoing. The decision of the WRC was upheld.

[24.05] *Twist DX Ltd v Armes[5]—UK Employment Appeal Tribunal—appeal from employment tribunal—Employment Rights Act 1996, s 43B—protected disclosure— whether information disclosed was capable of satisfying the relevant statutory definitions*

The claimant was a research scientist and was the managing director of Twist DX Ltd, a scientific research company, which was acquired by Abbot Laboratories, the second respondent to the proceedings before the employment tribunal. His wife, the second claimant, was the chief operating officer of Twist DX Ltd. In May 2018, the claimants were dismissed.

The claimant alleged that his dismissal was automatically unfair because it occurred by reference to a protected disclosure and health and safety concerns expressed by him, and was also unfair under ordinary unfair dismissal principles. He also claimed that he was subjected to a number of detriments for having made protected disclosures and/or raised health and safety issues. Essentially the claimant's case was that he was victimised and dismissed for raising issues about a product produced and marketed by the Alere companies, members of the same group of companies as the respondent, his former employer. The claimant claimed that he raised legal and regulatory issues with reference to that product and that he was penalised for doing so and ultimately was dismissed.

For the purpose of his whistleblowing and health and safety disclosure claims, the claimant claimed that he made seven disclosures, of which six were made in emails and one of which was made verbally. He claimed that his disclosures were qualifying disclosures as tending to show, within the meaning of s 43B of the Employment Rights Act 1996 (the 1996 Act):

(a) that a criminal offence has been committed, is being committed or is likely to be committed,

(b) that a person has failed, is failing or is likely to fail to comply with any legal obligation to which he is subject …

(c) that the health or safety of any individual has been, is being or is likely to be endangered … or

(d) that information tending to show any matter falling within any one of the preceding paragraphs has been, is being or is likely to be deliberately concealed.

5   *Twist DX Ltd v Armes* UKEAT/0030/20/JOJ.

He also claimed that his disclosures fell within s 100(1)(c) of the 1996 Act, which provides that an employee who is dismissed shall be regarded as unfairly dismissed if the employee brought to his employer's attention, by reasonable means, circumstances connected with his work which he reasonably believed were harmful or potentially harmful to health or safety.

The claimant's claims were denied by the respondents. They submitted that the disclosures did not disclose qualifying information and did not satisfy the relevant statutory definitions; nor were they protected under either of the statutory provisions on the basis that any such disclosure was not made to his employer, it was made to employees of other companies in the group. The respondents also denied that the raising of the concerns by the claimant was a reason, or the reason, for his dismissal or any other treatment about which he complained. They claimed that the claimant and his wife were dismissed because they had shown themselves to be 'antiethical and hostile' towards the group.

The respondents applied to the employment tribunal to strike out the claims and it refused to do so (exercising a jurisdiction available to the employment tribunal, but not available to the WRC in Ireland). The application to strike out was made on the basis that the claimant had no reasonable prospect of establishing that his pleaded disclosures were 'qualifying disclosures' under s 43B(1) or health and safety disclosures under s 100(1)(c). The respondents appealed to the EAT, which addressed a number of significant points with reference to the UK protected disclosures regime. The EAT stated that the statutory provisions should be read broadly, with regard to substance rather than form.

> The concepts of a *"qualifying disclosure"* and a health and safety disclosure therefore should not be interpreted so as to place onerous requirements on the worker if they are to qualify for protection … They should not be interpreted in a way which introduces technical requirements which, if unfulfilled by the worker, will leave them exposed despite the fact that they are sincere and may have had to pluck up courage to come forward in the public interest or, in the case of health and safety disclosures, in the interests of safety at work.

Turning to the protected disclosure question, the Court noted the decision of the EAT in *Williams v Brown AM*[6] where the EAT identified five issues arising in deciding whether an utterance by a worker amounts to a 'qualifying disclosure' as defined:

> First, there must be a disclosure of information. Secondly, the worker must believe that the disclosure is made in the public interest.* Thirdly, if the worker does hold such a belief, it must be reasonably held.* Fourthly, the worker must believe that the disclosure tends to show one or more of the matters listed in sub-paragraphs (a) to (f) [of s 43B of the 1996 Act]. Fifthly, if the worker does hold such a belief, it must be reasonably held. [* This is not required in Irish law.]

In this case, the EAT noted that the first, fourth and fifth of the questions were in issue in the appeal.

---

[6]   *Williams v Brown AM* UK EAT/0044/19/OO.

On the first question, the EAT noted that it must identify the information disclosed by the worker which is said to amount to a qualifying disclosure. The identification of the information is crucial because the statutory provisions require the employment tribunal to go on to consider whether the claimant's beliefs about that information fell within s 43B and, if the conclusion is that there was a qualifying disclosure, whether the disclosure of that information was a reason or the reason for the treatment complained of, depending on whether the complaint is victimisation or dismissal. The EAT noted that the leading authority on the first question is *Kilraine v London Borough of Wandsworth*,[7] where the Court of Appeal held that there is not a distinction between the making of an allegation and the disclosure of information. An allegation may disclose information depending on what was said by the worker and the context in which it was said. Evidence as to context is relevant and admissible.

The EAT noted that the information question is also linked to the question of the worker's beliefs, and the reasonableness of those beliefs. Determining the worker's beliefs is a subjective question based on evidence as to what the worker thought the evidence tended to show and is a question of fact.

As to the fourth question, ie, the claimant's beliefs about the information which was disclosed, the EAT noted that having identified the information which was disclosed, the employment tribunal should ask whether the claimant believed at the time of the alleged disclosure that the information tended to show one or more of the matters specified in paragraphs (a) to (f) of s 43B of the 1996 Act and, if so, which of those matters. The EAT noted that this was a subjective question. Furthermore, the employment tribunal must identify which limb or limbs of the definition (paragraphs (a) to (f)) are relevant. The answer to that question affects the 'reasonableness' question. By way of example, if the claimant says that he or she believed that the disclosed information tended to show that criminal offences were being or were likely to be committed, it is the reasonableness of that belief that must be considered. Finally, under this heading, the belief must be as to what the information 'tends to show' as distinct from it 'does show'. The EAT noted that the 'tends to show' test is a lower hurdle.

The fifth question is whether the claimant's belief is reasonable. The EAT noted that the fact that an employment tribunal might disagree with the claimant's view does not mean that the belief is necessarily unreasonable. It is well established that a belief might be reasonable even if it is wrong. There may be more than one reasonable view as to whether the belief is reasonable. The reasonableness of a belief actually held is for the employment tribunal to determine.

Following an extensive review of the authorities, the EAT concluded that a concern about actual or potential breaches of legal obligation must be stated or obvious or apparent as a matter of common sense. They are no more than evidential considerations in applying the statutory test, which is whether the worker's belief about the information was reasonable on the facts of the case.

---

7   *Kilraine v London Borough of Wandsworth* [2018] ICR 1850 (CA).

The EAT noted that in none of the authorities did the EAT overrule an employment tribunal which had found that there was a qualifying disclosure, despite a failure by the worker to identify in the disclosure the fact that they had an actual or potential breach of legal obligation in mind or, indeed, the precise legal obligations in question.

The conclusion of the EAT was that the extent to which it was apparent from the disclosure that the worker had the specified matters in mind is evidentially relevant to the question of whether they had the matters in mind at the time of the disclosure and whether any such belief about them was reasonable. The EAT also noted that the five requirements are 'evidentially exacting' for a claimant who bears the burden of proof. Furthermore, in a dismissal or penalisation claim, the worker must persuade an employment tribunal that the disclosure of the qualifying information was a reason or the reason for the treatment complained of.

The EAT concluded that the tribunal did not sufficiently apply its mind to what information, if any, was disclosed in the communications and whether that information was capable of being reasonably believed as showing the matters specified in paragraphs (a) to (f) of s 43B.

The EAT held that the employment tribunal had erred in law in failing to identify the information which was said to have been disclosed in each of the pleaded disclosures and to consider whether that information was capable of satisfying the relevant statutory definitions. The EAT concluded that six of the seven disclosures had no reasonable prospect of satisfying those definitions and would therefore be struck out, subject to the claimant having the opportunity to apply to amend his pleaded case within 28 days.

DETRIMENT

[24.06]   *Dobbie v Paula Felton t/a Felton's Solicitors[8]—UK Employment Appeal Tribunal—appeal from employment tribunal—protected disclosures—public interest—detriment—causation*

The claimant commenced an engagement with the respondent firm of solicitors in 2010 as a consultant. The claimant was substantially involved in work for client A, one of the most important clients of the firm. The claimant contended that he made three protected disclosures to the effect that client A had been overcharged, as a result of which he was subject to a number of detriments, the most significant of which was the termination of his consultancy agreement.

The claimant instituted proceedings in respect of the detriment and same was rejected by the employment tribunal on the basis that it had not been established that the claimant reasonably believed that the making of the disclosures was in the public interest, and also by reason of the claimant's failure to establish that the detriments complained of were caused by the disclosures.

---

8   *Dobbie v Paula Felton t/a Felton's Solicitors* UKEAT/0130/20/OO.

In considering the decision of the employment tribunal regarding whether the disclosure was in the public interest, the EAT found that the tribunal did not make any reference to the relevant authorities, nor in particular to the guidance set out in *Chesterton Global Ltd v Nurmohamed*.[9] Although this, in itself, was not an error of law, the EAT found that the following factors had not been dealt with in the judgment of the employment tribunal:

1. The identity of the alleged wrongdoer: as the respondents were a firm of solicitors, in terms of public interest, they were in a position 'subject to high requirements of honesty and integrity.
2. The nature of the wrongdoing: the overcharging was a breach of regulations which were put in place to protect the public and therefore was in the public interest.
3. The nature and extent of the interests affected by the wrongdoing.

The EAT accordingly concluded that the disclosures were in the public interest and upheld this aspect of the appeal.

The EAT went on to consider the detriment causation issue. The employment tribunal had held that the main reasons for the respondent's decision to terminate the consultancy contract were the claimant's insistence on being paid double his usual monthly fee for work on client A's account, a disagreement about the handling of the claimant's parents' litigation and concerns about the claimant's competence. The employment tribunal accordingly concluded that the disclosure of the information alleged to be protected disclosures 'had little influence' on the decision to terminate the consultancy agreement.

The EAT, in considering the test to be applied, noted the decision of the Court of Appeal in the leading case on this topic, *Fecitt v NHS Manchester (Public Concern at Work Intervening)*,[10] where the Court of Appeal of England and Wales stated that, in respect of detriment:

> Liability arises if the protected disclosure is a material factor in the employer's decision to subject the claimant to a detrimental act. I agree … that *Igen Ltd (formerly Leeds Careers Guidance) v Wong* [2005] ICR 931 is not strictly applicable since it has a European Union context. However, the reasoning which has informed the European Union analysis is that unlawful discriminatory consideration should not be tolerated and ought not to have any influence on an employer's decisions. In my judgement, that principle is equally applicable where the objective is to protect whistleblowers, particularly given the public interest in [e]nsuring that they are not discouraged from coming forward to highlight potential wrongdoing.

The claimant contended that the language used by the employment tribunal set a higher threshold than the *Fecitt* threshold, while the respondent contended that the employment tribunal was expressing the test in *Fecitt* but just with a slightly different wording.

The EAT, in terms that were critical of the employment tribunal, concluded that it could not read in its determination that the disclosure 'had little influence' as being the same as having had no material effect on the decision. The EAT concluded that

---

[9] *Chesterton Global Ltd v Nurmohamed* [2018] ICR 731.
[10] *Fecitt v NHS Manchester (Public Concern at Work Intervening)* [2012] ICR 372.

the employment tribunal had applied the wrong legal test and therefore erred in law in considering causation. The EAT concluded that the making of one or both of the protected disclosures (one of the three of them had been not relied on by the claimant) was an effective cause of the termination of the consultancy agreement. A detriment will be made out even if the agreement would have been terminated in any event, without the making of the disclosure. The possibility of the agreement being terminated absent the protected disclosure would be a matter that goes to remedy.

The EAT allowed the appeal on both grounds and remitted it for consideration by a differently constituted employment tribunal on the basis that it was not proportionate to await the availability of the same tribunal before the case could progress and by reason of the fact that the errors of law were fundamental to the decision reached.

[24.07]   *Watson v Hilary Meredith Solicitors Ltd and Hilary Meredith[11]—UK Employment Appeal Tribunal—Employment Rights Act 1998—whistleblowing—detriment—dismissal—causal link—waiver of without prejudice privilege*

The claimant was a solicitor, who joined the first respondent law firm as its chief executive officer and a statutory director. He had a contractual notice period of 12 months. With effect from 5 September 2017, the claimant and a colleague, the finance director, made protected disclosures to the second respondent. The disclosures related to the treatment of costs advances in the accounts and the treatment of unpaid disbursements in the accounts, meaning that the firm's accounts were misleading and the firm was in breach of its overdraft facility with the bank; there was also a breach of the Solicitors Regulatory Authority's accounts rules. The respondents accepted in advance of the hearing that the disclosures relating to disbursements were protected disclosures.

After the disclosures were made, the claimant gave notice of resignation, being 12 months' notice as per his contract of employment. Initially he was placed on garden leave but was subsequently requested to return to work, which he declined to do. Then there were negotiations with regard to a resolution of the matter between the solicitors for the respective parties. The claimant did not return to work and he was summarily dismissed by letter dated 17 October 2020.

The central issue in the proceedings before the employment tribunal was whether the dismissal, and associated detriments to which the claimant had been subjected, were materially influenced by the protected disclosures or whether, as the respondents had contended, the claimant had been dismissed because the second respondent was dissatisfied with him as she believed that his immediate resignation had made things worse, especially by unsettling others, and that he should have stayed on to help the business out of its difficulties.

The employment tribunal concluded that the protected disclosures had not materially influenced the decision to dismiss and that the claimant was dismissed because of the way that he behaved following the protected disclosures and that these actions could be severed from the protected disclosures themselves. Accordingly, the employment

---

[11]   *Watson v Hilary Meredith Solicitors Ltd and Hilary Meredith* UKEAT/0092/20/BA.

tribunal dismissed the detriment claim and concluded that the protected disclosures were not the reason or principal reason for the dismissal, as a consequence of which the automatic unfair dismissal claim was also dismissed.

On appeal to the UK EAT, the claimant contended that the employment tribunal failed to properly address the question of whether his dismissal had been materially affected by the disclosures and/or reached a perverse conclusion on the issue. There was also an appeal relating to the tribunal's refusal to order the respondents to disclose privileged documents beyond those disclosed voluntarily. Those documents arose out of the failed attempt to resolve the matter.

The EAT noted that the relevant law with regard to the causal link between a protected disclosure, and any detriment suffered as a consequence thereof, was set out in the Employment Rights Act 1998 at s 47B(i), which is in the following terms:

> A worker has the right not to be subjected to any detriment by any act, or any deliberate failure to act, by his employer done on the ground that the worker has made a protected disclosure.

The EAT noted that the meaning of an act done 'on the ground that' the worker has made a protected disclosure is well established. In order for a 'detriment' claim to be made out, the tribunal must be satisfied that 'the protected disclosure materially influences (in the sense of being more than a trivial influence upon) the employer's detrimental treatment of the claimant' (*Fecitt v NHS Manchester*).[12]

With reference to a causal link between a protected disclosure and dismissal, the EAT noted that the test is set out in s 103A of the Employment Rights Act 1998, and is in the following terms:

> An employee who is dismissed shall be regarded for the purposes of this Part as unfairly dismissed if the reason (or, if more than one, the principal reason) for the dismissal is that employee made a protected disclosure.

The EAT concluded that the employment tribunal did not err in law or act perversely in finding that neither the detriment suffered by the claimant nor the claimant's dismissal was materially influenced by his protected disclosure. The EAT noted that the appeal courts recognised that a distinction can be drawn between the protected disclosures themselves, on the one hand, and the way that they are made and their consequences, and the subsequent conduct of the person making the disclosure on the other. The EAT noted the decision in *Martin v Devonshires Solicitors*[13] where the Court concluded that there will be cases where an employer has dismissed an employee or subjected them to some other detriment in response to the doing of a protected act but the employer can, applying common sense and fairness, say that the reason for the dismissal was not the complaint as such but some separable feature of it. The most straightforward example 'is where the reason relied on is the manner of the complaint, but it can also apply where the reason relied on is related to the consequences of the complaint if they are properly and genuinely separable from the making of the complaint itself'.

---

12   *Fecitt v NHS Manchester* [2012] IRLR 64.
13   *Martin v Devonshires Solicitors* [2011] ICR 353.

The EAT found that the claimant's actions following the making of the protected disclosures could be severed from the protected disclosures themselves. The EAT noted that the employment tribunal gave reasons for this conclusion, including the fact that the second respondent did not at any stage criticise the claimant for making the disclosures, the second respondent was not at fault for the accounting problems which were the subject matter of the disclosures, the second respondent did not try to cover up the disclosures but acted immediately to investigate the issues raised and to notify the Solicitors Regulatory Authority, and for a period after the disclosures were made the second respondent maintained an amicable relationship with the claimant. Accordingly, the employment tribunal dismissed the claim and the EAT upheld this finding.

On the disclosure issue, the EAT noted that the three guiding principles of the law in this area are

1. if a party waives privilege, this waiver applies to all documents or communications concerned with the transaction;
2. a party cannot waive privilege 'in a selective way which is misleading or would give rise to unfairness', so if privilege is waived in relation to a document, the relevant party must also disclose any other documents which, were they not disclosed, 'would render the disclosed documents misleading or would give rise to unfairness'; and
3. waiver of privilege relating to 'one matter or document does not mean that the party has waived privilege on all of the privileged documents in its possession'.

The EAT concluded that the employment tribunal had correctly applied those principles and upheld its decision on the matter.

[24.08]   *Edinburgh Mela Ltd v Purnell[14]—UK Employment Appeal Tribunal— appeal from employment tribunal—whistleblowing—protected disclosure—protection against detriment—compensation for injury to feelings*

The respondent charity was the organiser of the Edinburgh Mela festival and the claimant was its director. Controversy arose with regard to governance and in particular term limits for board membership and the eligibility of board members for reappointment. The claimant raised those governance issues with the respondent's board. Board members reacted with hostility. At a board meeting, from which the claimant was excluded, allegations were made that he had been undermining the charity, and one board member, Mr K, sent him an email asking him to justify his concerns. As a result of the email, the claimant resigned and thereafter the board initiated an investigation into his expense claims and reported the claimant's alleged wrongdoing to the police. The police investigation took 17 months before concluding that no further action would be taken. The respondent charity also made statements to the press suggesting that it had suffered financial irregularities, causing suspicion to fall on the claimant. The claimant claimed constructive dismissal, dismissal by reason having made protected disclosures and detriment for having made protected disclosures.

---

[14]   *Edinburgh Mela Ltd v Purnell* [2021] UKEAT 0041/19/1906.

The employment tribunal found that the claimant had been constructively dismissed by reference to the email from Mr K. It found that he had made protected disclosures to the board with reference to governance issues and that the reason for the board's conduct was those disclosures; accordingly it allowed a claim of unfair dismissal by reference to the making of the protected disclosure. The tribunal also concluded that the claimant had suffered detriment by reason of the protected disclosures, the detriment including the facts that he was accused of financial irregularities, that his employment prospects had been severely damaged, and that he had been reported to the police and subjected to a lengthy and stressful investigation. The tribunal assessed the compensatory award based on loss of earnings to be just under £50,000 and considered that he suffered significant injury to feelings by reason of the police investigation and the damage to his reputation and awarded him £15,000 under that heading by reference to the middle *Vento* band. The respondent charity appealed, arguing that the tribunal had erred in concluding that the police investigation constituted a detriment and also contended that the award in respect of injury to feelings was excessive.

The EAT considered the concept of detriment extensively and noted that detriment should be broadly construed and judged from the viewpoint of the worker. If a reasonable worker might consider the relevant treatment to constitute a detriment, then there is detriment; a detriment can occur even after the employment has ceased. In determining whether the detriment is a result of the worker making a protected disclosure, the employer must show that the impugned conduct was not materially influenced by the protected disclosure. Detriment is a statutory tort and accordingly the usual principles of foreseeability apply in determining the extent to which an employer is liable for injury to feelings caused by the detriment.

The EAT agreed with the findings of the employment tribunal and concluded that the referral to the police was made without justification and that constituted a detriment. The EAT stated that such unjustified reporting of an employee would constitute a detriment, even if the employer thought it had good cause for making such a report. Notably, the EAT pointed out the employer's reasons for doing do 'might provide grounds for not concluding that the reason was the prohibited one of making a protected disclosure, but the detriment would still be established'.

The award in respect of injury to feelings was upheld and the appeal was dismissed.

[24.09]   *Martin v London Borough of Southwark and the Governing Body of Evelina School*[15]*—UK Employment Appeal Tribunal—appeal from employment tribunal— protected disclosure—disclosure of information—qualifying disclosure—detriment*

The EAT allowed an appeal against an employment tribunal decision which found that allegations made by the claimant, a teacher, in respect of excessive hours worked by him and his colleagues, were not protected disclosures as the issues raised were phrased as enquiries in emails to the Head Teacher, rather than disclosures of information tending to show a breach of a legal obligation. As a result, the tribunal did not have to consider the question of detriment. The claimant appealed to the EAT.

---

[15]   *Martin v London Borough of Southwark and the Governing Body of Evelina School* EA/2020/000432/JOJ.

The EAT found that the tribunal had failed to apply the statutory test and take the structured approach necessary to determine whether there had been a qualifying disclosure. It had omitted a number of essential components from its consideration. The EAT found that the tribunal should have considered each of the following elements in reaching its decision:

1. Had there been a disclosure of information?
2. Did the claimant reasonably believe that the disclosure was made in the public interest?
3. Did the claimant reasonably believe that disclosure tended to show a breach of a legal obligation?

The EAT allowed the claimant's appeal and remitted the case to a newly constituted employment tribunal.

[24.10] *Chief Constable of Greater Manchester Police v Aston[16]—UK Employment Appeal Tribunal—appeal from employment tribunal—protected disclosures in relation to investigation into misconduct, corruption and criminal offences*

The claimants were police officers who had brought a claim before the employment tribunal alleging that there had been protected disclosures in connection with their investigation into misconduct, corruption and possible criminal offences committed by a number of officers, including senior officers, of the police force. The tribunal held that the claimants' disclosures were indeed protected disclosures for the purpose of the legislation, and that the claimants had suffered detriment as a result of these disclosures.

The respondent appealed on the basis that the tribunal erred in finding a causal link between the disclosures and the detriment suffered, which the EAT rejected.

The respondent also argued that the tribunal ought to have dismissed one of the apparent detriments on grounds of 'judicial proceedings immunity', despite the fact that this had not been raised at the hearing. The EAT held that discretion should be exercised to allow a point to be raised for the first time at appeal. It held that the witness statement in separate proceedings before the employment tribunal was protected by judicial proceedings immunity, and as a result could not be considered a detriment. The EAT found that the fact the matter had not been raised amounted to an error and allowed the appeal on that issue.

DISMISSAL

[24.11] *Kong v Gulf International Bank (UK) Ltd[17]—UK Employment Appeal Tribunal—protected disclosure—detriment—unfair dismissal*

The claimant was employed by the respondent as head of Financial Audit. She prepared a draft audit report which raised concerns that a legal agreement relating to certain

---

[16] *Chief Constable of Greater Manchester Police v Aston* UKEAT/0304/19/RN.
[17] *Kong v Gulf International Bank (UK) Ltd* EA-2020-000357-JOJ and EA-2020-000438-JOJ.

financial products did not provide sufficient protection against certain risks arising from the involvement of non-bank counterparties. It was not disputed that the claimant's communications of her concerns about this and certain other matters amounted to protected disclosures. The respondent's head of Legal, who had been responsible for the impugned agreement, disagreed with the claimant's view. She went to the claimant's office and a discussion took place, following which there was an exchange of emails. The head of Legal considered that the claimant had impugned her integrity and raised the matter with the head of HR and others. The head of Legal indicated that she was very upset and could not see how she could continue working with the claimant. The head of Legal declined mediation. The head of HR, the CEO and the group chief auditor decided that the claimant should be dismissed. The claimant complained of detrimental treatment and unfair dismissal for having made protected disclosures. The complaint of detrimental treatment, relating to the conduct of the head of Legal, was out of time. The complaint of unfair dismissal for having made protected disclosures failed, but the claimant was found to have been ordinarily unfairly dismissed. The claimant appealed against the failure of the unfair dismissal arising from a protected disclosure complaint.

The EAT held that the employment tribunal had been correct to hold that the reason for dismissal was the motivation of the managers who took the decision to dismiss. The employment tribunal had properly considered the authorities when considering whether the principal reason for dismissal could properly be treated as separable and distinct from the making of the protected disclosure. It had properly concluded that, while the head of Legal's own conduct towards the claimant was materially influenced by the protected disclosure, the motivation of the managers who took the decision to dismiss the claimant was different. The employment tribunal had properly found that they were not motivated by the protected disclosures but by the view that they took of the claimant's conduct towards the head of Legal at the meeting and in particular in a subsequent email. They considered that the claimant had engaged in an unacceptable personal attack on the head of Legal's abilities and they considered that to be reflective of a wider problem with the claimant's interpersonal skills.

The letter of dismissal made reference to the claimant's conversation with the head of Legal which caused the head of Legal to conclude that the claimant was questioning her integrity, a view which was reinforced by the claimant's email that followed. The letter of dismissal asserted that the claimant's approach was entirely unacceptable and fell well short of the standards of professional behaviour expected and was contrary to the principles of treating colleagues with dignity and respect. This had prompted a wider review, identifying other incidents leading to the conclusion that key stake holders no longer wished to work with the claimant and trust and confidence in her had been lost. The claimant had unsuccessfully appealed against the dismissal using the respondent's internal appeals procedures.

The EAT noted that, in identifying a reason for a dismissal, the general principle is that the reason for dismissal is based on the facts known to, or beliefs held by the person or persons who took the decision to dismiss. There is however a limited exception where the facts or beliefs of another manager may be treated as the reason for dismissal instead. That exception was established by the decision of the Supreme Court in *Royal Mail Group Ltd v Jhuti*.[18] In *Jhuti*, a person in the management hierarchy above the dismissed employee decided to bring about her dismissal because of her protected disclosures and manufactured an invented reason, namely performance issues, which the dismissing manager then adopted, being unaware that it was not genuine. The EAT considered that the *Jhuti* exception is narrow and truly exceptional. This was confirmed in subsequent cases, namely *Simpson v Cantor Fitzgerald Europe*[19] and *University Hospital North Tees & Hartlepool NHS Foundation Trust v Fairhall*.[20]

Here, the head of Legal had not invented the fact that she was indeed upset to the extent that she was unable to continue working with the claimant. Accordingly, the *Jhuti* exception did not apply. The EAT noted that *Jhuti* was a case of positive invention whereas the present case was not remotely like that.

The EAT concluded that the employment tribunal had reached a properly reasoned conclusion on this point, based on the facts, which could not be disturbed. The EAT noted that the employment tribunal had found that the impugning of the awareness and integrity of the head of Legal at the meeting and then a follow-up email were the principal reasons for dismissal.

The appeal was dismissed.

[24.12] *Secure Care UK Ltd v Mott*[21]*—UK Employment Appeal Tribunal—appeal from employment tribunal—Employment Rights Act 1996, s 103A—protected disclosures—causation—material influence vs sole/principal reason test*

The claimant was employed by the respondent as a logistics manager. The respondent provided transport services, including the transport of persons detained under mental health legislation. His role was to accept transport assignments and deploy staff.

The claimant raised various concerns over staff shortages, long working hours, shift arrangements, adequate rest breaks, staff cover, breach of care quality regulations, health and safety law and working time regulations. Some, but not all, of these disclosures were accepted as 'qualifying disclosures' that were protected. He threatened to contact statutory bodies in relation to the staffing situation. The next day, he was advised that he was one of a number of persons at risk of redundancy and his access to IT systems was removed. A consultation process commenced, and the claimant was dismissed just over a month later by reason of redundancy.

The employment tribunal correctly identified that the applicable test for causation was that 'the reason for the dismissal is that the employee has made a protected disclosure'. However, in determining whether this test was met, the tribunal applied the 'material influence' test as set out in *Fecitt v NHS Manchester*,[22] ie, 'there is a causal link if the

---

18 *Royal Mail Group Ltd v Jhuti* [2019] UKSC 55.
19 *Simpson v Cantor Fitzgerald Europe* [2020] EWCA Civ 1601.
20 *University Hospital North Tees & Hartlepool NHS Foundation Trust v Fairhall* [2021] UKEAT 0150/20/3006.
21 *Secure Care UK Ltd v Mott* EA-2019-000977-AT.
22 *Fecitt v NHS Manchester* [2012] IRLR 64.

protected disclosure materially influences, in the sense of being more than a trivial influence, the employer's treatment of the whistleblower'. The employment tribunal ultimately found that the claimant's concerns regarding staffing levels had a 'more than trivial' impact on his selection for redundancy, and that 'the fact that the claimant had made protected disclosures had a material influence upon his selection for redundancy and eventual dismissal' and upheld his claim of unfair dismissal.

The respondent appealed to the EAT, which found that the wrong causation test had been applied by the tribunal. The *Fecitt* test applies to a claim under s 47B of the Employment Rights Act 1996 for subjecting a worker to detriment (excluding dismissal) on the ground that the worker has made a protected disclosure. The appropriate test for a claim under s 103A for dismissing an employee for making a protected disclosure is that the protected disclosure is the sole or principal reason for dismissal. The EAT noted that the *Fecitt* case had expressly considered the apparent anomaly of having different tests under the different sections of the Employment Rights Act 1996, and accordingly there was no doubt that the wrong test had been applied.

The EAT also found that the employment tribunal erred in law by not, when addressing causation, confining its assessment to the three 'qualifying disclosures'—rather, it had considered all the disclosures, including those that did not qualify for legislative protection, and the combined effect of such disclosures.

The EAT set aside the decision of the employment tribunal and remitted the case for re-hearing.

FREEDOM OF EXPRESSION/EUROPEAN CONVENTION ON HUMAN RIGHTS

[24.13] *Gawlik v Liechtenstein*[23]—*European Court of Human Rights— whistleblowing—European Convention on Human Rights, art 10—freedom of expression*

The applicant, Dr Gawlik, was a deputy chief physician in the only public hospital in Liechtenstein. He concluded, following review of the hospital's electronic files, that the chief physician, his line manager, had practised active euthanasia on a number of patients. The applicant communicated his suspicions to the President of a Parliamentary Control Committee and that person advised him to lodge a criminal complaint against the chief physician. The applicant lodged that complaint and the public prosecutor instituted criminal proceedings against the chief physician by reason of his suspected killing and his involvement in suicides. The applicant followed up to the effect that the chief physician had practised active euthanasia on a number of additional patients. The hospital commissioned an investigation and concluded that, if the applicant had examined the paper files, as distinct from the electronic files, he would have concluded that the suspicions of active euthanasia were unfounded.

---

[23]   *Gawlik v Liechtenstein* Application No 23922/19, [2021] IRLR 426.

Following the hospital's investigation, the applicant was suspended. The hospital commissioned an external investigation into the cases concerned, which concluded that there had been no active euthanasia. The applicant was thereafter summarily dismissed and the criminal proceedings against the chief physician were discontinued.

Following unsuccessful unlawful dismissal and whistleblowing proceedings in Liechtenstein, the applicant instituted proceedings before the European Court of Human Rights (the ECtHR) contending that his dismissal had breached his right of freedom of expression as provided for in art 10 ECHR.

The Court noted that the protection provided by art 10 extends to the workplace in general. The protection of art 10 applies not only to employment relationships governed by public law, but also those under private law. Furthermore, in certain cases, Contracting States have a positive obligation to protect the right to freedom of expression even in the sphere of relations between individuals.

The Court noted that, by reason of his statements regarding active euthanasia, the applicant was dismissed by the public hospital, a public law foundation, and that his employment relationship had been governed by private law. The Court observed that his dismissal had been endorsed by the Liechtenstein Constitutional Court. Accordingly, the Court concluded that the measure in question constituted an interference by a state authority with the applicant's right to freedom of expression as guaranteed by art 10. The Court noted its previous decisions, where it had held that the dismissal of an employee in a state-owned or -controlled company, whose employment relationship was governed by private law, could constitute an interference with the relevant employee's rights.

The Court went on to note that such interference would constitute a breach of art 10 unless it is 'prescribed by law', 'pursuant to a legitimate aim' under art 10.2 and is 'necessary in a democratic society' for the achievement of such aim.

In considering whether the dismissal met the first requirement of being 'prescribed by law', the Court noted that the dismissal was based on part of the Liechtenstein Civil Code, which authorises the termination of employment without notice for important reasons. Accordingly, the dismissal in this case was 'prescribed by law' for the purpose of art 10.2. The Court noted that was not contested by the parties.

Moving on to the second requirement, that of 'a legitimate aim', the Court noted that it was not disputed, and the Court agreed, that interference, namely the dismissal, had the legitimate aims of protecting the reputation and rights of others, ie the business reputation and interests of the hospital, including its interest in a professional working relationship based on mutual trust, and the reputation of the hospital's chief physician, the person against whom the allegations of euthanasia had been made.

Turning to the third requirement, whether the interference is 'necessary in a democratic society' for the achievement of the aim, the Court held that its task is not to take the place of the competent national authority but instead to review under art 10 the decisions they deliver within their power of appreciation. The Court has to determine whether the interference complained of was 'proportionate to the legitimate aim pursued' and whether the reasons offered by the national authorities to justify the interference were 'relevant and sufficient'. The Court has to satisfy itself that the national authorities applied standards which were in conformity with the principles enshrined in art 10 and that they relied on an acceptable assessment of the relevant facts. The Court noted that it had previously held that the signalling by an employee in the public sector of illegal conduct or wrongdoing in the workplace should, in certain circumstances, enjoy protection. Such protection might be appropriate where the relevant employee is the only person, or one of a very small number of people, who are aware of what is happening at work and is accordingly best placed to act in the public interest by alerting the employer or the public at large. The Court noted, however, that employees owe to their employer a duty of loyalty, reserve and discretion. The Court concluded that, when assessing the proportionality of the interference with an employees' right to freedom of expression in relation to the legitimate aim pursued, the Court in its case law has had regard to six criteria:

1. Particular attention is paid to the public interest involved in the disclosed information. The Court concluded that the information disclosed by the applicant, ie, his suspicion that the chief physician had repeatedly practised active euthanasia was of considerable public interest.

2. The authenticity of the information disclosed must be examined. The Court noted that freedom of expression carries with it duties and responsibilities and any person who chooses to disclose information must carefully verify, to the extent permitted by the circumstances, that it is accurate and reliable, particularly if the person concerned owes a duty of discretion and loyalty to the employer and there is a question of attacking the reputation of private individuals. The Court noted that courts in Liechtenstein had found that the reported suspicions of active euthanasia would have been apparent to the applicant had he examined the hospital's paper files as had been done by the experts appointed by the public prosecutor and the hospital. The Court did note that information disclosed by whistleblowers might be covered by the right to freedom of expression where the information subsequently proved wrong or could not be proven correct. However, if the protection is to be available, the person concerned must have complied with the duty to carefully verify to the extent permitted by the circumstances that the information was accurate and reliable. The Court observed that it had been found by the Liechtenstein courts that the applicant had known, as a doctor practising in the hospital, that the electronic files did not contain complete information on the patients' state of health. The Court accepted the findings of the courts in Liechtenstein that, had the applicant examined the paper files, he would have recognised immediately that his suspicions were clearly unfounded and that he had, accordingly, acted irresponsibly. The obligation to act responsibly applies, in particular, if the person who makes a complaint is a high-ranking and highly qualified employee who owes a duty of loyalty and discretion to his or her employer. The Court noted that the applicant could have consulted the paper files at any time and that the verification would not have been time consuming. In summary, the Court agreed with the domestic courts' finding that the applicant was obliged, but had failed, to engage in appropriate verification.

3. The Court must weigh the damage, if any, suffered by the employer as a result of the disclosure in question and assess whether such damage outweighs the interest of the public in having the information revealed. The Court considered that the allegation of active euthanasia having been practised at a state-run hospital was prejudicial to the hospital's business reputation and interests and to public confidence in the provision of medical treatment in what was the only public hospital in Liechtenstein. It was also prejudicial to the personal and professional reputation of the chief physician. The Court noted that, although the disclosures had initially been made privately, it was inevitable and it duly occurred that they became known publicly.

4. The Court has to determine, in the light of the duty of discretion owed by an employee towards the employer, whether the information was made public as a last resort following internal or private disclosure, unless it is clearly impracticable to disclose the information to a superior or other competent authority. The Court has to consider whether any other effective means of remedying the wrongdoing was available to the employee concerned. The Court noted that the Liechtenstein courts had left open the question as to whether the applicant, prior to raising his suspicions externally, should have attempted to raise them internally. The Court concluded that the applicant could not be expected to first raise his suspicions with the chief physician and that an alternative means of internal reporting had not been communicated within the hospital. Accordingly, the Court concluded that the applicant could legitimately proceed on the assumption that redress could not be obtained by way of internal disclosure. The Court left open the question of whether the applicant should have made disclosure to other potential recipients within the hospital.

5. The Court has to consider the motive behind the actions of the reporting employee in considering whether a disclosure should be protected or not. The Court cited as an example, a disclosure motivated by a personal grievance or personal antagonism or the expectation of personal advantage would not justify a strong level of protection. The Court noted that it is important to establish that the individual, in making the disclosure, acted in good faith and in the belief that the information was true and that it was in the public interest to disclose it and that no other more discrete means of remedying the wrongdoing were available. The Court observed that the Liechtenstein courts did not find that the applicant had acted out of personal motives and the Court did not doubt that the applicant, in making the disclosure, acted in the belief that the information was true and that it was in the public interest to disclose it.

6. In considering the proportionality of the interference, the Court must carefully analyse the severity of the sanction and, in particular, whether the penalty and its consequences were required. The Court noted that the applicant's dismissal without notice constituted the heaviest sanction possible under Liechtenstein law. The Court noted that the sanction had negative repercussions on his professional career and led to him and his family having to leave Liechtenstein because he lost his residence permit as a foreign national when he was dismissed. The Court also noted that the media coverage regarding the suspicions of euthanasia in the hospital must have had a negative impact on other employees in the hospital and in the health sector, in particular with reference to the disclosure to external bodies of suspicions of irregularities.

In light of the analysis set out above, the Court concluded that the applicant did not act with improper motives but he did raise suspicions of a serious offence with an external body without having carefully verified that the information he disclosed, which was of such public interest, was accurate and reliable. The Court concluded that the Liechtenstein courts were justified in their finding that the dismissal without notice, having regard to the prejudicial effect of the disclosure on the employer's and his colleagues' reputation, was justified. The Court concluded that the Liechtenstein courts had struck a fair balance between the need to protect the employer's and staff members' reputations and rights on the one hand and the need to protect the applicant's right to freedom of expression on the other. Accordingly, the Court concluded that the interference with the right to freedom of expression, in this case the right to impart information, was proportionate to the legitimate aim pursued and necessary in a democratic society. It followed that there had been no violation of art 10.

[24.14] *Halet v Luxembourg[24]—European Court of Human Rights—European Convention on Human Rights, art 10.1—freedom of expression—Luxleaks—whistleblowing*

The applicant was employed by PricewaterhouseCoopers (PwC) and, between 2012 and 2014, the applicant and another person disclosed to journalists many advance tax rulings and tax returns prepared by PwC, which were published in various media outlets (Luxleaks). That information revealed a practice over a 10-year-period from 2002 of 'highly advantageous' tax agreements between PwC, acting on behalf of multinational companies, and the Luxembourg tax authorities.

The applicant was given a criminal conviction and was fined €1,000 for disclosing to the media the confidential documents of his employer. The Luxembourg courts had concluded that the documents were of insufficient public interest to counterbalance the harm caused to his employer and that the applicant could not rely on the justification of whistleblowing in the domestic law of Luxembourg.

In the applicant's proceedings against the State of Luxembourg, the European Court of Human Rights (the ECtHR) concluded that it had to consider whether the Luxembourg courts had appropriately approached the matter having regard to the decision in *Guja v Moldova*.[25]

The ECtHR stated that *Guja* had established six criteria of relevance to this case. There was no dispute between the parties with regard to the applicability of the first four criteria, ie: (1) the disclosures had been of public interest; (2) the information disclosed had been true; (3) informing the public through the media had been the only realistic means of informing them; and (4) the applicant had acted in good faith. Disagreement arose concerning the fifth and sixth criteria, namely: (5) the balancing of the public interest in receiving the information against the harm caused to the employer by the disclosures; and (6) the proportionality of the penalty.

---

[24] *Halet v Luxembourg* (Application No 2188/18).
[25] *Guja v Moldova* (Application No 14277-04, 12 February 2008).

In terms of the fifth criterion, ie, that the general interest outweighed the harm caused to PwC, the Luxembourg courts held that this was not fulfilled. After extensive consideration, the Luxembourg Court of Appeal found that, although the information was liable to 'concern and shock people', the documents did not show anything that was 'vital, new or previously unknown'. The Luxembourg courts attributed greater weight to the harm caused to PwC, specifically damage to its reputation and the loss of client confidence in its internal security arrangements.

The Luxembourg Court of Appeal gave detailed reasons for its findings regarding the fifth criterion and accordingly the ECtHR would require strong reasons to substitute its own view for that of the domestic courts. The ECtHR held that the Luxembourg Court of Appeal examined all the evidence carefully and applied the *Guja* criteria properly; therefore the ECtHR had no reason to interfere with its decision.

As to the sixth criterion, the domestic courts had imposed a modest fine of €1,000 on the applicant, finding 'the disinterested nature' of the applicant's actions was a mitigating factor. The ECtHR noted that this was a 'relatively mild penalty' that would not have a 'real chilling effect on the exercise of the applicant's freedom or that of other employees, while encouraging those concerned to consider the legitimacy of their intended actions'. Accordingly, and having regard to the Contracting States' margin of appreciation, the ECtHR found that the domestic courts had struck a fair balance between the need to protect the rights of the applicant's employer on the one hand and the need to protect the applicant's freedom of expression on the other.

It followed that there was no violation of the freedom of expression provisions in art 10 of the Convention.

Chapter 25

Working Time

INTRODUCTION

[25.01] The European Court of Justice (ECJ) considered the question of annual leave entitlements between the date of dismissal and the date of re-instatement in *QH*, and, in the context of a premature termination of employment, in *WD*. In *BX v Unitatea Administrativ Teritoriala*, the ECJ considered whether mandatory vocational training constitutes working time.

Four decisions of the ECJ dealing with the question of 'stand-by' time are noted: *BX v Republica Slovenija*, *MG*, *DJ* and *RJ*. The EFTA Court considered whether travel time constitutes working time in *Sverrisson*. The ECJ had to consider the concept of minimum rest periods in circumstances where there were multiple contracts with the same employer in *Academia de Studii Economice din Bucureşti*. The ECJ considered the entitlement to parental leave in *XI*. Finally, the Labour Court decision in *O'Leary* is noted, which relates to a claim that an employee was not placed in the appropriate weekly working hours band.

ANNUAL LEAVE ENTITLEMENTS

[25.02] *QH v Varhoven Kasatsionen sad na Republika Bulgaria[1] and CV v Iccrea Banca SpA[2]—European Court of Justice—reference for preliminary ruling from Bulgaria and Italy—Directive 2003/88/EC,[3] art 7—protection of safety and health of workers—annual leave entitlements between date of dismissal and date of reinstatement*

The ECJ joined a request for a preliminary ruling from the Bulgarian courts and the Italian courts respectively in relation to the interpretation of art 7 of Directive 2003/88/EC (the Directive), which relates to the annual leave entitlements of workers.

The request for a preliminary ruling from the Bulgarian courts arose in the context of the unfair dismissal of a school employee, QH, and her subsequent reinstatement following a court finding that she was unlawfully dismissed. QH was dismissed again

---

[1] *QH v Varhoven Kasatsionen sad na Republika Bulgaria* (Case C-762/18).
[2] *CV v Iccrea Banca SpA* (Case C-37/19).
[3] Directive 2003/88/EC concerning certain aspects of the organisation of working time.

and brought an action in the Bulgarian civil courts, asserting that an employee who has been unlawfully dismissed and who is subsequently reinstated, may claim compensation in respect of unused paid annual leave for the period between dismissal and the subsequent reinstatement. This was appealed to the Bulgarian Court of Cassation, which ultimately rejected this assertion, finding that no such entitlement existed.

QH subsequently issued proceedings in the Bulgarian courts for compensation for the damage which she asserted to have sustained from the Court of Cassation's infringement of her EU rights. In particular she alleged that the Court of Cassation should have relied on art 7 of the Directive, in finding that she was entitled to paid annual leave for that period in which she was unable to take it as a result of her unfair dismissal—and to the extent that if there existed any doubt as to applying art 7, a preliminary ruling should have been made. Arising from this action for compensation, the following two questions were referred to the Court of Justice:

(1) Must Article 7(1) of [Directive 2003/88] be interpreted as precluding national legislation and/or case-law, according to which a worker who has been unlawfully dismissed and subsequently reinstated by a court decision, is not entitled to paid annual leave for the period from the date of dismissal until the date of his or her reinstatement?

(2) In the event that the first question is answered in the affirmative, must Article 7(2) ... be interpreted as precluding national legislation and/or case-law, according to which, in the event that the employment relationship is terminated once again, the worker in question is not entitled to financial compensation for unused paid annual leave for the period from the date of his or her previous dismissal until the date of his or her reinstatement?

In the Italian proceedings, an employee, CV, was reinstated following her dismissal arising from a collective redundancy process. Her employment was later terminated again—and she was again reinstated. She brought an action for the recovery of sums relating to annual leave, special leave and public holiday entitlements for the periods in which she was not working following her dismissals. This claim was rejected by the Italian courts on the basis that she had not performed any work during the reference period.

This finding was appealed to the Italian Court of Cassation, who referred the following question to the ECJ:

Must Article 7(2) of [Directive 2003/88] and Article 31(2) of the [Charter], taken separately where applicable, be interpreted as precluding provisions of national legislation or national practices pursuant to which, once the employment relationship has ended, the right to payment of an allowance for paid leave accrued but not taken ... does not apply in a context where the worker was unable to take the leave before the employment relationship ended because of an unlawful act (a dismissal established as unlawful by a national court by means of a final ruling ordering the retroactive restoration of the employment relationship) attributable to the employer, for the period between that unlawful act by the employer and the subsequent reinstatement only?

In relation to the first question referred by the Bulgarian courts, the ECJ found that an employee who is unlawfully dismissed and later reinstated is entitled to rely on their rights to paid annual leave acquired during the period of dismissal and reinstatement.

In so finding, the ECJ noted that art 7(1) is clear in providing that all workers must get at least four weeks annual leave. The ECJ stated that this is a fundamental principle of EU social law, and should not be interpreted restrictively.

Furthermore, the ECJ noted that art 7(1) has the dual aim of ensuring workers have adequate rest from work, and are able to enjoy a period of relaxation. However, the ECJ stated the entitlement to annual leave cannot be made conditional on having carried out paid work, as there may be certain circumstances in which workers cannot carry out work (such as being unable to work due to illness). Therefore, an employee who is unable to work due unlawful dismissal, and who is later reinstated, cannot be precluded from relying on their right to paid annual leave.

In relation to the second question from the Bulgarian courts, and the single question from the Italian courts, the ECJ noted that the right to be paid for annual leave also includes the right to an allowance in lieu of annual leave on termination of employment. The ECJ stated that the only two conditions attaching to this entitlement are that the employment relationship must be ended and the employee must not have taken their annual leave entitlements at the time of termination. Therefore, any national law which provides for no allowance in lieu of paid annual leave at termination of employment is precluded. Where an employee is dismissed following reinstatement (as arose in the circumstances at hand), they may claim compensation for annual leave not taken at the time of their new dismissal.

[25.03] *WD v job-medium GmbH, en liquidation*[4]*—European Court of Justice—request for preliminary ruling from Austria—Directive 2003/88/EC,*[5] *art 7— Charter of Fundamental Rights of the European Union, art 31(2)—annual leave—organisation of working time—premature termination of the employment relationship—health and safety*

The applicant was a former employee of the respondent who had not used all of his annual leave entitlements before his employment terminated. During his short period of employment between June and October 2018, he acquired the right to 7.33 days of annual leave. Upon termination, he remained entitled to 3.33 days of unused annual leave. Relying on a provision of local law, the respondent refused to pay him the equivalent of €322.06. The applicant brought a claim seeking payment of same, which was dismissed both by the court of first instance and on appeal in Austria.

Article 10 of the relevant Austrian provision (which is similar to the equivalent Irish provision), stated that on termination of employment an employee was entitled to 'a compensatory indemnity as compensation for leave corresponding to the duration of employment during the reference year in relation to the entire reference year' with a deduction made for any leave actually taken by an employee. Article 10.2 stated that no such compensation was due in circumstances where an employee 'terminates the employment relationship prematurely without cause'.

---

[4]   *WD v job-medium GmbH, en liquidation* (Case C-233/20).
[5]   Directive 2003/88/EC concerning certain aspects of the organisation of working time.

The Supreme Court of Austria, hearing the applicant's case on appeal on a point of law, referred two questions to the European Court of Justice relating to the interpretation of the Working Time Directive (Directive 2003/88). The Court asked whether a national law that permitted the non-payment of an allowance in lieu of annual leave not taken is incompatible with art 7 of the Working Time Directive and art 31(2) of the Charter of Fundamental Rights of the European Union in circumstances where the employee has unilaterally terminated the employment relationship early without cause.

It also asked that if a national law as described was not compatible with EU law, whether it is necessary to verify if the employee in question was unable to use his/her leave and if so, what the relevant criteria for verification were.

The ECJ noted, as a preliminary point, the fundamental importance of the right of every worker to be paid annual leave 'from which there may be no derogations'. It found that although Member States have discretion to introduce the conditions under which employees must exercise their right, preconditions could not be imposed limiting the application of this right.

The ECJ stated that the right to paid annual leave is a 'fundamental principle of EU social law' designed to provide employees with rest and relaxation and that the second aspect of this fundamental principle 'consubstantial with the right to paid annual leave' was the right to be paid in lieu of leave not taken on termination of employment when it is no longer possible to take a period of paid annual leave. It stated that the reason why the employment relationship terminated was inconsequential in this context and the relevant Austrian law was incompatible with established EU law rules.

Moving on to the Austrian Court's second question, the ECJ found that it was not necessary to verify why an employee may have been unable to take their annual leave entitlements during employment.

WORKING TIME—MANDATORY VOCATIONAL TRAINING

[25.04] ***BX v Unitatea Administrativ Teritoriala[6]—European Court of Justice— request for preliminary hearing from Romania—Charter of Fundamental Rights of the European Union—Directive 2003/88/EC[7]—organisation of working time***

The applicant was employed within the voluntary emergency service and worked eight hours a day and 40 hours a week. The applicant was required to undertake 160 hours of vocational training, of which 124 hours took place outside his normal working hours. The applicant sought an order for his employer to pay those 124 hours in overtime.

The Romanian Court referred the following two questions for a preliminary ruling:

(1) Is Article 2(1) of Directive [2003/88] to be interpreted as meaning that the period of time during which a worker attends mandatory vocational training courses after completing

---

[6] *BX v Unitatea Administrativ Teritoriala* (Case C-909/19).
[7] Directive 2003/88/EC concerning certain aspects of the organisation of working time.

his or her normal hours of work, at the premises of the training services provider, away from his or her place of work, and without performing any of his or her service duties, constitutes "working time"?

(2) In the event that the first question is answered in the negative, are Article 31(2) of the [Charter] and Articles 2(2), 3, 5 and 6 of Directive [2003/88] to be interpreted as precluding national legislation which, while establishing the need for employees to undertake vocational training, does not oblige employers to observe workers' rest periods in so far as concerns the time during which training courses are to be attended?

The Court noted that Directive 2003/88/EC relates to organisation of working time and not remuneration of workers, however, given that the question of remuneration in the main proceedings depended on the classification of a period as 'working time' or 'rest period' the Court considered it necessary to answer the questions referred.

In respect of the first question, the Court held that when a worker is required by their employer to attend vocational training, so as to better carry out their duties, with an undertaking contracted to the employer, that worker is 'at his or her employer's disposal within the meaning of Article 2(1) of Directive 2003/88'. Although the activity carried out by the worker during the training is not part of their normal duties, the worker is nevertheless still subject to their employer's instructions and so the training periods are still classified as working time.

It therefore concluded that the periods of vocational training be regarded as constituting working time within the meaning of the Directive 2003/88. In light of the answer to the first question the Court did not deem it necessary to answer the second question.

WORKING TIME—MILITARY

[25.05] *BK v Republica Slovenija[8]—European Court of Justice—reference for a preliminary ruling from Slovenia—protection of the safety and health of workers—organisation of working time—members of the armed forces—applicability of EU law—Treaty on European Union, art 4(2)—Directive 2003/88/EC,[9] art 1(3)—Directive 89/391/EEC,[10] art 2(2)—military activities—concept of 'working time'—stand-by period—dispute concerning the remuneration of a worker*

This case involved a dispute between the applicant, a former non-commissioned officer in the Slovenian army, and the Ministry of Defence of the Republic of Slovenia. The applicant took the case regarding the remuneration he was paid for certain on-call duties, which he performed regularly during his time in service.

---

8   *BK v Republica Slovenija* (Case C-742/19).

9   Directive 2003/88/EC concerning certain aspects of the organisation of working time.

10   Directive 89/391/EEC on the introduction of measures to encourage improvements in the safety and health of workers at work.

The Supreme Court of Slovenia asked the European Court of Justice (ECJ) two questions concerning the interpretation of Directive 2003/88/EC (the Working Time Directive):

(i) whether the Working Time Directive covers persons serving in the military and as such must their time be organised in accordance with the Working Time Directive, including on-call guarding duties which the applicant undertook during his service; and

(ii) whether the activities in question were in fact 'working time' for the purposes of the Working Time Directive.

The applicant performed uninterrupted guard duty seven days per month during which he was required to be present at the barracks where he was posted and contactable at all times. The duties involved periods of active surveillance and periods when he would only have to remain available to his superiors. The Ministry of Defence took the view that eight of those hours each day should be regarded as 'working time' (and remunerated as such at his basic salary). For the rest of the time the applicant was afforded an on-call allowance at 20% of his basic salary. The applicant argued he should be paid overtime for the periods which he was on call but not undertaking active duties.

The ECJ took the view that the applicant was a 'worker' for the purposes of the Working Time Directive. In view of art 2(2) of Directive 89/391/EEC (the Framework Directive) the ECJ held that the exclusions from the Working Time Directive must be interpreted strictly and that the legislative scheme underpinning the Working Time Directive was not intended to exclude whole proportions of the public from the scope, but only certain categories of activity in those sectors, by reason of their specific nature.

On this point, the ECJ stated that:

> certain activities which may be carried out by members of the armed forces, such as those connected, in particular, to administrative, maintenance, repair and health services, as well as services relating to public order and prosecution, cannot be excluded in their entirety from the scope of Directive 2003/88.

The ECJ held that operations performed by a member of military personnel are excluded from the scope of the Working Time Directive in the following, limited circumstances:

— where that activity takes place in the course of initial or operational training or an actual military operation; or

— where it is an activity which is so particular that it is not suitable for a staff rotation system which would ensure compliance with the requirements of that directive; or

— where it appears, in the light of all the relevant circumstances, that that activity is carried out in the context of exceptional events, the gravity and scale of which require the adoption of measures indispensable for the protection of the life, health and safety of the community at large, measures whose proper implementation would be jeopardised if all the rules laid down in that directive had to be observed; or

— where the application of that directive to such an activity, by requiring the authorities concerned to set up a rotation system or a system for planning working time, would inevitably be detrimental to the proper performance of actual military operations.

The ECJ held that it was a question for the referring Court as to whether the activities in the present instance came within those parameters.

On the question of whether the stand-by period could be regarded as 'working time' for the purposes of the Working Time Directive in determining the remuneration payable to the applicant, the ECJ held that (assuming the referring Court were to hold that the Working Time Directive was applicable to the duties undertaken by the applicant), then a stand-by period imposed on a member of the military which involves them being continually present at their place of work, where that place of work is separate from their home, must be regarded as working time.

However, the ECJ held that art 2 of the Working Time Directive must be interpreted as not precluding stand-by periods under which no actual work was performed from being remunerated differently to periods where actual work was performed. The ECJ further opined that the rates of pay applicable in such instances are a matter of national law; such national law, or a collective labour agreement, or an employer's decision which differentiates rates of pay, are permissible.

WORKING TIME—STAND-BY TIME

[25.06] *MG v Dublin City Council[11]—European Court of Justice—request for preliminary ruling from Ireland—Directive 2003/88/EC,[12] art 2—Organisation of Working Time Act 1997—working time—firefighter—stand-by time*

This case concerned a request for a preliminary ruling on the interpretation of 'working time', as defined in art 2 of Directive 2003/88/EC (the Directive).

The claimant, MG, was employed by Dublin City Council as a 'retained firefighter'. He operated under a stand-by system, under which during 'stand-by time' he had to be available to present at the respondent's fire station within a maximum of ten minutes (and had to endeavour to present within five minutes) of receiving an emergency call. In principle, all time (seven days per week and 24 hours per day) was designated as 'stand-by time', except for periods that were designated as leave periods and any periods which were notified to, and agreed by, the respondent in advance. The claimant was required to live a 'reasonable distance' from the fire station, so that he would be ready to respond as required during a period of stand-by time; however he was also permitted to take up alternative employment during that time and he carried out work as a self-employed taxi driver.

---

[11] *MG v Dublin City Council* (Case C-214/20).
[12] Directive 2003/88/EC concerning certain aspects of the organisation of working time.

The claimant claimed that the respondent was in breach of the Organisation of Working Time Act 1997 in failing to recognise stand-by time as working time. The respondent denied that stand-by time was working time, pointing to the fact that retained firefighters were not obliged to be in a particular place during that time and also that the only consequence of failing to present as required was a loss of remuneration.

The claimant was unsuccessful before the Workplace Relations Commission and appealed the determination to the Labour Court. The Labour Court referred the following questions, *inter alia*, to the ECJ:

1. Must Article 2 of [Directive 2003/88] be interpreted to mean that a worker, when [on stand-by] at a location or locations of his [or her] choosing without [being subject to a] requirement at any time while [on stand-by] to notify the employer of his or her location, but subject only to the requirement that the worker be able to respond to a "call in" within a desirable turn-out period of five minutes and a maximum turn-out period of ten minutes, is engaged in working time while [on stand-by]?
2. If the answer to [the first question] is in the affirmative, can a worker who is not restricted, other than by a requirement to respond to a call-in within a desirable turn-out period of five minutes and a maximum turn-out period of ten minutes, and who is able, without restriction, to be employed contemporaneously by another employer or to engage in business on his [or her] own account while [on stand-by], be regarded as engaged in "working time" on behalf of the employer in respect of which employment he or she is [on stand-by]?

In relation to the first and second questions, the Court noted that under art 2 of the Directive, the concepts of 'working time' and 'rest period' are mutually exclusive—time is either 'working time' or a 'rest period' and there is no 'intermediate category'.

The ECJ considered its case law on the categorisation of on-call/stand-by time, noting that it has held that:

> the concept of "working time" within the meaning of Directive 2003/88 covers the entirety of periods of stand-by time, including those according to a stand-by system, during which the constraints imposed on the worker are such as to affect, objectively and very significantly, the possibility for the latter freely to manage the time during which his or her professional services are not required and to pursue his or her own interests.

However, it noted that where the constraints imposed during such a period:

> do not reach such a level of intensity and allow him or her to manage his or her own time, and to pursue his or her own interests without major constraints, only the time linked to the provision of work actually carried out during that period constitutes "working time".

The ECJ held the facts that: the applicant had the opportunity of carrying out another professional activity during his 'stand-by time'; he did not have to be in a specific place during that time; and he was not obliged to take part in all operations he was called to attend, were all important factors and indicators that he was not so constrained in the management of that time so as to make it 'working time'. As such, the ECJ concluded that the applicant's 'stand-by time' did not constitute 'working time' within the meaning of art 2(1) of Directive 2003/88/EC.

[25.07] *DJ v Radiotelevizija Slovenija[13]—European Court of Justice—request for preliminary ruling from Slovenia—Working Time Directive,[14] art 2—working time—stand-by—constraints to manage time freely and pursue own interests*

This was a preliminary reference referred by the Slovenian courts to the ECJ regarding the interpretation of 'working time' as defined under art 2 of Directive 2003/88/EC (the Working Time Directive).

The employee in question, DJ, was employed as a specialist technician and carried out his duties in two transmission centres in Slovenia. He worked on a shift basis, along with one other technician. They worked in alternate shifts of 6 am to 6 pm, and 12 pm to 12 am. The technicians were provided with accommodation on one of the sites, as the circumstances were such that it was geographically impossible to return home on a daily basis.

DJ generally worked the shift from 12 pm until midnight, and his remuneration was based on this 12-hour shift. He received no remuneration from 12 am to 6 am, as this constituted his rest period. The contested period related to the period from 6 am until 12 pm, during which DJ was on stand-by. He was not required to be present on site; however, he was obliged to be contactable by phone and in a position to return to the transmission centre within one hour, if so required.

DJ was paid 20% of his basic salary during this period of stand-by, unless he was called in to carry out duties at the transmission centre—for which he was paid his normal rate.

DJ brought a complaint to the Slovenian courts, submitting that the time during which he was on stand-by constituted 'working time', regardless of whether or not he carried out any specific duties during this time. As such, this stand-by period constituted overtime, and he should therefore be remunerated accordingly.

His action failed at the first and second instance, and he ultimately appealed to the Supreme Court. The Supreme Court of Slovenia referred the following three questions to the ECJ:

1. must the period during which an employee is on stand-by, as in the circumstances at hand, constitute working time, for the purposes of art 2 of the Working Time Directive;

2. is the definition of stand-by affected by the fact that an employee resides in accommodation provided by the employer, in circumstances where it is geographically impossible for the employee to return home; and

3. would the answer to the above two questions be different in circumstances where the employee, whether by virtue of the location of the site or otherwise, is more restricted in the pursuit of their own interests during their free time, than they would be at home.

---

13   *DJ v Radiotelevizija Slovenija* (Case C-344/19).
14   Directive 2003/88/EC concerning certain aspects of the organisation of working time.

The ECJ examined all three questions together. It began its analysis by noting that the fundamental aim of the Working Time Directive is to guarantee minimum protection to employees in terms of their working hours by, for example, ensuring adequate rest periods, breaks and maximum working weeks.

Article 2 of the Working Time Directive defines working time as 'any period during which the worker is working, at the employer's disposal and carrying out his activity or duties, in accordance with national laws and/or practice'. Rest period is defined as 'any period which is not working time'.

The ECJ thereafter noted that, based on the jurisprudence of the ECJ, the concept of 'working time' for the purposes of the Working Time Directive:

> covers the entirety of periods of stand-by time, including those according to a stand-by system, during which the constraints imposed on the worker are such as to affect, objectively and very significantly, the possibility for the latter freely to manage the time during which his or her professional services are not required and to pursue his or her own interests.

The ECJ further elaborated on these 'constraints', and noted that any organisational difficulties experienced by the employee as a result of being on stand-by were not relevant for this assessment. Rather, relevant constraints included, for example, those constraints imposed by law, the employment contract and the system of dividing time. The ECJ further noted that other factors may be relevant in conducting this over-all assessment, such as the average frequency the employee is called into work and 'brevity of the time period within which he or she must ... undertake work, which ... requires him or her to return to his or her workplace'.

In this case, the ECJ held that the period of stand-by did not automatically constitute working time within the meaning of the Working Time Directive. However, it was open to the referring Court to find such time constituted working time, if, after analysing the facts of the case, it could be established that:

> the constraints imposed on that worker during that period are such as to affect, objectively and very significantly, the latter's ability freely to manage, during the same period, the time during which his or her professional services are not required and to devote that time to his or her own interests.

[25.08]   *RJ v Stadt Offenbach am Main*[15]*—European Court of Justice—request for preliminary ruling from Germany—Working Time Directive,*[16] *art 2— stand-by—working time—rest periods—objective and very significant constraints— opportunity to pursue personal and social interests*

This was request for a preliminary ruling from the German courts to the ECJ regarding the interpretation of art 2 of Directive 2003/88/EC (the Working Time Directive).

RJ, the worker at the centre of the proceedings, was a public official acting as a division commander firefighter. He also carried out the incident command service 'Beamter vom Einsatzleitdienst', (the BvE service). When carrying out the BvE service, he had

---

15   *RJ v Stadt Offenbach am Main* (Case C-580-19).
16   Directive 2003/88/EC concerning certain aspects of the organisation of working time.

to be reachable at any time during this stand-by period. He was required to have his service vehicle and uniform with him, and to be in a position to reach the Offenbach am Main town boundary within 20 minutes of being called to respond to an incident, using his traffic regulation privileges.

RJ carried out the BvE service approximately 10–15 weekends a year, and over a three-year period, he was required to respond to, on average, 6.67 alerts per year.

RJ brought an action to the German Administrative Court, arguing that the periods of stand-by during which he was carrying out the BvE service constituted working time, and he should be remunerated accordingly. In this regard, he argued that the stand-by system was such that he was required to return to work on very short notice, within a very short period of time and this constituted a 'significant restriction' on his free time.

Notably, the referring Court did observe that if this stand-by time was found to be working time, RJ would be working in excess of the maximum weekly time permissible under the Working Time Directive.

The German Court referred the following two questions to the ECJ:

1. Does the situation whereby an employee on stand-by is required to reach a town boundary within 20 minutes in a uniform and service vehicle constitute 'working time' for the purposes of the Working Time Directive, in light of the fact that while no physical location is prescribed by the employer, the employee's 'choice of location and … opportunities to devote himself to his personal and social interests' is significantly restricted?
2. When considering 'working time' for the purposes of the Working Time Directive, should account be taken of 'whether and to what extent a service call-out is generally to be expected during stand-by duty which is to be spent in a place not prescribed by the employer'?

The ECJ examined the questions together. It began by noting that the purpose of the Working Time Directive is to ensure the protection of the health and safety of employees, by guaranteeing minimum rest periods and adequate breaks, and stipulating maximum hours to be worked in a week.

Article 2 defines 'working time' as 'any period during which the worker is working, at the employer's disposal and carrying out his activity or duties, in accordance with national laws and/or practice', and 'rest period' as 'any period which is not working time'. The concepts are mutually exclusive and are to be defined in accordance with objective characteristics.

The ECJ noted that, when determining whether stand-by time constitutes 'working time' in circumstances where work is undertaken at a place separate from the worker's residence, the determining factor is 'the fact that the worker is required to be physically present at the place determined by the employer and to remain available to the employer in order to be able, if necessary, to provide his or her services immediately'. In such circumstances, following the jurisprudence of the ECJ, the whole period during which an employee is on stand-by constitutes working time, regardless of whether or not any actual physical work is carried out, as the employee is restricted from pursuing social and personal activities.

Furthermore, even where a worker is not required to remain at his workplace during the stand-by time, the whole period of stand-by time can still constitute working time where there are objective and very significant 'constraints imposed on the worker['s] … opportunities to pursue his or her personal and social interests'.

The ECJ noted that, when assessing these constraints for the purposes of determining if the time constitutes 'working time', only those constraints imposed by law, collective agreements and the employment agreement itself are to be considered. Organisational difficulties caused by decisions of the worker (for example, the location of the worker's residence as freely chosen by the worker), are not relevant.

The ECJ also referred to *DJ v Radiotelevizija Slovenija*,[17] where the ECJ found that the reaction time required by the worker, the consequences of this on the worker's abilities to plan recreational activities, and the frequency of the professional activities actually carried out during these stand-by periods are also of relevance.

In light of the above, the fundamental question for the national Court in determining whether the stand-by time constituted 'working time' was whether:

> RJ is subject to constraints of such intensity such as to constrain, objectively and very significantly, the ability that he has freely to manage, during those periods, the time during which his professional services are not required and to devote that time to his own interests.

The ECJ also observed that, in essence:

— the Working Time Directive does not address the remuneration of workers— therefore it is a matter of national law to determine how to remunerate for stand-by periods. It is open to Member States to distinguish, for the purposes of remuneration, between periods of stand-by in which work is actually carried out, and those where no work is conducted; and

— notwithstanding the fact that a stand-by period might be considered to be a 'rest period' for the purposes of the Working Time Directive, employers must still ensure the health and safety of their workers, and are precluded from scheduling stand-by periods to such an extent that they create a risk to the health and safety of their employees.

WORKING TIME—TRAVEL TIME

[25.09]   *Sverrisson v The Icelandic State[18]—EFTA Court—referral from Iceland—Directive 2003/88/EC[19]—working time—travel to a location other than a worker's fixed or habitual place of attendance—international travel*

The applicant was an aircraft mechanic, working as an inspector. His normal place of work was his employer's headquarters in Reykjavík. As part of his duties, he was also required to travel internationally and perform certain duties abroad, including outside the EEA. Together with other aircraft mechanics, the applicant requested that his

---

[17]   *DJ v Radiotelevizija Slovenija* (Case C-344/19), see **[25.07]**.
[18]   *Sverrisson v The Icelandic State* (Case E-11/20).
[19]   Directive 2003/88/EC concerning certain aspects of the organisation of working time.

travelling time be recognised in its entirety as working time from the time of departing his home until arriving at his final destination (ie his temporary lodgings).

The Reykjavík District Court referred the following questions to the EFTA Court:

(1) Should Article 2 of Directive 2003/88/EC be interpreted as meaning that time spent travelling by an employee in the service of, and at the behest of, his employer, to a workplace which is not the employee's regular workplace, is working time when it falls outside traditional daytime working hours.

(2) For the purpose of answering Question 1, is it of significance whether the journey made by the employee for the employer is made domestically or between countries?

(3) For the purpose of answering Question 1, is it of significance what form the work contribution takes during the journey?

In considering the matter, the EFTA Court noted that Directive 2003/88/EC (the Working Time Directive) does not provide for intermediate categories between working time and rest periods. The concepts are mutually exclusive. Accordingly, the EFTA Court found that it would have to consider whether the elements of working time were present. In particular, it focused on the following elements of working time:

(1) That the worker must be carrying out his activity or duties in the context of the employment relationship.

(2) That the worker must be at the disposal of the employer during that time.

(3) That the worker must be working during that period of time.

Addressing the first element, the respondent sought to compare the applicant's situation to circumstances where a worker travelled to work and returned to work from home. It sought to distinguish other EU cases on the basis that those cases involved work which did not have a fixed place of work (*Tyco* (Case C-266/14)) and where the worker travelled using a work vehicle to locations away from his fixed or habitual place of attendance (*Thue* (Case E-19/16)).

The EFTA Court rejected this contention and found that to do otherwise would distort the concept of working time and the objectives of the Working Time Directive. It determined that workers like the applicant, who undertook journeys to perform tasks specified by their employers at locations other than their fixed place of work must be considered as carrying out activities or duties in the context of the employment relationship.

Considering the second element, the EFTA Court noted that to be regarded as being at the disposal of an employer, the worker must be placed in a situation where they are legally obliged to obey the instructions of their employer and carry out activities for that employer. It observed that a major factor to be considered was whether workers could manage their time and pursue their own interests without major constraints. It noted that where an employer chose a particular route that mitigated the amount of freedom held by an individual, this could result in that travel time constituting working time. For example, during air travel, the employee could not spend their time freely as their time was limited. This was an inherent consequence of the method of travel chosen by the employer and accordingly the argument of the respondent that the worker was not at his employer's disposal as he was unreachable while travelling by air and not asked to perform a specific duty had to be rejected.

The Court also found it was an immaterial how frequently the employee had to travel to different workplaces, unless that was such as to change the place of work to a new or habitual place of attendance. The EFTA Court found that including necessary travel time was indispensable to meet the objectives of the Working Time Directive, and that it followed that travelling to and from a location that was not a fixed or habitual place of attendance must be considered an intrinsic aspect to the work of the employee.

Provided that there was a sufficient EEA connection to the employment relationship, the EFTA Court considered that the Working Time Directive could apply notwithstanding that travel was taking place outside the EEA. It was observed by the EFTA Court that travel to such countries involved significantly greater impact on an employee than travelling within the State, and that therefore it would undermine the meaning of the Working Time Directive were the rights to be suspended when they were most needed.

In conclusion, the EFTA found that 'the necessary time spent travelling, outside of working hours, by a worker to a location other than their fixed or habitual place of attendance in order to carry out his activity and duties in that other location, as required by an employer, constituted working time'. No assessment of the intensity of the work performed while travelling was required, and it was immaterial whether the journey was made entirely within the EEA.

DAILY REST PERIODS

[25.10]   ***Academia de Studii Economice din Bucureşti v Organismul Intermediar pentru Programul Operaţional Capital Uman—Ministerul Educaţiei Naţionale[20]— European Court of Justice—request for preliminary ruling from Romania—Directive 2003/88/EC[21] (Working Time Directive), arts 2(1) & 3—minimum rest period— multiple contracts with same employer***

This was request for on preliminary ruling on the interpretation of arts 2(1) and 3 of Directive 2003/88/EC (the Directive) from the Romanian courts.

The proceedings related to a financial dispute between the parties. The applicant ran a sectoral operational programme for human resources development; the respondent declared costs submitted to it by the applicant for certain salary costs with respect to the programme as ineligible, as they related to hours that exceeded the maximum number of hours an employee can work, as permitted under arts 3 and 6 of the Directive.

The European Court of Justice (ECJ) considered the following questions:

1.   Does 'working time' as contained in art 2 mean 'any period during which the worker is working, at the employer's disposal and carrying out his activity or duties' under a single individual contract, or under all employment contracts held by the worker with that employer?

---

20   *Academia de Studii Economice din Bucureşti v Organismul Intermediar pentru Programul Operaţional Capital Uman - Ministerul Educaţiei Naţionale* (Case C-585/19).
21   Directive 2003/88/EC concerning certain aspects of the organisation of working time.

2. Do the limitations imposed by art 3 (which require that employees have at least 11 hours rest in a 24-hour period) apply to individual contracts or to all employment contracts held by the employee with the same employer?
3. Can a public institution, in light of the direct application of art 3, sanction an employer for failure to comply with the limitations established therein?

The ECJ, in examining questions 1 and 2 together, noted that the right of workers to minimum rest periods is not only a rule of EU law, but is also protected by art 31(2) of the Charter of Fundamental Rights of the European Union, which should therefore inform any interpretation of the Directive.

In relation to the interpretation of art 3, the ECJ noted that it provides that 'every worker' is entitled to at least 11 consecutive hours rest in a 24-hour period. The Court held that the use of the words 'every worker' places an emphasis on the individual worker—and as such, a worker, regardless of how many contracts they hold with an employer, is entitled to this minimum rest period.

The Court further noted that the concept of 'working time' and 'rest period' are mutually exclusive. 'Working time' is defined in the Directive as 'any period during which the worker is working, at the employer's disposal and carrying out his activity or duties, in accordance with national laws and/or practice', with 'rest period' defined as 'any period which is not working time'. The Court noted that, when determining the periods in relation to a particular employee, the 'hours considered to constitute rest periods under one contract would ... be capable of constituting working time under another contract'. On this basis, the Court determined that all employment contracts held by employee must be examined together to ensure the minimum daily rest periods are provided.

The Court further noted that such an interpretation supported the objective of the Directive, namely to guarantee the harmonisation of national laws to ensure the health and safety of workers is protected. The Court also noted that the jurisprudence of the Court established that the employee is the weaker party in the context of an employment relationship—and, as such, if the Directive was to be interpreted as requiring multiple contracts to be assessed separately with a view to determining if art 3 has been complied with, the employee could be exposed to 'pressure from his or her employer intended to split his or her working time into a number of contracts, which would be liable to render those provisions redundant'.

Therefore, the Court held that, when determining compliance with art 3, all contracts of employment held by an employee with the same employer must be examined together.

Finally, the ECJ noted that the relevant national provision[22] provided that employees were entitled to at least 12 consecutive hours rest between two working days. This offered greater protection to workers than art 3. The ECJ held that there was no challenge to the compatibility of the national provision and it could be interpreted in

---

22   Romanian Labour Code, para 135(1).

conformity with art 3; as such, there was no requirement for the ECJ to answer the third question.

The Court concluded that, if an employee has multiple contracts of employment with the same employer, the minimum daily rest period provided for in art 3 'applies to those contracts taken as a whole and not to each of those contracts taken separately'.

PARENTAL LEAVE

[25.11]   *XI v Caisse pour l'avenir des enfants (Emploi à la naissance)[23]— European Court of Justice—request for preliminary ruling from Luxembourg— Directive 2010/18/EU[24]—Revised Framework Agreement on Parental Leave—social policy—parental leave*

The employee, referred to as XI, had been employed on two separate fixed-term contracts over 2012 and 2013 for teaching services in post-primary education. Thereafter, in 2014, she entered into a contract of indefinite duration. Between the two fixed-term contracts, she gave birth to twins. Three years later, having resumed employment, she submitted an application for parental leave. Her employer refused to grant parental leave on the basis that, when the twins were born, XI had not been in paid employment.

XI challenged this and the courts in Luxembourg upheld the decision until it was appealed to the referring Court which decided to stay the proceedings and ask the following question of the ECJ:

> Must clauses 1.1, 1.2, 2.1 and 2.3(b) of the framework agreement on parental leave ... be interpreted as precluding the application of a provision of national law ... which makes the grant of parental leave subject to the twofold condition that the worker is lawfully employed in a workplace and affiliated in that regard to the social security scheme, first, without inter-ruption for a continuous period of at least 12 months immediately preceding the start of the parental leave and, secondly, at the time of the birth or of the reception of the child or chil-dren to be adopted, compliance with that second condition being required even if the birth or reception occurred more than 12 months before the start of the parental leave?

In noting that the 1995 Directive was repealed and replaced by later Directives, the first conclusion the ECJ made was that 'it is necessary to reformulate the question referred as seeking, in essence, an interpretation of those clauses of the revised Framework Agreement'.

In response to the first question, the Court concluded that Member States may require a worker seeking parental leave to be employed for a period of at least 12 months preced-ing the parental leave, that 'the period [of employment] in question be continuous' and that 'the prior period of work immediately precedes the start of the parental leave'.

In response to the second question, the Court stated 'it cannot be inferred from those conditions governing the grant of a right to parental leave that the parents of the child

---

23   *Caisse pour l'avenir des enfants (Emploi à la naissance)* (Case C-129/20).
24   Directive 2010/18/EU implementing the revised Framework Agreement on parental leave.

in respect of whom that leave is sought must be workers at the time of the birth or adoption of that child' as the revised Framework precludes such an interpretation. The Court continued, noting that the right to parental leave 'cannot be interpreted restrictively', as excluding parents who were not working at the time of the birth or adoption would preclude them from taking parental leave in the future 'in order to reconcile their family and professional responsibilities'.

The Court concluded that, although Member States can require parents applying for parental leave to have been employed without interruption for 12 months prior to the start of the parental leave, they cannot require parents to have been in employment when the child was born or adopted.

BANDED HOURS

[25.12] *Aer Lingus Ireland Ltd v O'Leary*[25]*—Labour Court—appeal from Workplace Relations Commission—Organisation of Working Time Act 1997, s 18A—Directive 2003/88*[26]*—Interpretation Act 2005, s 5—banded hours*

This was an appeal by the respondent against a decision of an Adjudication Officer upholding the claimant's claim that the respondent had not placed her in the appropriate weekly working hours band. The claimant made an application to be placed on a banded hours contract on 21 March 2019. There was no dispute between the parties as regards the claimant's entitlement to be placed on banded weekly working hours in accordance with the provisions of s 18A of the Organisation of Working Time Act 1997 (the 1997 Act). The dispute centred on whether the respondent had placed the claimant in the appropriate band.

The claimant contended that the respondent miscalculated her entitlement to banded weekly working hours by failing to calculate time spent on annual leave during the reference period as working time within the meaning of the 1997 Act, and consequently the respondent failed to place her in the appropriately banded weekly working hours under the 1997 Act.

The respondent appealed the decision of the Adjudication Officer, in which the Adjudication Officer stated that s 18A should be interpreted with regard to ss 19 and 20 of the 1997 Act. The respondent submitted that this was not correct as a matter of law. It noted that s 18A created a new right to a statement of employment or employment contract which reflected the average number of hours worked per week when employees had a reference period. It further noted that the provision was a creature of Irish statute, rather than a provision to implement rights created or modified by the developments at a European level and on this basis, it was submitted that it was wrong to suggest that s 18A was linked to ss 19 and 20 of the 1997 Act or the rules established by Directive 2003/88.

---

[25] *Aer Lingus Ireland Ltd v O'Leary* DWT207.
[26] Directive 2003/88/EC concerning certain aspects of the organisation of working time.

The Labour Court accepted the argument that the protections under s 18A of the 1997 Act were unrelated to provisions derived from Directive 2003/88. It noted that the meaning of s 18A should be considered by reference to the 1997 Act, rather than to Directive 2003/88, but without undermining the protections guaranteed in the Directive.

In considering s 18A, the Labour Court found that the 'plain purpose of the provision' is to ensure the number of hours specified in the contract of employment reflect the employee's actual working week. It noted that failing to take into account annual leave would automatically defeat the plain purpose of the provision, because the 'mathematical means to average hours worked across a 12-month period' would guarantee a resulting average which did not reflect the average number of hours worked per week in any week during which she engaged in working time.

The Court determined that the meaning of the requirement to determine the average number of hours worked by an employee per week during the reference period could not be said to be clearly and unambiguously set out in the 1997 Act.

In circumstances where, in the view of the Court, the meaning of s 18A(4) of the 1997 Act appeared to be ambiguous and where a literal interpretation would, in the view of the Court, fail to reflect the intention of the legislature, it had regard to s 5 of the Interpretation Act 2005.

The Court concluded that the only reasonable means to ensure that the plain intention of the legislature could be achieved was by interpreting s 18A(4) so as to mean that the divider used to calculate the average number of hours worked by an employee per week during the reference period should be determined by excluding the number of weeks spent on annual leave in the period. Thus, in the reference period of 52 weeks, where an employee has had to spend, for example, four weeks on annual leave, the divisor for the purposes of s 18A(4) of the 1997 Act should be 52 less four weeks (ie, 48).

The Labour Court upheld the respondent's appeal and overturned the decision of the Adjudication Officer.

Chapter 26

Northern Ireland—2021 in Outline

INTRODUCTION

[26.01]   The disruption caused by the impact of the Covid-19 pandemic continued in 2021. The building housing the NI Industrial Tribunal and the Fair Employment Tribunal experienced a further period of closure from 19 January 2021 until a limited reopening on 2 March 2021. The backlog of cases caused by, among other things, the series of closures to the Tribunals' building throughout 2020 and 2021 has continued to cause significant delays to the Tribunal process. Despite this, there have been important NI Industrial Tribunal decisions issued in 2021. In *A v Department of Justice*,[1] for example, the NI Industrial Tribunal considered the issue of whether a prison officer who alleged that he was required to attend work before the commencement of his shift was entitled to be paid for that period. The NI Court of Appeal also delivered a useful judgment in *Balcetis v Ulsterbus Ltd and Translink*[2] regarding the role of an appellate court in the context of appeals against decisions of the NI Industrial Tribunal.

The UK Supreme Court delivered a number of highly significant judgments in the area of employment law in 2021, which will also be applicable to employers in Northern Ireland. In *Uber v Aslam*,[3] the UK Supreme Court unanimously dismissed Uber's appeal, finding that Uber drivers must be categorised as 'workers', with the accompanying entitlements under working time and national minimum wage legislation. In *Royal Mencap Society v Tomlinson-Blake; Shannon v Rampersad*,[4] the UK Supreme Court heard appeals from care workers who were seeking national minimum wage for periods of on-call time when they were on 'sleep-in shifts'. In a highly significant decision for care agencies and charities, the UK Supreme Court dismissed the appeals, finding that the care workers were not entitled to the national minimum wage during 'sleep-in shifts'. In *Asda Stores Ltd v Brierley*,[5] dealing with the issue of 'common

---

[1]   *A v Department of Justice* NIIT/23316/19.
[2]   *Balcetis v Ulsterbus Ltd and Translink* [2021] NICA 9.
[3]   *Uber v Aslam* [2021] UKSC 5; see **[5.08]** for full case digest.
[4]   *Royal Mencap Society v Tomlinson-Blake; Shannon v Rampersad* [2021] UKSC 8; see **[23.06]** for full case digest.
[5]   *Asda Stores Ltd v Brierley* [2021] UKSC 10; see **[4.40]** for full case digest.

terms' for the purposes of equal pay, the UK Supreme Court dismissed an appeal by Asda, confirming that the claimants, who were mostly female employees based in the retail section of the business, could properly compare themselves to the predominantly male workforce employed at the distribution depots.

The appeal against the NI Court of Appeal's landmark ruling in *Chief Constable of the Police Service of Northern Ireland, Northern Ireland Policing Board v Agnew*[6] was due to be heard by the UK Supreme Court in June 2021 but the case was reportedly removed from the court's listing at the joint request of the parties to facilitate mediation. Holiday pay cases waiting to be heard have been stayed until January 2022 pending the decision of the UK Supreme Court.

Legislative developments in the area of employment law have, expectedly, continued to be limited in 2021 as the Northern Ireland Executive focused its attention on the health, economic and social implications of the Covid-19 pandemic. However, on 1 June 2021, the Parental Bereavement (Leave and Pay) Bill was introduced, although it is envisaged that it could take until April 2022 for the new regulations to come into force.

UNAUTHORISED DEDUCTIONS FROM WAGES

[26.02]   *A v Department of Justice[7]—NI Industrial Tribunal—Employment Rights (Northern Ireland) Order 1996[8]—unauthorised deductions from wages— claimant not entitled to be paid for periods of early attendance at work before start of his shift*

The claimant had been employed as a custody prison officer by the Northern Ireland Prison Service, which is part of the Department of Justice. The claimant had alleged, as part of an internal grievance complaint, that he was required to be at the external gate of the respondent's premises 30 minutes before the start of his shift time to allow him time to travel through the site, change into uniform, show identification and walk to his post. As such, the claimant argued that he should be entitled to 30 minutes pay for each rostered day in respect of the period before his shift time commenced at his designated place of work within the prison site. The respondent's grievance investigation found that the claimant's contract was clear in its stipulation that a shift started when the claimant was in post and that time spent travelling to and from post while inside or outside the prison perimeter was not included. Further, the grievance investigation queried the claimant's assertion that he had attended work 30 minutes early to

---

[6]   *Chief Constable of the Police Service of Northern Ireland and Northern Ireland Policing Board v Agnew* [2019] NICA 32.
[7]   *A v Department of Justice* NIIT/23316/19.
[8]   Employment Rights (Northern Ireland) Order 1996 (SI 1996/1919 (NI 16)).

start shifts, finding instead that the evidence showed the claimant was arriving early (either ten minutes, seven minutes or 16 minutes) and leaving early, so that the times evened out.

The claimant subsequently presented a claim to the NI Industrial Tribunal alleging that the respondent had made unauthorised deductions from his wages contrary to Pt IV of the Employment Rights (Northern Ireland) Order 1996 (the 1996 Order) in that he had not been paid for a period of approximately 30 minutes on each rostered day of duty, during which period the claimant alleged that he had been required to be on the premises of the respondent and that during this period, he had been subject to the direction and control of the respondent. The respondent denied that there had been any unauthorised deductions.

The Tribunal found that the claimant had not established that he regularly attended 30 minutes early before the start of each rostered shift and furthermore he had not established that he had been required to either attend 30 minutes early or to work for 30 minutes in advance of the start of each rostered shift. However, the Tribunal noted that, in any event, the issue of alleged early attendance at the prison was not relevant, given the clear and specific terms of the claimant's contract of employment, which stipulated that shift times started only when the claimant was present at his designated workstation within the prison, not when he was present at the external gate or the main gate. Furthermore, it was noted that the claimant had worked for at least six years under that contractual arrangement without complaint, before he raised a grievance and lodged legal proceedings. Even if there had been any doubt about the clear contractual terms in this case, (and there was not), it was clear to the Tribunal that the claimant had affirmed those contractual terms by working without complaint for a period of at least six years.

While the Tribunal expressly sympathised with the claimant's position that he was not paid by the respondent until he reached his designated workstation within the prison complex, it found that the contract was clear and that the claimant had been paid in accordance with that contract. Significantly, the Tribunal held that its role was not to amend a clear and unambiguous contract which had been negotiated between parties and to substitute what one party may regard as a more 'equitable or fair arrangement'. The Tribunal clarified that it could only intervene under art 45 of the 1996 Order if the claimant had not been paid in accordance with his contractual terms, and that was not the position on the facts of this case. The unanimous judgment of the Tribunal was therefore that the claim of unauthorised deductions from wages contrary to the 1996 Order be dismissed.

This case is significant as the claimant had sought to test the boundaries of what is considered 'working time'. The case is likely to be of interest to other employers where employees attend the workplace prior to the formal commencement of their shift for the purposes of, for example, changing into uniform. The decision of the Tribunal highlights the importance of employers having clear and specific contractual terms in respect of this issue.

ROLE OF AN APPELLATE COURT

[26.03]   *Balcetis v Ulsterbus Ltd and Translink[9]—NI Court of Appeal—McCloskey LJ, Horner and O'Hara JJ—disability discrimination—unfair dismissal—appeals— role of appellate court is to determine questions of law and not to re-hear cases in substance*

The appellant commenced employment with Ulsterbus Ltd and Translink (the respondents) in a manual post in June 2008. In July 2014, the appellant was diagnosed with renal cancer and, consequently, he commenced a period of sickness absence. Between October 2014 and April 2016, he attended periodic occupational health examinations. In April 2016, an occupational health report confirmed that the appellant was fit to resume his previous work with effect from May 2016. The appellant disputed the outcome of the occupational health report and did not return to work.

From October 2016 to March 2017, several redeployment vacancies were offered to the appellant, without response. In October 2016, the appellant initiated a claim of disability discrimination, contending that he had been subjected to less favourable treatment on grounds of his disability. In April 2017, two formal meetings were held with the appellant to discuss his ongoing absence, to agree a date for his return to work and to discuss any adjustments of his duties. The appellant was advised in advance of the second meeting that a possible outcome of the meeting could be the termination of employment due to his continued refusal to return to work or to enter into any constructive discussion regarding alternative employment. The appellant indicated that he would never return to his substantive role and, when asked if there were any adjustments that would facilitate his return to work (either to his substantive role or an alternative role) he reiterated that he would never return to his substantive role. The appellant said that he would not discuss alternative work because he was preparing for the forthcoming NI Industrial Tribunal hearing. Having considered the available evidence, the respondents terminated the appellant's contract on 26 April 2017 (with notice) on the basis that his behaviour was unreasonable and that his absence could no longer be sustained. In July 2017, the appellant initiated a second NI Industrial Tribunal claim, namely unfair dismissal.

The Tribunal concluded that the appellant's claim that he was subjected to less favourable treatment on the ground of his disability had no evidential foundation. The respondents' assessment, made following extensive and appropriate enquiries, that the appellant was fit to return to work was held to be a reasonable one. The Tribunal found that the respondents acted reasonably thereafter in the steps which they took to explore the issue of the appellant returning to work and in their assessment that the appellant could safely return to his former post. The appellant's outright failure to engage in any way with the numerous alternative employment positions offered to him evidenced, in the view of the Tribunal, a lack of genuine interest in returning to work. The Tribunal held that the respondents' act of dismissing the appellant was based on the appellant's

---

[9]   *Balcetis v Ulsterbus Ltd and Translink* [2021] NICA 9.

conduct; such conduct was unreasonable, and the respondents' motivation was fair and reasonable. All claims were therefore dismissed accordingly.

The central basis of the appellant's appeal was that the Tribunal had conducted the proceedings unfairly and had violated the claimant's right to a fair trial. In setting out the relevant legal framework, the NI Court of Appeal referred to the recent decision in *Nesbitt v The Pallett Centre*,[10] which in turn referenced *Chief Constable of the Royal Ulster Constabulary v Sergeant A*,[11] where the relevant legal principles governing how an appellate court is to treat the conclusions reached by a tribunal were set out. *Sergeant A* held that the appellate court is confined to considering questions of law only and that it is not the role of the appellate court to conduct a rehearing on appeal. It was further held that a tribunal is entitled to draw its own inferences and reach its own conclusions. However profoundly the appellate court may disagree with the tribunal's view of the facts, it will not upset those conclusions unless: (i) there is no, or no sufficient, evidence to found them, which may occur when the inference or conclusion is based not on any facts but on speculation by the tribunal; or (ii) the primary facts do not justify the inference or conclusion drawn but lead irresistibly to the opposite conclusion, so that the conclusion reached may be regarded as perverse.

Applying these principles, the Court of Appeal found that the Tribunal's decision did not contain any material error of law. The Court noted that the Tribunal took into account all material evidence; it did not omit any material facts or considerations; nor did it misinterpret or misunderstand the evidence in any material fashion; there was ample evidence supporting its conclusions; it contained no material legal misdirection or misunderstanding of the law; and there was not the slightest hint of procedural unfairness. Accordingly, the appeal was dismissed and the decision of the Tribunal was affirmed.

This case reaffirms that the applicable threshold is 'elevated' when it comes to an appellant court interfering with the conclusions of the Tribunal and that prospective appellants should consider carefully whether any questions of law are engaged before pursuing an appeal.

HOLIDAY PAY

[26.04]   The appeal against the NI Court of Appeal's landmark ruling in *Chief Constable of the Police Service of Northern Ireland, Northern Ireland Policing Board v Agnew*[12] was due to be heard by the UK Supreme Court in June 2021 but the case was reportedly removed from the court's listing at the joint request of the parties so as to facilitate mediation.

---

[10]   *Nesbitt v The Pallett Centre* [2019] NICA 67.
[11]   *Chief Constable of the Royal Ulster Constabulary v Sergeant A* [2000] NI 261.
[12]   *Chief Constable of the Police Service of Northern Ireland and Northern Ireland Policing Board v Agnew* [2019] NICA 32, see *Arthur Cox Employment Law Yearbook 2019* at **[25.02]**.

It should be noted that the decision of the NI Court of Appeal leaves the Police Service of Northern Ireland facing a £40 million bill in respect of underpayment of holiday pay. Many other employers in Northern Ireland (particularly those with ongoing holiday pay claims) remain concerned about the prospect of potential holiday pay claims stretching back as far back as the introduction of the Working Time Regulations in 1998, given that the two-year backstop applicable in Great Britain does not extend to Northern Ireland.

The prospect of a potential settlement in the *Agnew* case will also be concerning to many employers in Northern Ireland given the existing inconsistency between the UK EAT decision in the case of *Bear Scotland Ltd v Fulton*,[13] and the NI Court of Appeal. It is not yet clear how this might affect the thousands of holiday pay cases currently registered with the NI Industrial Tribunal, which have been stayed pending the decision of the UK Supreme Court.

PARENTAL BEREAVEMENT

[26.05]   On 1 June 2021, the Parental Bereavement (Leave and Pay) Bill was introduced, although it is envisaged that it could take until April 2022 for the new regulations to come into force. This follows the introduction of similar legislation in Great Britain in April 2020. In Great Britain, parental bereavement leave is a period of one or two weeks' leave that may be taken at any time within 56 weeks of the death of a child. A child is anyone under 18, and includes a baby that is stillborn after at least 24 weeks of pregnancy. Employees taking parental bereavement leave may also be entitled to statutory parental bereavement pay if they meet the statutory eligibility criteria and provide the relevant notifications and evidence. Statutory parental bereavement pay is paid at the same rate as other statutory payments such as paternity pay, for one whole week or two whole weeks. Despite calls for a wider and more generous scope for the forthcoming NI legislation, it is anticipated that the position in NI will reflect the current provisions in Great Britain.

---

[13]   *Bear Scotland Ltd v Fulton* UKEATS/0047/13, see *Arthur Cox Employment Law Yearbook 2015* at **[30.04]**.

Index